A Constructive Christian Theology for the Pluralistic World

VOLUME 1

Christ and Reconciliation

CHRIST AND RECONCILIATION

Veli-Matti Kärkkäinen

William B. Eerdmans Publishing Company
Grand Rapids, Michigan / Cambridge, U.K.

Published 2013 by
Wm. B. Eerdmans Publishing Co.
2140 Oak Industrial Drive N.E., Grand Rapids, Michigan 49505 /
P.O. Box 163, Cambridge CB3 9PU U.K.

Printed in the United States of America

19 18 17 16 15 14 13 7 6 5 4 3 2 1

Library of Congress Cataloging-in-Publication Data

Kärkkäinen, Veli-Matti.
Christ and reconciliation / Veli-Matti Kärkkäinen.
p. cm. — (A constructive Christian theology for the pluralistic world; v. 1)
Includes bibliographical references and index.
ISBN 978-0-8028-6853-4 (pbk.: alk. paper)
1. Jesus Christ — Person and offices.
2. Reconciliation — Religious aspects — Christianity.
I. Title.

BT203.K36 2013
234′.5 — dc23

2012037319

www.eerdmans.com

Contents

Abbreviations

ANF — *The Ante-Nicene Fathers: Translations of the Writings of the Fathers Down to A.D. 325*. Edited by Alexander Roberts and James Donaldson et al. 9 vols. Edinburgh, 1885-1897. Public domain; available at www.ccel.org

CD — Karl Barth. *Church Dogmatics.* Edited by Geoffrey William Bromiley and Thomas Forsyth Torrance. Translated by G. W. Bromiley. 14 vols. Edinburgh: T. & T. Clark, 1956-1975. Online edition by Alexander Street Press, 1975

JBC — *Jesus beyond Christianity: The Classic Texts.* Edited by Gregory A. Barker and Stephen E. Gregg. Oxford: Oxford University Press, 2010

JWF — *Jesus in the World's Faiths: Leading Thinkers from Five Religions Reflect on His Meaning.* Edited by Gregory A. Barker. Maryknoll, N.Y.: Orbis, 2008

LW — *Luther's Works.* American ed. (Libronix Digital Library). Edited by Jaroslav Pelikan and Helmut T. Lehman. 55 vols. Minneapolis: Fortress Press, 2002

NPNF^1 — *A Select Library of the Nicene and Post-Nicene Fathers of the Christian Church.* 1st ser. 14 vols. Edited by Philip Schaff. Edinburgh, 1886-1890. Public domain; available at www.ccel.org

NPNF^2 — *A Select Library of the Nicene and Post-Nicene Fathers of the Christian Church.* 2nd ser. 14 vols. Edited by Philip Schaff and Henry Wace. Edinburgh, 1890-1899. Public domain; available at www.ccel.org

PG	Patrologia Graeca. Edited by J.-P. Migne. 162 vols. Paris, 1857-1886.
ST	Wolfhart Pannenberg. *Systematic Theology.* Translated by Geoffrey W. Bromiley. 3 vols. Grand Rapids: Eerdmans, 1991, 1994, 1998
WA	Weimarer Ausgabe (Weimar edition of Luther's works)

Unless otherwise indicated, all citations from patristic writers come from the standard series listed above.

Bible references are from Revised Standard Version unless otherwise indicated.

The Qur'anic references are from The Holy Qur'ān: A New English Translation of Its Meanings © 2008 Royal Aal al-Bayt Institute for Islamic Thought, Amman, Jordan. This version of the Qur'ān is also available online at http://altafsir.com.

Preface

The current book is one of the five volumes in the series titled CONSTRUCTIVE CHRISTIAN THEOLOGY FOR THE PLURALISTIC WORLD. This series conceives the nature and task of Christian systematic/constructive theology in a new key. Living as we are in the beginning of the third millennium in a world shaped by cultural, ethnic, sociopolitical, economic, and religious plurality, it is essential for Christian theology to tackle the issues of plurality and diversity. While robustly Christian in its convictions, building on the deep and wide tradition of biblical, historical, philosophical, and contemporary systematic traditions, this project seeks to engage our present cultural and religious diversity in a way Christian theology has not done in the past. Although part of a larger series, each volume can still stand on its own feet, so to speak, and can be read as an individual work.

The introductory chapter lays out this methodological vision in a more detailed way. That discussion will continue in a shorter form in the epilogue to this volume. Each subsequent volume continues honing the methodological approach, including specific issues related to specific topics at hand such as "method" in Christology in this volume.

For constructive Christian theology to speak to the issues, questions, and challenges of the pluralistic world, it has to open up to a dialogue with diverse voices from both inside and outside. On the one hand, the hegemony of aging white European and North American men — to which company I myself belong! — must be balanced and corrected by contributions from female theologians of various agendas such as feminist, womanist, and *mujerista;* women from Africa, Asia, and Latin America; other liberationists, including black theologians of the USA and sociopolitical theologians from South America, South Africa, and Asia; and postcolonialists, as well as others. Rather than considering the insights from these and similar traditions as "contextual" in the sense that they are shaped by the context — whereas "mainstream" views are not — and can therefore be incorporated into the conversation at the author's wish, as "ornaments" or means of enrichment, this project engages these contributions as equal conversation partners with traditional and contemporary systematic views. On the other hand, it is about time for Christian theology to break out from its ghetto and engage insights and contributions from other faiths. However, unlike naive pluralisms of Enlightenment traditions, this project believes that in order for the conversation to be meaningful, it is of utmost importance for each tradition to remain faithful to its core values, convictions, and beliefs. One does not have to be a postmodernist of any particular strand to realize that it is in the freedom and safety of a diversity of views — rather than in an artificial consensus — that personal testimonies and truth claims can be best presented and compared. That one remains faithful to one's own tradition does not of course mean an unwillingness to learn. A mutual dialogue is just that — a *mutual dialogue* in which one listens to and speaks with the other. Authentic dialogue does not seek to subsume the other under one's own way of understanding the world but rather, in the spirit of hospitality, makes room for the other.

The series plans[1] to include the following volumes: *Christ and Reconciliation, Triune God and Revelation, Creation and Humanity, Spirit and Salvation,* and *Community and Future.* The ultimate goal of the series is to provide a fresh and innovative vision of Christian doctrine and theology in a way that, roughly speaking, follows the outline, if not the order, of classical theology. Among contemporary constructive theologies, the German systematician Jürgen Moltmann's six-volume series Contributions to Theology shares some common interests in its approach. Rather than attempting a theological *summa* in the long and honored tradition of Christian theology, this multivolume series seeks to focus each volume on particular topics and look at them in the matrix of the whole.

While roughly following the typical systematic outline, theological ar-

1. When drafting the plan, I was reminded of the change in plan of Moltmann's Contributions to Theology series mentioned below. Originally it was meant to include five volumes, but during the process of development an additional volume on pneumatology emerged.

gumentation in this series also engages a number of topics, perspectives, and issues that are missing by and large in traditional and even most contemporary theologies. These include topics such as violence, race, environment, ethnicity, inclusivity, and colonialism. A constant engagement with religious and interfaith studies is a distinctive feature of this series. Depending on the specific topic, discussion may include sustained dialogues in other kinds of interdisciplinary settings including natural sciences, cultural studies, and behavioral sciences. The discussion of christological topics in the present volume calls for a sustained engagement of the current New Testament scholarship.

While it goes without saying that no single theologian possesses the needed learning and breadth of knowledge to execute this kind of project in the most ideal way, I am convinced that attempting such a project in itself may make a contribution to Christian theology. To no less a writer than G. K. Chesterton do we owe the famous — or infamous — saying "If a thing is worth doing, it is worth doing badly." This line comes from Chesterton's book *What's Wrong with the World* (1910) — a telling title also for a theological work! With this statement, Chesterton was not of course attempting to lower standards. The saying's wit lies elsewhere: Chesterton constantly defended the "amateur" over against the professional. The amateur, however, for Chesterton, did not mean a person who didn't know how to do something but rather a person who was totally dedicated to his or her cause. The British literary master speaks about the dilemma of the working mother, who has to decide whether to have her children brought up by "professionals" such as day-care providers or to bring them up herself; she would pour out love to the child. Not for nothing, the saying happens to be in part 4 of the book, entitled "Education: Or the Mistake about the Child"! Mother loves and takes care of her child out of love, not for money. That makes the real amateur. Mother does the things "worth doing" — even when perfect standards are not met!

I dedicate this volume to the "so great a cloud of" students from all five continents, men and women from all Christian traditions: those at Fuller Theological Seminary, a "theological laboratory" to learn from and engage global diversity and plurality, and also my students, past and present, in Thailand and Finland — and beyond.

As with so many other books, I owe greater gratitude than I am able to express to my Fuller Theological Seminary editor, Susan Carlson Wood. Suffice it to say that her impeccable editorial skills have again helped transform my "Finnish English" into American English! I also want to thank sincerely all my research assistants who have colabored in this project: Getachew Kiros, Leulseged Tesfaye, and Naoki Inoue helped identify some key sources in the beginning part of the work. Amy Chilton Thompson and David Hunsicker finished the meticulous checking of the accuracy of all references. Without the help of these doctoral students, representing three continents, the writing process would have taken much longer.

Introduction: A Methodological Vision in a New Key

On Doing Theology in a "Post-" World

Postmodern, postfoundationalist, poststructuralist, postcolonial, postmetaphysical, postpropositional, postliberal, postconservative, postsecular, post-Christian, post-? While contemporary theologians and philosophers share the deep desire of attempting to go beyond the old, they also are confused and ignorant about what that "beyond" might be! Leaving behind the "modern" does not necessarily take all postmodern theologians to the same place. Not every poststructuralist speaks of the "place" on the other side of the "structure" (of the language) in the same way. Most all postcolonialists remind us that the forces of colonialism are still at work in our world — they have just taken a different, and at times, more subtle and pervading, form. And so forth.

In light of this persisting confusion and desire "for beyond," it is not surprising that much of the energy in contemporary theology is devoted to the consideration of "method," whatever that term may imply in the beginning of the third millennium. Again, there is an irony here. Unlike our forebears — say the medieval writers of world-embracing theological *summae* — most everybody agrees that there is no single method available for systematic and constructive theology. However, as Jeffrey Stout ironically puts it, theologians are prone to clearing their throats to the point that they lose their audience.[1] Hence "the voice of theology"[2] is not heard in the public

1. Stout, *Ethics after Babel,* p. 163.
2. Chapter title in Stout, *Ethics after Babel,* p. 163.

sphere, nor even in church at times! "Academic theology seems to have lost its voice, its ability to command attention as a distinctive contributor to public discourse in our culture."[3] The Yale theologian Miroslav Volf echoes the concern of the Princeton philosopher-ethicist in complaining that "theologians have increasingly turned into methodologists."[4]

Like the poor, methodological concerns will be with theologians until the end! That doesn't, however, mean that all theologians view the task of tackling methodological issues similarly. Two "mainline" German theologians, Lutheran Wolfhart Pannenberg and Reformed Jürgen Moltmann, serve as representative examples. Whereas Pannenberg devoted the best part of his long, productive career to honing the method before launching his *summa,* the three-volume *Systematic Theology* (ET 1991-1998), Moltmann produced a number of important monographs on various topics of constructive theology and only at the end focused on methodological issues in his *Experiences in Theology* (ET 2000). Whereas Pannenberg crowned his theological work with a most tightly argued, comprehensive systematic presentation, Moltmann from the beginning resisted that kind of enterprise and only wanted to write individual volumes of his series Contributions to Theology (ET 1980-2000). Not only that, but the accounts of method by these two leading constructive theologians couldn't be more different. Pannenberg's massive *Theology and the Philosophy of Science* sets out a coherent and rational argumentation for theology as "the science of God," in the tradition of the medieval masters. In contrast, Moltmann's methodological work makes it clear that he never had a particular method to follow. Rather, for him, "theology was, and still is, an adventure of ideas. It is an open, inviting path."[5] Whereas for the Munich theologian only the rational arguments matter in theology,[6] for his Tübingen colleague, "*The road emerged only as I walked it.*"[7] Whereas Moltmann delights in experimenting with ideas with no desire to establish any kind of universal truth, but rather to engage a continuing dialogue,[8] Pannenberg argues that truth by definition has a universal orientation and thus, truth that is truth to one person only, cannot be truth to anyone.[9] And so forth.

3. Stout, *Ethics after Babel,* p. 163.

4. Volf, "Theology, Meaning and Power," p. 45.

5. Moltmann, *Experiences in Theology,* p. xv.

6. Pannenberg, "Faith and Reason," pp. 52-53. For a full-scale study, see Worthing, *Foundations and Functions of Theology as a Universal Science.*

7. Moltmann, *Experiences in Theology,* p. xv.

8. Moltmann, *Experiences in Theology,* p. xvii.

9. Pannenberg, *Anthropology in Theological Perspective,* p. 15.

Other differences and diversities with regard to "method" complicate any presentation of constructive Christian theology in our times. Thinkers drawn to various stripes of postmodernism, whether "deconstructive," as in much of the Continental traditions, or (more) constructive, as in Anglo-American approaches,[10] are wondering if any kind of pursuit of Christian vision is ultimately foundationalist in its epistemology, power-driven in its agenda, and hence, not only a useless enterprise but also counterproductive. Feminists, womanists, *mujerista* Latinas, and other female theologians from Asia, Africa, and Latin America have raised important questions of inclusivity and equality. Some wonder if traditional theology in any form is redeemable, especially when it comes to talk about God as "father" and Jesus as "son." Postcolonialists from different global contexts echo these concerns but are also voicing the opinion that the "power play" goes beyond the issues of sexism and has to do with all kinds of explicit and implicit abuses of power. For some of them, any presentation and argumentation of one religion's truth are trapped within a colonialist hegemony. Other liberationists have for a long time attempted to expose the various kinds of structures of oppression behind the Christian (and other religious) discourses. Liberationists tirelessly remind us that any theology that doesn't take a particular human experience, for example, the experience of the black or of the poor, as the beginning point, is not only not worth its name but also serves the interests of the powerful.

Add to the matrix of these kinds of challenges the pervasive and intense plurality of cultures, religions, ideologies, and worldviews, and one begins to fathom the uttermost difficulty of doing theology in and for the "post-" world. How could one even imagine arguing for the uniqueness of one Savior among many savior figures? How dare one present a particular vision of "salvation" as the only one? On what basis could one book of revelation be the key to ultimate questions of life and death in the midst of countless similar books? Religious identities are interwoven with national and ethnic ties. To be a Serbian is to be an Orthodox Christian — or a Muslim! To be an American is to confess Christian faith in an endless number of denominations — or, as has become evident in recent decades, to put one's trust in Jewish faith, either "orthodox," or "moderate," or "progressive." And so forth.

10. American Christian philosophers argue strongly for a distinctive and different nature of "Anglo-American" postmodernism from its European, particularly French, counterpart. See further, Murphy, *Anglo-American Postmodernity.*

Yet another challenge — or an opportunity, one can take it either way — is the vastly different worldview of our day when compared to any previous epoch in Christian history. We have moved a long way from the semi-mechanistic understanding of the world with fixed laws of nature governing the universe and substance-ontology with built-in dualistic explanations, including radical difference between subject and object, matter and spirit, and so forth. Our worldview is dynamic, interrelated, evolving, in-the-making. It relies on subtle and humble explanations, seeks to discern the relationality and mutual conditioning, and envisions holistic ways of understanding.[11] Not only has the worldview changed radically, but it seems to many that so has the philosophical and religious outlook that opens doors for "the new integration," as Philip Clayton puts it, which includes features such as the following:[12]

- multiple religious traditions
- diverse cultural traditions
- science and religion
- complicated ethical questions, from bioethics to new forms of human relationship
- the continuing struggle to integrate faith and politics
- the new opportunities for constructive dialogue between liberals and evangelicals within the one church
- the "lived integration" of one's corporate beliefs with one's corporate practice

So, how to do theology in a "post-world"? Or better: *whether* to do theology in this kind of environment. Rather than attempting a full-scale discussion of the account of the possibility, ways, and forms of Christian theology, this series continues developing "theological method" incrementally, step by step, as part of the material presentation of various themes and issues. In this introductory section, before a focused and specific orientation to the issues in the "method" of *Christology,* a brief outline of the vision of systematic/constructive theology at large will be attempted.

11. For a highly nuanced and insightful analysis, see Clayton, *Adventures in the Spirit,* pp. 22-37 particularly.

12. Clayton, *Adventures in the Spirit,* p. 260.

Changing Visions of Theology and the Question of the Truth of Christian Claims

In pre-Christian usage, the term "theology" appeared in three different types, namely, as "mythical" theology of the poets concerning the deities, as "political" theology of public life, and as "natural" theology as the inquiry into the nature of the deities.[13] Whereas the mythical talk about the divine things was embedded in myths and nonreflective beliefs, and political theology served the interests of the rulers, philosophical (natural) theology sought to speak of the deities in a way that would be in keeping with their true nature. Early Christian tradition, while for a long time suspicious of adopting the term "theology," took the developed Stoic meaning in which the theologian "is the divinely inspired proclaimer of divine truth and theology its proclamation"[14] instead of fables and myths.

In early Christian tradition, and indeed up until the falling apart of the Scripture principle[15] as the result of the Enlightenment and subsequent modernity,[16] the truth of Christian theology and doctrine was taken for granted. It was based, on the one hand, on the divine revelation as transmitted in the Bible, and on the other hand, as Saint Augustine established it conclusively, in God as its locus.[17] It was also agreed that the authority of the

13. This is the standard account of the meaning of theology in philosophical schools of the Stoa. Pannenberg, *Systematic Theology,* 1:1-2 (hereafter *ST*). See Moltmann, *Experiences in Theology,* p. 43. For Plato (*Republic* 379a.5-6) theology meant the *logos* of the song or speech of the poets announcing deities. In Aristotle (*Metaphysics* 1025a.19) theology (or as he first called it, "metaphysics") was one of the three theoretical disciplines. Unlike Plato, for Aristotle theology also meant the inquiry into the truthfulness of the *logos* (speech) of the deities.

14. Pannenberg, *ST* 1:1; for an extensive discussion, see Pannenberg, *Theology and the Philosophy of Science,* pp. 7-14 and passim.

15. See further, Pannenberg, *ST* 1:22, 26, and passim.

16. The recent historical and philosophical research into the meaning of the term "Enlightenment" rightly warns us to handle it with great care for many reasons: there were of course a number of Enlightenments, say in French, German, and British contexts; apart from the regional differences, there were competing and conflicting visions of what modernity may mean; and so forth. Hence, we should ask with Schmidt, "What Enlightenment Project?" See also Schmidt, ed., *What Is Enlightenment?;* Munck, *The Enlightenment;* Dupré, *The Enlightenment and the Intellectual Foundations of Modern Culture.*

17. Augustine, *On the Free Choice of the Will* 2.15. God is truth identical with Godself (2.12). Since God is the locus of the truth, there is the unity and coherence of all that is true. For the divinity of truth that makes it universally binding, see 2.10.

church and Scripture basically agree with each other and thus can be taken as "foundation." With the rationalism(s)[18] stemming from the Enlightenment with its introduction of the historical-critical methodology, theology lost its role as the "queen" of sciences. It sounds almost unbelievable to contemporary intuitions to be reminded that, indeed, there was a time when theology occupied the highest place of honor and authority in the academy! With the rise of modern universities beginning from the thirteenth century, theology was not only the highest academic discipline but also the normative one that told natural and other "secular" sciences what their presuppositions and results were.[19]

In the changing situation, theology reacted in more than one way. Those who were not content to merely hold on to the lost precritical mentality of the past after fundamentalism, influenced greatly by the post-Reformation Protestant Scholasticism (both Reformed and Lutheran), opted for a strategy in which the mere affirmation of truth, and thus conflict with science and growing secularism, could be avoided. Classical liberalism turned to "experience" and, under the tutelage of Friedrich Schleiermacher, defined the theological task as a human interpretation of human religious experience. The question of the truth of theological statements was thus set aside, and theology became hermeneutics of "piety." Along with this, God as the theme of theology was replaced by religion.[20]

In the twentieth-century theological landscape, some, most prominently Karl Barth, sought to redeem "neo-orthodoxy" by leveling a massive critique against classical liberalism (albeit, ironically, sharing some of its agenda, including the view of Scripture). Again, the question of the basis of the truth of Christian claims could be circumvented with appeal to divine revelation.[21] Postliberals saw promise in both classical liberalism and Barth

18. What I try to express in the plural is that there were of course various kinds of rationalism, say empiristic and rationalistic. For an enlightening discussion that also shows how artificial is the modernist distinction between "fundamentalism" and "liberalism," as they both share the Enlightenment epistemological foundationalism, albeit in somewhat different forms, see Murphy, *Beyond Liberalism and Fundamentalism.*

19. A highly insightful discussion with plentiful bibliography can be found in Zakai, "The Rise of Modern Science."

20. For an important historical and theological analysis and critique, see Pannenberg, *ST* 1, chaps. 2 and 3.

21. Of course, Barth's way of appealing to divine revelation is vastly different from that of the pre-Enlightenment strategy in his making a categorical distinction between revelation and Scripture. Yet, materially, it is the same kind of search for foundation.

— and were vehemently opposed to all forms of fundamentalism. Associated with Yale University, several theologians, most prominently the biblical scholar Hans Frei and historian of dogma George Lindbeck, sought to establish Christian faith as a unique form of rationality that would be accountable merely to its own conditions.[22] Hence, in lieu of the "cognitive-propositionalist" model, which takes theological statements as truth claims about objective realities, and the "experiential-expressivist" model, which "interprets doctrines as noninformative and nondiscursive symbols of inner feelings, attitudes, or existential orientations," Lindbeck proposed a "cultural-linguistic" model.[23] Taking a cue from the later Wittgenstein's turn to language, this model regards church doctrines neither "as expressive symbols or as truth claims, but as communally authoritative rules of discourse, attitude and action." Hence, it can be called a "regulative" or "rule" theory.[24] Frei's main contribution to the project is his refusal to look for the meaning and significance of biblical teachings "behind" the text as in historical-critical method's endless probing into the sociocultural and historical background as the key. This attempt has led, Frei opines, to "the eclipse of biblical narrative."[25] Rather than letting the world take over the biblical narrative, these Yale theologians "desire to renew in a posttraditional and postliberal mode the ancient practice of absorbing the universe into the biblical world."[26] The doctrinal "rules" aim merely — or at least predominantly — at the inner coherence of Christian thought. They are not interested in extratextual references.[27]

The obvious question to this postliberal approach is whether there is any way to negotiate between different — and at times deeply conflicting —

22. Materially, although in many ways radically different, another American movement, the Reformed epistemology of Alvin Plantinga, Nicholas Wolterstorff, and others, in rejecting evidentialism (which seeks to show "evidence" and thus "foundation" for the belief in God), relies on the inner rationality of Christian faith. In this case, it means taking the belief in God as a "self-evident" or self-justifying basis that cannot be supported by any appeal "behind" it.

23. Lindbeck, *Nature of Doctrine,* p. 16. Lindbeck also mentions yet another model (which he leaves unnamed), a sort of combination of the fundamentalistic "cognitive-propositionalist" and liberal "experiential-expressivist" one. The Roman Catholic Karl Rahner and Bernard Lonergan represent this attempt. In the remainder of his discussion, Lindbeck hardly comes back in a constructive way to this "model."

24. Lindbeck, *Nature of Doctrine,* p. 18.

25. Frei, *The Eclipse of Biblical Narrative.*

26. Lindbeck, *Nature of Doctrine,* p. 135.

27. See further Lindbeck, *Nature of Doctrine,* pp. 63-69 especially.

traditions and their narratives. An important attempt to address that liability and also build bridges between what used to be called "liberal" and "conservative" orientations, is Kevin J. Vanhoozer's "canonical-linguistic" proposal. His *Drama of Doctrine* seeks to defend the principle of *sola Scriptura* in a way that would fully affirm the linguistic turn — and, as the title expresses, envision Christian doctrine as a dramatic event. His leading thesis is that "the canonical-linguistic approach maintains that the normative use is ultimately not that of ecclesial *culture* but of the biblical *canon*."[28] Vanhoozer charts his epistemological course in the waters of postmodern rejection of foundationalism, critique of propositionalism, and celebration of plurality of meanings — and at the same time, doing everything in his power not to steer away from the primacy of canon and *sola Scriptura* as well as the existence of "objective" realities "out there" to which metaphors refer to ultimately. Vanhoozer chooses three nomenclatures that encapsulate his epistemological orientation: "postpropositionalist," "postconservative," and "postfoundationalist." This approach allows for metaphors, as metaphors say "more" rather than "less" than propositions. This is to say that metaphors convey some information but not only that — or that they convey information in a way propositions cannot. The use of metaphors fosters the possibility of "polyphonic truth," multiple meanings and imagination. It seeks actively to be contextual. Unlike many postmodernist and cultural-linguistic models, metaphors do not lose some kind of cognitive content. Furthermore, the meaning of the text is first of all the meaning intended by the author (in the case of Scripture, the divine author?). In sum: there is an "extratextual" reference to realities outside, such as the resurrection of Christ, in the midst of many meanings and many metaphors.[29]

While, oddly enough, Vanhoozer misses the dialogue with Pannenberg, it seems to me that, even with their in many ways disconnected and vastly different approaches to the task of theology, they share some common orientations. As the "science of God," theology for Pannenberg presupposes the existence of truth apart from human beings and human beings' social construction thereof. Sure, usually faith precedes theological reflection, but that does not establish the truth: "Personal assurance of faith always needs confirmation by experience and reflection."[30] That said, it is essential for the understanding of Pannenberg's approach to note that even though God, as

28. Vanhoozer, *Drama of Doctrine*, p. 16.

29. See Vanhoozer, *Drama of Doctrine*, particularly chap. 9.

30. Pannenberg, *ST* 1:50.

in classical tradition,[31] is the "object" of theology — and everything else in the created order *sub ratione Dei* (in relation to God) — God can only be approached indirectly, through humanity. We do not have a direct access to the divine because God is infinitely incomprehensible.[32] In keeping with human limitations, our grasp of truth is only provisional, as the biblical conception of truth — different from the Hellenistic view, which posits a fixed "truth" just to be discovered — is historical and thus evolving.[33] Consequently, only at the end of the process of history, at the eschaton, does the biblical God manifest himself as the One he promised to be.[34] The resurrection of Christ as a historical event is a major "proleptic" assurance but not yet certainty. Pannenberg rightly sees the deep dilemma, namely, that while "[t]heology deals with the universality of truth of revelation,"[35] human knowing is finite, partial, and provisional. As a result, this dynamic is built in with the task and matrix of theology.

Since other theological disciplines, most profoundly exegetical ones, have left out the pursuit of the question of truth and attune merely to the texts' historical and critical meaning, it is left for systematic theology to pursue and, if possible, establish the truth of Christian claims. Hence, for Pannenberg, systematic statements function in the forms of scientific hypotheses, to be tested, tried, and hopefully confirmed. Doing so means highlighting the importance of the category of anticipation.[36] Although subjective certainty or human experience cannot serve as a final arbiter, Pannenberg is not dismissing the importance of either[37] because, as said,

31. Thomas Aquinas, *Summa Theologica* 1a.1.7: "But in sacred science [doctrine, theology], all things are treated of under the aspect of God: either because they are God Himself or because they refer to God as their beginning and end. Hence it follows that God is in very truth the object of this science."

32. Pannenberg, *ST* 1:4-6; for a full discussion, see his *Theology and the Philosophy of Science,* pp. 297-326 particularly. For a careful anthropological grounding of theology (yet, different from Schleiermacher and other liberals), see also his *Anthropology in Theological Perspective,* pp. 11-23.

33. For an important early discussion on which Pannenberg builds everywhere in his argumentation, see his "What Is Truth?" pp. 1-27.

34. For a short statement, see Pannenberg, *ST* 1:54-55.

35. Pannenberg, *ST* 1:51.

36. Pannenberg, *ST* 1:8, 54, 56, 58. Not surprisingly, Pannenberg rejects the church consensus (pp. 12-17) or the subjective certainty (p. 36) or the faith of the theologian (pp. 376-78) as the basis for the establishment of truth.

37. For the role of "affective and practical verification," see *ST* 1:23, and for the role of experience in this regard, see p. 47.

having no direct access to God, theology must proceed via human experience of the world. Furthermore, everywhere in his methodological reflections, he speaks of the provisionality, fallibility, tentativeness, historicity, and limitations of human knowledge — so much so that at the end, he sees doxology as the ultimate "knowledge" of God as therein the "speakers rise above the limits of their own finitude to the thought of the infinite God." Then he adds, however, something essential, that "[i]n the process the conceptual contours do not have to lose their sharpness. Doxology can also have the form of systematic reflection."[38] In other words, with all his pursuit of "the truth of Christian doctrine as the theme of systematic theology,"[39] Pannenberg "accepts *the contested nature of theological truth claims*."[40]

Rightly, then, F. LeRon Shults, against common suspicions, calls Pannenberg's epistemology postfoundationalist rather than foundationalist. A postfoundationalist approach, as opposed to nonfoundationalist epistemology,[41] seeks "to engage in interdisciplinary dialogue within our postmodern culture while *both* maintaining a commitment to intersubjective, transcommunal theological argumentation for the truth of Christian faith, *and* recognizing the provisionality of our historically embedded understandings and culturally conditioned explanations of the Christian tradition and religious experience."[42]

Building on the work of the Princeton theologian J. Wentzel van Huyssteen,[43] the postfoundationalist approach hence attempts to critique the foundationalism of modernity, placing emphasis on the provisional and historical nature of human knowing, without leaving behind the goal of the truth as something that goes beyond one's own ghetto, as is the danger in some forms of nonfoundationalism. It calls for a nuanced and mutually conditioning negotiation between various "couplets," as Shults names them:[44]

- Interpreted experience engenders and nourishes all beliefs, and a network of beliefs informs the interpretation of experience.

38. Pannenberg, *ST* 1:55.
39. As he titles the first chapter in *ST* 1.
40. Clayton, *Adventures in the Spirit,* p. 28.
41. See Hauerwas, Murphy, and Nation, eds., *Theology without Foundations.*
42. Shults, *The Post Foundationalist Task of Theology,* p. 18.
43. Van Huyssteen, *Essays in Postfoundationalist Theology.*
44. Shults, *The Post Foundationalist Task of Theology,* p. 43; for a detailed discussion of each of these four couplets, see pp. 43-77.

- The objective unity of truth is a necessary condition for the intelligible search for knowledge, and the subjective multiplicity of knowledge indicates the fallibility of truth claims.
- Rational judgment is an activity of socially situated individuals, and the cultural community indeterminately mediates the criteria of rationality.
- Explanation aims for universal, transcontextual understanding, and understanding derives from particular contextualized explanations.

The present work argues that it belongs to the nature and inner structure of Christian theology to pursue the truth of its statements if it is based on the conviction that its "object" is God and everything in relation to God. If so, then it means that, unlike classical liberalism, theology cannot suffice to be merely a hermeneutics of human experience of religiosity, even though that kind of analysis is part of the wider theological task. Similarly, in contrast to postliberalism but in keeping with the stated goal of the canonical-linguistic approach, theology must be interested in both the intratextual and extratextual "basis" of its claims. This is to say that doctrinal statements are more than just "rules" that express the ecclesiastical practices. Certainly doctrinal statements function as rules, but not merely in that capacity. At the same time, theology may at times critique and deconstruct given ecclesiastical practices and "ways of speaking." The ultimate authority of such a theological task is the canonical Scripture, not only in the way Scripture is used in the church,[45] but also on the basis of the "authorial intention."

The epistemological vision of postfoundationalism as outlined above will guide the present project, accepting the provisional, historical, limited, and perspectival nature of knowledge — yet, in pursuit of God's truth that precedes such an inquiry. That kind of epistemological attitude is appropriate in correlation with God's truth, which will be fully manifested only at the end of history. The historical process does not establish the truthfulness of Christian claims (after process theology) but rather manifests and brings to light the eternal purposes of the triune God toward the reconciliation and eschatological fulfillment of the divine promises.

While pursuing the truth of Christian doctrine, theology can no longer rely on mere assertion or ecclesiastical authority as in Christendom,[46]

45. As yet another postliberal theologian argues: Kelsey, *Proving Doctrine.*

46. For useful critique, see Pannenberg, *ST* 1:10-11.

nor on the "retreat to commitment"[47] as in much of Barthianism. What about the vision of (the British) Radical Orthodoxy in this respect? Rather than attempting a Tillichian correlational approach in which the "secular" philosophy and culture sets the questions and theology provides answers on the basis of Christian tradition, Radical Orthodoxy — if I correctly understand their (intentionally?) obscure writings — rather robustly seeks to present the Christian "worldview" as the only alternative, and consequently theology as the "queen of sciences." While I applaud the desire to rediscover the public nature of Christian theology and the refusal to let social theory (Milbank) or other disciplines set the "foundation," I also find the unwillingness to engage in mutual dialogue with either "secular" academic disciplines or other living faiths an exercise in futility. Perhaps I do not grasp fully the movement's vision, but it seems to me that with all its distinctive features, materially it does not differ essentially from that of Barth or the Yale School, or even of Stanley Hauerwas, whose approach in some important ways resembles that of Lindbeck and Frei. In contrast, this current project agrees with Philip Clayton's listing of the conditions of the pursuit of truth as one of the major theses for the program of "critical faith" for the third millennium: "Theologians cannot simply presuppose the truth of the Christian tradition but must be concerned in an ongoing way with the question of the truth of their central assertions."[48] To do this task well, theology must engage in continuous ecumenical and interdisciplinary dialogue.

Constructive Theology in Search of a Coherent Vision

On the one hand, systematic theology as a theological discipline is a fairly new phenomenon, going back no further than 1727 and the important work published by Johann Franz Buddeus. The defining feature of systematic theology for Buddeus and others was its goal of a comprehensive presentation of Christian doctrine, particularly as presented in the Bible. But not only presentation of the doctrine but also explanation, proving, and confirmation were part of the systematic task. On the other hand, materially the roots go back to the very beginnings of Christian tradition, to great doctrinal works by the apologists, Irenaeus, Origen, and others, and later, during me-

47. See Bartley, *Retreat to Commitment,* for a penetrating analysis of this tendency in much of the mid-twentieth-century theology.

48. Clayton, *Adventures in the Spirit,* p. 22.

dieval times, to the grand *summae* and *sentences.* The nomenclature *sacra doctrina* was common in the medieval era. And then there are the great works of the Reformers, such as Calvin's *Institutes.*[49] These are all precursors to what we call "systematic theologies" today. Alternative current terms for systematic theology include "constructive theology" and "doctrinal theology." In this project, the terms "constructive theology" and "systematic theology" are used synonymously.

For the purposes of this short orientation to the way systematic/constructive theology will be attempted in this project, the following description serves as the starting point. Let us set it forth and then parse it in some detail:

> Systematic/constructive theology is an integrative discipline that continuously searches for a coherent, balanced understanding of Christian truth and faith in light of Christian tradition (biblical and historical) and in the context of the historical and contemporary thought, cultures, and living faiths. It aims at a coherent, inclusive, dialogical, and hospitable vision.

Constructive theology's nature as an "integrative" discipline points to its most distinctive feature in the current theological curriculum. It means that in order to practice well constructive theology, one has to utilize the results, insights, and materials of all other theological disciplines, that is: biblical studies, church history and historical theology, philosophical theology, as well as ministerial studies. Closely related fields of religious studies, ethics, and missiology also belong to the texture of systematic work. That alone is a tall order. But as the rest of the working definition implies, to do constructive theology well, one has to engage also nontheological and nonreligious fields such as natural sciences, cultural studies, and, as will be evident in this project, the study of living faiths (most importantly, Judaism, Islam, Bud-

49. In the eighteenth century systematic theology included dogmatics and moral theology, or in a more expanded form, apologetics and polemics. Polemics was later replaced with comparative symbolics, the study of ancient "symbols" (creeds) and current confessional statements of different denominations. Ecumenical theology later picked up that task. In its current usage, systematic theology has a fairly fixed place in the theological curriculum, along with biblical studies, church history or historical theology, philosophical theology, and pastoral or ministerial studies. Ethics has its own locus currently. See further, Pannenberg, *ST* 1:17-19, and for a longer discussion, Pannenberg, *Theology and the Philosophy of Science,* pp. 404-23 particularly.

dhism, and Hinduism). The use of materials and insights, at times even methods (such as exegesis or historiography), however, is guided by the principle according to which the systematician must listen carefully to related disciplines but also go beyond their inputs, domains, and questions. While it would be absurd for constructive theologians not to engage deeply and widely relevant OT, NT, and historical theological materials, it would also limit severely the constructive task if the theologian were bound with the questions, issues, contributions, and insights of those fields. The constructive theologian asks many questions — say, in relation to inclusivity, care for environment, or science — that the Bible and much of church history are silent about. At the end of the constructive task, however, the constructive theologian should make sure the proposal is in keeping with biblical revelation and, hopefully, with the best of tradition.

The ultimate goal of constructive theology is not a "system" of doctrine — hence, the nomenclature "systematic" is most unfortunate! Rather, it seeks a coherent and balanced understanding. In terms of the theory of truth, it follows the suit of coherence theory. One current way of speaking of coherence is to compare it to a web or a net(work).[50] That metaphor is fitting as it speaks of the coherence theory's attempt to relate every statement to the other relevant statements and ultimately to the "whole." The nomenclature "coherence," however, may mean more than one thing. When applied to the theological task, one can only think of inner coherence, namely, the relation of theological statements to the rest of Christian tradition. This is of course the program of the cultural-linguistic method. Mistakenly — or at least, oddly — Vanhoozer labels all coherence theory-laden theologies types of postfoundationalism, which only seek for intratextual coherence. He complains that the web image in itself limits the use of the metaphor to only this "inner coherence" approach, since "[i]n a web of beliefs, no one belief is more important than any other."[51] That, however, is not necessarily the case. Rightly the philosopher Nancey Murphy, who operates with Quine's web metaphor, is fully alert to the potential charges of relativism and combats them quite successfully.[52] To ex-

50. This usage goes back to the important essay by the epistemologist W. V. O. Quine, "Two Dogmas of Empiricism," pp. 20-46.

51. Vanhoozer, *Drama of Doctrine,* p. 293.

52. For a careful discussion of the problem of relativism and ways of overcoming it, see Murphy, *Beyond Liberalism and Fundamentalism,* pp. 98-108. Discussion partners from whom she draws significant resources are the philosopher of science Imre Lakatos and the ethicist Alasdair MacIntyre, among others. Where I differ from Murphy is that I

tend the web metaphor: granted there are no foundations, but there are "hooks" from which it hangs!

This project builds on the important conviction that coherence theory, when applied to theology, must check the "correspondence" of its statements to both inner and external statements.[53] Hence, Christian theology, whose "object" is God and everything else stemming from the creative work of God (God being the "all-determining reality"), operates with the widest possible notion of coherence. Pannenberg puts it succinctly: "Systematic theology ascertains the truth of Christian doctrine by investigation and presentation of its coherence as regards both the interrelation of the parts and the relation to other knowledge."[54] This dual, mutually conditioning task, while calling for the best use and resources of rational thinking, also necessarily makes that task provisional, historical, and limited: history is still unfolding, and thus — as the hermeneutic phenomenological philosopher Wilhelm Dilthey convincingly argued already at the end of the nineteenth century — to see how "parts" fit into the "whole," we have to wait until the End to finally establish it![55] Hence, the important category of anticipation in all theological argumentation.[56] Talk about postfoundationalist dynamic!

If the principle of coherence in the search for the truth of Christian doctrinal claims is taken seriously, it also means that by its very nature, constructive theology should seek to engage not only theological resources but also cultural, religious, sociopolitical, and other resources. Two tasks emerge out of this orientation: first, the challenge of cultural and social diversity, and second, the engagement of religions and their claims for meaning and truth.

---

call my epistemology postfoundationalist whereas she prefers the term "nonfoundationalist." However, in my understanding, hers is not nonfoundationalist because, among other things, she takes it for granted that for Christian tradition (via MacIntyre's view of "tradition") the Bible is authoritative; see p. 108.

53. For the importance of the idea of coherence in current understanding of the nature and tasks of systematic theology, see essays by N. M. Healy and A. N. Williams in the theme issue of *International Journal of Systematic Theology* 11, no. 1 (2009).

54. Pannenberg, *ST* 1:21-22; see also pp. 18-19.

55. For a detailed discussion, see Pannenberg, *Theology and the Philosophy of Science*, chap. 2.

56. See further, Pannenberg, *ST* 1:54-55; *Theology and the Philosophy of Science*, pp. 69-70; see also pp. 42-43 (in relation to Karl Popper), pp. 100-104 (in relation to Niklas Luhman), and so forth.

Theology in Search of an Inclusive Vision

> Christian difference is always a complex and flexible network of small and large refusals, divergences, subversions, and more or less radical alternative proposals, surrounded by the acceptance of many cultural givens. There is no single correct way to relate to a given culture as a whole, or even to its dominant thrust; there are only numerous ways of accepting, transforming, or replacing various aspects of a given culture from within.[57]

This remark by the Croatian-born Yale theologian Miroslav Volf, whose theology is shaped by wartime experiences in the Balkans, reminds us of the urgency of paying attention to particular contexts as a mandatory task for any theology worth its name. Not only is late-modernity/postmodernity speaking to that effect with its preference for locality, particularity, and difference over "globality," universality, and sameness, but also the dramatic re-formation of the Christian church at the global level issues the call. Theology, the way it has been conducted not only in the past but also by and large even in the beginning of the third millennium, has not paid attention to diversity nor been inclusive. It has preferred — often to the point of excluding and marginalizing the voices of the other — the voice of the powers-that-be, or the hierarchy, or the scholarly elite. The Cuban-born church historian Justo González laments that one of the fallacies of traditional Western philosophy and theology is the confusion of the universal with dominance. This marginalizes theologies from other contexts, as

> North American male theology is taken to be basic, normative, universal theology, to which then women, other minorities, and people from the younger churches may add their footnotes. What is said in Manila is very relevant for the Philippines. What is said in Tübingen, Oxford or Yale is relevant for the entire church. White theologians do general theology; black theologians do black theology. Male theologians do general theology; female theologians do theology determined by their sex. Such a notion of "universality" based on the present unjust distribution of power is unacceptable to the new theology. If the nature of truth is . . .

57. Volf, "When Gospel and Culture Intersect," p. 233. According to Volf, liberal accommodationism, postliberal traditionalism, and sectarian retreat are all unsatisfactory ways of accounting for the cultural challenge (pp. 233-36).

> both in its historical concreteness and in its connection with orthopraxis, it follows that every valid theology must acknowledge its particularity and its connection with the struggles and the vested interests in which it is involved. A theology that refuses to do this and that leaps to facile claims of universal validity will have no place in the postreformation church of the twenty-first century.[58]

The call for Christian theology in the "post-" world is to set inclusivity as a stated goal. Inclusivity allows for diverse, at times even contradictory and opposing, voices and testimonies to be part of the dialogue. Inclusive "theologies are multiperspectival, multidisciplinary, and multicultural."[59] Multiperspectivalism, the Malaysian-born, Chinese American, Pentecostal theologian Amos Yong reminds us, means "taking seriously the insights of all voices, especially those previously marginalized from the theological conversation — for instance, women, the poor, the differently abled or disabled, perhaps even the heretics!"[60]

Inclusivity is not blind to the limitations we all bring to the task. Rather, it builds trust and room for each and every one to face one's limitations. Unlike too many theologians, Moltmann in his *Trinity and the Kingdom of God* freely "recognizes the conditions and limitations of his own position, and the relativity of his own particular environment."[61] This acknowledgment, however, is an asset rather than an obstacle for doing a more inclusive theology. Speaking of himself in the third person, Moltmann remarks: "For him this means a critical dissolution of naïve, self-centered thinking. Of course he is a European, but European theology no longer has to be Euro*centric.* Of course, he is a man, but theology no longer has to be *androcentric.* Of course he is living in the 'first world,' but the theology which he is developing does not have to reflect the ideas of the dominating nations."[62]

The theological enterprise in search of an inclusive vision opens up to the grand challenge of the "macroreformation" — to use the striking label of González[63] — taking place before our very eyes as Christianity is moving from the Global North (Europe and North America) to the Global South

58. González, *Mañana,* p. 52.
59. Yong, *The Spirit Poured Out on All Flesh,* pp. 239-40.
60. Yong, *The Spirit Poured Out on All Flesh,* p. 240.
61. Moltmann, *Trinity and the Kingdom,* p. xii.
62. Moltmann, *Trinity and the Kingdom,* p. xii, emphasis in original.
63. González, *Mañana,* p. 49.

(Africa, Asia, Latin America). This demographic shift in itself has turned the tables:[64] by 2050, only about one-fifth of the world's three billion Christians will be non-Hispanic whites. According to Philip Jenkins's *The Next Christendom,* the most recent attempt to take stock of the changes, the typical Christian in the first decades of the third millennium is a nonwhite, nonaffluent, non-Northern person, more often female. "If we want to visualize a 'typical' contemporary Christian, we should think of a woman living in a village in Nigeria or in a Brazilian *favela.*"[65] Or, as the Kenyan theologian John Mbiti has put it, "the centers of the church's universality [are] no longer in Geneva, Rome, Athens, Paris, London, New York, but Kinshasa, Buenos Aires, Addis Ababa and Manila."[66] Jenkins calls this phenomenon "Christianity going south,"[67] and as such, "one of the transforming moments in the history of religion" — not only of Christianity — worldwide.[68] Therefore, as the Korean Methodist Jung Young Lee reminds us, due to the dramatic demographic shift, "Christianity is no longer exclusively identified as a Western religion. In fact, Christianity is already not only a world religion but also a world Christianity. This means Christianity cannot be understood exclusively from a Western perspective."[69]

What are the implications for the theological task that takes up such a challenge? The late Yale theologian Hans Frei, in his posthumous work *Types of Christian Theology,*[70] classified contemporary theologies in a continuum of five approaches. Theologies of the first approach, at one extreme, seem to ignore the special context in which they are operating and build solely on Christian tradition, believing that they are doing "universal" theology applicable to all at all times (most theologies done by white male theologians in Europe and North America are examples of this approach).[71] At the other

WHAT ABOUT THEOLOGIES/STRUCTURES THAT HAVE STOOD THE TEST OF TIME?

64. For a current, short statement, see Parratt, "Introduction," p. 1.

65. Jenkins, *The Next Christendom,* p. 2.

66. Quoted in Bediako, *Christianity in Africa,* p. 154.

67. This is the basic thesis of Jenkins, *The Next Christendom;* see e.g., p. 3; he explains his choice of "North"-"South" as the dominant pattern especially in chap. 1; that chapter also includes good bibliographical references. The basic statistical source is Barrett, Kurian, and Johnson, *World Christian Encyclopedia;* for global statistics, see pp. 12-15 especially.

68. Jenkins, *The Next Christendom,* p. 1.

69. Lee, *Trinity in Asian Perspective,* p. 11.

70. Frei, *Types of Christian Theology.* This scheme is used for example in Ford, "Introduction to Modern Christian Theology," pp. 1-15. For the relevance and limitation of Frei's typology, see Grenz, *Theology for the Community of God,* pp. 19-20.

71. The specific examples are mine, not Frei's.

end of the continuum are those that take the surrounding context so seriously that little of the distinctive Christian message can be discerned; elements in the Christian tradition are used only if they fit in the context (death-of-God theologies of the "secular" 1960s, neopagan feminist theologies, and some extreme contextualizations in Asian and African contexts, for example). Most theologies currently fall in between. The second approach, while it takes Christian tradition as norm, still tries to make it understandable to the surrounding culture. Perhaps right-wing evangelicalism falls in this category. Tillich may be an ideal example of the middle, or third, position, with correlation between culture and Christianity the aim. The fourth option takes a particular philosophy or worldview as its primary guide and interprets Christian faith in that light while still wanting to hold on to Christian faith as much as possible. Process theology and a number of liberation approaches come to mind as candidates here.

This typology is of course only heuristic, and placement of theologians or theological movements on the continuum is highly subjective. However, the template makes an important point for the purposes of this project: theology is by nature contextual, whether theologians or theological movements acknowledge it or not. It is not the case that theology done by predominantly white male theologians would be "neutral" while, say, trinitarian theology of the Tanzanian Roman Catholic Charles Nyamiti, who takes as the framework African ancestral traditions, would be "contextual." They are both context-laden — just differently context-laden. The latter approach is more intentionally seeking for connections with the particular context.

As a result of this macroreformation, theology in the third millennium ought to be done collectively in the world community, negotiating differences and seeking new ways of framing questions and answers. As González puts it:

> One characteristic of our macroreformation is that voices are being heard from quarters that have not been the traditional centers of theological inquiry, and from people who have not been among the traditional theological leaders. When mission theoreticians in past decades spoke of the "three selfs" as a goal for younger churches, they included self-support, self-government, and self-propagation. They did not envision self-interpretation or self-theologizing. They expected theology to continue being what it was, for the meaning of the gospel was fully understood by the sending churches, and all that the younger ones had to

> do was continue proclaiming the same message. At best, these younger churches were to recast the message in terms of their own culture.[72]

Doing theology in this way does not of course mean that Christian tradition is to be undervalued. That would be not only naive but also counterproductive. Much of contemporary theology in particular locations and contexts draws its energy from a careful, painstaking, and often tension-filled dialogue with and response to tradition. Theological tradition is the heritage of the whole church of Christ on earth, not only of the church in the Global North. Irenaeus, Augustine, Aquinas, Calvin, and Schleiermacher have contributed — and are contributing — to the growing living tradition of Christian theological reflection in all locations in our shrinking globe, albeit differently depending on the context. Therefore, this volume is also critical of those kinds of "contextual" or "intercultural" theologies that simply naively dismiss tradition and claim to begin from scratch, in other words, merely from the "context(s)." A landmark volume written by two leading Roman Catholic missiologists in the United States, titled *Constants in Context,*[73] accurately illustrates the need for Christian theology to negotiate the *constant* features of Christian beliefs and doctrines in changing, diverse, and often perplexing *contexts.* Christian theology has tried more than one way to "accommodate" the cultural challenge; some of the approaches have been less than successful.

The term "global," often used in these kinds of conversations, has to be handled with great care. What "global" means is that in the presentation and argumentation of constructive theology, voices, testimonies, and perspectives from around the world and from different agendas will be engaged. It is a communion of local conversations in interrelated dialogue. At the same time, we should be mindful of the danger that "global" smacks of modernity's preference for "universal," grand projects and concepts. One way to illustrate this dynamic is to coin a new word, tried by some contemporary speakers, namely, "glocal," a hybrid of "global" and "local."[74] The term was invented a

72. González, *Mañana,* p. 49. So also Kärkkäinen, *Pneumatology,* p. 147: "In our contemporary world, theology has the burden of showing its culture sensitivity. Theology can no longer be the privilege of one people group. Instead, it must be context specific as it addresses God and God's world in specific situations and in response to varying needs and challenges."

73. Bevans and Schroeder, *Constants in Context.*

74. See further, Dyrness and Kärkkäinen, introduction to *Global Dictionary of Theology,* pp. vii-xiv.

"glocal"

few years ago in the interdisciplinary debate about the meaning of "globalization"[75] and has been subsequently used by some Christian missiologists,[76] among others. The Reformed missiologist Charles Van Engen speaks to this issue: "In the twenty-first century, the church of Jesus Christ needs to become self-consciously what it in fact already is: a *glocal* church. . . . [A] healthy congregation of disciples of Jesus lives out its catholicity by intentionally and actively participating in Christ's mission that dynamically fosters the glocal interaction between the global and the local."[77]

The intentionally ambiguous and idiosyncratic meaning of "glocal" reflects appropriately the nature of this project's goal and ethos. The way constructive theology searches for "global" theology is by employing theologies that are authentically "local" in the sense of being reflective of particular locations. "Global" does not mean that we are envisioning the kind of "universal" theology that can speak to all places at all times. What is most distinctive about "global" theology is its diversity, richness, and plurality. Intentionally "contextual," "global," and "inclusive" theology — a "glocal" theology for the "post-" world of ours — seeks to present and argue for the truth of God in a coherent way that engages the whole catholic church of Christ, men and women, rich and poor, people from different ethnic and racial backgrounds. This "universal"[78] vision is in keeping with the endless richness, variety, and diversity of God's creative work and the needs of the kind of world we live in. In the religiously diverse world of ours, that task also calls for a careful and sustained engagement of living faiths and their claims to truth and meaning.

Theology in Search of a Dialogical Vision

Even though, as mentioned above, Pannenberg deplores the replacement in modern Protestant theology of the concept of God with the concept of religion — thus circumventing the question of the truthfulness of the Christian claims to the reality of God — he is not thereby dismissing the significance

75. See further, Tai and Wong, "Advertising Decision Making in Asia," pp. 318-19; Rosenau, *Distant Proximities.*

76. Subheading in Van Engen, "The Glocal Church," pp. 157-79.

77. Van Engen, "The Glocal Church," p. 157.

78. The term "universal" here has nothing to do with the modernist tendency to delete differences and subsume the other under one's own world explanation. Hence, it is put in quotation marks.

of religions and the study of them for Christian systematic theology. The most important reason for Pannenberg to include the study of religions and their insights as well as truth claims in the systematic task is that it is in the arena of the history of religions that the contestation of the reality of gods takes place. In that sense, religions have some kind of "revelatory" role to play. Hence, the task of pursuing the coherence of Christian doctrine necessitates the relating of truth claims to all reality; religions, certainly, play a crucial role in the experience of the world. As a result, Pannenberg boldly argues that since religious studies *(Religionswissenschaft)* in the aftermath of the Enlightenment have made the study of religions a "secular" discipline, rejecting categorically the possibility of the truthfulness of religions' claim to the existence and reality of God/gods/deities, a *theological* study of religions is a mandatory task. And Pannenberg boldly suggests that as long as no other theological discipline is doing the study of religions — except for missiology, but that merely for the "practical" reasons of preparing Christian ministers to operate in multifaith settings, rather than from a theological point of view — it is left to systematic theology to pursue it. The reason for systematic theology to be entrusted with that task, as opposed to, say, missiology or ministerial studies, simply is, as mentioned above, that in contemporary academic theology as it is pursued particularly in university settings, only systematic theology makes the truth of Christian doctrine a theological theme.[79] Astonishingly — and ironically — Pannenberg fails to redeem that promise as he lays out his theological *summa* as the comprehensive presentation of constructive theology![80] Of course, sadly enough, this

79. Pannenberg, *Theology and the Philosophy of Science,* p. 369: "Until religious studies develop into a theology of religions in the sense described here [i.e., that they allow for the possibility of the truthfulness of religions' claims for the existence of the deities], and so become the basic discipline of theology in general, this basic theological work must be accommodated provisionally within systematic theology." See also pp. 313-21, 324-25, 360-71, 420-21; and Pannenberg, *ST* 1, chap. 3. For an early programmatic essay, see his "Toward a Theology of the History of Religions," 2:65-118.

80. His excuse for not engaging religions in the preface to his first volume of *Systematic Theology* (p. xii) sounds lame at its best: "Those familiar with my book on theology and the philosophy of science will perhaps expect from me a presentation of Christian doctrine that does more to interact with other religious positions than is the case here. In this respect it should be noted that the classification of Christianity within the world religions and their conflicting truth claims is fundamentally posited. . . . As a result an express comparison with other religions might enter into the self-explication of the content of Christian revelation to a greater degree than it does in the following presentation. A systematic comparison between the competing conception of the world religions

German theologian does not differ from tradition or even contemporary practice of systematicians and other theologians. But at least Pannenberg has convincingly argued that an appropriate systematic task cannot be conducted apart from the engagement of other religions and their claims to truth and meaning.

The obvious "practical" reason for Christian theology to enter into a sustained dialogue with other religions is the prevailing diversity of religions. The introductory remarks by John Habgood, archbishop of York, to a compilation of essays on "interfaith and religious tolerance" (under the title *Many Mansions*) illustrate aptly the changed situation of religions in our world in the third millennium. "Other faiths used to belong to other lands. At home rival religious claims could safely be ignored. Or, if not ignored, patronized. The superiority of one's own faith was so evident that the alternatives could somehow be brought within its purview without posing any real theological or social threat. Today things are different. Different faiths are practiced cheek by jowl in most parts of the world."[81]

Other religions, which used to be distant, exotic topics for enjoyable conversation, if not a vague reality that could be totally ignored, have come much closer to us whether we live in the Global North or elsewhere. Religious plurality is not only "out there," but also in our backyards — or rather, in our front yards.[82]

In itself, the challenge of religious plurality is of course not new. Not only did the early church find herself proclaiming salvation in Christ among competing religions, but already in the Old Testament the faith of the people of God was threatened constantly by the faiths of the surrounding peoples. The Shema, the confession of Israel's faith, was fashioned among pressures from a legion of gods and goddesses: "The LORD is our God, the LORD is one!" (Deut. 6:4 NASB). Or think of the exchange between Christians and Muslims right from the beginning of the introduction of the latter faith to areas in which Christianity had already established itself. What makes the

---

is certainly a task that will more fully occupy systematic theology in the future. Perhaps in this field a particularly important contribution might be made to Christian theology by the Third World churches."

81. Habgood, "Preface," p. vii.

82. The missiologist and philosopher Harold Netland's comment may be — purposefully — an overstatement, but it is worth hearing. He argues that by the 1990s, the symbols of Hindu, Buddhist, and Taoist spirituality were so prevalent that it was increasingly difficult to distinguish "the East" from "the West." Netland, *Encountering Religious Pluralism*, p. 106.

current religious context unique is the intensity of religious communication and exchange. Whereas in the past the religious other could be ignored, nowadays that is not possible — let alone when we think of the radical transformation of the composition of the Christian church now that the majority of Christ's followers live in the Global South. It will soon be a commonplace for Christians to live in daily contact with followers of other living faiths, rather than in Christendom-cherished isolation.

That said, for the purposes of this brief prolegomenon to systematic theology, it is crucial to mention that as important and impending as the "practical" reason for engaging the religious other may be — in terms of establishing a pedagogical contact, helping Christians live in a civil way with the other, and preparing them to witness to Christ in the matrix of religious convictions — systematic/constructive theology could relegate that task to other theological disciplines such as missiology or ministerial studies unless the task materially belonged to its own domain. This project builds on the conviction argued above that in order for constructive theology to pursue the task of coherent argumentation of the truth of Christian doctrine, its claims must be related to not only the internal but also the external spheres. Religions certainly form an essential part of human experience and the experience of the world. In this process, the self-understanding of Christian faith may also be clarified and deepened — and if the engagement is done in an authentic and respectful way, the religious other may also benefit. A hospitable relating to the other not only makes space for a genuine presentation and identification of one's own position but also opens up for a careful listening to the testimonies and convictions of the other.[83]

For constructive theology to engage other religions and make their insights part of the systematic argumentation, an interdisciplinary approach is necessary. Three interrelated, yet distinct, disciplines come into play, namely, religious studies/comparative religions, theology of religions, and particularly comparative theology. Before introducing briefly these fields, we recall what was mentioned above: that systematic theology by its very nature builds on and engages critically contributions from several theological disciplines. Hence, widening the scope of the sources of contributions is not a materially different methodological choice from the past; it is rather a necessary refinement and expansion of methodological orientation.

Christian theology of religions seeks to reflect critically and sympathet-

83. See further, Kärkkäinen, "Dialogue, Witness, and Tolerance," pp. 29-33.

ically on the theological meaning of religions in the economy of God.[84] "Theology of religions is that discipline of theological studies which attempts to account theologically for the meaning and value of other religions. Christian theology of religions attempts to think theologically about what it means for Christians to live with people of other faiths and about the relationship of Christianity to other religions."[85] While in principle there could be theologies of religions from the point of view of any religion, say Islam, Christian tradition has so far excelled in this enterprise.[86] A growing number of theologians are becoming disenchanted with the potential of Christian theology of religions for many reasons, including that it tends to stay at too generic a level and that it may fail to engage the other from the perspective of that other's tradition, and so forth.[87] Hence, in recent years a complementary and more focused way of engaging in mutual dialogue of religious traditions is attempted under the rubric "comparative theology." Although the term has been used before,[88] in its current usage it is understood in two interrelated ways: as a branch of the history of religions that seeks to compare theologies from different religious traditions, and as a theological enterprise that studies two or more religious traditions on certain specific topics.[89] To accomplish its task, comparative theology gleans resources not only from Christian theology and theology of religions but also from comparative religions, which (along with the related but distinct fields of the history of religions and other disciplines in religious studies, phenomenology of religions, and social scientific study of religions) investigates "ideas, words, images and acts, historical developments — as found in two or more traditions or strands of tradition."[90]

Whereas comparative religion seeks to be "neutral" on faith commitments and look "objectively" at the features of religious traditions, and typically does not allow for the reality of gods/deities of religions, *comparative*

84. The Roman Catholic Jacques Dupuis preferred to name it "theology of religious pluralism." See his monumental work, Dupuis, *Toward a Christian Theology of Religious Pluralism.* See further, Dhavamony, *Christian Theology of Religions,* pp. 10-11.

85. Kärkkäinen, *An Introduction to the Theology of Religions,* p. 20.

86. For discussion of Muslim theology of religions in dialogue with Christian traditions, see Winkler, *Contemporary Muslim and Christian Responses to Religious Plurality.*

87. For a penetrating critique of theology of religions, see Fredericks, *Faith among Faiths;* Schebera, "Comparative Theology," pp. 7-18.

88. For historical antecedents and the way the term was used earlier, see further, Clooney, *Comparative Theology,* chap. 2.

89. Tracy, "Comparative Theology," p. 446.

90. Clooney, *Comparative Theology,* p. 9.

theology — "*comparative* and *theological* beginning to end — marks acts of faith seeking understanding which are rooted in a particular faith tradition but which, from that foundation, venture into learning from one or more other faith traditions. This learning is sought for the sake of fresh theological insights that are indebted to the newly encountered tradition/s as well as the home tradition."[91] Comparative theology is robustly Christian theology; it is committed to its traditions and contemporary expressions.

There is a deep, built-in dynamic between unwavering commitment to one's own tradition and bold openness for a dialogical engagement and learning from others. "In our religiously diverse context, a vital theology has to resist too tight a binding by tradition, but also the idea that religious diversity renders strong claims about truth and value impossible."[92] Hence, comparative theology, like Christian theology — as long as it is both *Christian* rather than a "pan-religious" mixing of aspects of insights from here and there[93] and *theological* rather than a sociological description of church practices or merely an analysis of human interpretations of human religiosity — is both an act of faith and a spiritual practice.[94] Thereby is not denied or compromised its status as an academic discipline, which follows the strict procedures and principles of any similar academic field in the humanities.

An important part of this task is to "inscribe within the Christian theological tradition theological texts from outside it, and to (begin to) write Christian theology only out of that newly composed context."[95] Different from the theology of religion's more generic approach, comparative theology makes every effort to consider in detail topics in religious traditions. "It is detailed, deeply reflexive, self-corrective in the course of its own investigation, even in regard to its basic questions, methods, and vocabulary."[96]

91. Clooney, *Comparative Theology,* p. 10. "Comparative theology must not be confused with comparative religion, since faith is a necessary and explicit factor in the former and not in the latter, where its influence might even be ruled out. But the fields need not be separated entirely, since comparative theology still has to measure up to expected disciplinary standards regarding the religions being compared" (p. 12).

92. Clooney, *Comparative Theology,* p. 8.

93. This is the fallacy of Smart and Konstantine, *Christian Systematic Theology in a World Context,* which seeks to develop a Christian-based more or less generic account of some key doctrinal themes. For a discussion and critique, see Kärkkäinen, *The Trinity,* chap. 16.

94. For fine insights, see Clooney, *Comparative Theology,* pp. 10-11.

95. Clooney, *Theology after Vedānta,* p. 7.

96. Clooney, "Comparative Theology," pp. 521-22.

One may hear the objection that it is only Christianity (and perhaps Judaism) that is "theological," strictly speaking. While as an academic discipline "theology" is by and large limited to the Christian sphere,[97] this is not to deny that in some qualified sense it is appropriate and useful to speak of "theologies" of different living faiths. Clooney makes the compelling case for such an opinion. He argues for Hindu theology and Hindu comparative theology, though without arguing that Hindu theology is exactly like Christian theology.[98] Hence, his choice of texts from various Hindu traditions presumes the possibility of making theological comparisons because "Hindu traditions such as Mimamsa[99] and Vedanta are best described as 'theological.'" Furthermore, not only do the faithful in each tradition have a "faith," but, to a growing extent, they are also aware of the growing diversity and thus the need to engage others.[100]

Scholars engaged in the enterprise of comparative theology come from two different backgrounds.[101] Some are trained as scholars of religions such as the two Catholics Francis Clooney (Hinduism) and James L. Fredericks (Buddhism, among others), whereas others are theologians, most notably the systematician and philosopher Keith Ward. This Oxford divinity professor has launched the most ambitious and wide-reaching project in comparative theology ever attempted by a theologian. His four-volume work focuses on revelation, creation and God, human nature, and community, and seeks to develop a robustly Christian account of these four key loci in intense and detailed dialogue with Judaism, Islam, Buddhism, and Hinduism. He rightly describes his project as "a systematic Christian theology, undertaken in a comparative context."[102] In other words, it is an "open orthodoxy," a faithful, open-minded, and developing construction of Christian faith.[103]

Systematicians and other theologians of course face the great challenge of overcoming lacunae in the detailed knowledge of religions. For example, Ward admits throughout his project that his knowledge of religions is lim-

97. See Moltmann, *Experiences in Theology,* p. 43.

98. Clooney, *Comparative Theology,* p. 78.

99. A liturgical ritual tradition in Hinduism.

100. Clooney, *Comparative Theology,* p. 78.

101. For an up-to-date and highly useful mapping out and analysis of most important contributions to comparative theology, see Clooney, *Comparative Theology,* chap. 3.

102. Ward, *Religion and Community,* p. 339. The final chapter of this final volume, chap. 14, offers another focused discussion of method, now in hindsight.

103. See further, Ward, *Religion and Revelation,* pp. 1-2. The remaining two volumes are: Ward, *Religion and Creation* and *Religion and Human Nature.*

ited in that it is based on careful reading of texts, along with some important personal contacts. In my case, only Buddhism — Theravada tradition, to be more precise — is familiar to me at a more personal and experience-based level from the years I spent in Thailand as a teacher of Christian theology. Even though I am fluent in Thai and can thus read many Buddhist writings inaccessible to Western scholars, I am still woefully an outsider. However, having a firsthand exposure to one specific tradition also translates into how one studies other traditions. As a continuing student of Hinduism, Islam, and Judaism, I read their texts differently from how I did before living with Buddhists as a young theologian.[104]

It goes without saying that my project naturally gleans from the method and insights of comparative theology as well as from the Christian theology of religions. In its use of those resources, this project rests on the conviction that a dialogical approach is an essential asset in the pursuit of truth, rather than denying differences. The latter fallacy stems from pluralisms that naively follow modernity's love for universal ways of explanation, coupled often with the highly dubious idea of the common core of religions. "Dialogue has to be about the question of truth, even if no agreement about the truth can be reached. For consensus is not the goal of the dialogue. . . . If two people say the same thing, one of them is superfluous. In the interfaith dialogue which has to do with what is of vital and absolute concern to men and women — with the things in which they place the whole trust of their hearts — the way is already part of the goal."[105] Moltmann rightly says that only those people are capable of dialogue — "merit dialogue," as he puts it — who "have arrived at a firm standpoint in their own religion, and who enter into dialogue with the resulting self-confidence." Thus, Moltmann continues, "it is only if we are at home in our own religion that we shall be able to encounter the religion of someone else. The person who falls victim to the relativism of the multicultural society may be capable of dialogue, but that person does not merit dialogue."[106]

Engaging not only the cultural diversity within the vastly globalizing

104. In my studying of religions I am greatly helped by my locations, as a scholar in a highly international divinity school with doctoral students coming from locations in which interfaith encounter is an essential part of religiosity. During the writing of this volume, a Vietnamese student is working on Buddhist-Christian-atheist relations, a Japanese student on Shinto-Christian views of Spirit/spirits, an Egyptian student on early Muslim-Christian polemics, and so forth.

105. Moltmann, *Experiences in Theology,* pp. 19-20.

106. Moltmann, *Experiences in Theology,* pp. 18-19.

Christian church but also the religious diversity is a laborious and in many ways annoying project as it takes theologians to the edge not only of their intellectual capacities but also of their emotional comfort zones. Clooney puts it well:

> If we are attentive to the diversity around us, near us, we must deny ourselves the easy confidences that keep the other at a distance. But, as believers, we must also be able to defend the relevance of the faith of our community, deepening our commitments even alongside other faiths that are flourishing nearby. We need to learn from other religious possibilities, without slipping into relativist generalizations. The tension between open-mindedness and faith, diversity and traditional commitment, is a defining feature of our era, and neither secular society nor religious authorities can make simple choices before us.[107]

Theology in Search of a Hospitable Vision

Theology, robustly inclusivistic in its orientation, welcoming testimonies, insights, and interpretations from different traditions and contexts, can also be a truly dialogical enterprise. It honors the otherness of the other. It also makes space for an honest, genuine, authentic sharing of one's convictions. In pursuing the question of truth as revealed by the triune God, constructive theology also seeks to persuade and convince with the power of dialogical, humble, and respectful argumentation.

Theology, then, becomes an act of hospitality, giving and receiving gifts. This is in keeping with the Christian vision of the triune God as the Giver and Sustainer of Life.[108] The basic Greek verb *didomi* appears over 400 times in the NT. It is used of both human and divine giving, and encompasses all levels, from most concrete to most abstract.[109] The Finnish ecumenist Risto Saarinen aptly notes: "Giving and receiving are basic human actions. In religious life, giving can also be portrayed as divine action. God is the supreme giver, whereas human persons remain receivers."[110] Among the

107. Clooney, *Comparative Theology,* p. 7.

108. An important discussion of the theme can be found in Newlands and Smith, *Hospitable God.*

109. For an insightful discussion, see Saarinen, *God and Gift,* pp. 36-45.

110. Saarinen, *God and Gift,* p. 1.

theologians who have developed the christological, trinitarian, and soteriological notions of gift most prominently, Martin Luther stands out.[111] Recent research on Luther's theology claims that the doctrine of justification is not the key to Luther's theology — even though it is the center of later Lutheranism — but rather his theology of love.[112] The implications of Luther's theology of God and its relation to love, gift, and hospitality will be studied in the context of the doctrine of revelation and of God.

Human giving always entails an element of faith: one never knows of the intentions of others[113] — or those of the recipient! No wonder many contemporary thinkers are seriously doubting if "hospitality" and "gift" are possible goals to attain. These scholars are also wondering if any intellectual enterprise such as constructive theology — particularly conducted with a view to pursuing the truth of "God," as is the case in this project — is anything but an act of hospitality. It rather smacks of imperialism, exclusivism, even violence.

All agree with Aristotle that gift is "something given without recompense" (*Topics* 125a18). But not everyone is convinced that is possible in our kind of world. Marcel Mauss's *Essay on the Gift,* originally published in 1924,[114] on the basis of anthropological observations of societies before monetary economy, is a profound analysis of the vicious circle that may result when persons and groups are driven into reciprocal "paying back" for the hospitality received. One's status, and thus the structure of hierarchy, may be dependent on the amount and quality of giving to others.[115] Jacques Derrida's *Given Time*[116] is a current massive attempt to deconstruct the whole notion of the possibility of gift. The reason is simply this: in our world, there is no way of giving a gift without the expectation of some kind

111. See the important essay by Sammeli Juntunen, "The Notion of 'Gift' (Donum) in Luther's Theology," pp. 53-69; see also Saarinen, *God and Gift,* pp. 45-57 particularly.

112. This is the basic thesis of Mannermaa, *Kaksi rakkautta;* Mannermaa, "Why Is Luther So Fascinating?" p. 3: "Luther's entire theology thereby takes on the character of a consistent theology of love."

113. See Saarinen, *God and Gift,* p. 6.

114. Mauss, *Essay on the Gift.* A useful introduction to basic philosophical, sociological, and anthropological issues of gift is Schrift, ed., *The Logic of Gift.* Helpful also is Caputo and Scanlon, eds., *God, the Gift, and Postmodernism.*

115. Whereas Mauss suggests that in contemporary society societal institutions such as a market economy or public welfare have replaced much of the traditional giving-network, Jacques Godbout *(The World of the Gift)* argues that even in our societies a system of gift giving exists, based on generosity rather than utilitarianism as in a market economy. Examples include Christmas gifts or blood donation.

116. Derrida, *Given Time: 1. Counterfeit Money.*

of reciprocity. This state of affairs makes the whole notion of gift impossible. Similarly, Derrida renders impossible any notion of hospitality. Even the most altruistically considered act of hospitality is interwoven with hidden notions of violence and power. To illustrate the subtle nature of the impossibility of hospitality, consider this example: with reference to *The Apology of Socrates,* in which the sage defends himself amidst the Athenians and judges, mentioning that he is a "foreigner" without knowledge of the language of the court, Derrida argues that the need of a foreigner to have translation in order for us to speak with him is an act of violence. Foreign language is "imposed on him by the master of the house."[117]

Derrida builds on the legacy of the Jewish thinker Emmanuel Levinas. With its preoccupation with ontological categories catering to understanding and mastering the world outside of us, Western philosophical tradition has violence and power built into its very structure. This means suppressing the otherness of the other.[118] Rather than philosophy thus conceived, ethics should be at the place of primacy. Rather than trying to deny or avoid or oppress the alterity, Levinas surmises that any encounter with the other puts us under the obligation of hospitality. This obligation is without any limits.[119] Indeed, Derrida radicalizes the principle of "unconditional hospitality" in contrast to conditional hospitality[120] to the point that we should "say yes to who or what turns up, before any determination, before any anticipation, before any *identification,*"[121] even if the guest "may be the devil"![122] Posi-

117. Dufourmantelle and Derrida, *Of Hospitality,* p. 15. He begins the dialogue in the book with this paragraph: "Isn't the question of the foreigner [*l'étranger*] a foreigner's question? Coming from the foreigner, from abroad [*l'étranger*]" (p. 3).

118. Levinas, *Basic Philosophical Writings,* p. 11. Levinas regards Martin Heidegger as the basic instigator for the obsession with "being" of modern Western philosophy.

119. See further, Peperzak, *To the Other,* p. 22. I am indebted to Boersma, *Violence, Hospitality, and the Cross,* p. 12, for this reference.

120. An example of conditional hospitality for Derrida is the classic manifesto of Kant, *Perpetual Peace;* "The Third Definitive Article of Perpetual Peace" defines the conditions of "universal hospitality" based on right: provided the guest behaves peaceably and understands that he or she can't stay there indefinitely (pp. 137-38). (The extended introduction by the translator [pp. 1-105!] is a highly interesting discussion that places Kant's essay in the religious, historical, and philosophical context.) A number of times Derrida engages and critiques the Kantian notion of "hospitality of right" and instead suggests his own notion of the hospitality of unconditionality; see, e.g., Dufourmantelle and Derrida, *Of Hospitality,* pp. 25-27.

121. Dufourmantelle and Derrida, *Of Hospitality,* p. 77.

122. Derrida, "Hospitality, Justice, and Responsibility," p. 70; in the beginning of

tively put, the "welcoming" has to be so much without conditions that there is not even an "invitation" — just a "surprise" at the coming of the guest. Derrida refers to the arrival of the Messiah who "arrive[s] whenever he or she wants. She may even not arrive."[123] The last sentence also betrays Derrida's distinctive eschatology.[124] Not that he expects a Jewish or a Christian Messiah to arrive; indeed, he doesn't expect any Messiah to come. That is his deconstructed eschatological "reserve," which for him symbolizes absolute openness not only to the guest but also to the future.[125] All this is to say that for Derrida (and Levinas), hospitality is an impossible concept. It will never realize itself, as it requires perfect conditions, and it never arrives.

Constructive Christian theology in search of a hospitable vision should consider carefully Derrida's warning. At the same time, his agnosticism concerning hospitality has to be subjected to constructive criticism. His warning is of course helpful in exposing the always-violence-driven nature of human exchange and the impossibility of gift giving in a total spirit of altruism. When giving something to someone, we always also exclude others from receiving gifts. Such are the conditions of the limited, fallen existence of ours. That said, it does not necessarily follow that *all* exchange is based on violence, nor that *no* gifts can be called gifts. The discussion of the doctrine of creation shows the value of all creation created good by the Creator. Creation is a profound gift. Furthermore, it is unrealistic to expect perfect quality from human persons who are less than perfect. We should be realistic rather than utopian. The notion of "gracing relationship" may be theologically and philosophically a more desirable and possible goal for human exchange and relations. It is a "relationship where both parties are recognized by each other as someone not determined by the conditions of one's own horizon, but rather as an Other, a relationship that is not part of the world and the concrete expectations (or anticipations) of the other. Hence, in such a relationship one is invited into the world of the other by means of an open invitation."[126] Such an open invitation and receiving of the other doesn't have to be perfect; it can still be ideal, a goal.

---

the dialogue, Derrida also helpfully explains his take on the term "deconstruction" (pp. 65-66 particularly).

123. Derrida, "Hospitality, Justice, and Responsibility," p. 70.

124. Rightly pointed out by Boersma, *Violence, Hospitality, and the Cross*, p. 30.

125. This is explained in Derrida, "Faith and Knowledge," p. 17; the abovementioned "Dialogue with Jacques Derrida" also refers (p. 68) to this essay (in its earlier lecture form from 1994) as a gateway to developing unconditional hospitality.

126. Henriksen, *Desire, Gift, and Recognition*, pp. 44-45.

Most importantly, there is a difference between the human and divine hospitality and gift giving. While the former is limited and imperfect, the latter is absolute and possible, as discussed in the context of the doctrine of God. Only the divine gift can be a "pure gift."[127] Only with the coming of the eschatological kingdom is it possible for men and women to participate in hospitality without the limits of the fallen world. When it comes to violence and hospitality, the relationship is more complex than Derrida's discussion implies. On the one hand, the concept of violence has to be defined more carefully; on the other hand, hospitality, rather than "welcoming" all forms of violence, should join forces with the resistance of the works of the "devil" and join in the pursuit of justice, love, and fairness.[128]

The theological vision pursued in this project, a coherent presentation of Christian truth that would be inclusive to the cultural and global diversity of Christ's followers and at the same time learn from and make a contribution to other living faith traditions — in other words, be an act of hospitality — is through and through dialogical, inviting, mutual. Moltmann captures succinctly some key aspects of this vision:

> [T]ruth is to be found in unhindered dialogue. Fellowship and freedom are the human components for knowledge of the truth, the truth of God. And the fellowship I mean here is the fellowship of mutual participation and unifying sympathy. . . . This free community of men and women, without privilege and without discrimination, may be termed the earthly body of truth. . . . [I]t is only in free dialogue that truth can be accepted for the only right and proper reason — namely, that it illuminates and convinces *as* truth. Truth brings assent, it brings about change without exerting compulsion. In dialogue the truth frees men and women for their own conceptions and their own ideas. . . . Christian theology would wither and die if it did not continually stand in a dialogue like this, and if it were not bound up with a fellowship that seeks this dialogue, needs it and continually pursues it.[129]

127. See the important discussion in Tanner, *Economy of Grace,* pp. 58, 63.

128. For a helpful discussion, see Boersma, *Violence, Hospitality, and the Cross,* pp. 35-38.

129. Moltmann, *Trinity and the Kingdom,* pp. xii-xiii, emphasis in original.

I. CHRIST

Few Christian theologians would oppose the claim that Christology, the doctrine of Christ's person and work, lies at the heart of Christian theology. As the Roman Catholic John P. Galvin puts it succinctly: "While no theology can confine itself exclusively to Christology, no Christian theology would be complete without serious reflection on Jesus Christ."[1] The keen interest in christological topics is not only confined to traditional theological academia. As the Nigerian theologian and bishop John Olorunfemi Onaiyekan remarks, the claim that "Christology is at the very heart of all Christian theology . . . is particularly true for African Christian theology."[2]

That said, the last two hundred years have also testified to ever-diversifying and intense debates about what is Christology, what are its main claims, and how to do Christology, so to speak, in the aftermath of modernity, and now in the dynamic matrix of modernity, postmodernity/later-modernity, globalization, and culture-religious diversity. The positive side effect of this debate has been an unprecedented interest and productivity in key christological topics, particularly in Protestant theology and, from the mid–twentieth century on, also in Roman Catholic theology.

In light of the short discussion on theological method in the introduction to this volume, it is a truism that there hardly is a chosen "method" of Christology. Proliferation of approaches, perspectives, and procedures is the order of the day. However — or perhaps: particularly for that reason — the

1. Galvin, "Jesus Christ," p. 256.

2. Onaiyekan, "Christological Trends in Contemporary African Theology," p. 356.

theological investigation into Christology has to begin with some remarks on the "method." In keeping with this methodological vision, the ensuing discussion of part I will begin with a careful look at the theological significance of Jesus' earthly life and ministry, focusing on the importance of the messianic ministry in deeds, words, and reaching out to the marginalized of the society (chap. 2). An integral part of that discussion is the investigation of the theological meaning of Jesus' earthly ministry in various local contexts such as in Africa and in varying life-situations and agendas, including those of women, black theologians, Latin American and other liberationists, as well as postcolonialists (chap. 3). Chapter 4 places the theological meaning of Jesus' ministry and emerging confession of faith in his person within the wider Jewish messianic context and seeks connections with and distinctive features from the OT messianic expectations.

Before launching the lengthier discussion of standard christological topics stemming from creedal traditions, a focused reflection on the meaning of Chalcedon is in order (chap. 5). The Christian confession of the deity and humanity of Jesus Christ, based on the historical and theological claim of his resurrection, will occupy chapter 6; that discussion both affirms the material content of the classical creeds and seeks to revise it in light of contemporary systematic, historical, and biblical research. The interrelated topics of incarnation and *kenosis,* preexistence, virgin birth, and sinlessness will be studied next (chap. 7). Chapter 8 focuses on the relation of Christ to Spirit/Spirit to Christ and its implications for understanding the person and ministry of the Messiah.

In light of its importance to the discussion of religious plurality and pluralisms, the topic of incarnation will be taken up again in chapter 9 with the focus on contemporary Christian efforts both in the Global North and Asia to make Christian confession of the divine embodiment more inclusive and capable of linking with other faiths. While engagement of other living faiths, where relevant, takes place throughout the discussion of this volume (as well as the rest of the series), the last, long chapter will focus on specific and concentrated dialogues with Jewish, Islamic, Buddhist, and Hindu traditions. That dialogue will be taken up again at the end of part II of this volume. (The detailed plan for part II will be presented in the beginning of that section.)

1. How to Do Christology

On the "Method"

The traditional methodological problem of Christology is simply this: "Should we begin with the basis in God and his initiative in sending the Son, or should we move on the plane of human reality, on which we must show that the event took place, if it really took place at all?"[1] The Christology "From Above" as presented in the NT simply begins with lofty titles related to Jesus Christ expressing belief in the divinity. The postbiblical traditions culminating in the classic creeds conceive the uniqueness of Jesus Christ through the lens of the preexistent divine Son of God in relation to God himself. With the mind-set of the Enlightenment, prepared by the anti-trinitarian and Socinian doubts toward the deity and preexistence of the Son, the Christology "From Below" emerged. In this approach, the historical Christ is the starting point and criterion.[2] Whether it culminates in the confession of the deity — and thus becomes "From Below to Above"[3] — was considered to be the matter of historical and critical investigation.[4]

1. Pannenberg, *ST* 2:277.

2. For a careful and well-informed investigation of the quest of the historical Jesus as it emerged in the aftermath of the Enlightenment, see C. Brown, *Jesus in European Protestant Thought (1778-1860).*

3. As Pannenberg (*ST* 2:279) prefers to call it. Here Pannenberg is quoting F. H. R. Frank's *Zur Theologie A. Ritschl's* (1888; 3rd ed. 1891), p. 27 n. 12.

4. There are of course various types of Christologies from below; see further, Pannenberg, *ST* 2:286.

The task of the From Below method is to test and justify christological statements by "inquiring into the actual inner necessity of christological developments in the NT and the continuation of this logic into the christology of the early church,"[5] especially as expressed in the creeds of the undivided church. Obviously, such conclusions also help sort out views orthodox and heretical. Of particular interest to us is whether the confessions of Chalcedon and preceding councils faithfully and appropriately develop the testimonies, narratives, titles, and incipient creedal traditions of the NT; otherwise, we are forced to conclude with Adolf von Harnack and others that the development of tradition is nothing but the "deterioration of dogma."[6] While Harnack's view is not followed by many in contemporary theology, there are weighty reasons why a From Below approach should not be abandoned: in the aftermath of the Enlightenment, merely affirming Jesus' divinity without rational argumentation would mean theology's capitulation before the court of reason; the uniquely Jewish and other historical bases of the person of Jesus would not be otherwise properly acknowledged; and, as Pannenberg puts it, a Christology From Above simply assumes "God's point of view," which is not accessible to us.[7]

The From Above approach is by no means the legacy of only the pre-Enlightenment noncritical tradition. It has had important followers in the twentieth century as well, even though for different reasons than tradition. In response to the failed nineteenth-century quest of the historical Jesus, which sought to establish the meaning of Jesus solely on the basis of historical knowledge, a counterproposal was raised to the effect of basing Jesus' significance on the *kerygma,* the proclamation of the church.[8] Rudolf Bultmann famously decried and dismissed any attempt to rest the assertion of faith on the shifting sands of historical evidence.[9] In systematic theology, Barth similarly rejected all notions of historical evidence not only as some-

5. Pannenberg, *ST* 2:282. Pannenberg makes the obvious note that in a monographic presentation, as in his earlier work *Jesus — God and Man,* the emphasis usually lies in the From Below whereas in his systematic presentation, particularly with its trinitarian undergirding, the From Above gets a fair accent.

6. As brilliantly presented and argued in his multivolume *History of Dogma.* The most famous statement of Harnack, often quoted and often misinterpreted, is: "*The Gospel, as Jesus proclaimed it, has to do with the Father only and not with the Son.*" Harnack, *What Is Christianity?* p. 154.

7. Pannenberg, *Jesus — God and Man,* p. 35.

8. The pacesetter here was Kähler, *So-Called Historical Jesus.*

9. Bultmann, *Jesus Christ and Mythology,* p. 84 and passim.

thing useless but also as counterproductive to what he took as the genuine notion of faith as trust.[10] Behind this distancing from historical study was the influence of the "existentialist-before-existentialism," Søren Kierkegaard's distinction between the "religion of Socrates," based on the immanence of the truth as self-knowledge, and the "religion of Jesus," based on the work and person of the Savior and Redeemer who remains paradox. It is faith rather than reason that matters.[11]

The distinction between the two approaches is not either-or but rather both-and; "the two lines of argument from above and from below are complementary."[12] It is rather the matter of methodologically beginning from below toward constructing a high Christology acknowledging that "material primacy belongs to the eternal Son, who has become man by his incarnation in Jesus of Nazareth."[13] The obvious danger of From Above divorced from the history of Jesus is the violation of the biblical insistence on Jesus as the way to the knowledge of God (John 14:6). Otherwise, an abstract view of God emerges rather than the Father of Jesus Christ. The danger of one-sided From Below is that it can at its best discover a generic nature of humanity rather than thinking "in terms of the God of the revelation in Christ as the basis of its interpretation of the coming and the special history of Jesus."[14] This method easily dissolves into mere "Jesuology" that dismisses the preexistent and exalted Christ altogether. That said, we shouldn't lose sight of the integral connection between anthropology and Christology[15] — if the Christian

10. Barth dismissed historical study because for him Jesus "is the End of History" and as "Christ, Jesus is the plane which lies beyond our comprehension." Barth was only interested in the "vertical," not the horizontal, level. Thus, he could conclude that "within history, Jesus as the Christ can be understood only as Problem or Myth." *The Epistle to the Romans,* pp. 29-30, with regard to Rom. 1:3-4. See also Brunner, *The Mediator,* p. 158.

11. Kierkegaard, *Philosophical Fragments,* pp. 11-27.

12. Pannenberg, *ST* 2:289. This reminds us of the obvious fact that the distinction between two kinds of approaches to Christology is not a distinction between "low" and "high" Christology. In a programmatic article Rahner rightly made a more nuanced distinction between five kinds of Christologies, namely, "Christology below," "Christology from below," "Christology from above," "Christology from below and from above," and "Christology above." "Die deutsche protestantische Christologie der Gegenwart," pp. 189-202. The "both-and" method is of course what Rahner names "Christology from below and from above," otherwise known as ascending Christology or Christology from below to above.

13. Pannenberg, *ST* 2:289.

14. Pannenberg, *ST* 2:290.

15. This is manifested in Pannenberg's ordering of his *Systematic Theology,* vol. 2, as

claim to the coming to flesh of the divine Logos is to be true.[16] On the other hand, for the *divine* Word rather than an elevated human consciousness or influence to become flesh, God is to be presupposed. Rather than being a matter of circular reasoning, it is the matter of reciprocal conditioning between *theo*logy and anthropology.[17] This christological orientation is an indication of the profound connection of humanity to God as discussed in the context of theological anthropology.[18] The mutual conditioning of From Below and From Above means that the historical investigation is in the service of the theological one. Moltmann puts it well, in keeping with his overall focus on the cross: "We shall attempt to achieve an understanding of the crucified Christ, first of all in the light of his life and ministry, which led to his crucifixion, and then in the light of the eschatological faith which proclaims his resurrection from the dead, and in so doing proclaims him as the Christ."[19] The mutual conditioning means to correct the long-standing bias in scholarship to "keep history and theology, or history and faith, at arm's length from one another."[20]

In this outlook, the old divide between the person and work of Christ also gets properly qualified. While the distinction should be maintained, it has to be maintained carefully and in a way that does not posit separation. Ontology and functionality cannot be distinguished in such a categorical way as older theology did, nor is it useful to do so. Who Jesus Christ is determines what he does; what he does reflects and grows out of who he is. The biblical testimonies contain very little abstract speculation of who Jesus is. The healing of the man at the pool of Bethesda is a telling example (John 5:2-15). The paralyzed man came to "know" Jesus only through his salvific works, healing and forgiveness ("Do not sin any more"; v. 14); what-

---

the first chapter (of three) on Christology, which follows the chapter on anthropology, is titled "Anthropology and Christology."

16. See further Moltmann, *Way of Jesus Christ*, p. 55 and passim, who speaks of "anthropological Christology" not as Jesuology but rather in a way of establishing and maintaining the integral connection between the history of Jesus and confession of Christ. Moltmann, like myself, is critical of such "anthropologization" of Christology that, as did classical liberalism, lost sight of the divinity, including the cosmic and transcendent dimensions of Christology.

17. See Pannenberg, *ST* 2:290-91.

18. In a masterful way Pannenberg (*ST* 2:292-93) finds a link to the philosophical concept of Logos, which was of course picked up by some NT traditions in the fact that as self-conscious beings we are religious beings.

19. Moltmann, *The Crucified God*, p. 112.

20. N. T. Wright, *The Resurrection of the Son of God*, p. 5.

ever little he knew of Jesus, he went out to proclaim good news about him (v. 15). Oscar Cullmann famously argued that the NT question "Who is Christ?" has little to do with who Jesus was and everything to do with "What is his function?"[21] This is only half true. It correctly affirms the starting point for discerning who Jesus is, namely, the experience of Jesus' salvific works.[22] It falsely rejects the mutual conditioning of functional and ontological explanations. Any statement about the task already implies something about the nature and vice versa. With all the suspicions against the Hellenistic tendencies of "ontologization" of the Christian message, contemporary biblical theology and systematic theology hold ontology and functionality tightly together.

One of the ways older theology made the distinction between the person and work of Christ was the typology of the threefold office of Christ as priest, prophet, and king. Pannenberg rejected the use of office because it separated the person from the work.[23] In his opinion, the person and work are so mutually related that this distinction — to which he gives some justification later in his career — has only "typological significance . . . [as it] expresses the fulfillment and consummation of the old covenant in the history of Jesus."[24] Furthermore, in his assessment, the use of offices misses the "relation between the work of the ascended Christ and that of the Spirit."[25] This judgment, however, needs some qualification and does not necessarily follow. Already Calvin, who of course helped solidify the use of offices in Protestant theology, does not miss the relationship between the ongoing work of Christ by the Spirit in his three offices.[26] While the integral connection between the person and work of the Christ[27] as well as the mutual relationship between Christ and Spirit is to be affirmed, I don't see any compelling rea-

21. Cullmann, *Christology of the New Testament,* pp. 3-4.

22. Cf. Emil Brunner's (*The Christian Doctrine of Creation and Redemption,* pp. 271-72) claim that the functional approach is the proper place to begin in the search to understand Jesus' unity with God. That said, Brunner himself by and large did not follow the From Below approach, but rather the From Above approach.

23. Pannenberg, *Jesus — God and Man,* pp. 128ff.

24. Pannenberg, *ST* 2:444-47 (446).

25. Pannenberg, *ST* 2:448.

26. Calvin, *Institutes* 2.15.1-6. For this reference I am indebted to McClean, "Anticipation," p. 198 n. 55. Similarly, Moltmann's creative use of the offices (to which he adds yet another, that of "friend") integrally relates the work of the Christ and that of the Spirit. *The Church in the Power of the Spirit,* pp. 114-20.

27. Famously expressed in Philipp Melanchthon's clause, "to know Christ means to know his benefits." Melanchthon, *Loci Communes Theologici,* p. 21.

son to deny the validity of the uses of the three offices as one way of highlighting the work of Christ.

The issue of From Below and From Above, along with the corollary topics mentioned here, has not lost its meaning in contemporary theology, nor is it at the center of the discussion of the "method" of Christology; it is safe to say, however, that by and large From Below in some form or another is followed by most. Indeed, rather than speaking of "method" in a technical sense, the current systematic/constructive theology discusses various issues widely related to the most viable "approach" to or perspectives on doing Christology.

Toward a More Dynamic Christology

"In every generation Christian theology is faced with the task of articulating the intuitions of the biblical tradition about the significance of Jesus Christ in a way that engages its own cultural context," F. LeRon Shults reminds us in the beginning of his exploratory investigation into contemporary implications and ramifications of Christology.[28] As mentioned above, the worldview of the beginning of the third millennium is radically different from the static, semimechanistic view of reality during the earlier periods of Christian history when the contours of classical Christology were hammered out. Not only more dynamic and elusive, but also robustly relational[29] — and thus mutually conditioning and conditioned — the contemporary view of reality offers new ways of giving account of traditional biblical and traditional formulations of Christology. Because of criticism against tradition's way of framing the Christian confession of Christ in a way that leads to a "static" and abstract account as well as lack of integral connection to the Spirit, dissatisfaction against the post-Enlightenment division of christological method into two camps (From Below/From Above), and the radically changing situation in the world and theology, new complementary, and often also competing, ways of conceiving the task of Christology have emerged. Before looking at those revised ways of accounting for a more relational and dynamic understanding, yet another important criticism against much of dogmatic Christology must be faced and responded to. That has to do with the lack of attention to the Jewishness of Jesus Christ.

28. Shults, *Christology and Science,* p. 1.

29. For a careful historical-philosophical retrieval of the rise of relationality, see Shults, *Reforming Theological Anthropology,* chap. 1.

Hence, a contemporary constructive Christology calls for a renewed account of the Jewish roots of the Christian confession of faith in the Messiah of Israel. Historically, unfortunately, this has not been the case, and therefore a correction is needed. Unlike traditional doctrinal theology — which often tended to operate with typological hermeneutics of some OT teachings — both traditional and contemporary systematic theology have not been too attentive to the relation of the NT Christology to its Old Testament roots. This development started early and was evident already in much of patristic theology.[30] This has divested theology of the integrally messianic dimension. Contemporary Jesus research as conducted by biblical scholars, however, shows a wide and variegated interest in the Jewishness of Jesus.[31] What has hindered the integration of these discoveries into systematic and constructive theologies is the fact that too often biblical and systematic disciplines have not engaged each other in the way they should.[32] Fortunately, the situation is changing rapidly. Among the systematicians, Moltmann is an exception to the rule by beginning his major monograph on Christology with a careful investigation of "Jewish messianology";[33] importantly, the subtitle of his christological monograph is *Christology in Messianic Dimensions.* Moltmann rightly takes the OT messianic hopes and metaphors as the presupposition of Christian theology of Christ, as the Christ is Israel's Messiah — even when it is the person of Jesus Christ who has divided Jews and Christians. Christian theology has to do everything to make sure the division does not degenerate into an anti-Jewish ideology.[34] The explanatory categories of the Jewish faith that provide the explanatory frameworks for the NT Christology are the genesis and development of the hope for the Messiah and the figure of the Son of Man (especially in Dan.

30. See further Moltmann, *Way of Jesus Christ,* pp. 69-70.

31. "Twentieth-century [NT] scholarship has at least one great advantage over its predecessors. . . . it has been realized that Jesus must be understood in his Jewish context." N. T. Wright, *Jesus and the Victory of God,* p. 5; also pp. 91-98, with plenty of references to current scholarship.

32. Among the biblical scholars, N. T. Wright particularly has been keen on the *theological* implications of his massive scholarship on the origins of Christian faith. Other such figures include J. D. G. Dunn and R. Bauckham in their respective ways.

33. Moltmann, *Way of Jesus Christ,* p. xv. Chapter 1 as a whole deals with the OT background. In this orientation, Moltmann follows his program introduced in *Theology of Hope* and further developed in many other publications such as his *Trinity and the Kingdom,* implying that Jewish/OT expectations and metaphors laid the presuppositions for all of Christian theology.

34. Moltmann, *Way of Jesus Christ,* pp. 1-2.

7:14).[35] It is highly important for Christian theology, both for its proper self-understanding and for its relation to the Jewish people, to reflect carefully on the Jewish roots of her faith.

In contrast to older static and abstract approaches,[36] Moltmann's *The Way of Jesus Christ* (orig. 1989)[37] embodies and points to several revisions under way for a more dynamic way of doing Christology. The title itself points toward an important shift away from a "static" two-nature approach of tradition toward an approach in which Jesus Christ is grasped "dynamically, in the forward movement of God's history with the world" (p. xiii). Consequently, the outline of the discussion is not structured according to the typical dogmatic topics — divinity, humanity, and natures — but rather according to a developing "process" (p. xiv) or various "moves" on the way of Jesus Christ from his birth to earthly ministry to cross to resurrection to current cosmic role to parousia. This kind of Christology, says the Tübingen systematician, "points beyond itself and draws people towards the future of Christ, so that they remain on Christ's path, and move forward along that path." Hence, it is also an eschatological Christology — and because the future has not yet arrived, it is provisional and based on promise (p. xiv). For "we walk by faith, not by sight" (2 Cor. 5:7). Christology "on the way" is by its nature biblical Christology, based as it is on the gospel story, thus a narrative Christology (p. xv). Biblical Christology focuses on the earthly ministry of Jesus much more than typical dogmatic presentations of Christ. Looking at the shape of both traditional and contemporary Christologies, we see a curious lack of focus on the earthly life and ministry of Jesus. Undoubtedly the Christology From Above with its focus on the coming of the preexistent Son into human flesh and the creedal neglect of the significance of Jesus' earthly life have contributed to this lacuna, which has to be corrected for the sake of systematic discussion. Liberation theologies as well as theologies from the Global South have rightly critiqued this omission and have begun to fill it in.

Moltmann reminds us that unless Jesus' earthly life is rediscovered in theology, what he calls "christopraxis" will be lost. Christopraxis — "christological theory that is concerned with the knowledge of Christ in his

35. For a careful theological analysis, see Moltmann, *Way of Jesus Christ,* pp. 5-27.

36. Shults (*Christology and Science,* pp. 1-2) makes the obvious remark: "Many traditional formulations of Christology rely so heavily on ancient concepts of substance or medieval concepts of jurisprudence that they seem irrelevant to the concrete concerns that shape late modern culture."

37. In-text page numbers in the following paragraphs refer to this work.

meaning for us today" — leads to discipleship and the appreciation of community in which the "practical" reflection on the teaching and life example of Jesus is being practiced (p. 41). "Christopraxis," Moltmann envisions, "inevitably leads the community of Christ to the poor, the sick, to 'surplus people' and to the oppressed . . . to unimportant people, people 'of no account'" (p. 43). Only then can we speak of the "therapeutic relevance of Christology." Whereas "apologetic Christology" rightly inquires into the grounds for putting belief in and sharing a testimony about Christ (1 Pet. 3:15), the therapeutic approach is soteriological Christology as it "confronts the misery of the present with the salvation Christ brings, presenting it as a salvation that heals" (p. 44). This approach honors the biblical unity of Christology proper and soteriology. In Christian tradition, rightly Christology has provided the basis of and contours for soteriology; that, however, should not make us blind to the integral unity and mutual conditioning of the two (p. 44).

Liberation Christologies and Christologies from the Global South by and large opt for a From Below approach basically for the same kinds of reasons Moltmann mentions. Their main concern is that traditional Christologies, with their focus on creedal traditions and the methodological debate between From Below and From Above, lead to christological discussions with no or little relevance to praxis. Womanist theologians have opted for the From Below approach that focuses on the "deeds of the historical Jesus and not the idealized Christ, in keeping with the liberative traditions of the religious community."[38] Yet they are less concerned about the traditional methodological questions in their pursuit of From Below insights in the service of liberation, inclusivity, and equality. Similarly, the African American theologian James H. Cone critiques classical Christology of the creeds for neglecting the grounding of the "christological arguments in the concrete history of Jesus of Nazareth." Consequently, Cone surmises, "little is said about the significance of his ministry to the poor as a definition of his person."[39] Because the Nicene Fathers were not slaves themselves, their Christology was removed from history and the realities of the world. Instead, they saw salvation in spiritual terms alone, this black theologian contends.[40]

As a corrective, liberation Christology has placed its main focus on the meaning of the historical Jesus who lived a real life under real human condi-

38. Terrell, *Power in the Blood?* p. 108.
39. Cone, *God of the Oppressed,* p. 107.
40. Cone, *God of the Oppressed,* p. 181.

tions. Interest in the historical Jesus leads to the study and appropriation of the Gospels.[41] Latin American liberationists usually prefer Mark and Luke to Matthew. But their interest in the Jesus of history differs from the quest of the historical Jesus among the theologians of classical liberalism. For the liberationists, the historical facts of the life of Jesus as such are not the focus, as in the main drive of the quest, but rather the understanding of the relevance of the history of Jesus to the struggles in Latin America. "*Understanding* Jesus, as opposed to recovering Jesus, requires holding together in creative fusion two distinct horizons: the historical Jesus of the Gospels and the historical context of contemporary Latin America."[42]

For the liberation Christologies to achieve their goal, not only the material presentation but also the method has to be reconsidered. The African American pioneer theologian Cone suggests six sources for black theology and Christology:[43]

1. Black experience: the totality of black existence in a white world of oppression and exploitation.
2. Black history.
3. Black culture: the self-expression of the black community in music, art, literature, and other kinds of creative forms.
4. Revelation: it is not only a past event but also God's present redemptive activity on behalf of blacks.
5. Scripture: in line with the neo-orthodox view, the Bible as such is not to be identified with revelation. The Bible is a testimony and guide to God who acts as the Liberator.
6. Tradition.

Cone's suggestion is hardly radical, nor highly innovative when compared to, say, the so-called Wesleyan Quadrilateral: Scripture, tradition, reason, experience.[44] The only added "source" of theology is the distinctively black experience and history. But isn't that the case by default in all theologies? White European male theologians or black female American theologians can hardly avoid filtering their theologies through their own life histo-

41. See, e.g., Sobrino, *Christology at the Crossroads,* p. 10.

42. Pope-Levison and Levison, *Jesus in Global Contexts,* p. 31.

43. Cone, *Black Theology of Liberation,* pp. 23-34.

44. "Experience" can hardly be classified under the same "sources" with the rest of the quadrilateral. Experience, as Paul Tillich (*Systematic Theology,* 1:42) has reminded us, is rather a medium through which all sources of theology are being received.

ries, experiences, and cultural-historical worlds.[45] What is significant about Cone's suggestion, however, is that black theology, and in this case Christology, should be unabashedly mindful of and make it a theological theme to also draw from black sources. This relates to the ongoing discussion of what is "global" theology. Rather than a modernist "universal" meaning, *global* refers to the "communion" of "local" interpretations in mutual dialogue with each other. In other words, the only "global" is "local."[46] That perspective both affirms the legitimacy of particular approaches and qualifies their claim to any kind of exclusivistic position. Along with that, fostering this particularity with regard to both method and material presentation from different types of liberationists (and other agendas) is important not only for the sake of *liberation* (and other "contextual") theologies, but also for the sake of all Christian theologies in general and Christologies in particular.[47] Specific liberation theologies are needed all the more as long as the "mainline" theology fails to include those motifs under the "normal" discussion. Here particularity does not foster exclusivism but rather inclusivity.

According to Moltmann, what really distinguishes this new dynamic and praxis-oriented approach from more traditional approaches[48] is "the transition from the metaphysical christology of the 'ancients' to the historical christology of modern times," and finally in our times, the "transition from the historical christology of modern times to a post-modern christology, which places human history ecologically in the framework of nature."[49]

45. For the importance of attuning to women's experiences as the source of theology, see Ruether, *Sexism and God-Talk,* p. 13. For an informed discussion of the role of "experience" in various women's theologies, see Peacore, *Role of Women's Experience,* chap. 1.

46. See further, Dyrness and Kärkkäinen, introduction to *Global Dictionary of Theology,* pp. vii-xiv.

47. L. Boff's liberationist presentation of the doctrine of the Trinity *(Trinity and Society)* is an illustrative example of a book that, although deeply liberationist, is meant for the whole church and thus engages the whole of Christian tradition. See the preface (p. v) to the Theology and Liberation Series, of which that book is the first installment.

48. The term "traditional" here does not mean the same as "old" but rather means an approach that is in keeping with Christian tradition of dogmatics. Hence, even most current Christologies such as those penned by Pannenberg, his student Stanley Grenz, and, say, Donald Bloesch (all of them to be engaged in what follows), differently from Moltmann, are structured and focus their discussion on traditional topics of two natures and their unity. (This is true even with regard to Pannenberg, who eschews the term "two-nature" Christology; materially, however, he follows that route, as is evident in his *Systematic Theology,* vol. 2, three chapters on Christology.)

49. Moltmann, *Way of Jesus Christ,* p. xvi.

Now, what might be the implications of the criticisms and challenges by liberationists and Moltmann to contemporary Christology? Undoubtedly, any Christology worth its salt must listen carefully to these calls to renew and expand its agenda. Unlike the traditional approach, a robust discussion of the earthly life of Jesus, including his teachings, miracles, pronouncing of forgiveness, and reaching out to those outside the covenant, will be attempted. The focus on Jesus' earthly life also gives us an opportunity to highlight the liberationist and therapeutic impulses, including the diverse ways of embracing the meaning of Jesus in various global and "contextual" settings. Similarly, the whole history of Jesus from birth to cross to resurrection to ascension will be included in theological investigation. Not all of that can be accomplished in this first part of the current volume; so part II, "Reconciliation," has to be seen as integrally related to the whole presentation of the Christian doctrine of Christ. That discussion will show that the doctrine of atonement and reconciliation not only has to do with "spiritual" salvation of individuals but also encompasses holistic healing in personal and communal dimensions and sociopolitical issues such as equality, peace, and ecological balance.

That said, a constructive critical remark is also in order. This "transition does not have to be a breach. Transitions can also place traditions within wider horizons, and preserve older perceptions by translating them into new situations."[50] That is, while the contours of contemporary Christology may differ quite significantly from the approach of the past, it does not mean leaving behind what Moltmann somewhat pejoratively calls "metaphysical" Christology and what liberationists of various stripes tend to ignore as irrelevant. Rather, a careful and detailed consideration and reworking of the traditional Christology of the Chalcedonian tradition will also be attempted, along with tackling the issues related to contemporary concerns such as liberation, equality, and resistance to violence. A careful consideration of the issues of the humanity and divinity of Jesus Christ as well as topics such as incarnation, preexistence, and sinlessness does not make Christology less relevant or less dynamic, nor make it theoretical and abstract. A contemporary Christology that holds tightly to the best of tradition and continues vibrant discussion of key theological themes can be dynamic and lively. The "metaphysical" questions belong to the core of Christian theology — liberationist, "global," and postmodern Christologies, not only to "traditional" theologies — lest Jesus be made merely a human figure

50. Moltmann, *Way of Jesus Christ*, p. xvi.

and "salvation" made a human enterprise to merely improve the conditions of this world. That kind of reductionistic account of Jesus Christ would bear little similarity to biblical and creedal traditions of the undivided Christian church, and hardly could serve as a resource for robust contemporary work for holistic salvation at all levels of human existence.

A rediscovery in contemporary theology of a major resource, whose roots go back to the earliest theologies of Christ, provides us a great asset in a more dynamic, comprehensive, and hopefully more relevant approach to Christology, namely, Spirit Christology. In their integral and thorough linking of Christ to the Spirit and of the Spirit to Christ, flourishing Spirit Christologies have not neglected the integral link in the Gospels between Jesus' temptations and ministry in terms of teaching, healings, exorcisms, and pronouncements of forgiveness and the work of the Father's Spirit in his life. In mainline theology, Protestant, Catholic, and Orthodox traditions, Spirit Christologies have emerged during the latter part of the twentieth century to give a theological account of these links. Furthermore, intuitively Pentecostal theology, with its focus on different roles of Jesus as Savior, Sanctifier, Healer, Baptizer-with-the-Spirit, and the Soon-Coming-Eschatological-King in the power of the Spirit, has also helped highlight the then and current ministry of Jesus.

The rise of various types of Spirit Christologies has helped theology to appreciate the mutual conditioning of the From Below and From Above approaches. In this outlook, "Jesus' history as the Christ does not begin with Jesus himself. It begins with the *ruach*/the Holy Spirit."[51] According to the Gospels, from the conception to the resurrection, Jesus' life is linked with the divine Spirit of his Father.[52] Consequently, the "historical account of his life is from the very beginning a theological account" because it links Father and Son.[53] The integral linking of Jesus to the Spirit means a necessary linking with his Father — if trinitarian canons are not to be compromised. The focus on Spirit Christology also helps make the necessary connection of the Jesus of the "past" and the Jesus of the "present" — who of course is one and the same person. "The experience of the Spirit evidently provides a differently sup-

51. Moltmann, *Way of Jesus Christ,* p. 73.

52. Jesus' birth (Matt. 1:18-25; Luke 1:35), baptism (Matt. 3:17; Mark 1:11; Luke 3:22; John 1:33), testing in the wilderness (Matt. 4:1; Mark 1:12; Luke 4:1), and ministry with healings, exorcisms, and other miracles (Matt. 12:28; Luke 4:18; 11:20) are functions of the Spirit. According to the Pauline tradition, Jesus was raised to new life by the Spirit (Rom. 1:4).

53. Moltmann, *Way of Jesus Christ,* p. 74.

ported logic of correspondence between the experience of Christ's presence and the remembrance of his history. . . . [The] experience of the risen Christ is the experience of the Spirit. . . . His [risen Christ] presence in the Spirit in the community of his people is presence 'since' his resurrection from the dead and his appearances in glory."[54] The following discussion seeks to combine Logos Christology and Spirit Christology, giving precedence to the former because that is the way tradition has developed and grown.

In sum: both the rise of Spirit Christology, cast in a proper trinitarian framework, and the dynamic, relational worldview help us see more clearly that the divide between From Below and From Above can only be held heuristically and cautiously. Indeed, "Christology is no longer forced to choose between beginning 'from below' or 'from above.' Neither of these is really possible. Every judgment made about the significance of Jesus Christ is embedded within a context already mediated by one's interpreted experience of tradition. Rational assessment of the historical Jesus operates within a web of beliefs about the relation of God to the world."[55]

One more move — indeed, a move in two stages — is critical and necessary for the construal of a relevant, adequate constructive Christology for the third millennium. That is the turn to intercultural/contextual and religious/interfaith diversity. Although there are separate studies on various aspects of intercultural (or global) issues such as African, Latin American, and Asian or liberationist and feminist or womanist or *mujerista* Christologies (to be engaged in what follows), no constructive Christian theology of Christ incorporates these diverse views into the primary theological discussion. The relegation of "contextual" theologies to separate studies makes them marginal and secondary. Thus, as is evident even in most recent constructive theology, systematic discussion can be safely conducted without any substantial reference to views from outside the male-dominated, mostly Euro–North American traditions.

Related to the cultural diversity is interaction between religions. As the Norwegian Islamist and Christian theologian Oddbjørn Leirvik reminds us, "there is a growing awareness that Christology has to be dealt with in the context of a dialogue with other world religions. Christ cannot be trapped inside the walls of the Church. Images of Jesus are part of global culture, Christian as well as non-Christian."[56] Hence, Leirvik continues, "the image

54. Moltmann, *Way of Jesus Christ,* pp. 77-78.

55. Shults, *Christology and Science,* p. 9.

56. Leirvik, *Images of Jesus Christ in Islam,* p. 3.

How is this possible if all religions have a fundamentally different image?

of Christ in world religions should be recognized as a necessary aspect of systematic theology."[57] This means that the dialogue with and engagement of views of other religions in systematic/constructive theology are not motivated primarily by the desire to establish a pedagogical contact, although the value of that should not be dismissed either. It simply belongs to the material and thematic presentation of systematic theology to relate its statements and claims for truth to other religions that advance similar claims in the context of their own traditions and beliefs.[58] Rightly, then, the Roman Catholic John Pawlikowski, deeply engaged in the dialogue with the Jews, argues that the task of the dialogue belongs to the theological task itself, on both Christian and Jewish sides.[59]

Again, although there are separate studies on the perceptions of Jesus Christ among religions, including comparisons and contrasts on key issues such as the role of Jesus in Christianity versus the role of the Prophet in Islam, no constructive theology incorporates interfaith resources into the main discussion. For the sake of interreligious work, it would also be fascinating to launch a collaborative study that would scrutinize whether any common interests and motifs exist between Christian, Muslim, and Buddhist "theologies" in terms of "method." In some way similarly to various Jesuses of Christian tradition, one could discern different Buddhas such as the "historical Buddha" of the oldest parts of the Pali Canon, the "hagiographic" and legendary Buddha of various biographies, and the Buddha(s) of popular devotion. Furthermore, there is the Mahayana tradition's view of multiple Buddhas and cosmic buddhahood.[60] What about the "historical" Prophet of Islam?[61] And so forth.

These methodological remarks will now give way to the tackling of the first major topic, namely, the theological significance of Jesus' earthly life and ministry.

57. Leirvik, *Images of Jesus Christ in Islam,* p. 4.

58. In the context of the discussion of theological method, the details of this argumentation will be fully worked out.

59. See, e.g., Pawlikowski, "Christology, Anti-Semitism, and Christian-Jewish Bonding," pp. 245-68; see also his important monograph *Christ in the Light of Christian-Jewish Dialogue.*

60. See Harris, "My Unfinished Business with the Buddha," p. 90.

61. For interesting discussions entitled "Historical Jesus, Historical Muhammad" and "Christ of Faith, Muhammad of Faith," see Leirvik, *Images of Jesus Christ in Islam,* pp. 224-32.

2. "A Prophet Mighty in Deed and Word": Jesus' Ministry

Earthly Ministry in Theological Perspective

In vain one looks for extensive discussions — or at times, even any discussion at all[1] — of the earthly life and ministry of Jesus in traditional and contemporary systematic theological discussions of Christology, unless those treatments of his earthly career are in the service of applying the from-below method on the way to the above.[2] There are remarks on virgin birth, especially in older dogmatic presentations, and occasional notes on miracles, either in terms of apologetics or modernist rebuttal of their possibility; but the lion's share of discussions goes to the events around the cross and resurrection. This all happens in the wider context of discussions of Jesus' divinity,

1. An illustrative example here is Bloesch, *Jesus Christ.* Not much better is Aquinas's detailed discussion of christological topics in the third part of *Summa Theologica.* Although after the detailed treatment of "Incarnation" (3.1-26) he devotes considerable space to "Life of Jesus" (3.27-59), including themes such as conception, birth, baptism, all the way to death, resurrection, and ascension, even in the section on "public life," he is focusing solely on topics that are of apologetic interest, namely, "the manner of his life," temptations, "doctrine," and especially miracles. The kind of interest evident in the Evangelists of the NT concerning his teaching, reaching out to the children, women, and other marginalized, and similar themes does not interest the Angelic Doctor.

2. The prime example here is Pannenberg, *Systematic Theology,* vol. 2, which speaks of the earthly life only as an expression of Jesus' obedience to the Father (in chap. 9) and of his proclamation as the manifestation of his relationship to the Father, in the context of establishing the deity of the man Jesus (in chap. 10).

humanity, and unity with God. What is strangely missing, as Moltmann aptly puts it in reference to ancient creeds, is interest in events between "born of the Virgin Mary" and "suffered under Pontius Pilate."[3] This is markedly different from the Gospels, in which the teachings, healings, exorcisms, pronouncements of forgiveness, table fellowship, and prophetic acts receive most of the space. The claim that the Gospels are nothing more than passion narratives with lengthy introductions[4] is true only up to a point — and as any half-truth, may also be misleading. Even the fact that when we go beyond the Gospels the NT narratives about Christ are less focused on the earthly life and more on the salvific and "spiritual" aspects of Christ, hardly legitimizes the virtual omission of the earthly life in later theology. Why should Paul and other non-Gospel authors of the NT offer yet another chronicle of the earthly life since there were already four such narratives![5]

Liberal Christology helped rediscover many aspects of Jesus' earthly ministry. However, its approach was plagued with severe theological and epistemological problems. In its reductionistic epistemology, it was led by its own logic to break off the integral unity of Jesus' ministry by carving out all notions of the miraculous — healings, exorcisms, and other mighty works. Furthermore, in its immanentist worldview, it could not see the integral link between the earthly ministry of Jesus and the announced eschatological kingdom. Hence, the Sermon on the Mount became nothing more than a fine piece of ethical teaching; its radically eschatological nature focused on the life under God's righteous rule was totally missed. Implications for Jesus' own person were also missed. As a result, Jesuologies rather than Christologies emerged. That approach is different from a theological focus on Jesus' earthly life as an integral part of the whole history of Jesus. It also differs from theologically grounded "anthropological Christologies" that — as with the Lutheran Pannenberg and the Catholic Rahner — forge an integral link between Jesus' humanity and Christology, between anthropology and theology.[6]

Over against the creeds' lack of focus on the earthly life of Jesus, Moltmann suggests an amendment, an addition to the creed after "born of the Virgin Mary" or "and was made man":

3. Moltmann, *Way of Jesus Christ,* p. 150.

4. Famously put forth by Kähler, *So-Called Historical Jesus,* p. 80 n. 11.

5. This argumentation should hold even in light of the fact that of course it is Paul rather than the Evangelists who is the earliest *writer* among the NT authors; when Paul penned his epistles, the oral tradition about Jesus was already in place.

6. Cf. the discussion on some similar motifs in Moltmann, *Way of Jesus Christ,* pp. 55-63.

Baptized by John the Baptist,
filled with the Holy Spirit:
to preach the kingdom of God to the poor,
to heal the sick,
to receive those who have been cast out,
to revive Israel for the salvation of the nations, and
to have mercy upon all people.[7]

New Testament scholars agree that Jesus initiated his public ministry in the context of the baptism of John the Baptist.[8] By submitting himself to baptism from John, Jesus in effect approved the public claim of the Baptizer as to the possibility of receiving forgiveness of sins not only in the cult of the temple but also there in the wilderness. Nothing less than a new exodus was being announced — and the opponents of John soon realized it.[9] In baptism, Jesus manifested his identification with the people, even the covenant people, in need of the baptism of repentance. Different from ritual lustrations common in the Jewish cult, John's baptism was a profound eschatological act, as "the eschatological sign of the conversion of all Israel."[10] Of old, his baptism has been seen as an anticipation of the "baptism" of suffering and death (Mark 10:38), thus also pointing to the cross and resurrection.

Jesus' baptismal event is a profound pneumatological and trinitarian event. Jesus, the Baptizer in the Spirit, was himself baptized by the Spirit as the Father's voice of approval was audible. The One on whom the Spirit descended in the form of the dove had a vision of open heavens, a profound sign of salvation and eschatological hope. The return of the Spirit after hundreds of years of absence meant nothing less than the return of Yahweh to visit his people, "the beginning of the end-time deliverance of men and women, the new creation and the manifestation of God's glory."[11] This cosmic and eschatological context notwithstanding, on the other hand we can say that by descending on Jesus, the Spirit underwent *kenosis,* self-emptying, not in terms of being limited in activity — the Spirit of Christ is also the Spirit of Yahweh, the life principle of all life in the cosmos — but rather in terms of "taking up its dwelling in this vulnerable and mortal human being

7. Moltmann, *Way of Jesus Christ,* p. 150.

8. In this vast area of NT research, Webb, *John the Baptizer and Prophet,* is as good a source as any.

9. See N. T. Wright, *Jesus and the Victory of God,* p. 160.

10. Moltmann, *Way of Jesus Christ,* p. 88.

11. Moltmann, *Way of Jesus Christ,* p. 92.

Jesus."[12] The universality of the divine Spirit and the particularity of the Spirit as the Spirit of Jesus Christ have to be confessed simultaneously and kept in a healthy dynamic.

Itinerant preacher and healer, Jesus was on the way most of the time; his route took him to private houses, synagogues, cities, and countryside fields, including occasionally non-Jewish surroundings. Moltmann's *The Way of Jesus Christ* is thus a most fitting title. Jesus was a man of prayer (Mark 1:21, 29; Luke 4:33, 38; Matt. 4:23; 9:35; etc.). His use of the Aramaic term *abba* denoted intimacy with his Father,[13] made available also to his followers. That he is a man of prayer and devotion — particularly the Gospel of Luke highlights Jesus' role as the institutor of prayer *(salah)* and almsgiving *(zakah)* — is also acknowledged in the Qur'an (19:31).

He broke national, religious (covenantal), cultural, and sexual barriers by associating with people not usually involved with a Jewish prophet. His challenging and "universalizing" of three key Jewish institutions, namely, Torah, temple, and banquet fellowship, were powerful acts of liberation. He assumed authority over the precepts of Torah, for example, concerning the Sabbath, and interpreted Sabbath as something that is meant for human beings rather than vice versa (Mark 2:23-28). He proclaimed the Court of the Gentiles in the Jewish temple a "house of prayer for all the nations" (Mark 11:17). Particularly his involvement with the "sinners," including table fellowship, the most profound sign of hospitality (Matt. 9:10-13; Mark 2:15-17; Luke 5:29-32; etc.), became a radical challenge to the religious establishment.[14] In that culture, as in many non-Western cultures even today, table fellowship is the most honorary and inclusive means of welcoming another person. Jesus also

> fought dehumanization by placing human need above even the most sacred traditions such as Sabbath purity (Mark 2:23-3:6). Therefore the

12. Moltmann, *Way of Jesus Christ,* p. 93. In Eastern Orthodox tradition, the theme of the *kenosis* of the Spirit is prevalent. See Lossky, *Mystical Theology of the Eastern Church,* p. 169.

13. The older interpretation of *abba* as a child's familiar address to father (as the English term "daddy") has been shown to be a misleading interpretation, and should not be taken to mean that therefore the term means little or nothing. It *does* denote unheard-of intimacy and closeness, not known in the OT. Although Moltmann (*Way of Jesus Christ,* pp. 142-45) seems not to be well informed of the newer research into the meaning of *abba,* his theological interpretation is profound and to the point.

14. See Levison and Pope-Levison, "Christology," p. 177.

> oppressed were conscientized in his presence. Blind Bartimaeus, whom the crowds silenced, was given voice and healed by Jesus (Mark 10:46-52). An unnamed woman with a flow of blood and no financial resources touched Jesus and subsequently "told him the whole truth" (Mark 5:25-34). Jesus fought sin by denouncing everything — whether religious, political, economic, or social — that alienated people from God and from their neighbor.[15]

Feminist theologians are rightly calling theology to return to the Jesus of the Gospels who was found to be "remarkably compatible with feminism," because in his ministry and behavior "the femaleness of the social and religiously outcast who respond to him has social symbolic significance as a witness against . . . patriarchal privilege."[16] The womanist theologian Kelly Brown Douglas surmises that mainline theology with its focus on incarnation and other classical topics has also made the ruling class totally blind to the sins of slavery and oppression. Jesus' "ministry to the poor and oppressed is virtually inconsequential to this interpretation of Christianity."[17]

The poor (Matt. 11:5; Luke 4:18) and the children (Mark 10:13-16 and par.) were especially dear to Jesus. Moltmann rightly speaks of the dignity of the poor — "the hungry, the unemployed, the sick, the discouraged, and the sad and suffering . . . the subjected, oppressed and humiliated people *(ochlos)*."[18] According to the womanist theologian Jacquelyn Grant, reading the Bible narrative about Christ, who was inclusive in his love toward women and other marginalized people in the society, black women found a Jesus they could claim, and whose claim for them affirms their dignity and self-respect. Jesus means several things to black people; chief among these, however, is belief in Jesus as the divine cosufferer who empowers them in situations of oppression. Black women "identified with Jesus because they believed that Jesus identified with them. As Jesus was persecuted and made to suffer undeservedly, so were they. His suffering culminated in the crucifixion. Their crucifixion included rapes, and husbands being castrated (literally and metaphorically), babies being sold, and other cruel and often murder-

15. Pope-Levison and Levison, *Jesus in Global Contexts,* p. 35.

16. Ruether, *Sexism and God-Talk,* pp. 135-37. Where I disagree with Ruether is that her call to return to the Jesus of the Gospels means leaving behind the Christ of "orthodox Christology," which in her understanding supports hierarchical structures and alignment with imperial powers (pp. 123-26).

17. K. B. Douglas, *The Black Christ,* p. 13.

18. Moltmann, *Way of Jesus Christ,* p. 99.

ous treatments. But Jesus's suffering was not the suffering of a mere human, for Jesus was understood to be God incarnate."[19]

The Korean-born theologian Andrew Sung Park looks at these and similar signs of identification with the people, particularly the weak and marginalized, through the key cultural concept of his first culture: *han.* That multifaceted concept denotes suffering and pain, "a sense of unresolved resentment against injustices suffered, a sense of helplessness, . . . a feeling of acute pain and sorrow in one's guts and bowels."[20] According to Park, not only the sufferings of the cross, but all of Jesus' life represented divine *han:* "Jesus' birth bespeaks of the han of God for the children of the poor. According to the birth story, there was no room at the inn and Mary delivered the baby in a manger (Lk. 2:7). . . . The han of God persists in the fact that there is no room available in the world for thousands of babies whom God has created. . . . Jesus' suffering for three hours on the cross was one thing; his many years' suffering . . . was a profound source of Jesus' han."[21]

In light of Jesus' inclusive reaching out to the marginalized of the community, it is problematic, although understandable in terms of folk piety, that physiognomic handbooks of the early centuries of Christian history portrayed Jesus as handsome and flawless.[22] That portrayal of course meant at the time that Jesus was separated from the disabled and "disfigured." Contemporary Christian theology of disability has to assess the biblical and historical traditions concerning disability in light of the principle of care and inclusivity Jesus showed to all persons regardless of their status or quality.

The Jesus movement was the movement of the poor;[23] the disciples were sent out barefoot without any provisions.[24] God was their only trust. Children were the ones who most sincerely and without any pretense embodied this trust. As much as the low and poor family background and social status of Jesus are admired in Christian tradition, not all other religions do so. The Chinese Buddhist scholar-monk Sheng Yen, who passed away in

19. Grant, "Womanist Theology," pp. 346-47.

20. Joh, *Heart of the Cross,* p. xxi. (Joh attributes this definition to Han Wan Sang but gives a mistaken reference to another author; I was unable to trace the original source.) A careful discussion of the many meanings of *han* can be found in Park, *Wounded Heart of God,* chap. 1 and passim.

21. Park, *Wounded Heart of God,* p. 125.

22. See further, Moore, *God's Beauty Parlor.*

23. This is another indication for Park (*Wounded Heart of God,* p. 125) of the experience of *han.*

24. See Theissen, *Sociology of Early Palestinian Christianity.*

2009, sought to defend the superiority of his own religion on the basis of the royal family roots of Shakyamuni (Gautama Buddha) vis-à-vis the lowly status of Jesus' background.[25]

Teacher with Authority — and Parables

Jesus of Nazareth was known as a prophet and teacher who could speak with power and authority. Totally different from the later liberal interpretations in which Jesus appears to be a kind ethical teacher cultivating the inner life of individuals and communities, the Jesus of the Synoptic Gospels announced a public message. The announcement was about the kingdom of God that "was a warning of imminent catastrophe, a summons to an immediate change of heart and direction of life, an invitation to a new way of being Israel."[26] Although public and "naked," his teaching came mostly in the form of the parables, which of course are open to more than one interpretation. Even when they operated with well-known OT and Jewish metaphors such as vineyards or sheep, Jesus' parables went way beyond the Jewish contours and spoke of the inbreaking in his own person of the righteous rule of God.[27] That said, Jesus' ethical teaching, particularly the Sermon on the Mount, has been greatly appreciated by some Jewish observers. The first Hebrew book on Jesus written in contemporary times, after almost two millennia of silence, by the Jewish historian Joseph Klausner, makes the most honoring comment on the Sermon on the Mount. Indeed, says Klausner, "[t]here is not one ethical concept in the Gospels which cannot be traced back to Moses and the prophets."[28]

As were his ministry and person at large, so his teaching in parables was open to more than one interpretation. The assessment of the above-mentioned contemporary (late) Chinese Buddhist critic of Christianity provides a radical counterexample of this Christian interpretation. He laments that Jesus preached to the masses only through parables and then explained their meaning only to the selected group of the inner circle. "His reason for

25. Yen, "Further Discussion of the Similarities and Differences between Buddhism and Christianity," in *JBC*, p. 250.

26. N. T. Wright, *Jesus and the Victory of God*, p. 172.

27. An insightful and useful summary of various dimensions of Jesus' parables and their use can be found in N. T. Wright, *Jesus and the Victory of God*, pp. 181-82.

28. P. Lapide, *Israelis, Jews, and Jesus*, p. 6, quoting from Klausner, *Jesus of Nazareth*, without page reference, unfortunately.

this was that he would only allow the mysteries of the kingdom of heaven to be known by his disciples. He would not let the masses know, for fear that if the masses knew, they would turn around and gain forgiveness."[29]

Undoubtedly the most significant feature of the person and ministry of Jesus in Buddhist interpretation is the teaching and compassion ministry of Jesus. Many recent Buddhist interpretations consider Jesus an enlightened teacher.[30] The Theravada Buddhist monk Ajarn Buddhadasa considered Jesus an apostle or prophet on par with Gautama. He opined that Jesus' message is enough for "salvation." The Vietnamese master Thich Nhat Hanh went so far as to say that "we are all of the same nature as Jesus," even though the manifestation of that nature takes a lot of study and effort.[31] All traditions of Buddhism highly value the teacher's role; this is in keeping with the three original vows of the tradition, namely, to take refuge in Buddha, *sangha* (community), and *dhamma* (teaching). The aspects of Jesus' teaching most highly valued by Buddhists include the Beatitudes, love of the enemy, the admonition to repay evil with kindness, and the stress on charity and equanimity.[32] The Qur'an also acknowledges Jesus' compassionate nature.[33]

29. Yen, "Further Discussion," p. 255.

30. So, e.g., G. A. Barker, introduction to *Jesus in the World's Faiths,* ed. G. A. Barker, p. 3. In this light, it is highly significant how in the canonical (Pali) tradition, Gautama Buddha himself embodies a number of characteristics similar to those of Jesus. We do not have reliable historical knowledge to write a life of Buddha; therefore, the following descriptions are "theological" interpretations of Gautama's life: Gautama embraced every kind of person indiscriminately; he showed honor to a leper; he accepted an invitation to a dinner by a prostitute; he spoke highly of a drunkard; he accepted into his discipleship a former murderer; he rejected the caste system; he affirmed the value of women; and so forth. For detailed canonical references to these incidents, see Schmidt-Leukel, "Buddha and Christ as Mediators," pp. 161-63.

31. José Ignacio Cabezón, "Buddhist Views of Jesus," in *JWF,* p. 16.

32. The Dalai Lama ("The Good Heart," in *JBC,* p. 258) says of the teaching in the Sermon on the Mount on turning the other cheek and similar acts of nonretaliation (Matt. 5:38-42), that those passages could be introduced into a Buddhist text and they would not be necessarily recognized as Christian writings at all! The subsequent teaching of Jesus on God's love and mercy toward all (5:43-48) reminds His Holiness of the important Mahayana text *The Compendium of Practices,* by the seventh-century Indian Buddhist philosopher Shantideva, as well as of another Mahayana text, *A Guide to the Boddhisattva's Way of Life,* by the same author. For an important commentary on the main teachings of Jesus from a Buddhist perspective, see His Holiness the Dalai Lama, *The Good Heart.*

33. Qur'an 19:32 says that Jesus was not "arrogant, unblest" (some other translations put it, not "arrogant, highhanded").

Jesus' nonviolence, not surprisingly, has elicited a number of positive responses among religions.[34]

What Buddhists find missing in Jesus' teaching is a focus on living beings other than humans as well as on wisdom and spiritual praxis, all key concerns for all Buddhist traditions. What is not only foreign but also repulsive to Buddhist views is Jesus' emphasis on the kingdom and eschatological rule of God as well as particularly the "*utter finality* of the Christian apocalypse" in terms of sealing one's destiny once and for all.[35] In sum, as long as Jesus as teacher stands alone, so to speak, without reference to the transcendent, absolute God the Father, Buddhists are able to admire his teaching. Zen Buddhist Daisetsu Teitaro Suzuki, well known for his engagement of Christian thinkers such as Thomas Merton (and Western thinkers such as Erich Fromm), puts it succinctly: "Jesus said, 'When thou doest alms, let not thy left hand know what thy right hand doeth; that thine alms may be in secret.' This is the 'secret virtue' of Buddhism. But when the account goes on to say that 'Thy Father who seeth in secret shall recompense thee,' we see a deep cleavage between Buddhism and Christianity."[36]

In the mainline, Buddhism, particularly the Theravada tradition, teaches that one should not be too active in intervening in another person's suffering in order to avoid interrupting the *kamma* and samsara-nature of reality. That said, the Mahayana traditions especially place an emphasis on the extraordinary passion of the Enlightened ones, seen in the Buddhist tradition of the extraordinary compassion of Gautama toward not only all sentient beings but also all other beings, and in the fact that in Mahayana history, Gautama is known not only as the teacher of wisdom but also as a magical healer and miracle-worker; his acts include passing through walls, flying, and walking on water. The Mahayana tradition also knows of self-sacrificial acts of healing and alleviation of other people's pain such as the story of Vimalakīrti. A virtuous Boddhisattva, he made himself sick, and in

34. The contemporary religious thinkers who have acknowledged and praised Jesus' nonviolence include the leading Pakistani Muslim thinker Gulam Ahmad Parwez (d. 1985), the Indian Hindu religious and political leader Mohandas Karamchand Gandhi (d. 1948), the Hindu religious teacher and former president of India, Sarvepalli Radhakrishnan (d. 1975), the Tibetan Buddhist His Holiness the Dalai Lama, and the Vietnamese Buddhist Thich Nhat Hanh. For some relevant excerpts, see *JBC,* pp. 127-30, 185-88, 196-99.

35. Cabezón, "Buddhist Views of Jesus," in *JWF,* pp. 20-21 (p. 21, emphasis in original).

36. Suzuki, *Introduction to Zen Buddhism,* p. 101.

the presence of Shakyamuni (Gautama) and his disciples explained that the reason there is sickness is ignorance and thirst for existence. To help fellow men and women realize it, he tied his own healing to the healing of others.[37]

Although Islam considers Jesus one of the "prophets," a highly respected title in that tradition, and even attributes miracles to him, Jesus' role as teacher is marginal in the Qur'an. Indeed, what the Qur'an emphasizes instead is that God teaches Jesus "the Scripture, and wisdom, and the Torah, and the Gospel" (5:110). The Gospel *([al-]Injil)* is a book given to Christ, and it contains guidance, admonition, and light; the Gospel confirms the Torah and Prophets (5:110; 5:46). In the Qur'anic understanding, Jesus has made lawful to the people of Israel some things forbidden before (3:50). The Hadith tradition includes a highly interesting parallel to the Gospel traditions: in the "semicanonical" Bukhārī collection, in the book on "Hiring" *(Kitāab al-ijāra)*, Muhammad is retelling the parable of laborers in the vineyard, speaking of the time preceding his own times: "The example of Muslims, Jews and Christians is like the example of a man who employed labourers to work for him from morning till night for specific wages."[38] There are a few other parallel teachings in the Hadith tradition, including prayer resembling closely the Lord's Prayer.[39] This is an indication of the creative adoption of Christian influences by early Islam.

Miracle-Worker

Not only prophet and teacher but also an itinerant "miracle-worker," healer and exorcist par excellence, is the figure of Jesus of Nazareth of the Gospels of the NT. In addition to other miraculous acts, all four Gospels narrate numerous healings and miraculous cures, and the Synoptic Gospels add to the picture the acts of deliverance and exorcisms.[40] Ironically, the recent third quest

37. The story can be found in *Vimalakīrti Nirdesa Sutra* 5.6-7; http://www2.kenyon.edu/Depts/Religion/Fac/Adler/Reln260/Vimalakirti.htm (accessed 10/12/2009).

38. Quoted in Leirvik, *Images of Jesus Christ in Islam*, p. 43.

39. See Leirvik, *Images of Jesus Christ in Islam*, p. 44.

40. The miracle tradition of the NT belongs to the earliest strata and thus cannot be eliminated without serious violence to the literary integrity of the Gospels. Particularly Mark, believed to be the earliest Gospel, builds his narrative almost totally on the miracle tradition. See Dunn, *Jesus and the Spirit*, p. 70, for a summary statement. See also Kasper, *Jesus*, p. 89. For the listing of the most important arguments in defense of the historical validity of most Gospel miracles stories, see pp. 90-91. With regard to exorcisms, a class of

of the historical Jesus has finally taken seriously and as integral to the person and ministry of Jesus the theme of the mighty deeds. Whereas the pre-Enlightenment theology took the miraculous acts as proof of the divinity of Jesus of Nazareth, the Enlightenment epistemology of the original quest bluntly rejected their factual and historical nature. At its best, classical liberalism took the miracles as "myths" elicited by the powerful encounter with Jesus; even if the mighty deeds never happened, they still were of great value in pointing to the influence of Jesus on his followers.[41] Both of these paradigms fail. Unlike the precritical interpretation, the key NT passages that speak of incarnation and divinity do not resort to miracles. And unlike the reductionistic modernist rejection of the miraculous, contemporary epistemology and worldview allow us to accept the possibility of the miraculous.[42] "It is prudent, methodologically, to hold back from too hasty a judgment on what is actually possible and what is not within the space-time universe. There are more things in heaven and earth than are dreamed of in post-Enlightenment philosophy, as those who have lived and worked in areas of the world less affected by Hume, Lessing and Troeltsch know quite well."[43]

With the spread of Christianity to the Global South, the historically recent phenomenon of the Enlightenment-based refusal to grant the possibility of the miraculous in theology has faced a major challenge. For people in Asia, Africa, and Latin America, the category of miraculous — however one understands it, say, in relation to the "natural" — is taken for granted.

---

miracles highly suspect in the modernist mind-set, Dunn (p. 44) goes so far as to say that Jesus' ministry as exorcist "belongs to the base-rock historicity of the gospels" and that even Strauss, the critic, took exorcisms as something historically fairly probable.

41. This modernist "demythologization" of miracles has to be differentiated from a careful historical-critical attitude that, while open to the possibility of miracles, may come to the conclusion that not all miracles recounted in the Gospels really happened but are rather theological or kerygmatic instances of the early church. In the contemporary culture the historical strictures after the post-Enlightenment historiography were of course not in place. That state of affairs might have left the biblical writers more leeway in fashioning their narratives about Jesus. See Kasper, *Jesus,* p. 90.

42. N. T. Wright, *Jesus and the Victory of God,* p. 188: "Few serious historians now deny that Jesus, and for that matter many other people, performed cures and did other startling things for which there was no obvious natural explanation." See also p. 194. Kasper (*Jesus,* p. 91) agrees. (Wright is a biblical scholar and Kasper a systematician.) Miracles are of course not limited to Christian sources. The existence of miracles in rabbinic and Hellenistic sources is of course well documented. For a brief discussion, see Kasper, p. 90.

43. N. T. Wright, *Jesus and the Victory of God,* p. 187. For an important study, see C. Brown, *Miracles and the Critical Mind.*

Among the several titles appropriate for Jesus Christ in the African culture along with the Ancestor — or, for example, the Chief[44] — one is certainly the Healer.[45] In Africa, health means not only lack of sickness but also well-being in a holistic sense. Sickness is not primarily a result of physical symptoms but also of deeply spiritual causes. Unlike their counterparts in the West, African Christians reject both the secularist worldview and missionaries' Western conceptions of reality and spirit. "Orthodoxy" has left Christians helpless in real life, and so an alternative theology has been needed that relates to the whole range of needs that includes the spiritual but is not limited to abstract, otherworldly spiritual needs. Indeed, for many African Christologists, healing is the central feature of the life and ministry of Jesus Christ. A parallel can be found between the figure of Jesus of the Gospels as the itinerant healer and the traditional African medicine man. Both practice a holistic form of healing on the physical, mental, and social levels, even on the environmental level.[46]

Of all Christian traditions, Pentecostalism and later charismatic movements have focused on the role of Jesus Christ as the healer. A rapidly growing "Pentecostalization" is going on in Africa with many traditional churches adopting Pentecostal-type worship patterns, prayer services, and healing ministries. A major attraction for Pentecostalism in African contexts has been its emphasis on healing. In these cultures, the religious specialist or "person of God" has power to heal the sick and ward off evil spirits and sorcery. This holistic function, which does not separate the "physical" from the "spiritual," is restored in Pentecostalism, and indigenous peoples see it as a "powerful" religion to meet human needs.[47]

Similarly, postmodern epistemologies typically have rejected the strictures of the Enlightenment view of reality. This is not to say that Christian theology should seek to return to the precritical mind-set nor that theological reflection should suspend judgment with regard to mistaken, unhealthy, or overenthusiastic embrace of the "supernatural." What the third quest has done is to help NT research come to a place in which the key element of the Gospels' narrative of Jesus' ministry is not being eliminated or explained away due to an allegedly "critical" mind-set.

44. See, e.g., Wessels, *Images of Jesus*, pp. 11-12.

45. For an important recent discussion, see Tennent, *Theology in the Context of World Christianity*, pp. 109-22.

46. See further, Kole, "Jesus as Healer?" pp. 128-50.

47. See further, A. H. Anderson, "The Gospel and Culture," pp. 220-30.

The term "miracle" is foreign to the worldview of the Gospel writers.[48] Instead, the terms used in the NT include "*paradoxa,* things one would not normally expect; *dunameis,* displays of power or authority; *terata* or *semeia,* signs or portents."[49] The only word used in the Gospels that comes close to the Western term "miracle" is *thaumasia,* "marvels." The critical difference between the biblical worldview and our term "miracle" is that there is no overtone of invasion from another world in the Bible; rather, the mighty deeds happen "*within* what we could call the 'natural' world . . . and which seems to provide evidence for the active presence of an authority, a power, at work, not invading the created order as an alien force, but rather enabling it to be more truly itself."[50] As mentioned above, precritical theology took miracles as the proof of Jesus' deity. In response to the Enlightenment, Christian apologetics took up the task of defending the possibility of miracles since now they were seen as the way to negotiate the uniqueness and excellence of Christian religion vis-à-vis religions with no such claims or claims less weighty. This attitude grew out of the response to David Hume and others who argued that should the miracles of the Bible be shown to not be true, then not only Christianity but also other religions with similar claims could be considered to be of little or no value. As Tom Wright rightly puts it: the posing of questions from both of these camps, namely, "a non-miraculous 'Christianity' on the one hand, and a rearguard anti-critical reaction on the other . . . [seems] a little lame."[51]

What contemporary theology rightly is interested in is the meaning of

48. According to the classic definition of David Hume (*An Enquiry concerning Human Understanding,* p. 114), "A miracle is a violation of the laws of nature; and as a firm and unalterable experience has established these laws, the proof against a miracle, from the very nature of the fact, is as entire as any argument from experience can possibly be imagined." As a response to this appeal to "supernatural," Friedrich Schleiermacher (*On Religion,* pp. 48-49) went to the other extreme by insisting that any "natural" event originating in God be called miracle. Although I understand the theological and philosophical desire to soften (in Schleiermacher's case, reject) the natural-supernatural distinction, going this far makes any talk about miracles senseless.

49. N. T. Wright, *Jesus and the Victory of God,* p. 188.

50. N. T. Wright, *Jesus and the Victory of God,* p. 188. Kasper (*Jesus,* p. 92) makes the important observation that theologically it is not possible to think that God would replace this-worldly causality: "If he were on the same level as this-worldly causes, he would no longer be God but an idol. If God is to remain God, even his miracles must be thought of as mediated by created secondary causes. They would otherwise be like a meteor from another world."

51. N. T. Wright, *Jesus and the Victory of God,* p. 188.

the mighty deeds for Jesus' ministry and his person. As mentioned, in the Gospels the mighty deeds are not a means of "proving" the deity of Jesus but rather — as with OT prophets and charismatic leaders — an indication of the power of God at work. Thereby, the mighty deeds also indicate God's approval of the ministry of Jesus. Rather than done by *Beelzebub*, the mighty deeds are the function of the Spirit of God (Mark 3:20-30) — they are God's business. The favorite terms *terata* and *semeia* should be taken in their basic meaning, namely, as "signs." They point to God's power at work for salvation and deliverance vis-à-vis contestation to the contrary, in arguments that the miracles had their origin in the opposing evil forces. Similarly to the parables, the mighty deeds, including exorcisms, point to the coming of the kingdom of God: "But if it is by the Spirit of God that I cast out demons, then the kingdom of God has come upon you" (Matt. 12:28). At the same time, the mighty works were also linked with the OT and its prophetic fulfillment[52] in the way of restoring to membership and community those who, through sickness or possession of evil spirits, had been excluded. There is evidence that in addition to the burden of physical pain, ill people such as the blind, deaf, and lame might not have been included in the covenant people.[53] These "healing miracles must be seen clearly as bestowing the gift of *shalom*, wholeness, to those who lacked it, bringing not only physical health but renewed membership in the people of YHWH."[54] His healing bodily contact with people considered "untouchable," such as the woman with bleeding (Mark 5:24-34), meant that he "dispelled a false ideology, the oppressive body/soul dualism, which can be especially destructive to women. . . . Jesus challenged the ideology that women's bodies were polluted by refusing to consider that he became unclean by touching her."[55]

The healing ministry of Jesus is a robust statement about the all-inclusiveness of God's salvation; it includes the physical and emotional as well as the spiritual.[56] The miracles of feeding and stilling the storm, in addition to being tangible ways of meeting human needs, also carry overtones of covenant renewal and exodus.[57] Healings also were signs of profound sympathy, of cosuffering (Matt. 14:14), similar to giving leadership to confused

52. See further Kasper, *Jesus*, p. 97.

53. See Wenham, "Christ's Healing Ministry," pp. 115-26.

54. N. T. Wright, *Jesus and the Victory of God*, p. 192; also p. 189.

55. Levison and Pope-Levison, "Christology," p. 178.

56. See further Moltmann, *Way of Jesus Christ*, p. 104.

57. N. T. Wright, *Jesus and the Victory of God*, p. 193, with a listing of relevant OT passages.

people (Mark 6:34; Matt. 9:36) or providing food for the hungry (Mark 8:2; Matt. 15:32). Finally, healings and other acts of restoration — linked as they are with the coming of the kingdom of God — are also eschatological signs: the restoration and renewal taking place in healings, deliverances, and other mighty works refer to the expectation of the coming fulfillment of all promises of the righteous and loving God. Raising people from the dead was a profound sign of the victory over death. Exorcisms bespeak the ultimate victory of God over all evil forces.

In sum: the miraculous acts are thus an integral part of the story and ministry of Jesus; there "is no dividing line, enabling us to bracket off" them from the rest of his ministry, teaching, pronouncing forgiveness, reaching out to the outcasts and others.[58] Against the prejudice of the Enlightenment mind-set, even exorcisms belong integrally to Jesus' ministry. The same *exousia* (authority, power) present in his words (Mark 1:22) is present in the expulsion of demons (v. 27). These unclean spirits recognize Jesus for the person he was, "the Holy One of God" (v. 24). People gathered around Jesus for exorcisms as well as healings (Luke 4:40-41; 6:18 par.). There are absolutely no exegetical, nor theological, reasons for the kind of patchwork thinking so uncritically and naively practiced for two centuries of earlier NT scholarship!

Any consideration of the earthly life and ministry of Jesus leads one to acknowledge the robust Spirit Christology of the Gospels. Everywhere Jesus' ministry is referred to the Spirit; conversely, the Spirit at work is Christ's Spirit, the Spirit of Yahweh, Father of Jesus Christ. An integral biblical Spirit Christology helps contemporary systematicians to focus in a profound way on the earthly life of Jesus, including healings, deliverances, and other mighty works. Pneumatological Christology — or christological pneumatology — also means going back to the messianic expectations of the OT. In Jesus Christ the *ruach* Yahweh is now at work bringing about the salvific, restorationist, and eschatological purposes of God.[59] Spirit Christology also helps theology hold on to the whole history of Jesus and the place of earthly ministry therein: "If Christ is present now in the eternal Spirit of God, then his history must have been determined by this Spirit from the very beginning."[60]

58. So also N. T. Wright, *Jesus and the Victory of God,* p. 189.

59. Moltmann (*Way of Jesus Christ,* p. 74) rightly remarks that the pneumatological dimension and therefore the relation to the OT messianic background were missed at Nicea.

60. Moltmann, *Way of Jesus Christ,* p. 77.

Miracles are of course known and acknowledged in other religious traditions as well. What makes Islam unique is that, on the one hand, the Qur'an does not chronicle any specific miracle performed by Muhammad since the miracle of the Qur'an itself — as the Word of God — is by far the biggest and most important miracle. On the other hand, the Qur'an recounts several miracles of Jesus, such as healing the leper and raising people from the dead.[61] For example, in Muslim Persian literature written in Urdu, Jesus' role as healer is remarkable, including but not limited to emotional healing of a lover.[62] The Qur'an also knows miracles such as shaping a living bird out of clay based on the apocryphal gospels.[63] A remarkable miracle is the table sent down from heaven spread with good as the divine proof of Jesus' truthfulness as the spokesperson for God and the divine providence (5:112-115). Muslim commentary literature, poetry, and popular piety contain many different types of accounts and stories of Jesus' miracles that lead to a high regard for the personality and prophethood of Jesus. For the most well-known Muslim poet, the thirteenth-century Persian Sufi Jalaluddin Rumi, the miraculous birth and life of Jesus with a ministry of miracles, including healings and resuscitations, also become the source of inspiration for spiritual rebirth. His highly influential *Mathanawi,* also called the Qur'an in Persian language, praises Jesus for his power to raise the dead and for his wisdom.[64]

The high praises given to Jesus as well as the acknowledgment of the divine proof of truthfulness, however, do not mean in any sense of the word that Jesus would thereby be considered divine on the basis of miracles. Miracles belong to the repertoire of prophets, and they attest to their authenticity. Neil Robinson summarizes the meaning of miracles assigned to Jesus in the Qur'an in a way that helps Christian theology put them in perspective in re-

61. For a dramatic later tradition and chronicle of Jesus raising the dead, see the well-known tale by al-Tha'labi (d. 1035 C.E.) in *JBC,* pp. 106-7, where Jesus prays to Allah and raises the dead woman.

62. See further, Mir, "Islamic Views of Jesus," p. 115.

63. Qur'an 5:110 is an illustrative example: God himself is speaking to Jesus: "thou didst shape of clay as it were the likeness of a bird by My permission, and didst blow upon it and it was a bird by My permission, and thou didst heal him who was born blind and the leper by My permission; and how thou didst raise the dead by My permission." Other Qur'anic references to Jesus' miracles include 2:87, in which Jesus is strengthened by the Holy Spirit and given signs to support his teaching, and 4:63. Healings are also recorded in 3:49. For a useful discussion of Jesus' miracles in the Qur'an, see N. Robinson, *Christ in Islam and Christianity,* chap. 14.

64. Relevant excerpts are available in *JBC,* pp. 113-14.

lation to Muslim theology: "[I]t is clear that the Qur'ran's attribution of unprecedented miracles to Jesus is not a cause of embarrassment to the Muslim commentators. On the contrary, from their point of view, since Jesus is a prophet the miracles which God vouchsafes him must be sufficiently great to convince those to whom he is sent. Hence in common with popular Muslim piety the commentators tend to exaggerate the miraculous rather than play it down."[65]

Most Hindus and Buddhists are open to what the Western mind-set would call a miracle. Only a few isolated Hindus such as Dayananda Saraswati, the founder of the reformist movement of Arya Samaj, *qua* Hindu, would echo the kinds of rationalistic doubts common among the modernist Western thinkers. Saraswati sought to demythologize and at times even ridicule biblical claims to miracles in the life and ministry of Jesus, including incarnation.[66] When it comes to Buddhism, particularly Mahayana traditions are well familiar with miraculous stories of Gautama Buddha and other Enlightened ones. However, what is radically different among Buddhist thinkers is the interpretation of the meaning of miracles. The capacity to perform miracles points to the fact that Jesus was an extraordinary individual, but it does not point to deity nor to the link with the kingdom of God as outlined above. A typical Buddhist way of regarding Jesus' miracles would be to call them "common accomplishments," common in the sense that they can be accomplished by both Buddhists and non-Buddhists. What makes them especially valuable in Buddhist estimation is that they were done for the benefit of others.[67] That said, even those Buddhist thinkers and masters who highly appreciate Jesus' life, ethics, ministry, and compassion still take issue with the way Christian theology considers the role of Jesus. The Christian claim to the divinity of Jesus and the claim of the unique incarnation of God in him are totally foreign and utterly difficult claims for Buddhism.[68]

The Jewish appraisal of the NT claims to the miracles of Jesus is more complex and complicated. They are routinely considered to be "magic." The

65. N. Robinson, *Christ in Islam and Christianity,* p. 154.

66. Of miracles Saraswati said: "No learned man can believe these things; as they are against the evidence of the senses, the laws of nature. It is the credulity of ignorant men and savages to put faith in them, but not the civilized and learned people. . . . [Miracles] are believed by those who are mentally blind and financially fat to be caught in the priest's trap." *English Translations of the Satyarth Prakash,* p. 471, reproduced in *JBC,* p. 169.

67. See Cabezón, "Buddhist Views of Jesus," in *JWF,* p. 19.

68. Cabezón, "Buddhist Views of Jesus," in *JWF,* pp. 16, 21.

eleventh-century rabbi Solomon ben Isaac's judgment of Jesus as a "magician" and a "perverter of the people" is an illustrative example here. That judgment is backed up by the (Jewish) extracanonical tradition.[69] An interesting point here is that the Talmud states (in the mouth of a rabbi) that for the Sanhedrin, men are chosen who are not only wise but also "are well versed in magic,"[70] and that Jewish tradition is suspicious about an effort to establish one's credentials on the basis of miracles since, as Deuteronomy 13 reminds us, a (messianic) pretender may excel in miraculous acts and yet lead astray the people of God.

As mentioned above, the importance of the earthly life of Jesus — including his reaching out to sinners and other marginalized persons; his teaching of the righteous rule of God that turns the sociopolitical, cultural, and religious tables upside down; his powerful works of healing, exorcisms, and nature miracles — came to be marginalized in Christian tradition. At the same time, with the spread of Christianity (back!) to Africa and Asia, as well as Latin America, and the mushrooming of new expressions of Christian indigenous communities, interest in his earthly ministry is picking up. Furthermore, as mentioned above, women theologians of various stripes as well as liberationists and postcolonialists have demanded a closer look at the meanings of Jesus in relation to liberative, emancipatory, and inclusivistic needs. While this turn to his earthly life does not have to mean leaving behind the classical questions of Christology on topics such as preexistence, "two natures," or virgin birth, the contemporary world mandates such an expansion of theological discussion of the meaning of Christ. The next chapter attempts to do so by turning specifically to "global" and "contextual" interpretations on the way to developing a more dynamic account of christological doctrine for the third millennium.

69. P. Lapide, *Israelis, Jews, and Jesus,* p. 88; extracanonical texts referred to, among others, are Babylonian Talmud *Sanhedrin* 106a and *Yalkut Shimoni* 766.

70. Babylonian Talmud *Sanhedrin* 17a; see P. Lapide, *Israelis, Jews, and Jesus,* p. 89.

3. Jesus in the Matrix of Diverse Global Contexts and Challenges

The Emergence of "Global" Testimonies to Christ

With the rise of narrative theologies and the rediscovery of the meaning of symbols, metaphors, images, as well as stories and testimonies as "sources" and materials for theology,[1] global[2] systematic theology is better equipped to transcend a hopeless parochialism. What I mean is this: until recent years, systematic theology has at its best tolerated interpretations of Christology from outside the mainstream academic quarters, that is, mostly Euro-American and predominantly male theologians. Toleration has meant paying lip service to the role of "exotic" interpretations of Christ stemming from the soil of Africa, Asia, Latin America, and nondominant cultures in the Global North. At the same time, these interpretations have been marginalized, put in separate volumes and essays — apart from the "serious" dogmatic and systematic works. How many systematic theological presentations of Christology — or any other theological loci, for that matter — are

1. For a useful, nuanced discussion, see Fiddes, "Concept, Image and Story in Systematic Theology," pp. 3-23.

2. The term "global" theology — often used along with "intercultural" and "contextual" — does not refer to a modernist idea of "universal" theology in which all particularities and differences are being deleted. Rather, the term means something opposite to that erroneous notion: it refers to the communities of local conversations that engage, enrich, and challenge each other. A detailed consideration of the nature, place, and challenges of "global" theologies in systematic theology will be conducted in the volume on theological method.

there, even in the beginning of the third millennium, in which Charles Nyamiti of Kenya, Gustavo Gutiérrez of Peru, C. S. Song of Taiwan, James H. Cone of the U.S. African American community, and, say, Kwok-pui Lan representing the postcolonialist tradition are included as equal contributors in the discussion along with Augustine, Aquinas, Luther, Schleiermacher, and Barth?[3] Yet all these theologians, and many more, have written quite a lot on Christology, and their writings are readily available in English.

As with any theologies of Christ, these are occasional and "contextual" in the sense that they emerge from specific cultural, social, personal, and religious locations. That, however, is the case for all so-called mainstream theologies as well. Anselm's interpretation of the incarnation in *Cur Deus Homo* is no less "contextual" in its linking with high medieval hierarchic European culture than Schleiermacher's classical liberal Christology of the nineteenth century. Irenaeus's *Christus Victor* account of Christ's overcoming of powers from the patristic era is no less "contextual" than the sociopolitical liberationist construction of Christ's meaning that Gustavo Gutiérrez offers in the twentieth century. The only difference between traditional/mainstream theologies and current, specifically global/contextual/intercultural or liberation theologies is the level of awareness and intent: whereas in the past, theology was not able — or willing — to acknowledge its deep involvement with the local context, many current theologies make contextuality a theological theme. By doing so, these newer approaches are not necessarily less applicable to contexts outside their own than are typical male theologians' Euro-American interpretations.[4]

Like Christians in Asia and Latin America, Africans have struggled to discover and make legitimate their distinctive interpretations of Christ: "For too long, embracing Christ and his message meant rejection of African cultural values. Africans were taught that their ancient ways were deficient or even evil and had to be set aside if they hoped to become Christians."[5] Yet, "Jesus was in Africa even before the rise of Christianity," in that his family found a hiding place in Egypt and one of the first converts was Ethiopian,

3. For a useful discussion of global interpretations, see Levison and Pope-Levison, "Christology," pp. 180-85.

4. Acknowledging the danger of the particularity of local metaphors of Christ and the fear of their irrelevance to outsiders to African cultures, many African Christians in interviews mentioned that they prefer those taken directly from the Bible. Stinton, *Jesus of Africa,* pp. 123-26, 130-35; I am indebted to Tennent, *Theology in the Context of World Christianity,* p. 131.

5. Schreiter, "Jesus Christ in Africa Today," p. viii.

among other early allusions.[6] Furthermore, much of early Christian theology in general and Christology in particular was shaped by North African theologians such as Tertullian, Cyprian, and Augustine![7]

Due attention to African Christologies is even more important in light of the centrality of Christology to all theology in Africa.[8] "If it is true that Christology is at the very heart of all Christian theology, it is particularly true for African Christian theology."[9] Furthermore, today, as is well known, Africa is the "most" Christianized continent with the significant presence of not only traditional Christian churches but also African Instituted (or Initiated) Churches with highly contextualized spirituality as well as rapidly growing Pentecostal-charismatic movements. It is only to the detriment of global theological scholarship and the church that African testimonies, teachings, and insights into Christ have been almost totally ignored so far.

Rediscovery and Reconstruction of Titles of Jesus Christ

Whereas in traditional Christology, the "titles" of Jesus Christ played a significant role, as theology was following the "From Above" method and took even the loftiest designations such as "Son of God," "Son of Man," "Lord," and similar titles at face value, in contemporary critical Western scholarship that approach has by and large been marginalized. That is not the case with Christians in many locations in the Global South. Some leading African theologians have made much of the relevance of the key NT titles to their

6. Wessels, *Images of Jesus,* pp. 98-99 (98).

7. True, by the time of the Islamic invasion in the seventh century, both Christian theology and churches had virtually disappeared from African soil, and it took until the beginning of the modern missionary movement in the nineteenth century for Christianity to be reintroduced on any significant scale to Africa. This sweeping historical note, however, is not meant to dismiss the sporadic presence of Christianity in Africa between these two periods; the Portuguese reintroduced Christianity to the Congo before the time of the Reformation and so forth.

8. As recently as the latter part of the twentieth century, several leading African theologians lamented the lack of a distinctively *African* Christology. Mbiti, "Some African Concepts of Christology," p. 51; Appiah-Kubi, "Jesus Christ," p. 56; for Setiloane, see Wessels, *Images of Jesus,* pp. 109-10.

9. Onaiyekan, "Christological Trends in Contemporary African Theology," p. 356. So also, e.g., Vähäkangas, "African Approaches to the Trinity," p. 69: "Christology is at the center of African theology today. The majority of writings on African theology that could be classified as doctrinal theology deal with Christology."

context. They have discerned parallels between the New Testament teaching concerning Jesus Christ and the traditional African worldview and beliefs.[10] The ancient idea of *Christus Victor,* the powerful Christ who rose from the dead and defeated the opposing powers, is obviously relevant to the African search for power. The victorious Christ is able to overcome the spell and threat of spirits, magic, disease, and death, and to transform the culture of fear into a culture of hope and joy.

The idea of Jesus Christ as the Son of God corresponds with several tribal beliefs; the title "Servant of God" is similarly found in some African societies; and several other christological titles such as "Redeemer," "Conqueror," and "Lord" have parallels in African cultures. According to John Onaiyekan, the NT title "Son of God" is understandable in the African context in that the idea of God having a son sent to the world makes good sense for a culture used to divinities and the Supreme Being. The title "Lord" denotes authority and power in the same way as the title "Oluwa l'oke," the "Lord on the hills" of the people of Kabba, one of the Yoruba tribes. Even though the idea of Savior is not so prevalent in most African cultures, it is not totally foreign to them either, as is evident in the Yorubas' expectation of the divinities *(orisha)* to save them. "Redeemer" is welcomed as he who rescues them from the enslavement of the evil forces that surround them.[11]

Various African cultures have created a myriad of other titles, symbols, and metaphors that highlight various aspects of Christ's personality, relation to us, and work. Bantu Christians have called Christ "Chief,"[12] another metaphor with NT allusions (see also "captain," Heb. 2:10 KJV). There are several facets to Christ as the chief. Christ is called Chief by the Bantus because he has conquered and triumphed over Satan and thus is a hero (cf. Col. 2:15). The figure of the Bantu chief is closely associated with the role of hero. Christ is also called Chief because he is the son of the Chief, of God. The belief that God is the Chief of the whole universe is part of Bantu religion. That Christ is the Son of God Bantus have learned from Christian revelation.

For a culture that looks at personality in vitalistic, dynamic terms, the idea of incarnation opens up new horizons: "Incarnation is the highest fulfillment of personality as understood by the African. For the African, to

10. See Mbiti, *Bible and Theology in African Christianity.*

11. For a useful and succinct discussion of these and other titles, see Nyamiti, "African Christologies Today," pp. 3-23.

12. Kabasele, "Christ as Chief," pp. 103-15.

achieve personality is to become truly human and, in a sense, authentically Black; hence, the incarnate Logos is the Black Person par excellence. There is, therefore, no genuine blackness or negritude outside him."[13]

Not only particular titles and metaphors but more widely, for many Africans, the Gospels' narrative about the life of Christ is already a local theology. Several episodes in the life cycle of Christ, such as birth, baptism, and death, have meaning to Africans who celebrate and honor crucial turning points of life with the help of various rites. Jesus was initiated according to Jewish tradition at birth, when he was circumcised. Christ was dedicated in the temple, and his growing into puberty, and later into adulthood in a Jewish culture, was marked by rites of passage from one life stage to another not unlike the life-cycle rituals in most African communities. Even Jesus' washing the feet of his disciples at the Last Supper is seen as an initiatory gesture: Jesus, the Master, initiates his followers into his own lifestyle. As such, Christ acts as the Head and Master of initiation: having been made perfect, he becomes the Head of those who obey him (Heb. 5:9). In general, African Christology discovers in Christ's life a gradual movement toward a goal, toward perfection, as mentioned in Hebrews 5:8.

Christ as Ancestor

While the theme of ancestry is not limited to theologies from Africa,[14] a distinctive feature of African theologies in general and Christologies in particular is the use of ancestors as a theological resource.[15] "In many African societies ancestral veneration is one of the central and basic traditional and even contemporary forms of cult."[16] Obviously the idea of Christ as Ancestor is more meaningful to the typical African than, say, Logos or Messiah or *Kyrios.* It allows the culture of Africa to bear on the understanding of faith in Christ.

13. Nyamiti, "African Christologies Today," p. 5.

14. From an Asian perspective, see, e.g., Lee, "Ancestor Worship," pp. 83-91; Phan, *Christianity with an Asian Face,* pp. 135-45.

15. For representative examples, see Bediako, *Jesus in African Culture;* Bediako, *Christianity in Africa,* pp. 84-86; Kabasele, "Christ as Ancestor and Elder Brother," pp. 116-27. For a helpful overview and assessment, see Vähäkangas, "Trinitarian Processions," pp. 61-75.

16. Nyamiti, "African Ancestral Veneration," p. 14, cited in Vähäkangas, *In Search of Foundations for African Catholicism,* p. 171 n. 106.

Charles Nyamiti, the author of the widely acclaimed *Christ as Our Ancestor* (1984), succinctly summarizes the significance of the ancestor theme for the African context:[17]

- kinship between the dead and the living kin;
- sacred status, usually acquired through death;
- mediation between human beings and God;
- exemplarity of behavior in community; and
- the right to regular communication with the living through prayer and rituals.

An important characteristic of the sacred status of the ancestor is also the possession of "superhuman vital force" deriving from the special proximity to the Supreme Being. That gives the ancestor the right to be a mediator.

The Ghanaian Kwesi Dickson reminds us of the significance of the role of ancestors in representing the sense of community and the "concept of corporate personality," a theme familiar from the OT.[18] The ancestors, as well as those not yet born, are regarded as part of the community, and by their presence they express the solidarity of the community. The spirits of the ancestors use their power for the well-being of the community; this is consistent with the fact that not all dead become ancestors, but primarily those who have lived a good, virtuous life or served as leaders of the community. Ancestors are certainly lower in status than God, but higher than humans. They are called upon at the important moments of life.[19] A relational, familial version of the ancestral theme is Christ as "Brother Ancestor,"[20] a metaphor having links with the naming of Jesus Christ as "our brother" in the book of Hebrews (2:10-12).[21]

According to Bénézet Bujo of the Democratic Republic of the Congo (formerly Zaire), the idea of Jesus as the "Proto-Ancestor," the unique ancestor, the source of life and highest model of ancestorship,[22] rather than being a superficial concession to the existing culture, is a legitimate way to bring

17. Nyamiti, "The Trinity," p. 41.

18. Dickson, *Theology in Africa,* p. 170; see also pp. 172-74.

19. Fulljames, *God and Creation in Intercultural Perspective,* p. 47.

20. Nyamiti, *Christ as Our Ancestor,* pp. 74-76.

21. Similarly, the Vietnamese Peter C. Phan (*Christology with an Asian Face,* pp. 104-15) proposes the title "eldest Son" as a metaphor for Jesus.

22. Bujo, *African Theology in Its Social Context,* p. 79. For the ancestral theme, see pp. 79-121 especially.

home the central idea of Word becoming flesh (John 1:14).[23] If we look back on the historical Jesus of Nazareth, we can see in him not only one who lived the African ancestor-ideal in the highest degree, but also one who brought that ideal to an altogether new fulfillment. Jesus worked miracles, healing the sick, opening the eyes of the blind, raising the dead to life. In short, he brought life, and life force, in its fullness. He lived his mission for his fellow humans in an altogether matchless way, and furthermore, he left to his disciples, as his final commandment, the law of love.[24]

Ancestorship helps explain not only the role of Christ but also that of the whole Trinity: "The Father has the fullness of eternal life and begets the Son. They live for each other in a total and vital union, mutually reinforcing their common life. The vital power goes out from the Father to beget the Son and finally returns to the Father." This vital union that produces the interaction between Father and Son is nothing else than the Holy Spirit, the bond between the Father and the Son.[25] Theologically, it is highly significant that Nyamiti draws parallels between the ancestral relationship on the human level and the inner life of the triune God. He maintains that there is an ancestral kinship among the divine persons: the Father is the Ancestor of the Son, the Son is the Descendant of the Father. These two persons live their ancestral kinship through the Spirit whom they mutually communicate as their ancestral "Oblation" and Eucharist. "The Spirit is reciprocally donated not only in token of their mutual love as *Gift* but also on behalf of the homage to their reciprocal holiness (as *Oblation*) and gratitude to their beneficence to each other (as *Eucharist,* from the Greek: *eucharistein* 'to thank')."[26]

Linked with the title of "Ancestor" is that of "Kinsman." For Saint Paul, the biblical Christ is "the first-born of all creation" (Col. 1:15). Born of God (John 1:13), in participation with our Kinsman, we have the hope of becoming "children of God" and thus acquiring the status of kinship with Jesus. The African kinship leads to a relationship of strong solidarity not only horizontally among living members, but also vertically with those who have gone before, the deceased members of the community.

Commensurately, the role of Christ as the one who existed before all (Col. 1:15) and, having emptied himself (Phil. 2:7), became one of us (Heb. 2:14-18), is as the mediator between God the Father and creation. Since ev-

23. Bujo, *African Theology in Its Social Context,* p. 83.
24. Bujo, *African Theology in Its Social Context,* p. 79.
25. Bujo, *African Theology in Its Social Context,* p. 86.
26. Nyamiti, "African Christologies Today," p. 11.

erything was created through Christ (Col. 1:16), the incarnation, the coming to flesh of an eternal God (John 1:14), is the supreme example of the union between God and the world. Christ's resurrection as the sign of the defeat of the power of death (1 Cor. 15:26; 2 Tim. 1:10) and evil (1 Cor. 15:57) is the sign of hope for this culture that naturally looks beyond death even though fearing it. To the Ewe-Mina, Christ represents *Jete*-Ancestor, the source of life. "An ancestor is, according to the Ewe-Mina, co-fecundator of birth and is capable of providing to many newly born children the necessary vital energy for his apparition in them. Christ as *Jete*-Ancestor means that he is the Ancestor who is the source of life and the fulfillment of the cosmotheandric relationship in the world."[27]

Critical Western scholarship should not dismiss these contextual interpretations as precritical inventions but rather take them as legitimate interpretations of the churches of the continent that is now the "most Christianized" of all. In principle these interpretations do not differ methodologically and materially from current efforts by feminists and other female theologians and, say, postcolonial theologians to reenvision the meaning of Christ against and within a particular cultural context and agenda. The richness and multiplicity of biblical metaphors, symbols, and titles of Jesus Christ in the NT alone legitimize this kind of enterprise. Although particular and occasional, these images, pictures, metaphors, and titles can also help the whole global church to grasp something new and fresh in the meaning of Jesus Christ for today. A potential liability of the ancestral and similar metaphors of Christ in African theologies is the Arian tendency. Ancestors are not gods, even though they are highly regarded.[28] Yet another liability, acknowledged by both African[29] and other[30] theologians, to use Luther's terminology, is the "theology of glory." The theme of suffering, "theology of the cross," may easily be neglected. As long as theology is mindful of these potential liabilities, the theological and spiritual use of these kinds of titles should be acknowledged and fostered.

27. Nyamiti, "African Christologies Today," p. 5.

28. So also Tennent, *Theology in the Context of World Christianity,* p. 131.

29. Pobee, *Toward an African Theology,* p. 97.

30. Tennent, *Theology in the Context of World Christianity,* p. 131.

Jesus, the Liberation, and Empire

One of the complaints of liberation theologians and theologians from the Global South is that traditional theology is too quick to move away from careful consideration of Jesus' earthly life and ministry and toward abstract speculations of Chalcedonian "metaphysical" Christology. Jesus' role as social critic, challenger of prejudices and conventional ways of society, as well as his table fellowship with the marginalized do not loom large in that kind of Christology. The Roman Catholic Peruvian Gustavo Gutiérrez's *Theology of Liberation* was one of the first works of a new style of theology, namely, "liberation theology." In that book Gutiérrez argued that what is most distinctive about liberation theologians is the perspective from which they engage in theological reflection. Liberation theologians take as their point of departure the experience of the poor and the struggle of the marginalized for liberation. Gutiérrez rightly insists that the turn to liberation, rather than being an optional move, is rather "a question *about the very meaning of Christianity and about the mission of the Church.*"[31]

The most recent Jesus research has highlighted the social, political, and ideological importance of Jesus' radical egalitarianism. According to John Dominic Crossan, that is "something infinitely more terrifying than (contemporary democracy)."[32] There is an important link with Buddhist tradition here. It, too, began as a reformist movement, albeit of a different kind. Whereas Jesus targeted his criticism mainly against social structures and religious practices that marginalized and oppressed the weaker classes of the society, Gautama's desire was to renew Indian religious beliefs and practices in search of a new ethical approach. Buddha was not uninterested in social issues, but neither were they at the forefront of his thought.[33] The important similarities between the two founders of religious traditions include the following: "The Buddha opened up the religious life . . . to members of society who had hitherto been denied it: members of the lowest castes, and women especially. The Buddha and Jesus were also exponents of a kind of theological reform that emphasized the interior life over external ritual action."[34]

A growing number of Christian theologians from various contexts and

31. Gutiérrez, *A Theology of Liberation,* p. xi.

32. Cited in Cabezón, "Buddhist Views of Jesus," in *JWF,* p. 17.

33. For an important discussion, see Queen and King, eds., *Engaged Buddhism.*

34. Cabezón, "Buddhist Views of Jesus," in *JWF,* p. 18.

agendas — female theologians in search of sexual equality, other liberationists looking for sociopolitical and economic equality, and postcolonialists with the desire to unmask the injustices of colonialism — are asking whether the principles of inclusivity, openness, justice, equality, and reconciliation promised by the righteous rule of the heavenly Father are being discussed and highlighted in traditional Christologies. As the Roman Catholic Robert Schreiter aptly puts it: "If any single area of theology is especially poised to raise questions about the nature and practice of inculturation, it is surely christology. The fact of the Incarnation itself places us already on a series of boundaries: between the divine and the human, between the particular and the universal, between eternity and time."[35] Thus, before engaging the complicated and complex matrix of doctrinal developments in Christology, we must take a careful look at Jesus' role as liberator.

"Can a Male Savior Save Women?"

The feminist Rosemary Radford Ruether's now classic question, "Can a male savior save women?"[36] has become a clarion call for a liberationist questioning of traditional Christologies by women of various agendas, (white) feminists, (African American) womanists, (Latina) *mujeristas,* and women from Asia, Africa, and Latin America.[37] The Roman Catholic feminist Elizabeth Johnson laments the "[n]ormative speech about God in metaphors that are exclusively, literally, and patriarchally male"[38] because that usage begins to shape our view of reality. Over the years, the faithful begin to imagine and feel that "God is male, or at least more like a man than a woman, or at least

35. Schreiter, "Foreword," p. xi.

36. Ruether, *To Change the World,* pp. 45-56.

37. "Even with all their diversity, feminist, womanist, and *mujerista* theologies have one thing in common: they make the liberation of women central to the theological task." Fulkerson, "Feminist Theology," p. 109. While united in the central task of liberation, women's voices in theology no longer form a united front but rather display the kind of variety that can be expected of any theology in the beginning of the third millennium. Therefore, to speak of "feminist" theology in generic terms is quite misleading. The term "feminist" refers to white women's approaches, while "womanist" is for African American women, and *mujerista* for Latina women. The proliferation of views is enhanced by the emergence of women's voices from Africa, Latin America, and Asia. The fact that white women's voices are heard most often is simply because other women's voices on the topic of the Trinity are not yet widely available.

38. E. Johnson, *She Who Is,* p. 44.

more fittingly addressed as male than as female."[39] The root cause for these unfortunate effects is literal-mindedness that also leads to exclusivity and thus patriarchalism. For the moderate feminist Johnson, the option is not to deny the legitimacy of male symbols but rather to balance them with female ones. Female images are needed to both challenge and correct the prevailing structures of patriarchalism[40] in introducing alternative symbols and metaphors of the divine, "discourses of emancipatory transformation."[41] After all, as all theology has always insisted, "the holy mystery of God is beyond all imagining."[42]

In keeping with this "turn to metaphors," the rediscovery of a holistic, inclusive view of Christ and human beings means celebrating one human nature, yet multidimensional, in an interdependence of multiple differences, neither "a binary view of two forever predetermined male and female natures, nor abbreviation to a single ideal, but a diversity of ways of being human: a multipolar set of combinations of essential human elements, of which sexuality is but one."[43] In a brilliant sentence Johnson turns the maleness of Jesus into a way of constructive critique against patriarchalism and exclusion: "the heart of the problem is not that Jesus was a man but that more men are not like Jesus, insofar as patriarchy defines their self-identity and relationships."[44]

Alongside this, Johnson proposes qualifying and balancing the usage of the Logos metaphor in a more inclusive way in Christology. Whereas in the NT, Logos is linked with Jesus of Nazareth, its OT background could also be found in the concept of Wisdom. Both Spirit *(ruach)* and Wisdom *(hokmah)* are "symbols of God's energy involved in universal cosmic quickening, inspiring the prophetic word of justice, renewing the earth and human heart."[45] Especially in the Wisdom literature, *hokmah* is a highly developed personification of God's presence, and Johnson finds its use in the Bible suggestive of many female traits such as "sister, mother, female beloved, chef and hostess, preacher, judge, liberator, establisher of justice, and a

39. E. Johnson, *She Who Is*, pp. 5, 36-37.

40. E. Johnson, *She Who Is*, p. 33; see also pp. 4-5.

41. E. Johnson, *She Who Is*, p. 5, see also pp. 8-9, 17, 31.

42. E. Johnson, *She Who Is*, p. 45. Here Johnson refers to Aquinas, *De Potentia*, q. 7, a. 5: "Since our mind is not proportionate to the divine substance, that which is the substance of God remains beyond our intellect and so is unknown to us."

43. E. Johnson, *She Who Is*, p. 155.

44. E. Johnson, *She Who Is*, p. 161.

45. E. Johnson, *She Who Is*, p. 94.

myriad of other female roles."[46] While there is no consensus among the commentators if *Sophia* (the Greek term for Wisdom) is best depicted as a male or female symbol, Johnson finds credible the option that holds that Sophia is a female personification of God.[47] Along with other titles, "Divine Sophia" can be utilized in speaking of Jesus Christ, alongside "Logos." Furthermore, importantly, Johnson notes that many of the actions attributed to "Jesus-Sophia" involve preaching, ingathering, confronting, as well as dying and rising, activities that are as much female as male. In all these activities, Jesus-Sophia is also linked with the female figure of personified Wisdom. Wisdom categories by their own force help expand the traditionally too-limited view of Christ to encompass cosmic dimensions including "belief toward a global, ecumenical perspective respectful of other religious paths." Sophia also bespeaks justice and peace, having incarnated and thus identified with suffering humanity.[48]

Not all are convinced that the "masculinist predominance of Logos-centered theology" can be redeemed.[49] Some feminists have lost all hope of Jesus Christ being able to "symbolize the liberation of women," so much so that, "In order to develop a theology of women's liberation, feminists have to leave Christ and Bible behind."[50] Other feminists and postcolonialist female theologians have critiqued Johnson's attempt to negotiate a more balanced account of Christology and theology by tapping biblical and Christian historical tradition's resources. Grace M. Jantzen does not see any possibility for redeeming biblical and traditional ways of speaking of the divine form; instead she urges women to "begin deliberately to project the divine according to our gender, as men have always done according to theirs."[51] Jantzen further surmises that the traditional account of incarnation is only partial since it is confined only to one sex, the masculine. Hence, there is "room for other incarnations, other trinities, other sexualities."[52]

46. E. Johnson, *She Who Is*, p. 87.

47. E. Johnson, *She Who Is*, p. 91. With reference to female theologians such as Elisabeth Schüssler Fiorenza, Johnson argues that Jewish wisdom writers — unlike the classical prophetic traditions — were not afraid of employing the goddess traditions of the surrounding cultures to bring home the idea of a female side of God (p. 93).

48. E. Johnson, *She Who Is*, pp. 165-67 (166).

49. This formulation comes from Joh, *Heart of the Cross*, p. 93. Joh herself does not fully support this criticism.

50. Goldenberg, *Changing of the Gods*, p. 22; see also Hampson, *After Christianity.*

51. Jantzen, *Becoming Divine*, p. 15; I am indebted to Joh, *Heart of the Cross*, p. 93.

52. Jantzen, *Becoming Divine*, p. 17.

Theologically and practically, Johnson's approach is far more viable. Considering Logos Christology male-oriented is a claim that lacks proper nuancing. True, in biblical tradition, the Word-made-flesh is found in the male. From the historical and cultural point of view, that "choice" is fully understandable. For better or for worse, the contemporary culture was based on the predominance of the masculine sex, as it was for all religions' "founders" and holy men. The Logos concept itself, however, has nothing masculine about it, any more than feminine, for that matter. This is not a statement about grammatical pronouns but about a theological principle: Logos as the universal principle of reality, adopted and adapted by some biblical writers, is beyond sexism. Furthermore, should the incarnation have happened in the form of female sex, the corresponding problem would be how to include the male sex. Hence, replacing male-dominated talk about the divinity with female-dominated talk is not only unnecessary but also a thoroughly counterproductive exercise. It would sharpen rather than help resolve the issue of lack of inclusivity. A true human being can only exist as either male or female. Both sexes are fully human beings, created in the image of God. Thus, either male or female has the capacity to fully represent the human person and humanity. Consequently, the unfortunate argument in the Roman Catholic *Inter Insigniores*[53] that it takes a male priest to represent Christ is utterly mistaken: "The doctrine that only a perfect male form can incarnate God fully and be salvific makes our individual lives in female bodies a prison against God and denies our actual, sensual, changing selves as the locus of divine activity."[54] The suggestion of multiple incarnations as a way to qualify the incarnation of the Logos in the man Jesus of Nazareth does not fit Christian tradition and systematic coherence of Christian doctrine, as will be discussed in detail in the section on incarnation below.

Whereas traditional feminist Christology seeks to find ways to make the maleness of Jesus less exclusivistic, the postcolonial approach goes further in its project of "Engendering Christ."[55] While Ruether's question "Can a male savior save women?" "implicitly consents to the fact that the savior is male, and the question then becomes what has a male savior to do with women," postcolonialists wonder what would happen if they "problematize the gender

53. Declaration on the Admission of Women to the Ministerial Priesthood, chap. 5 particularly.

54. Brock, "The Feminist Redemption of God," p. 68.

55. Title of chapter 7 in Pui-lan, *Postcolonial Imagination.*

of the savior."[56] Hence, "marginalized images of Jesus/Christ" have been proposed, including the "Theological Transvestite" and "Jesus as Bi/Christ."[57] The Jewish theologian Susannah Heschel has proposed the former hybrid concept in her effort to "destabilize Christian theology and create a space for Jewish self-definition."[58] Standing on the border of two religions, Judaism and Christianity, Jesus thus challenges the self-understanding of both traditions. Thus, the queer concept of transvestite, which combines male and female features, is suggested as a proper metaphor.[59] The latter metaphor of "bi-" comes from the influential work of the Argentinian Marcella Althaus-Reid, who wants to include in theology and Christology sex and sexuality along with gender. For her it is not enough to have that discussion in gay and lesbian theologies. In her view, even liberation theologies suffer from masculinist and heterosexual assumptions. Her proposal of Bi/Christ is not about alleged sexual activity but rather about "people's sexual identity outside heterosexualism and 'a pattern of thought for a larger Christ outside binary boundaries.'"[60]

The problem with these kinds of constructions of engendering is total lack of support in Christian tradition, both biblical and historical. Reconstructing the history of Jesus Christ is not at the interpreter's will apart from any kind of historical point of reference. Methodologically it would mean losing all contours. There are also material reasons for rejecting these reinterpretations of Christ. Bisexuality does not represent more inclusively men and women than the traditional view of incarnation. A small, tiny minority of humanity (bisexuals) do not represent the whole of humanity any better than one-half of humanity (men — or women). For most men and women who define their identity along the lines of either female or male sexuality,

56. Pui-lan, *Postcolonial Imagination,* pp. 169-70.

57. The first phrase in quotation marks in this sentence is a subheading in Pui-lan, *Postcolonial Imagination,* p. 174; the discussion of the two hybrid concepts of Jesus appears on pp. 179-82. I am indebted to Pui-lan for bibliographic references in the following two footnotes.

58. Cited in Pui-lan, *Postcolonial Imagination,* p. 179, from Heschel, "Jesus as a Theological Transvestite," pp. 188-97.

59. Others who have followed this suit include McLaughlin, "Feminist Christologies," pp. 138-42. Behind the application of the queer theory to Christology is the insight of the classic study of transvestites by Marjorie Garber (*Vested Interest,* p. 11), who suggests the notion of "third" in order to transcend the conventional binary thinking of sexual roles.

60. As paraphrased by Pui-lan, *Postcolonial Imagination,* p. 181; citation comes from Althaus-Reid, *Indecent Theology,* p. 117.

bisexuality hardly represents inclusivity even though it denotes hybridity. Finally, there are weighty cultural reasons for rejecting these kinds of hybrid constructs of Christ: in most cultures of the world, a transvestite "savior" would be anathema. This does not mean capitulating to cultural pressures but rather reading the cultural clues.

Black Christ?

James Cone defines liberation in his *Black Theology of Liberation* to mean "that the community of the oppressed will recognize that its inner thrust for liberation is not only *consistent with* the gospel but *is* the gospel of Jesus Christ."[61] Since the Christ of the dominant forms of Christianity is presented as a white Christ tailored to the values of modern white society, there is a need for a black Christ, this black theologian surmises. "If Jesus Christ is to have any meaning for us, he must leave the security of the suburbs by joining blacks in their condition. What need have we for a white Jesus when we are not white but black? If Jesus Christ is white and not black, he is an oppressor, and we must kill him. The appearance of black theology means that the black community is now ready to do something about the white Jesus, so that he cannot get in the way of our revolution."[62] Later on, Cone softened his rhetoric against the "white Christ," granting that his early theology was too much a reaction to the theology of the dominant class rather than a distinctively black theology. But even then, he continued to hold the opinion that the *"norm of all God-talk which seeks to be black-talk is the manifestation of Jesus as the black Christ who provides the necessary soul for black liberation."*[63]

Cone's standpoint joins the long conversation among African American religious thinkers and theologians concerning the necessity and meaning of a black Christ/Messiah. As early as 1829, Alexander Young's "Ethiopian Manifesto" referred to the appearance of a black Messiah. The first book to set forth a detailed presentation of the meaning of a black Messiah for African American theology was Howard Thurman's *Jesus and the Disinherited* in 1949. Thurman's approach draws heavily from *African* experience of African American Christology. It combines creatively biblical and historical ideas of

61. Cone, *Black Theology of Liberation,* p. 1.
62. Cone, *Black Theology of Liberation,* p. 117.
63. Cone, *Black Theology of Liberation,* p. 38.

Jesus as the Messiah with the cosmic and mystical notions of Christ, thus also making robust connections with early Christian traditions. Thurman's main question asks, what is the significance of Jesus for people "against the wall," and why has the "white" religion of Christianity been so impotent to deal with this problematic? Unlike Cone's, Thurman's Christology does not make a direct reference to political activism but rather refers to the idea of the kingdom of God in Jesus "in us." Its emphasis lies in the role of Jesus the Messiah in bringing about liberation by being a mediator between the forces of evil, the effects of sin, and the powers of redemption. Here salvation is still essentially spiritual, though it is not relegated totally to the future, as that escapist tendency of white Christianity is a major target of criticism.

Albert Cleage's *Black Messiah* from 1968 is the first book to promote a politically and socially activist orientation and thus resembles closely Cone's Christology. Cleage's most controversial claim is that Jesus of Nazareth, as a member of his people, was literally black. He insists that the Bible was written by black Jews. He also argues that Jesus identified himself with the ultranationalistic Zealot movement, which was committed to bring about a black nation of Israel. Not only white scholars but also most black theologians distanced themselves from that hermeneutic. A moderate counterpart appeared two years later: Tom Skinner's *How Black Is the Gospel?* Different from Cleage's, Skinner's "black Messiah" is beyond racial divisions. Christ is liberator but does not identify with any particular color of people. Jesus' only allegiance was to his Father and the kingdom of God he preached.[64]

J. Deotis Roberts's *Black Theology in Dialogue* (1987) represents an intentionally moderate and dialogical orientation, building also on the correlational model of Tillich. The term "black Messiah" should be understood symbolically, as the historical Jesus cannot be shown to be black racially. Roberts's task is "psychocultural," that is, to restate the teaching about the universal Christ in such a way as to particularize God's redemptive act for a specific group. Christ is the Redeemer of all, but also of each and every specific group. The central idea here is the relation between the black Messiah and the "Christ of faith." The black Messiah is a mythical construct that helps to overcome the negative associations of being black. But ultimately,

64. Many other black Christologies fall between the extremes of Cleage and Skinner. A moderate viewpoint is represented in Roberts, *Black Theology in Dialogue,* which, as the name suggests, seeks to facilitate dialogue with whites and blacks about the meaning of Christ. Significantly, Roberts utilizes Tillich's correlational and dialogical approach to theology. The term "black Messiah" should be understood symbolically.

the black Messiah has to give way to a "colorless Christ." The black Messiah is particular, while the Messiah of the Bible is universal. There is a dialectical relationship between the particular and universal Christ: the universal Christ is particularized for the sake of the particular people of the black race, while the particular black Christ points to the universalization of Christ for all people. The ultimate goal of the black Messiah is reconciliation of all. Hence, Christ is the reconciler of both blacks and whites.

The nuanced and insightful christological interpretation of Roberts makes it possible both for blacks and for whites to affirm the idea of black Christ/Messiah as a contextual interpretation, similar to, say, the African title of the Ancestor. This interpretation has a liberating effect as it, on the one hand, facilitates a real identification of African Americans with a Christ "who looks like them" and sympathizes with their special needs and plight. On the other hand, this interpretation does not foster the violence, antagonism, or exclusivism present in the Christology of Cleage or the young Cone. Furthermore, Roberts's theology also helps negotiate the status of the historical Jesus and the relation of that to the Christ of faith.

The Face of Jesus in the Poor

Speaking of his personal experience as a *Mexicano*, Roman Catholic student of theology Virgilio P. Elizondo reminisces about his frustrations when studying theology in the United States: "[We] shared the scandal, the outrage, and the anger at our respective churches . . . with . . . orthodox theologies . . . [with] no knowledge of the suffering of the millions of Lazaruses all around them. We shared the frustration with schools of theology and theologies . . . who ignore the needs for the poor and dispossessed of this world and continue to read Scripture and the Christian tradition from within the perspective of the rich, the nicely installed, and the powerful of the world."[65]

To respond to the many charges against the complacency toward the issues of poverty and social inequality, the term "integral liberation" was coined by the Latin American Roman Catholic bishops in the so-called Puebla Document subsequent to the Medellín conference in 1968. It denotes Jesus' liberating ministry that takes into consideration different dimensions of life — whether social, political, economic, or cultural — and the whole web of factors affecting human life. Gustavo Gutiérrez has called this libera-

65. Elizondo, "Foreword," p. 10.

tionist orientation a "theology from the underside of history."[66] The idea of integral liberation insists that "spiritual" and "earthly" belong together and can never be divorced from each other, as has often happened in classical theology. To fight economic and political injustice is a spiritual act. Jesus himself made explicit the link between his own ministry and the coming of the kingdom: "But if it is by the finger of God that I cast out demons, then the kingdom of God has come upon you" (Luke 11:20). Those that Jesus delivered, the sick, the demon possessed, those outside the covenant community, became signs of the coming kingdom and its power of liberation and reconciliation. It is a "world in which the creative plan of God is finally fulfilled; where hunger, poverty, injustice, oppression, pain, even disease and death have been definitively overcome; it is a world from which evil has been rooted out forever."[67]

According to the Brazilian Leonardo Boff, there are two current approaches to Christology. The "sacramental approach" aims to offer a reinterpretation of Christology in terms of classical dogmas and concepts with some liberationist orientation. Boff thinks that even though it is helpful in its acknowledgment of the need for liberation, this type of Christology falls short in its analysis of the Latin American context and is not able to remedy its massive social and political challenges. The second type of liberation Christology is called a "socioanalytical presentation of Christology." This is genuinely liberationist in that it not only offers an incisive analysis but also attempts sociopolitical structural change. This type of liberation theology makes critical use of the tools of social and political sciences and is not afraid to borrow from socialist or Marxist analyses of society. In this latter approach, social, economic, and political liberation is seen as constitutive of the preaching of the kingdom of God. In light of the socioanalytical approach, for example, the exploitative nature of capitalism with the corollary problem of economic dependency is exposed and measures are taken to counterattack. Socioanalytical Christology aims for liberating *orthopraxis* (literally, "right action") rather than *orthodoxy* (literally, "right worship," though the current meaning is "right belief").[68]

Orthopraxis and orthodoxy are not supposed to be exclusive of each

66. Gutiérrez, *The Power of the Poor in History,* p. 169.

67. Bonino, *Room to Be People,* p. 41.

68. L. Boff, *Jesus Christ Liberator,* pp. 269-78. Leonardo's brother, Clodovis Boff, speaks of the "socioanalytic mediation" of theology, a robust interaction with social sciences as an aid to analyze appropriately sociopolitical conditions for theology. C. Boff, *Theology and Praxis.*

other. Rather there is a mutual conditioning. The encounter with the poor illustrates this principle of mutuality. Access to God is not attained primarily through cultic worship or religious observance, but through service to the poor and the oppressed. Liberationists have rightly argued that Christ's presence is to be found among the poor. Therefore, the poor become a christological criterion, not in an exclusive sense (maintaining that Christ is present *only* in the poor) but in an inclusive way, stating that Christ is present *at least* among the poor and the outcasts. The One who himself was poor, and who became poor for all people, is even after his resurrection and ascension to be found amidst the poor. The *kenosis,* self-emptying, of Jesus Christ offers the poor a restitution of their dignity before God, and consequently before other men and women. Küster rightly interprets this foundational idea of liberation Christology: "The adoption of the generative theme of the presence of Jesus Christ in the suffering of the poor and oppressed in liberation theology is to some extent a modern version of Luther's basic hermeneutical principle 'that God is to be found only in suffering and cross.' The liberation theologians 'call things by their right names' [a saying of Luther with regard to the right perspective on reality given by the theology of the cross]."[69]

The affirmation of the presence of Christ in the midst of the poor is significant because today, as in Jesus' time, the poor and outcast make up the majority of the world's population. The Spanish-born Jesuit liberationist who served decades in Latin America, Jon Sobrino, rightly concludes: "If Christianity is characterized by its universal claims, whether made on the basis of creation or of the final consummation, what affects majorities should be a principle governing the degree of authenticity and historical verification of this universalism. . . . Otherwise, the universality it claims will be a euphemism, an irony, or a mythified ideologization."[70] A significant majority of the "common people" of the world — in the midst of whom Jesus of Nazareth mostly ministered during his earthly life — are poor and marginalized. The Korean *minjung* ("masses of people") theologian Byung Mu Ahn hence issues a call to Christian theology to free the "Christology of the Kerygma" from Western enslavement and put the living Jesus in contact with the common people. The "real" Jesus lived with the poor, the sick, and the women, healing them, feeding them, and defending them. Unlike the "Christ of the Kerygma," Jesus does not remain seated, immovable on his

69. Küster, *The Many Faces of Jesus Christ,* p. 55.

70. Sobrino, *Jesus in Latin America,* p. 141.

unshakable throne within the church.[71] Similarly the Indian liberationist A. P. Nirmal, who coined the term "Dalit theology" in the beginning of the 1980s, reminds us that Jesus himself was a "Dalit" — the lowest class in the Indian caste society, indeed, a large group of people without any kind of caste status. In his "Nazareth Manifesto" (Luke 4:16-18), Nirmal remarks, Jesus promised liberation to all prisoners.

That said, the potential liabilities of the "turn to the poor" as the locus of christological presence need to be acknowledged — and they are obvious. On the one hand, this turn may end up glorifying poverty as an access point to the divine. However, there is nothing to be glorified in poverty. Human beings need to have their basic needs met. Hence, a poor person is not necessarily more noble than a richer neighbor. Poverty is one of the social and economic problems to be tackled rather than honored. Likewise, poverty in itself does not make a person Christian or Christ's follower. Faith in Christ and obedience to his commands do. This is not to deny the significance of voluntary giving up of one's privileges for the sake of God's kingdom, as illustrated profoundly in the lives of the religious who dedicate themselves to such lifestyles. But even those Christians do it as Christians in their desire to take discipleship seriously.

With these qualifications in mind, we should fully affirm the call from various contexts of liberation theologies — African American, Latin American, and Asian — to develop Christologies that facilitate and nurture robust sociopolitical activism, on the basis of the hope for the coming of the righteous kingdom of God and on the basis of Jesus' own example. Even the most recent christological discussions in academic theology, with few exceptions such as that of Moltmann — unless they are intentionally liberationist — are totally oblivious to the needs for liberation, reconciliation, justice, and peace. In light of biblical teachings and the overwhelming needs of contemporary life, that state of affairs is not only deplorable but also scandalous. As much as liberation Christologies have contributed to the Christian awareness of these themes, it is not enough to relegate topics of liberation to specialized theological investigations. As long as that is the case, "mainline" theologians can safely go about their work as if nothing had changed. Only when Christian systematic and constructive theology makes liberation a theological theme can the situation change. That said, the separation between dogmatic (traditional) and liberationist Christologies should be re-

71. Ahn, "Jesus and the People (Minjung)," pp. 163-72. See further, Chung, ed., *Asian Contextual Theology for the Third Millennium.*

jected. Concentrated and deep reflection on the dogmatic and systematic implications of Christology in no way leads to complacency in praxis; on the contrary, a proper account of the meaning of Jesus Christ both for this world and for the world to come takes continuing doctrinal reflection.

The Quest of the Hybridized Jesus

The term "hybrid" has been launched by postcolonial thinkers, including Christian theologians, to speak of the bewildering diversity of societies and communities of the third millennium in terms of cultures, nationalities, races, identities, and other such markers that used to be easily identifiable. Currently, we discern national, cultural, racial, and sexual multiplicities. "The international blurs into the national. 'We' do not quite know who is 'us' and who is 'them.' Neither race nor language can any longer define nationality."[72] Hence, the postcolonial theorist Homi K. Bhabha launched the terms "interstitial perspective" to denote the in-between spaces, borderlands, and "interstitial subjectivity" to refer to the complex and undefined ways of seeing identities.[73] The subway in a metropolitan area, "like a great subterranean serpent . . . in the maze beneath the city," full of people of different and mixed colors, races, suits, languages, dialects, and other characteristic features, may well serve as a fitting metaphor.[74]

Why should Christian theology of Christ be concerned about and interested in the postcolonial notion of hybridity? There are at least two important reasons — beyond the more general observation that at all times Christian theology, in order to transcend its own ecclesiastical borders, has engaged existing philosophical and cultural phenomena. First, the "ancient church was born a hybrid of the Jewish religion with the plurality of cultures mingling within the Roman Empire. . . . Today, another global hybridity, with both its wounds and its potentiality, is again redefining Christianity" as the church grows and expands, particularly in the Global South.[75] The beginning of Christianity in Asia is a telling example of hybridity. Even though "it was on a hill in Asia, at the far western edge of the continent, that Jesus

72. Keller, Nausner, and Rivera, eds., *Postcolonial Theologies,* p. 1.

73. Bhabha, *The Location of Culture.*

74. "The Subway" is the first subheading in Keller, Nausner, and Rivera, eds., *Postcolonial Theologies,* "Introduction," p. 1.

75. Keller, Nausner, and Rivera, eds., *Postcolonial Theologies,* p. 4.

said to his disciples, 'Go ye into all the world and preach the gospel' (Mark 16:15),"[76] and even though Jesus was Asian — western Asian, to be more precise — it is also true that "it was in *Roman* Asia that Jesus Christ was born." Like the Greeks that preceded them, the Romans were intruders in the continent.[77] This means that Jesus lived under colonialism and under hybridity when it comes to cultures, politics, identities, and allegiances. Second, Christology "offers as its central doctrine the symbol of a divine/human hybrid, at once mimicking and scandalizing the operative metaphysical binaries of the time."[78] Hence, Kwok Pui-lan has launched the phrase in the subheading to this section, "The Quest of the Hybridized Jesus," after the classic work of Albert Schweitzer, *The Quest of the Historical Jesus*![79]

A profound current example of a hybrid interpretation is Jesus as an Afro-Asiatic Jew. Behind this conjecture is the conviction that the Semitic Hebrews are less a race and more a mixed crowd of people, including those of African descent.[80] Similarly, the metaphor of Jesus as the "Corn Mother" is one of the ways to release American Indians from the "cultural frame of reference that necessitated self-denial and assimilation to the language and social structures of the conqueror."[81] The First Nations' theologian George Tinker develops this image by linking the Johannine preexistent Logos in its historical existence with symbolic-mythological themes of American Indian culture. Like the Johannine Christians who looked for the Logos that is not necessarily limited to male figures, Indians are looking for the mythic image of the Corn Mother who transcends conventional binary sexual limitations. The Corn Mother's suffering and self-sacrifice provide food and sustenance for the people. Tinker finds the vicarious suffering of the Corn Mother to be a critical link with the figure of Jesus Christ in the Bible.[82]

The concept of hybridity pushes Christian theology beyond its comfort level and reminds it of the need to continually appreciate the complexity and subtle nature of diversity built into the biblical narrative of Christ and the subsequent history of the global Christian tradition. If nothing else, the notion of hybridity makes contemporary theology uneasy about being stuck with conventional interpretations and formulations of Christ. This does not

76. Moffett, *History,* 1:4.
77. Moffett, *History,* 1:6.
78. Keller, Nausner, and Rivera, eds., *Postcolonial Theologies,* p. 13.
79. Pui-lan, *Postcolonial Imagination,* p. 170.
80. Baker-Fletcher and Baker-Fletcher, *My Sister, My Brother.*
81. Tinker, "Corn Mother," p. 139.
82. Tinker, "Corn Mother," pp. 151-52.

mean leaving behind the doctrinal guidelines as set forth in the creedal tradition, but rather calls for commitment to continuous reevaluation and reconsideration of current formulations with regard to their faithfulness to tradition and current cultural, social, political, and religious diversity. Hybridity prompts questions such as this one: What are the implications of hybridity for affirming the central claims of the Chalcedonian formula?

Christ and Empire

Whereas liberation theologies of various stripes focus on sexism, poverty, other socioeconomic problems, and political oppression, postcolonial theologies attempt to look at these and similar kinds of issues against the wider horizon of colonialism in its different forms. Hence, "Postcolonial Feminist Rethinking of Jesus/Christ"[83] considers typical feminist theology to be reductionist and counterintuitive as it thinks that "the central problems of Christianity were that the savior was male and that the foundational Christian symbol was androcentric."[84] A postcolonial framing of the issue is wider and more complex. For Kwok Pui-lan,

> the central question is, How is it possible for the formerly colonized, oppressed, subjugated subaltern to transform the symbol of Christ — a symbol that has been used to justify colonization and domination — into a symbol that affirms life, dignity, and freedom? Can the subaltern speak about Christ, and if so, under what conditions?
>
> . . . Alternatively, if we need to ground our reflections in the culture and religiosity of our people, how can we avoid the pitfalls of cultural essentialism, nativism, and nationalistic ideologies? What makes it possible to say something new about Jesus/Christ?[85]

The postcolonial critique of other kinds of feminist Christologies is in need of qualification. It smacks of a "colonialistic" attitude of superiority to hear one group of theologians tell others that their concerns are not valid or are "mistaken." True, feminist and other women's Christologies might have been caught up with the problem of the maleness of Jesus and thereby ne-

83. Subheading in Pui-lan, *Postcolonial Imagination,* p. 169.
84. Pui-lan, *Postcolonial Imagination,* p. 168.
85. Pui-lan, *Postcolonial Imagination,* pp. 168-69.

glected the wider global-political-economic ramifications of many women's oppression. But isn't that justified and a corrective for those women in whose lives the androcentric problem lies at the heart? Commensurately, Asian women construct Christologies differently from European women because their concerns and motifs are different.

At the center of postcolonial Christology is the unmasking of the ways traditional Christianity has allegedly used the uniqueness of Christ in justifying the colonialization project. Or to put it more provocatively: "How does the Aryan Christ contribute both to the colonialization of the Other living outside Europe and also to the oppression of the Other living inside Europe — the Jews?"[86] Christian theologies have been slow to respond to the challenge of the imperium, admits the Latino theologian Virgilio P. Elizondo:

> Theologies, churches, and preaching seem more concerned with helping people feel good about being in this world with all its hedonistic tendencies than with calling individuals and nations to a true conversion to the way of Jesus of Nazareth. There seemed to be more concern with the Christ of Glory who could justify the glories of our United States way of life than with Jesus of Nazareth who lived and died as a scandal to all the respectable, religious, and fine people of *this world!* The churches have often presented the Glory of Christ more in terms of the glories and glitter of this sinful world, thus preventing the true light of the Glory of Christ from illuminating the darkness of our present society.[87]

Why should theology, particularly systematic theology, be mindful of power issues? Simply because the figure of Christ has been used both by Christian and by secular authorities in a way that has supported and facilitated colonialist enterprises. In that light, as the Sri Lankan–born theologian R. S. Sugirtharajah complains, "what is striking about systematic theology is the reluctance of its practitioners to address the relation between European colonialism and the field."[88] It belongs to the domain of systematic theology as much as to any other theological discipline to critically unpack hidden power structures.

86. Pui-lan, *Postcolonial Imagination,* p. 169.

87. Elizondo, "Foreword," pp. 10-11, emphasis in original.

88. Sugirtharajah, "Complacencies and Cul-de-sacs," p. 22. For a theological account of colonialism, see Keller, Nausner, and Rivera, eds., *Postcolonial Theologies;* for two important postcolonial Christologies, see Pui-lan, *Postcolonial Imagination;* Joh, *Heart of the Cross.*

At the end of the fifteenth century when South America was discovered under the leadership of Christopher ("The Christ-Bearer") Columbus and taken over by the *conquistadors* (Spanish soldiers), the figure of Christ was introduced to the first nations of the continent. The Christ presented to the Indios represented the side of the powerful and the ruler. This was the beginning of lengthy suffering by the Indians as they "have been economically exploited, culturally destroyed and alienated, and raped in matters of religion." In too many cases, the figure of Christ presented from the point of view of the power holders served the interests of oppression and suppression.[89] While the figure of the suffering and dying Christ, so dramatically displayed and re-presented in Catholic folk piety even centuries afterward, consoled those oppressed, it did not necessarily elicit the hope that would inspire people to rise to the occasion.

> The two images [of Christ presented to the Indios] are to some degree two sides of the one coin of colonialist propaganda. The dying or dead Christ is an offer of identification in suffering, without arousing hope — the resurrection is distant. Even today, in the popular Catholicism of Latin America, Good Friday is the greatest day of celebration. The other side, Christ the ruler, is embodied in the Spanish king and the colonial rulers, to whom the Indios are to bend the knee in veneration. In both cases the christology degenerates into an instrument of oppression. At an early stage resistance against it grew.[90]

According to Justo L. González, an American Hispanic liberation theologian, very early in Christian history the interpretation of Christ became tuned in with the wishes and hopes of the ruling class, and the role of Christ as the one who identifies with the outcasts, the poor, and the oppressed lost its dynamic:

> Great pains were taken to mitigate the scandal of God's being revealed in a poor carpenter. His life and sayings were reinterpreted so as to make them more palatable to the rich and powerful. Innumerable legends were built around him, usually seeking to raise him to the level that many understood to be that of the divine — that is, to the level of a

89. For political and religious motifs behind the conquest, see Wessels, *Images of Jesus*, pp. 58-61 (61).

90. Küster, *The Many Faces of Jesus Christ*, p. 42.

> superemperor. Art depicted him as either the Almighty Ruler of the universe, sitting on his throne, or as the stolid hero who overcomes the suffering of the cross with superhuman resources and aristocratic poise.[91]

Not only in Latin America, but also in many parts of Asia, "It was largely colonization and evangelization in tandem that brought and propagated the western understanding of Jesus. . . . Not only was it foreign to Asia, it was also an understanding which was polemical against non-Christian religions, disrespectful of indigenous cultures and insensitive to the injustices which colonialism brought about."[92] The shadow of the "European Jesus" superimposed by the colonialists of the past centuries is a continuous challenge to Asian theologians as they are in the process of rediscovering the "Asian faces of Jesus"[93] — and this in the midst of religious plurality and rampant poverty. In the words of the Sri Lankan Aloysius Pieris, "The Asian context can be described as a blend of a profound religiosity (which could be Asia's greatest wealth) and an overwhelming poverty."[94]

Contemporary theology has to consider carefully the abuse of the symbol of Christ in Christian history in light of biblical intuitions. The cosmic Christ of the NT does not rule with tyranny or subjugation, but rather as the one who, as the agent of creation, brings about reconciliation (Col. 1:15-22) and peace (Eph. 2:14). The victorious royal "Lion of Judah" rules as the "Lamb" who was slain and has shed his blood for others (Rev. 5:5-6). "To him who sits upon the throne and to the Lamb be blessing and honor and glory and might for ever and ever!" (v. 13). The acts and attitudes of those who have "want[ed] to pervert the gospel of Christ" (Gal. 1:7) must be judged in light of the righteous rule and standards of the true gospel. Theology has its part to play in this renunciation of anti-Christian acts. That process of repentance and returning to gospel values, however, should eschew all forms of hypocrisy and lack of balanced judgment. The missionaries and other Christians who carried Christ to the continents of Asia, Africa, and

91. González, *Mañana,* p. 140.

92. De Mesa, "Making Salvation Concrete and Jesus Real Trends in Asian Christology," p. 1.

93. Cf. Sugirtharajah, ed., *Asian Faces of Jesus.*

94. Pieris, "Western Christianity and Asian Buddhism," p. 75. Statistically, the number of Christians in Asia range from less than 1 percent (Japan and Thailand, among others) to a few percent at most, with the exception of the predominantly Roman Catholic Philippines (about 85 percent Christian) and more recently South Korea (less than a third Christian) and China (estimations vary widely from 50 to 70 million or so).

Latin America were by and large driven by pious and sincere desire to sacrifice their lives for Christ and other people. Their legacy, thus, has to be put in perspective. At the same time, we who write and teach theology particularly in the abundant, resourceful, and still colonializing Global North, should carefully scrutinize the nature of our "carrying of Christ" in our neighborhoods and beyond. We must root out hidden power motifs, attitudes of selfishness, unwillingness to lay down our lives for the sake of Christ, and similar manifestations of "a different gospel" (Gal. 1:6) in our midst.

We have discussed in some detail the various facets of Jesus' earthly ministry in its various forms, from teaching to healing to exorcism to pronouncement of forgiveness to reaching out to the marginalized — in other words, the embodiment and manifestation of God's righteous rule in his person as the obedient Son served its coming in the power of the Spirit — and how it has been appropriated in rich ways and forms in diverse global contexts. The next large task is to delve into the details of doctrinal formulations both in tradition and in contemporary theology. As mentioned, that task is in no way antagonistic to a robust attention to Jesus' earthly life and ministry. Nor is the doctrinal work insignificant for a better understanding of his meaning and ministry. Indeed, Jesus' teachings, ministry, and liberative work can only gain ultimate meaning against the horizon of Christian confession of him as the Son of God, the second person of the Trinity. Commensurately, the dogmatic confession of faith in Jesus the Christ has to be anchored in his life as the obedient Son in his earthly life and ministry. Christology From Below and From Above presuppose and demand each other. We placed extensive focus on his earthly life first to correct tradition's neglect of it.

4. Messiah and the Kingdom

The Reconfiguration of the Messianic Hopes

N. T. Wright has persuasively argued that Jesus understood his messianic task in terms of the *"reconstitution of Israel"* and thus "believed himself called to work as a prophet, announcing the world of Israel's god to his wayward people, and grouping around himself a company, who . . . would be regarded as the true people of YHWH." Even in the eyes of outsiders, he was perceived to be a prophet because of his teaching and actions, including mighty deeds, miracles, and announcement of forgiveness and warnings of judgment.[1] Here the link between the OT messianic expectations and their fulfillment and embodiment in Jesus is properly highlighted. The prophetic aspect also finds important correlations in the Islamic view of Jesus and the Prophet.

At the center of Jesus' teaching, pronouncements of forgiveness, healings, exorcisms, and identity was the kingdom of his Father, the righteous rule of Yahweh. Jesus fully shared and let come to bear on his life the imminent rule of God (Matt. 6:33), based on the expectations of Israel expressed for example in many psalms (e.g., 96 and 97). Behind the demand of the kingdom is the unreserved loyalty to the uniqueness of Yahweh (Deut. 6:4).

1. N. T. Wright, *Jesus and the Victory of God,* pp. 169, emphasis in original, 196; see also pp. 473-74. For the context and background of prophethood in Israel at the time of Jesus, see chap. 5. For the relation of Jesus as prophet to *the* prophet of Deut. 18:18-19, see p. 163.

The coming rule was already present to those who received his message and repented (Matt. 5:20; 7:21).

Theologically, of primary interest is not only the way Jesus embraced the Jewish hope for the coming of the righteous rule and made it a leading theme in his own life but also the way he radically revised and reoriented it. The reconfiguration and expansion happened in the light of his own coming in relation to his Father.[2] This is the key to his universal relevance and his role as the Savior of the nations as well.

There is continuity and discontinuity here, the acknowledgment of which is essential to Christian theology: "[W]hen Jesus spoke of the 'reign' or 'kingdom' of Israel's god, he was deliberately evoking an entire story-line that he and his hearers knew quite well; second, . . . he was retelling this familiar story in such a way as to subvert and redirect its normal plot. . . . The basic announcement carries, by implication, the complete story in its new form."[3] Unlike the merely future-oriented Jewish hopes, the kingdom became both present reality, which was already dawning in his own personhood, and something awaiting future consummation. "The particular dynamic of Jesus' message of the *basileia,* then, is that the rule of God is imminent but that it also emerges from futurity as present."[4] This dynamic is aptly illustrated in the book title of G. E. Ladd, *The Presence of the Future.*[5]

Also important is that the hope for the kingdom was divorced from nationalistic, racial, or geographical connotations and made a universal theme with a view to the whole of humanity, including even cosmic renewal.[6] The anticipatory nature comes to the fore in his healings, which were "signs" (in the parlance of the Gospel of John) of the eschatological wholeness and shalom: exorcisms, which signaled the overcoming of evil; revised interpretation of the Law as manifestation of the Fatherly love of God over tradition;[7] and pronouncement of forgiveness to sinners as indication of the inclusion of the Gentiles in the covenant promises of salvation. As an anticipation of the future eschatological fellowship that also included the nations, forgiveness was already pronounced to those willing to subject their lives to the righteous demands of the kingdom of God (Matt. 8:11 par.).

2. See further, Pannenberg, *ST* 2:326-34.

3. N. T. Wright, *Jesus and the Victory of God,* p. 199.

4. Pannenberg, *ST* 2:330; see also pp. 326-34.

5. With the subtitle *Eschatology of Biblical Realism.*

6. N. T. Wright, *Jesus and the Victory of God,* pp. 215-19; see also Pannenberg, *ST* 2:326-34.

7. See further, Pannenberg, *ST* 2:333-34.

The orientation to the present and coming rule of God meant that Jesus was an eschatological (or apocalyptic) prophet.[8] In that light, one of the current interpretations of Jesus' role by scholars associated with the Jesus Seminar such as John Dominic Crossan and Burton Mack, who highlight one-sidedly the sapiential (wisdom) rather than prophetic and apocalyptic themes, has to be deemed totally failing. That view would make the idea of the kingdom totally this-worldly,[9] a claim one supposes had been left behind once and for all after the collapse of the original quest. Highlighting the eschatological nature of the rule of God helps bring the theme of resurrection and its confirmatory role into the picture. According to the NT testimonies and mainline Christian interpretation, it was the resurrection — an idea deeply imbedded in Jewish intertestamental apocalypticism (and yet also revised in the light of Jesus' rising from the dead) — that confirmed the deity of the Messiah of Israel in the person of Jesus of Nazareth.

So far we have used the term "Messiah" as if its meaning were obvious and there would be unanimity about it. Far from that — in contemporary scholarship the meaning of the term "messiahship" is widely debated, particularly its significance and meaning in relation to Jesus Christ. Of course, in a systematic study it is not possible to delve into the myriads of details of biblical scholarship concerning this issue. Yet no systematic argumentation can operate without a careful scrutiny of biblical scholars' work. This systematic argumentation operates with the claim that "[f]rom its very earliest days, the community of Jesus' followers regarded him as Messiah."[10] According to Acts 2:36, "Let all the house of Israel therefore know assuredly that God has made him both Lord and Christ, this Jesus whom you crucified." Indeed, "Early Christianity was through and through *messianic*, and, in line with many hints and promises from the biblical and post-biblical literature, the early Christians believed that the Messiah, whose name they now knew, was the true *lord* of the world."[11]

8. See further, N. T. Wright, *Jesus and the Victory of God*, pp. 251-58 and passim.

9. For a careful critique and assessment, see N. T. Wright, *Jesus and the Victory of God*, pp. 210-20.

10. N. T. Wright, *Jesus and the Victory of God*, p. 486 (and see literature referred to there); so also Moltmann, *Way of Jesus Christ*. For opposing views among biblical scholars, arguing for some type of "nonmessianic" interpretation, see N. T. Wright, *Resurrection of the Son of God*, pp. 554-55; Bird, *Are You the One?* pp. 25-26 (part of the "nonmessianic" argumentation has to do with the question, to be discussed below, of the "messianic awareness" of Jesus, which of course is a different issue in many ways).

11. N. T. Wright, *Resurrection of the Son of God*, p. 553; so also, e.g., p. 554.

How is it then understandable that the Jews, whose Messiah Jesus of Nazareth was claimed to be, by and large rejected him? What was there in this Christian presentation of the Messiah that was resisted and opposed? Here biblical scholarship speaks with much agreement. Three basic viewpoints lay the foundation for the consideration of this important issue. First of all, rather than one defined formulation of messianic hopes, the OT and Second Temple Judaism present a number of competing messianic hopes. This is acknowledged by both Christian and Jewish scholars.[12] Second, unlike theological tradition, contemporary biblical scholarship unanimously agrees that messiahship in Second Temple Judaism and in the time of Jesus did not connote divinity.[13] This is of course not to deny that in Christian parlance, the Greek title "Christ" became a major title for the divinity and that it was also linked with the highest NT title, namely, *Kyrios* (the Lord), as in Acts 2:36. What the claim says is that in the Jewish ears of Jesus' contemporaries, "Messiah" was not a divine title.[14]

Third, and here we come to the crux of the issue for the current discussion: whatever the content of the various messianic hopes of Second Temple Judaism, definitely they were in sharp conflict with the way these hopes were claimed to be "fulfilled" in the Messiah of the Christian interpretation.[15] Jewish hopes included in some form or another overthrow of foreign occupants and their judgment and destruction, the purging of Jerusalem of Gentiles, the gathering back to the land of the dispersed people of God, and such deeply held eschatological beliefs. Here obviously is the riddle and the "stumbling block" of the crucified Messiah of Christians. In the words of N. T. Wright,

> What nobody expected the Messiah to do was to die at the hands of the pagans instead of defeating them; to mount a symbolic attack on the Temple, warning it of imminent judgment, instead of rebuilding or cleansing it; and to suffer unjust violence at the hands of the pagans instead of bringing them justice and peace. The crucifixion of Jesus, understood from the point of view of any onlooker, whether sympathetic

12. For detailed discussion and literature, see N. T. Wright, *Jesus and the Victory of God,* chap. 11; Bird, *Are You the One?* chap. 2; for a nuanced and useful discussion by a leading American Jewish scholar, see Kogan, *Opening the Covenant,* chap. 2.

13. See the useful and nuanced discussion in Kogan, *Opening the Covenant,* chap. 2.

14. Hence, the century-long debate about the "messianic secret" going back all the way to Wilhelm Wrede should be cast in a different light.

15. See further, N. T. Wright, *New Testament and the People of God,* pp. 307-20; N. T. Wright, *Jesus and the Victory of God,* pp. 481-86.

or not, was bound to have appeared as the complete destruction of any messianic pretensions or possibilities he or his followers might have hinted at.[16]

Now, the inevitable question before Christian theologians is simply this: Why did the first Christians come to the conclusion, against all evidence, as it were, that indeed Jesus was Messiah, particularly in light of the fact that he "had been scourged, dragged through the streets and executed" and that "his execution was in public, increasing the shame and the sense of utter and devastating victory for the pagans"?[17] The shorthand answer is that, in light of the resurrection of Jesus that was taken by the first Christians as divine vindication, the messianic hopes of Israel, rather than being abandoned, were radically reconfigured. On the one hand, much of the OT messianism was reembraced, including the universal lordship (hence the combination: Messiah and Lord). On the other hand, as already hinted at above when discussing the reconfiguration of the meaning of the kingdom of God, foundational revisions were adopted. Four such revisions are most significant: first, the loosing of ethnic specificity; second, instead of military campaign, confrontation of evil was expected; third, the rebuilding of the temple would take place in the form of new community; and fourth, the justice and peace imagined and hoped for by the Jews would consist of God's own righteousness over the whole of creation.[18]

The fact that the first Christians claimed to be witnesses to his bodily resurrection — namely, that "Israel's god had raised Jesus from the dead"[19] — is the only reason that theologically and also historically explains the emergence of the belief in Jesus as the Messiah. The meaning and importance of resurrection as the way to establish the belief in Jesus as the Messiah and as the *Kyrios,* which led to the more fully formulated confession of the deity of Christ as the second person of the Trinity as expressed in creedal traditions, have to be investigated in detail below. Similarly, the implications of the emergence of the radically reconfigured interpretation of Messiah in Christian faith to the current Christian-Jewish dialogue also have to be investigated in detail below.

16. N. T. Wright, *Resurrection of the Son of God,* pp. 557-58.

17. N. T. Wright, *Resurrection of the Son of God,* p. 559.

18. N. T. Wright, *Resurrection of the Son of God,* pp. 562-63. For important discussion, see also N. T. Wright, *The Climax of the Covenant,* chaps. 2 and 3; *New Testament and the People of God,* pp. 406-9; *Jesus and the Victory of God,* chap. 11.

19. N. T. Wright, *Resurrection of the Son of God,* p. 563.

Messianic Awareness

Interestingly enough, the Jewish historian Joseph Klausner opined that "there can be no doubt" that "Jesus was convinced that he was the Messiah," because "otherwise he would have been nothing more than an evil impostor and deceiver."[20] Most contemporary Christian scholars, ironically, disagree with him! It is commonly argued that to say Jesus was recognized as Israel's Messiah who is also the Messiah of the nations is not to say that Jesus of Nazareth considered himself to be the Messiah. This takes us to a corollary, the highly contested debate about whether the earthly Jesus claimed authority to his person before the resurrection. Pannenberg says no because he stresses so much Jesus' role as the obedient human person[21] — and because his Christology operates with the idea of the human Jesus rather than Christ/Logos as the subject of the one person. This is also the way Pannenberg explains the "messianic secret," the fact that Jesus intentionally withdrew from identifying himself with the messianic expectations until his trial (Matt. 26:64; 27:11 par.).[22] The question for Pannenberg is about the fact that there is no doubt that his audience did acknowledge authority in his teaching and works of miracles (Mark 1:27).

The question can also be formulated in this way: Did the earthly Jesus realize who he was? In other words, what can we say of his awareness of vocation and identity? There are two interrelated, yet distinguishable, questions here — which are not often distinguished as they should be. The first level has to do with whether Jesus was aware of his messiahship and God-given vocation. As mentioned above, contemporary biblical scholarship unanimously agrees that messiahship in the Second Temple Judaism and in the times of Jesus did not connote divinity.[23] The second level, then, has to

20. Cited in P. Lapide, *Israelis, Jews, and Jesus,* p. 6, without page reference.

21. Pannenberg, *ST* 2:327-31. Pannenberg also argues forcefully that there is no need to refer to Jesus' sense of authority because the future coming of the kingdom, "[t]ransition from the future to the present arises out of the matter itself, out of the content of the proclamation of Jesus, out of the claim of the oneness of God upon the present of the hearers" (p. 331). Even though I acknowledge the value of this insight, in my view this fails to do full justice to the Gospel accounts that imply a sense of authority.

22. Pannenberg, *ST* 2:335-37. Along with the majority of scholarship, based on the classic work of William Wrede *(The Messianic Secret),* Pannenberg also refers to the political connotations of Jewish messianic expectations as the reason for rejecting them (p. 334).

23. For contemporary discussion and literature, see N. T. Wright, *Jesus and the Victory of God,* chap. 11; Bird, *Are You the One?* chap. 2.

do with whether and in what sense Jesus was (or became) aware of his divine nature (in the sense that postbiblical tradition formulated it in terms of the divine Son, the second person of the Trinity).[24]

So much of twentieth-century biblical scholarship has taken it as axiomatic that the earthly Jesus could not have had any meaningful awareness of his messianic calling and especially divinity, that the question was thought to be settled without much debate.[25] Building on that tradition, Pannenberg, even though he represents a high Christology in contrast to most of the above-mentioned biblical scholars, surmises that Jesus' identity as the divine Son was "ambivalent,"[26] indeed, the human Jesus was not aware of his identity "from the very outset."[27] That is not to deny the gradual deepening and intensification of Jesus' awareness of unity with God as his life unfolded.[28] (The concept of anticipation, of course, is an important way for Pannenberg to reconcile Jesus' denial of messianic consciousness before resurrection and his acknowledgment thereafter.)

A significant strand of the most recent biblical scholarship has come to challenge this consensus and acknowledge the possibility of Jesus' self-awareness of his identity. As a counterproposal to the denial of self-awareness by a whole generation of scholarship, Wright has marshaled evidence of the messianic vocation and Jesus' role as the representative of his people.[29] One of the many weighty supporting arguments is Jesus' acting as if he replaced the temple and Torah.[30] Indeed, Jesus believed that the core Jewish hopes of the return of Yahweh to Zion and defeat of evil "were com-

24. In contemporary literature the question of Jesus' self-awareness is often referred to as the "Christology of Christ."

25. A noted example is Marcus J. Borg, who claims to believe that Jesus was the Son of God and savior of the world, but cannot imagine that Jesus thought the same of himself; see, e.g., Borg, *Meeting Jesus Again for the First Time.*

26. Pannenberg, *ST* 2:373.

27. Pannenberg, *ST* 2:389.

28. Cf. Pannenberg, *ST* 2:383-84.

29. N. T. Wright, *Jesus and the Victory of God,* pp. 132, 465-67, and passim. Those who materially agree include Bird, *Are You the One?;* Witherington, *Jesus, Paul, and the End of the World,* pp. 170-77; Charlesworth, *The Historical Jesus,* p. 110; C. A. Evans, "Assessing Progress in the Third Quest of the Historical Jesus," p. 44 (he summarizes leading views of this quest). Found at http://www.craigaevans.com/Third_Quest.rev.pdf; page numbers refer to the online version. Wright mentions a number of other important scholars who "have been happy to affirm that Jesus believed himself to be, in some sense, Messiah" (p. 488 n. 35), including Ben Meyer, Sanders, Harvey, Witherington, and Hengel.

30. N. T. Wright, *Jesus and the Victory of God,* pp. 646-47.

ing true in and through himself."[31] This awareness culminated in Jesus' determination to go to Jerusalem "to die."[32] More convinced about the authenticity of Son of Man and similar statements on the lips of Jesus, these scholars conclude that there is no reason to reject the messianic consciousness of the pre-Easter Jesus[33] — as church tradition before critical studies had held universally.

Even N. T. Wright, with his passionate mounting of evidence for the messianic consciousness, falls short of arguing that on the *historical* basis it would be possible to establish necessarily Jesus' awareness of divinity (as in Christian tradition).[34] However, important elements in his argument clearly support the possibility of the consciousness of divinity. Wright rightly ridicules the reluctance of scholars to acknowledge any capacity or willingness to concede theological thinking by Jesus. Now that more recent scholarship agrees that the Gospel writers were "*theologians*" rather than "artless chroniclers or transcribers" who "thought deeply and creatively about the Jewish scriptures, about Israel's god, about the achievement of this god in completing the story of those scriptures in Jesus," why should Jesus himself be denied the possibility of careful theological thinking and reflection on his own personality and vocation — even as "some greater, more original, more subtle mind"? This is not of course another failing exercise, after the liberal "lives of Jesus" model, into the psychology or inner biography of Jesus, he rightly warns us. This is a historical claim.[35] Furthermore, Wright highlights the emergence of worship of Jesus as divine from very early on and the rise of the Christian community that has no parallel in history. How probable is it that the followers of the condemned and crucified Messiah would form and expand the community, especially when the "founder" was absent, apart from the reference to the deep-seated faith in the divinity of Christ, based on resurrection and ascension? Importantly, the resurrection alone would not have given such a meaning to the risen Christ had such meaning not been

31. N. T. Wright, *Jesus and the Victory of God,* p. 652.

32. N. T. Wright, *Jesus and the Victory of God,* pp. 553, 593, and the careful argumentation in chap. 12. This is not to deny that "Within Jesus' prophetic and messianic vocation, we can trace the outlines of a deeper vocation that would remain hidden" (p. 645).

33. See particularly the carefully argued work of Bird, *Are You the One?*

34. N. T. Wright, *Jesus and the Victory of God,* pp. 652-53.

35. N. T. Wright, *Jesus and the Victory of God,* pp. 478-81 (479, emphasis in original). As a parallel example Wright refers to Saul of Tarsus and John the Baptist, who historians acknowledge had a deep sense and awareness of their vocation, based on the NT records (p. 480).

there before that, during his earthly life.[36] None of these important theological and historical viewpoints of course necessarily lead to the assumption of Jesus' own consciousness of divinity. What they do is support that possibility and make it plausible.

The question of Jesus' awareness of messiahship and particularly of divinity is of course intimately related to the postbiblical developments of Christian tradition, first and foremost as they led to the creedal formulations. Hence, a constructive critical assessment of the achievements and liabilities, as well as the continuing value for theology and faith, of Chalcedonian (and Nicene-Constantinopolitan) traditions will be investigated next. Thereafter, we can delve into the key christological doctrines and claims that stemmed from Chalcedon and were fine-tuned and debated in subsequent theological debates.

36. N. T. Wright, *Jesus and the Victory of God*, pp. 486-88.

5. The Chalcedonian Tradition: A Horizon for Understanding Christ

Classical christological traditions are based on the creedal traditions, the so-called two-nature Christology, culminating in the definition of Chalcedon in 451. A patchwork of earlier pronouncements, particularly from Cyril of Alexandria against Nestorius and from Pope Leo I against Monophysite (Eutychian) views, the creed advocates more strongly the interpretations of the Christian West, including the legacy of Tertullian, Hilary of Poitiers, and Augustine.[1] According to Leo's *Tome*, "the properties of either nature and substance . . . came together in one person . . . both natures retain[ing] their own proper character without loss." This guarantees the unity of the one person and affirms the famous *communicatio idiomatum* ("communication of proper qualities") formula.[2] Tradition presupposed that in the NT both divine and human attributes are predicated of one subject, Christ (the divine Word, Logos), as seems to be the case in passages such as Acts 3:15 and John 17:5, among others. Furthermore, Chalcedon also affirmed the Nicean faith in its preamble.[3]

Chalcedon takes great pains in affirming, on the one hand, the true humanity and deity of Jesus Christ and, on the other hand, both the unity and duality of this God-man. These affirmations could only be defined neg-

1. On the continuing debates in the Christian East following Chalcedon, see Pelikan, *Emergence of the Catholic Tradition*, pp. 266-77.

2. Leo I, "Letter [XXVIII] to Flavian Commonly Called *Tome*," 3; also 4; *NPNF*[2] 12:40-41.

3. For the whole text, see, e.g., *NPNF*[2] 14:262-65.

atively with the help of four terms: "unconfusedly," "immutably," "indivisibly," and "inseparably." Even though distinguished, the two "natures" in one person are not to be separated nor conflated; in other words, divinity and humanity cannot be a mixture that would lead to a "third nature."[4] Logos, the divine Word, is the "subject" of the Incarnate One, expressed in tradition with the help of the term "hypostatic union" (Cyril's favorite term, which, even though it does not appear in Chalcedon, lies behind its affirmations). The use of the much-debated *theotokos* title for Virgin Mary is an indication of the application of the *communicatio idiomatum* clause.

One of the terms widely used in Christian traditions, primarily in trinitarian considerations, but also in Christology, is *perichoresis,* "mutual indwelling."[5] In this formula, the divinity and humanity of Jesus Christ inhere, mutually indwell each other, without separation, without mingling of natures. True, this conceptual apparatus has been used in tradition as a "theological black box . . . as a means of filling a conceptual gap in reflection upon . . . the hypostatic union in the Incarnation."[6] The term *perichoresis* thus is materially saying the same as *communicatio idiomatum.*[7]

The Liabilities and Problems of Chalcedonian Tradition

Even though Chalcedon is, as Pelikan pointedly puts it, "an agreement to disagree," it also is "a statement of the theology of preexistence, kenosis, and exaltation."[8] How do we assess its merits and liabilities in our contemporary setting? Do we have to stick with its formulations to be "orthodox"? What would the development of Chalcedon entail and mean? A number of complaints and criticisms have been leveled against the two-nature, "incarna-

4. Already Tertullian (*Against Praxeas* 27 in *ANF* 3:624) saw this kind of view as erroneous.

5. For a technical note on how the term *perichoresis* is applied and understood in trinitarian and christological contexts, see Swinburne, *The Christian God,* p. 209 n. 20. It might be significant that the term itself was first used in relation to Christology rather than the Trinity, although, as said, it was in the context of the trinitarian considerations that it came to be used most prominently in later tradition. Gregory of Nazianzus in his *Epistle 101* and elsewhere used it first, and it was subsequently picked up by Maximus the Confessor and others. See further, Crisp, *Divinity and Humanity,* p. 4.

6. Crisp, *Divinity and Humanity,* p. 1.

7. For a useful historical and theological discussion of *perichoresis* and *communicatio idiomatum,* see chap. 1 in Crisp, *Divinity and Humanity.*

8. Pelikan, *Emergence of the Catholic Tradition,* p. 266.

tional" Christology of Chalcedon. The criticisms can be grouped under the following categories.

In many quarters of the theological world a suspicion has arisen whether the development of dogma, rather than being a matter of clarification of incipient NT ideas about Christ, is an aberration — or, as the liberal church historian A. von Harnack named it, the "deterioration of dogma."[9] However, this simplistic and erroneous interpretation hardly can be taken seriously.[10] The Chalcedonian Christology has also been blamed for political bias, namely, deriving its ethos from the church's alliance with the powers-that-be of the Constantinian empire.[11] The feminist Rosemary Radford Ruether, among others, has articulated the charge that the "orthodox Christology" of the first Christian centuries helped the marginal religious sect evolve "into the new imperial religion of a Christian Roman Empire."[12] That charge, however, has been successfully combated by the historical observation that it was the non-Chalcedonian Arian party that was more prone to look for earthly power sympathies and agendas.[13]

No more convincing is the charge that the Chalcedonian Logos Christology led to the "patriarchalization of Christology" that in turn led to the hierarchical view in which, "just as the *Logos* of God governs the cosmos, so the Christian Roman Emperor, together with the Christian Church, governs the political universe."[14] This is a problematic and naive statement on more than

9. Over against that view, Harnack set forth a presentation of original, simple Christianity in his *What Is Christianity?* The same kind of suspicion can also be found in Dewart, *The Future of Belief.*

10. Pannenberg, *ST* 2:379: "It should now be clear that the history of Christological development in primitive Christianity does not consist of a disconnected sequence of heterogeneous ideas that were later attached to the person of Jesus and had nothing to do materially with his historical figure." For a careful discussion of the Greek, particularly Aristotelian, philosophy and worldview behind the formulations, see McIntyre, *The Shape of Christology,* pp. 87-96 especially.

11. A fairly sophisticated, yet in my understanding, failing, current such view is held by the Anabaptist Denny Weaver in his attack against all notions of "violent atonement" (satisfaction and penal substitution theories) and in defense of other views such as the patristic *Christus Victor* theory, which, in his analysis, fell into disfavor because of Chalcedon's and Nicea's sympathies with the power of Rome. Weaver, *Nonviolent Atonement,* pp. 86-91 especially.

12. Ruether, *Sexism and God-Talk,* p. 122.

13. See the important essay by G. H. Williams, "Christology and Church-State Relations in the Fourth Century."

14. Ruether, *Sexism and God-Talk,* p. 125.

one account. First of all, it grossly exaggerates the role of doctrine in the ascendancy of Christian religion into the place of power. Complex political, including ecclesio-political, forces were in place. Second, it ignores the fact that the development of Christian doctrine was in itself a long, winding, and complex process; hence, attempting to discern one leading motif, such as desire to enforce power structures, can hardly be supported by historical evidence. Third, this feminist explanation neglects the fact that even though the Christian church (more so than Christian doctrine per se) has been used by the empire for earthly power plays, and the church has not always resisted that desire on the basis of the gospel, that abuse can hardly be made a standard and rule. Finally, even if it were true that Chalcedonian tradition was used in such an unchristian way, it does not necessarily mean that there could not be a right use of the ecumenical statement of the undivided church.

At the heart of many complaints about and challenges to two-nature Christology stands the concept of "nature" as applied to Jesus the Christ. It is a major challenge — and to many, an insurmountable obstacle — to continuing to employ the framework of incarnational Christology of tradition. The term "nature" in Latin and Western ontological usage means something akin to "substance." "Substance," however, is something "self-subsistent," apart from relations. It is also immutable, not subject to change. Neither one of these premises, namely, nonrelationality and nonalterability, serves well christological — or other *theo*-logical — purposes.[15] Schleiermacher famously eschewed all talk about "nature" in reference to Jesus and God because for him the term denoted the summary of all that is finite existence, which, of course, does not apply to the deity.[16] Consequently, he rejected the tradition's notion of *communicatio idiomatum,* communication of properties of each nature, as something that would cancel the union altogether; the union between the human and the divine is that of the person.[17]

Many wonder if the two-nature Christology by default tends to shift focus from the "lowliness" of Jesus, his suffering and anguish, to his divinity, exaltation, and triumph.[18] As long as the human nature assumed by the eternal Logos is conceived as a nonpersonal human nature, it is difficult to think of a particular human person. For many contemporary minds, this kind of assumed human nature may not look much different from "the human gar-

15. For helpful reflections, see Henriksen, *Desire, Gift, and Recognition,* p. 209.
16. Schleiermacher, *Christian Faith,* §96.1, p. 392.
17. Schleiermacher, *Christian Faith,* §97.5, p. 413.
18. Moltmann, *Way of Jesus Christ,* p. 52.

ment of the eternal Son."[19] Moreover, it is challenging to see any kind of identity between that kind of generic human nature and ours. A related issue is whether the assumption of sinless human nature can be taken as a statement about genuine human nature. This question will be taken up below in our discussion of the traditional doctrine of sinlessness.

Several of these problems go back to the exquisite difficulties in finding a satisfactory way to link the two natures with each other. Too often, traditional Christology has attempted to differentiate between the two natures on the basis of general — even static — metaphysics rather than the particular history of Jesus the Christ himself. This tendency leads to nonpersonal models of explanation and tends to turn off the notions of true, vulnerable human nature: "His faithfulness is transformed into a substantial immutability, his zeal, his love, his compassion — in short, his 'pathos,' his capacity for feeling — are supplanted by the essential apathy of the divine. The passion of his love and its capacity for suffering can no longer be stated."[20]

A significant weakness of Chalcedonian Christology is the lack of focus on the whole history of Jesus the Christ; in other words, its horizon is hopelessly narrow. A glaring omission is the silence in the creeds of everything that has to do with the earthly life of Jesus, including his compassion, teaching, healings, exorcisms, and pronouncements of forgiveness. As Moltmann chidingly points out, in the creeds, "there is either nothing at all, or really no more than a comma, between 'and was made man, he suffered' or 'born' and 'suffered.'"[21] The rediscovery of the integral link between anthropology and Christology has made many contemporary theologians weary of the two-nature model. Pannenberg is of course a grand example. He warns us against the tendency in tradition to take the two natures as standing "ontologically on the same level" and yet having "nothing to do with one another apart from their union" in one person.[22] This doesn't give a proper account of the humanity of Jesus. In early Christology, this weakness was intensified with the effort to establish Jesus' humanity primarily in terms of the virgin birth instead of the whole history of Jesus.[23]

Liberation theologians of various sorts have harshly critiqued the

19. Moltmann, *Way of Jesus Christ,* p. 51.

20. Moltmann, *Way of Jesus Christ,* p. 53.

21. Moltmann, *Way of Jesus Christ,* p. 150.

22. Pannenberg, *ST* 2:385.

23. Pannenberg, *ST* 2:383-85. The dangers of independent humanity (Nestorianism) or no full humanity at all (Monophysitism) loom large in early tradition in Pannenberg's estimation.

christological formulations of Nicea and Chalcedon, along with classical atonement theories, which "investigated the meaning of Jesus' relation to God and the divine and human natures in his person, but failed to relate these christological issues to the liberation of the slave and the poor in the society."[24] According to James Cone, the generic categories of "divinity" and "humanity" lack ethical content and can easily lead to practice in which religion supports the hegemony of the empire, as happened with Constantinian Christendom.[25] According to the Episcopalian womanist Kelly Brown Douglas, for many black Christians the Nicene-Chalcedonian confession is not important or relevant. They are rather interested in the ministry of Jesus as described in the Gospels. Yet that does not mean that therefore the creed should be left behind; it is held as an important, if not normative, conversation partner.[26]

Many critics of Chalcedon wonder if it can be saved from being equated with mythological parallels in gnosticism and religions. Myths about gods ascending and descending abound in religions. Notwithstanding some thematic parallels, the NT narrative of Logos, however, does not present a gnostic redeemer myth[27] in which a deity visits the earth for a while and then returns to the heavenly realm — not to mention the fact that such gnostic myths are later than the NT narrative. In these myths, deities do not become human beings. The narrative in Philippians 2:7-11 underlines not only the true humanity of Jesus but also his obedience and self-sacrifice; thus for Paul "the emphasis is not on the transition from one phase to another, but on the humility, obedience, and selflessness of Christ."[28] Unlike ancient mythologies, bishops at Ephesus (431), both Eastern and Western, following Clement of Alexandria, agreed: "Neither do we say that his flesh was changed into the nature of divinity, nor that the ineffable nature of the Word of God was laid aside for the nature of flesh; for he is unchanged and absolutely unchangeable, being the same always, according to the Scriptures. For although visible and a child in swaddling clothes, and even in the bosom of his Virgin Mother, he filled all creation as God, and was a fellow-ruler

24. Cone, *God of the Oppressed,* p. 104.

25. Cone, *God of the Oppressed,* p. 107.

26. K. B. Douglas, *The Black Christ,* pp. 111-13.

27. As J. A. T. Robinson (*Human Face of God,* p. 163) seems to imply as he speaks of "a Gnosticizing version of the distinctively Christian message." Gerhard Friedrich ("Der Brief an die Philipper," p. 151) strongly rejects this interpretation. I am indebted to Schwarz, *Christology,* p. 235, for these exact references.

28. Schwarz, *Christology,* p. 234.

with him who begat him, for the Godhead is without quantity and dimension, and cannot have limits."[29] In other words, in Christian understanding God became human rather than changed into a human. And even after the ascension, the glorified Lord bears the marks of the incarnation.[30] A careful look at the relation of the Christian doctrine of incarnation to Hindu views of avatars as incarnations of deities will be taken up below.

Finally, a host of Enlightenment-born christological interpretations deem it necessary to go beyond not only the thought forms and affirmations but also the basic intent. In that understanding, the focus shifts from the descent of the Logos in incarnation to the humanity of Jesus as the essence of christological reflection. For Schleiermacher, Jesus was the perfect human being[31] — whom, curiously, he preferred to call "Christ" in his dogmatics — and it was Jesus' activity or vocation that formed the basis of Christology rather than, as in tradition, Jesus' being.[32] The same kind of approach, which leads to the dismissal of Jesus' divinity in the Chalcedonian sense, is evident in the rest of classical liberal Christology. Albrecht Ritschl shines here as a good example: in his estimation the uniqueness of Jesus is the "new and hitherto unknown relation to God," which makes him the highest form of revelation. Consequently, Jesus could be compared to other such figures in religions, whether in Zoroastrianism, Buddhism, Islam, or Judaism.[33]

The Continuing *Relative* Value of the Christology of the Creeds

The acknowledgment of these weaknesses and lacunae does not warrant leaving behind the Chalcedonian model of explanation. Rather, the task of contemporary theology is to correct, expand, and reorient Christology, building critically on the basis of tradition and also using the Chalcedonian formula as the minimum — and relative, as is any human device — crite-

29. The Epistle of Cyril to Nestorius with the XII. Anathematisms, in "Council of Ephesus," in *NPNF*[2] 14:202.

30. See further, Bloesch, *Jesus Christ*, pp. 54-55.

31. For Schleiermacher (*Christian Faith*, §94.2, p. 388), "the human God-consciousness becomes an existence of God in human nature"; see also 92, p. 374; 97.3, p. 409.

32. Schleiermacher, *Christian Faith*, §93.1, p. 377.

33. Ritschl, *Christian Doctrine of Justification and Reconciliation*, par. 44; pp. 385-90 particularly (386).

rion.[34] Many of the problems mentioned above go back to the use of the terms "person" and "nature" in an abstract sense. However, they are to be defined and regulated ecclesiastically and theologically. These words are used specifically, and can only be understood in that particular sense and context. They are not intended to mean that this is everything the Christian church says of Christ; thus, the need for continuing constructive theology. Nor is it the case that everyone means — or even, originally, meant — the same thing with these terms.[35] The approach of this discussion takes seriously these challenges and believes that the main intent of Chalcedon could and should be maintained. I feel great sympathy for the statement of Dietrich Bonhoeffer: "The Chalcedonian Definition is an objective, but living, statement which bursts through all thought-forms."[36]

Of old, this creed has been called the Chalcedonian "definition." However, as Sarah Coakley brilliantly notes, it is less a definition in the modern sense of the word and more — building on the etymology of the Greek term for definition, *horos* — a "horizon."[37] The many meanings of *horos*, "horizon," "boundary," "limit," "standard," "pattern," and "rule," remind us of the way early Christianity understood and employed a creedal statement: it was a "rule of faith" *(regula fidei)*. The term "rule" here means guidance, limits, standards, and boundaries that help the community of faith to rule out heretical views and point to the shared consensus even when everything — or often, many things — in the rule is not exactly defined.[38] This is not to say, after the postliberal understanding of doctrine of George Lindbeck and like-minded scholars, that therefore the "doctrine" is not understood to refer to something that really happened.[39] It is rather to say that Chalcedon speaks

34. Even Pannenberg, particularly in his *Systematic Theology*, grants the continuing legitimacy of the traditional affirmation even when he doesn't like to use the explanatory model of two natures.

35. See Galvin, "Jesus Christ," p. 271.

36. Bonhoeffer, *Christ the Center*, p. 92; I am indebted to Bloesch, *Jesus Christ*, p. 70.

37. Coakley, "What Does Chalcedon Solve?" p. 160.

38. The term "symbol" for early creeds served the same function (and cannot be read in the "thin" sense of contemporary usage).

39. A proposal echoing the epistemology of the Yale School, even though, in my understanding, independent from it, is that offered by Richard Norris. According to his view, the drafters at Chalcedon were neither equipped (not being "professional theologians") nor specifically inclined to construct precise theological formulations; the result, rather, is a patchwork of clauses from well-known sources behind the creed. Thus, the Definition is hardly more than "a paradigm" that provides of Christ "essentially a transcription and an account of a pattern of predication." Norris, "Chalcedon Revisited," pp. 149-51 (151);

of — and we should continue speaking of its affirmations in terms of — something believed to have really happened in a way that can only be expressed as a rule of faith, rather than, in the spirit of modernity, as a highly accurate, "scientific" analysis. This is what Karl Rahner was aiming at in his programmatic and widely renowned essay written several decades ago titled "Current Problems in Christology." The late Jesuit theologian reminds us that every theological formula, including Chalcedon, is "beginning and emergence, not conclusion and end." Theological formulation is a "means . . . which opens the way to the-ever-greater-Truth."[40] This helps put the Definition in the right perspective:

> We shall never stop trying to release ourselves from it, not so as to abandon it but to understand it, understand it with mind and heart, so that through it we might draw near to the ineffable, unapproachable, nameless God, whose will it was that we should find him in Jesus Christ and through Christ seek him. We shall never cease to return to this formula, because whenever it is necessary to say briefly what it is that we encounter in the ineffable truth which is our salvation, we shall always have recourse to the modest, sober clarity of the Chalcedonian formula. But we shall only really have recourse to it (and this is not at all the same thing as simply repeating it), if it is not only our end but also our beginning.[41]

In the final analysis, the question of the continuing value of the Chalcedonian formula is a wide-ranging hermeneutical decision. A related question is the genre of the Definition itself. Its basic affirmation, namely, the coming together of the divine and human in an irreversible yet distinguishable unity, can be appropriately called a mystery and metaphor. It is mystery in the sense that it goes beyond human capacity to understand. It is paradox in the sense that it is a statement against our expectations. However, it is not paradox in the sense of being so much against reason that it is a contradictory or senseless statement.[42] Finally, it is metaphor in the sense defined

Coakley ("What Does Chalcedon Solve?" pp. 145-52), to whom I am indebted, offers a careful exposition and critical engagement of Norris's proposal; her conclusions seem to be very similar to mine.

40. Rahner, "Current Problems in Christology," p. 149; see also p. 150.

41. Rahner, "Current Problems in Christology," pp. 150-51.

42. For a careful consideration of these two meanings of paradox (and a related term, "riddle"), see Coakley, "What Does Chalcedon Solve?" pp. 154-56.

above: a picture of reality that goes beyond ordinary language, yet depicts events that have happened. So, it is a "true" metaphor.

Is the Chalcedonian Definition, thus, to be taken "literally"? Yes, as long as we clarify how that nomenclature is to be understood. Somewhat surprisingly, in recent years several Christian philosophers trained in the current analytic-philosophical tradition such as Thomas V. Morris and David Brown have insisted on the need to understand the christological confession in the literal sense.[43] With their emphasis on the literal sense of the confession's claims, both writers wish to combat that kind of "metaphorical" approach to Christology put forth by Hick and others that undercuts the historical and "factual" meaning of the terms. But what does the term "literal" mean here? The many meanings of the term are usefully clarified by yet another philosopher of language, William Alston, who distinguishes between the primary or obvious meaning of "literal" as "true" and its cognate meanings of "precise," "specific," "empirical," and "ordinary."[44] With regard to Chalcedon, the first, primary meaning as true can and should be affirmed; the related meanings were hardly in the minds of the drafters or the audience of the Definition. That passion for "scientific" accuracy is the concern of post-Enlightenment mentality and does not stick with the premedieval mind-set. Both the biblical writers and patristic theologians took the statements about Jesus the Christ as true, but they didn't have the burden of "proving" their historical, philosophical, or scientific accuracy. (This is not to deny the at-times highly sophisticated analytic and philosophical acumen of patristic writers, but even that does not stem from the concerns of modernity.)

Consequently, the genre of the Definition is not a detached, "objective," systematic explanation of the details of how to understand "nature" or "union" or similar key terms. Rather, as a rule of faith, it is a "grid" through which reflections on Christ's person must pass. Exactly as such it only says so much, and even of those things it sees important to delineate, it does not say everything. Indeed, it leaves open a host of issues, including the most obvious one: What do "human" and "divine" nature consist of?[45] Behind Chalcedon, similar to all rules of faith in early Christianity, is the soteriological intent. Having confessed belief in the God-man, Jesus the Savior, Christians

43. Morris, *The Logic of God Incarnate*, pp. 17-18; D. Brown, *The Divine Trinity*, pp. 102-3. I am indebted to an insightful discussion in Coakley, "What Does Chalcedon Solve?" pp. 156-59.

44. Alston, *Divine Nature and Human Language*, pp. 21, 25, 44.

45. See further, Coakley, "What Does Chalcedon Solve?" pp. 161-63.

naturally wanted to say as much as they could about the person and "nature" of the Savior. Coakley summarizes all this well:

> It does not . . . intend to provide a full systematic account of Christology, and even less a complete and precise metaphysics of Christ's makeup. Rather, it sets a "boundary" on what can, and cannot, be said, by first ruling out three aberrant interpretations of Christ (Apollinarism, Eutychianism, and extreme Nestorianism), second, providing an abstract rule of language *(physis* and *hypostasis)* for distinguishing duality and unity in Christ, and, third, presenting a "riddle" of negatives by means of which a greater (though undefined) reality may be intimated. At the same time, it recapitulates and assumes . . . the acts of salvation detailed in Nicea and Constantinople.[46]

Although in no way a "precise metaphysics," Chalcedon — as well as any Christology worth its salt — entails some "foundational" metaphysical claims. In their widest framework, as statements concerning the origin, purpose, and fulfillment of the created cosmos, Christian christological claims cannot, and should not, suspend metaphysical consideration. "The universal claim of Christological belief can be represented appropriately only against the most extensive horizon conceivable." Consequently, the Catholic systematician Walter Kasper rightly notes that the "Christian is so to speak compelled to become a metaphysician on account of his faith."[47] Hence, the common charge against classical Christology's alleged metaphysical imprisonment has to be reconsidered. Indeed, no Christology — not even the so-called nonmetaphysical ones — is a matter of "Whether metaphysics?" but rather of "What kind of metaphysics?"

An important afterword to the discussion of the criteriological role of Chalcedon — especially in light of global Christianity — is the continuing legacy of so-called non-Chalcedonian Christologies. It is impossible to understand the history of Christianity in the largest continent of the world, Asia, without acknowledging the crucial role played by two christological "schools" that deviate from the Chalcedonian tradition, namely, Nestorianism and Monophysitism.[48] Nestorianism was *the* theological cause for the

46. Coakley, "What Does Chalcedon Solve?" p. 161.

47. Kasper, *Jesus*, pp. 20-21.

48. For the complicated and complex dispute between the two Eastern theological centers, Alexandria and Antioch, which produced these two "heresies," see Pelikan, *The Spirit of Eastern Christendom*, chap. 2.

first major division in the church, between the Christian East and West, Europe and Asia, after the patristic era.[49] The Nestorian "two-nature" Christology was greatly interested in the human nature of Christ, allegedly because "it had long been known for its care for the poor and hungry" and therefore saw it fitting to "emphasize Christ's humanity, for only a completely human Christ could be an ethical and moral example."[50] Christianity was introduced to China by the Nestorians in the first half of the seventh century, when the land was ruled by the powerful Tai Tsung of the Tang dynasty. The "two-nature" Christology was preached in the most influential country of that time[51] until the mid–ninth century, when an imperial edict virtually banned Christianity (and Buddhism).[52] While a number of Christian communities in central and east Asia fell under the power of the Mongols and thus Islam, the Christian church slowly established itself in many places in central Asia and India and then returned to China — again with the Nestorians — in the eleventh century.[53] In the thirteenth century, the Nestorians had an archbishop in Peking (the Mongol capital), and early in the fourteenth century the Nestorian patriarch is reported to have had twenty-five metropolitans in China, India, Turkestan, Kashgar, and elsewhere.[54] This is all to say that the Nestorian interpretation of Christ has been immensely influential in the history of the largest continent of the world.

The other "heresy" in the eyes of the advocates of the Chalcedonian creed, Monophysite Christology, has similarly exercised a significant role in many parts of Asia. An instrumental role in the later consolidation of Monophysitism was played by the West Syrian Jacobite churches in the eighth and ninth centuries. While having their earliest strongholds in Africa (Egypt and Ethiopia), Monophysites soon gained influence beyond Syria in Asian regions such as Armenia, and even in Persia, as the influence of Nestorianism began to fall off in Persian Asia.[55] Monophysitism also found its way to India in the seventeenth century in the form of the (Jacobite) Syrian Orthodox Church. It is a continuing ecumenical challenge to the current

49. Appropriately, Moffett, *Christianity in Asia,* vol. 1, names the discussion of Nestorianism "The Great Schism."

50. Moffett, *Christianity in Asia,* 1:171.

51. Of course, the Arab empire was the other world power at the time.

52. Latourette, *A History of Christianity,* 1:324-25.

53. Latourette, *A History of Christianity,* 1:401-2.

54. Latourette, *A History of Christianity,* 1:591.

55. For the spread of Monophysitism in Persia, see Moffett, *Christianity in Asia,* 1:243-47.

global church to negotiate these diverging interpretations of Christ, both of which have been labeled heretical by the mainline tradition.

Having examined at some length the continuing relative value of the ecumenical creedal "horizon" in Christology, we now take up several key Chalcedonian doctrinal formulations, including the "two natures," divinity and humanity, incarnation, preexistence, sinlessness, and virgin birth, in order to assess their basis and value in light of biblical, historical, and contemporary concerns and contributions. Ultimately, a constructive contemporary formulation will be attempted for each of these classical doctrines with a view to their capacity to speak to contemporary Christian diversity and religious plurality.

6. Resurrection and the Identity of Jesus Christ

Resurrection as the Confirmation of Jesus' Deity

According to Paul, Jesus was "designated Son of God in power according to the Spirit of holiness by his resurrection from the dead" (Rom. 1:4). The supreme significance of the resurrection to Christology lies in the fact that not only the title Son of God but basically all titles used in the early church stem from the Easter event, including the Redeemer of Israel (Luke 24:21), the Lord of universal rule (Rom. 10:9), and the Savior of the nations (15:9).[1] Importantly enough, with regard to the work of salvation, Paul argues that resurrection was the event of justification of Jesus' work of salvation (Rom. 4:25).

In Christian tradition, several proposals have been set forth as likely candidates for establishing the deity of Jesus, such as sinlessness, teaching "with authority" (Mark 1:22, 27), his death on the cross, and Jesus' own claims to messiahship.[2] While important in themselves as ways of affirming

1. See further, Moltmann, *Way of Jesus Christ,* p. 170.

2. Cf. Schleiermacher (*Christian Faith,* p. 385), who took sinlessness as the result and manifestation of "the constant potency of His God-consciousness" and as such "a veritable existence of God in Him." This statement is not meant to say that Schleiermacher thereby affirmed the deity of Jesus in the way tradition does. On teaching "with authority," see Adolf von Harnack (*What Is Christianity?* p. 55), who located Jesus' uniqueness in his "core" teachings of the fatherhood of God, infinite value of the soul, and the kingdom of God as the community of love. This is not to say that Harnack affirmed the deity of the Son in keeping with tradition. On his death on the cross, cf. Matt.

the significance and uniqueness of Jesus' personality and ministry, none of these proposals has the capacity to constitute his deity. Even though human history knows no persons without sin, potentially finding one wouldn't make that person a god, any more than would the most insightful and wonderful teaching per se. Jewish history knows a number of self-made messiahs who issued all kinds of claims without any basis in history or personality. Death on the cross in itself is not any kind of unique event in human history; at its best, crucifixion could make Jesus a (failed) self-made messiah after a host of other such figures in the Jewish milieu or, say, an innocent martyr.[3]

We are thus left with resurrection as the most appropriate candidate for establishing Jesus' deity. Even that, alone, however, can hardly do so. Rightly, doubts have been raised such as those presented by Schleiermacher, who argued that the early "disciples recognized in Him the Son of God without having the faintest premonition of His resurrection and ascension." Consequently, current disciples can do the same because for Schleiermacher faith was grounded on Jesus' influence, the "impression that such a being of God indwells Him."[4] The explanatory power of the resurrection as the way to establish Jesus' deity is dependent on both historical and theological premises. Historically, it is necessary to be able to show the credibility and reasonableness of the event as a historical event. Otherwise, the NT claim to its indispensable role as the ground of faith can hardly be sustained (1 Cor. 15:13-17 especially). That task will be taken up below. Along with the historical task, its theological explanatory power has to be carefully developed. Barth has masterfully summarized the theological meaning of resurrection:

> [T]he resurrection of Jesus Christ is the great verdict of God, the fulfilment and proclamation of God's decision concerning the event of the cross. It is its acceptance as the act of the Son of God appointed our Representative. . . . It is its acceptance as the act of His obedience which judges the world, but judges it with the aim of saving it. It is its acceptance as the act of His Son whom He has always loved. . . . In this the res-

yet w/pretense that 'messiah' would reign forever.

27:54: "Truly this was the Son of God!" And Jesus' own claims to messiahship have been the cornerstone of conservative theology; see, e.g., Erickson, *Christian Theology,* 2:684-88.

3. See further, Grenz, *Theology for the Community of God,* pp. 251-56.

4. Schleiermacher, *Christian Faith,* p. 418. At the moment, we can leave aside the fact that Schleiermacher's reasoning is faulty on several accounts: he ignores the fact that the Gospels are of course written in light of the resurrection rather than "before" it; that Jesus' significance hardly can be established merely or even primarily on the basis of his influence on us; and so forth.

> urrection is the justification of God Himself, of God the Father, Creator of heaven and earth, who has willed and planned and ordered this event. It is the justification of Jesus Christ, His Son, who willed to suffer this event, and suffered it to the very last. And in His person it is the justification of all sinful men, whose death was decided in this event, for whose life there is therefore no more place. In the resurrection of Jesus Christ His life and with it their life has in fact become an event beyond death: "Because I live, ye shall live also" (Jn. 14:19).[5]

Four interrelated theological tasks are essential to develop and clarify the confirmatory theological role of resurrection. First, it is necessary to establish an integral link between resurrection and Jesus' own claims. In his teaching and announcement, Jesus set forth the claim to Sonship. That claim called for future confirmation. That came on the day of Easter, and it was thus interpreted by the early church (Acts 13:30, among other passages). Negatively, resurrection meant the repudiation of the charge that Jesus had made himself equal to God and was thus guilty of blasphemy (Mark 14:61). By not making himself equal with God (Phil. 2:8), he humbled himself and at resurrection was vindicated by his Father.[6]

Second, there must be an integral link between resurrection and the whole history of Jesus. Throughout Jesus' ministry and proclamation there was an anticipation of divine confirmation that turned out to come first in his resurrection and soon after in his ascension, as a "confirmed anticipation" of the kingdom in the eschaton. This gives a "proleptic character" to his appearance and ministry. It has to be shown that it was the crucified Messiah who was raised to new life, the one who prior to his crucifixion issued the claims to being the Son sent by his Father. In other words, what came to manifestation with the raising of Jesus from the dead, had to be implicitly and thematically there already in his life and ministry. In critical dialogue with Bultmann and Barth, for whom, in somewhat different ways, resurrection was a "disclosure" of something that was hidden, Pannenberg contends that resurrection is more than that; it is a "determination" or "confirmation":[7]

5. Barth, *CD* IV/1, p. 309; the whole §59 is a comprehensive explanation of the theological meaning of resurrection against the parable of Jesus as the prodigal son having been judged and raised to new life by his Father in the Spirit.

6. See Pannenberg, *ST* 2:363-64.

7. Pannenberg, *ST* 2:345.

> The Easter event certainly shed a new light on the death of Jesus, on his earthly ministry, and therefore on his person. But that does not mean that even without the event of the resurrection these would have been what they are when seen in its light. We depreciate the Easter event if we construe it only as a disclosure or revelation of the meaning that the crucifixion and the earthly history of Jesus already had in themselves. Only the Easter event determines what the meaning was of the pre-Easter history of Jesus and who he was in his relation to God.[8]

In other words, resurrection "dispelled and removed the ambiguity that had earlier clung to the person and history of Jesus."[9] Confirmation means that what was confirmed at the event of resurrection was something that was there already in the beginning of the history of Jesus.[10]

If Bultmann and Barth are too soft in speaking of the confirmatory role of the resurrection, too thick an account of resurrection would entail the dangerous belief that Jesus was "made" divine at the resurrection.[11] That would be of course nothing but a version of adoptionism. Hence, the Pauline expression "designated Son of God" (Rom. 1:4) has to be read in a way that avoids this error. Among the current NT scholars who champion traditional Christology, the historicity of the resurrection, and Jesus' self-awareness of his identity, there is a strange reluctance to link resurrection and messianic identity — or even resurrection and incarnation.[12] Whatever the motive behind this move, I don't find it justified either biblically or theologically. Clearly, for Paul, among other things, resurrection meant the establishment of divine Sonship as discussed above. And whatever else resurrection may mean, its key theological role is the theological confirmation of Jesus' divinity, as also discussed above. This is not to deny in any way the importance of linking resurrection (and death) with the whole history of Jesus; indeed, that is a theologically necessary task as explained above.

Third, having established the necessary link of resurrection with the

8. Pannenberg, *ST* 2:345.

9. Pannenberg, *ST* 2:345-46; see also p. 283.

10. Pannenberg, *ST* 2:282-83; Pannenberg, *Jesus — God and Man,* p. 137.

11. Pannenberg's use of the term "retroactive" in speaking of the confirmatory role of resurrection could potentially raise this concern. Particularly in *ST* (2:365, 303 n. 2) he makes sure that is not the case.

12. See Bird, *Are You the One?* p. 65. I don't fully understand what he means by his idea of divine Sonship being "transposed" rather than "triggered" by the resurrection; so also basically N. T. Wright, *Resurrection of the Son of God,* pp. 23-26.

whole history of Jesus, we must also look at the dynamic discontinuity. We should appreciate the dynamic nature of Christ's resurrection as something that, on the one hand, is an event in continuity with the whole history of Jesus and that, on the other hand, also represents something radically new. There is the contradistinction between death and life, darkness and light, hope and hopelessness. This contradistinction lies at the heart of the Christian idea of revelation: "The fundamental event in the Easter appearances then manifestly lies in the revelation of the identity and continuity of Jesus in the total contradiction of cross and resurrection, of god-forsakenness and the nearness of God."[13] Or to put it another way: there is both continuity and discontinuity between the risen Christ and Christ before Easter. The risen Christ is the crucified one. On the other hand, "with his resurrection from the grave something had taken place akin to the original creation, and indeed transcending it. It was not just a miracle within the creation, but a deed so decisively new that it affected the whole of creation and the whole of the future."[14]

The fourth theological task relates to the integral link between resurrection and eschatological expectations behind the event of Jesus (as well as the NT as a whole). For the resurrection to deliver on this theological task, it has to be shown that resurrection fits in and links with the apocalyptic expectation that forms the background of the event of Jesus, namely, that with the raising of the Messiah, the new age, the righteous rule of God, was dawning (Mark 1:15 par.). "The resurrection is God's declaration that through his ministry, Jesus had indeed inaugurated the divine reign. In him God is truly at work enacting his eschatological purpose."[15] As the breaking forth of life through death, resurrection represents something radically new; it is an "event of fulfilled redemption [that] . . . issues in a new creation beyond the corruptible processes of this world, on the other side of decay and death . . . in the fullness of a new world and of a new order of things."[16] Resurrection is nothing less than "healing, lifting up and projection of human being into a new order of things."[17] Only this way can we avoid the error of making resurrection synonymous with resuscitation, a miracle that in biblical times

13. Moltmann, *Theology of Hope,* p. 199.

14. Torrance, *Space, Time, and Resurrection,* p. 36.

15. Grenz, *Theology for the Community of God,* p. 260. Grenz's otherwise good discussion of the theme fails to acknowledge the importance of the link with the whole history of Jesus as he only mentions the claims and apocalyptic expectation.

16. Torrance, *Space, Time, and Resurrection,* p. 86.

17. Torrance, *Space, Time, and Resurrection,* p. 86.

happened to a few persons such as Lazarus. In the NT witness, the resurrection of Christ, while a onetime decisive event, is also an "event of cosmic and unbelievable magnitude"[18] in that it signals the consummation of history and creation in the coming of the righteous rule of God. Rightly, then, the Uruguayan liberationist Juan Luis Segundo, in *An Evolutionary Approach to Jesus of Nazareth,* argues that the resurrection of Jesus as the "primordial" event is nothing less than the recapitulation of the universe, an eschatological sign of coming consummation. Building on Pauline theology, Segundo argues that believers, having been delivered from under the power of fear of death and even when facing suffering, are liberated for service and solidarity with others.[19]

Part of the redemptive nature of resurrection and the related event of ascension is also the "*redemption of space and time*."[20] Space and time as creational acts of God will not be suspended nor abrogated but healed and, in anticipation of the coming of God's eternity into time, taken up by God. The Johannine Jesus' resurrection appearances (John 21), as much as exegetical disputes should be taken into careful consideration, may be pointers to this healing of space and time.[21] The eschatological dimension of the resurrection also reminds us of the integral link between creation and new creation: the redemption of space and time also bespeaks the healing and renewal of nature. The same God who in the first place created the heavens and earth is going to show his faithfulness in renewing creation.[22]

Above, it was argued that for the resurrection to serve in its confirmatory role, its integral link with the whole history of Jesus must be established. There is a need to expand that horizon and reflect on the implications of the relation of the establishment of the deity at resurrection to what goes beyond Jesus' earthly life. "The confirmation of his message by the God who raised him to life says not merely that Jesus acted with divine power but also that God is from all eternity the One whom Jesus proclaimed him to be."[23] Before that task is taken up, one important theme requires clarification, namely, the historical basis of the resurrection, without which the theological task outlined here cannot work.

18. Torrance, *Space, Time, and Resurrection,* p. 31.

19. Segundo, *An Evolutionary Approach to Jesus of Nazareth,* pp. 111-14 particularly.

20. Torrance, *Space, Time, and Resurrection,* p. 90, emphasis in original.

21. See further, Torrance, *Space, Time, and Resurrection,* pp. 90-91.

22. For a robust discussion of this theme, see Moltmann, *Way of Jesus Christ,* pp. 246-73.

23. Pannenberg, *ST* 2:367.

Resurrection as Historical and Eschatological Metaphor

The biblical idea of resurrection is without parallels in religions. Of course, religions know myths of gods rising and dying.[24] That, however, is far from the idea of Christ's resurrection, which is not a cyclic process of becoming but rather a historical act of God.[25] No wonder the Gentile audience found the claim to resurrection incredible (Acts 17:32). The background of the Christian idea of resurrection can be found in Jewish eschatology.[26] A remarkable link with the Hebrew Scriptures is the expression "on the third day." According to the Jewish NT scholar Pinchas Lapide, this expression, far from being primarily a temporal expression, contains "a clear reference to God's mercy and grace which is revealed after two days of affliction and death by way of redemption"[27] (Gen. 22:4; 42:18; Exod. 19:16; Jon. 1:17; Esther 5:1; Hos. 6:2). Lapide also lists a number of features in the earliest written testimonies to the claim of resurrection (1 Cor. 15:3-8) that bear the marks of established tradition (and passing of tradition) rather than one's own thoughts.[28] Lapide's conclusion thus is: "The resurrection of Jesus on that Easter Sunday and his appearances in the following days were purely Jewish faith experiences. Not one Gentile saw him after Good Friday. Everything that the Gentile church heard about the resurrection came only from Jewish sources because he appeared after Easter Sunday as the Risen One exclusively to Jews."[29] On the ba-

24. For a meticulous study of ideas about life beyond death in ancient paganism, see N. T. Wright, *Resurrection of the Son of God,* chap. 2.

25. Torrance, *Space, Time, and Resurrection,* pp. 26, 30-31.

26. For a succinct discussion, see Pannenberg, *ST* 2:347-50; for a detailed treatment with massive documentation, see N. T. Wright, *Resurrection of the Son of God,* chap. 3 on the OT, and chap. 4 on postbiblical Judaism. Torrance (*Space, Time, and Resurrection,* pp. 28-30) finds roots of the Christian idea of resurrection in the OT, including Yahweh's faithfulness to covenant, which implies supporting covenant partners both in life and death; the motif of restoration through judgment in prophetic literature; and, linked with restoration, the promise of a Savior to be raised up from among the people.

27. P. Lapide, *Resurrection of Jesus,* p. 92.

28. P. Lapide, *Resurrection of Jesus,* pp. 98-99.

29. P. Lapide, *Resurrection of Jesus,* p. 123. Unlike Lapide, another Jewish scholar, Kogan (*Opening the Covenant,* pp. 117-18), does not see any convincing reasons to believe that Jesus Christ rose from the dead. On the other hand, he says that, should that have happened, it would in no way threaten Jewish faith. He also surmises that the reason for his refusal to believe in Jesus' resurrection has nothing to do with unwillingness to accept the possibility of miracle nor with the denial of the belief in resurrection (apart from the Christian interpretation of Jesus) belonging to Jewish faith.

sis of a careful analysis of the NT accounts of the resurrection and in light of Jewish traditions concerning resurrection, Lapide surprisingly comes to the conclusion that it is a historical event. Ironically, he critiques a number of contemporary Christian theologians for statements concerning resurrection that are "abstract" and fail to express a final opinion in an unambiguous way.[30] Instructive here is the change of position of a noted Christian theologian who has participated widely in Jewish-Christian dialogue, A. Roy Eckhardt. Whereas at first he was compelled to deny the resurrection either physically or spiritually in order to avoid triumphalism or a repudiation of Judaism, in his major work on Christology, *Reclaiming the Jesus of History,* he came to see resurrection at least in "an extrabodily or spiritual sense" as an idea in keeping with Jewish hopes.[31]

The radical revision of Jewish eschatological hope is its focus on one individual before the end of this age. Jewish theology doesn't know that, not even with regard to the Messiah.[32] Early Christianity saw in the resurrection of Jesus the beginning of the end times, culminating in the resurrection of all.[33] This means that "for its final verification, the Christian message of the resurrection of Jesus needs the event of an eschatological resurrection of the dead."[34] In other words, resurrection is both a historical and an eschatological concept.

The language of resurrection in the Bible and in theology is metaphorical. Terms such as "raising" have as their point of reference a wakening from sleep. "Metaphorical" in this context, however, does not mean that therefore it is not historical or factual. What it means is that *any* theological talk by its very nature is metaphorical, not only talk about resurrection — or say, atonement.[35]

Even though a real event, resurrection is not like any other event we know of. Not accidentally, the NT links the raising of the crucified Jesus to the Spirit. This is in keeping with the biblical idea of all life as the function of the Spirit of God. Jesus was raised to new life; indeed, Paul speaks of this

30. P. Lapide, *Resurrection of Jesus,* p. 129. He cites from Bultmann, Rahner, Willi Marxsen, Herbert Braun, and others.

31. Eckhardt, *Reclaiming the Jesus of History,* pp. 211-15 (211); I am indebted to Kogan, *Opening the Covenant,* p. 103.

32. N. T. Wright, *Resurrection of the Son of God,* p. 28; Pannenberg, *ST* 2:350-51.

33. 1 Cor. 15:12-21; *1 Clement* 24:1; *Barnabas* 5:6.

34. Pannenberg, *ST* 2:350-51.

35. For details, see discussion of metaphor and analogy in the doctrine of God above.

permeation by the Spirit in the most dramatic way, calling the Risen One "spiritual body" (*sōma pneumatikon;* 1 Cor. 15:44).[36]

Resurrection is both an event that happens in history and an event that goes beyond (but not against) history;[37] it is a *"new kind of historical happening."*[38] On the one hand, it is important that Christian theology not lose the connection of this unique miraculous act to the earthly and historical realities of this world. Otherwise, gnosticism follows and the holistic nature of salvation with a view to the resurrection of the body is blurred. On the other hand, it is equally important to insist on its eschatological and, in that sense, "nonhistorical" nature. In it was inaugurated the beginning of the end, the dawning of God's righteous rule and the renewal of creation. That said, however, we should be critical of the way Moltmann juxtaposes the crucifixion as a "historical" event and resurrection as an "apocalyptic happening." He rightly calls attention to the dynamic between the historical and the apocalyptic. But he falsely presupposes that they belong to totally different planes of reality and thus resurrection cannot be considered a historical act as well.[39] On the contrary, it is precisely in its historical nature that resurrection affirms the possibility of life beyond death, not in terms of returning to life again subject to decay, but as a transitioning to new life without end.

The affirmation of resurrection as a historical event in terms of bodily resurrection (which also has both an eschatological and a "spiritual" nature) is a claim hotly contested in contemporary scholarship. N. T. Wright surmises that in biblical scholarship in the twentieth century, a "dominant paradigm" has arisen that has severely critiqued the traditional understanding of resurrection as a historical event. There are several main theses of that paradigm: in the Jewish context, resurrection may mean so many different things; Paul, the earliest Christian writer, believed in a "spiritual" rather than

36. See further, Pannenberg, *ST* 2:346-47.

37. See further, Fuller, *Easter Faith and History,* pp. 145-47 particularly.

38. Torrance, *Space, Time, and Resurrection,* p. 88, emphasis in original.

39. Moltmann, *Way of Jesus Christ,* p. 214. "Anyone who describes Christ's resurrection as 'historical,' in just the same way as his death on the cross, is overlooking the new creation with which the resurrection begins, and is falling short of the eschatological hope. . . . Since resurrection brings the dead into eternal life and means the annihilation of death, it breaks the power of history and is itself the end of history." Oddly enough, with all his criticisms of Barth's "de-historizing" tendencies in speaking of Christ's resurrection, as evident in *CD* IV/1, §59, Moltmann's de-historization does not materially differ from Barth's "category of divine history," as Moltmann calls it; for Moltmann's critical discussion of Barth, see *Way of Jesus Christ,* pp. 230-32.

a bodily resurrection; the earliest Christians came to affirm resurrection traditions such as the empty tomb only in hindsight on the basis of their belief in Christ's exaltation/ascension/glorification, which makes resurrection narratives in the Gospels later inventions to bolster such belief; the accounts of "seeing" Jesus are but hallucinations and/or conversion experiences after Paul's experience on the Damascus road; and finally, whatever happened to Jesus' crucified body, certainly it was not "resuscitated" or "raised from the dead."[40]

The various objections to the historicity of the resurrection usually rest on one of three main lines of argumentation: first, that there is no access to such historical knowledge; second, that there is no analogy for such a resurrection; and third, that there is no evidence.[41] Let me take them up one at a time. Willi Marxsen has famously articulated the claim that instead of the history of resurrection we have access only to the beliefs in resurrection of the disciples. Bultmann's claim that resurrection is not a historical event of the past but rather an experience or event in the hearts of the disciples follows this line of argumentation.[42] Strangely, Marxsen rejects the testimony of the Gospels and considers only the noncanonical *Gospel of Peter,* which chronicles Jesus' coming out of the tomb; even that, in Marxsen's estimation, cannot deliver reliable historical information. Hence, to call resurrection "historical" is not meaningful nor justified.[43] The obvious counterargument is that Marxsen's view represents a typical positivistic objection according to which things such as raising people from the dead do not happen. This epistemological rule, of course, breaks its own rules — going beyond its area of competence. "Ruling out as historical that to which we do not have direct access is actually a way of not doing history at all,"[44] objects N. T. Wright,

40. N. T. Wright, *Resurrection of the Son of God,* p. 7.

41. I am following here the broad outline presented in N. T. Wright, *Resurrection of the Son of God,* pp. 16-20.

42. Bultmann, "New Testament and Mythology," pp. 39-42. It is highly interesting that in earliest postbiblical theology, the sensing of the exquisite difficulties in convincing particularly the pagan audience of Jesus' resurrection led some theologians to develop metaphorical explanations that sought distance from a historical conception. Thus, *1 Clement* speaks of every new day as resurrection (24:3), or the growing of plants from the seed (24:4), or even the myth of the phoenix (25)! In the second century, however, against the spiritualizing tendencies of the Gnostics, the defense of the bodily resurrection became a strong apologetic theme as evident in Athenagoras, *The Resurrection of the Body.* I am indebted to Pannenberg, *ST* 2:352.

43. Marxsen, "The Resurrection of Jesus," pp. 15-50.

44. N. T. Wright, *Resurrection of the Son of God,* p. 16.

who sees it mandatory to clarify the notion of "historical." The term itself has several meanings, such as history as "event," "significant event," "provable event," "writing-about-events-in-the-past," or as "what modern historians can say" about the topic.[45] Obviously, Marxsen's rejection of the historicity of Jesus' resurrection rests on an unnuanced use of the term "historical": from the fact that in his estimation no one has written about resurrection, he deduces that it is not a provable event, and therefore, a modern historian cannot accept it.[46] Marxsen's denial of access to the historicity of the resurrection is thus as "provable" as is his underlying epistemology. Many current-day historiographers, not only those of a postmodernist slant, would strongly disagree with Marxsen.

The charge that there is no analogy to resurrection goes back to the programmatic essay by Ernst Troeltsch in 1898, "Historical and Dogmatic Methods in Theology."[47] According to it, an analogical corresponding happening is required to qualify an event as historical. Troeltsch is not necessarily denying the possibility of the event of resurrection as positivists would do; he is just insisting on the necessity of having an analogy from our own experience in order to write history in the modern sense. That cannot, of course, be provided with reference to Jesus' resurrection, which is a onetime event. Being a onetime event, however, does not disqualify it from being a historical event. Nor does the historicity of the event call for an "indubitable certainty" after Cartesian epistemology. The possibility of dispute always remains. But that is the case with virtually all historical claims. Furthermore, the possibility of the historical happening of an event such as resurrection is part of the wider question as to what we suppose *can* (or cannot) happen in reality. If we believe that the dead can in no case rise, then resurrection is a settled issue (cf. 1 Cor. 15:13).[48] Wright adds the important note that should we follow categorically the analogy rule of Troeltsch, then we could not say anything about the rise of the early church, which is a historical happening deriving from the resurrection and has no analogy in the history of religions and our experience. "Never before had there been a movement which began as a quasi-messianic group within Judaism and was transformed into the sort of movement which Christianity quickly became."[49]

45. N. T. Wright, *Resurrection of the Son of God,* pp. 12-13.

46. See N. T. Wright, *Resurrection of the Son of God,* p. 16.

47. Troeltsch, "On the Historical and Dogmatic Methods in Theology [1898]," pp. 728-53.

48. See Pannenberg, *ST* 2:360-63; Moltmann, *Way of Jesus Christ,* p. 244.

49. N. T. Wright, *Resurrection of the Son of God,* p. 17.

The objection to the historicity of resurrection because of lack of real evidence can be — and has been — presented in many ways. A significant movement in NT scholarship of the past generation, often labeled as post-Bultmannian, came to focus on the tradition-historical investigation of the Gospels and, in this case, their account of the resurrection. This simply means that scholars sought to examine hypothetical stages by which the Gospels came into existence. The "results" of these investigations betray such a diversity of opinions and orientations that this fact alone should make us suspicious of its recommendations.[50] A more contemporary approach is represented by the well-known Jesus researcher John Dominic Crossan. In many ways, his approach is not unrelated to the tradition-historical method. Differently from that, however, Crossan's main focus is on hermeneutical suspicion regarding political and power-driven motifs in shaping resurrection traditions, instead of pastoral and theological motifs at the center of post-Bultmannian study. In Crossan's hermeneutics, the this-worldly oriented, alternative-lifestyle-driven early Christian movement is truncated into a "collection of power-seeking factions."[51] Consequently, no historical evidence is available through those amended narratives.[52]

It goes without saying that these hypothetical reconstructions of the Gospel narratives of resurrection are just that, *hypothetical.* They fail badly, however, because there is a lot of historical evidence about the coherence and unity of the views of resurrection among various early Christian communities. This unity is the defining feature. At the core of that shared conviction was the belief in the bodily resurrection of the crucified Christ.[53] At the same time, mere rejection of any evidence hardly suffices as an explanation of the beginning of the radically new religion, Christianity. And the efforts of tradition historians fail in weighing the significant evidence that other scholars have found in support of the possibility of the historicity of the resurrection.

The two main pillars of evidence for the historicity of the resurrection are the appearances of Jesus to a great number of eyewitnesses and the

50. For a representative discussion, see Luedemann, *The Resurrection of Jesus.*

51. As characterized by N. T. Wright, *Resurrection of the Son of God,* p. 19.

52. Crossan, *The Historical Jesus,* pp. 395-416; Crossan, *Birth of Christianity,* pp. 550-73.

53. Summarized succinctly by N. T. Wright, *Resurrection of the Son of God,* pp. 209, 476-77, based on a most detailed scrutiny of various NT texts and testimonies. On the centrality of the resurrection in early Christianity, see C. A. Evans, *Resurrection and the New Testament,* p. 40; I am indebted to Wright, p. 210.

empty tomb tradition.[54] Rather than "visionary experiences,"[55] as in hallucinations or other psychological projections, there are good reasons for maintaining the appearances as actual encounters. Similarly, the empty tomb tradition was not contested by the contemporaries — even though its validity as a historical claim was widely doubted by many twentieth-century biblical scholars.[56] Had the claim to the empty tomb been a fabrication, how could the preaching about the resurrected Christ have taken place in Jerusalem, the place of execution and burial?[57] In that sense not only the resurrection but also the empty tomb is a public event.[58]

In sum: the belief in the physical resurrection of Jesus from the dead is not necessarily a matter of faith totally apart from historical investigation and rational reasoning, and certainly not a modern fundamentalist invention, as a leading Jesus scholar recently has pejoratively labeled it![59] That said, the limits of historical inquiry alone should be acknowledged. No amount of historical evidence or logical reasoning is meant to establish indubitable certainty beyond questioning. And certainly, no amount of historical investigation in itself leads to the establishment of the divinity of the Crucified One. Rowan Williams reminds us that in our preoccupation merely with the "facts" of res-

54. For a detailed investigation, see Pannenberg, *Jesus — God and Man,* pp. 88-106. Materially similar arguments can be found in R. E. Brown, *The Virginal Conception and Bodily Resurrection of Jesus,* pp. 92-124.

55. For Edward Schillebeeckx (*Jesus,* p. 369), Easter appearances can be understood as conversion experiences after Saul's experience in Acts 9; yet he is not thereby saying that they are simply conversion experiences.

56. See, e.g., Bultmann, *The History of the Synoptic Tradition,* pp. 287-89 particularly.

57. Pannenberg, *ST* 2:356-59. "There is no trace of any contention against Christians that the body was still in the tomb" (p. 358). This is not to say that there was no debate or circulating rumors, such as the one recorded in Matt. 28:13, according to which some Jews claimed that Jesus' disciples had stolen the body in the night — or later ones such as the one mentioned by Tertullian (*The Shows* [or *The Spectaculis*] 30; *ANF* 3:91) that it was the gardener who removed Jesus from the tomb in order that "his lettuce might come to no harm from the crowd of visitants"! (For the Tertullian reference, I am indebted to Schwarz, *Christology,* p. 97.) These rumors, however, are just that, *rumors,* and do not offer a substantive denial of the empty tomb tradition.

58. Contra Moltmann (*Way of Jesus Christ,* p. 215), who in his support of the nonhistorical ("apocalyptic") understanding of resurrection juxtaposes the two events, considering crucifixion as a public and resurrection as a nonpublic event: "Jesus was crucified publicly and died publicly. But it was only the women at his tomb in Jerusalem, and the disciples who had fled into Galilee who learnt of his 'resurrection.'"

59. Strangely enough, that's what Crossan (*Birth of Christianity,* p. xviii) contends.

urrection, the event itself as "good news *now* almost disappears."[60] The same happens, of course, with the opposite danger, evident in Bultmann, who makes resurrection only an inspiring kerygmatic message, "faith in the word of preaching," devoid of any historical contours.[61]

In the final analysis, following T. F. Torrance, we have to say that the "incarnation and the resurrection really are *ultimates* which must be accepted, or rejected, as such, for they cannot be verified or validated on any other grounds than those which they themselves provide" and are, as such, "the basic and all-embracing miracles upon which the Christian Gospel rests."[62] That statement, however, has to be handled with care since it can easily lead to a misguided understanding of the complex and mutually conditioning relation of history and theology, history and faith. The self-verifying or self-validating nature of resurrection to which Torrance refers must not be understood in terms of avoiding careful historical investigation. That danger is evident in the work of Yale School founder, biblical scholar Hans Frei, for whom historical investigation of the resurrection is blocked by its being the ground of faith.[63] That blockage, of course, raises the question of on what basis we should take Christ's resurrection rather than, say, the Prophet's teaching or Gautama's experience as the "ground." This is a closed epistemological circle.[64]

Among Jewish New Testament scholars, as discussed above, Pinchas Lapide affirms the historicity of Jesus' resurrection. In the introduction to Lapide's book on resurrection, the American Lutheran theologian Carl E. Braaten asks why the Jewish scholar is not Christian, as he believes in Jesus' resurrection. The answer is simply that for him it doesn't prove that Jesus is the Jewish Messiah. What, then, is its meaning to Lapide? It means that "Jesus belongs to the *preparatio messianica* — the line of the great patriarchs and prophets of Israel — pioneering the full salvation of the future kingdom which God will establish through the Messiah in the last days."[65] That for Christian theology resurrection is a crucial element in the affirmation of Je-

60. R. Williams, *Resurrection,* p. 110; for this reference and the next, I am indebted to Migliore, *Faith Seeking Understanding,* p. 192.

61. Bultmann, "New Testament and Mythology," p. 41.

62. Torrance, *Space, Time, and Resurrection,* p. 22.

63. Frei, *Theology and Narrative,* chaps. 2; 8; 9 (I am indebted to N. T. Wright, *Resurrection of the Son of God,* p. 21). There is similarity in this respect with the Reformed epistemology.

64. See further, N. T. Wright, *Resurrection of the Son of God,* pp. 21-22.

65. Braaten, "Introduction," p. 17.

sus' divinity does not of course mean in itself that in the logic of Jewish religion the same principle is at work.

In sum, the theological claim of Jesus' divinity is based on the historical claim to Jesus' resurrection from the dead. When combined with the earthly Jesus' claims to Sonship, the resurrection lends credibility and validity to the creedal clarification and formulation of the deity of Jesus Christ, in the context of the trinitarian doctrine. More than that, the resurrection is also linked with the theological claim for the humanity of Jesus.

The Unity of Jesus Christ with Humanity

Whereas older Christology had the question of the deity at the center, in recent times the focus has been the question of the humanity of Jesus.[66] It might be significant that the same kind of "turn to the humanity" of Jesus is to be discerned widely among some important Muslim interpreters of Jesus.[67] Whereas in older theology the starting point of affirming Jesus' humanity was the union of the Logos with the human Jesus at the incarnation, in contemporary theology it is customary to begin with the affirmation of the humanness of Jesus of Nazareth and inquire into how this "low" Christology came to be developed into a "high" one. James D. G. Dunn is a representative mainline scholar in this respect. In his widely acclaimed *Christology in the Making* (1980), he took as the established starting point the opinion that in contrast to the earliest low Christology, the high Christology is the function of Hellenized effects and comes to manifestation only in John and Hebrews but not in Paul. Paul, according to Dunn, stuck with low Adam Christology.

66. That it has been so for some time is evident in the comment by Baillie, *God Was in Christ,* p. 11.

67. The Christian Islamicist Fr. Jomier of the Dominican Institute of Oriental Studies in Cairo, Egypt, summarizes the works on the personality of Jesus of four leading Egyptian Muslim thinkers, including Khālid Muhammad Khālid (d. 1996): "in the Middle Ages, this Muslim sympathy showed itself towards Jesus as a wonder-worker, ascetic and mystic, today it seems rather to seek the deeply human side of the doctrines of Christ. In the Middle Ages, Jesus was seen as a prophet who had fought against the formalism of the doctors of the Law and had reminded men of the duty to live an interior religion, the religion of the heart. In . . . [these four works], on the contrary, Jesus' struggle against the Pharisees appears firstly as that of natural conscience and justice in the face of hypocrisy and clericalism. In the Middle Ages, Jesus was seen in regard to God. In these [contemporary] works, He is seen rather in regard to men and humanity." In "Christ Seen by Contemporary Muslim Writers," p. 10, quoted in Leirvik, *Images of Jesus Christ in Islam,* p. 193.

For Paul, steeped in Jewish traditions, "incarnational" Christology after the later tradition was not a possibility.

Unlike Dunn, Pannenberg (as will be discussed in more detail below) locates the deity of Jesus in his humanity and discerns high Christology in Paul and of course the rest of the NT. This is Pannenberg's correction to what he sees as the weakness of tradition, namely, the capacity to affirm Christ's genuine humanity. At the same time, Pannenberg, unlike Dunn and mainstream biblical scholars, many of whom are much more "liberal" than Dunn, also materially affirms what Chalcedon does — full deity and humanity in one person — even when Pannenberg prefers not to use that terminology or frame of reference. In Pannenberg's theology, Adam Christology is a statement not about low Christology but rather about the connection between creation and Christology as well as about communal and universal implications of Christology.

What are we to think about the starting point and strategy for affirming the fellowship and unity of Jesus the Christ with humankind in our contemporary situation? With all its benefits, including the importance of the diversity of testimonies to Jesus in the NT and its development as a process, Dunn's approach is problematic. It mistakenly makes the whole idea of incarnation a matter of later Hellenization of the gospel. In that, it echoes the now dismissed approach of Harnack concerning dogma as deterioration of the gospel and more importantly the post–World War II biblical scholarship's reluctance to believe that the "real" Jesus can be found in the NT Gospels exactly because the various tradition-historical developments already tampered so much with the Gospels. Dunn's approach also suffers from the integral and full confession of the deity of the man Jesus; it is strong in the affirmation of Jesus' humanity of course.

For these and other reasons to be mentioned in the following, particularly with regard to the topic of preexistence, my argument follows the logic started above with regard to the centrality of the resurrection. I argue that the affirmation of not only the deity but also the humanity of Jesus is clarified in and based on the resurrection. Even though I do not fully agree with Pannenberg's locating the deity of Jesus in the human nature, I wholeheartedly endorse his affirmation of full humanity and argue that Chalcedonian-based dynamic Christology is not as vulnerable to the dangers of truncated humanity as is often remarked. I also think that a healthy dose of Spirit Christology may help in establishing the humanity of Jesus, following in the footsteps of the Gospel writers. Furthermore, a careful affirmation and investigation of the topic of incarnation, following the method from-below-to-above, help clarify both Jesus' humanity and its relation to his deity. As part of the affirmation of the incarnation, in order to avoid adoptionism, a robust doctrine of preexistence is needed, as well as the relation of virgin birth to incarnation and the theological meaning of virgin birth.

The question about the humanity of Jesus simply has to do with this question: "in what sense, if any, can we meaningfully use the word 'god' to talk about the human Jesus, Jesus as he lived, walked, taught, healed, and died in first century Palestine?"[68] In affirming the true humanity of Jesus Christ, we are claiming that "in this historical life we find not only the true deity, but also essential humanity." As such, Jesus is also "the exemplar of creaturely fellowship" with the eternal God.[69] That said, it is essential to keep in mind that in the question of the deity of Jesus, his unity with God, we are not dealing with a generic concept of divine nature in isolation. We are speaking of the deity of the man Jesus.[70] The traditional incarnational Logos Christology has at times drifted into abstract and generic ways of explaining the apparent "paradox" of the union of divine and human.

A potential approach is the way classical tradition has formulated the nature of the "human personhood" of the Incarnate One, that is, in terms of *anhypostasis* and *enhypostasis*, formally ratified at the Second Council of Constantinople in 553. The term *anhypostasis* means that Jesus' human nature lacks its own personality in the sense that he can be said to have his "person" *(enhypostasis)* in the divine Logos. When *anhypostasis* is translated as "impersonal," one may be easily led to think that therefore Jesus' human nature was not "real." That is not what tradition says. The formula is just meant to safeguard the "hypostatic union" of two natures, in other words, to reject the view that Jesus' personality would exist apart from the union with the Logos.[71]

68. N. T. Wright, "Jesus and the Identity of God," p. 42.

69. Grenz, *Theology for the Community of God*, p. 272.

70. Pannenberg, *ST* 2:325.

71. For an authoritative discussion, see Barth, *CD* I/1, pp. 162-65 especially. F. LeRon Shults makes much of the fact that *historically* it can be shown that Barth's alleged patristic use of this formula is rather a much later Protestant Scholastic invention. Hence, Barth would have misconstrued the ideas of Leontius of Byzantium, to whom we owe the formula. Although Shults's innovative claim may be of great interest to Barth students (especially in light of the fact that this formula plays an important role in his Christology), for my contemporary systematic usage, it has hardly any implications. What is undisputed is that post-Chalcedonian Christology "ratified" the usage of this term. Shults, "A Dubious Christological Formula," pp. 431-46; Shults, "Anthropology and Christology," chap. 7. For a useful discussion of the complicated history and (re)interpretations of the formula, see Crisp, *Divinity and Humanity*, chap. 3.

Closer attention should be given to the relation of the man Jesus to his Father, which came to the fore first in his public ministry and proclamation and culminated in the cross and especially resurrection.[72] This route is from-below-to-above and honors both the plot of the Gospel narratives and the current methodological preference in Christology. The Gospel writers, as mentioned, show remarkable interest in various aspects of the earthly life of Jesus. Rather than beginning from abstract speculations as to how the divine and human as abstract constructions can come together in one person — which are legitimate questions of later theology based on the creeds — the economic approach seems to give a naive (in a good sense of the term) and innocent description of the human person who lived under normal human conditions. To those belong development and growth (Luke 2:40). Even the more "theological" account of John's Gospel speaks of Jesus as weary and thirsty (John 4:6-7). Jesus showed human emotions such as sorrow (11:35) and anguish (12:27). Jesus struggled in trying to accept God's will (Matt. 26:39), including prayer life (Heb. 5:8-9). Jesus underwent temptations (Matt. 4:1-11). While a host of other Gospel and NT testimonies could be added, suffice it to summarize with the statement from the book of Hebrews (4:15) — a clause that also found its way into the creed — that Jesus was tempted in every way as we are except that he never committed a sin.

The dangers to Logos Christology and traditional "high" Christology presented by Docetism — or Apollinarianism — as if the deity lurked behind the guise of humanity, must be countered with the robust narratives of the NT. Instructive here is the approach of those biblical authors who represent high Christology and yet, at the same time, go to pains in presenting a true human being, Jesus of Nazareth. The prologue of John's Gospel, which begins with the Logos Christology affirming the unity of the Word with God and his agency in creation and revelation ("light"), makes the astonishing statement that the Logos became *sarx*, "flesh." Later the Gospel tells us that *sarx* lacks everything spirit has (John 3:6) and is ineffective spiritually (6:63). *Sarx* denotes not only human frailty and sinfulness but also the self-sacrifice and suffering of the Son of Man (6:51-56). Similarly, the book of Hebrews, which opens with a profoundly high christological statement about the Son, the word spoken by the Father, as the Father's true reflection and heir, the keeper of the universe and the agent of reconciliation, now seated on the

72. That, however, is not necessary even in the Chalcedonian framework as long as the specific and unique nature of the Logos's union with Jesus of Nazareth is kept in mind.

right hand of God (Heb. 1:1-4), goes on to speak of Jesus as the one who "had to be made like his brethren in every respect," including suffering and temptations (2:17-18). Like any human being, "In the days of his flesh, Jesus offered up prayers and supplications, with loud cries and tears, to him who was able to save him from death" (5:7); he could only learn "obedience through what he suffered" (5:8).[73]

A necessary step in the establishment of the true humanity of Jesus is that record in the Gospels and other earliest testimonies. That alone, however, is hardly sufficient for the specific task of establishing the human nature of the one confessed Son of God (denoting his divinity). The Gospel testimonies can only get us to the establishment of Kant's idea of the "Son of God" as the archetype of moral perfectness, or Schleiermacher's view of Jesus as the "ideal human" in whom there was the fully developed and perfect God-consciousness, or Tillich's construction of Jesus as the bearer of the New Being.[74] Even Bonhoeffer's idea of Jesus as the "man for others" could be constructed on the basis of these materials.[75] What is noteworthy about these NT narratives of Jesus' humanity is that they are not meant to establish an ideal humanity but rather support the truth that "Jesus participated in our existential humanness."[76] This is the needed starting point From Below.

Whereas the oneness of Jesus with humanity can be gleaned from the historical records in the NT, the uniqueness of the humanity of Jesus the Christ can only be established on the basis of the resurrection. The full establishment of the humanity of Jesus Christ is to be referred to the confirmatory role of the resurrection. Resurrection vindicated not only his divine status as the Son who was sent by his Father but also his earthly ministry: "The implied claim of Jesus for his own person — namely, that the future of God is present in and by him — no longer seems to be human arrogance in the light of the Easter event."[77] Only in light of the resurrection can we also establish Jesus' humanity as the paradigm for all human existence.[78] Only resurrection confirms his claims to true humanity, similar to his claims to be the one sent by his Father. "God must either confirm the opinion of his op-

73. For insightful discussion, see Schwarz, *Christology,* pp. 234-35.

74. Kant, *Religion within the Limits of Reason Alone,* pp. 54-59; Schleiermacher, *Christian Faith,* pp. 367, 424-25; Tillich, *Systematic Theology,* 2:97.

75. This nomenclature occurs frequently in Bonhoeffer, *Letters and Papers from Prison.*

76. Grenz, *Theology for the Community of God,* p. 281.

77. Pannenberg, *ST* 2:365.

78. Grenz, *Theology for the Community of God,* p. 281.

ponents who considered him a great sinner or acknowledge that Jesus is in truth the embodiment of true humanity. God's response came in the resurrection. By raising Jesus from the dead, God declared that this man is indeed the paradigmatic human he claimed to be. This event, therefore, marks God's declaration of the correctness of Jesus' unique claim concerning his humanity."[79] Resurrection brings to manifestation and confirmation the role of Jesus as the true revelation of God as in this human life the true face and identity of God is to be seen (John 14:6). Part of the revelation of God was the nature of true humanity as dependence, service, and even ultimate self-offering to the Father: he died as he had taught (Mark 8:34-38; 10:35-45). The difference between Socrates or Jewish martyrs and Jesus' life testimony is that only his life was validated by his Father as the expression of the humanity of the Son of God.

When considering the resurrected humanity of Jesus the Christ, Christian theology has to hold on to two poles, as discussed above: continuity and discontinuity. On the one hand, it was the crucified who was raised to new life; on the other hand, it was an act of raising into new life:

> We must understand the paradigmatic nature of Jesus' humanness in an ontological sense. Through the resurrection, Jesus reveals the transformed ontological reality that we will one day become. In raising him from the dead, God transformed Jesus' earthly, bodily existence into the glorious, incorruptible state to which the early witnesses to the risen Christ gave testimony. But this transformed humanness is precisely God's design for us. . . . "And just as we have borne the likeness of the earthly man, so shall we bear the likeness of the man from heaven" (1 Cor. 15:49). . . . The transformed humanness which now characterizes the resurrected Jesus reveals that God intends that we too live eternally as spiritual-physical beings.[80]

Having established the deity of the man Jesus and the humanity of Jesus the Christ on the basis of the resurrection and in the context of the whole trinitarian history of Jesus, we must continue reflections on the topic that typically in Christian theology falls under the term "incarnation." In other words, we will consider the unity of the deity and humanity in this one person. Before that, however, I would like to clarify the topic of the human-

79. Grenz, *Theology for the Community of God*, p. 282.
80. Grenz, *Theology for the Community of God*, p. 283.

ity of Jesus the Christ in dialogue with the important reconstruction of, and alternative to, the Chalcedonian formula by Pannenberg.

Whereas tradition locates the deity of Jesus the man in the person of Christ/Logos, Pannenberg locates the deity in the humanity of Jesus. According to Pannenberg, the obedient Son did not seek his own glory but rather subjected himself to the service of the Father's kingdom. Pannenberg makes here the brilliant observation that it is precisely in this distinguishing himself from the Father, "in this subordination to the rule of the one God [that he is] the Son."[81] In other words, as the heading in the chapter on the deity of Jesus Christ puts it: "The Self-Distinction of Jesus from the Father as the Inner Basis of His Divine Sonship."[82] By thus submitting himself to the Father, the earthly Jesus also avoided the crime of making himself equal to his Father. Pannenberg's focus on the inner logic of obedience and its relation to the divine Sonship is a needed correction to tradition's exquisite difficulties in accounting for the self-emptying of Jesus. Self-emptying in this outlook, rather than being an exercise in renunciation of divine attributes, is the refusal to equate oneself with the Father. This manifests his "divine essence as the Son."[83] Furthermore, Pannenberg's insistence on basing the human Jesus' self-distinction from his Father in the inner-trinitarian relations links not only the economic and immanent Trinity but also the preexistence, incarnation, and earthly life: "[W]e cannot separate the eternal dynamic of self-distinction (the *logos asarkos*) from its actualization in Jesus Christ (the *logos ensarkos*)."[84]

This is all good and important. Yet Pannenberg's view also has to be subjected to criticism and correction. His relocating the deity solely to the human life of Jesus the man, instead of tradition's locating it in Logos/Christ, while not totally satisfactory, is neither heretical in light of tradition. His affirmation of preexistence alone safeguards the German theologian from violating the intention and main motif of tradition, namely, the identity of Jesus as the eternal Son of God in union with the Father (and the Spirit).[85] Pannenberg's view helps avoid one of the major problems of the traditional incarnational model, that is, the true humanity of the incarnated Son. On the other side, it goes too far in making the deity solely the matter of

81. Pannenberg, *ST* 2:373.

82. Pannenberg, *ST* 2:372.

83. Pannenberg, *ST* 2:377.

84. Pannenberg, *ST* 2:63. It is significant that this clause appears in the context of the discussion of creation and the role of the Logos therein.

85. See also Pannenberg, *ST* 1:319-27.

the humanity of Jesus and thus fails to establish a thick account of divinity. This of course has implications for the work of salvation: the death on the cross is merely the death of the human Jesus,[86] who only by the account of resurrection will be shown to be the Son of God. The abiding and necessary teaching of Chalcedon is that both the life and death of Jesus Christ are the joint work of the divine and human natures in one person. Chalcedon presents the identity and union as "constituted by the incarnation of the eternal Son who takes on the human nature, which is individuated as the human Jesus. . . . In contrast, Pannenberg finds the identity of the Son and his unity with the Father as constituted by the life of Jesus."[87]

McClean brilliantly notes that as a Lutheran theologian Pannenberg presents an inverted version of his own tradition's christological formulation. It is instructive to look at the debate to gain a more precise understanding of how to best define the humanity of Jesus. The key to the Lutheran two-nature Christology is the robust use of the ancient *communicatio idiomatum* formula, particularly its idea of *genus maiestaticum,* according to which the divine attributes such as ubiquity are predicated to the human nature. This view leads easily to difficulties in the affirmation of genuine humanity, and the danger of Monophysitism emerges.[88] This was rightly critiqued by the Reformed party.[89] What makes the Lutheran Pannenberg's view interesting is that whereas in Lutheranism the distinguishing of the human nature from the divine is the challenge, in his theology, in which the humanity of Jesus is the locus of divinity, the discernment of divinity is challenging, and therefore, the joint work in salvation of the divine-human Savior is in doubt.[90]

The Chalcedonian teaching doesn't necessarily truncate the genuine humanity, nor does the application of *communicatio idiomatum* when it is done concretely rather than in the abstract. True, the Chalcedonian formula gives precedence to the divine Logos, who is the acting subject of the person of Jesus, but it also insists on the hypostatic union as "free grace." That humanity and divinity are "asymmetrically related" helps avoid the danger of

86. Pannenberg, *ST* 1:314: "To be dogmatically correct, indeed, we have to say that the Son of God, though he suffered and died himself, did so according to his human nature."

87. McClean, "Anticipation," p. 159.

88. As rightly noted by the Lutheran Dietrich Bonhoeffer, *Christology,* pp. 93-95.

89. For details and documentation, see Pelikan, *Reformation of Church and Dogma,* pp. 355-59.

90. McClean, "Anticipation," pp. 179-80.

lumping them together and prevents a statement about the lack of authenticity of the human nature.[91]

The way the NT develops the idea of the humanity of Jesus is with reference to Adam typology going back to the primal history in Genesis. This is a profound statement of the faithfulness of God to his creation and creatures: as long as the Creator God is the same as the Redeemer God revealed in the coming to humanity of Jesus, the faithfulness of God can be established.[92] The new Adam Christology develops the ongoing function of the risen and ascended Lord as the founder and paradigm of a new humanity. "The New Man from Above," in contrast to the failed first Adam, came to be "The Author of a New Humanity."[93] Two key Pauline passages bring this idea, which is implicit in many places in the NT, to culmination: Romans 5:12-21 and 1 Corinthians 15:45-49. Whereas the first Adam embodies disobedience, pride, and sin, the second Adam brings obedience, humility, and grace. It is highly significant to pick up the communal, and in many ways cosmic, orientation of the new Adam typology. This is in keeping with the NT expression "in Christ," which denotes the location of the whole people of God in Christ, not only, or even primarily, of each individual Christian. To highlight the communal dimension, Pauline literature at times uses the new Adam typology metaphorically, as in Ephesians 2:14-15, which speaks of Jesus creating "in himself one new man" out of the Gentiles and Jews.[94] This widening and opening up of the relevance of Jesus' person as the new Adam beyond the contours of Jewish nationalistic faith are the key to the universal embrace of the gospel by all nations.[95] As such, this act anticipates the eschatological consummation of all people of God under one God, a theme to be developed in ecclesiology.

The community orientation and reconciliation and unity-effecting teaching of the new Adam typology have profound implications for the issues of equality, inclusivity, and the value of each human being. The issue of the humanity of Jesus in relation to the divine Logos is further clarified in reflections on the doctrine of the incarnation and related issues of virgin birth and sinlessness.

91. Webster, "Incarnation," p. 224. I am indebted to McClean, "Anticipation," p. 180, for this reference.

92. Pannenberg, *ST* 2:297.

93. Subheadings in Pannenberg, *ST* 2:297 and 304, respectively.

94. See the careful exposition in Grenz, *Theology for the Community of God*, pp. 285-86.

95. See further, Pannenberg, *ST* 2:297.

7. "The Word Became Flesh": Incarnation and Preexistence

The doctrine of the incarnation and the corollary doctrines[1] of preexistence and virgin birth are all different ways of speaking about the unique relation between Jesus' divine origin and his human existence. All of them also have analogues in the history of religions and living faiths. In Tibetan Buddhism, the Dalai Lama, and in Hinduism, various avatars are considered to be manifestations of the deity.[2] In Christian tradition, there is very little similarity with the Gnostic or later religious notions of gods appearing and disappearing.[3]

Although it has become a commonplace to insist that the idea of incarnation sits better in the theology of Johannine literature (John 1:14, 18; 14:7; 1 John 4:2), this claim should not be taken as denying the existence of the idea also in Paul.[4] Think of passages such as 1 Corinthians 8:6 and Colossians 1:15-17, which seem to speak of the role of the Son as the agent of creation and redemption; Philippians 2:6-8, the famous *kenosis* passage; and references to the sending of the Son by his Father (Gal. 4:4-6; Rom. 8:3).[5]

1. Typical of systematic argumentation, any reflection on incarnation must seek to relate to a number of other key doctrines such as God, creation, humanity, atonement, soteriology, and so on.

2. See further, Schwarz, *Christology,* p. 230.

3. Perhaps the closest analogue — yet with significant differences — is the "Jewish idea of Wisdom as God's agent or emanation." Finlan, *Problems with Atonement,* p. 117.

4. One of the reasons that Pauline thoughts on the incarnation have been underdeveloped or at times virtually dismissed is the fierce debate about whether in Paul there is teaching of the preexistence of the Son.

5. For a detailed exegetical and theological analysis of key Pauline passages, see Fee, "St. Paul and the Incarnation," pp. 62-92.

Incarnation and preexistence are mutually related teachings. If the former is affirmed without the latter, adoptionism follows.[6] Similarly, any talk about the *Christian* view of incarnation without the presupposition of the deity of Christ — which would lead, as in the Gnostic *Gospel of Philip,* to the affirmation of every human person's divinity — results in an impasse.[7]

Incarnation is an act of salvation. Thus it belongs integrally to the discussion of atonement and soteriology as well. Yet it does not determine a specific view of atonement theory.[8]

Before inquiring into the meaning and an appropriate doctrinal formulation of the incarnation, the foundational question of whether incarnation is fitting to the divine will be raised. In other words, What are the prospects and conditions of an almighty God becoming embodied in the world he has created?

The Divine Embodiment

Thomas Aquinas begins his discussion of incarnation in the third part of *Summa Theologiae* (3.1.1) by asking if it is a "fitting idea" for God to become human: "Since God from all eternity is the very essence of goodness, it was best for Him to be as He had been from all eternity. But from all eternity He had been without flesh." Other potential objections include the infinite difference between the divine and human, including the observation that God fills the whole universe and is hardly to be "contained" in a human life. Furthermore, he notes that "a body is as distant from the highest spirit as evil is from the highest good." However, the Angelic Doctor comes to the conclusion that indeed, it is most fitting for God to become human because "[t]o each thing, that is befitting which belongs to it by reason of its very nature. . . . But the very nature of God is goodness," Thomas says, and refers to Dionysius (*Divine Names* 1), and hence to the essence of goodness belongs the desire to communicate itself to others (again, with reference to Dionysius, *Divine Names* 4). More than that, God is indeed the highest good-

6. Cf. the famous statement by Martin Hengel (*The Son of God,* p. 71): "*[T]here was an inner necessity about the introduction of the idea of pre-existence into christology*" (emphasis in original). Hengel means by this a reference particularly to the OT history in which lesser revelations through angels, prophets, and other special people were already in place as an anticipation of the full revelation in Christ.

7. See further, Finlan, *Problems with Atonement,* p. 4.

8. Finlan, *Problems with Atonement,* pp. 4, 118-19.

ness and thus it is befitting "to communicate itself in the highest manner to the creature, and this is brought about chiefly by 'His so joining created nature to Himself that one Person is made up of these three — the Word, a soul and flesh,' as Augustine says (*De Trin.* xiii)." In support Aquinas lists several reasons:

1. The union with humanity did not change God, who is the same from eternity; rather, human nature, which is mutable, was united with the divine.
2. Although it is not fitting for human nature to be united with the divine, it is fitting for God in his goodness, for the sake of salvation, to have union with the human nature.
3. It is fitting for God the Creator to be united with human nature, albeit different from divine nature, the author of which God himself is.
4. As Augustine also teaches, God's becoming human did not mean that thereby he lost his power and status as the one who fills the whole universe.

The Christian philosopher Richard Swinburne has taken up these and related observations of Aquinas and made a compelling case for the logic and rationale of the embodiment of the divine. He refines and develops the reasons to include these: since human nature is good, it is fitting for God to assume it; by doing so, God shows great appreciation of human nature and bestows great dignity to it; the assumption of human nature is also a mighty evidence of the divine love; the divine embodiment shows humans the proper way of life; although God in principle could save human beings in any other way,[9] the assumption of human nature is the highest way. Finally, Swinburne also links incarnation to suffering: the divine shares in the suffering of humanity when in the embodied form.[10]

Embodiment is an underlying Christian principle that goes beyond

9. This observation helps theology avoid prescribing necessity to incarnation, as seems to be the case with Anselm (see *Cur Deus Homo* 2.5). It is better to think, along with Thomas, that in principle God could have saved humankind using any other tactics but that God chose to be united with the human nature. It is significant that the theology of eleventh-century Rāmānuja, of the Vaishnava tradition of Hinduism (followers of Vishnu), argues that karma does not apply to deities who descend to help humanity. Rather, divine embodiment happens out of freedom and out of compassion. See further, Clooney, *Hindu God, Christian God,* p. 112.

10. Swinburne, *The Christian God,* pp. 218-20.

but is not unrelated to the salvific purposes of the "Word became Flesh" in Jesus of Nazareth. Moltmann rightly says that in the creative works of God, "Embodiment is the end of all God's works."[11] This is a "postulate which sets human reality in the history and surrounding field of God's creation, reconciliation and redemption. . . . According to the biblical traditions, embodiment is the end of God's works in creation. . . . According to the biblical traditions, embodiment is also the end of God's work of reconciliation: 'The Word became flesh. . . .' By becoming flesh, the reconciling God assumes the sinful, sick and mortal flesh of human beings and heals it in community with himself."[12] Indeed, avers Moltmann, "embodiment is also the end of the redemption of the world, the redemption which will make it the kingdom of glory and peace. 'The new earth' completes redemption (Rev. 21), and the new 'transfigured' embodiment is the fulfillment of the yearning of the Spirit (Rom. 8)."[13] The principle of embodiment is not only an essential theological observation but also the way to a right understanding of human life and society on this earth: "These works of God in creation, reconciliation and redemption also surround and mould the living character of created, reconciled and redeemed men and women. . . . We arrive at the theological perception of the truth of the human being in the arc that reaches from his physical creation to the resurrection of the body."[14]

The Reformed theologian William A. Dyrness speaks of embodiment as one of the three "normative categories" in the articulation of the theological reality of our life in the world, categories that also correspond to the trinitarian approach to life, faith, and theology. The other two are agency and relationality. God as lover of the world is committed to the world and thus seeks to make contact. Relationality and commitment are intertwined. Hence, agency emerges: "[t]he mutual exchange of the ideal relationship, even the intimate fellowship with God, is realized and expressed by our life in the world." Love manifests itself not only in speaking but also in doing. God's deeds suggest the third category, embodiment. Having created a world in which human life and life in general are physical — embodied — God's loving reaching out to the world takes the shape of embodiment, incarnation.[15]

11. Title for chap. 10 of Moltmann, *God in Creation,* with reference to Friedrich Oetinger.

12. Moltmann, *God in Creation,* pp. 244-45.

13. Moltmann, *God in Creation,* p. 246.

14. Moltmann, *God in Creation,* p. 246.

15. Dyrness, *The Earth Is God's,* pp. 16-22 (20).

The divine embodiment in Christian tradition thus is a "homecoming": "God's being at home in the world, a situation which even the sin cannot efface, leads to God's full identification with creation in the incarnation of Jesus."[16] On this basis, Luther could say that God

> himself must be present in every single creature in its innermost and outermost being, on all sides, through and through, below and above, before and behind, so that nothing can be more truly present and within all creatures than God himself with his power. For it is he who makes the skin and it is he who makes the bones; it is he who makes the hair on the skin, and it is he who makes the marrow in the bones; it is he who makes every bit of the hair, it is he who makes every bit of the marrow. Indeed, he must make everything, both the parts and the whole.[17]

Embodiment is not an idea that belongs only to Christian faith. Jesuit expert on Hindu-Christian relations Francis X. Clooney speaks to this issue in his important discussion entitled "Making Sense of Divine Embodiment":

> Many Christian and Hindu theologians agree that there is a God, maker of the world, and that there is only one such God, possessed of certain superlative qualities and likely to act in certain proper ways. Though God is mystery, God can be known well enough that he can be named. . . . Many of these same theologians . . . also hold that there are advantages and problems connected with asserting further that the God who makes the world could or should also have a body, as a necessary instrument for making things or for other kinds of activities in the world.[18]

That said, not all Hindu and Buddhist theologians agree that it makes sense to speak of God's embodiment in the world (neither do all those theologians agree on the existence of god, and even if they do agree, the conceptions of what makes the divine vary).[19] Some Vedic traditions, particularly those related to the Mimamsa branches,[20] see various difficulties in assigning bodily nature to the divine, such as that the deities seem not to be eating

16. Dyrness, *The Earth Is God's,* p. 22.

17. WA 23:133; *LW* 37:58.

18. Title of chap. 4 in Clooney, *Hindu God, Christian God;* quote p. 94.

19. For examples among some Hindu thinkers, see Clooney, *Hindu God, Christian God,* chap. 2.

20. This tradition emphasizes ritual and rites and thus ritual theology.

food offered to them in ritual and that they are unable to attend more than one ritual event at a time.[21] On the contrary, there are Vedanta theologians who, using logic similar to that of Christian theologians, argue for the necessity of deities undergoing divine embodiment. Curiously enough, texts in the Uttara Mimamsa Sutras adopt this position ultimately because the gods also need "salvation" by the right insight into the Brahman. Once embodied, the deities encounter similar kinds of troubles in the pursuit of right knowledge as human beings do and hence turn to learning meditation practices and similar devices to enhance liberation.[22]

With sweeping generalizations it can perhaps be said that whereas the Hindu path of Vaishnavism (of Vishnu God) makes divine embodiment in terms of avatars an important element in the path of liberation and "salvation," the path of Shaivism (of Shiva God) is far less occupied with that idea. The Christian doctrine of incarnation hence speaks more easily to the followers of Vishnu, particularly in relation to the two most important "incarnations" of Vishnu, namely, Krishna and Rama.[23] That said, it is important to acknowledge for the sake of a fruitful dialogue that "[b]oth Śaiva and Vaiṣṇava theologians may find the Christian emphasis on the uniqueness of the Incarnation and the importance of Christ's suffering needlessly literal-minded, perhaps a diminishment of divine dignity and in any case an instrument of polemic." These traditions also oppose linking suffering to the embodied deity.[24] This topic will be taken up in more detail below.

Speaking of the wider context of embodiment and its link with incarnation is not to compromise the traditional Christian insistence on the particularity of the incarnation, God-become-human, in the historical figure of Jesus Christ. On the contrary, it is to make that particular and unrepeatable act of God more meaningful in the wider context of the whole history of the triune God's salvific works. In this wider framework of the understanding of

21. As discussed in *Purva Mimamsa Sutras* 9.1.4-10; see Clooney, *Hindu God, Christian God,* pp. 95-96.

22. See Clooney, *Hindu God, Christian God,* p. 96.

23. This is not to say that Shaivism does not know divine descents; yes, it does. Indeed, there is the common belief in twenty-eight incarnations of Shiva, among whom one, namely, Lakulīśa, the alleged founder of the ancient sect of Pāśupatas, is prominent. Yet Shaivism by and large does not pay much attention to avatars. For detailed discussion of differences between the two main Hindu traditions, based on original texts, see Clooney, *Hindu God, Christian God,* pp. 101-23; for a useful discussion, see also chaps. 6 and 7, respectively, in Kulandran, *Grace in Christianity and Hinduism.*

24. Clooney, *Hindu God, Christian God,* p. 125.

embodiment, there is an important link between Christian faith and some other theistic traditions.

Above, it was mentioned that incarnation is about salvation. At the same time, it is essential for Christian theology, in order to see the continuity of the divine economy with the holistic nature of salvation, to discern the integral link of incarnation to creation.

Incarnation, Creation, and Humanity

Theologically it is of utmost importance to discern the way early theology established the link between incarnation and creation of the world, including the creation of humanity in the image of God. Athanasius's *On the Incarnation of the Word* thus argues in the very beginning that it is "proper for us to begin the treatment of this subject by speaking of the creation of the universe, and of God its Artificer, that so it may be duly perceived that the renewal of creation has been the work of the self-same Word that made it at the beginning. For it will appear not inconsonant for the Father to have wrought its salvation in Him by Whose means He made it" (1.1).[25] It is important for Athanasius to establish the doctrine of the incarnation on the basis that the same God who "made the universe to exist through His word" (3.1) also made human beings in his image, "as it were a kind of reflexion of the Word" (3.3). Seeing the lostness of humankind, the Father sent the "Word of the Father . . . [who] alone of natural fitness was both able to recreate everything, and worthy to suffer on behalf of all and to be ambassador for all with the Father" (7.5). In a most remarkable statement, Athanasius summarizes the integral connection between creation, creatures, and incarnation: "For this purpose, then, the incorporeal and incorruptible and immaterial Word of God comes to our realm, howbeit he was not far from us before. For no part of Creation is left void of Him: He has filled all things everywhere, remaining present with His own Father" (8.1).

Many other similar voices in early theology materially say the same, such as Maximus the Confessor: incarnation "is the great and hidden mystery; this is the blessed end on account of which all things were created. This

25. So also 4.1-2: "You are wondering, perhaps, for what possible reason, having proposed to speak of the Incarnation of the Word, we are at present treating of the origin of mankind. But this, too, properly belongs to the aim of our treatise. 2. For in speaking of the appearance of the Saviour amongst us, we must needs speak also of the origin of men, that you may know that the reason of His coming down was because of us."

is the divine purpose foreknown prior to the beginning of created things."[26] The two theologians are complementary; each presents the same truth from a different point of view. Whereas Athanasius begins from creation to speak for incarnation, Maximus begins from incarnation to speak of creation.

Earlier, Irenaeus, in vehement opposition to a number of heretical views, spoke of the incarnation as the act of the preexistent Word, the agent of creation, "who was also always present with mankind" and came to be "united to His own workmanship, inasmuch as He became a man liable to suffering" (*Against Heresies* 3.18.1). Incarnation made it possible for the human being, having been created in God's image, to find communion with God; Irenaeus, famously, explains this with the help of the "recapitulation" idea based on Ephesians 1:10: "Wherefore also He passed through every stage of life, restoring to all communion with God. . . . God recapitulated in Himself the ancient formation of man, that He might kill sin, deprive death of its power, and vivify man; and therefore His works are true" (3.18.7).[27] All this is to say that "His hospitality submits to the historical and temporal particularities of human existence with all its limitations and exclusions, even to violence and death itself. God's hospitality is . . . a creational and incarnational hospitality."[28]

The integral link between creation, creaturelihood, and incarnation then means that the Word "came to his own [possession]" (John 1:11). The continuation of the Johannine verse, "his own people received him not," says the "unheard-of aspect of this fact . . . that by creation we belong to the Logos and are thus 'his own.'"[29] Hence, this linking with Logos can be established also from the viewpoint of theological anthropology: that we humans are "religious by nature" (a point established in the volume on theological anthropology) means that human awareness is transcendent awareness, "openness" to God. This openness makes it possible for us to grasp the Infinite over against and embracing the finite. The sharing in the Logos who is also the principle of differentiation and distinction, as taught not only by the Greek philosophy of Heraclitus and the Stoics but also by the trinitarian theology of creation, forms the basis of the linking of creation to incarnation.[30]

26. Maximus the Confessor, *Questions to Thalassius* 60; PG 90, 620, cited in O'Collins, *Jesus Our Redeemer,* p. 36.

27. In *Against Heresies* 2.22.4, Irenaeus details carefully how the Word really underwent all phases of human life — from infancy to old age — in order to heal and restore.

28. Boersma, *Violence, Hospitality, and the Cross,* p. 187.

29. Pannenberg, *ST* 2:292.

30. See further, Pannenberg, *ST* 2:292.

In the words of Pannenberg, seen from "the standpoint of our relation to the Logos, the appearance of Jesus Christ may be understood as the completion of creation."[31]

Along with Pannenberg,[32] another contemporary theologian who vigorously highlights the importance of anthropology to incarnation is Rahner. Behind Rahner's anthropological orientation is his foundational idea that, as created by God, the human person is "the event of a free, unmerited and forgiving, and absolute self-communication of God." This is because "God . . . has already communicated himself in his Holy Spirit always and everywhere and to every person as the innermost center of his existence."[33] Consequently, human nature is the most fitting vessel to be united with the divinity.[34] Incarnation, according to this Jesuit, can thus be understood as the "free, unmerited, unique, and absolutely supreme fulfillment of what humanity means." This view renders incarnation as a mystery that "makes sense," rather than an unintelligible, contra-rational paradox.[35] In other words, Rahner understands "creation and Incarnation as two moments and two phases of the *one* process of God's self-giving and self-expression, although it is an intrinsically differentiated process."[36] But to combat the obvious error of expanding the concept of incarnation beyond the history of Jesus of Nazareth, Rahner notes that the incarnation of God is the one supreme case of the fulfillment of reality.[37] In that light, and rightly understood, Rahner can say that anthropology is "defective Christology,"[38] mean-

31. Pannenberg, *ST* 2:293.

32. It is significant that the first of three chapters in Pannenberg's *Systematic Theology,* vol. 2, is titled "Anthropology and Christology" (chap. 9).

33. Rahner, *Foundations,* pp. 116, 139, respectively.

34. This is what Rahner famously calls his "transcendental" Christology: it is "Christology which asks about the a priori possibilities in man which make the coming of the message of Christ possible" (*Foundations,* p. 207).

35. Rahner, "Jesus Christus, III.B.," 5:956; cited in Pannenberg, *ST* 2:293. Behind Rahner's turn to creation and anthropology in explaining incarnation is also his linking of theology, including Christology, with evolutionary science as discussed brilliantly in his "Christology within an Evolutionary View of the World," pp. 157-92. A number of theologians (and scientist-theologians) such as Teilhard de Chardin, Arthur Peacocke, and Denis Edward have in recent decades considered christological topics, especially incarnation, through the lens of evolutionary science. For a lucid, exploratory discussion, see Shults, *Christology and Science,* chap. 2.

36. Rahner, *Foundations,* p. 197.

37. Rahner, "On the Theology of Incarnation," p. 109.

38. Rahner, "Current Problems in Christology," p. 164 n. 1.

ing that the creation of human beings points to and receives its culmination in the coming-to-humanity of the Logos. Rahner's summative statement is worth quoting at length:

> The Incarnation of the Logos (however much we must insist on the fact that it is itself an historical, unique Event in an essentially historical world) appears as the *ontologically* (not merely "morally," an after-thought) unambiguous goal of the movement of creation as a whole, in relation to which everything prior is merely a preparation of the scene. It appears as orientated from the very first to this point in which God achieves once and for all both the greatest proximity to and distance from what is other than he (while at the same time giving it being); in that one day he objectifies himself in an image of himself as radically possible, and is himself thereby precisely given with the utmost truth; in that he himself makes most radically his own what he has created.[39]

The Korean theologian Jung Young Lee makes the unfortunate and theologically suspect proposal that in order for theology not to subsume creation into redemption,[40] the Chalcedonian *homoousios* clause must be rejected and, by that, the equality of the Son with the Father. Lee's concern is that Christian theology has so one-sidedly assigned redemption to the Son and creation to the Father that if the Johannine statement "I and the Father are one" (John 10:30) is taken literally, it means equating the creature (Jesus) with the Creator (Father). Rather, he oddly insists that "Christ is subordinate to the creator, and his work as savior and redeemer is one part of the work of God as creator."[41] This is to correct a fatal mistake in traditional theology and Christology, namely, the subsuming of creation into redemption. The fallacies of this proposal are obvious: beyond the fact that it rejects the foundational ecumenical agreement, it also makes trinitarian subordinationism a rule and ignores the fact that in attributing specific tasks in the world to particular trinitarian members, theology is still holding fast to the principle of the unity of the works of the triune God *ad extra*.

39. Rahner, "Current Problems in Christology," p. 165.

40. Lee, *Theology of Change*, pp. 86-87, claims that in Christian theology the saving work has been "attributed exclusively to the Christ and the creative work to the Father. Almost all past theology disjoins the doctrine of salvation from that of creation, giving the impression that the creation was a discrete event occurring prior to salvation." So also Lee, *Trinity in Asian Perspective*, pp. 86-87, among others.

41. Lee, *Theology of Change*, p. 88; see also Lee, *Trinity in Asian Perspective*, p. 88.

So far in this discussion, we have moved from the integral link between creation and incarnation to the link between the creation of human beings (anthropology) and incarnation. According to Rahner, the reverse is also the case: when the Logos became a human being in Christ, it meant that "he assumed a human history" because, in that human history is part of the history of the world, centered and based in Christ, Christ assumed it all. In the world created by God everything is related. Hence, assuming humanity, the Logos assumed the whole of history.[42] A corollary result is that the coming together of humanity and divinity, finite and infinite, matter and spirit, because of the unity of God's creative works in all their multiplicity and because of the orientation to transcendence of the human "spirit," "[t]his essential difference must not be misunderstood as an essential opposition or as an absolute disparity and mutual indifference between the two."[43] In insisting that the Logos became "flesh" (John 1:14), Christian theology is also saying that matter was included in the incarnation.[44] Against dualistic Gnosticism, the early church's theology linked tightly "the new man from heaven" with "the earthly man of the first creation."[45]

That is all good, and necessary to establish, namely, not only an integral link between creation and incarnation but also incarnation as the fulfillment of creation in general and the creation of humanity in particular. More must be said in this context, however. We should ask the foundational question: Why did the incarnation happen? Tradition has given two answers. The first, obvious answer is that the incarnation of the Son was necessitated by human sin and disobedience; this question was profoundly addressed by Anselm's *Cur Deus Homo* and the whole history of "atonement theories." The second answer is that "God intended the incarnation of the Son of God from eternity. His intention was formed together with the idea of the world" in terms of preparation for the coming of the Son to humanity.[46] According

42. Rahner, "Current Problems in Christology," p. 167; for the integral linking of everything in creation, from the point of view of Christology, see Rahner, *Foundations*, pp. 181-82.

43. Rahner, *Foundations*, p. 184.

44. Rahner, *Foundations*, p. 196, says it even more strongly: "The fundamental assertion of Christology is precisely that God became *flesh*, became matter."

45. Pannenberg, *ST* 2:297.

46. Moltmann, *Trinity and the Kingdom*, p. 114. Of the second answer, Moltmann — in my opinion, mistakenly — takes Barth's discussion of creation in *CD* III as the prime example. A far better example for Moltmann, however, would be Rahner, as explained above; Moltmann's own theology, of course, is another shining example of that

to Moltmann, in the first answer creation only has a functional value rather than its own remaining value. In the second outlook, the incarnation of the Son completes creation. In the first, human sin and obedience are the "reason" for the coming of the Son; in the latter they are its "occasion."[47] During the height of the medieval period, the Dominican and Franciscan schools famously articulated and argued for these two positions. Whereas for Saint Thomas and his followers the main reason for the coming of the Word in flesh was our salvation,[48] under the influence of John Duns Scotus, the Franciscans did not make incarnation dependent on the Fall but rather made it necessary for God's claiming of his kingdom through the coming of Christ.[49]

The distinction between "reason" and "occasion" helps correct and balance the impression that the two answers to the question of "why incarnation" are exclusive of each other in the way Moltmann seems to put them and that we should go with the latter option. Indeed, they mutually require and complement each other. It is here where the approach of Rahner and Moltmann (and to a lesser extent, of Pannenberg) should be critiqued and balanced in light of tradition. The difference between Athanasius and Rahner, to use them as types, is that whereas for the former, human lostness and disobedience seem to be the main explaining motif for the incarnation, along with God's mercy,[50] for the latter the human need seems to be missing. The statements from Athanasius cited above, as much as they underscore the importance of linking incarnation with creation, also speak everywhere of the human lostness and need for the Savior to come and die and be raised

---

answer. Indeed, Barth is not a typical representative of this view because, as I will show in what follows, his theology brings together both answers to the "why" of incarnation.

47. Moltmann, *Trinity and the Kingdom*, pp. 114-15.

48. In *Summa Theologica* 3.1.3 Thomas ponders this question in light of different opinions and finally ends up supporting the above view mainly on the basis of scriptural support: "everywhere in the Sacred Scripture the sin of the first man is assigned as the reason of the Incarnation." Thomas tackled this issue in several other places and acknowledged the force of other views on the reason for the incarnation as well; for documentation, see Weinandy, *In the Likeness*, p. 135 n. 1.

49. See Weinandy, *In the Likeness*, p. 136 n. 2.

50. Athanasius, *On the Incarnation of the Word* 6.5-6: "For it were not worthy of God's goodness that the things He had made should waste away, because of the deceit practised on men by the devil. Especially it was unseemly to the last degree that God's handicraft among men should be done away, either because of their own carelessness, or because of the deceitfulness of evil spirits"; see also #4-6 on the lostness and #3 on God's mercy.

from death for our salvation. For Athanasius, incarnation alone,[51] apart from the rest of the history of Jesus including suffering, cross, resurrection, and ascension, would not do. Even for Irenaeus, with all his stress on the relation of incarnation to creation and anthropology, the human condition is the ultimate reason for the coming to humanity of the Logos.[52] In Barth's theology, the two answers to the need for incarnation come together in a profound way, as the following representative citation from his exposition of creation clearly brings to light:

> When God speaks He reveals Himself as the Creator who by His activity, as this takes place by His Word, unfolds the history which according to the witness of the whole Bible is directed toward the reconciliation and finally toward the redemption of the world, and will reach its goal in the incarnation, crucifixion and resurrection of this Word of His. It is by His Word, by which He is the Creator, that in this history He also becomes the Reconciler, and at the culmination of this history, declared as such, will finally be the Redeemer.[53]

The incarnation is not a passing moment in the divine life. If it were, the event would be closer to ancient mythologies in which deities change into human beings (and may again "go back" to the divine mode of being).[54] As the Athanasian Creed says, the incarnation happened "not by conversion of the Godhead into flesh, but by taking of that manhood into God."[55] In that sense we can speak of "permanent incarnation." To speak of incarnation implies that something "new" entered the divine life.[56] This of course is not to speak of the "change" in God in a way that would compromise God's de-

51. This is the feeling from G. Daly, "Theology of Redemption in the Fathers," pp. 137-39; I am indebted to Boersma, *Violence, Hospitality, and the Cross,* p. 123 n. 27.

52. *Against Heresies* 3.18.2. "2. For as it was not possible that the man who had once for all been conquered, and who had been destroyed through disobedience, could reform himself, and obtain the prize of victory; and as it was also impossible that he could attain to salvation who had fallen under the power of sin, — the Son effected both these things, being the Word of God, descending from the Father, becoming incarnate, stooping low, even to death, and consummating the arranged plan of our salvation."

53. Barth, *CD* III/1, p. 115.

54. See further, Bloesch, *Jesus Christ,* pp. 54-55.

55. In *Historic Creeds and Confessions,* p. 6.

56. For careful reflections on this issue in light of the doctrine of the Trinity, see Rahner, *Foundations,* pp. 212-24, especially 219-23, and Rahner, "On the Theology of Incarnation," pp. 105-20.

ity, but rather to speak of God's own choice from eternity to be united with humanity, created in his own image.

With its linking of incarnation to the Word/Logos, Christian theology came thereby to forge the link between the Jewish and OT world as well. Even for the early apologists, with all their efforts to make the Christian doctrine understandable to the Greeks, the continuity with the OT faith was of central concern. The link between the Word of the Johannine prologue and the OT teaching of the *dabar Yahweh,* become flesh in the person of Jesus of Nazareth, thus represents both continuity and discontinuity. Most Jewish contemporaries of the NT times rejected the Christian claim to "God in Christ" in the person of the Jewish rabbi. Reasons might have been many. Simply put, the "vast majority of Jews at the time who knew of Jesus rejected this claim, probably because they found no particular reason to accept it. Jesus may have been a notable rabbi; he may even have been a prophet, as many Jews apparently believed (Mark 8:22; Matt. 21:6), but there was simply no evidence for a claim of divinity."[57] For most Jews the claim to the resurrection did not function as such.

The way Christian tradition has spoken of the divine embodiment within the structures of this created reality in the person of Jesus of Nazareth has to do with the idea of two "natures" in one "person." What is the meaning of that central Christian formula? How can we best understand it at the beginning of the third millennium when our worldview has significantly changed from substantialist to relational and dynamic?

Two "Natures" in One "Person"

The difficult question that has haunted Christian theology since the beginning is the most obvious: how to even begin to speak of the coming together of the infinite (divinity) and finite (humanity) in one and the same person. All the parallel thoughts in the OT such as the presence of Yahweh/glory of God in the temple or at the mountain and other similar divine manifestations are just that, manifestations.[58] They say nothing like what the idea of the hypostatic union means to say. "The incarnation involves a divine being who

57. Kogan, *Opening the Covenant,* p. 115.

58. Num. 24; 1 Kings 8; Ezek. 10, and numerous other similar references can be mentioned here. See further, Dearman, "Theophany, Anthropomorphism, and the *Imago Dei,*" pp. 31-46. See also Segal, "The Incarnation," pp. 116-39.

is by definition eternal, without body, and unlimited in power, knowledge, and presence (i.e., omnipotent, omniscient, and omnipresent) personally taking up an existence that is temporal, partly material, and thoroughly limited in power, knowledge, and presence. Through the incarnation God, who is pure Spirit, assumes (and not merely creates and conserves) matter; the eternal God personally enters time."[59] Schleiermacher famously put forth the modern objection: "one person is to share in two quite different natures."[60]

Beginning from the early apologists,[61] an appealing way to resolve the issue of the joining together of the divine and human has been to allow a distinction between what the human nature is and can do and what the divine nature is and can do. In the patristic theology leading up to Chalcedon, the problem was often tackled in relation to questions such as how to explain the miracles or suffering and death of the one person. Theodore of Mopsuestia, with his Nestorian leanings, and others were trying to explain the logic in terms of attributing miracles to the divine nature and suffering and death to the human nature.[62] This view of course endangers the unity of the one person and can be interpreted in a way that supports Nestorian heresy (which is understandable in light of the fact that Antiochenes were thereby combating the emerging Apollinaristic heresy). A much more nuanced contemporary attempt to reconcile the unity of the one person in the context of divinity and humanity is that of O'Collins: "It would be a blatant contradiction in terms to attribute to the same subject at the same time and *under the same aspect* mutually incompatible properties. But that is not being done here. With respect to his divinity Christ is omniscient, but with respect to his humanity he is limited in knowledge. Mutually exclusive characteristics are being simultaneously attributed to him *but not within the same frame of ref-*

59. O'Collins, "Incarnation," p. 6.

60. Schleiermacher, *Christian Faith,* p. 393. A typical example of contemporary objection comes from Cupitt, "The Finality of Christ," p. 625. For these references, I am indebted to O'Collins, "Incarnation," p. 7. Emil Brunner's *(The Mediator)* simultaneous stern rejection of two-nature Christology as a function of foreign Hellenistic influence and unabashed confession of Jesus Christ as true man and true God raises the obvious question: Is that enough? Shouldn't that kind of confession be "filled in" with some more precise formulations?

61. See, e.g., Justin Martyr, *Dialogue with Trypho* 68 for struggling with the obvious incredibility of such an idea among the Jews. Similarly, Origen (*Contra Celsum* 4.14) tackles this issue in light of objections coming from the learned Greeks.

62. For detailed discussions, see Pelikan, *Emergence of the Catholic Tradition,* pp. 243-46 and passim; and J. N. D. Kelly, *Early Christian Doctrines,* chaps. 11 and 12.

erence."[63] Now, the key is the added note on "under the same aspect" and "not within the same frame of reference." This means that there is a distinction but not separation between the "incarnate Son of God *qua* divine and *qua* human [which] seems to deliver belief in the incarnation from falling under a ban from the principle of contradiction."[64] But does it? It can be objected that this is not much different from speaking of, say, "round squares." Couldn't one speak of circles as "four sided" *qua* squares and round *qua* circles. No, one cannot; these logical contradistinctions cannot be spoken of like that "within the same frame of reference" and "under the same aspect," in this case, as geometrical entities. In Christ's case, the talk of divine and human nature in one person seems to be possible without necessary logical contradistinction because there are two natures, different from each other.[65] Needless to say, this kind of abstract logical reasoning can at most make a negative argument to support the potential intelligibility of the talk about "two natures" in "one person." Left alone, that argument however stays abstract and not very useful.

In the same context, O'Collins also refers to the argument by Stephen Evans[66] according to which we are in a proper place to decide what is proper to the human and divine natures only *a posteriori,* after the incarnation. In other words, should we be convinced by virtue of other considerations of the possibility and facticity of the Word becoming flesh, its occurrence gives us assurance in hindsight that in this specific case we may think of the coming together of finite and infinite. This is indeed what Barth saw so clearly: "The meaning of His deity — the only true deity in the New Testament sense — cannot be gathered from any notion of supreme, absolute, non-worldly being. It can be learned only from what took place in Christ. Otherwise its mystery would be an arbitrary mystery of our own imagining, a false mystery. It would not be the mystery given by the Word and revelation of God in its biblical attestation, the mystery which is alone relevant in Church dogmatics."[67]

Instead of too much logical reasoning concerning the possibility of the

63. O'Collins, *Christology,* p. 240, emphasis added.

64. O'Collins, "Incarnation," p. 8. In Aquinas (whom O'Collins does not mention in this context), one can find fairly similar attribution of some things to Christ *qua* God (omnipotence) and other things to Christ *qua* human (limited power). *Summa Theologica* 3a.13.1.

65. O'Collins, "Incarnation," p. 8.

66. C. S. Evans, *Historical Christ and the Jesus of Faith,* pp. 125-26; O'Collins, "Incarnation," p. 9.

67. Barth, *CD* IV/1, p. 177.

divine and human "natures" joining together, one has to approach the divine mystery in concrete, particular terms. Two moves are important here to balance and correct classical tradition, namely, the turn to a "From Below to Above" approach, which is here in keeping with the NT testimonies, and the turn to the concrete person of the incarnate Lord. Stanley Grenz makes the useful observation that even in the two key passages in the NT on which the Chalcedonian incarnational Christology is anchored — Philippians 2:5-11 and John 1:14 — there hardly is an abstract description of the divine Logos suddenly descending on a man Jesus of Nazareth. Paul does not even mention Logos! Paul's point is that the historical person Jesus refused to clutch his divine prerogatives and instead chose the path of the obedient servant, all the way to the point of death on the cross. His exaltation by the Father was the result of his obedient life as a whole.

What about John? Doesn't he speak of the preexistent Logos who became flesh? Yes, he does, but, Grenz argues, not exactly in the way classical tradition has framed the issue. Rather than highlighting any specific moment in Jesus' life, even the virgin birth, which in tradition soon became the locus of incarnation, John "appeals to eyewitnesses who observed our Lord's earthly life. On the basis of personal observations of Jesus' life (not his birth), these persons bear testimony to the incarnation: The Word became flesh and lived for a while among us. We have seen his glory, the glory of the one and only Son, who came from the Father, full of grace and truth (John 1:14)." In other words, incarnation for early witnesses was "a theological declaration of the significance of the Master's earthly life." In that sense, the confession "the Word became flesh," rather than a presupposition, is the conclusion on Jesus' person on the basis of his whole history.[68]

This methodological insight is conducive to a turn to the concrete, particular person of Jesus Christ as the Incarnate One rather than a focus on the possibility and intelligibility of the divine-human union as a general universal principle. The Christian confession presents a particular mystery of faith that claims that the Word became flesh in Jesus of Nazareth. In this exercise, we may be helped by the Neo-Chalcedonian tradition, theological developments in the Eastern Church, building on the legacy of Cyril of Alexandria, which came to culmination in the Second Council of Constantinople in 552. Brian D. Daley lifts up the leading contemporary theologian Leontius of Byzantium — whose reflections on the union of the natures are often highly sophisticated and technical — as a prime example of a thinker who did not be-

68. Grenz, *Theology for the Community of God*, pp. 309-11 (310).

gin with the consideration of divinity or humanity in itself but focused on their union in the particular historical person of Jesus of Nazareth. He takes the unity of soul and body in the human person as the appropriate metaphor of the way two seemingly incompatible entities come together and work as in a "hypostatic union."[69] Borrowing from the Aristotelian concept of relationship, the Byzantine theologian surmises that it is possible for the soul to be united with the body without losing its transcendence. That said, to avoid saying too little Leontius reminds us of the important fact that in Christ's case the union is "substantial" rather than "relational" alone.[70] Rather than trying to truncate the infinite differences of natures, he argues that if there were not "something incommunicable in the union, rooted in the very greatness of the divine nature, there would be no condescension in the divine love for humanity, but only a natural joining of what is lofty with what is humble."[71]

In Neo-Chalcedonian theology, "The one Jesus Christ is the *datum*, the presupposition, given in Scripture and the doxology of the Church; the starting-point for christology is the single ascriptive subject of the Gospel narratives and the praise of the community."[72] Rather than trying to resolve the paradox of the being or ontology of the God-man, these theologians concentrated on the question: "What does it *mean to say* 'the Logos became flesh'?"[73] Thus, the Neo-Chalcedonian approach attempts to avoid undue abstract speculations and to focus on the person of Jesus Christ. In this outlook, then, "It is said of this single subject that he created the world and died on a cross, that he healed by a word of command and hungered, thirsted, and grew weary."[74] That is of course much closer to the economic way the NT speaks of Jesus Christ as a whole, united person who taught, healed, showed compassion, got weary, was thirsty, suffered, died on the cross, and ministered and taught again after the resurrection.

An essential technical tool in Neo-Chalcedonian thought is the terminological distinction between *ousia/physis* ("essence/nature") and *hypostasis/ prosopon* ("person[?]"/"person"). Rather than using terminology in a fixed and rigid way, it might be better to see it in terms of rhetoric and "usage." When speaking of "what" Christ is, the terminology of "essence," *ousia,* is

69. Leontius of Byzantium, *Contra Nestorianos et Eutychianos* 4 (PG 1285C-9B), cited and translated in Daley, "Nature," p. 168.

70. Leontius, *Epilysis* 4 (PG 86, 1925C), in Daley, "Nature," p. 169.

71. Leontius, *Epilysis* 8 (PG 86, 1940C), in Daley, "Nature," p. 167.

72. Yeago, "Jesus of Nazareth," p. 166.

73. Yeago, "Jesus of Nazareth," p. 167.

74. Yeago, "Jesus of Nazareth," p. 167.

proper; when speaking of "who" Christ is, then "person," *prosopon,* is the right choice. Some things are appropriate when we speak "according to nature" *(physis),* what Christ is, whereas other things are more appropriately addressed "according to person," who Christ is.[75] This useful distinction comes to the fore in the writings of Saint Maximus the Confessor, in whose theology the Neo-Chalcedonian school comes to the fullest expression: "Things united according to one and the same ousia or nature . . . are in every case of the same ousia with one another and different in hupostasis."[76] The converse is also true: "On the other hand, things united according to one and the same hupostasis or person, that is, things making up one and the same hupostasis by virtue of union, are of the same hupostasis with one another and different in ousia."[77] Maximus illustrates these two registers of speaking with reference to the identity and distinction between human body and soul. The specific features that mark off a person's body and soul as his "coming together by virtue of union, characterize and at the same time mark off from other humans the hupostasis made up of them, that of Peter, for example." But at the same time, "these features do not mark off the soul of Peter from his own body. For both, soul and body, are identical *(tautos)* with one another, by the principle *(logos)* of the one hupostasis made up of them by virtue of union. For neither of these actually exists on its own, separate from the other."[78] This is the basis of affirming, in this case, the unique identity of soul and body in the one person of Peter. So, now the full paragraph from Maximus with implications to Christ:

> Thus it is in the case of the human soul and body. For the features which mark off someone's body from other bodies, and someone's soul from other souls, coming together by virtue of union, characterize and at the same time mark off from other humans the hupostasis made up of them, that of Peter, for example, or of Paul. But these features do not mark off the soul of Peter from his own body. For both, soul and body, are identical *(tautos)* with one another, by the principle *(logos)* of the one hupostasis made up of them by virtue of union. For neither of these actually exists on its own, separate from the other, before their composi-

75. Yeago, "Jesus of Nazareth," pp. 167-68.

76. Maximus the Confessor, "Letter 15," in Yeago, "Jesus of Nazareth," p. 168; all translations are by Yeago, to whom I am also indebted for all these references to Maximus.

77. Maximus the Confessor, "Letter 15," in Yeago, "Jesus of Nazareth," p. 169.

78. Maximus the Confessor, "Letter 15," in Yeago, "Jesus of Nazareth," p. 170.

> tion *(synthesis)* to produce the species. For the production *(genesis)*, the composition, and the constitution *(symplerosis)* of the species by virtue of their composition, are simultaneous with one another.[79]

It may not be too far-fetched to see in this dynamic description of the sameness and difference through a relational approach similarities with the emphasis of some contemporary postmodern writers on the need to appreciate in the Chalcedonian formula not only the unity/sameness but also the real difference between the two natures. In the words of the philosopher J. K. A. Smith, Chalcedon "provides an alternative way for understanding difference, or better, the *relation* between differences. In the Chalcedonian model we see a certain mutuality — a play of differences that permits relation without either reducing the terms to the Same or asserting a radical incommensurability that precludes connection."[80]

Lee offers an interesting proposal in that his approach is Son-driven: "I will begin with God the Son because the dual nature of Christ is a key to understanding the divine Trinity. Moreover, God the Son represents the fulfillment of the trinitarian principle through the incarnation."[81] The Son is the way to know the Father, and therefore the inductive method, ascending from the historical manifestation in the world of the Father in the Son, is a preferred method over the traditional deductive one.[82] This Asian Christology is based on the foundational principle of *yin-yang*, which is for Lee a superb way of explaining the mystery of two natures: "The relationship between Christ's divinity and humanity is like the relationship between *yin* and *yang*. Just as *yang* cannot exist without *yin* nor *yin* without *yang*, the humanity of Jesus cannot exist without the divinity of Christ nor the divinity of Christ without the humanity of Jesus."[83]

Applying the *yin-yang* symbolic, which is cosmo-anthropological (rather than only anthropological, as in the West), to the doctrine of the incarnation helps link it with creation, Lee argues. "The incarnation of God in human form must therefore be considered as part of the cosmic process."[84]

79. Maximus the Confessor, "Letter 15" in Yeago, "Jesus of Nazareth," pp. 169-70.

80. Smith, "The Call as Gift," p. 225; I am indebted to Henriksen, *Desire, Gift, and Recognition*, p. 211 n. 9.

81. Lee, *Trinity in Asian Perspective*, p. 19. The methodological choice is also illustrated in the order of discussion: chap. 4 on Son, chap. 5 on Spirit, and chap. 6 on Father.

82. Lee, *Trinity in Asian Perspective*, p. 70.

83. Lee, *Theology of Change*, p. 98.

84. Lee, *Trinity in Asian Perspective*, pp. 71-72 (72).

The *yin-yang* symbolic also helps negotiate the mystery of fullness and emptying evident in passages such as the Philippians 2 hymn, to which Lee finds parallels in Taoist philosophy.[85] Similarly, this approach helps make sense of the maleness and femininity as well as individuality and community of the Son.[86] Lee also uses this inclusive Asian way of thinking to probe the mystery of death and resurrection, a profound dialectic of death and life, life and death.[87] The undergirding principle behind all these reflections is the replacement of an "either-or" duality with a "both-and" inclusivity and the idea of *yin* and *yang* as both limiting and complementing each other, opposing as well as embracing each other. We have a good example in the notions of singularity and plurality. While Christ is an individual (individuality), Christ is also community (plurality) rather than either one or the other.

That said, the Asian *yin-yang* symbolic has only limited value. As a heuristic device, it may help us speak of the mutual conditioning, interpenetration *(perichoresis)* of the human and divine natures.

In some ways the Neo-Chalcedonian effort to shift focus from an abstract negotiation of the coming together of two natures to the question of the person of Jesus Christ as incarnate anticipates the wider shift in theology: "In many ways one can say that the ancient attempts to define someone's nature were predecessors to more modern questions of identity."[88] The key to proper understanding of Christ's unique existence is his *personal* unity and relationship to God and to humanity. This is not to say that that question is hostile to or dissociated from the questions of ontology.[89] It is to say that the personal unity should be the main gateway and end point of

85. Lee, *Trinity in Asian Perspective,* pp. 73-74.

86. Lee, *Trinity in Asian Perspective,* pp. 78-82.

87. Lee, *Trinity in Asian Perspective,* pp. 82-87.

88. Henriksen, *Desire, Gift, and Recognition,* p. 203.

89. In that sense, I am not following all the way those contemporary theologians who argue that ontological and personal explanations are contradictory or irreconcilable. Thus Gogarten, *Die Verkündigung Jesu Christi,* p. 500. Schleiermacher, famously, also rejected talk about nature because it is used in christological talk in total opposition to normal usage. *Christian Faith,* §96.1, p. 392. Nor am I persuaded by those contemporary approaches that, in their fear of the too-fixed and static nature of the term "nature" *(physis),* attempt an approach to the two-nature problem via the idea of human nature as not-yet-finished, in other words, as something emerging. My objection to this view does not violate the talk about the evolving development of human identity as conducted in the context of theological anthropology; my resistance has to do with applying this to a christological framework. For such a proposal, see Macquarrie, *Jesus Christ in Modern Thought,* p. 385.

christological reflections. Leaving all ontological language behind subjects Christology to the dangers of merely functional or ethical notions, thus compromising the key idea behind the *hypostatic union* formula, which is to say that there is some kind of "essential" and irreversible union between divinity and humanity.[90]

Shifting the focus from nature to person also has the great advantage of gleaning from the significant developments in contemporary understanding of "person[hood]" in terms of relationality and communion theology. Identity, which is of course linked with "person[ality]" in contemporary understanding, as discussed in the context of the Trinity, is relational in contrast to the older substance ontology.

Part of the doctrine of the two "natures" in hypostatic union has to do with the classical question of self-emptying: the divine Logos took upon himself not only the generic nature of humanity, but also the form of the slave. Not surprisingly, Christian tradition has tried several tactics in its effort to make sense of that essential Christian confession.

He "Emptied Himself"

Pannenberg makes the important observation that, quite early, patristic thought made a shift to equating the incarnation of the Logos with the birth of Jesus. Apart from the fact that the theme of virgin birth is marginal in the NT, this shift helped bring about a change in the theological understanding of incarnation. However, in Paul's Adam typology (Rom. 5 and 1 Cor. 15) and in his reference to the sending of the Son, as well as in the key Johannine passages (John 1:14; 1 John 4:2), the theme of virgin birth is missing. Instead, the "reference is to the totality of his life and work." Similarly, the Johannine sayings about the sending of the Son (John 3:16) speak of passion and death rather than birth.[91]

90. Cf. Henriksen, *Desire, Gift, and Recognition,* pp. 210-12 and passim; he attempts to maintain the principle of *hypostatic union* but believes it can be formulated otherwise. I applaud Henriksen's sincere desire, writing as he is from a postmodern perspective, to develop an alternative formulation in order to preserve the insistence on the true divinity and humanity of the one person of Jesus Christ even if I am not convinced his proposal is clearly articulated in order to offer a real solution.

91. Pannenberg, *ST* 2:301-2 (301). In two important passages in the NT the virgin birth and the sending of the Son, incarnation, are closely related. In Luke 1:35, the child to be born is said to be "the Son of God" as the Holy Spirit will come upon his mother and

The reason we cannot equate incarnation with the birth of Jesus is that then the whole life and history of Jesus would not matter. Not only would that seriously hinder the full establishment of Jesus' humanity but it would also make the incarnation of the Logos an "external" affair. In the eyes of the NT writers, Jesus' human life mattered. There is no need to list again the many NT references mentioned above in establishing the full humanity of Jesus. Suffice it to recall two important points here. The Lukan saying of the growth of the boy Jesus in "wisdom and in stature, and in favor with God and man" (Luke 2:52) is a paradigmatic statement about the subjection under normal human conditions of evolution and development. Not only the body and intellectual and other mental powers but also his identity and personhood developed along the lines of a normal human being.[92] Furthermore, the way NT writers such as the author of Hebrews speak of the shaping of Jesus' character in order for him to be "a merciful and faithful high priest" (Heb. 2:17b) sounds dangerously semiheretical to those for whom the incarnation was "fixed" at conception/birth. As our "brother," Jesus shared in the lot of those who suffer from the "fear of death" (2:14-15). He had to be "tempted as we are" (4:15) to be able to "deal gently" (5:2) with the weakest of us. Indeed, he was subject to weakness and "learned obedience through what he suffered" (5:7-9). Having "offered up prayers and supplications, with loud cries and tears" (5:7), his prayer was answered, but not in a way that saved him from passion and death! Finally, the author of Hebrews makes a statement that really tests the contours of classical Christology: the "pioneer of their salvation [was made] perfect through suffering" (2:10); through the process of having been "made perfect he became the source of eternal salvation to all who obey him" (5:9)! And to add to the complexity and freshness of this biblical exposition, the terms "Jesus" and "Christ" are being used interchangeably!

Classical tradition has had a hard time in fully making sense not only

---

"the power of the Most High will overshadow" her. The main focus of this statement probably is to assure us that Jesus was the Son of God from the very first rather than becoming such at the baptism or resurrection (as in adoptionism); Gal. 4:4 is another significant linking of the coming of the Son and birth: "God sent forth his Son, born of woman, born under the law." Here the emphasis is on the subjection to the Mosaic Law of the one who was born; this is important for Paul, who in this epistle considers carefully the role of the Law in relation to the old and new covenants.

92. For the importance of life experiences and experience of the world for the development of human personality, see our discussion of theological anthropology, particularly Pannenberg's insights.

of the humanity of Jesus but also — and particularly — of his "emptying," the *kenosis* (Phil. 2:7).[93] The point about the emptying is neither renouncing nor even temporarily turning off the use of divine powers — which of course, when taken to its logical end, would lead to the heretical denial of the full divinity of the incarnated Son — but rather the voluntary submission of the earthly Jesus to his Father's will, as a number of Johannine sayings (John 5:19, 30, 36, among others) and the sayings from Hebrews quoted above affirm. "Obedient subordination to the Father characterizes Jesus as the Son."[94] Unlike the first Adam, the will of the new Adam totally corresponded to the will of God as "an expression of his free agreement with the Father."[95] By doing so, Jesus as a man differentiated himself from the Father. As a creature, Jesus set himself below his God and thus assumed the place that belongs to the human being.[96]

The rejection of Monothelitism in favor of the "two-will" doctrine[97] meant that the "'human nature' of the Logos possesses a genuine, spontaneous, free, spiritual, active centre, a human selfconsciousness, which as creaturely faces the eternal Word in a genuinely human attitude of adoration, obedience, a most radical sense of creaturehood."[98] In other words, to continue rejecting not only Monothelite but also Monophysite heresies after the Chalcedonian tradition, we must be able to "allow the Lord to appear . . . as true Man . . . who, standing before God on our side in free human obedience, is Mediator, not only in virtue of the ontological union of two natures, but also through his activity, which is directed to God (as obedience to the will of the Father) and cannot be conceived of *simply* as God's activity in and through a human nature thought of as purely instrumental, a nature, which in relation to the Logos would be, ontologically and morally, purely passive."[99]

The self-surrender to the death on the cross and the cry, "Father, into thy hands I commit my spirit!" (Luke 23:46), was the ultimate point of his self-distinction and self-emptying. Looking back from the perspective of

93. Still a definitive exegetical study is Martin, *Carmen Christi.*

94. Rahner, "Current Problems in Christology," p. 161.

95. Pannenberg, *ST* 2:315-16 (316).

96. See Pannenberg, *ST* 1:309-10.

97. For this decision made at the Second Council of Constantinople (533) and theological issues, see Pelikan, *Emergence of Catholic Tradition,* pp. 340-41; Pelikan, *The Spirit of Eastern Christendom,* pp. 68-75.

98. Rahner, "Current Problems in Christology," p. 158.

99. Rahner, "Current Problems in Christology," p. 161.

the resurrection, which helped confirm the authenticity of the earthly Jesus' claims to the Sonship, we must conclude that this self-distinction corresponds and is fully in keeping with the eternal, preexistent Son's relation to the Father. That said, "the self-emptying of the Preexistent is to be understood as a renunciation not of his divine essence but simply of any equating of himself with the Father."[100] Rather than being something contrary to the divine nature of the Son, refusal to "count equality with God a thing to be grasped" (Phil. 2:6), this act is rather the "activation" of his deity. Barth saw this in a profound way: "in this condescension, He is the eternal Son of the eternal Father."[101] In other words, Jesus' self-emptying, his making himself dependent on the will and love of his Father, is in keeping both with the true divinity of the Son as revealed to us and with the true humanity as created by God.

This is nothing unnatural but rather is in keeping with the nature of humanity as contingent and dependent. Not only the heretics, such as the Socinians, of the sixteenth century saw in the self-emptying of Jesus the denial of his deity, but even orthodox Protestants could relate the voluntary subjection under the Father's will only to Jesus' humanity. Pannenberg rightly says that with their "evasive answer the older dogmatics was missing the point that Jesus shows himself to be the Son of God precisely in his self-distinction from God."[102]

The interpretation of the *kenosis* of Jesus by some Buddhist commentators who know Christian tradition well has some thematic similarities with these less-than-satisfactory ways of trying to negotiate the self-humiliation of Jesus in relation to his divinity. Masao Abe's reflection entitled "Kenotic God and Dynamic Sunyata" pays special attention to Jesus' refusal to cling to being divine and instead divest himself of the divine status and become fully human. That for him speaks of something similar to the Buddhist notion of "emptiness" *(sunyata)*. In this process, Abe sees the dynamic and paradoxical logic of God's transcendence and immanence. Following this self-negation is the exaltation (Phil. 2:9-11).[103] The problem from the Chalcedonian perspective is that this interpretation is not able to hold on to the simultaneous divinity and humanity of the incarnate Jesus.[104]

100. Pannenberg, *ST* 2:372-75, 377 (377).

101. Barth, *CD* IV/1, p. 129; see also the profound insights on pp. 177, 179.

102. Pannenberg, *ST* 1:309-10 (310).

103. M. Abe, "Kenotic God and Dynamic Sunyata," pp. 3-65.

104. Here I cannot agree with the conclusion of James L. Fredericks (*Buddhists and Christians*, pp. 93-94), according to which Abe is able to follow the logic of Chalcedon by

The so-called kenotic Christologies of the nineteenth century set out to find an alternative — in many ways commonsense-driven — account of the meaning of *kenosis.*[105] There is more than one version of those attempts, and there are also varying assessments of their orthodoxy.[106] At the heart of kenotic theories is the attempt to interpret the humanity and divinity of Jesus Christ in terms of some kind of self-limitation of the use of divine attributes during incarnation. Kenotists typically base their negotiating on the distinction between the "essential" and "relative" (nonessential) attributes of the divine being. Hence, they argue that whereas at the incarnation the essential attributes such as holiness and love were retained, the relative attributes of omnipotence, omnipresence, and omniscience were renounced for the time being.[107] The Congregationalist P. T. Forsyth denied that those attributes were renounced; they were rather "retracted from the actual to the potential."[108] Although kenotic interpretations can affirm the humanity of Jesus, they share obvious problems in affirming his divinity; however, they can hardly be called heretical unless, as in extreme cases, they end up renouncing not only divine attributes but also the divine nature.[109] Not only do the kenotic views have a real hard time in establishing the full deity of the Incarnate One, they also seem to miss the point of self-emptying as explained above.[110]

---

taking "the entire drama of the incarnation and resurrection of Christ as a doctrine of God's *simultaneous* and paradoxical transcendence and immanence through *kenosis*" (p. 94, emphasis added). Instead, I do not read Abe's interpretation of the hymn of Phil. 2 as able to affirm this; rather, it seems to me this Buddhist reading follows the logic of divine, then human, and then again divine.

105. For an informed and theologically insightful discussion, see Crisp, *Divinity and Humanity,* chap. 5.

106. It is not uncommon to find judgments of heresy passed on kenotic Christologies at-large (Swinburne, *The Christian God,* pp. 230-33). There are also those who consider kenotic Christologies as alternative orthodox ways of affirming what Chalcedon is saying. See S. T. Davis, *Logic and the Nature of God.* In contemporary constructive theology many are favorably utilizing and recasting the kenotic idea in relation to other systematic topics as well, as is evident for example in Polkinghorne, ed., *The Work of Love.*

107. This view goes back to the Lutheran Gottfried Thomasius. Bloesch, *Jesus Christ,* p. 61.

108. Cited in Bloesch, *Jesus Christ,* p. 61.

109. Bloesch (*Jesus Christ,* p. 61) first calls kenotic views heretical and then, on the same page, grants that as long as one is not speaking of renouncing the divine nature, kenotic views can also be orthodox.

110. I don't really see in what ways Bloesch's (*Jesus Christ,* p. 61) view differs from

Dependency, contingency, and reference to the other characterize human nature; that is presented to us most purely and innocently in Jesus' humanity. In that sense — and only in that sense — it can be said that "[t]he human nature of Jesus is subordinate to his divine nature" exactly because this subordination "does not mean the cancellation of humanity but the realization of true humanity."[111] To the human nature belong limitations; God, on the contrary, is infinite. The current theological understanding of human nature and personhood as something ec-static, always in reference to the beyond, to God, supports this same view.

When Jesus' human nature is cast in a trinitarian framework, we can also reflect on the dependency and limitations of it from the perspective of his relation to the Spirit. Jesus attributed his power to the Spirit given to him by his Father (Matt. 12:28; Luke 4:18; 11:20).[112] In that outlook, the earthly Jesus was dependent on the Spirit for his ministry, teaching, and miracles, as well as for overcoming temptations. "In becoming dependent, the Son surrendered the independent use of his divine attributes in incarnation. The Word became flesh and exercised power through the Spirit, not on its own. The Son's self-emptying meant that Jesus was compelled to rely on the Spirit."[113] The role of the Spirit in relation to the Logos as the way of explaining the presence of the divine in the man Jesus calls for greater clarification, which will be taken up below.

The relation of the Christian doctrine of Christ's self-emptying to similar-sounding ideas of emptiness in Buddhist (and to some extent, some Hindu) traditions will also be investigated below.

"Yet Was without Sin": Sinlessness

In Christian tradition prior to the time of the Enlightenment, by and large, the sinlessness of Jesus was unequivocally affirmed. This belief was based in NT statements such as Hebrews 4:15, which says that Jesus "in every respect has been tempted as we are, yet without sin" (so also 7:26; 9:14; 1 Pet. 2:22; 1 John 3:5; 2 Cor. 5:21). At Chalcedon, the view was reaffirmed. The thick ac-

---

the kenotic interpretations he considers inadequate: "Against the kenoticists I contend that the exalted one and the humiliated one are the same. The divine attributes are not renounced by Christ but are concealed in the humiliated Christ."

111. Bloesch, *Jesus Christ,* p. 73.

112. Luke 11:20 employs the Jewish metaphor of "the finger of God" for the Spirit.

113. Pinnock, *Flame of Love,* p. 88.

count of Jesus' sinlessness came to be expressed technically as *non posse peccare* (not able to sin), which says more than the thinner expression *posse non peccare* (able not to sin).[114] Early theologians were well aware that with the affirmation of the sinlessness also came the affirmation of the different nature of Jesus' humanity from our empirical nature — yet that was not seen as threatening but rather as facilitating the redemptive work of Jesus Christ.[115] The basis for the affirmation of sinlessness, apart from biblical references, was seen in Jesus' total obedience and moral perfection, as well as his immutable union with God.[116] Until recently, there was a virtual consensus about the way the Fathers thought of Christ: that he assumed fully the human nature in its unfallen rather than in its fallen state.[117] Currently, alternative readings have been suggested that seek to show evidence that indeed, from the early centuries onward, the majority view has been that he assumed the fallen nature.[118] Some commentators seek to stick with both options and hold them together at the same time.[119] This hermeneutical dilemma helps us understand the diversification of views in later theology.

Because of a looser understanding of the union of the two "natures" of Christ, Nestorius came to compromise or at least reformulate the classic view of sinlessness. Having affirmed that Jesus took human likeness "in order to abolish the guilt of the first man and in order to give to his nature the former image which he had lost through his guilt," Nestorius comes to underscore the assumption of sinful nature to the point that the classic view is

114. For a classic modern discussion, see, e.g., Shedd, *Dogmatic Theology,* pp. 330-31.

115. See, e.g., Irenaeus, *Against Heresies* 5.14.3; Tertullian, *On the Flesh of Christ* 16.

116. Origen, *De Principiis* 2.6.3-4: "But to whom is it more becoming to be also one spirit with God, than to this soul which has so joined itself to God by love as that it may justly be said to be one spirit with Him? That the perfection of his love and the sincerity of his deserved affection formed for it this inseparable union with God, so that the assumption of that soul was not accidental, or the result of a personal preference, but was conferred as the reward of its virtues"; see further, Pannenberg, *ST* 2:306.

117. For a useful discussion of the meaning of "fallen" and "unfallen" in relation to sin and the Fall in Christian tradition, including the notion of "original sin," see Crisp, "Did Christ Have a *Fallen* Human Nature?" pp. 270-88.

118. The most vocal contemporary writer who argues for the necessity of affirming the assumption of the fallen nature is the Roman Catholic Thomas Weinandy, in his *In the Likeness.* In a less radical way, the idea was carefully studied and presented by Torrance, *The Trinitarian Faith.*

119. This is the way the Orthodox Bishop Kallistos Ware is arguing: Ware, "The Humanity of Christ," p. 4, cited in Kapic, "The Son's Assumption of a Human Nature," pp. 158-59 n. 16.

rejected: "For this [cause] also he took a nature which had sinned, lest in taking a nature which was not subject unto sins he should be supposed not to have sinned on account of the nature and not on account of his obedience." That said, Nestorius also reminds us that, despite the assumption of sinful nature, "he stood firm in thoughts of obedience."[120] Not surprisingly, the Fifth Ecumenical Council of Constantinople (553) rejected similar kinds of ideas related to Theodore of Mopsuestia as heresy.[121]

In the aftermath of the Enlightenment, a number of ways of either rejecting or revising the doctrine emerged. Although Schleiermacher eschewed any attempt to prove the sinlessness of Jesus, he took sinlessness as the result and manifestation of "the constant potency of His God-consciousness," and as such "a veritable existence of God in Him."[122] The excommunicated Presbyterian of the nineteenth century Edward Irving was one of the first modern theologians to virtually reject the idea of sinlessness because of his emphasis on Christ's bearing of our sinful and fallen humanity.[123] From a more orthodox point of view, Dietrich Bonhoeffer came to reformulate sinlessness materially the same way. Because Jesus "became involved in the predicament of the whole flesh" of ours, "He was not the perfectly good man."[124] Reinhold Niebuhr could not affirm sinlessness mainly because he was seemingly unable to reconcile that with real humanity and temptations. At the most, he could affirm the sinlessness of Jesus as some kind of "symbolical reality."[125] Without necessarily truncating the doctrine, Moltmann asks — in the context of speaking of problems in classical two-nature Christologies — whether the assumption by the Logos of a human nature without sin would make also the human nature immortal (if, as assumed, death is the consequence of sin, however one may want to negotiate that causality).[126]

Among contemporary theologians, Karl Barth most famously reformulated the doctrine in light of his strong insistence on identification with humanity. It was axiomatic for him to affirm that "the Word was made 'flesh' means first and generally that He became man, true and real man, participating in the same human essence and existence, the same human nature

120. Nestorius, *The Bazaar of Heracleides,* bk. I, part 1, 68.

121. "The Decretal Letter of Pope Vigilius," *NPNF*², 14:322.

122. Schleiermacher, *Christian Faith,* p. 385.

123. See Gunton, "Two Dogmas Revisited," pp. 359-76.

124. Bonhoeffer, *Christology,* p. 112. I am indebted to Bathrellos, "Sinlessness of Jesus," p. 113.

125. Niebuhr, *Nature and Destiny of Man,* 2:70-95.

126. Moltmann, *Way of Jesus Christ,* pp. 51-52.

and form, the same historicity that we have."[127] The "flesh" *(sarx)* assumed by the Word "is the concrete form of human nature marked by Adam's fall, the concrete form of that entire world which, when seen in the light of Christ's death on the cross, must be regarded as the old world already past and gone, the form of the destroyed nature and existence of man as they have to be reconciled with God."[128] Barth is critical of the tendency of early theology to soften and compromise the real identification with sinful human nature because of the sinlessness doctrine. All the way to Protestant orthodoxy, Barth saw this tendency at work. The Roman Catholic Thomas Weinandy has materially argued along the same lines.[129] Against Gregory of Nyssa and later, similar thinkers, Barth insists that our human nature is not good.[130] In Barth's theology of incarnation, 2 Corinthians 5:21 looms large as he interprets it in a way that affirms Jesus' assumption of our sinful human nature liable to God's judgment and wrath.[131]

From a very different perspective than mainstream theology, religious pluralists such as John Hick bluntly reject the whole idea of the sinlessness of Jesus. Hick finds him guilty, for example, of racial prejudice (Mark 7:27) and use of violence in the temple (Matt. 21:12); after all, Hick surmises, there is no way to historically prove a human person's sinlessness.[132] Not surprisingly, Jewish tradition denies the sinlessness of Jesus.[133] The Buddhist Soho Machida offers an intriguing suggestion that Jesus as the Son of Man was burdened with original sin and thus died to atone for his own sin. Machida takes the Buddhist notion of karma as materially identical with the Christian notion of original sin.[134]

The question of the historical basis for the affirmation of Jesus' sinlessness, apart from the ramifications of thinkers such as Hick, should not be

127. *CD* I/2, p. 147.

128. *CD* I/2, p. 151.

129. Weinandy, *In the Likeness,* pp. 17-18 and passim.

130. *CD* I/2, p. 153.

131. *CD* I/2, pp. 153-56 and passim. In *CD* II/1, in the section in which he speaks of God's "no" at the cross and "yes" in the Easter event, Barth similarly emphasizes the need to speak of Jesus' identification with sinful, condemned human nature (pp. 397-98).

132. J. Hick, ed., *Metaphor of God Incarnate,* pp. 77, 110.

133. The acknowledgment of Jesus' culpability, as with any other Jew, did not mean he wouldn't be counted a true Jew. Often rabbis applied to Jesus the talmudic principle: "Even though [the people] have sinned, they are still [called] 'Israel'" (Babylonian Talmud *Sanhedrin* 44a [http://www.come-and-hear.com/sanhedrin/sanhedrin_44.html#44a_2], accessed January 31, 2011).

134. Machida, "Jesus, Man of Sin," pp. 60-61.

taken lightly. Any more than deity or humanity, sinlessness cannot be merely affirmed in contemporary theology. An important reminder here is that Jesus' opponents were not convinced at all that he was sinless. Charges leveled against him included not only lifestyle-related issues such as gluttony — a vice totally improper for a religious teacher — but also the most serious of all in the Jewish context, namely, blasphemy.[135] Hence, the affirmation of the sinlessness in the "From Below to Above" approach is not so much the conclusion from his life, as important as it is, but more importantly an inference from resurrection that confirmed his claims. "Rather than being a foundation for faith, therefore, our declaration that Jesus was sinless is dependent on faith"[136] in resurrection. Mere sinlessness doesn't of course make the human person divine; but God, by definition, cannot sin. Apart from the resurrection, even the claim that having been filled with the Holy Spirit from his conception made him sinless probably would not be enough.[137]

At work in the affirmation of the sinlessness of Jesus is the same kind of dynamic relationship between continuity and discontinuity that characterizes the question of the relation of the resurrected body to our human body. On the one hand, soteriologically, it has to be insisted that however one negotiates the assumption of human nature, whether fallen or unfallen, the salvific effect of the work of atonement cannot be compromised. In other words, if Jesus were sinner in the same way we are, he could not save us. That is, of course, the rule of faith going back to the Fathers. On the other hand, similarly following the patristic rule, only that which was assumed can be healed. This means that if Jesus' humanity is so much different from ours that, in his incarnation, earthly life, death on the cross, resurrection, and ascension, our human nature, including fallenness, was not assumed and healed, our salvation is in jeopardy. In sum: the question of sinlessness, which first of all is a soteriological question,[138] has to remain in the dynamic field of affirming both identification with us and uniqueness. Early theology clearly let the soteriological considerations take the upper hand. In no case was it willing to think of Christ's identification with us in a way that would make him a creature in need of salvation himself. Later theology has felt much more intensely the need to let the identification be understood in a robust way, including the assumption of the fallen nature.

135. See further, Davidson, "Pondering the Sinlessness of Jesus Christ," p. 374.

136. Grenz, *Theology for the Community of God*, p. 252.

137. As Bloesch (*Jesus Christ*, p. 73) claims.

138. See Weinandy, *In the Likeness*, p. xiii.

The difference in viewpoints regarding the assumption of either unfallen or fallen human nature comes to the fore in the hermeneutics of key NT passages, particularly Romans 8:3.[139] What is the meaning of the expression "in the *likeness* of sinful flesh"? Is *homoiomati* an indication of dissimilarity (his flesh was similar to but not really the same as ours) or similarity, including fallenness?[140] Other hermeneutical tasks related to this verse and similar ones such as Galatians 4:4 include the weighing of the validity of the recent suggestion by the Catholic theologian Vincent Branick, according to which the "sending" of the Son by God in Paul normally entails subjection or contamination; that view would support the idea of the assumption of fallen human nature.[141] It seems to me this question cannot be resolved with the help of hermeneutical and exegetical considerations alone.

Terminologically, it is useful to distinguish between Jesus' sinlessness *de facto* and *de jure*. That Jesus was in fact without sin is affirmed by the orthodox view. The *non posse peccare,* however, seems to be saying also the latter — that Jesus was *necessarily* sinless. If so, was he then also immune to temptations? No serious interpretation of Jesus' temptations, widely attested not only in the Gospels but also elsewhere in the NT, considers temptations "a mere charade, as if he simply went through the motions of being tempted to give us a good example, without feeling any pull whatsoever from temptation."[142]

The theological consideration of the possibility of reconciling the doctrine of sinlessness and the full humanity of Jesus must begin with the consideration of the original nature of human nature. The true humanity of the created person who exists in the form of the image of God does not of course entail sinfulness. Our fallen humanity rather represents corruption.[143] Similarly, the concept of sin has to be clarified. Whatever else it is,

139. Other passages bearing directly on this question include 2 Cor. 5:21 and perhaps 2 Cor. 8:9. Mainline opinion in exegetical studies is that although Jesus did not personally sin, his humanity is similar to ours but not identical; see, e.g., Cranfield, *The Epistle to the Romans*, pp. 370-82.

140. It seems to me that it may be saying too much to draw the conclusion from Paul's use of this term in other contexts (such as Rom. 1:25; 5:14; 6:5) that "Paul consistently used 'likeness' to denote appropriate correspondence or congruity" in terms of affirming "Jesus' radical conformity to and solidarity with our sinful flesh *(sarx)*" (Weinandy, *In the Likeness*, pp. 79-80).

141. Branick, "The Sinful Flesh of the Son of God (Rom 8:3)," pp. 247-48.

142. O'Collins, "Incarnation," p. 14.

143. See Bloesch, *Jesus Christ*, pp. 73-74.

including "rebellion" against the Creator of fellow human beings or "transgression" of divine law, at its core it is a relational term. "Sin primarily consists in parting company with God. Likewise salvation is the result of the reestablishment of this relationship."[144] In the fallen humanity, the reason for the broken relationship with the Creator has to be found in "a deep ontological, existential and structural deformation and depravity of man's very being."[145] This is a statement by a contemporary Eastern Orthodox theologian rather than, say, a traditional Reformed thinker, and it represents well the ecumenical consensus in classical tradition. That statement is different from thinner accounts of sinfulness as found in heretical movements such as Socinianism or in the theology of classical liberalism. Apart from nuances, these views differ from tradition in that they make someone a sinner by account of sinful acts, whereas tradition considers sinful nature the basis for sinfulness.[146] Bathrellos makes the important observation that only the revisionist modernist view of sin makes it possible to attribute a sinful and fallen human nature to Christ and at the same time consider him sinless because of lack of sinful acts.[147] Or to put it differently: in the case that Jesus Christ bore also the fallen human nature, it is hard not to make a connection between that and "original sin," however that difficult concept is to be understood in contemporary theology. That conclusion would be fatal to any kind of affirmation of hypostatic union.[148]

Putting together the two universally agreed Christian theological statements explained above, namely, the exclusion of sin as the ontological element of human nature and the notion of sin as the breaking off of a relation between Creator and human beings — as well as the earlier remarks in the context of the self-emptying of Jesus Christ on the contingency of humanity on God — the conclusion by the Orthodox theologian D. Bathrellos makes a profound point: "[A]uthentic humanity is humanity in God. Humanity

144. Bathrellos, "Sinlessness of Jesus," p. 114.

145. Bathrellos, "Sinlessness of Jesus," p. 115. On the basis of relationality Bathrellos also critiques Barth's view in which the assumption of sinful, fallen human nature is taken as the profound expression of solidarity. This Orthodox theologian argues that because sin is a thoroughly antirelational concept, it cannot be taken as the basis for establishing a relation, in this case solidarity (pp. 124-25 n. 9).

146. A useful historical and theological tracing of the shift from classical to modernist views of sin can be found in Pannenberg, *ST* 2:231-75.

147. Bathrellos, "Sinlessness of Jesus," p. 115.

148. See the careful discussion in Crisp, "Did Christ Have a *Fallen* Human Nature?" pp. 270-88.

cannot be thought of as something complete and self-contained prior to and independently of God — let alone against him. Unity with God *is* a defining characteristic of authentic humanity, without which the latter is not what it really is. This is why sin, which consists exactly in alienation from and in opposition to God, does not make us more but less human. Sin is a privation that distorts and minimizes our humanity."[149]

Consequently, rather than asking first how a pure, sinless humanity of Jesus Christ can represent humanity, we have to wonder how our fallen humanity can still be said to represent humanity. Rather than Jesus becoming "more like" us, we should become more like him (2 Cor. 3:18).

In both paradigms — the assumption of either fallen or unfallen human nature — which of course are not so much contradictory as they are a matter of emphasis, the question still remains about how any kind of affirmation of sinlessness can be reconciled with genuine humanity when it comes to questions such as temptations. An appealing way to negotiate the possibility of sinlessness comes from the philosopher T. V. Morris, who surmises that perhaps the human consciousness of Jesus wasn't fully aware of his perfect goodness. In other words, the metaphysical impossibility of sinning (gods do not commit sins!) did not trump the full force of facing temptations in his humanity.[150] The obvious problem with this creative solution is not only its hypothetical nature, having not much support in tradition, but also, materially, the risk of some kind of "Nestorian" understanding of the "split" of the one person(ality) of the incarnated Christ. Hence, to speak of what "earthly consciousness" does in distinction from "divine nature" seems to imply that it is not the "person" himself (in Jesus' case) but something "else" — perhaps an abstract concept of "nature" — that is responsible for sin. Most thinkers, on the contrary, would probably argue that it is as *persons* we act, either to commit a sin or to do a noble act.[151]

To say that Jesus was fully engaged in the human predicament should begin with the acknowledgment that as human he was deeply affected by the effects of the fallen world, without himself participating in sinful acts. More than that, "Jesus was born in a fallen and sinful world. He lived under the same conditions as we do. He was faced with the various forms of evil that

149. Bathrellos, "Sinlessness of Jesus," p. 117.

150. Morris, *The Logic of God Incarnate*, pp. 153-62; for criticism, see Werther, "The Temptation of God Incarnate," pp. 47-50. I am indebted to O'Collins, "Incarnation," pp. 14-15, for these references.

151. O'Collins, "Incarnation," p. 15.

dominate this world and with the pain and suffering that they impose upon their victims." Ultimately, Jesus also had to undergo death and fear of death, human experiences linked with the Fall and sin.[152]

What about temptations? Before anything else, we have to acknowledge the difference between the horizon of the Synoptic Gospels and later Christian tradition in terms of the main focus of temptations. Whereas Christian tradition has struggled in trying to understand the authenticity of temptations against the affirmation of sinless nature, the Gospels make the temptations a matter of Jesus' relation to the Father. All three temptations raise the question of "If you are the Son of God . . ."[153] So, temptations are about obedience. Beyond that, the difference between Jesus and us is that temptations in humans originate from within the fallen nature (James 1:14), whereas in Jesus' case, from outside. That said, that is not to deny the force of temptations. Only think of the Fall narrative of Genesis 3: the impetus to disobey must have come from outside for persons prior to the Fall, including for the first couple. Furthermore, with regard to Jesus, although coming from outside, the temptations had a real contact point with his human nature given his hunger after forty days of fasting. The same can be said of the temptation in Gethsemane to sway from the way of obedience as a result of fear and the felt violence from the mob.[154]

As discussed above, the Bible links growth, development, and learning to the human nature of Jesus Christ (Luke 2:52; Heb. 5:8). Doesn't that also imply that in Jesus Christ we see not only the pure, unadulterated human nature but also a holy human nature, the "'mature' and eschatological Adam . . . the highest possible embodiment of holiness that has ever existed and will ever exist, because its unity with God the Logos and its relationship with the Father and the Spirit is the closest possible"?[155]

If these considerations make the argumentation lean toward *non posse peccare,* necessary sinlessness, is thereby the true freedom of Jesus Christ being compromised? In other words, can one be authentically free and "not able to sin"? The Sixth Ecumenical Council (681), the third one held at Constantinople, dealt with this issue, affirming the previously ratified view of the two wills of Christ. Jesus' sinlessness could not be defined in terms of denying the freedom of the human will. The free and voluntary

152. Bathrellos, "Sinlessness of Jesus," pp. 117-18 (118).

153. See incisive remarks in Moltmann, *Spirit of Life,* pp. 61-62.

154. Bathrellos, "Sinlessness of Jesus," p. 119.

155. Bathrellos, "Sinlessness of Jesus," p. 120.

submission to the Father's will was the way to define his sinlessness.[156] One also has to subject to criticism the view that freedom entails the possibility of sin. In that case, God of course would not be free! As Augustine argued, "the will that cannot sin at all is more free than the will that can either sin or not sin."[157] The reason for this is the widespread patristic idea that only the will that is not firmly and unreservedly established on good has the possibility ("freedom") to sin. The potentiality of not sinning as the ultimate manifestation of human freedom, reflecting the divine freedom from all sin, is of course an anticipation of the eschatological renewal in which, following Christian tradition, *non posse peccare* as a gift becomes the feature of the human state. The freedom of Jesus Christ was not predetermined, semiautomatic submission but rather true freedom *in God.* Freedom essentially is a relational concept; misuse of freedom, sinning, means breaking the relationship.[158]

In the framework of Spirit Christology, we will see in the affirmation of Jesus' sinlessness also the manifestation of his true humanity as contingent and dependent, in submission to the righteous will of his Father:

> [The earthly Jesus] had to rely on the Spirit's resources to overcome temptation. . . . He suffered real attack in the temptations and was not play-acting. It was not through confidence in his own power that he put himself at risk. Victory over temptation was not achieved in his own strength. He overcame sin by the power of God and in so doing modeled the lifestyle of faith for us all. Jesus surrendered himself in trust and conquered the powers of evil by the Spirit, as we all must. . . . His sinlessness was really due to his relation with the Spirit, not his own deity. . . . He conquered in the power of the Spirit.[159]

So far the fitness, possibility, and conditions of the doctrine of divine embodiment — incarnation — have been investigated by looking at the two central corollaries: self-emptying and sinlessness. According to received tradition, classical Christianity affirms that in the one person of Jesus Christ, in a hypostatic ("personal") union, two natures, divine and human,

156. "The Definition of Faith" of the Sixth Ecumenical Council (480-81), in *NPNF*[2] 14:493-95.

157. Cited in Pannenberg, *ST* 2:258 n. 287. I am indebted to Bathrellos, "Sinlessness of Jesus," p. 125 n. 16, for pointing me to this passage.

158. See Bathrellos, "Sinlessness of Jesus," p. 121.

159. Pinnock, *Flame of Love*, p. 88.

coexist perichoretically. The human nature assumed by the Logos is manifested in Jesus of Nazareth in its purest and most original form, in loving and willing obedience of the Son to the Father, child to the parent, indeed to the point of ultimate self-sacrifice for the sake of our salvation and the hope of the whole cosmos. Along with a full affirmation of the identification of the human Jesus with our humanity, that identification avoids sinfulness as sin does not belong to the essence of human nature. On the contrary, in the new Adam the children of the first Adam see for the first time their goal and destiny.

Now, in order for the classical Christian notion of the incarnation to make sense, the doctrine of preexistence must be assumed, or else the idea of divine embodiment hardly makes any sense. Not surprisingly, in recent times a growing number of theologians doubt whether the creedal notion of the preexistence of the second person of the Trinity is warranted by (mainstream) NT witness and whether it is either a necessary or a useful formulation. Even for those like the current author who hold tightly to the traditional creedal doctrine, the affirmation of preexistence is a major theological and philosophical challenge. To that topic we turn next.

"He Came Down from Heaven": Preexistence

In Christian tradition, the doctrine of preexistence means that the second person of the Trinity, the Son of God, became human in Jesus of Nazareth. Tradition doesn't of course teach that the man Jesus existed in any real sense before the incarnation but that God the Son existed prior to the incarnation. The Nicene-Constantinopolitan Creed testifies to this: "Who for us men and for our salvation came down from heaven and was incarnate by the Holy Ghost and the Virgin Mary, and was made man."[160] Preexistence and incarnation thus belong together and mutually presuppose each other.

It took early Christian theology some time to formulate its view of the nature of preexistence as there was vacillation between a purely ideal preexistence, as existing in the mind of God, and "real" ("personal") preexistence. Ideal means that whoever or whatever is deemed preexistent was in the mind and intent of God before it appeared on earth. Ideal preexistence had roots in Judaism, where some of the rabbis taught that seven things existed in the mind of God before they appeared on earth, in-

160. *NPNF*^{2} 14:163.

cluding Torah and the Messiah.[161] Complicating the issue was the creaturely nature of the preexistence of Wisdom (Prov. 8:22-23); in other words, it seemed like it did not take a divine being to be said to preexist.[162] Tertullian's view of the eternal generation of the Word[163] made a significant contribution to the solidification of the doctrine of preexistence in early Christian theology. At the same time, in the hands of later theologians this kind of idea may also be used, differently from Tertullian himself, to support a nonpersonal preexistence of the Logos.

The doctrine of preexistence was not the result of early Christianity's encounter with Hellenism as earlier scholarship claimed.[164] It arose out of the early church's Jewish roots.[165] Justin Martyr identified the preexistent Christ with the angel of the Lord of the OT, and Novatian concluded that Abraham's visitor on the eve of Sodom's destruction was the same preexistent Christ. This is not to say that Jews of the period would have been comfortable with any really preexistent being sharing any measure of deity with God the Father. After all, the claims Christianity makes in conjunction with this doctrine are what made Christianity a different religion from Judaism.[166]

161. See further, Hengel, *The Son of God,* p. 69. For an important discussion of the differences between ideal and personal preexistence, see Hamerton-Kelly, *Preexistence, Wisdom, and the Son of Man.*

162. See Pannenberg, *ST* 1:265.

163. Tertullian, *Against Praxeas* 7.

164. This is the famous thesis of A. von Harnack, who made a distinction between the Hebraic and Greek views of preexistence. In his view, Paul's was much closer to the latter. *History of Dogma,* pp. 318-32. The rejection of Harnack's view in current theological scholarship (in favor of the Hebraic origin of preexistence) does not mean ignoring the Hellenistic influences, as is evident particularly in Origen's "two-stage" conception of incarnation (not unique in early theology). The first stage of the incarnation of the Logos was the assumption of the untainted human soul of Jesus (in its undeserved clinging with the Logos in contrast to all other souls who failed to do so) in eternity; and the second stage, the assumption of a human body in the virgin conception. (Behind Origen's thought is of course the Greek idea of the eternity of the [human] soul.) Origen, *De Principiis* 2.6.2-6.

165. This has been shown convincingly in the massive study of Gottfried Schimanowski, *Weisheit und Messias.* On the other side, it seems to me that H. R. Mackintosh (*The Doctrine of the Person of Jesus Christ,* pp. 449-54 particularly), having first acknowledged the obvious similarities between the Jewish/Hebraic and Christian notions of preexistence, also reminds us of differences, the latter being focused solely on Christ, the Son.

166. McCready, "He Came," p. 421. So also Hurtado, "The Origins of the Worship of Christ," p. 5.

Unlike classical tradition, contemporary biblical scholarship has cast serious doubts on the doctrine of preexistence, and many wonder if the view has much solid biblical support at all.[167] The view of the majority of contemporary biblical scholars, followed by a number of systematicians, used to be that the teaching of preexistence can only be found developed in John, whereas Pauline and other NT traditions contain at the most only ambiguous references.[168] J. D. G. Dunn has articulated this claim in a most sophisticated way.[169] Dunn's scrutiny of relevant NT texts leads him to the conclusion that the only NT document to express a belief in Christ's real preexistence is John's Gospel. In his reading of the Synoptic Gospels, there are no hints of this belief. What Paul and the author of Hebrews affirm can at the most be named an "ideal" preexistence. The reason Dunn is not recognizing the traditional idea of preexistence even in the most important Pauline passage, Philippians 2:6-7 (which he grants on the surface seems to be teaching it),[170] is that he interprets that and similar Pauline passages through the lens of Adam Christology. This "second Adam" interpretation (on the basis of Gen. 3) not only does not require preexistence; it may even be counterproductive. Dunn surmises that the *morfe* of God (Phil. 2:7) denotes Adam as he was created in the image ("form") of God and the counterpart in the same verse, the "form of a slave," was Adam's status after the Fall. Neither use of "form" implies deity or preexistence.[171] Not only the classical doctrine of preexistence but also the incarnation is ruled out as the most viable reading of this key Pauline passage.

But is the dismissal or marginalization of the thought of preexistence in the NT by Dunn and other biblical scholars a valid conclusion? Hardly. Exegetes as different as N. T. Wright, the "evangelical" Gordon Fee, and the Jesuit Brendan Byrne, among others, have taken another careful look at the scholarly results and methods and come to the conclusion that the thought

167. For a massive up-to-date discussion and critical engagement, see McCready, *He Came Down from Heaven,* pp. 11-199 (on biblical studies), pp. 201-33 (on postbiblical Christian tradition), pp. 257-307 (on modern and contemporary theology).

168. For a succinct discussion, with full bibliographic references to contemporary biblical and systematic scholarship, see Byrne, "Christ's Pre-existence," pp. 308-11 (Byrne himself advocates the traditional view).

169. Dunn has presented his ideas in a number of places; the main locus of course is his *Christology in the Making.* For other places, see, e.g., the succinct discussion in *Romans 1–8,* p. 278.

170. Dunn, *Christology in the Making,* p. 114.

171. Dunn, *Christology in the Making,* pp. 119-20 particularly.

of preexistence is widely attested in the NT canon, way beyond the Gospel of John — once regarded as the culmination of slow development.[172] Hence, this new paradigm, as formulated by Byrne, concludes that the meaning of Philippians 2:6-8 (and similar passages) "makes most sense in terms of an 'invasion' from the divine sphere into the human,"[173] after the traditional interpretation. It is significant that even such critical systematicians as Pannenberg who used to be hesitant to grant the idea of preexistence (because of its Hellenistic origin), now argue for the idea of preexistence in the NT. The thought can be found not only in Philippians 2:6-8 but also in the statements about Christ's part in creation (1 Cor. 8:6), and perhaps in his activity in the life of Israel (1 Cor. 10:4). The sayings of the sending of the Son into the world (John 1:14; 3:17; Gal. 4:4; Rom. 8:3; 1 John 4:2) make sense only if the One sent preexists his birth on earth. To the same category of evidence in the NT must of course be added Colossians 1:15-17, Hebrews 1:2, and a number of (other) references in the Gospel of John.[174]

That said, it is also true what Byrne adds, namely, that in the final analysis the full affirmation of the doctrine of preexistence (which, as mentioned above, in early theology took some time to develop into its creedal form) is not only a hermeneutical matter of dealing with certain texts. Ultimately that doctrine is a systematic topic and also has everything to do with soteriology.[175] On the way to constructing a contemporary systematic view of the doctrine of preexistence in the context of Christology, a careful dialogue with revisionist views in twentieth-century theology is in order.

As mentioned above, Tertullian's idea of the eternal generation of the Son could be developed into a nonpersonal conception. A "latter-day variant"[176] of Tertullian's idea has emerged in contemporary theology in the

172. The key phrase of Phil. 2:6b, "did not consider being like God something to exploit for selfish gain" (Byrne's translation), is studied very carefully in critical dialogue with all major studies in N. T. Wright, *Climax of the Covenant,* pp. 56-98; see also Byrne, "Christ's Pre-existence," pp. 314-20; for a comprehensive study of all the main Pauline references, see Fee, "St. Paul and the Incarnation" pp. 62-92 (as the title indicates, Fee focuses on the question of preexistence particularly from the perspective of incarnation).

173. Byrne, "Christ's Pre-existence," p. 318. This doesn't exclude an allusion to Adam typology, as Dunn mistakenly alleges, but rather means that both an Adam reference and teaching of the incarnation/preexistence are in place here; see N. T. Wright, *Climax of the Covenant,* pp. 59, 90-94; Byrne, "Christ's Pre-existence," pp. 320-21.

174. Significantly, Pannenberg (*ST* 2:369) regards all these references as evidence of the wide attestation in the NT.

175. Byrne, "Christ's Pre-existence," p. 311.

176. O'Collins, "Incarnation," p. 4.

thinking of Piet Schoonenberg. Resisting the idea of personal preexistence, this Catholic theologian surmises that the Son only became "person" at the time of conception and thus existed from all eternity in some "nonpersonal" state. By extension, the same can be said of the Spirit, who allegedly became "person" only at the moment of the glorification of Jesus.[177] This kind of interpretation, however, leads into many insurmountable problems. It of course endangers any solid classical doctrine of the Trinity. The second person of the Trinity, rather than being "person" in any classical theological sense of the word, becomes a divine presence or influence. Furthermore, it makes too much of salvation history. Although history matters, it doesn't matter so much that the infinite is established only with the help of the finite. In other words, even when we speak of salvation history, how could the infinite God be dependent for existence on historical finite realities?[178] Similar kinds of criticisms can of course be leveled against the Hegelian idea of making incarnation not only the destiny of the world process but — at least in some way — the divine destiny; this thought again would make the happening in the world the presupposition of the "fullness" of God.[179] Aquinas's way of considering the incarnation as "fitting" instead of "necessary" is the needed counterbalance.[180]

Another progressive Catholic, K.-J. Kuschel, who has offered a massive study of interpretations of preexistence in modern theology,[181] considers preexistence an "unfortunate theological coinage" because it encourages us

177. Schoonenberg, *The Christ;* in his "Spirit Christology and Logos Christology," pp. 350-75, Schoonenberg seeks to clarify his position and also respond to criticisms by fellow Catholic theologians.

178. Several leading Catholic theologians interpret the Dutch theologian's views in a way that the immanent Trinity seems to come to existence only by virtue of events in salvation history. Kasper, *The God of Jesus Christ,* p. 276; O'Collins, "Incarnation," pp. 4-5. In a later essay, Schoonenberg is a bit more nuanced ("Trinity — the Consummated Covenant," p. 114): "In the salvation history before Christ the distinction between God and the Logos was already present. In the incarnation, however, this distinction became fully interpersonal, a distinction between Father and Son." (He also says basically the same about the Spirit.) Even then, it seems to me his original view holds: speaking of "personal distinction" in need of becoming "fully interpersonal" hardly clarifies an already confusing and complex view!

179. Similarly, O'Collins, "Incarnation," p. 17.

180. Thomas Aquinas, *Summa Theologica* 3.1.1, 2; see D. Brown, "'Necessary' and 'Fitting' Reasons in Christian Theology," pp. 211-30. I am indebted to O'Collins, "Incarnation," pp. 17-18.

181. Kuschel, *Born before All Time?*

to believe that the person of Christ can be split into the two phases of "eternal [preexistent] Son" and "temporal [incarnated] Son." It is necessary, says Kuschel, to hold together both Jesus' origin in time and his origin in the eternity of God.[182] What Kuschel says in the latter sentence is of course true, whereas what he mentions in the former sentence is not. The doctrine of preexistence is not a matter of time. It is a matter of logical priority. The priority envisaged in the "pre-" is not a matter of time but a priority that has to do with eternity, the timeless existence of God.[183] O'Collins rightly says: "Pre-existence means rather that Christ *personally* belongs to an order of being other than the created, temporal one. His personal, divine existence transcends temporal (and spatial) categories. . . . Eternity transcends time but without being apart from it."[184]

With his desire to marginalize the belief in preexistence, John Knox, as opposed to biblical scholars with whom he dialogued, did not hesitate to attribute to Paul belief in Christ's preexistence. However, the way Knox thinks Paul came to the affirmation is only partially adequate. He thinks that preexistence was an early consequence of belief in Jesus' resurrection. "[T]he post-resurrection status of Christ led directly and immediately to the affirmation of his pre-existence."[185] Contemporary theology, on the contrary, shouldn't consider preexistence as a literal doctrine but rather as a vehicle for telling us a story, namely, that God was in Christ "in the whole of the human career from conception through death."[186] It is hard to say exactly what he means; what is evident is his refusal to hold on to the traditional, personal view of preexistence. Apart from this inadequate conclusion, the lasting value of Kuschel's position is that it establishes the important link to resurrection. The confirmation by the Father of the earthly Jesus' claims to equality with God at the resurrection means that "the Son was linked to the Father before the beginning of the earthly existence of Jesus. . . . If the relation to the historical person of Jesus of Nazareth in eternity characterizes the identity of God as Father, then we must speak of a preexistence of the Son, who was to be historically manifested in

182. Kuschel, *Born before All Time?* p. 496.

183. Byrne, "Christ's Pre-existence," p. 311.

184. O'Collins, *Christology*, pp. 249-50. That said, it is also true that in another sense, preexistence is of course related to the considerations of time. This has to do with the issues of whether God is outside time (as mainline tradition maintains) or in time. For useful reflections, see Crisp, "Jenson on the Pre-existence," p. 29.

185. Knox, *The Humanity and Divinity of Christ*, p. 11.

186. Knox, *The Humanity and Divinity of Christ*, pp. 107-8 (108).

Jesus of Nazareth, even before his earthly birth."[187] Simply put, the affirmation of Jesus' divinity requires the doctrine of the personal preexistence of Christ.[188]

For classical liberals, preexistence is either a myth or something ideal. For Schleiermacher, what distinguished Jesus from other humans was "the constant potency of his God-consciousness, which was a veritable existence of God in him." Recommending belief in "inspiration" instead of incarnation, he presented Jesus as a God-filled man, not the God-man.[189] Among twentieth-century theologians, John Macquarrie materially follows this interpretation. To him "Christ pre-existed in the mind and purpose of God."[190] Hence, he bluntly rejected the doctrine of preexistence "as mythical," and also considered it antithetic to true humanity.[191] J. A. T. Robinson's revisionist view also gleans from classical liberalism in that Christ "completely embodied what was from the beginning the meaning and purpose of God's self-expression."[192] Religious pluralists such as John Hick adopt the liberal view and make it an asset in attempting to relate to religions and religious plurality. Hick explicitly places himself in the tradition of Schleiermacher, Strauss, and Harnack.[193] For Hick, Jesus was "a human being extraordinarily open to God's influence" who was metaphorically "'incarnating' the divine purpose for human life."[194] Consequently, at the center of the influence and meaning of Jesus lie a "universally relevant religious experience and ethical insights of Jesus" apart from doctrinal strictures of tradition and churches.[195]

The problem with liberal and pluralistic interpretations is the random and artificial reinterpretation of tradition, both biblical and historical, which then also leads to the denial of Christ's divinity and, as a result, the doctrine of the Trinity. Furthermore, the traditional idea of incarnation is impossible without preexistence.

Christian tradition until recent times has thought of preexistence only in the sense of the preexistence of the divine nature. The idea of the pre-

187. Pannenberg, *ST* 2:367-68.
188. See O'Collins, "Incarnation," p. 3.
189. Schleiermacher, *Christian Faith*, §97; McCready, "He Came," p. 422.
190. Macquarrie, *Jesus Christ in Modern Thought*, p. 57.
191. Macquarrie, *Jesus Christ in Modern Thought*, p. 145.
192. J. A. T. Robinson, *Human Face of God*, p. 179.
193. J. Hick, ed., *Metaphor of God Incarnate*, p. 18.
194. J. Hick, ed., *Metaphor of God Incarnate*, p. 12.
195. J. Hick, ed., *Metaphor of God Incarnate*, p. 13.

existence of the human nature was not only not affirmed[196] but at times considered to be dangerous or even heretical. The heretical suspicion might have been due also to the thought's connection with advocates otherwise considered marginal, such as some Radical Reformers, Emanuel Swedenborg, and the nonconformist eighteenth-century Isaac Watts.[197] Only in the latter part of the twentieth century has there been a resurgence of the belief in the preexistence of the human nature of Jesus among mainline theologians.[198] Barth towers here as the defining figure. The background to Barth's thought can be found in his mature theology of the "Humanity of God," from 1956. Unlike the past, Barth admits, his mature "evangelical" theology now acknowledges the importance of the humanity of God in a new, fresh way.[199] Indeed, earlier he had laid the foundation for robust talk of the human nature of the preexistent Lord with his reworked Reformed doctrine of election in which Jesus Christ is both the "electing God" and "elected man."[200] The Son of God took upon himself the identity of Jesus Christ even before the creation of the world as "the uncreated prototype of the humanity which is to be linked with God."[201] Of course, this does not mean existence in flesh before birth but rather that "the incarnation happened in eternity before all time, and its occurrence in time is a transition from concealment to publicity. . . . Because humanity is already latent within God, because God is already characterized by vulnerability and dependency in the fellowship of the holy Trinity, he can assume the humanity of Jesus Christ without contradicting his own nature."[202]

The benefit of such an idea — speaking of the preexistence of the human nature in this sense — is that it makes incarnation and the coming into human form of the Son of God less a paradox and more an event in keeping with the original creational purposes of God. It is also a powerful statement of the identification with humanity of the almighty God in his Son. "Humanity" in this context means "individuality, embodiment, vulnerability and dependency."[203] The obvious danger is of course that it may potentially compromise the new-

196. So, e.g., Bloesch, *Jesus Christ*, p. 13; Crisp, "Jenson on the Pre-existence," pp. 27-28.

197. Bloesch, *Jesus Christ*, pp. 136-37.

198. Bloesch (*Jesus Christ*, pp. 137-38) lists the following advocates in contemporary theology besides Barth: Klaas Runia, Robert Jenson, Ray Anderson, and Wilhelm Vischer.

199. Barth, "The Humanity of God," pp. 37-38 particularly.

200. *CD* II/2, p. 145.

201. *CD* III/2, p. 155.

202. As Bloesch (*Jesus Christ*, pp. 138-39) helpfully explains Barth's thought.

203. Bloesch, *Jesus Christ*, p. 141.

ness of incarnation and its role in response to human sin and rebellion.[204] Whether one chooses to speak of the preexistence of the human nature or not — and in light of the tradition's refusal to do so, one could easily try to find other ways of expressing the same truth of incarnation — the way another Reformed theologian and interpreter of Barth, Ray Anderson, defines the idea is both accurate and useful: "[T]he relation of Jesus as the obedient Son to God as loving and sending Father has its origin within the very being of God's existence. This is what is meant by the 'pre-existence' of Jesus of Nazareth in the form of the divine Son of God before the historical event of incarnation. There is no pre-existence as such of Jesus the male Jew, born of Mary."[205]

This observation takes us to yet another corollary affirmation of the classical creedal tradition of Christ, namely, virgin birth. Above it was mentioned that Christian tradition came to see virgin birth as a way to explain incarnation; in that context it was also argued why that linking is not useful theologically (as it leads to the undermining of the whole history of Jesus and it also lacks biblical support). What, then, is the continuing meaning and significance of the affirmation of virgin birth, or virginal conception of Jesus, as it should be formulated, strictly speaking?

"Born of the Virgin Mary"

Although direct references to virgin birth in the NT are scarce (Matt. 1:18-22; Luke 1:26-36), belief in the supernatural virginal conception of Jesus soon became a universally held view in early Christian theology, including creedal traditions.[206] What this tradition is saying is that there was a supernatural conception of Jesus by the Holy Spirit in the Virgin Mary apart from normal sexual intercourse (Matt. 1:18-22). Of course, the interests of the Gospel writers are not "scientific" as ours are.[207] Yet everything in the Gospel records indicates that the early Christians took the statement about virgin birth as God's miraculous act. When early creeds included the statement "born of

204. See further, Bloesch, *Jesus Christ,* p. 139.

205. R. S. Anderson, "The Incarnation of God in Feminist Christology," p. 307.

206. The first early Father to speak of the virgin birth — although in the context of atonement rather than incarnation — was Ignatius of Antioch, *To the Ephesians* 19. He mentions the virginity of Mary as one of the "three celebrated mysteries" along with the birth and death of her son. The Apostles' Creed says, "Who was conceived by the Holy Ghost, born of the Virgin Mary" (in *Historic Creeds and Confessions,* p. 3).

207. See Schwarz, *Christology,* p. 238.

the virgin Mary," the emphasis was more on the true humanity of the one who "suffered under Pontius Pilate"; hence, the creedal statement is materially saying the same as Paul's "born of woman" (Gal. 4:4).[208]

Not until the rise of the quest of the historical Jesus was there a widespread rejection or radical reinterpretation of the traditional belief in virgin birth.[209] In *The Life of Jesus Critically Examined,* Strauss offers detailed scrutiny and rebuttal of the "orthodox position." Against tradition, he surmises that the mention of the "Holy Spirit" and "the power of the Most High overpower[ing]" the virgin refers not to the Holy Spirit as the third member of the Trinity but rather to the more general divine "agency upon the world, and especially upon the man." Furthermore, Strauss concludes that it simply is not possible for a new human being to emerge apart from the sexual union of man and woman — generation without sexual union can happen only among some lower-level animals! Among other arguments against traditional belief is the scarcity of NT allusions to virgin birth. Strauss also notes that the traditional assumption of the need for virgin birth to establish Jesus' impeccability for the sake of our redemption rests on false assumptions, including the one that exclusion of paternal influence doesn't exclude all human co-agency in the conception.[210] In keeping with his methodological choice, Strauss concludes that both "supernaturalists" who choose to believe in virgin birth in the traditional sense and "naturalists" or rationalists who seek to find a natural explanation miss the point. Strauss's own choice is to consider the narrative of virginal conception as a myth that, although it is not historically true, expresses some important spiritual truths. In keeping with stories in Jewish and other religious environments of the divine origin of great persons, for Strauss the myth of virgin birth speaks of the extraordinary influence of Jesus' life.[211] Not surprisingly, conservative segments of the church reacted vehemently. The later fundamentalist movement listed belief in virgin birth (understood in the traditional sense) among the "five fundamentals" to be affirmed and believed.[212]

208. Schwarz, *Christology,* p. 238.

209. For a useful history, see Boslooper, *Virgin Birth.*

210. Strauss, *Life of Jesus,* pp. 130-31; see also the whole §26 (from which these pages under the heading "Criticism of Orthodox Position" are taken).

211. Strauss, *Life of Jesus,* pp. 140-43. Schleiermacher (*Christian Faith,* p. 405) seems to follow basically Strauss's line of argumentation: the "general idea of a supernatural conception remains . . . essential and necessary, if the specific pre-eminence of the Redeemer is to remain undiminished."

212. "2. It is an essential doctrine of the Word of God and our Standards, that our

Contemporary mainline NT scholarship does not regard the virgin birth as a historical event but rather as a "theological" one,[213] for example, in terms of the symbol of total human surrender to God of the human being as embodied in Mary's attitude.[214] Materially not much different is the Jungian interpretation in which virginal conception is only "true" psychologically, as in a psychic vision.[215] Another fairly typical way of "explaining" the virgin birth was suggested recently by an ecumenical group of scholars who surmised that "the 'catalyst' for the notion [of the virginal conception] might have been that Jesus was born prematurely (i.e., too early after Joseph and Mary came to live together — cf. Mt. 1:18), a 'fact' which was interpreted by his enemies in terms of his illegitimacy, and by Christians in terms of having been miraculously conceived."[216] Even though the same "Conclusions from the Study" report suggests that "[t]he tenuousness of this hypothesis was acknowledged,"[217] it still strikes one as odd that a study group composed of Roman Catholics, Protestants, and Anglicans could agree on this kind of statement.

Often NT scholarship seeks to explain the virgin birth as another version of a myth after contemporary pagan religions. The problem in those assertions, not usually acknowledged by the supporters of those views, is that in the NT there is no hint of sexual impregnation by a male deity as in the myths. What makes the NT and Christian claim to virgin birth dramatically different from similar kinds of legends in Near Eastern and Hellenistic religions is that in those contexts, "there is always a sexual element present, a divine marriage, for instance, in which a divine male in human or other form impregnates a woman." This is of course missing in the NT account, which speaks of nonsexual virginal conception.[218] Indeed, according to Raymond

---

Lord Jesus Christ was born of the Virgin Mary." In "The Doctrinal Deliverance of 1910" of the Presbyterian Church (USA); PCA Historical Center, Archives and Manuscript Repository for the Continuing Presbyterian Church (http://www.pcahistory.org/documents/deliverance.html). Accessed July 30, 2010.

213. Räisänen, "Maria/Mariafrömmigkeit," 22:118.

214. Rahner, "Dogmatische Bemerkungen zur Jungfrauengeburt," p. 157; I am indebted for this reference to Schwarz, *Christology,* p. 237 n. 81.

215. Jung, *Psychology and Religion,* p. 6; I am indebted to Bloesch, *Jesus Christ,* p. 107, for pointing me to this reference.

216. "Chapter 10: Conclusions from the Study," in R. E. Brown et al., eds., *Mary in the New Testament,* p. 291.

217. R. E. Brown et al., eds., *Mary in the New Testament,* p. 291.

218. Schwarz, *Christology,* p. 85, with reference to R. E. Brown, *Birth of the Messiah,* pp. 522-23.

Brown, differences are so profound that he maintains there "is no clear example of *virginal* conception" in the ancient world.[219] Nor does Judaism offer a clear parallel even though early Christian exegesis took Isaiah 7:14 and reconfigured it to build a bridge (Matt. 1:23).[220] On the other hand, finding parallel stories in religions would not in principle invalidate the Christian claim to its truthfulness[221] — any more than, say, finding healings or other miracles in other religious traditions would invalidate healings and miracles in the Bible.

No other contemporary theologian has stressed the theological importance of virgin birth as much as Barth. The main discussion of the theme, significantly enough, has been placed in the very beginning of *Church Dogmatics* (I/2), which actually forms the work's prologue. The immediate context of the discussion is "The Mystery of Revelation," the title for §15. The preamble to this section helps set the subsection on virgin birth, "The Mystery of Christmas," into a proper theological framework in Barth's thought: "The mystery of the revelation of God in Jesus Christ consists in the fact that the eternal Word of God chose, sanctified and assumed human nature and existence into oneness with Himself, in order thus, as very God and very man, to become the Word of reconciliation spoken by God to man. The sign of this mystery revealed in the resurrection of Jesus Christ is the miracle of His birth, that He was conceived by the Holy Ghost, born of the Virgin Mary."[222]

Barth remarks that in light of a fairly weak and not unambiguous biblical attestation, the belief in this dogma must be a matter of systematic reflection.[223] For Barth, virgin birth is a "mystery," a narrative not to be explained nor understood. The narratives of the virgin birth speak of its "inconceivability, . . . its character as a fact in which God has acted solely through God and in which God can likewise be known solely through God." As such, these "New Testament passages about the Virgin birth draw a boundary line around the reality of Jesus Christ," marking it as a work of God, not to be explained nor understood by the human mind but rather revered as mystery.[224] As God's work, it is also a judgment of human self-righteousness; God did what humans cannot.[225] In Barth's thinking, "the

219. R. E. Brown, *Birth of the Messiah,* p. 523, emphasis in original.

220. For detailed discussion, see R. E. Brown, *Birth of the Messiah,* pp. 534-35.

221. This is aptly noted by Kierkegaard, *Journals and Papers,* 1:124.

222. *CD* I/2, p. 122. The discussion of virgin birth is found on pp. 172-202.

223. *CD* I/2, pp. 174-76.

224. *CD* I/2, p. 177.

225. *CD* I/2, p. 188. Although Barth's idea of the "judgment" of humanity — in

Virgin birth is paralleled by the . . . miracle of the empty tomb. These two miracles belong together." These two "miracles" are different from other miracles in that they mark off Jesus' history and origins from the rest of reality.[226] That said, on the basis of a careful analysis of the clause "born of the Virgin Mary," Barth emphasizes both God's total initiative in that no male collaboration was needed ("virgin") and its nature as a real event in our world ("Mary"), against Gnostic and other heretical views (such as that of Valentinus, rejected as Docetistic). And yet, even as a "natural" event in that sense, "it is not grounded upon the continuity of events in this world nor is it to be understood in terms of it."[227]

Even though in the NT there is not yet a direct link between virgin birth and preexistence, early in Christian theology that link came to be established. Early theology thus said it was Logos, the preexistent word of God, that was conceived in the Virgin Mary. The statement from Justin Martyr is illustrative: "[T]he Word who is the first-birth of God was produced without sexual union, and . . . He, Jesus Christ, our Teacher, was crucified and died, and rose again."[228] This is a legitimate development of incipient NT ideas. Indeed, virgin birth is a historical and theological symbol of the uniqueness of Jesus in terms of being a true human being but one who had a divine origin. The further development in early theology toward the affirmation of Jesus' sinlessness in terms of virgin birth, on the contrary, is both unnecessary and problematic, as will be discussed below. Nor has the virgin birth anything to do with marginalizing, let alone blaming, sexuality and normal human birth as sinful.[229] Theologically it is important to note that the passages in the NT that speak of preexistence do not speak of virgin birth. On the other hand, there is no legitimate reason to juxtapose these two events in a way that they become irreconcilable, as has become typical in the NT studies[230] and in some systematic theologies.[231] Doesn't it make more sense

terms of highlighting human incapacity and divine power in the bringing forth of the Savior — could be affirmed, his curious idea of the difference of male and female in the sexual production (the former being active and the latter passive receiver) should be rejected theologically, anthropologically, and with regard to the implications for equality of the sexes (pp. 188-92).

226. *CD* I/2, p. 182.

227. *CD* I/2, pp. 185-87 (187).

228. Justin Martyr, *First Apology* 21.

229. See helpful discussion in R. E. Brown, *Birth of the Messiah,* p. 530.

230. Bultmann, "New Testament and Mythology," pp. 34-35.

231. Pannenberg, *Jesus — God and Man,* p. 143.

to treat preexistence and virgin birth as complementary assertions about Jesus being the Son of God, having divine origin? That said, it is not right to think of preexistence "pushing back" the time of the beginning of Jesus' Sonship. These are not statements about temporality but of ontology. "While Jesus' earthly origin is an act of God, through his ontological union with God Jesus always has been and always will be."[232]

The equation of the incarnation of the Logos and the establishment of the union of deity and humanity with the virginal conception[233] of Jesus has the effect of minimizing the role of Jesus' earthly life in obedience to his Father and especially the resurrection as the way to establish Jesus' divinity.[234] It is significant that in none of the key NT passages for the incarnation of the Logos (John 1:14; 1 John 4:2; Phil. 2:6-9) is there any mention of virgin birth. Only in Luke (Luke 1:35) can one discern the link. But even there, theologically we could see "testimony to the fact that Jesus was the Son of God from the very first and did not become so later, whether by his baptism or his resurrection,"[235] as in adoptionistic views. Rather than incarnation being based on virgin birth, theologically we must look at virgin birth in the context of the whole history of Jesus Christ. Only in light of what followed can it be said that the birth of Jesus was virginal conception by the divine power.[236] The theological significance of the virginal conception is not self-evident, as is the case with the Islamic affirmation of the virginal conception of Jesus, the view of which, however, leads to the denial of the deity and incarnation in the Christian sense. Even in Christian tradition, heretics such as the Arians believed in virginal conception and yet ended up with views failing to affirm the deity.[237]

Like Pannenberg, who ridicules any talk about virgin birth, apart from theological considerations, as a form of "gynecology,"[238] Barth, in sharp dis-

232. Schwarz, *Christology,* p. 237.

233. This tendency goes back as far as Ignatius, *To the Ephesians* 18; in 19 Ignatius speaks of the virginity of Mary as well as the birth and death of her child as "three mysteries." For the views of the Fathers who in some way or another established the idea of two origins of Christ with reference to begottenness in eternity from the Father and birth from the Virgin Mary in incarnation, see Boslooper, *Virgin Birth,* p. 42.

234. Rightly criticized by Pannenberg, *ST* 2:301-2, 383.

235. Pannenberg, *ST* 2:302.

236. Pannenberg, *ST* 2:302. In line with his anthropology, Pannenberg also makes the important point that no one is the full person at the moment of birth. We "become" persons by virtue of our life history (pp. 302-3).

237. See Bloesch, *Jesus Christ,* p. 99.

238. Pannenberg, *ST* 2:318; Barth, *CD* I/2, p. 183.

agreement with E. Brunner, rejects the view of the narrative of virgin birth as a "biological" explanation.[239] Virginal conception is first of all a statement about the divine intervention[240] — the power of the Most High at work — in bringing about the Savior. Rightly, then, Moltmann reminds us that the birth of Jesus is a theme of pneumatology. It was through the Spirit that the announcement and conception took place. "Conceived by the Holy Spirit, born of the Virgin Mary" is "a way of saying that God *alone is the Father of Jesus Christ.*"[241] Against the Jewish messianic expectations, the Spirit's agency in the virginal conception shows clearly the fulfillment of the OT expectation of the Son of God being filled with the Spirit.[242] The Messiah was expected to be Spirit-filled, as especially the songs of Second Isaiah so profoundly illustrate. That statement is not meant to downplay the humanity of the infant born. On the contrary, the point of the nativity story is to say "that God is bound up with Jesus of Nazareth not fortuitously but essentially."[243] Seen from human perspective, Mary embodies the "proper human attitude of humble reception" of God's work in her life. It is also an expression of the exclusiveness of commitment to the one God. Mary's submission and obedience are anticipation of the same attitude of her Son in relation to his heavenly Father.[244]

In criticism of earlier tradition, contemporary theology rightly has to correct some misconceptions popular in piety and faith regarding the theological importance of virginal conception. These inadequate views include the establishment of Jesus' sinlessness for alleged lack of sinful paternal influence (the heavenly Father being the only father). This explanation is totally foreign to the NT. More important theologically, that position betrays two mistaken anthropological views, namely, that in human conception the role of the

239. *CD* I/2, p. 183.

240. Contra Brunner (*Dogmatics,* 2:355), there is no reason to object to virginal conception on the basis that it would truncate the true humanity of Jesus. Indeed, Irenaeus opposed the Gnostics, who denied the true humanity of Jesus, with the doctrine of virgin birth! Boslooper, *Virgin Birth,* pp. 33-34.

241. Moltmann, *Way of Jesus Christ,* p. 82, emphasis in original.

242. Moltmann, *Way of Jesus Christ,* p. 85.

243. Moltmann, *Way of Jesus Christ,* p. 84.

244. Pannenberg, *ST* 2:319; see also the useful discussion in Bloesch, *Jesus Christ,* pp. 97-99. Oddly enough, the feminist theologian Rosemary Radford Ruether (*Sexism and God-Talk,* p. 154) turns the tables and surmises that the human submission of Mary is the condition for the divine intervention; in other words, without Mary's submission, the virgin birth couldn't have happened! Affirmation of human cooperation hardly necessitates or leads to such an understatement of divine capacities!

(earthly) father could be excluded, and that, even if it could be, that would help safeguard the infant from the influence of the Fall (as that influence was supposed to come mainly from the father).[245] Other inadequate views of virginal conception prevalent in tradition include the proof of the biblical prophecy. The exegetical reconsideration of the key passage in Isaiah 7 alone would make the appeal to the evidence problematic. At the same time, there is no reason to reject or downplay the OT types that point to God's miraculous intervention such as the bringing forth of a child by barren Sarah. The late moderate evangelical theologian Stanley J. Grenz summarizes well the theological meaning and role of the tenet of virgin birth:

> Although not conclusive, the arguments in favor of the historical nature of Jesus' virgin birth also tip the scales in the affirmative direction. Our earlier discussion [leaves] us with the impression that the link between the virgin birth and other doctrines is not strong. . . . The weakness of the connection between the virgin birth and other doctrines leads to an important theological conclusion. While being an important doctrine, the virgin birth is not christologically indispensable. Christology does not rise or fall with the historicity of the virgin birth in the way that it is dependent on Jesus' historical resurrection. The confession that Jesus was born of a virgin coheres well with the twin christological affirmation that Jesus is fully divine and fully human. But rather than confirming these assertions, it provides an additional substantiation for what we have already concluded on other historical grounds, namely, on the basis of Jesus' claim concerning his identity as confirmed in his resurrection. With this in view, we see the wisdom in Rahner's distinction between a ground of faith and an object of faith. The virgin birth does not function as the ground of faith; it is not the historical foundation of our christological confession. Instead, it is an object of faith — an article of the faith we confess.[246]

In Christian theology and piety, Mary is rightly honored as the "mother of God" *(theotokos)*.[247] Mary plays a unique role in the salvation

245. Not only many Fathers such as Ambrose, Augustine, and Gregory of Sinai took the virginal conception as the condition for the sinlessness of Jesus, but even later teachers of the church, including Luther; for Luther, see Althaus, *Theology of Martin Luther,* p. 160. Rightly, Schleiermacher (*Christian Faith,* §96, pp. 403-4) rejected this view.

246. Grenz, *Theology for the Community of God,* pp. 324-25.

247. Affirmed at the Council of Ephesus (431, e.g., in Cyril's anathemas [#1] against

history and thus should be honored appropriately.[248] Rightly, Pannenberg notes that the dignity of Mary as *theotokos* remains whatever the results of the continuing debates among biblical scholars as to the historicity of the infancy stories. The creedal statements about Mary have little to do with the role of Mary per se and everything to do with Christology,[249] as is evident in the statements on *theotokos* against Nestorius. In light of the fact that there is no theological teaching about Mary in the NT in terms of her as "mother of Christ,"[250] Christian theology has to appraise critically and sympathetically the traditions about Mary that emerged early in Christian theology; that discussion will be taken up in ecclesiology.

In terms of interfaith issues, both Islam[251] and some occasional Buddhist writers[252] affirm the importance of Jesus' virgin birth. But as said, for neither Islamic nor Buddhist thinkers does that affirmation have anything to do with the divine status of the child born.

This chapter has investigated in some detail key christological affirmations of the creedal tradition of the undivided church. Those creeds, while being structured around the trinitarian logic, tend to look at the person and work of each of the trinitarian members apart from the work of the other two. Hence, for example, creation is assigned to he Father; the role of the Son as the agent of creation as well as that of the Spirit as the energy and life principle are not mentioned. When it comes to the second article, that of Christology, the same principle applies. Even though early Christianity was profoundly trinitarian in its spirituality and ethos even before the canons of the *doctrine* of the Trinity were hammered out in the Nicene-Constantinopolitan Creed, the trinitarian outlook is not present in the discussion of christologi-

---

Nestorius; *NPNF*[2] 14:312) and at the Second Council of Constantinople (553) in the Capitula II (14:453).

248. For the ecumenical significance of holding on to this binding ecumenical tradition between Roman Catholics, Orthodox, and Protestants, see Bloesch, *Jesus Christ,* p. 99.

249. Moltmann, *Way of Jesus Christ,* p. 80: "It is for Christ's sake that his mother Mary is remembered and venerated."

250. Moltmann, *Way of Jesus Christ,* p. 78.

251. The most extensive discussion of the virgin birth in the Qur'an is 19:16-36; the parallel account is in 3:42-59. For a careful discussion, see N. Robinson, *Christ in Islam and Christianity,* chap. 15.

252. One of the rare Tibetan Buddhist writings about Jesus (before the contemporary Dalai Lama), *The Crystal Mirror,* by the eighteenth-century Thuken Chökyi Nyima, highlights the importance of the miraculous birth of "the teacher Jesus or world protector" (in *JBC,* p. 232).

cal themes. While this state of affairs is understandable for a short symbol of faith such as that of Chalcedon, whose main goal was to combat a number of heretical notions, systematic/constructive theology has the mandate to work out a trinitarian account of Christ and his work. Hence, the next chapter will investigate and reflect upon the integral linking of Jesus Christ to the Spirit of the Father. This is but paying special attention to the economic narrative of the NT.

8. Jesus and Spirit: "Logos Christologies" and "Spirit Christologies"

The Tradition of Spirit Christology

Whereas in the NT and in earliest Christian theology, the most common way of speaking of the presence and activity of God in Jesus Christ had a reference to the Spirit,[1] soon Christian tradition opted for incarnational Christology with the concept of Logos as the way of explanation. Whereas the Synoptic Gospels present a thoroughgoing Spirit Christology, Paul and John, having this as a premise, put forth *"a christological doctrine of the Spirit."*[2] The oldest christological formula spoke of Jesus in terms of the dynamic of "after the flesh" and "after the Spirit," as is evident in 1 Timothy 3:16 and 1 Peter 3:18.[3] The former denotes human weakness and frailty as evident in Jesus' humiliation; the latter refers to divine transcendence, power, and eternity. This scheme was used in the earliest postbiblical sources such as Ignatius's letters and *2 Clement,*[4] and was also found in Tertullian, among

1. Rosato, "Spirit Christology," p. 424. For a useful scrutiny of biblical and patristic Spirit Christologies, see Balthasar, *The Spirit of Truth,* pp. 48-51 and 37-40, respectively.

2. Moltmann, *Spirit of Life,* p. 58, emphasis in original; see also p. 59.

3. J. N. D. Kelly, *Early Christian Doctrines,* p. 138; Rosato, "Spirit Christology," p. 430.

4. Ignatius, *To the Ephesians* 7: "There is one Physician who is possessed both of flesh and spirit; both made and not made; God existing in flesh; true life in death; both of Mary and of God; first passible and then impassible"; *2 Clement* 9:5; see further, J. N. D. Kelly, *Early Christian Doctrines,* pp. 142-45, which lists as other representative early exam-

others.[5] Thus, the earliest Christologies can be called Spirit Christologies. They sought to explain the unique presence and efficacy of the divine in Jesus Christ with reference to the Spirit of God. It can also be named a "pneumatological Christology" or — correspondingly — a "christological pneumatology."[6]

Regarding the notions of "after the flesh" and "after the Spirit," an important shift happened in the Fathers that helps explain the rapid ascendancy of the Logos explanation instead of the Spirit. Whereas these phrases in the NT have to do with two successive stages of Christ's life, from early patristic theology onward they refer to two simultaneous principles of being, humanity and divinity.[7] Indeed, in Tertullian we see that the Spirit-flesh model is explained in terms of two "substances," which leads to the use of Logos as the way of explaining the deity.[8] Pannenberg explains this shift stemming from Tertullian (*Against Praxeas* 27) and others such as Melito, in an accurate way: "The way was thus prepared for the later two-natures doctrine of the church's christology, which developed, therefore, out of the twofold evaluation of Jesus as according to the flesh and according to the spirit. Because of a possible 'dynamic' [adoptionistic] misunderstanding of the description of the deity that was present in Jesus as 'spirit,' however, the end of the 2nd century saw 'Logos' coming into more common use for the deity of Jesus. It increasingly replaced 'spirit' in this context."[9]

The danger of adoptionism loomed large in early Christology;[10] that is the reason why some contemporary theologians, such as Pannenberg earlier in his career, tended to be very critical of the whole idea of Spirit Christology. There is no denying the existence of several types of adoptionistic (especially Ebionite) Spirit Christologies in early theology. The safest way — and the orthodox way in light of later creedal formulations — to safeguard Spirit

ples, among others: *1 Clement* 22:1; *2 Clement* 9:5; Hippolytus, *Refutation of All Heresies* 9, 12, 17; Cyprian, *On the Vanity of Idols* 11.

5. Tertullian, *Against Praxeas* 27.

6. Moltmann, *Way of Jesus Christ,* pp. 73-74.

7. See Coffey, "Spirit Christology and the Trinity," pp. 315-16.

8. See further, J. N. D. Kelly, *Early Christian Doctrines,* pp. 150-51 especially.

9. Pannenberg, *ST* 2:382.

10. Monarchianist Christologies serve as examples here in their attempt to hold on to the "sole monarchy" of the Father while acknowledging the divine power at work in Jesus; see Pannenberg, *Jesus — God and Man,* pp. 116-20; for a careful discussion of the Ebionite version of adoptionism in this regard, see Rosato, "Spirit Christology," pp. 431-35.

Christologies from the danger of adoptionism was to solidify the doctrine of preexistence.[11]

In addition to the danger of adoptionism, there were other important reasons for the rapid ascendancy of Logos Christology at the expense of the Spirit-*sarx* interpretation. Whereas the Jewish milieu was familiar with talk about Messiah under pneumatological categories, the Greco-Roman world was far less so. Instead, the concept of Logos as the principle of reality was well known in ancient philosophy, going back all the way to the sixth century B.C.E. or even further. Furthermore, different from biblical use and our contemporary use of the term "spirit," the Hellenistic view of *pneuma,* influenced profoundly by Stoic philosophy, had in its background the idea of some kind of materiality (as the finest stuff). That conception did not sit well with the Christian theology of God (and led to the understanding of God's spirituality as mind by early theologians) or as a way of explaining the divine presence in Christ. Hence in this chapter, we have focused first on the Logos theology for the simple reason that most of the Christian reflection on christological topics is to be found there. Having done so, it is important now to revisit Spirit categories and see how that explanatory model would relate to, correct, and balance incarnational Christology.

Unlike in contemporary debates, early theological tradition hardly saw Spirit and Logos Christologies as alternatives. Consequently, Spirit Christology was not seen as an alternative to incarnation but rather as a complementary way of explaining the unique presence of God and the coming together of the divine and human in a person.[12] That the Spirit Christology could be found in writers such as Tertullian, mentioned above, who also was one of the great architects of Logos and two-nature Christology (or "two-substance" Christology, as he preferred to call it),[13] is a cue to affirming the complementary nature of these two models of explanation.

Similarly, unlike in current debates, the turn to the Spirit was not seen

11. For details, see J. N. D. Kelly, *Early Christian Doctrines,* pp. 143-44 (143); see also Pannenberg, *ST* 2:381-82.

12. See Haight, "Case for Spirit Christology," pp. 276-77.

13. In Tertullian, *Against Praxeas* 5 and 6, can be found the famous statements about the Logos (or Wisdom or Reason) who became united with Jesus at the incarnation, as preexisting with God before everything was created. Tertullian underscores the "personal" nature of the Logos. For various aspects of his theology of incarnation, see *On the Flesh of Christ,* which contains both a vehement rebuttal of heretical views that rejected the true humanity of Christ and the unity of the Logos with flesh.

as a denial of incarnation but rather as its affirmation.[14] Scripture sees the whole earthly life of Jesus, from birth (Luke 1:35) to baptism (Mark 1:10 par.)[15] to anointing (Luke 4:18-21) to ministry (Matt. 12:28; Luke 4:14, 18) to testing (Luke 4:1) to self-offering at the cross (Heb. 9:14) to raising to new life (Rom. 1:4; 8:11), as the function of the Spirit — so much so that at the end Paul can say that the resurrected Christ became a "life-giving spirit" (1 Cor. 15:45). As the Son of God, he is "a Spirit-creation."[16] It is too often ignored that the basic nomenclature in Christian tradition, Jesus *Christ*, links the person spoken of to the OT idea of the Messiah *(masiah)*, the "Anointed" *(Christos)*, the Spirit-bearer (cf. Isa. 11:2), in other words, the man of the Spirit. The Orthodox Nikos Nissiotis puts it succinctly: "Christ can never be separated from the Spirit of God. His Incarnation and resurrection are the work of the Giver of Life, the Paraclete."[17] As the Anointed One, Jesus Christ is a "public person" similar to OT types of the anointed prophets, priests, and kings.[18]

This linking of the Messiah to the Spirit is a theme thoroughly embedded in the theology of the OT and the Jewish roots of Christian faith. Already on the first page of the Jewish Bible, the *ruach* Yahweh appears as the life-giving principle that brings about new life over the primal chaos (Gen. 1:2). With the vitality of the same life-giving Spirit, Yahweh creates the first human being (2:7). All life in the cosmos is brought about and maintained in life with the energy of this same Spirit:

> When you [Yahweh] send your Spirit [*ruach*],
> they are created,
> and you renew the face of the earth. (Ps. 104:30 NIV)

Similarly, when Yahweh "take[s] away their breath [*ruach*], / they die and return to the dust" (v. 29 NIV). The prophetic books see an integral connection between the Messiah and the Spirit; the messianic figure is anointed and empowered by the Spirit of God (Isa. 11:1-8; 42:1-4; 49:1-6). Rightly, then,

14. See Moltmann, *Way of Jesus Christ*, p. 74.

15. The coming of the Spirit at Jesus' baptism was an occasion for a number of profound pneumatological accounts in later theology, as evident, e.g., in Cyril of Jerusalem, *Catechetical Lectures* 3.11-14; Ambrose, *Of the Holy Spirit* 3.1.1-6; Bede, *Commentary on the Acts of the Apostles*, pp. 102-3 (on Acts 10:38a).

16. Kasper, *Jesus*, p. 251.

17. Nissiotis, "Pneumatological Christology as a Presupposition of Ecclesiology," p. 236.

18. Kasper, *Jesus*, p. 253; see also Pinnock, *Flame of Love*, pp. 79-82, 85.

Moltmann reminds us that "Jesus' history as the Christ does not begin with Jesus himself. It begins with the *ruach*/the Holy Spirit."[19] In that sense it can also be said that the workings of the Spirit precede those of the Son.[20] Hence, there is no subordinating the Spirit under the Son. With the coming of the Messiah in the person of Jesus Christ, the eschatological promise of the pouring out of the Spirit (Joel 2:28-32) has begun. The one "baptized in the Spirit" at the Jordan becomes the baptizer with the Spirit (Matt. 3:11). When after the resurrection and ascension, Christ is present through his Spirit, it also means that "his history must have been determined by this Spirit from the very beginning."[21]

From the perspective of the divine Spirit and him "condescending" in the person of the man Jesus of Nazareth, we can also talk about the *kenosis* of the Spirit, "which emptied itself and descended from the eternity of God, taking up its dwelling in this vulnerable and mortal human being Jesus."[22] The Spirit who descends upon the Messiah and anoints him is no self-referential person, but as theological tradition cautiously has called him, the "shy" person of the Trinity. The Russian Orthodox Vladimir Lossky, speaking of the *kenosis* of both the Son and the Spirit, says of this "mystery of the self-emptying" the following: "If in the *kenosis* of the Son the Person appeared to men while the Godhead remained hidden under the form of a servant, the Holy Spirit in His coming, while He manifests the common nature of the Trinity, leaves His own Person concealed beneath His Godhead. He remains unrevealed, hidden, so to speak, by the gift in order that this gift which He imparts may be fully ours, adapted to our persons."[23]

Contemporary Spirit Christologies

Not surprisingly, a diversity of approaches to Spirit Christology has emerged in contemporary theology, particularly during the past few decades with the

19. Moltmann, *Way of Jesus Christ,* p. 73. The Benedictine Kilian McDonnell ("The Determinative Doctrine of the Holy Spirit," p. 151) rightly emphasizes that a robust Spirit Christology can only be maintained if "the Spirit belongs to Jesus constitutively and not merely in a second moment."

20. Moltmann, *Spirit of Life,* pp. xi, 60. On the "messianic expectations of the Spirit" in the OT, see pp. 51-57.

21. Moltmann, *Way of Jesus Christ,* p. 77.

22. Moltmann, *Way of Jesus Christ,* p. 93.

23. Lossky, *Mystical Theology of the Eastern Church,* p. 168.

coming of the pneumatological renaissance in general and enthusiasm over Spirit Christologies in particular. Not everyone agrees with the argumentation above, namely, that Spirit Christology and Logos Christology ought to be seen as complementary and mutually conditioning.[24] In contrast to the view advocated here, there are approaches that can be named "replacement" models. Those models seek to replace Logos Christology with Spirit Christology.[25]

The replacement model is represented by both biblical theologians and systematicians. The main claim is the rejection of the traditional notion of incarnation and trinitarian distinctions after classical doctrine; instead, the Spirit is understood as divine influence or inspiration. According to Dunn, we can speak of "the 'divinity' of the *historical* Jesus . . . only . . . in terms of his experience of God: *his 'divinity' means his relationship with the Father as son and the Spirit of God in him.*"[26] Hence, Dunn surmises that in Jesus' own understanding "inspiration and empowering" are the main categories of the relationship to the Spirit.[27] Consequently, "it is only this transcendent otherness of Jesus' consciousness of God which enables it to link up with Christologies 'from above,' which, if we may put it thus, allows the approach 'from below' to be called 'Christology.'"[28] As discussed above, Adam Christology is a key to Dunn's hermeneutics of NT Christology. In his reworked two-stage Christology, the historical Jesus represents and identifies with the fallen and failing first Adam, whereas the last Adam in Pauline theology is represented only by the risen Christ. The way Jesus is instituted into his role as last Adam is resurrection rather than a preexistent state or incar-

24. An indication of the wide diversity of the views is the assessment of some (earlier) contemporary theologians to whom the whole concept of Spirit Christology seems to denote by default something adoptionistic, nontrinitarian, thus heretical or at least highly suspect; for an example, see Hunter, *Spirit Baptism,* pp. 212-30.

25. Two slightly different typologies have been suggested recently. Sammy Alfaro (*Divino Compañero,* chap. 2) distinguishes three types: "replacement" (Lampe, Newman, Dunn), "revisionist" (Haight, Schoonenberg), and "complementary" (Pinnock, Suurmond). The terms are self-explanatory; in relation to my typology, the first and second are combined. Ralph del Colle suggests two ways of making a distinction. In *Christ and the Spirit,* p. vii, he simply speaks of "trinitarian" (e.g., Coffey and himself) or "post-trinitarian" trajectories (e.g., Dunn, Lampe, Newman), whereas in "Spirit-Christology," pp. 97-98, the division is between a revisionary post-Chalcedonian alternative (Lampe, Newman, Haight) and an orthodox Spirit Christology (Coffey, Moltmann, and himself).

26. Dunn, *Jesus and the Spirit,* p. 92, emphasis in original. Materially, and indeed almost verbatim, he says the same, for example, in "Rediscovering the Spirit (1)," p. 50.

27. Dunn, *Christology in the Making,* p. 138.

28. Dunn, *Jesus and the Spirit,* p. 92.

nation.[29] When it comes to the earthly Jesus, what really matters in his humanity is unreserved obedience to the Father, which thus reverses the path of disobedience of the first Adam.[30] At the end, Dunn makes the curious turn in which he virtually and materially equates Jesus Christ and the Spirit.[31] The way he explains this transformation is that "Jesus has given personality to the Spirit — his personality. The impersonal Spirit, like the impersonal Logos, is now identified with Jesus and bears his personality. In other words, as the Spirit is the divinity of Jesus, so Jesus is the personality of the Spirit."[32] Rightly, then, Dunn himself raises the question of how appropriate it is to talk about the Trinity rather than the Biunity. At best, he leaves the question open.[33] The problems with Dunn in light of tradition and the argumentation in this chapter are obvious, and they are all interrelated: identification of Christ and Spirit,[34] failure to establish the divinity of Jesus

29. Dunn, *Christology in the Making,* p. 108.

30. E.g., Dunn, *Christology in the Making,* p. 113.

31. Dunn, *Jesus and the Spirit,* pp. 322-26, includes a number of phrases in which the equation is evident, such as that *"Paul equates the risen Jesus with the Spirit who makes alive"* (p. 322) or *"If Christ is now experienced as Spirit, Spirit is now experienced as Christ"* (p. 323). Here Dunn is following a long trajectory that goes back all the way to the definitive work on pneumatology by Hermann Gunkel of the nineteenth century. According to Gunkel, despite the gradual release in biblical studies of the notion of "spirit" from the abstract and human-driven limitations of idealistic philosophical tradition with the focus on the extraordinary and supernatural *Wirkungen* (effects) of the Spirit and the Spirit's link to Judaism and OT background, the relationship between the risen Christ and the Holy Spirit remained ambiguous and indefinite. Scholars known for the identification of the two include Adolf Diessmann, Albert Schweitzer, and Wilhelm Boussett. Although Gunkel himself did not equate the two in granting to Christ's activity a greater sphere than to that of the Spirit, the way he distinguished the two, namely, in relation to "power" and "person" (with regard to *pneuma,* the "supernatural is derived from a *divine* power," whereas regarding *Christos,* "it is derived from a divine person who has this power in himself"), is not satisfactory. Gunkel, *Influence of the Holy Spirit,* p. 115, emphasis in original. For a brief insightful discussion with full documentation, see del Colle, *Christ and the Spirit,* pp. 141-43.

32. Dunn, "Rediscovering the Spirit (1)," p. 52.

33. Dunn, "Rediscovering the Spirit (1)," pp. 52-53. Hence he argues that the Christian cannot "experience" the Trinity, only the Spirit. Thus, he only approves the trinitarian *taxis* of Spirit, Son, and Father.

34. Another profound example of this tendency coming from a Reformed systematician is Hendrikus Berkhof's strongly modalistic pneumatology in *The Doctrine of the Holy Spirit.* For the identification of Spirit as the action of the exalted Christ, see p. 21 and passim; and for the identification of the Spirit with God, see p. 116. True, he doesn't make a total equation, but the modalistic tendency is a leading motif.

and consequently the Trinity[35] as well as the incarnation.[36] Christology in keeping with tradition has to be able to maintain trinitarian distinctions throughout the whole history of Jesus Christ from preexistence to incarnation to resurrection to cosmic rule to parousia and new creation.[37] Dunn fails to achieve that goal.

Geoffrey Lampe and Paul Newman advocate the replacement model materially quite similarly to Dunn. Lampe is deeply critical of the project of "hypostatization" prevalent in Chalcedonian tradition and issues a passionate call to return to what he considers the highly metaphorical and economic language of the early Fathers. Hence, terms such as "Word," "Wisdom," and particularly "Spirit" are "quasi-poetical" in nature rather than metaphysical and are "expressive of God in relationship to men."[38] That allows him to define the meaning of Jesus by saying that "God indwelt and motivated the human spirit of Jesus in such a way that in him, uniquely, the relationship for which man is intended by his Creator was fully realized."[39] The most Lampe is willing to say is that the "deeds and words" of Jesus, who "was genuinely a man," "were done and said divinely: that his Person mediates true God to man."[40] This is the unity of will and operation in contrast to the substantive unity of tradition.[41] In keeping with this approach, Lampe is reluctant to

35. Del Colle (*Christ and the Spirit,* p. 146) rightly calls Dunn's view modalistic.

36. The only way Dunn wants to speak of incarnation is with reference to Wisdom/Word, which can be understood as "God's self-manifestation" rather than a hypostatic entity after the Chalcedonian interpretation. Indeed, Dunn contends that speaking of "*Christ* as himself pre-existent, coming down from heaven, and so forth, has to be seen as metaphorical; otherwise it leads inevitably to some kind of polytheism." To avoid this, he chooses to speak of Jesus as "the person/individual whom God's Word *became*." Dunn, "Incarnation," p. 47.

37. So also del Colle, *Christ and the Spirit,* p. 146. As discussed above, Piet Schoonenberg also fails to stick with this rule, as in his interpretation Jesus "becomes" Christ only at the resurrection, and the Spirit "divine" only at Pentecost. For a succinct explanation, see his "Spirit Christology and Logos Christology," pp. 350-75; "Trinity — the Consummated Covenant," pp. 111-16.

38. Lampe, *God as Spirit,* pp. 36-37. Lampe also uses the term "projection" in reference to the doctrine of preexistence and linking of Jesus with Logos (p. 141).

39. Lampe, *God as Spirit,* p. 11.

40. Lampe, "The Holy Spirit," p. 123.

41. Not convincingly, Lampe ("The Holy Spirit," p. 124) claims that this position is in keeping with the Chalcedonian formula of "without separation and without confusion" when looked at through the lens of Cyril's concept of "one theandric energy." Lampe fails to acknowledge the obvious fact that reference to Cyril's notion is valid only when taken out from the context of his whole theology, which did materially affirm Chalcedon.

continue speaking of preexistence and the divine status at the right hand of the Father.[42] Different from Dunn and tradition, Lampe claims even resurrection should not be the focus but rather the "encounter today with the active presence of God the Spirit who was in Jesus."[43]

Like Dunn, Newman contends that the only way to speak of the "divinity" of the earthly Jesus is by the presence of the Spirit. However, it is better not to speak so, in order to avoid the danger of polytheism or idolatry, he adds.[44] Unlike most theologians, Newman freely acknowledges the possibility and even necessity of an adoptionistic position; he simply concludes that Jesus cannot be simultaneously human and divine.[45] Rightly, then, it can be said that for Newman the relation of Christ to God is merely "relational" rather than "ontological."[46] Not surprisingly, Newman describes incarnation in terms of inspiration.[47] Ralph del Colle accurately identifies the main problems with Lampe, and those also apply materially to Newman: first, truncation of trinitarian hypostatic distinctions; second, the conflation of the Holy Spirit with the risen Christ; and third, "a thorough demythologization of all the christological loci" from preexistence to parousia. Del Colle insightfully sees this replacement of traditional trinitarian Christology being reflected liturgically in prayer, which should not be directed "to Christ" but to God "through Christ."[48]

An Integral Linking of Spirit and Christ

In its desire to retrieve and rediscover the resources of Spirit Christology, contemporary theology cannot merely go back to the original form in the NT and early patristic theology. Current theological reflection must take into account and assess the value to Spirit Christology of the long and variegated Logos tradition and the solidification of the doctrine of the Holy Spirit in the context of the trinitarian doctrine. Not only in the NT but also in the early centuries thereafter, there was a lot of ambiguity and vacillation

42. Lampe, *God as Spirit,* p. 33.

43. Lampe, *God as Spirit,* p. 152.

44. P. W. Newman, *Spirit Christology,* p. 217.

45. P. W. Newman, *Spirit Christology,* p. 217.

46. Habets, "Spirit Christology," p. 208.

47. P. W. Newman, *Spirit Christology,* p. 184.

48. Del Colle, *Christ and the Spirit,* p. 163; the reference to prayer is Lampe, *God as Spirit,* pp. 162-65.

about the nature and role of the Spirit. Often the Spirit merely denoted divine power and efficacy rather than a "personal" presence, as was affirmed finally in Constantinople (381). In light of these considerations, the main task for contemporary theology is simply this: how to best combine and keep together the two traditions and explanatory models of Logos and Spirit Christology. It can be argued that a model that is able to incorporate both is superior to the explanatory power of only one and does better justice to tradition.[49]

Fortunately, in the contemporary theological milieu the pressing needs of the early Christian centuries that led to the virtual dismissal of Spirit Christologies are no longer factors. Rightly, then, the late Canadian Baptist theologian Clark H. Pinnock issued a passionate call for a new integration of both models:

> Let us not diminish the importance of the Spirit for Christology. Logos Christology is not the whole story; indeed, if we exaggerate it we may eclipse the mission of the Spirit and effect its subordination to that of the Son. Among other risks, we may strip the self-emptying of the Son of its radicalness and even put his true humanity in jeopardy. At least the early church had an excuse for favoring Logos Christology. There was an apologetic advantage to Logos Christology then, but not today. There is no reason for us to continue to let Logos Christology dominate and marginalize other dimensions.[50]

Different from the replacement models — in light of the affirmation that Spirit and Logos Christologies are not meant to be alternatives but rather are complementary ways of explanation — it is argued here that the orthodoxy and propriety of both Christologies have to be checked in light of the ecumenical creeds, particularly the Nicene and Chalcedonian.[51] There is "only

49. I echo here the approach of Coffey, "Spirit Christology and the Trinity," pp. 316-17. His essay offers a sophisticated and to some extent idiosyncratic way of combining the two models through the lens of Wisdom. I am not following his lead in this respect. It seems to me that a more humble and modest approach that refuses to put these two traditions in contradistinction suffices without any specific way of trying to subsume them under an "umbrella" model of explanation.

50. Pinnock, *Flame of Love,* p. 91.

51. See Haight, "Case for Spirit Christology," pp. 274-76. Haight is often mistakenly named, to use the terminology above, as the advocate of the replacement model (see, e.g., del Colle, *Christ and the Spirit*).

one instance in history where the Spirit found acceptance in a unique way, totally, undistorted and untarnished — in Jesus Christ. In the power of the Spirit he was wholly a mould and receptacle for God's self-communication through the Logos."[52] Whereas traditional theology, not only Western scholasticism but also contemporary Eastern Orthodox tradition represented by Vladimir Lossky,[53] quite categorically distinguishes the two "missions" of the Son and Spirit in the one divine economy, it is more useful to speak of christological and pneumatological dimensions of the one divine economy.[54] This is not merely a matter of fine-tuning theological expressions but is an intentional attempt to link the work of the Spirit and Christ in an integrated whole. While the "two-mission" approach does not of course reject such linkage, it also can be understood in a way that lacks robust integrity.

The linking of Logos and Spirit Christology in this way best helps theology stick with a robust confession of both the uniqueness and universality of Jesus Christ. On the one hand, only in him are there the presence and activity of the Spirit without measure (John 3:34); on the other hand, this unique, unrepeatable presence bespeaks universality since it is the culmination of all that the Spirit of God represents from the beginning of history. It is often claimed that whereas Logos represents particularity in that there is a hypostatic union only in the life of one historical person, Jesus Christ, the Spirit represents universality. That is only half true, and as any such contention, may also be misleading. Both biblically and theologically, Logos and Spirit represent both universality and particularity. While it is true that the Spirit is a cosmic energy everywhere in creation, the NT speaks of *Christ's* Spirit, which bespeaks particularity. Wherever the cosmic and universal Spirit is at work, there is always a reference to Christ, and through Christ also to the Father. In other words, the presence of the Spirit is trinitarian in nature. And while it is true that Logos came to dwell personally, hypostatically only in one historical person, as the beginning of John's prologue tells us, this Logos not only was with God, but was God, the very principle of creation. There is thus a robust universal element to Logos, the Word, as well. In the OT, the Word of Yahweh as much as the Spirit of Yahweh as a (semi)divine entity is also universal. Holding tightly to Logos and Spirit Christology has the capacity of affirming both the particularity and universality of Christ.

52. Kasper, *Jesus,* p. 267.

53. Lossky, *Mystical Theology of the Eastern Church,* pp. 156-73 particularly.

54. This is indeed what John Zizioulas does (*Being as Communion,* pp. 123-42), and on this point critiques Lossky's approach.

Yet another reason why Spirit Christology is needed to complement Logos Christology is its capacity to bridge the disjuncture between Christ's person and work. Put in other words: this is to seek a balance between "identity without relevance" and being "relevant without an identity." Logos Christology comes to mind with regard to the former and Spirit Christology can fall into the trap of the latter.[55] In a balanced outlook, Christ, the Anointed, presents both the unique culmination of the presence of the Spirit and its source for the salvation of all: "Just as Jesus Christ is, on the one hand, the goal and culmination of the presence and operation of the Spirit of God, so on the other he is also the starting-point for the sending, the mission, of the Spirit. In Christ the Spirit has, as it were, finally attained his goal, the new creation."[56] The efficacy of Christ and the efficacy of the Spirit work together and mutually presuppose each other.[57] Especially theologians in the Christian East have emphasized this integral link between the Son and the Spirit. In the words of the Cappadocian Gregory of Nyssa, "For as between the body's surface and the liquid of the oil nothing intervening can be detected, either in reason or in perception, so inseparable is the union of the Spirit with the Son; and the result is that whosoever is to touch the Son by faith must needs first encounter the oil in the very act of touching; there is not a part of Him devoid of the Holy Spirit."[58] Consequently, it is in the power of the creative Spirit that Jesus also brings "health and liberty for enslaved men and women into this sick world."[59]

A promising example of an integral link between *theologia* and *oikonomia* in the context of a grassroots-level Spirit Christology is Pentecostal spirituality. Pentecostalism represents a unique way of framing Spirit Christology. Against the common misunderstanding, at the heart of Pentecostal spirituality is not a pneumato-centrism but rather Christocentrism. To be more precise, it is a thoroughly pneumatological-charismatic Christocentrism in which Jesus is perceived in five interrelated roles: Savior, Sanctifier, Baptizer with the Spirit, Healer, and Soon-Coming Eschatological

55. Del Colle, *Christ and the Spirit,* p. 8.

56. Kasper, *Jesus,* p. 256; so also del Colle, *Christ and the Spirit,* p. 3.

57. Moltmann, *Spirit of Life,* p. xi.

58. Gregory of Nyssa, *On the Holy Spirit against the Followers of Macedonius; NPNF*² 5:321. (There are no subdivisions, chapters, or paragraphs marked in the document; hence, only pages in *NPNF*² 5 are given here.) The same integral link between Spirit and Son can be found in many much-later theologies, for example, Sibbes, "A Description of Christ," pp. 17-19.

59. Moltmann, *Way of Jesus Christ,* p. 73.

King.[60] It is believed that Jesus Christ ministers in the power of the Spirit in these roles. Jesus saves, sanctifies, heals the body, baptizes with the Holy Spirit, and will usher in the eschatological kingdom.[61] In this model — granted, it needs theological clarity and sophistication — the "person" and "work" of Christ are intertwined; similarly, a mutual conditioning and collaboration between Spirit and Christ are in play.[62] Undoubtedly, one of the reasons for the rediscovery in ecumenical theology of the importance of Spirit Christology has to do with the lively spirituality of the Pentecostal and charismatic renewals of the last century.[63]

Spirit Christology also helps forge a link with Wisdom Christology, the roots of which go deep into the OT. In Israel, as is well known, Spirit *(ruach)* and Wisdom *(hokma),* along with the Word *(davar),* are closely related. Moltmann makes the brilliant — and obvious — observation that both Spirit and Wisdom are feminine modes of the divine appearance.[64] That insight highlights the liberationist aspect of Spirit Christology via Wisdom categories.[65] In recent years feminist theology has argued the case for preferring a Wisdom Christology over the Son Christology that has traditionally held sway. Elizabeth Johnson in particular has rightly drawn attention to the prevalence of Wisdom categories in biblical literature and especially in the presentation of the person and work of Jesus in the Gospels.[66] Although I do not find it useful to attempt yet another replacement, this time between "Son" Christology and "Wisdom" Christology, I look forward to further work by women theologians on the link between Spirit, Son, Wisdom, and

60. The definitive study on which later interpreters build is Dayton, *Theological Roots of Pentecostalism.*

61. From the perspective of Spirit Christology and in critical dialogue with other contemporary views, see Alfaro, *Divino Compañero,* pp. 29-46.

62. A number of contemporary Pentecostal theologians argue for the mutuality of Logos and Spirit Christologies. See, for example, Habets ("Spirit Christology," p. 229), who makes every effort to maintain "the twin concepts of both the filiological and the pneumatological aspects of Christology." Similarly Amos Yong (*Spirit-Word-Community,* p. 53) builds on Irenaeus's idea of the "two hands of God" (*Against Heresies* 4.20.1) as well as the ancient concept of *perichoresis* in speaking of the mutuality of Christ and the Spirit in terms of the "mutuality of partners in a dance."

63. So, e.g., Rosato, "Spirit Christology," p. 423.

64. Moltmann, *Way of Jesus Christ,* p. 74.

65. Wisdom is of course a well-attested OT theme that may illumine the NT christological categories. The definitive study here is Edwards, *Jesus the Wisdom of God.*

66. E. Johnson, "Jesus, the Wisdom of God," pp. 261-94, esp. 276-89; E. Johnson, *She Who Is,* pp. 94-98.

Logos. For the simple reason that the biblical canon includes all these orientations, a reductionist weighing of one approach over another seems to be just that: *reductionist.*

Be that as it may, one of the impetuses for the reemergence of Spirit Christology in contemporary theology has to do with liberationist, multicultural, and other "contextual" concerns and opportunities. Speaking of the reasons for the rediscovery of the turn to the Spirit, Philip Rosato makes the important point that "Christian theologians, engaged in a multifaceted dialogue with other cultures and ideologies, are groping for an effectual [pneumatological] Christological paradigm which is both identical with their tradition and relevant to the empirical, socially critical, and future-oriented outlook of modern man."[67] The linking of Christ's work with his person as well as Christ's saving work with the dynamic empowering through various charisms naturally helps combat social and political issues in a more adequate manner. A related issue is the pressing need for Christology to empower and inform pastoral theology and ministry; a rigid, at times somewhat abstract, Logos approach calls for a dynamic, more "tangible" Spirit orientation as complementary.[68]

A robust trinitarian Spirit Christology carries a lot of potential for interfaith encounters and interreligious issues. Christ and Spirit cannot be set in opposition. "Christocentrism" and the turn to the Spirit cannot be considered as alternatives. An integral Spirit Christology holds both together and, as mentioned above, helps negotiate in a more appropriate way the complex dynamic of the universality and particularity of Jesus Christ. The yields of Spirit Christology — christological pneumatology and pneumatological Christology — are brought to bear on the continuing discussion in this volume regarding revised interpretations of incarnation and similar challenges of religious pluralism and interfaith encounters.[69] To those topics we turn next.

67. Rosato, "Spirit Christology," p. 423.

68. Rosato, "Spirit Christology," p. 423.

69. For the Spirit Christology's potential for interfaith encounters, see Haight, "Case for Spirit Christology," pp. 280-82.

9. Contra Pluralism

Revisionist Interpretations of Incarnation

Incarnation as Divine Presence and Influence

Toward the end of his massive two-volume *Life of Jesus Critically Examined,* David F. Strauss raised the question that subsequently has haunted the minds of many post-Enlightenment thinkers, namely, whether the manifestation of the divine should be restricted to one individual in history or is rather to be understood as realized in the whole human race.[1] Strauss himself of course opted for the latter, and a whole host of twentieth-century religious pluralists have followed suit. The pluralistic hermeneutics in Christology is a major intra-Christian challenge to any notion of traditional, particularly Chalcedonian, doctrine.

The roots of contemporary pluralistic[2] and other similar revisionist interpretations can be found not only in Strauss or the earlier radical Enlightenment-based rethinking of the nature of religion in general and Christianity in particular, but also in the philosophical tradition of Strauss's teacher, G. W. Hegel. Whereas Hegel's thoughts on God and (a highly idiosyncratic reworking of the doctrine of) the "Trinity" are complex and perhaps not thoroughly internally coherent,[3] in his *Phenomenology of the Spirit,*

1. Strauss, *Life of Jesus,* pp. 779-81; this paragraph (151) comes under a telling heading: "The Last Dilemma."

2. The chapter title is inspired by Larson, "Contra Pluralism," pp. 303-26.

3. For an important investigation, see Hodgson, "Hegel's Christology," pp. 23-40.

this German philosopher puts forth a theory of incarnation that focuses on the universal presence of the divine in all humankind. As is well known, in the context of his idealistic philosophy focused on the Absolute Spirit, the fundamental content of religion, manifested most purely in Christianity, is the idea of incarnation: "this becoming human of divine essence . . . is the simple content of the absolute [or Christian] religion."[4] Hence, "In Hegel's theory God appears as human thinking; even Jesus incarnates God's presence in this way. The incarnation thus becomes a rational truth instead of a supernatural mystery. But since rational truths are universal in scope, applying to all instances of the phenomena they describe, divine incarnation should occur wherever human thinking occurs. Hegel's position would then imply a universal incarnation rather than a unique one restricted to Jesus alone."[5] Strauss continued this line of thinking and affirmed the incarnation of God in all human beings.[6]

Similarly, other classical liberals materially either rejected or radically revised the idea of incarnation. Schleiermacher's dictum that "He alone is destined gradually to quicken the whole human race into higher life"[7] hardly is in keeping with classical tradition. More recent attempts to cash out the implications of liberal reinterpretation of incarnation include the controversial manifesto of Bishop J. A. T. Robinson, which speaks of incarnation as "a breakthrough of cosmic consciousness."[8] In keeping with the title of his well-known work, the incarnation is hardly more than *The Human Face of God.* To call incarnation "critical" to our salvation is merely a semantic move since in Robinson's view there are other faces of God among religions. Both historical contours of a particular historical person and metaphysical notions of an eternal Logos assuming humanity are replaced by symbolic notions of God's love manifested.[9] The problems with these revisionist attempts to understand incarnation have less to do with the lack of faithfulness to Chalcedon — all humanly crafted creeds are just that, *human* creeds — and everything to do with the historicity and significance of God's unique, unrepeatable act in Jesus Christ, the Word-Made-Flesh. If, on the basis of the resurrection from the dead, the claims of Jesus of Nazareth can

4. Cited in Jamros, "Hegel on the Incarnation," p. 278 (his translation from the original *Phänomenologie des Geistes,* 405.14-16).

5. Jamros, "Hegel on the Incarnation," p. 277.

6. Strauss, *Life of Jesus,* pp. 779-81.

7. Schleiermacher, *Christian Faith,* §13, p. 63.

8. J. A. T. Robinson, *Human Face of God,* p. 204.

9. J. A. T. Robinson, *Human Face of God,* p. 239 and passim.

be considered genuine and validated as to the unique Sonship — implying the intelligibility of the Christian doctrine of the triune God as the true God — then the ideas of incarnation as universal presence and influence of the divine not only say too little but also say something different.

Taking up Strauss's question mentioned in the beginning of this chapter, the Jesuit Gerald O'Collins contends that any consideration of the topic of incarnation in Christian theology and tradition has to clarify whether the reference is to "a unique event: namely, the second person of the Trinity being born into history to live, teach, die, and then rise gloriously from the dead — all with a view to inaugurating a radical new relationship between human beings and God" or to "something [that] should be understood as 'myth,' merely a non-historical, religious truth about ourselves."[10] This Catholic theologian further argues that to interpret the NT statements about the sending of the Son who became a human being (Rom. 8:3; Phil. 2:6-8; Heb. 1:2; John 1:14) and the similar affirmations in the Nicene-Constantinopolitan Creed in a "revisionist way" — say, merely as "myth" or "as *simply* statements expressing deep truths about ourselves" — "means that those ancient writers were either deliberately deceptive or else extraordinarily incompetent."[11] These kinds of interpretations end up advocating a low Christology in which Jesus hardly differs from other Spirit-bearing noble human beings. These interpretations, then, for better or for worse, end up presenting a Christology foreign to received Christian tradition. The value of that kind of reworked view in relation to the religious other is doubtful.

The question of the uniqueness and universality of Christ's incarnation has everything to do with the way Logos, the divinity, and Jesus, the man, are being linked with each other. Patristic and creedal traditions, ironically, and against their will, contributed to the loosening of the contours. Traditional Christology runs a danger of considering Logos and its activity apart from the Son, Jesus. What did Logos do before the incarnation? "Thereby we separate what for the New Testament cannot be divided; we objectify what in the New Testament is a christological title describing the significance of Jesus. Because *Logos* is a title for Jesus, there is no other *Logos* or Son except Jesus of Nazareth. When we speculate about the *Logos* apart from Jesus' historical life, we lose the significance of the term as a christological title."[12] In other words, the failure to link the Logos (of John 1)

10. O'Collins, "Incarnation," p. 1.
11. O'Collins, "Incarnation," p. 2.
12. Grenz, *Theology for the Community of God*, p. 309.

to the man Jesus of Nazareth may have opened the door to making the function of the Logos more or less independent.

Whereas contemporary pluralistically oriented approaches have made it a leading theological theme to differentiate between the more universal sphere of Logos and its more particular manifestation in the life of Jesus of Nazareth, John Cobb's version of process Christology offers a middle way. On the one hand, he treats Logos as if it were a cosmic or universal principle that has had a number of manifestations in arts, theology, the Freudian concept of "conscience," and so forth.[13] Speaking of "Christ as the Logos *incarnate* in the world as creative transformation" certainly smacks of Hegelian and Straussian influences.[14] On the other hand, unlike pluralists, Cobb maintains that "Christ is indissolubly bound up with Jesus."[15] He even maintains that "unless the power of creative transformation discerned in art and theology is also the power that was present in him and that continues to operate through his word, the affirmations [about the manifestations of Logos in arts and elsewhere] . . . cannot stand."[16]

Rather than pushing away the centrality of Christ as pluralists such as Hick would do, Cobb attempts to widen the meaning of Christ as "creative transformation," manifested in areas such as the arts, cosmic realities, psychology, and future hope, which so far have been marginal in traditional Christian interpretations.[17] Ultimately, this is to find a better way to relate to other religions. Following process thought, which rejects all notions of "substance," Cobb cannot of course subscribe to the creedal confession of *homoousios* (of the same "essence"). The way he attempts to express the current meaning of the ancient formula, gleaning also from his earlier work *The Structure of Christian Existence,* means that the incarnation of the Logos would be manifested in the constitution of selfhood, in a way that "the 'I' in each moment is constituted as much in the subjective reception of the lure to self-actualization that is the call and presence of the Logos as it is in continuity with the personal past. This structure of existence would be the incarnation of the Logos in the fullest meaningful

13. Cobb, *Christ in a Pluralistic Age,* pp. 82-83; more widely part 1.

14. Cobb, *Christ in a Pluralistic Age,* p. 97; interestingly enough, Cobb admits that — because he has been collaborating with "two Hegelians," namely, Pannenberg and Thomas Altizer (as different as their theologies are from that of Cobb himself!) — there are Hegelian soundings in his thought (pp. 14-15).

15. Cobb, *Christ in a Pluralistic Age,* p. 62.

16. Cobb, *Christ in a Pluralistic Age,* p. 97.

17. See especially Cobb, *Christ in a Pluralistic Age,* p. 61.

sense."[18] Although for Cobb, Logos "is incarnate in all human beings and indeed in all creation,"[19] it is only in Jesus that the presence of God is incarnated in the way explained above. Other human beings experience "the new possibility ['lure'] provided by the Logos as challenging it from without," and they conform to it in varying degrees.[20]

In some sense, Cobb's contemporary interpretation of incarnation is not saying materially something radically different from what thinkers such as the early apologist Justin Martyr were testifying about the Logos, namely, that "he is the Word of whom all humankind partakes."[21] What is different, however, between the process interpretation and tradition has to do with the casting of the incarnation of Logos in terms of the constitution of self and the loosening of the relation of Logos to Christ and Jesus. Indeed, the relation of Logos to Christ, Jesus, and the metaphor of "the creative transformation" remain confused and highly unnuanced.[22] Hence, it calls for more clarity, including its relation to classical trinitarian doctrine as well.

Incarnation as Metaphor and Myth

Through the wide influence of Strauss, the concept of myth[23] became a crucial hermeneutical device in the post-Enlightenment milieu in which miracles and other supernatural events such as the historical incarnation of Jesus could not be taken at face value. Different from the first generation of advocates of the quest of the historical Jesus such as Hermann Reimarus,[24] to whom myth was equated with fraud and lie, Strauss, after a careful and nuanced consideration of viewpoints between "orthodox"/"supernatural-

18. Cobb, *Christ in a Pluralistic Age,* p. 140.

19. Cobb, *Christ in a Pluralistic Age,* p. 138.

20. Cobb, *Christ in a Pluralistic Age,* p. 139.

21. Justin Martyr, *First Apology* 46. In the same vein, Clement of Alexandria (*Stromata* 6.5) makes the Law for the Jews and philosophy for the Greeks function in a parallel way "as a tutor to lead them to Christ"; this was due to the presence of Logos behind the true Gentile wisdom.

22. Interestingly, this is at the heart of Hick's criticism of Cobb's Christology. J. Hick, "Critique," pp. 158-60; so also McIntyre, *The Shape of Christology,* p. 213.

23. For a useful discussion of myth in earlier and contemporary theology, see Bloesch, *Jesus Christ,* pp. 120-31.

24. Reimarus presented this view most vocally in an essay "On the Aims of Jesus and His Disciples" (1778), described as "one of the greatest events in the history of criticism" by Albert Schweitzer (*Quest of the Historical Jesus,* p. 15).

ists" and "rationalists"/"naturalists," concluded that notwithstanding the historical factual nature, myths are an essential and legitimate — although to a modern person in many ways problematic — way of the Gospel writers to communicate about the superb influence of the historical Jesus. Whereas the orthodox end up creating incredible explanations to support the historical and factual nature of the NT stories, the rationalists simply come to dismiss the whole religious message of Jesus, or go to extremes in trying to find a natural explanation for the miracle story told. Strauss's middle way is to embrace the concept of myth as a vehicle for gaining insight into the religious message and influence of Jesus.[25] Narratives of incarnation, or virgin birth, or resurrection, rather than being historical records, are rather *stories* about such important religious events.

The leading religious pluralist of our times, John Hick, not only builds on this legacy but also sharpens and revamps it with a view to rapidly growing religious, cultural, and worldview plurality.[26] Unabashedly he represents "low Christology" in which incarnation means that all human beings, who only differ from each other in degree, are "Spirit-filled, or Christ-like, or truly saintly."[27] This Hick calls "mythical" or metaphorical understanding, as presented in his monograph *The Metaphor of God Incarnate: Christology in a Pluralistic Age.*[28]

To negotiate the uniqueness and historicity of incarnation, Hick makes two interrelated epistemological turns. First, he divides the differences between seemingly contradictory claims of various religions into three categories: "historical conceptions," such as the Christian belief in the death of Jesus on the cross vis-à-vis the Qur'anic interpretation of the death of someone

25. See the long introduction, titled "Development of the Mythical Point of View in Relation to the Gospel Histories," in Strauss, *Life of Jesus,* pp. 39-92. A more contemporary follower of much of Strauss's thought with regard to myth is of course R. Bultmann ("New Testament and Mythology," pp. 1-44, 191-211) and his many followers. On the other side of the theological spectrum, I find it interesting that Barth, with all his aversion to liberal tradition, did not reject the notion of myth. Although understandably more cautious than the great liberal, in his reflections on the historicity of creation stories, Barth basically granted the legitimacy of the mythical element, which, however, he replaced with a materially similar kind of concept of "saga." Barth, *CD* III/1, p. 81; see also pp. 81-94.

26. The now classic, important work that elicited a number of responses is J. Hick, ed., *Myth of God Incarnate.*

27. Cited in O'Collins, "Incarnation," p. 2 (and wrongly attributed to J. Hick, "Incarnation," p. 205; I have been unable to find the original reference).

28. The summary is in Crisp, *Divinity and Humanity,* pp. 155-56.

else in Jesus' place, could be resolved only if there were enough factual evidence.[29] "Transhistorical" (or "quasi-historical") claims, such as those regarding resurrection and reincarnation, can hardly be convincingly arbitrated at all. The only way to deal with those kinds of issues in a sensible way is to have an attitude of mutual respect and acceptance.[30] The conflicts concerning the "conceptions about the Ultimate Reality," such as Yahweh, Shiva, Vishnu, Allah or Brahma, Tao, nirvana, sunyata, or Dharmakaya, seem to be totally impossible to resolve. Hick's only advice is to treat each one of them as complementary.[31] Hence, the point of the first epistemological turn is to remind us that the more deeply religious language goes into the beliefs and ideas, the more complicated and complex is the arbitration between varying and conflicting claims.

The second turn for trying to ease the conflict between contradictory truth claims is to appeal to the mythical nature of religious language. The "myth" is based on "metaphor," which means that we speak "suggestive of another."[32] In other words, metaphors that are not meant to be taken at face value still convey meaning but in terms of eliciting emotions and associations familiar to a group that shares the common context of meanings. In an important sense, myth is an expanded metaphor. Even though myth is not literally true, it "tends to evoke an appropriate dispositional attitude."[33] Its purpose is to change our attitude and thus influence our thinking in a real way. The story about Buddha's flight to Sri Lanka, the creation story of the Old Testament, or the legend of the dance of Shiva functions like that.[34] As long as myths are understood literally, conflicts arise as a result, but if they are treated mythologically, they function in a way in "separate mythic spaces" and do not end up being in contradistinction with each other.[35]

29. J. Hick, "On Conflicting Religious Truth Claims," pp. 485-91; J. Hick, *An Interpretation of Religion,* pp. 363-65.

30. J. Hick, *Problems of Religious Pluralism,* pp. 89-95; J. Hick, *An Interpretation of Religion,* pp. 365-72.

31. J. Hick, *Problems of Religious Pluralism,* pp. 90-95; J. Hick, *An Interpretation of Religion,* p. 374.

32. J. Hick, *Metaphor of God Incarnate,* p. 99. Hick is well aware of the debates among various approaches to the definition of myth, but he basically follows the conventional definition.

33. J. Hick, *An Interpretation of Religion,* pp. 99-104, 348; see also Amnell, *Uskontojen Universumi,* pp. 79-81.

34. J. Hick, *An Interpretation of Religion,* pp. 103, 347-72.

35. J. Hick, *An Interpretation of Religion,* p. 15.

Rather than inquiring into the truth of the myth, one should rather ask whether it functions accordingly in that life situation and context for which it is created.[36] Speaking specifically of key Christian doctrines such as Trinity and incarnation, Hick opines that Christian doctrines are in the "nature of theories."[37] Rather than factual notions, he sees "religious doctrines as products of human thinking."[38]

In keeping with this linguistic and epistemological turn, in Hick's view traditional talk about incarnation has to be "demythologized" and set in harmony with other major religions. What incarnation is all about is making real the presence of the divine to all men and women. It is not about a god becoming a human being; that kind of idea is totally repulsive to contemporary people.[39] In mythical interpretation, Christ is depicted as the embodiment of divine love, complementary to what is revealed about the divine in Buddhism in the intense experience of the release from suffering or in Hinduism as the source of life and purpose. The Logos for Hick transcends any particular religion and is present in all of them.[40] Talk about incarnation thus is not indicative but rather expressive.[41] Hick illustrates this with reference to how two lovers express themselves to their beloved. Even though expressions such as "I love you more than anybody else" seem to be absolutistic in nature, they are not exclusive; other lovers may freely use them as well, and still they are true in their own context and for the purpose they were meant.[42]

When inquiring into the origins of the Christian doctrine of incarnation and the divine Sonship of Jesus, Hick makes the obvious point that the "son of God" was a familiar metaphor within Judaism. Thus, Jesus is called "Son of God" in the sense that the ancient Hebrew kings were called "son of God."[43] In later Christian tradition, as Hebrew poetry hardened into Latin prose, "the metaphorical son of God was transformed in Christian thinking

36. J. Hick, *An Interpretation of Religion,* pp. 267-68. Amnell (*Uskontojen Universumi,* pp. 92-95) rightly notes that Hick's use of myth bears obvious similarity to George Lindbeck's description of the "expressive-symbolic" category.

37. J. Hick, "Recent Development," p. 1.

38. J. Hick, "Recent Development," p. 2.

39. See, e.g., J. Hick, *Problems of Religious Pluralism,* p. 14.

40. J. Hick, *God Has Many Names,* p. 75; J. Hick, *Christian Theology of Religions,* pp. 22-23.

41. J. Hick, *God Has Many Names,* p. 78; Amnell, *Uskontojen Universumi,* pp. 108-9.

42. Amnell, *Uskontojen Universumi,* pp. 119-20.

43. J. Hick, "Islam and Christianity."

into the metaphysical [literal] God the Son, second person of a divine trinity."[44] In the same manner, Hick affirms, the term "incarnation" should be interpreted metaphorically. "The sense in which I use it is its metaphorical meaning. In English we often use the word 'incarnate' as a metaphor. We might say, for example, that Winston Churchill incarnated the British will to resist Hitler in 1940 — meaning that he embodied it, that it was expressed in him in an exemplary way. In this metaphorical sense, whenever a human being carries out God's will in the world we can say that in that action His will becomes incarnate, or embodied, on earth."[45]

Hick's metaphorical/mythical and pluralistic account of Christology can be summarized in this way:[46]

1. Jesus did not teach that he himself was God incarnate.
2. The Chalcedonian two-natures doctrine of the person of Christ cannot be expressed in a religiously adequate fashion.
3. The historical and traditional two-natures doctrine has been used to justify great evils, such as wars, persecution, repression, and genocide.
4. The notion of incarnation is better understood as a metaphor rather than as expressing some literal, metaphysical truth about the person of Christ.
5. The life and teaching of Jesus challenge us to live a life pleasing to God. Jesus is the Lord who makes God real to Christians.
6. This metaphorical understanding of the incarnation fits with a doc-

44. J. Hick, "Islam and Christianity."

45. J. Hick, "Islam and Christianity." Even in these most recent writings Hick is appealing to two theologians (Donald Baillie and Geoffrey Lampe) who are advocates of a Spirit Christology that falls short of trinitarian canons and a Christology that employs the more generic idea of "incarnation" as God's influence. Paradoxically — in light of radical changes in NT scholarship — writing in 1998, Hick supports the use of Baillie's interpretation with reference to Rudolf Bultmann's statement that Baillie's *God Was in Christ* was "the most significant book of our time in the field of Christology." J. Hick, "Trinity and Incarnation," p. 205. Furthermore, even though Baillie and Lampe rejected (or radically revised) the classical Chalcedonian Christology (and as a corollary implication, also the Trinity), Hick considers even these two as much too "exclusivistic." He does not agree with them in considering God's action in the life of Jesus as a supreme and unique one. Thus, while for Baillie the "paradox of grace" in Jesus is "absolute," and for Lampe "God's inspiration" is "perfect," Hick believes these suppositions cannot be followed. See J. Hick, "Recent Development," pp. 14-20; see also J. Hick, "Trinity and Incarnation," pp. 204-10.

46. As summarized succinctly in Crisp, *Divinity and Humanity*, pp. 155-56.

trine of religious pluralism, whereby Christ's life and teaching are seen as one example of the religious life that can also be found, in different ways and forms, in other major world religions.

Hick's reformulated Christology suffers from a number of theological, historical, and epistemological liabilities that also tend to lead to lack of hospitality, even to "imperialistic" and violent notions toward the other. Let me take up these liabilities one at a time. First, in reference to O'Collins's remarks above whether theological talk about incarnation refers to "a unique event" of the Word becoming flesh or to something "non-historical, understood as 'myth,'"[47] Hick's view has to be judged as failing to present a viable Christian position. In defense of the classical position, in which only one unique historical incarnation is confessed, the Catholic Reformer St. John of the Cross made the profound observation — when expositing the meaning of God's "speaking" in his Son of Hebrews 1 and the coming of the "word" of John 1 — that having spoken and uttered the Word, everything God wanted was said. There is nothing to add![48] Apart from the many debates surrounding Chalcedonian-driven classical Christology, as O'Collins strongly argues, it presupposes some kind of "historical," "realist," and "personal" understanding of the christological claims. With regard to the doctrine of preexistence, a necessary corollary doctrine of incarnation, he summarizes: "The personal pre-existence of the Word, Wisdom, or Son of God is a necessary element in any orthodox affirmation of the incarnation or 'the Word becoming flesh' (John 1:14). By personally pre-existing 'before becoming flesh,' the Word can mediate creation . . . , be 'sent by the Father,' become incarnate . . . and take on the human condition through the power of the Holy Spirit. Belief in Jesus' divinity stands or falls with accepting his *personal* pre-existence within the eternal life of the Trinity."[49]

Second, consequently, Hick breaks all the contours of classical trinitarian doctrine.[50] Hick rightly notes that in the doctrinal system in which Christian thought was embedded from the beginning, the doctrines of incarnation, atonement, and Trinity cohere together — and he intentionally does not want to side with that view since, again rightly, it leads to the affir-

47. O'Collins, "Incarnation," p. 1.

48. St. John of the Cross, *Ascent of Mount Carmel* 2.22.4-5, pp. 163-64, as referred to in O'Collins, "Incarnation," p. 22.

49. O'Collins, "Incarnation," p. 3.

50. For a critical discussion of Hick's theology in light of the Trinity, see S. T. Davis, "John Hick on Incarnation and Trinity," pp. 251-72.

mation of Christ's uniqueness![51] Hick presents a modalistic view of the Deity based on what he also calls "inspiration" Christology:

> An inspiration Christology coheres better with some ways of understanding trinitarian language than with others. It does not require or support the notion of three divine persons in the modern sense in which a person is a distinct center of consciousness, will, and emotion — so that one could speak of the Father, the Son, and the Holy Spirit as loving one another within the eternal family of the trinity, and of the Son coming down to earth to make atonement on behalf of human beings to his Father. An inspiration Christology is, however, fully compatible with the conception of the trinity as affirming three distinguishable ways in which the one God is experienced as acting in relation to, and is accordingly known by, us — namely, as creator, redeemer, and inspirer. On this interpretation, the three persons are not three different centers of consciousness but three major aspects of the one divine nature.[52]

In line with his metaphorical understanding of religious talk, Hick conceives the doctrine of the Trinity "not as ontologically three but as three ways in which the one God is humanly thought and experienced."[53] In Hick's view, this kind of modalistic version of the doctrine of the Trinity has parallels with other religions such as Islam's threefold name of God as omnipotent creator and ruler of the universe, God as gracious and forgiving, and God as intimately present to us.[54] While the question of to what degree and in what sense parallels to the Christian doctrine of the Trinity are acceptable will be investigated in the discussion of the Trinity, suffice it to note here the failing trinitarian basis of Hick's inspiration Christology.

My third uneasiness with Hick's proposal has to do with his "turn" to metaphorical and mythical language. Now, in itself that turn hardly is problematic. Indeed, as the discussion above on Christ's resurrection testifies and particularly the discussion below on the doctrine of atonement will testify, Christian doctrinal language is always and also must be metaphorical. How else could finite and fallible human language speak of the eternal, infinite

51. J. Hick, "The Non-Absoluteness of Christianity," p. 30; J. Hick, "Rethinking Christian Doctrine," p. 90.

52. J. Hick, "The Non-Absoluteness of Christianity," p. 32; see also *An Interpretation of Religion,* pp. 170-72, 271-72.

53. J. Hick, *Metaphor of God Incarnate,* p. 149.

54. J. Hick, "Rethinking Christian Doctrine," p. 98.

mystery! Even the term "myth" is not necessarily antagonistic to classical Christology, rightly configured. Although a fuller discussion, as mentioned, will be relegated to the context of atonement, we mention here that the main principle of the nature of doctrinal language is metaphor: metaphor is not necessarily a nonhistorical way of speaking of divine acts in history, but rather, it is a way of "saying more" about something that human language can only capture in part. That is, to capture more fully the mystery of incarnation — or the resurrection or atonement, for that matter — Christian theology attempts to use also what I call "true metaphors," metaphors that have a historical basis for doctrinal claims while acknowledging the fallibility, limitedness, and tentative (hypothetical) nature of them. In that light Hick's turn to metaphors in order to leave behind all historical contours is a failing exercise, not only because it is in strict violation of creedal tradition but also because it blocks the dialogue. Dialogue with Hickian Christology would not be a particularly interesting or useful exercise since then the other is not talking to any established tradition (such as Chalcedon) but to an individual Christian thinker who basically only represents himself.

This brings me to the fourth concern, which has to do with Hick's rereading of the development of Christian dogma. That claim, however, is nothing more than a return visit to the storehouse of classical liberalism and the original quests, an exercise deemed unsatisfactory by most all contemporary scholars. Above we noted that classical liberalism by and large sided with Harnack's highly tenuous postulation in which doctrinal development was nothing but the "deterioration of dogma." Materially that view hardly can be maintained, and has been rejected by most. Methodologically it is utterly unsatisfactory since it wrongly assumes that — in the spirit of the first generation of the quest of the historical Jesus advocates — we could have a "pure" and unadulterated access to the real Jesus of history. Although maintaining such a utopian dream might have been somewhat more excusable for the scholars of the eighteenth and nineteenth centuries, for anyone writing at the end of the twentieth century, in the aftermath of a number of new quests, it simply does not make sense. One does not have to subscribe to any particular type of postmodern epistemology to know that a categorical distinction between the "real" and interpretation-laden Jesus is a myth, and nothing else.

Finally, against his own announcements, Hick's Christology is neither hospitable nor embracing the other but, rather, is imperialistic and "exclusive"; hence it also blocks the dialogue rather than fosters it. Borrowing from the Jewish philosopher Emmanuel Levinas, Hick subsumes the other under his own frame of explanation and does not let the other be other. That is violence.[55] Many critics have rightly noted that ignoring the self-understanding of adherents of religions means nothing less than violating their religious rights. It is "elitistic" and "imperialistic."[56] Alister McGrath goes so far as to call it "intellectual Stalinism."[57] While more irenic, John Cobb expresses materially similar kinds of grave concerns.[58] The religious scholar Peter L. Berger asks in this context what gives the modern interpreter a superior knowledge concerning ancient religions.[59] Put otherwise: What makes the contemporary interpreter take it for granted that the old view is "wrong" whereas the new one is "right"?

Let me illustrate these concerns from a recent exchange between Hick and a leading Muslim scholar and cleric, Muzammil H. Siddiqi.[60] In response to Hick's assertion that all religions be considered merely human, and thus fallible and limited, responses to the Ultimate Reality (the divine), Siddiqi argues that for him and Islam, there is also the divine initiative alongside and before the human response. "I as a Muslim who holds the prophetic tradition seriously find [Hick's claim] unsatisfactory to say the least."[61] The Muslim cleric also takes issue with Hick's refusal to grant any criteria to negotiate the value and superiority of any religion in relation to others. Siddiqi insists, "We must have some principles for judgment and evaluation."[62] Ironically, but perhaps not surprisingly, at the end Siddiqi does approve Hick's Christology. "I like John Hick's discussion on Christology. John knows quite well that his book *The Myth of God Incarnate* is very

55. For the reasoning on why Levinas considers ethics as "first philosophy," and hence the responsibility toward the other, as well as the importance of letting the other be other, see Levinas, "God and Philosophy," pp. 127-45. As the title of the essay implies, behind this logic is his particular understanding of God (through the lens of a post-metaphysical philosophy). For a succinct and useful exposition of Levinas's key ideas in this respect (and in relation to his doctrine of God), see the preface and introduction to Levinas, *Of God Who Comes to Mind.*

56. Amnell, *Uskontojen Universumi,* p. 63.

57. McGrath, "Conclusion," p. 206.

58. Cobb, *Beyond Dialogue,* pp. 38-44.

59. Several authors have raised this question: Berger, *The Heretical Imperative,* pp. 119-20; Amnell, *Uskontojen Universumi,* p. 90.

60. He is imam and director of the Islamic Society of Orange County in California, and professor of Islamic Studies at California State University. See Siddiqi, "A Muslim Response," pp. 211-13.

61. Siddiqi, "A Muslim Response," p. 211.

62. Siddiqi, "A Muslim Response," pp. 211-12.

well received by Muslims. The Christology proposed by John Hick can serve as a good subject for dialogue between Muslims and Christians."[63] However, the price paid for gaining acceptance of a *Christian* interpretation of Christology is high and counterproductive. The violation of the principle of hospitality and the otherness of the other coupled with the radical rejection of one's own tradition and thus religious identity hardly engenders fruitful dialogue, which is the ultimate goal of Hick's work! The Roman Catholic theologian of religions Gavin D'Costa concludes that the modernist epistemology behind Hick's and similar kinds of pluralisms is hostile to real differences in its insistence on sameness and universality: "Despite their [pluralists'] intentions to encourage openness, tolerance, and equality they fail to attain these goals (on their own definition) because of the tradition-specific nature of their positions. Their particular shaping tradition is the Enlightenment. . . . The Enlightenment, in granting a type of equality to all religions, ended up denying public truth to any and all of them."[64]

D'Costa laments that even though pluralists "present themselves as honest brokers to disputing parties," they conceal "the fact that they represent yet another party which invites the disputants actually to leave their parties and join the pluralist one," namely, liberal modernity. Therefore, ironically, pluralists end up being "exclusivists." Hick's view D'Costa calls "liberal intolerance."[65] Hence, D'Costa contends, the "hidden gods" of modernity should be unmasked![66] The alternative to pluralism is of course not inhospitable exclusivism. D'Costa calls for a robust and unabashed tradition-based (Christian tradition, that is, and in his case, Roman Catholic, more specifically) dialogue with and engagement of the other: "The other is always interesting in their difference and may be the possible face of God, or the face of violence, greed, and death. Furthermore, the other may teach Christians to know and worship their own trinitarian God more truthfully and richly."[67] Pluralisms fail exactly because they water down real differences among religions and regard all of them as the same below the surface. Hick's pluralism leads to the denial of otherness and difference. He "demythologizes" the differences away so that the religions can be fitted into his system. Consequently, it does not take the dialogue with the other seriously since basically all reli-

63. Siddiqi, "A Muslim Response," p. 213. For the references to Siddiqi's essay, I am indebted to my student Reda Samuel.

64. D'Costa, *Meeting of Religions,* pp. 1-2.

65. D'Costa, *Meeting of Religions,* pp. 20, 22, 24.

66. D'Costa, *Meeting of Religions,* pp. 1-2.

67. D'Costa, *Meeting of Religions,* p. 9.

gions teach the same thing, differing doctrines notwithstanding. As a result, pluralism denies the self-definitions of particular religions and from a distance tells the followers of other religions what is the truth.

For a genuine dialogue to happen, the three cardinal virtues modernity lifts up but fails to deliver — equality, justice, and tolerance — must be reconfigured. For D'Costa, openness becomes "taking history seriously," rather than dismissing it as pluralism seems to do. Differences do matter and should not be suspended. Tolerance, rather than denying the tradition-specific claims for truth — which in itself, ironically, is one more truth claim among others — becomes the "qualified establishment of civic religious freedom for all on the basis of Christian revelation and natural law." Equality becomes the "equal and inviolable dignity of all persons," which naturally leads to taking the other seriously, dialoguing with the other with willingness to learn from the other and teach the other.[68]

The Uniqueness of Christ Revisited

"Relationally Unique"

The two leading Roman Catholic pluralists, Paul F. Knitter and Raimundo Panikkar, both in their own respective ways, have offered a revised understanding of incarnation and uniqueness. Knitter, who later in his career turned robustly to a liberationist theology of religions (to be discussed below), started by echoing the views of Hick and similar pluralists, in turning to a theo-centric Christology as the key to "a more authentic dialogue."[69] Rather than approaching the question of religions from the standpoint of Jesus Christ as the normative norm — the standpoint of classical orthodoxy — Knitter came to focus on the theo-centric consciousness of Jesus Christ and his preaching of the coming of the kingdom of God. That turn, he believed, was aided by the insight that biblical Christology be taken "seriously" but not "literally," the reason being that the christological statements are "myth" rather than definitive, final statements of fact. Hence, as mysteries, they "must be understood ever anew."[70] While it was appropriate for the

68. D'Costa, *Meeting of Religions,* p. 9.

69. Significantly enough, this is the title for part 3, Paul Knitter's own proposal, in *No Other Name?* p. 169.

70. Knitter, *No Other Name?* pp. 180-81.

early church to define the uniqueness of Christ in an exclusive manner, this is neither necessary nor helpful for us as we encounter the challenge of religions, Knitter opines. He suggests that the transcendental Christologies of the early church councils would be better off if reinterpreted along functionalist lines: the purpose of the doctrine of incarnation is to be a medium of God's self-communication rather than a way of emphasizing the particularity of a literal divine descent.[71]

On the basis of these considerations, Knitter comes to the conclusion that Jesus Christ is "unique" in that he is an authoritative revelation of God, but there may be other savior figures among other religions. This for Knitter does not undermine the Christian's commitment to Christ — nor of course make him willing to "convert others" — but renders one's faith in Christ "more intellectually coherent (better theory) and more practically demanding (better praxis)."[72] The implications for interreligious dialogue, which Knitter wholeheartedly recommends to all, are these:

> Christians, in their approach to persons of other faiths, need not insist that Jesus brings God's definitive, normative revelation. A confessional approach is a possible and preferred alternative. In encountering other religions, Christians can confess and witness to what they have experienced and come to know in Christ, and how they believe this truth can make a difference in the lives of all peoples, without making any judgments whether this revelation surpasses or fulfills other religions. In other words, the question concerning Jesus' finality or normativity can remain an open question.[73]

From the Buddhist side, a materially similar kind of defense of Jesus' "relative uniqueness" among the savior figures of religions is offered by Tanabe Hajime of the Kyoto School. His highly sophisticated irenic reasoning sought to present Buddhist philosophy in the framework of European philosophical traditions. In his "Demonstratio of Christianity" Hajime argues that the long and winding road to the final affirmation of the doctrines of the Trinity and the deity of the Son of God in itself should remind us of the complexity of these issues. Beginning from what he calls the "Trinity of love" and basing it on the mutuality of the love of God and love of the neigh-

71. Knitter, *No Other Name?* p. 186.
72. Knitter, *No Other Name?* p. 200.
73. Knitter, *No Other Name?* p. 205.

bor, Hajime wonders if we could "then convert the uniqueness of the son of God into the many-ness of the existential community and reduce it to 'the one which is identical to the many and the many which are identical to the one.'" This way he believes can affirm both the unique character of Jesus as the founder of the religion and his universality among the religions.[74]

Knitter's proposal suffers from many of the same problems Hick's does, although this Catholic theologian's views earlier in his career tended to be less radical. The turn to theo-centric Christology contradicts not only the biblical insistence on Jesus as the way to knowing God who is the Yahweh of the OT but also the doctrine and intuitions of creeds. It also opposes the classical trinitarian canons as it is not possible to confess belief in the Trinity if Jesus Christ is not the Son, the eternal counterpart to the Father (and Spirit). The linguistic gimmick of taking NT statements "seriously" but not "literally" is an ambiguous turn at its best. It raises the obvious question as to the meaning of "serious." It is a clever rhetorical device but leaves its theological and philosophical value undefined. Its value for a robust dialogue is also limited as it does not allow the representatives on the Christian side to present their own views in an authentic and open way. One wonders if, similar to Hick's theology of religions, there is the unwritten expectation that the other party is not allowed to express its "true" beliefs and deep commitments but, for the sake of dialogue, is to water them down.

A Cosmotheandric and Advaitic Christological Vision

The theology of the "Hindu-Catholic"[75] Raimundo Panikkar is highly unique among the pluralists in many ways. For him Trinity is not an obstacle to dialogue to be ignored, as in Hick and Knitter, but rather a central Christian vision that may be the key to the dialogue with the other.[76] Trinity is "a junction where the authentic spiritual dimensions of all religions meet."[77]

74. Tanabe Hajime, "The Demonstratio of Christianity," in *JBC*, pp. 245-46.

75. The often quoted autobiographical comment according to which Panikkar "left" Europe as a Christian, "found" himself as a Hindu, and "returned" as a Buddhist, fittingly illustrates this diverse background and varied orientations. Panikkar, *The Intrareligious Dialogue*, p. 2.

76. Rightly, Vanhoozer (*Trinity in a Pluralistic Age*, p. 58) says Panikkar "is the exception that proves the rule, a pluralist who *does* invoke the Trinity and who believes it to be at the heart of all human religions."

77. Panikkar, *The Trinity*, p. 42.

For Knitter, Trinity is saying something all religions are expressing in their own unique ways. While not to be equated, as in typical pluralistic understandings, but rather honored in their diversities, what religions envision is something Panikkar chooses to name "cosmotheandrism." The root terms here are obviously "God," "human," and "cosmos." Whatever else "cosmotheandrism" means, it refers to the coming together of God, humanity, and the world. Panikkar gives this definition: "The cosmotheandric principle could be formulated by saying that the divine, the human and the earthly — however we may prefer to call them — are the three irreducible dimensions which constitute the real, i.e., any reality inasmuch as it is real."[78] Incarnation, hence, looms large in Panikkar's vision, and particularly the kind of cosmically oriented embodiment evident in some NT passages such as Colossians 1:15-20, and in some Fathers such as Irenaeus and Athanasius. Trinity, while a distinctively Christian way of speaking of cosmotheandrism, is not an exclusively Christian reality. "It simply is an unwarranted overstatement to affirm that the trinitarian conception of the Ultimate, and with it of the whole of reality, is an exclusive Christian insight or revelation."[79] Christianity can learn from others, but it also has a significant role to play in leading "to the *plenitude* and hence to the *conversion* of all religion."[80] In the final analysis, the end of this process (and the goal of Christianity) is "humanity's common good." Christianity "simply incarnates the primordial and original traditions of humankind."[81]

Along these lines, in his most significant christological monograph, the revised version of *The Unknown Christ of Hinduism* in 1981, he moved definitely toward a pluralistic version of Christology. In that book, he rejects all notions of Christianity's superiority over or fulfillment of other religions by arguing that the world and our subjective experience of the world have radically changed since the Christian doctrine concerning Christ was first formulated. Panikkar's revised understanding is based on the distinction between the universal Christ and the particular Jesus. This is the key for him to

78. Panikkar, *The Cosmotheandric Experience,* p. ix. Elsewhere (Panikkar, "The Myth of Pluralism," p. 217) he puts it this way: "There is a kind of *perichoresis,* 'dwelling within one another,' of these three dimensions of Reality, the Divine, the Human and the Cosmic — the *I,* the *you* and the *it.*" Kajsa Ahlstrand's (*Fundamental Openness,* p. 134) paraphrasing is as good as any: "There is no God without Man and the World. There is no Man without God and the World. There is no World without God and Man."

79. Panikkar, *The Trinity,* p. viii.

80. Panikkar, *The Trinity,* p. 4.

81. Panikkar, "The Jordan, the Tiber, and the Ganges," p. 102.

an "authentically universal" Christology. "Christ is . . . a living symbol for the totality of reality: human, divine, and cosmic."[82] With Catholic theology he affirms that the Logos or Christ has been incarnated in Jesus of Nazareth. But he departs from orthodoxy by denying that this incarnation has taken place solely and finally in Jesus. Arguing for the opposite of what he argued in the first edition of *The Unknown Christ of Hinduism,* in which he posited a unity between Christ and Jesus, he now rejects it. According to his revised Christology, no historical form can be the full, final expression of the universal Christ. The universal symbol for salvation in Christ can never be reduced to a merely historical personhood, he argues. Panikkar claims that "Christ will never be totally known on earth, because that would amount to seeing the Father whom nobody can see."[83] The saving power of Jesus, indeed, is to be found in the fact that he embodies a reality that is beyond every historical form, the universal Christ. As a "a living symbol for the totality of reality," Christ represents an intimate and complete unity between the divine and the human. The meaning of the confession "Christ is God the Son, the Logos" for Panikkar is that Christ is both symbol and substance of this nondualistic unity between God and humanity.

In order not to leave behind but rather to consolidate the trinitarian conditions of his pluralistic Christology, Panikkar utilizes a major Asian epistemological resource, the Hindu term *advaita,* which means "nonduality" (literally: not two).[84] According to Panikkar, "there are not two realities: God *and* man (or the world). . . . Reality itself is theandric; it is our own way of looking that causes reality to appear to us sometimes under one aspect and sometimes under another because our own vision shares in both."[85] Applied to the ancient problem of unity and diversity in the trinitarian God, the advaitic principle implies that Father and Son are not two, yet "they are not one either: the Spirit both unites and distinguishes them."[86]

The advaitic logic, so Panikkar assumes, gives him resources to also radically reformulate not only the trinitarian doctrine but also the place of Christ therein, including his incarnation and self-emptying. Father is "Nothing," similar to the Buddhist notion of the emptiness and the Chris-

82. Panikkar, *Unknown Christ of Hinduism,* p. 27.

83. Quoted in Knitter, *No Other Name?* p. 156.

84. Fittingly, then, Ewert H. Cousins names it "Panikkar's Advaitic Trinitarianism," in *The Intercultural Challenge of Raimon Panikkar,* pp. 119-130; for the term "advaitic," see especially p. 120.

85. Panikkar, *The Trinity,* p. 75.

86. Panikkar, *The Trinity,* p. 62.

tian apophatic way, the way to approach the Absolute without name.[87] There is no "Father" in himself; the "being of the Father" is "the Son." In the incarnation, *kenosis,* the Father gives himself totally to the Son. Thus the Son is "God."[88] Panikkar believes this understanding is the needed bridge between Christianity and Buddhism as well as advaitic Hinduism. What *kenosis* (self-emptying) is for Christianity, nirvana and sunyata are for these two other religions. "God is total Silence. This is affirmed by all the world religions. One is led towards the Absolute and in the end one finds nothing, because there *is* nothing, not even Being."[89]

Panikkar's version of pluralism and his way of negotiating the role of Jesus Christ among religions from a Christian perspective are superior in many ways to the efforts of his Catholic colleague Knitter and Protestant counterpart Hick. The elevation of the Trinity to the center of theology and dialogue, his effort to resist pluralism's subsuming of the other under one's own framework, and his openness to some form of high Christology are all assets in a Christian attempt to encounter the other. The liabilities are also important to consider. In the context of the doctrine of the Trinity, the question whether Panikkar is indeed representing an authentically *Christian* version will be investigated in detail. Here the focus is on his Christology.

Pannikkar's liability is getting rid of historical contours even though, unlike many pluralists, he neither supports the idea of the common core of all religions nor argues for leaving behind some kind of uniqueness of Jesus Christ. His making reference to the Christ principle without any concern for an approach "From Below" is nothing other than trying to rehabilitate the "From Above" method, in other words, defining the meaning of Christ apart from historical contours and then reading the narrative of the Gospels in light of this preconceived "theology." While in principle it is of course possible to expand the Christic principle beyond the figure of Jesus of Nazareth, one pays a high price: historical and theological criteria are left behind, and one operates in a milieu in which personal opinions count as much as historical investigation. Occasionally he himself seems to acknowledge the danger of separation by speaking to the importance of not letting Jesus and Christ be too much divorced from each other, but for the purposes of not making the Jesus of history a stumbling block to dialogue, he emphasizes the universality of the Christ principle at the expense of the

87. Panikkar, *The Trinity,* p. 46.
88. Panikkar, *The Trinity,* pp. 45-47.
89. Panikkar, *The Trinity,* p. 52.

particularity of the historical figure of Jesus. In my reading of Panikkar's corpus, he leaves the question open and is willing to live with ambiguity. While the danger of "historicism" may be real in some quarters, for Panikkar the danger is the opposite. His Christ has a strong tendency to separate from historical contours.

What does it mean to say the Son is the "real" God after the *kenosis* of the Father? And how is that statement to be related to Jesus of Nazareth? Panikkar's Christology and thus his trinitarianism seem to share the typical weaknesses of "theo-centric" approaches to the theology of religions, according to which the significance of Jesus is diminished in favor of the concept of God. This move, however, while typical of pluralistic approaches, works against the trinitarian idea of the equality, unity-in-diversity of the three divine persons. Holding on to the trinitarian doctrine (even in his unique way) seems to be very problematic if the Christic principle is divorced from history and salvation history. Especially in light of the fact that in Panikkar's trinitarian doctrine the Son is the whole focus of deity, his pluralistically constructed Christology creates internal contradiction. Panikkar's exegesis in support of his Christology does not convince. He interprets the Johannine saying that no one comes to the Father except through the Son (John 14:6) to mean that the Father does not exist except through and in the Son.[90] I understand Panikkar's motive here — to relate the Father of Christianity to the godhead in the Buddhist concept of nirvana and sunyata[91] — but I fear he is mispresenting both Buddhist and Christian sources. Dogmatically also, Panikkar's claim that the Son is the focus of the Trinity is unacceptable. Ironically his is too "christocentric" an approach! The NT teaching is clear that even the Son's equality to the Father never implies taking the place of the Father but rather serving the coming of the Father's kingdom.

Neither is his epistemological turn convincing. Certainly as an Asian theologian, it is appropriate and useful for him to look for Asian resources. But the problem is that he seems to be applying the *advaita* principle to Christian theology in a quite uncritical way. First of all, it might be the case that a principle such as that, more than just an external device, is deeply embedded in the philosophical, religious, and cultural matrix of its origin and hence, when used in a different framework, has to be handled with great care. More importantly, it seems to me that Panikkar calls forth an advaitic

90. Panikkar, *The Trinity*, p. 47.
91. Panikkar, *The Trinity*, p. 47.

principle whenever serious logical or other intellectual problems are being encountered. Resorting to either the advaitic or mystical principle can also become an exercise in avoiding the core problem. G. J. Larson, in a recent appraisal of Panikkar's pluralism, puts this basic problem in perspective by saying that Panikkar's "notion of pluralism becomes unintelligible in a two-valued (truth-falsehood) logic, inasmuch as the principle of the excluded middle is violated," and therefore "the notion of pluralism so formulated is as self-defeating as any formulation of relativism and as tripped up by the problem of self-referentiality as any formulation of universalism or absolutism."[92] I think Panikkar confuses rather than clarifies the truth issue by his statement that "to understand is to be convinced," as the title of one of his essays puts it.[93] Convinced of what? one has to ask. What Panikkar means by this is that rather than positing common, taken-for-granted criteria of meaning and validity, on the "religious" plane, understanding what a statement means is the same as acknowledging its truth. If so, one cannot really understand the views of another if one does not share them. But how do we then assess the truthfulness (in any traditional sense of the term) of religious statements?[94]

An important step in some current pluralistic theologies of religions is the turn to liberation as the ultimate goal of religions in general and Christian religion in particular. Knitter's influence looms large over this field.

Liberation and Religious Pluralism

As mentioned, the mature Knitter turned to considering carefully the relationship between liberation and pluralism. His way of negotiating the role of Jesus Christ among religions is more interesting than that of Hick since he seeks to take seriously the "other," both the "religious other" and the "suffering other."[95] The mature Knitter attempts to bring together the two disciplines of liberation theology and the theology of religions and sees that as the key to dialogue and, more importantly, to collaboration between religions. Like liberationists, Knitter "experienced the fundamental option for

92. Larson, "Contra Pluralism," p. 72.

93. Panikkar, "Verstehen als Überzeugtsein," p. 134.

94. For an incisive assessment of Panikkar's view of truth, see Krieger, "Methodological Foundations for Interreligious Dialogue," pp. 201-3.

95. Knitter, *Jesus and the Other Names,* p. 3; see also pp. 15-20.

the oppressed not simply as an option but a demand,"[96] which as a result seeks "a globally responsible, correlational dialogue among religions."[97]

In his programmatic essay "Toward a Liberation Theology of Religions," Knitter agreed with Arnold Toynbee that religion is necessary to overcome society's selfishness and injustice. This means that the liberation movement requires not merely religion, but religions (plural). For example, for a liberation theology to accomplish its huge task amidst Asian poverty, it needs help from all religions, not just Christianity. "A purely Christian theology of liberation . . . suffers the dangerous limitation of inbreeding, of drawing on only one vision of the kingdom."[98]

In Knitter's vision of the future of the theology of religions, a liberation perspective contributes in several ways. The "hermeneutics of suspicion," the main methodological orientation of liberationism, is to be adopted in the theology of religions, too. This helps us acknowledge the extent to which our biblical and theological interpretations are conditioned by our own interests. The liberation theologies' preferential option for the poor has the capacity of becoming the norm for the theology of religions as well. Instead of positing a common core for all religions — in the spirit of Toynbee and others — one may take the status of the poor as the criterion. Furthermore, the liberation theologies' soterio-centric (salvation-oriented) approach gives the theology of religions the right goal, which is to advance the coming of the kingdom of peace and justice.[99] Knitter summarizes his vision succinctly:

> For Christians, that which constitutes the basis and the goal for interreligious dialogue, that which makes mutual understanding and cooperation between the religions possible (the "condition of the possibility"), that which unites the religions in common discourse and praxis, is *not* how they are related to the church (invisibly through "baptism of desire"), or how they are related to Christ (anonymously or normatively), nor even how they respond to and conceive of God, but rather, to what extent they are promoting *Soteria* (in Christian images, the *basileia*) — to what extent they are engaged in promoting human welfare and bringing about liberation with and for the poor and nonpersons.[100]

96. Knitter, *Jesus and the Other Names,* p. 10.

97. Section title in Knitter, *One Earth, Many Religions,* p. 16.

98. Knitter, "Toward a Liberation Theology of Religions," p. 180.

99. Knitter, "Toward a Liberation Theology of Religions," pp. 183-88.

100. Knitter, "Toward a Liberation Theology of Religions," p. 187, emphasis in original.

What, then, is the uniqueness of Jesus Christ in this liberationist theology of religions? Knitter locates the uniqueness of Jesus in his capacity to elicit a proper incentive and response to promoting the welfare of all persons, especially of the poor and underprivileged. Jesus' special meaning can be found in that "the reality of God cannot be truly experienced and known unless one is actively, historically, materially engaged in loving one's neighbors and working for their betterment in this world."[101] This we might call "relational uniqueness," which is inclusive of others, not exclusive. In contrast to the official Roman Catholic position, which he calls a "constitutive Christology," Knitter's representational Christology speaks of Jesus as "a *decisive/definite* and as *universally meaningful* embodiment or manifestation of God."[102] Utilizing the classical theological categories, Knitter does not regard Christ as *norma Normans non normata,* a norm that norms all others but is not normed itself, but rather as *norma Normans et normata,* a norm that norms others but can also be normed itself.[103]

For Knitter, suffering and eco-balance are givens; they are common to all inhabitants of the earth. "Suffering has a universality and immediacy that makes it the most suitable, and necessary, site for establishing common ground for interreligious encounter."[104] With regard to ecological well-being, Knitter calls on science for help and argues that the contemporary scientific narrative of the origins of the world may indeed serve as a "common creation myth" and a "common ethical story." Knitter believes that ethical standards to further the well-being of both the people and the environment can be "worked out by international ecological groups, especially non-governmental." Unless the religions and peoples of the earth can respond to suffering and ecological threat, there is no hope for the future.[105]

Hence, epistemologically, praxis has to be prioritized over theory. Indeed, the praxis becomes the criterion for the "truth," that is, the promotion of eco-well-being is the criterion for the truth: "If followers of various religious traditions can agree in the beginning that whatever else their experience of truth or of the Divine or of Enlightenment may bring about, it must always promote greater eco-human well-being and help remove sufferings

101. Knitter, "Christian Salvation," p. 43.

102. Knitter, *Jesus and the Other Names,* p. 53, with reference to Ogden, "Some Thoughts," pp. 9-10.

103. Knitter, *Jesus and the Other Names,* p. 169 n. 9.

104. Knitter, *One Earth, Many Religions,* p. 89.

105. Knitter, *One Earth, Many Religions,* pp. 119-23 especially.

of our world, then they have a shared reference point from which to affirm or criticize each other's claims."[106]

Calling religions to work together for the betterment of this planet and life therein is something all (theistic) religions echo. In Christian religion that call goes beyond the level of the need to be nice to one's neighbor. Jesus' own example in reaching out to all people and calling them to submit their lives under a "universal" ethic of love and respect, as well as concrete neighborly caring, certainly points in that direction. The rampant religious violence alone in our world should make the call for collaboration a high priority to all religious persons and communities. My concern has to do with the way Knitter grounds and issues that call. Although it might be debated whether Knitter's mature eco-liberationist interpretation of Christology is still pluralistic, it seems to me it is. It is just differently pluralistic from his earlier, more commonsensical view. Its subtext is the modernist illusion of the common core of religions and the need to circumvent the centrality of any particular standpoint (uniqueness of Christ in this case). Knitter's liberationist proposal raises a number of epistemological questions. They center on the question of criteria of truth. Bluntly dismissing the cognitive (doctrinal) content in preference of praxis — be it as noble a goal as liberation — is only to defer the question of criteria.[107] A related question asks of Knitter, what is the meaning of *soteria*, "salvation"?[108] Paraphrasing A. MacIntyre, the question simply reads: "Whose Salvation? Which Liberation?" What are the criteria for discerning when the goal is reached? To assume that different religions with vastly differing views of "salvation" and "liberation" just agree with each other is an unbelievably naive assumption. One does not have to be an ethicist to begin to mount the questions, doubts, and concerns. Truth simply does not emerge from praxis. Praxis is guided and shaped by one's understanding of truth. There is a mutually conditioning relationship here.

Alongside epistemological questions, assumptions in Knitter's proposal are both unfounded and naive. Assuming that the mere work in collaboration among religions would make the adherents dismiss deep confessional and doctrinal differences hardly is an intuitive idea, and even if it is, it hardly has much support in the kind of world in which we live. Speculating, one could ask: What about after finishing the work? Once liberation is

106. Knitter, *One Earth, Many Religions*, p. 127.

107. See further, Vroom, *No Other Gods*, pp. 171-72.

108. Noted by critics such as Fredericks, *Faith among Faiths*, pp. 124-25.

achieved — or to be more modest, once the work toward liberation is put in place — what do we do with deep confessional differences?

A further unfounded and problematic assumption behind Knitter's turn to liberation is that the traditional focus on doctrine necessarily hinders one from the work of liberation. In other words, one either "does doctrinal Christology" or one "practices liberationist Christology." Again, this hardly is the case and can be shown to be a false premise in light of centuries-long work for liberation in various forms among the most sincere, Chalcedonian-bound Christians from different Christian traditions and communities.

10. Jesus Christ among Religions

The discussion of pluralistic Christian theologies of religions in the previous chapter was a fitting bridge to the current chapter, the last discussion in part I, which is focused on the relation of Christian confession of Christ to other religious traditions and their claims to truth and salvation. As explained briefly in the introduction, the current constructive theological project utilizes resources and methods of both theology of religions and comparative theology. The former, when done from the Christian perspective, investigates the relation of Christian tradition to other faith traditions as well as the meaning of religion in the divine economy. That conversation rarely engages any particular interfaith encounters unless to illustrate an example, nor does it usually focus on any specific topic shared between two (or more) religions. Comparative theology, on the other side, while at its best assuming results and insights from the theology of religions, seeks to investigate in some detail specific theological topics common to two or more religious traditions. Hence, the Christian and Hindu notions of incarnation would be a typical theme for a comparative theology approach.

The previous chapter was an exercise in the Christian theology of religions, whereas the current one engages comparative theology. It will engage each of the four living faiths — Judaism, Islam, Hinduism, and Buddhism — with regard to specific, focused topics of interest. Since religions are different, the topics arising in interfaith encounters are also different. Even with regard to a specific Christian doctrine such as Christology, Islam, whose tradition knows well the figure of Jesus Christ, and say, Judaism, which *should* know him but by and large just ignores Jesus, approach the encounter with

Christian theology from different vantage points. Similarly, the two leading Eastern religions, Hinduism and Buddhism, while sharing much more in common with each other, pose their own specific challenges and promises to that task.

Speaking of, say, Christian-Hindu encounter is a huge and in many ways both problematic and questionable concept, not only because Hinduism, as is well known, is in itself a hybrid concept, a Western construction, but also because there are so many different Hindu traditions. True, it is much better and probably more useful when speaking of a theological exchange between two specific religions to try to focus on a limited topic than to generalize about interfaith matters, just speaking of religions in general (which is the serious liability of the generic theology of religions). Yet, it still calls for much specification and limitation. Not all Hindus — any more than Christians, for that matter, as the overly long discussion of key christological themes in this volume indicates! — speak with one voice. Hence, to make the discussion manageable and useful, the following interfaith discussion aims at severely limited, specific, and focused investigations. The topics have been selected with good reason to assume that they derive from the inner logic of the dialogue partners and, as mentioned, are based on their relation, if any, to the traditions about Jesus Christ.

The investigation seeks to consult the definitive and representative sources of each tradition. From the Christian side, the constructive/systematic development of key christological themes above serves as the basis. With regard to Jewish tradition, whose authoritative Scripture is Torah, shared by Christians, the main dialogue partners are leading modern thinkers beginning from the nineteenth century who started engaging the figure of Jesus Christ, consulting also the great Jewish medieval resources. Merely attempting an exegesis of key texts of Torah hardly leads anywhere; the contemporary Christian-Jewish dialogue has to listen carefully to the leading historical and contemporary interpreters of the Jewish tradition. The dialogue with Muslim tradition builds heavily on a careful study of key Qur'anic passages; that choice hardly calls for further justification. Furthermore, because of historical reasons, due to the emergence of Islam in the seventh century C.E., as a result of which a vigorous interfaith exchange took place for several hundred years, some of the key resources from that time and their interpretations will be consulted as well. Those debates happen to focus on Christology (and Trinity) and are thus extremely relevant to the purposes of this investigation. In the case of Hindu tradition, rather than attempting a systematic study of the philosophical Vedanta texts (of the Upanishads), which by and large are unknown to most Hindus, the "common Bible" of Bhagavad-Gita will be consulted along with some key historical and contemporary Hindu scholars of various traditions. With the Buddhist tradition, because of the lack of a definitive "canon" — the closest to which comes the huge collection, in the Theravada tradition, of *Tipitaka*, from which a couple of key writings such as Anguttara Nikaya will be consulted — some leading modern and contemporary Buddhist thinkers from various traditions will be engaged.

This chapter engages other living faiths with regard to topics relevant to and arising out of the previous discussion that also relate integrally to the dialogue partner. At the end of the discussion on reconciliation (the last chapter of part II), the question of the nature, role, and conditions of Christian salvation among religions will be carefully investigated. As mentioned, on top of that, throughout the volume short interfaith exchanges take place where relevant and useful. The results of those exchanges will not be repeated in these two chapters unless there is a specific reason to do so.

Because the affinity of Christian tradition with the mother tradition, Judaism, is so obvious, that faith will be engaged first. Thereafter, it is natural to investigate the relationship between Muslim and Christian interpretations of Christ for the reason that, unlike other faiths except Judaism, the role of Jesus Christ is well known. Thereafter, the two Eastern traditions will be studied.

The Jewish Messiah — the Christian Messiah

The Jew — between the Jews and Christians

"When one asks the basic question of what separates Jews and Christians from each other, the unavoidable answer is: a Jew." This is the striking way the Jewish NT scholar, deeply engaged in dialogue with Christians, Pinchas Lapide begins his book on Christian-Jewish dialogue on Christology. He continues: "For almost two millennia, a pious, devoted Jew has stood between us, a Jew who wanted to bring the kingdom of heaven in harmony, concord, and peace — certainly not hatred, schism, let alone bloodshed."[1] Yet, during the past two millennia, another Jewish theologian, Susannah Heschel, reminds us, "Jews rejected the claim that Jesus fulfilled the messi-

1. P. Lapide, *Resurrection of Jesus,* p. 30.

anic prophecies of the Hebrew Bible, as well as the dogmatic claims about him made by the church fathers — that he was born of a virgin, the son of God, part of a divine Trinity, and was resurrected after his death."[2]

It is one of the grand ironies of Christian history that for the first eighteen hundred years or more, Jewish theologians by and large ignored Christianity and particularly its claim that Jesus is the Messiah. The irony is even sharper when, as Lapide remarks, there is no denying the existence of a "Hebrew gospel" in all four of the Christian Gospels as seen in vocabulary, grammar, and semantic patterns. Yet, we had to wait "till the twentieth century for more Hebrew literature about Jesus, written in the same land of Israel, by the descendants of the same sons of Israel who made up the original audience of all the sermons of the Nazarene."[3] At the same time, until that time, "Jews' perceptions of Jesus were predominantly disparaging."[4] The few writings by Jews on Jesus before that were mostly ignored by Christians, even in medieval Europe where Jewish-Christian disputations took place here and there. The most important early Jewish source on Christ, *Toldot Yeshu* (fifth or sixth century?),[5] radically alters the Gospel narratives and in general advances a highly polemical and mocking presentation. For example, Jesus' miracles are attributed to sorcery or other similarly forbidden sources. More irenic is the fifteenth-century examination of the Gospels by Profiat Duran, but at the same time, it argues forcefully that Jesus only called for adherence to Torah and refused to claim divinity. The genius of the argumentation of the leading medieval Jewish theologian, the thirteenth-century Moses Maimonides — routinely compared to Saint Thomas Aquinas in Christian tradition — is that not only Christianity but also Islam is part of the divine plan to prepare the world for the reception of the message of the biblical God. Maimonides' assessment of Jesus himself is less complimentary, as he regards the Nazarene as a "wicked heretic."[6]

In the rabbinical writings — highly formative for most brands of Jewish traditions — there is a definite and direct rebuttal of the claim to the di-

2. Susannah Heschel, "Jewish Views of Jesus," in *JWF,* p. 149.

3. P. Lapide, *Israelis, Jews, and Jesus,* pp. 3-4.

4. Cook, "Jewish Perspectives on Jesus," p. 215.

5. For contemporary significance of *Toldot Yeshu,* see Bammel, "Christian Origins in Jewish Tradition," pp. 317-35.

6. This paragraph is based on Heschel, "Jewish Views of Jesus," in *JWF,* pp. 149-51. For an informed discussion of three Jewish theologians of Christianity from three different time periods, namely, Menachem Ha Me'iri (d. 1315), Moses Mendelssohn (d. 1786), and Elijah Benamozegh (d. 1900), see chap. 3 in Kogan, *Opening the Covenant.*

vine Sonship of Jesus, "a blasphemy against the Jewish understanding of God." The Christian doctrines of the incarnation, atonement through the cross, and of course the Trinity, among others, "remained alien to normative Judaism and taboo to the rabbis."[7] That said, it is significant that even with the harshening of tone in later levels of Talmud, the opposition was less targeted against the historical figure of Jesus of Nazareth and more against what was considered to be the Pauline Christology and the subsequent patristic and creedal tradition. That became the focal point of opposition, at times even anger, among the formative Jewish writings.[8]

Somewhat similarly to early Muslim polemicists, medieval Jewish writers such as the legendary Rabbi Saadia Gaon (d. 942) in his famous "Book of Beliefs and Opinions" paid close attention to different christological traditions among different churches and came to the conclusion that it was impossible to arrive at a single, uniform picture of Jesus.[9] The subtext of this observation is of course not to highlight only the inconsistency of Christian theology of the Messiah but also its self-contradictory nature.

In the aftermath of the Enlightenment, and with the newly opening opportunities for Jews to participate in the wider European societies, interest in Jesus emerged, partly to help justify Judaism as a religion. Another famous Moses, namely, Mendelssohn, hence painted a picture of Jesus as a thoroughly Jewish religious figure, so much so that, "closely examined, everything is in complete agreement not only with Scripture, but also with the [Jewish] tradition."[10] Similarly influential nineteenth-century Jesus scholar Abraham Geiger[11] and the famous liberal rabbi of Stockholm, Sweden, Gottlieb Klein, at the turn of the twentieth century stressed the thoroughly Jewish nature of Jesus and his self-understanding.[12] Encouraged by the quest of the historical Jesus and classical liberalism's subsequent interest in the "real" Jesus, divorced from the layers of dogmatic and creedal traditions,

7. P. Lapide, *Israelis, Jews, and Jesus,* pp. 76-77.

8. P. Lapide, *Israelis, Jews, and Jesus,* p. 77.

9. See P. Lapide, *Israelis, Jews, and Jesus,* p. 86.

10. Mendelssohn, *Jerusalem,* p. 134, cited in Heschel, "Jewish Views of Jesus," in *JWF,* p. 151.

11. The contribution of one of the leading Jewish scholars is analyzed in Heschel, *Abraham Geiger and the Jewish Jesus.* Other prominent Jesus scholars include Heinrich Graetz, Levi Herzfeld, Joseph Derenbourg, Leo Baeck, Joseph Eschelbacher, and Felix Perles, among others, as listed in Heschel, "Jewish Views of Jesus," in *JWF,* p. 152.

12. See further, Hagner, *The Jewish Reclamation of Jesus;* Hagner, "Paul in Modern Jewish Thought."

the Jewish quest for Jesus as a Jew was energized. Different from the "Jewish Jesus" paradigm, the first modern study on Jesus written in Hebrew, by Joseph Klausner, *Jesus of Nazareth: His Life, Times, and Teaching,* presented him as a Pharisee who "departed the boundaries of Jewish nationhood, implying that Jews who reject Zionism, end up like Jesus, as Christians."[13]

There were two agendas or at least effects of the modern Jewish reclamation of Jesus. First, there was the task of correcting the mispresentation of earlier Jewish sources: "During late antiquity and the Middle Ages, Jews had commonly caricatured Jesus as a sorcerer who had attempted to beguile the Jewish people and lead them astray. The modern Jewish scholarly reassessment stripped away such earlier misconceptions, restored respectability to Jesus' image, and then reclaimed him as a Jew who merited a rightful place in Jewish literature alongside those of ancient Jewish sages."[14] Second, although the emphasis on Jesus' Jewishness was in keeping with the Christian quest, the Jewish search for the Jewish Jesus also wanted to develop "a counterhistory of the prevailing Christian theological version of Christianity's origins and influence."[15]

Among the Christian students of Jesus Christ, the recent decades have brought about an unprecedented interest in the Jewishness of Jesus, beginning with the first generation of the "New Perspective" in the 1970s. Conversely, it is remarkable that some contemporary Jewish scholars are now arguing that what happened with the rise of Christianity was not "the parting of ways" and that Judaism was not the "mother" religion out of which the younger religion emerged. Rather, both religions emerged simultaneously within the matrix of the Mediterranean world.[16]

Is Christology Inherently Anti-Semitic?

Anti-Semitism has a sad and long track record in Christian tradition. It goes all the way from the church fathers (John Chrysostom, Jerome, Augustine) to Reformers (Luther) to twentieth-century theologians (Karl Adam), and includes even the highest-ranking leaders such as numerous popes. "What one learns from this record is that subtle, powerful, essentially murderous

13. As paraphrased by Heschel, "Jewish Views of Jesus," in *JWF,* p. 156.
14. Cook, "Jewish Perspectives on Jesus," p. 224.
15. Heschel, "Jewish Views of Jesus," in *JWF,* p. 152.
16. Segal, *Rebecca's Children;* Becker and Reed, eds., *The Ways That Never Parted.*

inner-connections exist between Christian self-witness *and* theological derogation of Judaism *and* political oppression of Jews."[17] Alone, the destruction of Jerusalem by the Gentiles in 70 C.E. should have led Christians to reach out to their suffering Jewish brothers and sisters in sympathy and love — yet, it did not! In repentance and humility, coupled with sympathy and love for their Jewish brothers and sisters, the Christian church must take full responsibility for these violent acts and attitudes.

More than the acknowledgment of this sad history of violence against the Jews, there is a suspicion among many current Christian theologians that something in Christian faith makes it inherently anti-Semitic. Particularly Christology has been named as the source of that attitude. These thinkers consider the New Testament and the way Christian theology has interpreted it inherently anti-Semitic. The most vocal among those critics is the feminist Rosemary Radford Ruether, who wrote *Faith and Fratricide: The Theological Roots of Anti-Semitism.*[18] "Theologically, anti-Judaism developed as the left hand of christology."[19] Ruether wonders if it is possible to confess Jesus as Messiah without at the same time saying that "the Jews be damned."[20] She opines that because anti-Judaism is intimately intertwined with the christological hermeneutic of the early church, the only way to purge it is to radically reconceive Christology along two lines. First, faith in Jesus as the Christ must be understood as proleptic and anticipatory rather than final and fulfilled; and second, Christology must be understood paradigmatically rather than exclusivistically: "The cross and the resurrection are contextual to a particular historical community."[21] Hence, in this outlook, Jesus' paradigmatic role should be abandoned in order to avoid a supersessionist Christology.

Ruether's presuppositions and charges against the NT are sweeping and unnuanced, and ignore different types of christological trajectories and traditions and their complex and complicated development in the canon. A quick look at the conflicting and contradictory "results" of the tradition-historical criticism of the NT should make one hesitant in making sweeping

17. Idinopulos and Ward, "Is Christology Inherently Anti-Semitic?" pp. 194-95. According to P. Lapide (*Israelis, Jews, and Jesus,* p. 81), "In the period from the fourth to the sixteenth century no fewer than 106 popes and 92 Church councils issued anti-Jewish laws and regulations."

18. Ruether, *Faith and Fratricide;* chap. 2 focuses on the anti-Jewish materials in the NT.

19. Ruether, *To Change the World,* p. 31.

20. Ruether, *Faith and Fratricide,* p. 246.

21. Ruether, *To Change the World,* p. 43.

claims about causes of development of ideas! The Jewish scholar Thomas A. Idinopulos and the Christian Roy Bowen Ward carefully investigated Ruether's claims and concluded that "the appearance of anti-Judaic thought in certain documents in the New Testament does not lead to the conclusion that anti-Judaism is necessarily the left hand of Christology." They looked carefully at the parable of the vineyard in Mark 12, which Ruether considers a showcase for inherent anti-Jewishness and the beginning of anti-Semitism in the NT, and they come to contest Ruether's interpretation.[22] A critical investigation of the seemingly most anti-Jewish passage in the Pauline corpus, 1 Thessalonians 2:14-16 ("the Jews, who killed both the Lord Jesus and the prophets"), another key passage for Ruether, similarly does not support her reasoning. First of all, the interpretation of that passage is full of problems and unanswered questions of which Ruether seems to be ignorant. One of her omissions is that in the Thessalonian correspondence Paul is talking to a Gentile audience rather than to the Jews; in Romans, Paul clarifies in no uncertain terms his understanding of the continuing special status granted to the chosen people. Idinopulos and Ward conclude:

> It is difficult to understand how Ruether can conclude that "Judaism for Paul is not only *not* an ongoing covenant of salvation where men continue to be related in true worship of God: it never was such a community of faith and grace." It is only Gentiles, not Jews, that Paul characterized as those who "knew not God." Paul himself boasts of his Jewishness and can even say that "as to righteousness under the law [he was] blameless" (Phil 3:6). He never says that Judaism was a false worship of God; rather, he claims that a new righteousness has been revealed (Rom 1:17; 3:21; 10:3) which causes him to move into a new phase in the history of salvation. Nor does his acceptance of the gospel lead him to deny the holiness of the law (Rom 7:12) nor the election of the Jews (Rom 11:28). It is difficult to see how Paul is any more anti-Judaic than other Jewish sectarians such as those at Qumran, who like Paul, believed that God was doing a new thing in the history of salvation. Unlike the Qumran sectarians who expected the destruction of "Mainstream" Jews (whom the sectarians considered apostate), Paul hoped for/expected the salvation of all Israel (Rom 11:26).[23]

22. Idinopulos and Ward, "Is Christology Inherently Anti-Semitic?" p. 196.

23. Idinopulos and Ward, "Is Christology Inherently Anti-Semitic?" pp. 198-99; citation in the text from Ruether, *Faith and Fratricide,* p. 104.

There is also an important difference between the time prior to and the time following the destruction of Jerusalem in 70 C.E., which according to common theological wisdom has to do with the worsening relations between the Christian church and the Jews. Whereas in the earlier part of the NT ("earlier" in time of writing), such as most of the Pauline correspondence, there is very little in terms of attributing the death of Jesus to Jews, in the Christian writings after the disaster, motivated by Christians' desire to distance themselves from the Jews and so show evidence of alliance with Rome, the tone gets harsher. The apocryphal *Gospel of Peter* relates the crucifixion in a way that basically removes the Romans from the scene and leaves the responsibility for it to the Jews.[24] Even if the nuances of this common interpretation may be debated, it cannot be ignored as Ruether does. Yet another historical observation has to be considered before charging the birth of anti-Semitism to the NT; it is that anti-Jewish attitudes precede Christianity. The Jewish thinker Salo Baron speaks for many when he states the commonplace fact that "almost every note in the cacophony of medieval and modern anti-Semitism was sounded by the chorus of ancient writers."[25] This is of course not to absolve Christians of the guilt of anti-Semitism, far from that. But it is to put the question under consideration in perspective.

In criticizing the unnuanced attribution of anti-Jewish attitudes to the NT, I do not deny the "hardening of attitudes"[26] toward the Jews in Matthew nor the quite negative presentation of the Jews in the Gospel of John (however the dating of these documents goes). This criticism of Jewish people, usually their religious leaders, must be put in proper perspective. The Matthean critique of the Jewish people, especially in chapter 23, is not necessarily different from nor untypical of the harsh criticism of one Jewish group by another Jewish group at the time.[27] Even when the whole people is addressed, usually the target of the criticism is the religious and/or political leadership that is deviating from the will of God.

The NT scholar Raymond Brown reminds us that at first "there was

24. So, e.g., Pearson, "I Thessalonians 2:13-16," pp. 79-94; see also Idinopulos and Ward, "Is Christology Inherently Anti-Semitic?" p. 199.

25. Baron, *A Social and Religious History of the Jews*, p. 194, cited in Idinopulos and Ward, "Is Christology Inherently Anti-Semitic?" p. 200. For a careful discussion of anti-Semitism before Christianity and its continuation apart from Christianity, see Flannery, *The Anguish of the Jews*.

26. Ruether, *Faith and Fratricide*, p. 75.

27. R. E. Brown, *Introduction to the New Testament*, p. 222; for a detailed discussion, see L. T. Johnson, "New Testament's Anti-Jewish Slander," pp. 419-41.

nothing anti-Jewish in depicting the role of the Jewish authorities in his death: for Jesus and his disciples on one side and the Jerusalem Sanhedrin authorities on the other were all Jews." Only later was the passion narrative "'heard' in an anti-Jewish way." The change into the predominantly Gentile composition of the church of course was a main factor here.[28] Brown also remarks that a careful comparison of the Gospel narratives of crucifixion oscillates between making the Romans (Gentiles) responsible for and executors of crucifixion, and blaming the Jewish authorities.[29] Hence, it is an unfounded charge by Ruether that John's Gospel makes the blame of the Jews "very close to what will become the charge of 'deicide,'"[30] namely, that the Jews are "murderers" of God's Son — even though that accusation became a commonplace throughout history in the mouths of Christians!

The American Lutheran theologian Carl E. Braaten warns that, as an overreaction to compensate for the long history of anti-Semitism such as that found in Ruether, Christian theology now "relativizes the gospel down to one of many ways of salvation, that surrenders the exclusive place of Christ in doing 'theology after Auschwitz,' and that lays the blame of hatred of the Jews on a so-called [Christian] *theological* anti-Semitism."[31] In Braaten's estimation Ruether ends up "throwing out the christological baby with the anti-Judaic bath in Christian tradition."[32]

Has the Messiah Come?

Moltmann aptly sets the stage for contemporary consideration of the role and meaning of Messiah between these two religions: "The gospels understand his [Jesus Christ's] whole coming and ministry in the contexts of Israel's messianic hope. Yet it is the very same messianic hope which apparently makes it impossible for 'all Israel' to see Jesus as being already the messiah."[33] Hence, every Christian theology of Christ should seek to consider and respond, if possible, to the Jewish no to the NT Messiah. The re-

28. R. E. Brown, *Introduction to the New Testament,* pp. 166-67.

29. R. E. Brown, *Introduction to the New Testament,* p. 39; see also R. E. Brown, *Death of the Messiah,* pp. 388, 396, 831-39.

30. Ruether, *Faith and Fratricide,* p. 114.

31. Braaten, "Introduction," p. 23. It is significant that this statement is part of his introduction to the Jewish writer P. Lapide's book on resurrection.

32. Braaten, "Introduction," p. 23.

33. Moltmann, *Way of Jesus Christ,* p. 28.

sponse of contemporary Jewish counterparts is understandable in light of the vastly differing views of messianism as discussed above in relation to Second Temple Judaism and the first Christians. Martin Buber formulated the Jewish objection in 1933 in dialogue with the NT scholar Karl-Ludwig Schmidt:

> We know more deeply, more truly, that world history has not been turned upside down to its very foundations — that the world is not yet redeemed. We *sense* its unredeemedness. The church can, or indeed must, understand this sense of ours as the awareness that *we* are not redeemed. But we know that that is not it. The redemption of the world is for us indivisibly one with the perfecting of creation, with the establishment of the unity which nothing more prevents, the unity which is no longer controverted, and which is realized in all the protean variety of the world. Redemption is one with the kingdom of God in its fulfillment. An anticipation of any single part of the *completed* redemption of the world . . . is something we cannot grasp, although even for us in our mortal hours redeeming and redemption are heralded. . . . We are aware of no centre in history — only its goal, the goal of the way taken by the God who does not linger on his way.[34]

Many other Jewish thinkers have expressed the same sentiment. In the words of Schalom Ben-Chorin, the Jewish mind is "profoundly aware of the unredeemed character of the world," which means that the "whole of redemption" has not yet taken place since the Messiah has not yet arrived.[35] Behind the Jewish no to the Christian claim for the arrival of the Messiah is hence a different kind of concept of redemption. Rightly or wrongly, the Jewish theology considers the Christian version of redemption "happening in the spiritual sphere, and in what is invisible,"[36] whereas for the Jewish hopes, it is the transformation happening in the most visible and concrete ways, including the removal of all evil.

34. Buber, *Der Jude und Sein Judentum,* p. 562, cited in Moltmann, *Way of Jesus Christ,* pp. 28-29. See also Buber, "The Two Foci of the Jewish Soul," pp. 28-40. For an informed discussion of Buber's views in this respect by a contemporary Jewish theologian, see Kogan, *Opening the Covenant,* pp. 90-95.

35. Ben-Chorin, *Die Antwort des Jona,* p. 99, cited in Moltmann, *Way of Jesus Christ,* p. 30.

36. Scholem, "Zum Verständnis der messianischen Idee," p. 7, cited in Moltmann, *Way of Jesus Christ,* p. 30.

Without downplaying, and certainly not dismissing, this profound difference in understanding of what the coming of Messiah and the ensuing redemption mean, Moltmann poses the question to the Jewish counterpart that needs to be asked here. This is the "Gentile" question to the Jews: "*[E]ven before* the world has been redeemed so as to become the direct and universal rule of God, can God already have a chosen people, chosen moreover *for the purpose of this redemption?*" Furthermore: "Does Israel's election not destroy Israel's solidarity with the unredeemed humanity, even if the election is meant in a representative sense?" All this boils down, says Moltmann, to the simple and profound query: "can one already be *a Jew* in this Godless world?"[37] Another important counterquestion — or, more irenically: invitation to mutual dialogue — has to do with the one-sided, if not reductionistic, interpretation by Jewish theology of the Christian hope for redemption. As will be discussed in detail in the section on many dimensions of redemption and reconciliation, Christian theology is not bound to limit redemption only to the inner personal and invisible notion. Christian eschatological hope, focused on the crucified and risen Messiah who now rules with the Father and Spirit, includes the total transformation of the world, a foretaste of which has already come in this messianic age.[38] Yes, regarding the expectation and totality, a difference still continues: whereas the Jewish theology discerns the coming of Messiah as the fulfillment of all hopes for redemption, Christian tradition — slowly and painfully, as the NT eschatology shows — came to understand the coming of Messiah in two stages. That difference must be acknowledged and honored but doesn't have to form a block to continuing dialogue.

Is the idea of God taking human form absolutely unknown to Jewish faith? While most Jews think so, some current theologians are willing to look for parallels such as "God walking in the garden" (Gen. 3:8), or the Lord appearing to Abraham in the form of the angel sharing a meal (Gen. 18), or Jacob's wrestling match with a man of whom he says, "I have seen God face to face" (Gen. 32:24, 30), or Israelite leaders under Moses claiming that they "saw the God of Israel" on the mountain (Exod. 24:9-11). The Jewish scholar Michael S. Kogan draws a conclusion from these kinds of texts: "For Jewish believers, then, the thought may come to mind that, if God can take human form in a series of accounts put forward in one's own sacred texts, one would be unjustified in dismissing out of hand the possibility that the same God

37. Moltmann, *Way of Jesus Christ,* p. 30.

38. See further, Moltmann, *Way of Jesus Christ,* pp. 30-32.

might act in a similar fashion in accounts put forward in another text revered as sacred by a closely related tradition."[39] This is of course not to push the similarities too far; the differences are obvious, particularly in light of Christian creedal traditions that speak of the permanent "personal" (hypostatic) union of the human and divine in one particular person, Jesus of Nazareth. But it is to point to the possibility for early Christians to make such claims while still not leaving behind the confession of faith in the unity of the God of Israel.

Over the resurgence of interest in Jesus among Jewish scholars and the heightened Christian interest in the Jewishness of Jesus looms large the shadow of the horrors and crimes of the Holocaust.[40] It is a continuing task for Christian theology to more fully understand how it was ever possible for such a horrendous ethos to develop in "Christian" soil. What Christian theology in general and Christology in particular must resist is any notion of imperialism, whether in terms of political hegemony and crimes against the Jewish people as under the Nazi regime, or in terms of "realized eschatology" claiming the eschatological glory and rule already now. The Messiah confessed in Christian theology is the crucified one "who heals through his wounds and is victorious through his sufferings . . . the Lamb of God, not yet the Lion of Judah."[41] This kind of "theology of the cross" makes it possible for Christian theology to tolerate and appreciate the Jewish no rather than assuming, as has happened in Christian history, that God has abandoned the people of Israel because of their reluctance to acknowledge the Messiah.

> The Christian "yes" to Jesus' messiahship, which is based on believed and experienced reconciliation, will therefore accept the Jewish "no," which is based on the experienced and suffered unredeemedness of the world; and the "yes" will in so far adopt the "no" as to talk about the total and universal redemption of the world only in the dimensions of a future hope, and a present contradiction of this unredeemed world. The

39. Kogan, *Opening the Covenant*, p. 115. For a highly promising and constructive essay on Jewish views of incarnation, see Wolfson, "Judaism and Incarnation," pp. 239-53.

40. For the role of Christian theology behind the events leading to the Holocaust, see Klein, *Anti-Judaism in Christian Theology*. For a historical and theological account, see also Idinopulos, "Christianity and the Holocaust," pp. 257-67. See also the important essay by Greenberg, "Judaism, Christianity, and Partnership after the Twentieth Century," pp. 25-35.

41. Moltmann, *Way of Jesus Christ*, p. 32.

> Christian "yes" to Jesus Christ is therefore not in itself finished and complete. It is open for the messianic future of Jesus. . . . This means that it cannot be an excluding and excommunicating "yes," not even when it is uttered with the certainty of faith.[42]

A systematic account of the redemption in Christ and its rejection by the people of the Messiah needs to be worked out in the context of the doctrine of reconciliation. Similarly, in the context of ecclesiology, the relation of the Christian church to Israel and the question of the continuing legitimacy of the rightly configured mission to Israel have to be investigated in detail.

A dialogue about Messiah and other corollary christological issues between Christians and Jews is meaningful only if there is mutual trust to allow both parties to represent their positions faithfully.[43] The challenge to the Jewish faith is to stop "constructing Jewish conceptions of Jesus . . . and try to confront Christian claims about him as we [Jews] actually hear them from Christians." That said, it is also important for Christian theologians to acknowledge that the "Jews . . . cannot and should not see Jesus through the eyes of Christian faith, but . . . try to understand that faith in the light of" their own.[44] This does not mean that the Jews do not have the right to comment on Christian doctrines and views of Jesus; yes, they do. That is an opportunity also for Christians to learn more about their own faith. Nor does this mean that Christians should refrain from presenting Jesus as the Messiah to all men and women, Gentiles as well as Jews. Similarly, Jewish counterparts should be granted the same right to defend their no to Christian interpretation.

Only such an encounter may also open up new ways of looking for thematic and material parallels in the midst of foundational differences. A patient, common search of both real differences and potential common themes does not necessarily promise "results" but is a process to which all believers, regardless of religion, are called. This is wonderfully represented in the following statement from the Jewish theologian Michael S. Kogan:

42. Moltmann, *Way of Jesus Christ,* pp. 32-33.

43. My uneasiness with Christian theologians, as well informed as they are about Jewish theology and the conditions of the dialogue, such as Clark Williamson *(A Guest in the House of Israel),* is the turn to "low Christology" (in this case, building on the process tradition), which is not in keeping with the mainline Christian tradition and thus, in my mind, does not represent well a Christian position.

44. Kogan, *Opening the Covenant,* p. 112.

> But Jews do not ask Christians in the dialogue to give up core doctrines. How would Jews respond if Christians who have problems with Zionism demanded that Jews give up the theological claim that God has given us the land of Israel? . . . [T]he divine bestowal of the Holy Land is a core doctrine of Israelite faith that cannot be given up for the sake of the dialogue or to suit anyone's preferences. . . . Similarly, the incarnation and resurrection are essential experiences of Christian faith. In Christ the transcendent God comes down to earth as, in the gift of land to God's people, the Holy One acts in the world and its history. These doctrines are parallel concretizations of the divine activity crucial to the respective faiths.[45]

Jesus in Light of Islamic Interpretations

Vatican II's *Nostra Aetate* sums up the general Muslim perception of Jesus: "Though they do not acknowledge Jesus as God, they revere Him as a prophet. They also honor Mary, His virgin Mother; at times they even call on her with devotion."[46] That said, Christian-Muslim relations are plagued — and hopefully enriched — by a number of ironies. "It is a curious fact of history that whilst Muhammad has been frequently criticized in western and Christian writings, Muslims hold the central figure of Christianity in high esteem." Not only that, but "Islam is the only religion other than Christianity that *requires* its adherents to commit to a position on the identity of Jesus"![47] Indeed, "[in] the Islamic tradition, Jesus ('Isa) was a Muslim,"[48] which accounts for titles such as *The Muslim Jesus*[49] for an anthology of sayings and stories about Jesus in Islamic tradition.

One would imagine, then, a deep mutual interest in the meaning of Jesus Christ. However, "The question of Christ's image has been a sensitive one in the history of Christian-Muslim apologetics and dialogue. One might ask

45. Kogan, *Opening the Covenant,* p. 102. In another context Kogan (p. 111) adds: "the dialogue ought not to require either participant faith to dismantle itself or to deny age-old core beliefs. We have inherited symbols, concepts, and creeds that tell us who we are and how we fit into the divine scheme of things."

46. *Nostra Aetate* #3.

47. Gregory A. Barker and Stephen E. Gregg, "Muslim Perceptions of Jesus: Key Issues," in *JBC,* p. 83.

48. Meshal and Pirbhai, "Islamic Perspectives on Jesus," p. 232.

49. Khalidi, *The Muslim Jesus.*

whether it has ever been a real issue for dialogue. Most attempted dialogue in this field has been overruled by an apologetic or polemical bias on both sides." This is the way the Norwegian Islamist and Christian theologian Oddbjørn Leirvik begins his important study *Images of Jesus Christ in Islam.*[50] Behind this uneasiness is the principle of the "self-sufficiency" of the Islamic canonical tradition (Qur'an and Hadith). It simply is the case that the Islamic tradition presents a radically different picture of Jesus Christ.[51] That both the canonical tradition and the rich and variegated later commentary tradition speak of Jesus Christ so much[52] can of course potentially build a bridge. But because that tradition paints such a remarkably different portrait of the personhood and theological meaning of the Christian Savior, the dialogue becomes an utterly challenging exercise. Not surprisingly, many observers seriously doubt if any "practical results" can come from this dialogue.[53]

The ambiguity about Jesus has characterized Muslim-Christian exchange from the beginning.[54] There were problems on both sides. On the Christian polemical side, from the beginning of the encounter a handful of arguments have persisted, often used in an uncritical and unnuanced manner against any Muslim interpretation of Jesus: (1) What the Qur'an says of

50. Leirvik, *Images of Jesus Christ in Islam,* p. 1.

51. Leirvik, *Images of Jesus Christ in Islam,* p. 1. Behind the Muslim reluctance to consider the Christian view of Christ is also the widespread deep suspicion that Christians let the emperor formulate and corrupt the gospel and Christology.

52. There are roughly 100 references or allusions to Jesus in the Qur'an. A detailed listing and discussion can be found in Cragg, *Jesus and the Muslim,* chap. 2; a useful, thematic summary of these can be found in Leirvik, *Images of Jesus Christ in Islam,* pp. 20-24. The main titles assigned to Jesus in the Qur'an are Īsā (16 times), each time linked with *ibn Maryam,* the son of Mary; Christ/Messiah (11), messenger (3). Other attributes include servant, prophet, word, spirit. Leirvik, p. 23.

53. Balić, "Image of Jesus in Contemporary Islamic Theology," p. 7.

54. For the purposes of this discussion, there is no way to go into detail about differing Islamic schools (Sunni, Shi'ite, and Sufi, to name the most obvious ones). What makes this more general discussion more justified is that generally speaking the two main traditions, Sunni and Shi'ite, speak in a fairly similar way of Jesus Christ. That has to do with especially the earlier commentators, classical Muslim theologians, whose works are still immensely important. If there is any difference, it has to do with the fact that in comparison with the Sunnite commentators, the Shi'ites usually are less comfortable with the idea of the uniqueness of Jesus. See further, N. Robinson, *Christ in Islam and Christianity,* pp. 176, 191. For specifically Shi'ite interpretations, see, e.g., Leirvik, *Images of Jesus Christ in Islam,* chap. 4; Robinson, chap. 7 (which also includes the Sufi views) and chap. 16. The major differences can be found between main schools and Sufi; for that see, e.g., Leirvik, chap. 5.

Jesus is hopelessly distorted. (2) There are clear mistakes in the Qur'anic presentation of Jesus. (3) Muhammad received much of his information from heretical or otherwise suspect sources. (4) Some elements of the Qur'anic presentations of Christ are more "Christian" than Muslims suppose, including pointers to Jesus' divinity and the affirmation of his death on the cross.[55] A typical Muslim engagement for a long time was to add to the existing references in the Qur'an and Hadith mainly on the basis of Christian legends and Gospel materials, including gospels not ratified by Christians, especially the *Gospel of Barnabas,* whose influence even today is immense in anti-Christian polemics.[56] This development culminated in the mystical Sufi spirituality and continues. Some contemporary Muslim theologians have also utilized historical-critical tools of NT studies to discredit key christological beliefs.[57]

Although a serious dialogue has to acknowledge and carefully weigh these kinds of challenges, the reasons for continuing and deepening Muslim-Christian dialogue are integrally related to the matrix of both traditions. In this exchange more is at stake than just the need to make pedagogical contact for the sake of better relations:

- Christology is the heart of Christian theology, and must be taken seriously as a central point of reference in the self-understanding of the church. For the church, there is a need continually to rethink the question of Christology in an Islamic context — as part of the more general task of a contextualized theology.
- Christology is in fact dealt with as an issue from the Muslim side — both in Muslim polemics, medieval and modern, and in more dialogical contributions from Muslims.
- Christology is not an isolated subject, but touches upon fundamental issues in anthropology and theology as well as in ethics. This is true both for Christians and, in a different sense, for Muslims.[58]

55. These are conveniently listed and discussed in detail in N. Robinson, *Christ in Islam and Christianity,* chap. 2.

56. For a useful discussion, see Leirvik, *Images of Jesus Christ in Islam,* pp. 132-44.

57. See further, Leirvik, *Images of Jesus Christ in Islam,* p. 2.

58. Leirvik, *Images of Jesus Christ in Islam,* p. 222.

On the Conditions of a Dialogue

In many ways it is not fair nor useful to compare Jesus Christ to Muhammad. First of all, even though Christ is of course named a "prophet"[59] in the Qur'an, it is Muhammad who is the "seal of the prophets" and thus occupies a unique role. That said, unlike Christian faith, which is determined by belief in Christ, Islam is not based on Muhammad but rather on Qur'an and Allah. Neither Christ nor Muhammad in Islamic interpretation is divine; only God is.[60] The closest parallel to Christ in Islamic faith could be found in Christ's role as the living Word of God, in relation to the divine revelation of the Qur'an.[61] (In the dialogue between Islam, Christianity, and Judaism, a topic well worth careful consideration would be whether not only the Qur'an and the Word but also the Jewish Torah would function as parallels.)[62] However, in the Hadith collections a number of sayings seek to clarify the relation between Muhammad and Jesus. Among them is the important, oft-quoted, and highly respectful statement by Muhammad of Jesus: "Prophets are brothers in faith, having different mothers. Their religion is, however, one and there is no Apostle between us (between me and Jesus Christ)."[63] As is well known, Muhammad's own relation to Christianity and Christian tradition in general, especially in the early phases of his career, was fairly positive and constructive.[64]

Because neither the person nor the work of Christ is in any way as cen-

59. It may be significant that in the Sunni Hadith collection Bukhārī, which almost gained canonical status, most of the references to Jesus occur in "The Prophets" *(Kitāb al-anbiyā')*.

60. In some strands of Islam, particularly in the esoteric Sufism, the veneration of Muhammad goes way beyond the established tradition, making him not only an embodiment of "Perfect Man" but also a carrier of divine light and expression of divine attributes. In the popular cult of this tradition, no less than 201 names of Muhammad play a central part (cf. 99 beautiful names of Allah). See further, Leirvik, *Images of Jesus Christ in Islam*, p. 47.

61. Hence the heading "The 'Christ of Islam' Is the Koran," in Imbach, *Three Faces of Jesus*, p. 87. See further, Balić, "Image of Jesus in Contemporary Islamic Theology," p. 1.

62. "Torah and Christ are both seen, respectively, as Word of God." Kogan, *Opening the Covenant*, p. 31.

63. Shahih Muslim, *Kitāb al-Fadā'il*, book 30, chap. 37, quoted in Leirvik, *Images of Jesus Christ in Islam*, p. 38. For sayings clarifying the relation between Muhammad and Jesus, see Leirvik, pp. 37-38.

64. For a useful discussion, see N. Robinson, *Christ in Islam and Christianity*, chap. 4.

tral to Islam as it is to Christianity, the portrayal of Jesus in the Qur'an is set in a different context.[65] Jesus is put in the line of a number of OT prophets beginning with Moses and Abraham. Furthermore, Mary's role is much more prominent in the Qur'anic presentation. Both of the two main suras that contain the most references to Jesus, 3 and 19, are named after Mary.[66] Even the fact that Jesus is a miracle-worker in the Qur'an, unlike Muhammad, does not imply that therefore he should be lifted up higher than the Prophet of Islam; the miracles wrought by Jesus are similar to those performed by Moses and other such forerunners of Muhammad.[67] In other words, the most the miracles can do for Jesus is to confirm his prophetic status; they cannot confirm his divinity.[68] Even the fact that Jesus is described as sinless in Hadith and legendary tradition whereas it is not quite certain if Muhammad is — although in the Shi'ite tradition all imams are! — does not make Jesus superior.

Along with post-Enlightenment Christian theology's heightened focus on the humanity of Jesus Christ vis-à-vis the divinity in tradition, contemporary Muslim interpreters of Jesus Christ have similarly come to appreciate the humanity in a more profound sense. Of course, Muslims never did interpret Jesus Christ as divine; however, in the Middle Ages, Muslim thinkers often bore a more elevated picture of Jesus as a prophet. The Pakistani-born bishop of the Church of England Michael Nazir-Ali makes the pointed remark that many of the traditional and contemporary Islamic Christologies seem to find a lot in common with Christian interpretations of Jesus that work with "low Christology," basically reducing Jesus' significance to his role as a human person.[69] The American Jesus Seminar's view of Jesus would be an example.

65. That said, there are a number of parallels between the two "founders" of religions as carefully delineated in N. Robinson, *Christ in Islam and Christianity,* chap. 5. For a standard, masterful study, see Parrinder, *Jesus in the Qur'an.*

66. "The House of Imrān" (Mary's father's house; sura 3) and "Maryam" (sura 19).

67. The early and medieval Muslim polemics paid special attention to Jesus' miracles and sought to relativize their value by comparing them to similar kinds of acts of other prophets. Particular attention in this exercise was given to those OT miracles that had to do with command of nature, transformation of objects such as the budding of Moses' rod, and restoration to life as performed by Elijah and Elisha. The end result of this polemical reasoning was that Christians' taking the miracles of Jesus as an indication of divinity would lead to assigning similar status to many other prophets. D. Thomas, "Miracles of Jesus," p. 229; the whole essay is a most useful discussion of this topic.

68. See D. Thomas, "Miracles of Jesus," p. 240.

69. Nazir-Ali, *Frontiers in Muslim-Christian Encounter,* p. 25.

Of course, the Qur'an contains nothing like the NT Gospel narratives. Instead, there are a number of references to key events in Jesus' life from conception to earthly ministry to death/resurrection to his eschatological future (the last theme is dealt with in much more detail in Hadith tradition). The eschatological allusions are hardly clear, yet they are highly meaningful to both religions. Especially 4:159 is open to many interpretations, depending on how one interprets the events of the cross and resurrection, which we will discuss below in the context of the work of Christ.

The only title that is uniquely reserved for Jesus in the Muslim tradition is Messiah (e.g., 4:171). It is, however, difficult to determine the distinctively Islamic interpretation of that term. It is significant that the same sura that calls Jesus "Messiah" also names him as "a spirit from Him" (God, obviously). Christian theology has been aware of and interested in Muslim interpretations of this important passage; John of Damascus of the seventh century, in the last chapter of *De Haeresibus (On the Heresies)*, discusses this passage.[70]

In Christian tradition, of course, Messiah, the Anointed One, is integrally connected with the Spirit of God. As said, the connection, if any, in Muslim tradition is an unresolved question. What is clear is the direct linking in the Qur'an with the life-giving power of creation (as in connection with Adam in 15:29). "Christ himself is seen as a creation of the life-giving spirit, but at the same time as a privileged vehicle of the spirit, aided by the Holy Spirit in his mighty signs (2.253)."[71] Although it would be tempting to read these and similar descriptions, which have clear Christian parallels, through the lens of Christian theology, the warning by the Finnish NT scholar Heikki Räisänen is worth hearing: "The Qur'an must be explained by the Qur'an and not by anything else." Hence, in the Qur'anic interpretation, "Jesus became an example and a precursor of Muhammad, a guarantor of Muhammad's message who had experienced similar things."[72] Ultimately, the highest status granted to Jesus in the Qur'an is the "highest" predecessor of Muhammad — something like the Baptist to Jesus himself![73]

70. The last chapter of *De Haeresibus* (100/101) is unusually long. See further, Merrill, "John of Damascus on Islam," pp. 88-89.

71. Leirvik, *Images of Jesus Christ in Islam,* p. 24. The highly influential thirteenth-century mystic Ibn al-Arabi's *Bezels of Wisdom,* a reflection on the twenty-seven perfect men mentioned in the Qur'an who achieved a unique realization of the divine, highlights the importance of the reception of Jesus, which makes him different from other human beings. Ibn-al-Arabi, *The Bezels of Wisdom,* pp. 174-79, cited in *JBC,* pp. 116-19.

72. Räisänen, "Portrait of Jesus in the Qur'an," p. 124.

73. See Leirvik, *Images of Jesus Christ in Islam,* pp. 29-30. So also N. Robinson,

That said, Räisänen cautiously finds parallels between some NT portraits of Jesus and Jesus in the Qur'an. The Lukan Christology with the focus on subordination of Jesus to God as exemplified in his voluntary submission under God's plan (Acts 2:22-23) and servanthood (Acts 3:13; 4:27) provides such parallels.[74]

A tempting way to try to ease the tension between two vastly different portraits of Jesus in these two religions would be to "water down" the NT account of Jesus — for the sake of the dialogue. The classic work in Christian-Muslim relations by Kenneth Cragg, *The Call of the Minaret,* warns of that orientation. It recommends that for the sake of a genuine dialogue, Christians should present Jesus to Muslims in the fullness of his personality as it is revealed in the Gospels.[75] This means that Christians are required to present Jesus to Muslims in the fullness of both his humanity and his divinity. "To concentrate only on elements in Jesus that Muslims can at once accept is to fail Jesus himself," Cragg asserts.[76] Thus, to be content with only Jesus the prophet-teacher would not do justice to the Muslim's need.[77] Beginning with the NT narrative of Jesus helps Muslims experience Jesus as did the first disciples. Of course, "A simple reassertion of the Christian doctrine of Christ will not suffice," without a conscious effort to face honestly the difficulties Muslims face in trying to understand the Christian interpretation.[78]

For the sake of a fruitful dialogue, both parties face the challenge. Here the recommendation from the Roman Catholic Hans Küng is worth following. Beginning from the narrative of the historical Jesus of the Gospels, he reminds us of the need to acknowledge the difference between Christian and Islamic interpretations. He advises Christians not to read Christian mean-

---

Christ in Islam and Christianity, p. 40; Robinson (p. 37) rightly reminds us that "the Qur'anic representation of Jesus serves to legitimise Muhammad by giving the impression that he was doing what Jesus had done before him." Qur'an 61:14 is a striking example of this.

74. Räisänen, "Portrait of Jesus in the Qur'an," p. 127. Where Räisänen's argumentation seems much weaker is the contrasting of Luke with the presentation of Jesus by John, the latter allegedly focusing mostly on the preexistent Christ and identification with God. True, those themes are more robustly present in John, but at the same time, the Johannine Christology also contains many features that speak of voluntary submission and subordination, such as talk about "my God and your God" (John 20:17). See further, Leirvik, *Images of Jesus Christ in Islam,* pp. 28-29.

75. Cragg, *Call of the Minaret,* pp. 258-60.

76. Cragg, *Call of the Minaret,* p. 258.

77. Cragg, *Call of the Minaret,* p. 259.

78. Cragg, *Call of the Minaret,* p. 258.

ings into the Qur'an: "The Qur'an should be interpreted *from the standpoint of the Qur'an,* not from that of the New Testament or the Council of Nicaea or Jungian psychology. For the Qur'an, Jesus is a prophet, a great prophet, like Abraham, Noah, and Moses — but nothing more. And just as in the New Testament John the Baptist is Jesus' precursor, so in the Qur'an Jesus is the precursor — and highly encouraging example — for Muhammad."[79]

On the other hand, Küng advises Muslims to evaluate Jesus on the basis of the historical sources of the Gospels: "If we on the Christian side make an effort to reevaluate Muhammad on the basis of Islamic sources, especially the Qur'an, we also hope that for their part the Muslims will eventually be prepared to move toward *a reevaluation of Jesus of Nazareth on the basis of historical sources* (namely the Gospels) as many Jews have already been doing."[80] The implication that the Qur'an gives a faulty picture of Jesus, however, is a deeply troubling challenge to devout Muslims. It goes way beyond the unwillingness to reconsider one's own interpretative framework. A leading Muslim thinker, the American-based Seyyed Hossein Nasr, in dialogue with Küng, made this point in a most pointed way: "To suggest that the Qur'ān had the wrong Christology makes absolutely impossible any dialogue with Islam. . . . It must always be remembered that for Muslims the Qur'ān, the whole Qur'ān, and not only parts of it, is the Word of God."[81] Against Küng's historical interpretation of Muhammad's prophecy, Nasr says, "One should be very clear on this point and on the role of the Prophet in the process of the revelation of the Sacred Text. It is because of this Islamic belief in the nature of the Qur'ān as the direct Word of God that any consideration of the Prophet of Islam as having learnt this view of sacred history and Christology from Jewish and Christian sources is the greatest blasphemy in the eyes of Muslims."[82]

79. Küng, *Christianity and World Religions,* p. 110, emphasis in original.

80. Küng, *Christianity and World Religions,* p. 111, emphasis in original. Küng considers the image of Jesus in the Qur'an incomplete and different from the historical Jesus of the Gospels. "The portrait of Jesus in the Qur'ān is all one-sided, too monotone, and for the most part lacking in content, apart from monotheism, the call to repentance, and various accounts of miracles." Küng, "Christianity and World Religions," p. 88. I am indebted to my student Reda Samuel for this reference.

81. Nasr, "Response to Hans Küng's Paper," p. 100. For Küng's contribution to the public debate held at George Washington University in 1984, see *Muslim World* 77 (1987).

82. Nasr, "Response to Hans Küng's Paper," p. 99.

The Divinity of Jesus

The proper way to begin to consider the deity of Jesus in Islam is with a reminder of the foundational belief in Islam that Muhammad is not divine but human. The poem of the thirteenth-century Egyptian Al-Busiri, *Qasidah Burdah,* makes the point in a polemical way:

> Renounce what the Christians claim concerning their prophet,
> Then praise him [Prophet Muhammad] as you will, and with all your heart.
> For although he was of human nature,
> He was the best of humanity without exception.[83]

A contemporary Muslim scholar sets the question of the divine Sonship and deity of Jesus in proper perspective: "Jesus the 'Christ,' the 'eternal logos,' the 'Word made flesh,' the 'Only Begotten Son of God' and second person of the trinity has been the barrier separating the two communities [Muslims and Christians]."[84] This judgment is consonant with Muslim tradition going back to the beginning. Take one example from the highly respected twelfth-century medieval figure al-Ghazali: in his celebrated *Ninety-nine Beautiful Names of God,* he bluntly speaks of "errors" of Christians who say of ʿIsa (Jesus) that "he is God." Saying this is similar to looking into the mirror and imagining that the colors seen are the colors of the mirror itself![85]

When investigating this issue, it is hard to establish exactly how much early Muslim thinkers knew of the details of established orthodox tradition when they began to engage Christian claims about Jesus and the Trinity.[86] On the Christian side, the first Christian writer to discuss Islam, John of Damascus (d. 749), in *dār al-islām* showed an extensive understanding of Islam and its main beliefs. Two of John's writings contain an account of Islam: "The Heresy of the Ishmaelites," in his *De Haeresibus (On Heresies),* and *Disputatio Saraceni et Christiani (Dialogue with a Saracen).*[87] One striking

83. Al-Busiri, *Qasidah Burdah,* chap. 3, lines 29-32, trans. Abdal Hakim Murad, cited in *JBC,* p. 115.

84. Ayoub, "Jesus the Son of God," p. 65.

85. In *JBC,* p. 111.

86. A common Muslim assessment is this: "It is hardly necessary to argue that neither the Qur'ān nor early Muslim traditionists were aware of the theological doctrines of the church fathers and church councils in their debate with Christians, but they were aware of Christian piety, liturgy, and worship" (Ayoub, "Jesus the Son of God," p. 66).

87. English translations of these texts were first published by Rev. John W. Voorhis

point in John's account is his perception of the Qur'anic Christology. In *On Heresies* John shows an accurate awareness of the Qur'an's portrait of Jesus. He knew well what the Qur'an affirms about Christ, such as that "Christ is a Word of God and His Spirit" (4:169), that Christ "was born without seed from Mary, the sister of Moses and Aaron" (19:29), and that Christ is "a prophet and a servant of God" (43:59). John was also aware of the Qur'an's denial of Jesus' crucifixion. Thus, according to the Qur'an, John affirms, the Jews "crucified Him in appearance only (Qur'an 4:156); but the Christ Himself was not crucified, nor did He die, for God took Him into heaven unto Himself (Qur'an 4:156) because He loved Him."[88] In *Dialogue with a Saracen,* John used this Qur'anic account of Christ, especially the two titles the Qur'an uses to describe Jesus — God's Word and His Spirit — to defend and prove Jesus' divinity.[89] A complicating factor here is that Christian tradition did not of course always speak in one voice — even after Chalcedon. By the time of the rise of Islam, especially the Eastern Christian tradition was deeply divided into different groups and orientations, some affirming, others resisting or revising, key Chalcedonian formulae.[90]

As mentioned above, the virgin birth of Jesus is affirmed in the Qur'an in many places. Two aspects of that discussion are relevant to the consideration of Jesus' divinity. According to Qur'an 21:91, God "breathed into Mary and caused her to become pregnant with Jesus."[91] The second is related to God's *word* that, according to the Qur'an, God cast (sent forth) to Mary. Al-

in the *Muslim World* 24 (1934): 391-98, and vol. 25 (1935): 266-73. These translations were based on the Greek text of PG 94 (1864), cols. 764-73; sec. 101, Latin text in parallel columns. The same English translations of these two texts were reprinted in N. A. Newman, ed., *Early Christian-Muslim Dialogue,* pp. 133-68. The current study will consult Newman's work. For secondary studies on these texts, see, in addition to the introductions of the editions of the previous studies, the excellent study by Sahas, *John of Damascus on Islam;* and also Sweetman, *Islam and Christian Theology,* part 1, vol. 1, pp. 63-66.

88. Newman, *Early Christian-Muslim Dialogue,* p. 139.

89. Newman, *Early Christian-Muslim Dialogue,* pp. 144-47; for the Qur'anic "Spirit Christology," see the careful discussion in Schumann, *Jesus the Messiah in Muslim Thought,* pp. 14-18.

90. For the history of the church in the Middle East until the rise of Islam, see Goddard, *A History of Christian-Muslim Relations,* pp. 11-17; see also Griffith, *The Church in the Shadow of the Mosque,* pp. 129-40.

91. The manner of expression is important in Qur'an 21:91 and has striking parallels with Christian tradition: "And the one who guarded her virginity, so We breathed into her of Our spirit. And We made her and her son a sign for all the worlds." The same idea, almost verbatim, can be found in 66:12.

though the Qur'anic *tafsir* does not speak in one voice about many details in these accounts, including the exact meaning of the reference of "Our spirit," whether to the angel Gabriel or to God, and the relation of the "spirit" here to the Qur'anic reference where Jesus is called "a spirit from Him" (4:171), from the point of view of Christian theology the idea of the agency of the divine Spirit in the virgin conception is significant. Alongside the Spirit, there is also a reference to the word in the conception of Jesus. In one of the most significant passages about Jesus in the Qur'an, 4:171, the reference to "spirit" and the coming of Jesus as the "word" are connected: "The Messiah, Jesus son of Mary, was only a messenger of Allah, and His word which He conveyed unto Mary, and a spirit from Him."[92] Again, there are exegetical debates in the Islamic *tafsir*, not least concerning the meaning of the word being "conveyed" and, of course, the meaning of the term "word" itself in reference to Jesus. Notwithstanding those debates, from the perspective of Christian theology, two important points follow: the linking of the coming of Jesus into the world via the agency of the Spirit and Word as well as the birth of Jesus through the pure, obedient Virgin Mary without the intervention of a male parent. Those two, however, should be put in perspective. No more than similar statements in Christian theology do these Muslim references seek to establish the divinity of Jesus. They are meant to speak of the high status as a religious figure of Jesus, the son of Mary. It is important to remember that in the very same passage in the Qur'an (4:171) in which the reference to the Spirit and Word occurs, there is also one of the strongest denials of the Trinity and the divine Sonship of Jesus: "So believe in Allah and His messengers, and say not 'Three' — Cease! (it is) better for you! — Allah is only One God. Far is it removed from His Transcendent Majesty that He should have a son. His is all that is in the heavens and all that is in the earth. And Allah is sufficient as Defender."

Although assumed everywhere, the Qur'an contains only a handful of direct references to the Christian claim of Jesus as the Son of God and his divinity. It bluntly denies those claims (4:171; 5:17, 72, 73, 116; 9:30; 19:35).[93] A related Qur'anic denial is the idea that Allah had a son (2:116; 4:171; 10:68; 17:111; 18:4; 19:35, 88; 21:26; 23:91; 39:4; 43:81; 72:3). The main arguments in these pas-

92. Jesus is also called "a Word from God" (or "from Him") in another important passage: 3:45.

93. Behind (some of) these statements is also the need to combat the Jewish interpretation according to which Ezra was considered the Son of God (however that was understood theologically).

sages for not having a son are God's transcendence and the fact that Allah already possesses everything that is in the world: "He hath no needs! His is all that is in the heavens and all that is in the earth" (10:68). In general the idea of God begetting is denied at the outset (37:152; 112:3; among others). The idea of sonship is also denied in the Qur'an because it is seen linked with Allah having a consort (6:101, among others).

Incarnation

To their credit, early Muslim polemicists and commentators were fairly well aware of the many different interpretations and nuances among various Christian interpretations of incarnation. Indeed, these early Muslim thinkers often considered the nuances in Christian interpretations more carefully than usually happens in contemporary debates, as Muslims tend to treat Christian interpretations of Christ without much nuancing between very different types. In the past, the three Christian "schools" of Melkites, Nestorians, and Jacobites were carefully analyzed by several Muslim writers for their differences in negotiating the "two natures."

The Muslim rebuttals of the Christian doctrine of the incarnation of Jesus Christ, as presented in the *anti-Christian* Muslim literature during the first centuries — in light of the Muslim understanding of what the Christian doctrine was teaching — can be classified under two broad sets of arguments.[94] First, incarnation is inconsistent with both Muslim and Christian Scripture. With regard to Muslim Scripture, Muslim scholars quoted Qur'anic passages that refute Jesus' divinity (e.g., 5:72, 73) while employing Qur'anic passages that speak of the mere humanity of Jesus (e.g., 5:75). As for the Bible, Muslim scholars devoted considerable attention to the sayings that speak of Jesus' humanity, such as his being the son of David and Abra-

94. This paragraph is based on a careful analysis of twelve leading Muslim anti-Christian writers who reproduced fifteen defining texts in Arabic from the beginning to the end of the tenth century, by an Egyptian doctoral student at Fuller Theological Seminary. These Muslim writers varied in denominational and theological affiliations, styles and purposes of writing, and also emphases and concerns. Writings include standard texts such as *The Letter of al-Hāshimī* by ʿAbd Allāh ibn Ismāʿīl al-Hāshimī, *Kitāb al-Radd ʿalā al-Naṣārā (The Book of the Refutation of the Christians)* by Al-Qāsim ibn Ibrāhīm al-Rassī, and Abū ʿUthmān al-Jāḥiẓẓ's *Kitāb al-Radd ʿalā al-Naṣārā (The Book of the Refutation of the Christians).* Samuel, "The Incarnation in Arabic Christian Theology from the Beginnings to the Mid–Eleventh Centuries."

ham (Matt. 1:1) and that he ate, drank, slept, traveled, rode a donkey, suffered, and died; similarly, his need to pray (Matt. 26:39; 27:46; John 17), his temptations, his ignorance, and so forth were included in this way of reasoning, as well as the highly contested claim that according to John 14:16 Jesus foretold the coming of Muhammad, the Paraclete. These were all meant to show that God-man incarnation is not compatible even with Christian Scripture. On the other hand, Muslim commentators also downplayed the importance of Christian interpretation of a few passages in which they saw direct claims to Jesus' divinity.[95] Second, these early Muslim commentators argued that the Christian doctrine of incarnation is inconsistent with Muslim and Christian teachings at large. On top of this argumentation was the central Muslim idea of *tawḥīd,* the oneness of God, which by default rejects all notions of not only incarnation but also the corollary Christian doctrine of the Trinity. *Tawḥīd* was seen as taught not only by the Qur'an but also by the Bible, especially the OT (Deut. 6:4).

A related concern among Muslim commentators is the incompatibility of incarnation with God's transcendence, affirmed firmly in both faiths. The idea of God becoming flesh violates in Muslim sensibilities the principles of God's glory and greatness. Hence, it is unworthy for a sovereign God to be human. According to the Christian Cragg, however, "the crucial question has to do with the nature of the 'greatness' we affirm."[96] "The question between us is not about *whether* there is God's stake in our humanity but *how* far it might go in what it entails within the divine power and whether what we have in Jesus might or might not be the measure of the answer."[97] Does the incarnation or the *kenosis* of God oppose God's greatness? On the contrary, Cragg argues, it is in Jesus Christ, the Word made flesh, that what Muslims desire to assert regarding God's greatness is in effect. It is in Jesus Christ, "God in Christ," that God achieved his intention toward humanity. "For is that sovereignty truly sovereign if it fails to take action against the empire of ignorance and evil in humankind?" Cragg asks.[98]

Furthermore, Jesus' physical conception and birth as part of the doctrine of incarnation were seen as incompatible with both Christian and Muslim teachings. A logical problem here is the exact moment the two na-

95. Some commentators even declared that they found in the Bible about 20,000 verses that suggest Jesus' humanity, and less than 10 allusions that were used to support Jesus' divinity!

96. Cragg, "Greater Is God," p. 38.

97. Cragg, *The Arab Christian,* p. 288.

98. Cragg, *Call of the Minaret,* p. 264.

tures were united, whether in conception or birth or afterward. A final Muslim concern about the incarnation is that it involves itself in *Shirk*, the greatest sin of all, associating with God what should not be associated with him. By believing in "God in Christ," Christians are somehow "deifying" a creature, the man of Nazareth.

Is there a way to negotiate or soften the impasse without unduly compromising the core teachings of both traditions? Kenneth Cragg has widely argued that one such attempt could be built around the central Christian idea of "God in Christ" (2 Cor. 5:19).[99] That idea, rather than the "Word made flesh" (John 1:14), may provide some stimulus and avenues for mutual rethinking. He wonders if there is "not a Christian sense of God in Christ truly compatible with the Islamic awareness of divine unity." And, he asks if, conversely, there is "not an Islamic sense of Christ compatible with the Christian understanding of divine self-revelation." The first response has to merely be that there hardly exists such a convergence. And more importantly, whether or not it can be found, it cannot be based on anything but "the inner authenticity of their respective apprehension of the divine."[100] If the reasoning is based on something else, it can only result in a poor apologetic and an even worse "dialogue." Some have attempted to find the convergence in a forced Christian reading of the Qur'anic passages that speak of Jesus as "a spirit from God" or "a word from God," as discussed above. Muslim interpretation of those passages does not yield any divinity, and thus a Christian understanding of incarnation; even if, in an unlikely event, there could be found exegetical or hermeneutical reasons in the study of these kinds of passages toward a more Christian understanding, the theological structure and inner self-understanding of Islam hardly allow that.[101]

Instead, Cragg suggests that the idea of "God in Christ" — which can be expressed as "having been sent" from God (John 3:16) — may find a better hearing in Islam when related to the central Qur'anic idea of the prophets and the Qur'an itself as the Word of God having been sent. "*Rasūl*, the 'sent one,' is of course the fundamental definition of the prophet in Islam. *Rasūliyyah*, or 'mission from God,' is the agency of the Qur'an on earth. Such *Rasūliyyah* is culminatory, in the Islamic belief, of a sequence of divine

99. He summarizes the main argumentation succinctly in an essay titled "Islam and Incarnation," pp. 126-39. Another important source is the chapter titled "The Decisive Faith: 'God in Christ,'" in his *Jesus and the Muslim*. See also his *The Weight in the Word;* Cragg, *Muhammad in the Qur'an.*

100. Cragg, "Islam and Incarnation," p. 126.

101. See further, Cragg, "Islam and Incarnation," pp. 126-27.

address to the human situation, [through] a long succession of prophets and messengers." In other words, both religions speak of the divine mission, sending. Despite their profound differences, Cragg surmises that the idea of the divine and human interpenetration is there, "and, in that interpenetration, the real involvement of the divine in the temporal and the constant concern about the genuine mandate of the eternal."[102] Both "human aegis" and "divine fiat" are at work here, somewhat similar to the Christian understanding. Although Muhammad is always considered to be short of divinity, given his role as the "instrument" in the process of *Tanzil,* the reception of the Qur'an, the Word of God, "The Quran, as divine word, is intensely a human phenomenon, and takes its place in human history."[103]

That Muhammad or even the Qur'an is not considered "divine" is not to downplay its unique mediatorial role for humanity to know God's will, in order to "submit," be a Muslim; rather, this hesitancy has everything to do with the protection of the source of revelation and sending in God, the unity of God.[104] It is of course ironic — and promising for the dialogue with Islam — that along with the doctrine of incarnation, affirmation of "God in Christ" because of sentness, Christian theology from the beginning had to fight against idolatry in the form of either contemporary mystery cults with myriads of gods and goddesses or the emperor cult. Christian faith is strictly monotheistic, as is Islam. This defense of monotheism, based on the transcendence and majesty of God, Cragg helpfully reminds us, "is far from being a divine dissociation from [hu]mankind."[105] The Muslim idea of sentness of course confirms that Christian claim.

Although Cragg's creative reasoning hardly convinces many Muslims, its gains are twofold. First, it helps continue conversation that, as mentioned, is not based on a cheap and useless compromise but rather seeks to operate on the basis of the inner logic of both traditions. Second, it helps Christians understand better the inner logic of Muslim monotheism and its relatedness to their own faith.

102. Cragg, "Islam and Incarnation," pp. 127-28. Speaking of this interpenetration, Cragg also daringly uses the term "association," well aware of the dangerous connotations when having to do with *Shirk,* the main Muslim charge against Christians for allegedly compromising the unity of God with the doctrine of the Trinity.

103. Cragg, "Islam and Incarnation," 131.

104. Cragg, "Islam and Incarnation," pp. 128-32 (131).

105. Cragg, *Jesus and the Muslim,* p. 198.

Jesus and Buddha

Unlike the relationship with Islam, the interaction between the Jesus traditions and the Buddhist traditions has not been wide and deep until the twentieth century. The reasons are many and variegated. First is the sheer geographical fact that when the Christian faith was born, Buddhist movements were locating themselves in areas of the world distant from Christian mission.[106] Before the twentieth century, by far the most significant interaction between the two religions took place in China during the Tang Dynasty in the latter part of the first millennium in the form of Nestorian Christianity. Second, there are also thematic and material reasons for the "silence about Jesus" between Buddhism and Christianity. The topics addressed by those Buddhists who engaged Christianity included creation/codependent origination, sin/karma, heaven/nirvana, and the notions of the ultimate reality in both traditions. The third reason is deeply cultural-religious and doesn't easily make sense to the contemporary Western mind-set. Particularly in Theravada tradition, given the fact that Buddha taught no fewer than forty-five years, establishing a solid and coherent tradition to follow, the teaching ministry of Jesus — comprising only three years at most and not yielding any kind of systematic and organized body of tradition — does not easily gain much respect. Finally, a complex set of colonial factors lurks behind the suspicion and indifference among Buddhists toward Jesus. Related to this is the fact that the Buddhist attitude toward Christianity, whether hostility or indifference or desire to engage and incorporate, often seems to be the function of how much pressure the Buddhist people felt from "Christian" nations in any given location and context.[107]

In terms of life history, there are obvious similarities between Shakyamuni (Gautama) Buddha and Jesus of Nazareth. This much can be said even if the historical details of Gautama's life are very scarce, including the lack of precise dating of his birth.[108] Both founders of religions had miraculous elements attached to their birth, including cosmic signs and phenomena, as well as ominous threat; both of them faced temptations, one in the forest, the other in the desert; both became itinerant preachers and teachers

106. The strong Buddhist areas include China, Tibet, Japan, Thailand, Vietnam, and other areas of that part of Asia. Buddhism engaged the religions of the area, including Confucianism, Taoism, and Shintoism.

107. See further, Donald S. Lopez Jr., "Jesus in Buddhism," in *JBC*, pp. 266-71.

108. For a concise and useful historiographical and material discussion, see Nagao, "Life of the Buddha," pp. 1-31.

who also were considered miracle-workers; both were men of prayer and meditation; and so forth.[109]

Potentially the Mahayana tradition's stress on the transcendent and "salvific" presence of Buddha might find bridges with Christian faith more easily. The major difference, however, has to do with its vision of multiple Boddhisattvas vis-à-vis Christian faith's focus on one single savior.[110] In sum: "That Jesus prayed to a deity that is self-caused, self-existent, and independent of the created world conflicts with both the notion of co-independent origination as well as the non-dualistic goal of a self merged with all consciousness."[111] The seventeenth-century Buddhist monk and scholar Ouyi Zhixu of China presented weighty criticisms of some key aspects of the Jesus tradition, including the incomprehensibility of the idea of the "Lord of Heaven" having been born as a human being. Zhixu compares the Christian idea of the preexistence and incarnation of Jesus with the Buddhist teaching of *trikaya* ("three bodies of Buddha") and finds it a poor plagiarization of Buddhist belief.[112]

Silence, rather than aggressive polemics, is the defining characteristic of Buddhist reaction to Jesus. However, Buddhist critics of Jesus and the faith originating with him are not totally lacking. A onetime convert to Christianity in Japan, Fabian Fucan, during the short period of flourishing of Christian faith at the end of the sixteenth and beginning of the seventeenth century, resorted to the kinds of criticism well known from other religions, including the illicit status of Mary. He also ridiculed the coming of Jesus at such a late moment of history, namely, five thousand years after the beginning of the world — according to the Christian calendar; a related point of criticism was that the traditional Christian counting of time differed drastically from the Japanese and Chinese histories with their vast periods of time. Furthermore, Fucan concluded that because followers of Jesus "are preaching a doctrine wicked and contrary to the Way of the Sages . . . the wise ruler has decided to stamp out" them from Japan.[113]

With all their appreciation of Jesus' ethical life, ministry, and teaching, "the single most problematic aspect of Jesus' identity is his portrayal by

109. For a lucid exposition and discussion, see Lefebure, *The Buddha and the Christ,* chap. 2.

110. See further, Gregory A. Barker, "Buddhist Perceptions of Jesus: Key Issues," in *JBC,* pp. 217-19.

111. Barker, "Buddhist Perceptions of Jesus," in *JBC,* p. 220.

112. Ouyi Zhixu (no title provided), in *JBC,* pp. 229-30.

113. Fabian Fucan, "Deus Destroyed," in *JBC,* pp. 223-26 (226).

Christians as God," says the leading Tibetan Buddhist scholar and practitioner José Ignacio Cabezón. He specifies the problem in this way: "The problem lies not in the claim that Jesus is the incarnation or manifestation of a deity. What I find objectionable is (a) the Christian characterization of the deity whose incarnation Jesus is said to be, and (b) the claim that Jesus is unique in being an incarnation."[114] That the idea of incarnation in itself is not a problem for Buddhists is based on the belief prevalent among all Mahayana Buddhists that the universe is populated by enlightened beings who, having attained the buddhahood, have the capacity to incarnate for the welfare of others. Not all Mahayana adherents are willing to grant to Jesus the status of the manifestation of a deity, say after "Wisdom" *(Sophia)*, but many would accede to the possibility of such a belief.

To consider Jesus as incarnate on the basis of his extraordinary teaching, miracles, and ethical life is not to say that therefore he "possessed the quality of maximal greatness (enlightenment), that is, that he was a Buddha."[115] In many respects, Jesus might be better compared with Boddhisattva, a Buddha-in-the-making, as it were, who for the sake of others is willing to suffer and postpone one's own enlightenment (as happens in Mahayana traditions).[116] In the Pure Land tradition, similarly, Jesus can be respected as a Boddhisattva, a compassionate being who helps others, a manifestation of Amitabha.[117] Even then there is no ultimacy to the role of Jesus after the Christian tradition.[118] Between the Theravada tradition and Christian interpretation of Jesus there are even wider differences, as Theravada does not emphasize the idea of enlightened manifestations of the divine incarnating for the benefit of others. What matters in the oldest Buddhist tradition is the following of *dhamma*, the way of training *(vinaya)*, and *sangha*, the community in which assistance may be received from others, but which has no salvific effect.[119]

Behind the Buddhist refusal to grant a salvific role to Jesus lie a number of doctrinal presuppositions. In Buddhist thought, every sentient person is responsible for his or her destiny. Suffering, the ultimate cause that neces-

114. Cabezón, "Buddhist Views of Jesus," in *JWF*, p. 21.

115. Cabezón, "Buddhist Views of Jesus," in *JWF*, pp. 21-22 (22).

116. See Gross, "Meditating on Jesus," pp. 45-47.

117. Amitabha is the original Sanskrit name for the central Buddha in Pure Land; it means literally "Infinite Light." In Japanese, the title is *Amida*. See further, Alfred Bloom, "Jesus in the Pure Land," in *JWF*, p. 31.

118. See further, Bloom, "Jesus in the Pure Land," in *JWF*, pp. 31-32.

119. Sister Ajahn Candasiri, "Jesus: A Theravadan Perspective," in *JWF*, p. 25.

sitates "salvation," is caused by each and every person, and consequently one cannot refer to another source of deliverance apart from one's own efforts. The idea that salvation of men and women would be dependent on any historical event such as the cross is totally unknown to Buddhism. Furthermore, Buddhism includes no temporal end to the continuing path of salvation, not even physical death. Mere belief or doctrine cannot save the human person; only effort toward enlightenment may lead to the end goal.[120]

Behind the differences between Buddhist and Christian notions of the "Savior" — including that of the Pure Land tradition, which comes closest to Christianity — are their approaches to the question of faith and history. As argued above with regard to both incarnation and resurrection, the reliability of historical claims, while not sufficient in themselves, is necessary for the validity of Christian faith. That is not the case with Buddhist traditions. Particularly for Mahayana (including Pure Land) traditions, the stories and happenings "are mythical beyond any history with which we are familiar."[121] Furthermore, all Buddhist traditions grant the existence of multiple Buddhas,[122] whereas Christian tradition of course denies many Christs.

The Buddhist Rita M. Gross makes the insightful observation that Christian tradition tends to "locate truth in the messenger, whereas Buddhism tends to focus on the message." This is linked with the fact that Christian tradition has a tendency "to personify the ultimate while Budddhists tend toward nonpersonal metaphors about ultimate reality."[123] Further complications for Buddhist acknowledgment of Jesus as divine come from Christian trinitarian teaching. If Christ is divine, that means one has to acknowledge the God of the Bible. To begin with, Buddhists are not willing to approve the notion of a creator God, one who has no beginning in time, and other corollary Christian theistic notions.[124]

Incarnation in Buddhist Perspective

What about the doctrine of incarnation? Are there any parallels or similar motifs between the two religions and the founding figures? This line of questioning also gives us an opportunity to refine the typical Western tendency to

120. Cabezón, "Buddhist Views of Jesus," in *JWF*, pp. 23-24.
121. Bloom, "Jesus in the Pure Land," in *JWF*, pp. 35-36 (36).
122. See Gross, "Meditating on Jesus," p. 45.
123. Gross, "Meditating on Jesus," p. 44.
124. See Cabezón, "Buddhist Views of Jesus," in *JWF*, pp. 22-23.

make Buddhism less a religion and more an ethical system, particularly when it comes to Theravada tradition — the implication being, as mentioned above, that whereas in Christian faith Christ is the center, in Buddhism the role of the founder is not. Anyone who knows Buddhism in its everyday manifestation — even in the Theravada form — knows how highly Buddha is venerated. I am not thinking here of Buddhism only in its folk-religious form, which often is almost exclusively "animistic," but also in its textual traditions. The story of Brahman Dona in Pali Canon is an illustrative example. Having found Buddha's footprints, in his amazement and awe Dona went to ask Buddha of their origin. Buddha explained that they do not belong to a deva (celestial being) nor a spirit nor a human being since all those forms of existence still are stuck within the bounds of samsara leading to rebirths. Instead, Buddha has transcended all that — and that's what makes him *Buddha!*[125]

The state of buddhahood is also the key to the Buddhist notion of incarnation, whose relation to Christian doctrine merits some consideration for the sake of interfaith learning and encounters. Resisting the temptation to remain silent after the enlightenment, Buddha, filled with compassion, decided to teach and minister for the sake of the well-being of other sentient beings.[126] In an important, oft-quoted saying, Buddha makes an identification with Dhamma: "He who sees Dhamma . . . sees me; he who sees me sees Dhamma. Truly seeing Dhamma, one sees me; seeing me one sees Dhamma."[127] Interestingly enough, the editor/translator of this text, Maurice O'Connell Walshe, adds this note: "A famous quotation. It has been compared with Christ's words: 'I and my Father are one' (John 10:30)." One could also think of the relation of Jesus to the Word/Logos. It has been rightly noted that by this statement, Buddha seems to be pointing toward himself, to the Dhamma.[128] Indeed, Buddhist tradition speaks of the kind of "visible Dhamma" in terms of the life of the person who has freed himself or herself totally from hatred, delusion, and greed. This is nothing less than "visible nirvana."[129] Mahayana tradition further developed and expanded the idea of the

125. Anguttara Nikaya 4, 36 ("Tipitaka: The Pali Canon," edited by John T. Bullitt).

126. For the narrative about encountering the divine Brahma as a result of which Buddha decided to show compassion and teach, see Majjhima Nikaya 26. In the Pali Canon, there are also several stories about Mara, the main tempter seeking to silence Buddha after his enlightenment.

127. Samyutta Nikaya 22.87.

128. Schmidt-Leukel, "Buddha and Christ as Mediators," p. 155.

129. See Anguttara Nikaya 3.54-56; I am indebted to Schmidt-Leukel, "Buddha and Christ as Mediators," p. 155.

continuing presence of Buddha in the world, as a "temporally limited manifestation of a supra-mundane and virtually eternal Buddha-reality"[130] for the sake of the enlightenment of others.[131] Here there is an unmistakable parallel with the Hindu idea of incarnation as expressed in Bhagavad-Gita.[132]

The final form of the (Mahayana) Buddhist doctrine of incarnation is the idea of *trikaya,* three bodies: first, "Transformation Body," the earthly Buddha, a transient and illusionary form of existence; second, "Enjoyment Body," the form of existence for the sake of others; and third, "Dhamma Body," the ultimate form of existence that indeed is no longer a "form" of existence but formless. In other words, the last "body" transcends the form and laws of existence. It is inconceivable and ineffable.[133] Although there are some interesting similar motifs between the Buddhist and Christian doctrines of incarnation, including the ascent-descent/descent-ascent dynamic, "salvific orientation," and the dialectic between the "historical" and "suprahistorical" forms of existence, even a cursory look reveals profound differences, many of which have already been alluded to above.

Perry Schmidt-Leukel accurately locates the ultimate and defining issue in any search for commonalities in the Buddhist and Christian understanding of incarnation and "Savior." That has to do with the meaning of the source to which both incarnations refer. Briefly put: Is Jesus Christ's relation to the Father/God similar to Gautama Buddha's relation to Dhamma (assuming the validity for Buddhists of the identity between Buddha and Dhamma, as discussed above)? Different from the more optimistic expecta-

130. Schmidt-Leukel, "Buddha and Christ as Mediators," p. 157.

131. See the important statement in Lotus-Sutra, the most important and widely used text in the Mahayana world, in chap. 15: "21. So am I the father of the world, the Self born, the Healer, the Protector of all creatures. Knowing them to be perverted, infatuated, and ignorant I teach final rest, myself not being at rest. 22. What reason should I have to continually manifest myself? When men become unbelieving, unwise, ignorant, careless, fond of sensual pleasures, and from thoughtlessness run into misfortune, 23. Then I, who know the course of the world, declare: I am so and so, (and consider): How can I incline them to enlightenment? how can they become partakers of the Buddha-laws?" *Saddharma-Pundarika* 15:21-23.

132. *Bhagavadgita* 4:6-8: "Though I am eternal, imperishable, and the Lord of all beings; yet I (voluntarily) manifest by controlling My own material nature using My Yoga-Maya. . . . Whenever there is a decline of Dharma and the rise of Adharma, O Arjuna, then I manifest (or incarnate) Myself. I incarnate from time to time for protecting the good, for transforming the wicked, and for establishing Dharma, the world order."

133. Schmidt-Leukel, "Buddha and Christ as Mediators," pp. 157-59, contains useful bibliographic references to the three-body doctrine.

tions of the Christian scholar Schmidt-Leukel[134] and those of a group of Buddhist thinkers[135] — all of whom also refer to the key concept of *upāya*, the "skilful means," which helps negotiate inconceivable and ineffable issues by regarding all teachings as provisional — I am much less assured of the compatibility of God and Dharmakaya. The differences between the concepts of God and Dharmakaya are many and profound: one is personal, the other is not; one is Creator, the other is not; and so forth. The other main problem I have with these in many ways useful and insightful attempts is that they end up focusing too one-sidedly on the human nature of Jesus in incarnation, referring only to his obedience and service to the Father and ignoring the fact that in Christian theology, incarnation is also a deeply trinitarian event. *God* becomes human; it is not only that the human Jesus serves the kingdom of his Father.[136]

Sunyata and Self-Emptying

Not surprisingly, perhaps the most promising connecting point between (Mahayana) Buddhism and Christology can be found in the correlation of the main concepts of sunyata and self-emptying of Christ. Notoriously difficult to translate and even more notoriously hard to understand, sunyata literally means "(absolute) nothingness." However, it is not "empty nothingness," since it is what in Western terms should be called the ultimate reality. It is only "empty" in terms of being "entirely unobjectifiable, unconceptualizable, and unattainable by reason or will."[137] For the sake of dialogue with

134. Schmidt-Leukel, "Buddha and Christ as Mediators," pp. 166-75. His assessment is more open-ended and inquiring than that of the three Buddhist thinkers mentioned in the next note. He also reminds us of the need for Christians to avoid any notion of idolatry when speaking of Dharmakaya as well as stick with the biblical idea of love as the essence of God (rather than the Buddhist notion of detachment) (p. 170).

135. Bloom, "Shin Buddhism," pp. 17-31 (Pure Land Buddhism); M. Abe, "A Dynamic Unity in Religious Pluralism," pp. 163-90, 225-27 (Zen Buddhism); Makransky, "Buddhist Perspectives on Truth in Other Religions," pp. 334-61 (Tibetan Buddhism).

136. That tendency is clearly evident in Schmidt-Leukel, "Buddha and Christ as Mediators," pp. 167-69.

137. M. Abe, "Kenotic God and Dynamic Sunyata," p. 50. For an insightful and careful attempt to clarify the meaning of sunyata to the Western and Christian mind-set, by a Christian systematician, see Ott, "The Convergence," pp. 127-34 particularly. For a fuller, highly insightful discussion by a leading Christian Buddhist expert, see Waldenfels, *Absolute Nothingness.*

Christians, Masao Abe of the Japanese Kyoto School outlines what he calls the "positive meanings of Sunyata":[138]

- Regardless of any distinctions such as those between self and other, or human and divine, "everything without exception is realized *as it is* in its *suchness*." Although distinctions are not eliminated, distinctiveness and sameness "are fully realized."
- "Sunyata indicates *boundless openness* without any particular fixed center. Sunyata is free not only from egocentrism but also from anthropocentrism, cosmocentrism, and theocentrism."
- It also means something like "things as they are," or "'naturalness,' not as a counterconcept to human agency, but as the primordial or fundamental naturalness underlying both human beings and nature."
- "In Sunyata, not only the interdependence and interpenetration but also the mutual reversibility of things is fully realized."
- Most importantly, it contains the two key characteristics of *prajna* (wisdom) and *karuna* (compassion).

Commenting on "one of the most impressive and touching passages in the Bible," Philippians 2:5-8, Masao Abe makes two important observations: he notes, first, the "abnegation of Christ as the Son of God," and second, that this self-emptying "indicates the self-sacrificial love of Christ for humankind," as a manifestation of the "unfathomable depth of God's love." Well informed of the debates in Christian tradition concerning whether Christ really emptied himself of the divine nature or only forwent certain attributes of divinity, this Japanese Buddhist strongly opines that the abnegation was full and thoroughgoing. By that he means that a radical transformation took place as "the Son of God abandoned his divine substance and took on human substance," all the way to the cross. Another major revision to received Christian tradition by the Buddhist commentator is the replacement of preexistence, in which Christ was originally divine, with, as in chronological sequence, an interpretation of *kenosis* in which "Christ as the Son of God is *essentially* and *fundamentally* self-emptying or self-negating." Hence, the traditional Christian interpretation of the preexistent Logos of John 1 needs to

138. M. Abe, "Kenotic God and Dynamic Sunyata," pp. 52-57. The standard scriptural reference is the "definition" in the Heart Sutra: "Form is Emptiness, Emptiness is form. Emptiness does not differ from form, and form does not differ from Emptiness" (http://www.sacred-texts.com/bud/tib/hrt.htm, accessed 2/2/2011).

be revised because, according to Abe, we can speak of Christ only in terms of how he is revealed to us; there is no way of speaking of the Son of God "apart from us." Finally, in the logic of sunyata, Abe provides this Buddhist revisionist view of Christ: "The Son of God is not the Son of God (for he is essentially and fundamentally self-emptying); precisely because he *is not* the Son of God he *is* truly the Son of God (for he originally and always works as Christ, the Messiah, in his salvational function of self-emptying." Along the same lines, *homoousios* should be interpreted not only in terms of "consubstantiality" but also as "one function" or "nondual function" of self-emptying.[139]

Furthermore, Abe sees an integral link between the human self and Christ's self-emptying, to be more precise, the existential problem of the self and what Christ did. This is based on Gospel sayings such as Matthew 10:39, which issues a call to lose life in order to find it, and the Pauline sayings that convey materially the same message (Rom. 6:11; 2 Cor. 4:10). Similarly to the total abnegation of Christ, Christians are called to a "complete death of our ego-self."[140]

The self-emptying is followed by the exaltation of Christ (Phil. 2:9-11). Referring to Barth, Abe emphasizes the need to complete the theology of the cross with the theology of glory.[141] Why Abe makes this turn, I am not quite sure; at least he does not elaborate on the significance of Christ's exaltation to this interpretation. However, somewhat counterintuitively, in this same context he reminds us that any notion of Christ's preexistence, even in light of the exalted status, should be dismissed. Surprisingly, he appeals to rational reasons and "antireligious ideologies," such as the current atheistic "scientism," as he calls it![142]

Now, having argued for the complete and thoroughgoing *kenosis* of Christ, Abe takes the discussion a step forward in relating it to the question of the *kenosis* of God.[143] Against Christian tradition that is not willing to

139. M. Abe, "Kenotic God and Dynamic Sunyata," pp. 32-33.

140. M. Abe, "Kenotic God and Dynamic Sunyata," p. 34.

141. Abe ("Kenotic God and Dynamic Sunyata," p. 34) cites Barth, *CD* IV/1, p. 558.

142. M. Abe, "Kenotic God and Dynamic Sunyata," pp. 35-36; on pp. 25-31 he offers a critical rebuttal of "scientism" and other antireligious ideologies, including a sustained dialogue with Nietzsche.

143. Abe ("Kenotic God and Dynamic Sunyata," p. 36) begins the discussion with Moltmann's question: "What does the cross of Jesus mean for God himself?" (in *The Crucified God*, p. 201). He carries on a conversation with Moltmann throughout the essay. For Moltmann's highly appreciative remark on Abe's interpretation of the hymn in Phil. 2, see Moltmann, "God Is Unselfish Love," p. 116.

speak of "the incarnation of God himself,"[144] Abe surmises that to speak of "the kenosis of God is a crucial issue for our dialogue." Or else, "the self-emptying of the Son of God is inconceivable." God's *nature* as love as well as God's *will* to reach out to sinners demand this.[145] A problem in Christian theology that for Abe seems to hinder such complete abnegation of God is the persisting dualism. This deep dualism has much to do with incarnation as a whole, "a dualism of God and the other, the infinite and the finite, immutability and change, within and without, and so forth."[146] Behind this dualism is not only the lack of a concept such as sunyata but also the typical Western logic's "either-or" reasoning rather than the dynamic "both-and" reasoning, one may surmise. Abe's conclusion about the *kenosis* of God, then, reads like this: "God's self-emptying must be understood not as partial but as total to the extent that God's infinite unrelatedness has no priority over relatedness with the other and that God's self-emptying is dynamically identical with God's abiding and infinite fullness."[147] Such a self-emptying, Abe avers, overcomes the Nietzschean dismissal of God's self-sacrifice "for nothing" in that this abnegation is "God's self-sacrifice for absolutely 'nothing' other than God's own fulfillment." This absolute *kenosis,* furthermore, helps Christian tradition transcend its monotheism and thus share with "Buddhism the realization of absolute nothingness as the essential basis for the ultimate."[148]

Wisely enough, this Buddhist thinker anticipates typical Christian objections to his reinterpretation of *kenosis,* incarnation, and God. There is, first, the danger of pantheism, and second, the obvious denial of Jesus' uniqueness. Pantheism does not follow, at least in the form of Spinoza's philosophy in which God is identified with nature/world *(dues sive natura),* avers Abe, since according to the sunyata logic, God is both personal and imper-

144. Citation from Küng, *Does God Exist?* p. 685, in M. Abe, "Kenotic God and Dynamic Sunyata," p. 36; Abe also cites from pp. 690-91, which deny that Christian theology can speak of a "crucified God" in any strong sense.

145. M. Abe, "Kenotic God and Dynamic Sunyata," p. 37, with reference to Nishitani, *Religion and Nothingness,* p. 59. Abe seeks to find support for his idea of the full *kenosis,* that is, "death of God," in the writings of Rahner, including his essay in *Sacramentum Mundi* (vol. 2 [London: Burns and Oates, 1969], pp. 207-8 [208]), which says that "Jesus' death belongs to God's self-utterance." That, however, hardly makes the same point as Abe's "strong" claim for the death of God.

146. M. Abe, "Kenotic God and Dynamic Sunyata," p. 38.

147. M. Abe, "Kenotic God and Dynamic Sunyata," p. 38.

148. M. Abe, "Kenotic God and Dynamic Sunyata," pp. 39-40.

sonal rather than one substance. "In the completely kenotic God, personality and impersonality are paradoxically identical." Neither does the denial of the uniqueness of Christ follow, responds Abe. Through the total abnegation, "God fully identifies with the crucified Christ on the cross"; the same applies to Christ's resurrection. Rather than thinking of Christ's incarnation as one among many, the Japanese Buddhist wonders why we couldn't apply the total identification of God in Christ to everything in reality. "Can we not legitimately say that each and every thing in the universe is also an incarnation of God together with Jesus Christ on the cross and his glorious resurrection?"[149]

Several Christian theologians have responded to Masao Abe's highly creative and constructive interpretation.[150] Marjorie Suchocki rightly remarks that in a Christian framework, Trinity is the way to affirm both otherness and diversity on the one hand and unity on the other hand. "The Christian story is that the internal perichoretic relations of what is called the immanent trinity yield the external perichoretic work of the economic Trinity." Hence, she replies that major Christian tradition has rightly resisted pantheism: Trinity tells us that God is god and we are not god. Yet, divine and human are integrally related. Furthermore, in Christian tradition, inner-trinitarian relations are not interpreted according to the principle of radical self-emptying. "To the strong contrary, the coinherence signified by perichoretic union is one that requires the irreducible otherness within the trinitarian structure."[151]

Pannenberg not only wonders what really is the meaning of Abe's talk about the seemingly contradictory (at least to Western logic) notion of emptiness not only emptying everything else but also itself, but christologically more importantly, he wonders if in the context of Christian theology one can speak of Christ's emptying himself in terms of "*essentially* and *fundamentally* self-emptying or self-negating." I agree with his judgment that, yes, we should speak of Jesus Christ, the Son of God, in this way; according to Philippians 2:8, the self-emptying was so radical that it led to the death on the cross. Differently from Abe, however, this did not mean that he ceased to be the Son of God. Furthermore, when Paul speaks of Jesus taking the form of a servant (v. 7), it means that Jesus differentiates himself as a human from God in obedience and so serves the Father. Unlike in sunyata, distinctions

149. M. Abe, "Kenotic God and Dynamic Sunyata," p. 41.

150. For the wider interfaith dialogue, the Jewish response by Richard L. Rubenstein ("Holocaust, Sunyata, and Holy Nothingness," pp. 93-112) is highly interesting; that response also engages some insights of Christian theology as part of the discussion.

151. Suchocki, "Sunyata, Trinity, and Community," p. 145.

remain. For this statement to make sense, unlike Abe, mainline Christian theology takes preexistence as a necessary dogmatic assertion, as discussed above. Finally, it is one thing to say that Christ's *kenosis* leads — must lead, as Abe opines — to the *kenosis of* God, and another to say that its "origin" is in God. For the self-emptying of God, Pannenberg contends, "there is not the slightest evidence in Paul's letter to the Philippians, nor in any other place in the New Testament."[152] According to the biblical testimony — and in the context of the trinitarian theology of reconciliation developed above — the Father suffers in the self-sacrifice of the Son, but the Father does not undergo self-sacrifice, not emptying. In the Christian view, the abnegation of the Father would have been disastrous as that would have hindered the raising of the Son from the dead through the Spirit. Mainline Christian tradition also rejects the pantheistically oriented view of the incarnation of Christ in relation to everything in reality.

Pannenberg's summative comment on Abe's constructive interpretation makes a valuable point: "[T]he notion of kenosis is of limited value in Buddhist-Christian dialogue, though I recognize its merit in providing inspiration for the initial phase of that dialogue. . . . [I]n contrast with Buddhist emptiness the Christian idea of kenosis presupposes an agent, the Son, in relation to another agent the Father, whose action is not kenotic." Instead, Pannenberg surmises that a more promising common point could perhaps be found in the Christian conception of the mutuality of love between the trinitarian persons, "which can be conceived of as suprapersonal thought becoming manifest only in the trinitarian persons. This field of perichoretic love, of mutual indwelling, is the one divine essence that the three persons share and in which the Christian mystic participates by sharing in the sonship of Jesus and thus in his spiritual relation to the Father."[153] Yet, even here there is, as Pannenberg also rightly observes, the important difference between "emptiness" and the remaining distinctions and the quality of "existence," we might say. In the discussion of the concept of God, the question of emptiness in relation to the Christian doctrine of God has to be investigated. As Pannenberg rightly points out, in relation to Abe's views, the most foundational question involves whether there is a "god" (whether personal or nonpersonal) distinct, if not separate, from the finite human world.[154]

152. Pannenberg, "God's Love and the Kenosis of the Son," pp. 247-48.

153. Pannenberg, "God's Love and the Kenosis of the Son," p. 250.

154. See Pannenberg, "God's Love and the Kenosis of the Son," pp. 245-46 particularly.

Christ and Avatars

Christianity and India, the home of "Hinduism,"[155] are no foreigners to each other historically. Whatever scholarly disputes remain, it is probable that as early as the first century there was a Christian presence in India. Syrian Christianity is believed to have been present beginning from the fourth century, and so forth. However, no evidence of Hindu perceptions of Jesus survives from those early days. We have to wait until the seventeenth century or so for the first Hindu response to Christ through the missionary activity from Spain, Portugal, and Holland to southwest India. But even then, we are speaking of Christians' recording of reports by Indians. The most notable such reports come from the Danish Lutheran Bartholomaeus Ziegenbalg (d. 1719). Not until the nineteenth century do we have firsthand Hindu responses to and interpretations of Christ.[156] The earliest modern Hindu interpretation of Jesus was offered in the early nineteenth century by Raja Ram Mohun Roy, who focused on Jesus' ethical meaning and denied divine incarnation.[157]

Perhaps unexpectedly, during the heights of the colonial enterprise beginning from the end of the nineteenth century, there emerged a new wave of interpretations of Christ that were deeply rooted in the religious (Hindu) soil of Asia and that pointed to an authentic Asian Christology. It was part of the so-called Indian Renaissance or neo-Hindu reform. The contemporary Indian theologian Stanley J. Samartha, one of the ablest interpreters of this renaissance, describes the Christ acknowledged by neo-Hinduism as an "unbound" Christ. What he means is that while many Indians attached themselves to the person of Jesus Christ — who reflects the features of Hindu avatars (incarnations of Hindu gods such as the famous Krishna or Vishnu) — they also detached that person from the institutional church, which for them did not rep-

155. It has become a commonplace to begin studies on any aspect of Hinduism by pointing out that such a thing never existed! "Hinduism" is a fairly late scholarly (and popular) construction, in many ways misleading or at least in need of many qualifications. A useful guide to and discussion of theological purposes is Lipner, "Ancient Banyan," pp. 109-26.

156. In traditional Brahmanical (Sanskrit) texts there are almost no Hindu interpretations of Muslims either, although Muslims have been in India from the beginning of the second millennium C.E. In general, Brahmanical thought was dismissive of foreign religions until the nineteenth century. P. J. Griffiths, "Hindu Perceptions," p. 191.

157. For a useful survey and discussion of main figures, see Neufeldt, "Hindu Views of Christ," pp. 162-75.

resent the quintessence of Christ's religion.[158] For Keshub Chunder Sen, the Hindu teacher of the nineteenth century, Christ was regarded as the focus of personal devotion *(bhakti)*. Jesus was no stranger to Asians, but rather one of them. Sen summed up his Christology as a "doctrine of the divine humanity." The essential component of Christ's divinity was his oneness with the Father. Christ is "as a transparent crystal reservoir in which are the waters of divine life. . . . The medium is transparent, and we clearly see through Christ the God of truth and holiness dwelling in him."[159]

Several Hindu writers were turned on by the social teachings of Christ but did not make a personal commitment to him. In his *Sermon on the Mount according to Vedanta,* Swami Prabhavananda calls this sermon the "essence of Christ's Gospel."[160] His spiritual teacher Swami Prahmananda had taught him to regard highly Christ's teaching; indeed, the teacher had seen Jesus in a vision. During his first days in the monastery of the order of Sri Ramakrishna, on Christmas Day, the monks were advised to "meditate on Christ within and feel his living presence." "An intense spiritual atmosphere pervaded the worship hall," Swami Prahbavananda reminisces, which led to the realization for the first time that "Christ was as much our own as Krishna, Buddha, and other great illumined teachers whom we revered."[161] Following this introduction, the book gives an elaborate and highly appreciative exposition of and correlation with some Vedanta teaching of the Sermon on the Mount. Swami Vivekananda of the Ramakrishna order similarly elevated Jesus among the highly revered figures of Buddha and Krishna, generally believed to be the incarnation of Vishnu. The twentieth-century Radhakrishnan held a similar view. Mahatma Gandhi's Jesus is an ethical teacher who expresses the ideal of a new community and way of life in the Beatitudes and other teachings. In those teachings, Gandhi saw the same principles that guided his own pacifistic fight for the liberation of the Indian people, namely, *satyagraha* (the search for truth) and *ahimsa* (nonviolence). As deeply as Gandhi was committed to the teaching of Jesus, especially the Sermon on the Mount, he was never ready to make a personal commitment to the person of Christ, let alone the community of the Christian church.[162]

158. For a short statement and sources, see Dupuis, *Jesus Christ,* p. 15.
159. Cited in Dupuis, *Jesus Christ,* p. 24; *Chunder Sen's Lectures,* p. 290.
160. Prabhavananda, *Sermon on the Mount according to Vedanta,* p. 7.
161. Prabhavananda, *Sermon on the Mount according to Vedanta,* pp. 8-9.
162. Gandhi, *The Message of Jesus Christ.*

Finally, there are Hindus who have become Christians but insist they have remained Hindus. The best known of these is Brahmabandhab Upadhyaya, who became a Catholic by way of first receiving an Anglican baptism. Upadhyaya's spirituality is based on a deep personal experience of the person of Jesus the Son of God, who becomes at once his guru and his friend. Whether Jesus was divine or not is not the point; what matters is that Christ claimed to be the Son of God. As a monk, Upadhyaya also understood Jesus Christ in terms of *advaita,* the Hindu mystical experience.[163]

The creativity and potential of the christological portraits in neo-Hindu reform are beautifully reflected in the different, yet complementary, titles of current interpreters, namely, Raimundo Panikkar's *Unknown Christ of Hinduism* and M. M. Thomas's *Acknowledged Christ of the Indian Renaissance.*[164] Yet another facet of the Indian portrait of Christ — in keeping with Roman Catholic theology — is offered by the title of the famous missionary John N. Farquhar, *The Crown of Hinduism* (1913), in which he presented a case for Christianity as something complementary to rather than exclusive of Hinduism.

By and large — with few exceptions, often related to the colonialist history — Hindu perceptions of Jesus are positive. This is similar to Buddhist views and different from a number of Jewish and Islamic views. With sweeping generalizations, the Hindu perceptions, including the twentieth-century ones, can be described in this way: "Jesus is a rational teacher of universal values; (2) Jesus is an incarnation of God among other incarnations; and (3) Jesus is a spiritual teacher. These positions are not, of course, mutually exclusive."[165]

What makes the mutual dialogue between Hindus and Christians both promising and challenging is that there are few, if any, doctrinal boundaries that are exclusively Hindu or required of followers to belong. Add to that a bewildering variety of beliefs, rites, rituals, "favorite" local gods and goddesses — and you get a feel of a "religion" very different from most other living faiths. Even the most well-known Hindu insistence on Brahman as the ultimate reality has never been fully and consistently held by all Hindus. Similarly, the question of whether there are 330,000,000 gods and goddesses

163. For a brief discussion, see Kavunkal, "The Mystery of God in and through Hinduism," pp. 28-30.

164. For an autobiographical account, see M. M. Thomas, "My Pilgrimage in Mission," pp. 28-31.

165. Gregory A. Barker and Stephen E. Gregg, "Jesus in Hinduism: Closing Reflection," in *JWF,* p. 202.

— as the standard way of putting it goes — or just 1, is a matter of continuing debate! Most Hindus still believe that there are "personal" *(saguna Brahman)* and "impersonal" *(nirguna Brahman)* natures to the divine.

One further complicating factor in the Hindu-Christian encounter is the profound philosophical and worldview difference between the two; this also applies to Christian-Buddhist relations in many contexts. A dominant strand of Indian philosophy is *advaita,* "nondualism" (lit. "not-two"), which is focused on a dynamic understanding of unity.[166] Following this logic makes any "literal" and exclusive talk about two natures of Christ or incarnation or reconciliation utterly challenging.

The Divinity of Jesus in Hindu Estimation

Among the Hindu commentators are those who consider Jesus of Nazareth a mere human teacher, albeit a highly respected and honored one. These interpreters of Christ also reject the belief of Jesus as the incarnation of God.[167] Materially these interpretations echo many of the views of classical liberalism.

There are also those such as Keshub Chunder Sen. Replacing the doctrine of the Trinity with the Biunity of Father and Spirit, Sen falls short of regarding Jesus as the divine incarnation, but does highly regard his "sonship" as an embodiment of the ideal of God's Son. Hence, Jesus provided for us a perfect example of "Divine Humanity."[168] Sen testifies that he would "go to my Christ to learn what a son ought to be . . . [as] Christ teaches me human-

166. Among Indian Christian theologians, as discussed above, Raimon Panikkar has intentionally utilized the advaitic logic. There are also nonadvaitic strands of Hinduism that focus on the divine transcendence in distinction from immanence. Yet it seems to me that even then, the all-pervasive *logical* orientation to nonduality is still in place in a way foreign to most people outside Asia.

167. As mentioned above, Raja Ram Mohun Roy was one of those who rejected belief in Jesus as the divine incarnation. Indeed, he also rejected the popular Hindu belief in incarnations such as the great heroic figure Ram whose life is recounted in *The Ramayana.* Behind Roy's attitude was his effort to contribute toward a social and education program that found religious beliefs to be superstitious and counterproductive. See his writing (pseudonymous letter) in Jogendra Chungder Ghose, ed., *The English Works of Raja Ram Mohun Roy,* vol. 1 (Calcutta: Srikanta Roy, 1901), pp. 287-90, reproduced in *JBC,* pp. 159-62.

168. Editors' explanation as an introduction to *Chunder Sen's Lectures,* pp. 25-27, reproduced in *JBC,* pp. 165-66 (165).

ity," whereas "God teaches me Divinity." However, Sen's Jesus not only teaches about humanity in classical liberalism's immanentist, merely ethical sense, he also teaches the "Worship of Humanity." In that sense we can bow before Jesus as we bow before the Divine: "Humanity when touched and inspired by Divinity is indeed worthy of the profoundest reverence." Put another way, we can speak of "Brother-worship" rather than the "worship of our Father." No wonder, Sen admits, this is "[a] strange doctrine"! Hence, we can speak of Jesus as "an incarnation of Brotherhood" but not of Fatherhood. According to Sen, there is an "eternal distinction. The Brother was born, he is called the 'begotten Son'; but the Father is the unbegotten, unborn, uncreate [*sic*] God, the Creator of all, Himself uncreated."[169]

Sen's revisionist interpretation of Christ materially echoes many of the important challenges early Christians faced in their efforts to define more carefully the christological canons, including the highly technical distinction between nuances of "begottenness" and its distinction from "having been born." Against Arians and others whose reasoning capitalized on the intuitive idea of the "son" being in some sense inferior or secondary to the "father," and the difficulty for strict monotheists to grant plurality in the one godhead, Christian orthodoxy only slowly and painfully came to the Nicean-Constantinopolitan and Chalcedonian "agreement." Hence, although Sen's interpretation clearly falls outside the received Christian tradition, a careful engagement of these kinds of views in a patient mutual dialogue would benefit both traditions.

Many contemporary Hindu interpreters of Jesus, perhaps a majority of them, are willing to grant divine status to Jesus Christ, something parallel to Krishna, the avatar of Vishnu.[170] That said, important qualifications

169. Cited in *JBC,* pp. 165-66.

170. With all his expertise in world religions, it seems to me Hans Küng ("A Christian Response," pp. 277-78) is overstating his case when, speaking of the relationship between Jesus and Krishna, he states: "In *Krishna* we are dealing with a historical person, . . . with an authentic *human being (vere homo).* At the same time we see in him the *revelation of the one God (vere Deus).* This means that for Hindus, too, the one God has revealed himself at a certain time and in a certain place. And for Hindus, too, there is within a cyclical world process a decisive intervention by God, which, as in the case of Krishna, has a sort of eschatological character for his world period." There are a number of problems here; let me just list some: the historicity of Krishna should be understood differently from that of Jesus of Nazareth; the context of the question of revelation in traditional Christianity and Hinduism is vastly different; the unity with God in Hinduism and Christianity cannot be equated; and so forth.

and clarifications are in order. It is a commonplace in Hindu thought to believe that some dimension of the human being is divine. In some current Advaita Vedanta forms, "this amounts to saying that the divine is simply the human name for some absolute principle of reality whose ultimacy lies in its alone being the real." The possibility of realization of the divine lies within the reach of any human being; however, in most cases that does not happen. Jesus is one among those in whom the realization of the divine came to happen.[171] Hence, Jesus' importance lies in his role as the symbol of the potential of the realization of the divine in the human person. In that outlook, even the cross may be appropriated as the form of an ultimate self-sacrifice, "in the metaphysical sense of the sacrifice of the ego to the all-pervasive divine."[172]

Chakravarthi Ram-Prasid goes so far as to make this summative statement of contemporary Hindu christological estimations: "It is probably right to say that the aspect of earlier Hindu views of Jesus that retains influence now is the recognition of Jesus as unquestionably divine in some way. There is hardly any systematic theorization of Jesus in which he is dismissed as a charlatan or as a 'mere' human being or as having no spiritual significance whatsoever."[173] Over against the dearth of contemporary academic[174] and "official" interpretations, the popular interest in Jesus is mushrooming, as can be seen in pictures and symbols all over in India.

There are strands of Hinduism such as Chaitanya Vaishnavism, founded in West Bengal by the fifteenth-century Christian reformer Chaitanya (whose teachings are currently being disseminated by the Hare Krishna movement, founded by A. C. Bhaktivedanta Swami), that consider Jesus as Guru. Chaitanya focused on love and devotion rather than on doctrine, particularly toward Krishna, the avatar of Vishnu. The ultimate goal of this pursuit is *uttama bhakti,* active love and desire for God. Avatars, divine embodiments, empowered with divine *shakti* (power), help revive the devo-

171. Chakravarthi Ram-Prasad, "Hindu Views of Jesus," in *JWF,* p. 85. In non-advaitic views, the distinction between the transcendent God and humanity is preserved although the human being is considered to have some dimension of the divine.

172. Ram-Prasad, "Hindu Views of Jesus," in *JWF,* p. 85. It is clear without saying that this appreciation of self-sacrifice has nothing to do with the Christian interpretation of atonement in which Jesus dies for the sins of others.

173. Ram-Prasad, "Hindu Views of Jesus," in *JWF,* p. 86.

174. One has to remember that the study of religions (including comparative study of religion) is not part of the contemporary academic life in India. This has everything to do with the effort to uphold a secular government and way of life.

tion to the Lord. Jesus is one of those divinely empowered incarnations.[175] That devotion shares unmistakable parallels with the long tradition of Christian mysticism.

If possible, even higher status is granted to Jesus in *The Gospel of Sri Ramakrishna,* written by the nineteenth-century great Bengalese guru Ramakrishna Paramahansa. He claimed to have a number of mystical encounters with Jesus, one time so deep that he felt like "Christ possessed his soul." When on the fourth day following this experience he saw a vision of Christ, "a voice rang out in the depths of Sri Ramakrishna's soul: 'Behold the Christ who shed His heart's blood for the redemption of the world, who suffered a sea of anguish for love of men. It is He, the Master Yogi, who is in eternal union with God. It is Jesus, Love Incarnate.'" One of his disciples comments: "Sri Ramakrishna realized his identity with Christ, as he had already realized his identity with Kali, Rama, Hanuman, Radha, Krishna, Brahman, and Mohammed. . . . Thus he experienced the truth that Christianity, too, was a path leading to God-Consciousness."[176] The Christian reader of Sri Ramakrishna's experiences and interpretations of Christ must exercise caution in not misinterpreting them. His talk about the shedding of "heart's blood for the redemption of the world" or the equation of Jesus with God does not translate into any kind of Christian theology of atonement nor make Jesus exclusively unique among similar religious leaders mentioned above. It is highly instructive that his disciples at times equated him with Jesus, seeing both of them standing in the line of special prophets such as Muhammad, Buddha, and Krishna (the incarnation of Vishnu).[177] Also noteworthy is that the most famous disciple of Ramakrishna, Sami Vivekananda — best known for his influential speech at the first World's Parliament of Religions in Chicago (1893) and as the founder of Vedanta Societies — wrote the highly honoring preface to the (unfinished) Bengali translation of Thomas à Kempis's *Imitation of Christ.*[178]

Bede Griffiths makes the obvious but important point that whereas in Hinduism the unity between the avatar and the Deity is union without dis-

175. For a succinct discussion, see Amanda Mills, "Jesus: Emissary of Divine Love," in *JWF,* pp. 100-107.

176. *The Gospel of Sri Ramakrishna,* p. 34, reproduced in *JBC,* p. 173. Goddess Kali, at the Dakshineswar temple near Calcutta, was the focus of Ramakrishna's spiritual devotion.

177. For text sample from *The Gospel of Sri Ramakrishna,* see *JBC,* pp. 175-77.

178. *The Complete Works of Vivekananda,* 8:159-60, reproduced in *JBC,* pp. 177-79. It is reported that while traveling on his teaching trips, Vivekananda carried with him only two books, the Bhagavad-Gita and *The Imitation of Christ.*

tinction, in Christian tradition there is unity-in-distinction.[179] Otherwise, the classical rule of the distinctiveness of Father, Son, and Spirit in their inner eternal love relationship would not follow. For Hindus, in contrast, the union means identity.

Hence, a closer look at the complex issue of uniqueness is in order. However, before that, closer scrutiny of the important topic of incarnation and avatars is attempted. The question of "atonement" will be discussed later in the context of the doctrine of reconciliation.

Incarnation and Avatars

With all the differences and diversities in Hindu traditions, it is safe to say that in classical Hinduism,[180] the one Brahman in its "manifested" *(saguna)* form is known as the Hindu Trimurti,[181] namely, Brahma (the "Creator God"), Vishnu (the "Preserver God"), and Shiva (the "Destroyer God" [and/or "Completer God"?]). As it is the task of Vishnu to make sure the universe and its order will not be destroyed in an undue manner, through various forms of avatars, Vishnu intervenes in the affairs of the world. This "descent," as the word literally means, can be expressed in terms of the word "incarnation," as the often-cited passage in Bhagavad-Gita (4.7-8) renders it:

7. Whenever, O descendant of Bharata, there is decline of Dharma, and rise of Adharma, then I body Myself forth
8. For the protection of the good, for the destruction of the wicked, and for the establishment of Dharma, I come into being in every age.[182]

The purpose, hence, of the "coming down" of God is the establishment of *dhamma,* the right order, "righteousness" (as it is rendered in some English translations). It has little to do with the Christian notion of atonement.

179. B. Griffiths, *Vedanta and Christian Faith,* pp. 54-55.

180. Roughly speaking, beginning from the time of the Upanishads (1000-6000 B.C.E.) down, and as presented in a concise form in the most popular and treasured Scripture, Bhagavad-Gita (around 400 B.C.E.), "Bible" of the common folks in India, which is a philosophical dialogue between the god Krishna and the warrior Arjuna.

181. The relation of this Hindu "trinity" to Christian trinitarian doctrine will be investigated in the context of the doctrine of God.

182. Trans. Swami Swarupananda, http://www.sacred-texts.com/hin/, accessed February 3, 2011.

It has everything to do with what we might call enlightenment (true knowledge, right insight?) in our terminology. As Sandy Bharat puts it: "The purpose . . . is to help people return to the Source [Brahman, 'ultimate reality'] by remembering their true Selves and so be free from *avidya* (ignorance) and its conditioning. It is avidya that keeps one in the spell of *maya* (delusion) and separated from God. Most Hindus believe that, to help people return to the Source, Truth is revealed through descents of divine beings."[183] Or: "Avatars come then to bring a new or renewed revelation of Truth, expressed through the example of their lives. This enables people to know that they can change and become like the avatars."[184] Chapter 4 in Gita, in which the above-quoted important statement about the divine descent is found, can be titled "The Way of Renunciation of Action in Knowledge," which is a (divine) solution to the human effort in "The Way of Knowledge" of chapter 2 and "The Way of Action" in chapter 3. The divine descent is both the aid, as it were, and the way of renunciation of the *yogic* path on the way to a fuller realization.

Hindu mythology includes numerous accounts of incarnations. Among those, an established doctrine widely shared by various Hindu strands is *daśāvatāra,* ten incarnations of Vishnu beginning from a fish and tortoise and continuing all the way to Rama and Krishna, the two most cherished avatars of all, and finally to the Buddha. The last one-to-be-waited-for is Kalkī at the end of this degenerate era.[185] Of the multiplicity of incarnations, an illustrative example is the possibility of multiple avatars of the one and same figure such as Krishna. Based on Vedic teaching and embraced by even contemporary Hindu piety, six such incarnations are often discerned: Purusa Avatars, Lila Avatars, Guna Avatars, Manvantara Avatars, Yuga Avatars, and Satyavesa Avatars.

Furthermore, unlike Christian tradition, it is customary for Hindu thought to conceive of avatars in degrees, from a partial to a fuller to a fullest measure of incarnation. Srila Prabhupada, the founder of the International Association for Krishna Consciousness,[186] says it is also therefore understandable that, in contrast to the traditional Christian view of incarnation of the divine in one particular person at a certain point in history in a particu-

183. Bharat, "Hindu Perspectives," pp. 250-51.

184. Bharat, "Hindu Perspectives," p. 255; so also Yuketswar, *The Holy Science,* p. 32.

185. A reliable, nontechnical exposition is offered by Sharma, *Classical Hindu Thought,* pp. 6-7, 82-86.

186. Prabhupāda, *Bhagavad-Gita as It Is,* p. 69, cited in Bharat, "Hindu Perspectives," p. 251.

lar place, Hindu religion not only speaks of multiple "descents" of the divine but also speaks of them in universal terms.

> The Incarnation is a symbol of universal integration. The Divine Incarnation is the individual symbol of a universal purpose. Divine Incarnations are considered apparently as individuals but really they are universals. We are told often that they walk on earth with their feet planted on the physical level, but their heads move in the heavens. The Incarnations are universal beings and they are super-human in their knowledge and power. The distinction between an ordinary individual and a Divine Incarnation is this, that while the individual is confined in its consciousness to the operations of the sense faculties, the mind and the intellect, the Incarnation has an intuitive perception of the inter-relatedness of all things and there is a vision of the Absolute perpetually before the eyes of the Incarnation, notwithstanding the fact that it appears to have descended to the level of the particular individuals.[187]

At first reading these kinds of texts would suggest that for Hinduism, the avatars are nonindividualistic and nonhistorical. That is not always the case. Rather, in a Hindu framework, the descent of the divine is not merely — and perhaps we should say: not primarily — focused in individuals in certain locations in a particular point of time. Hence, it seems to me that Sandy Bharat's contention that "a sense of hypostatic union and anti-docetism is affirmed by some of Hinduism's great preceptors,"[188] although a

187. Krishnananda, *Philosophy of the Bhagavadgita,* p. 99 (www.swami-krishnananda.org) (accessed February 3, 2011). Similarly, e.g., Radhakrishnan, *The Recovery of Faith,* p. 117: "The Incarnation is not an historical event which occurred two thousand years ago. It is an event which is renewed in the life of everyone who is on the way to the fulfillment of the destiny."

188. Bharat, "Hindu Perspectives," p. 252. True, there are statements that seemingly support Bharat's judgment, such as the one she cites in this context from Paramahansa Yogananda (*Man's Eternal Quest,* p. 295): "They [Hindu *avatāras*] have their weaknesses, their struggles and temptations, and then, through righteous battle and right behavior, they attain victory. . . . A Christ and a Krishna created perfect by God, without any effort of self-evolution on their part, and merely pretending to struggle and overcome their trials on earth, could not be examples for suffering humans to follow." This statement, however, has to be put in perspective: rather than a "Son of Man" who not only embodies the life of total identification with sinful and suffering humanity, culminating in the vicarious death on the cross, after the Christian interpretation, the *avatāras* in Hindu religion is more like an example to be imitated. Of course, the theme of *The Imitation of Christ* is

friendly Hindu gesture, is an overstatement from the point of view of Christian theology.

Like the Christian Raimon Panikkar, Hindus customarily make a distinction between Jesus and Christ. The title Christ appeals to them as it speaks of universal application. The founder of the Self-Realization Fellowship and one of the ablest communicators to the West of Hindu religion, Paramahansa Yogananda (d. 1953) says this well: "There is a difference of meaning between *Jesus* and *Christ.* Jesus is the name of a little human body in which the vast Christ Consciousness was born. Although the Christ Consciousness manifested in the body of Jesus, it cannot be limited to one human form. It would be a metaphysical error to say that the omnipresent Christ Consciousness is circumscribed by the body of any one human being."[189] In this framework, "Christ" does not mean a particular individual but rather "the state of realization of Truth." Hence, each and every one of us can become Christ.[190]

Revisiting the "Uniqueness" of Jesus Christ

Most Hindu traditions have a strong inclusivistic orientation. This comes to the fore in the often-quoted Rig Veda saying: "To what is One, sages give many a title."[191] As discussed above, most Hindus would be ready to affirm the divine status of Jesus Christ, and he is counted among other such figures. The truthfulness and beauty of other traditions are often openheartedly affirmed. Yet there is also the awareness that, say, the value of Jesus, as high as it is, in some sense may be inferior — or at least is not superior — to the Hindu religion.[192] In some sense, the typical Hindu view resembles the Roman Catholic fulfillment theory of religions but perhaps in a more radicalized form: everything good and true is being affirmed, yet with the expectation that the "fullness" may be found in one's own religion.

---

part of the matrix of Christian theology of salvation, but that is not all — and, divorced from the "divine initiative," it has no final value in itself in traditional Christian interpretation. The details of this argumentation, of course, have to be worked out in the section on atonement/reconciliation.

189. Yogananda, *Man's Eternal Quest,* p. 297.

190. Abhedananda, *Vedanta Philosophy,* p. 40.

191. Rig Veda 1.164.46. The whole verse goes: "They call him Indra, Mitra, Varuṇa, Agni, and he is heavenly nobly-winged Garutmān. To what is One, sages give many a title they call it Agni, Yama, Mātariśvan."

192. See further, P. J. Griffiths, "Hindu Perceptions," p. 194.

Hence, finding parallels between the incarnation of Jesus and Hindu avatars, and even granting divine status to Jesus, does not make him unique in the Christian sense. In denial of the traditional and mainline Christian interpretation in which Jesus Christ is the unique, historically based divine intervention, Hindus insist that the divine intervenes in and interpenetrates human life constantly, in various ways. Over against the Christian view of "God-as-human" (the Word made flesh), the Hindu formula is "God-in-human." In this Hindu outlook, "the divine and human are ultimately identical, or the divine is the spark of potential in the human, or something else. . . . In all of them, everyone is potentially divine, and Jesus is an outstanding . . . embodiment of the human who has realized his divinity." Consequently, Hindu interpretation of Jesus knows no idea of atonement after Christian tradition. Similar to Judaism and Islam, there is no original sin to begin with; rather, similar to Buddhism, there is the law of karma. This is not to deny the profound significance of the *idea* of self-sacrifice for others, as long as it is stripped of all notions of Christian "atonement."[193]

The only way in the Hindu framework to speak of the "uniqueness" of Jesus is to link it with oneness, the underlying oneness of all, as explained in the often-cited formula from Chandogya Upanishad (6.2.1): "In the beginning . . . there was that only which is . . . one only, without a second. Others say, in the beginning there was that only which is not, . . . one only, without a second; and from that which is not, that which is was born."[194] This kind of uniqueness, however, is not the same as the traditional Christian "exclusive" uniqueness of Jesus Christ. The Hindu thought makes Jesus "unique" among other "unique" manifestations of the Divine.

Keshub Chunder Sen speaks for many Hindus[195] when he wants to

193. Ram-Prasad, "Hindu Views of Jesus," in *JWF,* p. 88. For the theme of self-sacrifice, see further, J. W. Douglas, "From Gandhi to Christ," pp. 101-8.

194. Trans. Max Mueller, http://www.sacred-texts.com/hin/sbe01/sbe01120.htm (accessed February 2, 2011); see Ravi Ravindra, "Jesus is Not an Idol," in *JWF,* pp. 96-97.

195. This list would include a number of well-known Hindu figures, such as Vivekananda and Mohandas Gandhi. Said Vivekananda: "We are all Christians; we are all Mohammedans; we are all Hindus; or all Buddhists. No matter if a Buddhist is a Chinaman, or is a man from Persia, they think that they are brothers, because of their professing the same religion. Religion is the tie, [the] unity of humanity." Cited in *JBC,* p. 182. And Gandhi uttered this often-quoted saying: "I believe that He [Jesus Christ] belongs not solely to Christianity, but to the entire world; to all races and people. It matters little under what flag, name or doctrine they may work, profess a faith, or worship a god inherited from their ancestors." Cited in *JBC,* p. 188.

"repudiate the little Christ of popular theology" that is in keeping with the traditional Christian exclusive uniqueness. Sen, who, as mentioned, rejects Jesus as divine incarnation, still speaks of Jesus in the highest possible terms but in the context that bespeaks universality and inclusivity, building on the biblical and Christian teaching, as he sees it: "Wherever there is intelligence, in all stages of life . . . there dwells Christ, if Christ is the logos. . . . Do they [the church fathers] not speak of an all-pervading Christ? Do they not bear unequivocal testimony to Christ in Socrates? Even in barbarian philosophy and in all Hellenic literature they saw and adored their Logos-Christ." Therefore, Sen strongly argues that he wants to "stand up for a greater Christ, a fuller Christ, a more eternal Christ, a more universal Christ." Indeed, he goes so far as to say: "I plead for the eternal Logos of the Fathers, and I challenge the world's assent. This is the Christ who was in Greece and Rome, in Egypt and India. In the bards and the poets of the Rig Veda was he. He dwelt in Confucius and in Sakya Muni [Gautama Buddha]. . . . He is not the monopoly of any nation or creed." On this basis, Sen confesses and believes in "Jesus Christ an Asiatic."[196] The Christian responses to, and qualifications of, positions such as that of Sen were dealt with above in the discussion of pluralistic and revisionist Christian understandings of the incarnation and uniqueness of Jesus Christ.

As discussed above in the context of Jewish-Christian dialogue, the constructive approach to interfaith dialogue cannot mean mindless renunciation of the distinctive features of one's faith. A number of current approaches not only recommend that but take it for granted. Bharat's uncritical and unnuanced charge that "Christian exclusivist claims, backed by colonial and contemporary mission, that Jesus Christ is the only divine incarnation, have hindered Hindu-Christian dialogue" is a half-truth at its best.[197] Of course, there are Christians and "missionaries" who are not thoughtfully considering the similarities and differences between Christian and Hindu claims. That said, it is utterly naive — and in many ways colonial — to take any serious, considered Christian claim to the uniqueness of Christ and his incarnation as an expression of blind exclusivism. A dialogue without the freedom and encouragement for participants to remain faithful to their traditions' position is neither useful nor interesting. If all such attempts are labeled "blind exclusivism," I fear that behind such modernist naivete is the "speck" in the eye of the beholder.

196. *Chunder Sen's Lectures,* vol. 2, in *JBC,* pp. 167-68.
197. Bharat, "Hindu Perspectives," p. 253.

For the sake of clarification and progress, it is essential to remind both Christians and Hindus of the true differences in the understanding of the deity of the "Savior(s)," incarnation, and the intervention of God. Rather than either tradition giving up its own dearly held convictions, a genuine dialogue calls for a patient, at times painful, and always rewarding mutual exchange. Why is it that Hindu partners, in this case, are never required by the Christian "pluralistic" counterparts to give up their allegedly "inclusive" standpoint and so approach the traditional Christian stance? Why is it that Christian "pluralists" always take it for granted that Christian traditionalists are ill-informed, prejudiced, and stuck with their own limited views whereas the other is "liberal," open-minded, and embracing of the other?[198]

198. I fear the "liberals" and "pluralists" of the Global North who are most vocal in those charges do not have much experience in living with people of other faiths. A brief "scholarly" trip to, say, India as an outsider hardly makes one acquainted with the culture in a way that some of us who have had to undergo the painful and delightful experience of not only surviving culture shock but also learning a new language, settling one's family in a strange territory, building up relationships, and living out one's faith in a multicultural environment, have experienced. Even then, we who have had such experience are woefully "outsiders"! Hopefully, however, in a more modest and more self-critical way.

II. RECONCILIATION

In the introductory discussion of the "method" in Christology, it was noted that while the traditional distinction between the work (atonement) and person (identity) of Christ should be handled with great care, for pedagogical and heuristic purposes it continues to be utilized — if not for other reasons, then because of the need to take up one major topic at a time! Although the first part of the volume focused on topics that usually are categorized under the person of Christ, even a cursory look back at the discussion reveals that some key themes investigated, such as incarnation and resurrection, are certainly deeply soteriological as well. Hence, those themes will be taken up again as the discussion demands, as we now turn specifically to the topic of reconciliation.

While no single word in the biblical canon refers to the trinitarian work of the salvation of humankind and the whole creation, Christian tradition uses "atonement" most frequently. Other umbrella terms include "reconciliation," "redemption," and simply "salvation."[1] That said, most theologians would agree that "atonement" in one sense is more limited than the other three terms mentioned and basically focuses on the means of salvation; hence the term "atonement theories" used in classical discussions (as a way of explaining *how* salvation is brought about).[2]

Older discussions of atonement usually focused on the suffering and death of Christ on the cross. They also dealt with incarnation when incarna-

1. The terms "reconciliation" and "redemption" also can be used in a more limited, technical way, as the ensuing discussion will show.

2. See further, O'Collins, "Redemption," p. 5 n. 4.

tion was seen as an integral part of the salvific act. The life, ministry, miracles, and preaching of Jesus were not typically highlighted. It was also typical for the investigations to focus, at times almost exclusively, on the christological dimensions; the role of the Father was brought to the picture either in terms of the "object" of atonement or as counterpart to the Son. The Spirit's role was not crucial.

In contemporary treatments of atonement, a number of orientations both challenge and complement earlier approaches. This discussion will look at the work of salvation through the trinitarian framework as a salvific event and process, initiated and completed by the joint work of Father, Son, and Spirit. Add to that the radically changed worldview of late modernity with the turn to relationality and a dynamic understanding of reality discussed above, intensifying globalization of the world with cultural diversity and hybridity, and the interaction with other living faiths.[3] These and similar philosophical, cultural, scientific, religious, and theological developments urge contemporary systematic/constructive theology to do what it has done throughout the centuries — to interpret salvation in Christ through the lens of its current thought forms. In keeping with this, themes such as violence, power, and inclusivity, as well as sociopolitical dimensions, will also be brought to bear on the discussion, along with the truthfulness of Christian claims of salvation in the midst of other religions.

As a corrective to earlier juridical, often individualistic and at times "static" ways of interpreting the work of salvation, Adam Kotsko recommends a "social-relational" perspective in which relationality and communal aspects are appropriately acknowledged.[4] Along the same lines, Moltmann warns us of the danger of an individualistic reading of atonement tradition and its "spiritualization," which divorces it from earthly realities and relegates it only to the eschaton: "Admittedly, in the past the Christian doctrine of salvation was often applied solely to the eternal situation of human beings in God's sight, in order that eternal salvation might be related to the fundamental existential situation of men and women: their separation from God, their transience, finitude and mortality. This meant that often enough this doctrine ignored the actual, practical human situation, in its real misery."[5]

3. Kotsko, *The Politics of Redemption*, p. 3. He titles chap. 1 "Thinking Relationally."

4. For a useful exploratory discussion of the influence of cultural and philosophical frameworks on the development of atonement theories throughout history up until late modernity, see Shults, *Christology and Science*, chap. 3.

5. Moltmann, *Way of Jesus Christ*, p. 45.

Over against this reductionist account of salvation, we need to speak of reconciliation in holistic terms: "In the theological sense, salvation is whole salvation and the salvation of the whole, or it is not God's salvation; for God is 'the all-determining reality.' It is therefore more appropriate to present the salvation which Christ brings in ever-widening circles, beginning with the personal experience of reconciliation and ending with the reconciliation of the cosmos, heaven and earth."[6] Hence, a holistic and hospitable account of atonement as the gift from the triune God will be attempted.

The first chapter to follow (11) seeks to look carefully at the growth of Christian traditions of reconciliation, both biblical and historical (traditionally named atonement theories). In the investigation of both biblical and historical perspectives, every effort is made to be sensitive to the amazing richness and diversity of views. For the sake of systematic/constructive analysis, the growth of traditions will be assessed as to their liabilities and problems, as well as their continuing value for the contemporary needs of the globalizing and religiously pluralistic world. A key task therein is to relativize and qualify, as well as make more inclusive, the "atonement theories" of tradition in light of the biblical diversity. Before launching the construction of a contemporary theology of reconciliation in chapter 13, the chapter before that (12) will take up an issue whose relevance by and large went unnoticed in tradition but that in recent years has moved to the center of attention, namely, violence. Rumor is out there that any notion of a sacrificial death of the Son of God on the cross is hopelessly violent and oppressive. Any theology of reconciliation worth its salt must tackle this issue in a robust way. The constructive proposal of reconciliation seeks to develop a fully trinitarian account of reconciliation, drawing from not only the discussion of biblical and historical developments in chapter 11 but also from the results of key themes dealt with in part I.

Chapter 14 continues the outlining and discussion of the constructive theology of reconciliation with a special focus on how the Christian church as reconciled community can live out and work toward the reconciliation of men and women with God as well as among themselves, including their communities. In other words, what are the missionary implications for the church's life? That discussion will naturally lead into the last chapter of the volume (15), which again focuses on interfaith encounters and follows the principles and procedures established in chapter 10 above.

6. Moltmann, *Way of Jesus Christ,* p. 45.

11. Atonement Traditions

Biblical Metaphors and Symbols

The saving significance of the life, death, and resurrection of Jesus Christ is undoubtedly the center of the Gospels and to a large extent the rest of the NT. Two remarks are in order to help appropriately orient the reader of these NT testimonies. First, even though the Evangelists devote more space to Jesus' life, ministry, and teaching, the plot of the narrative clearly culminates in the cross and resurrection; thus the lasting value of the famous words of M. Kähler in terms of the Gospels being "passion narratives with extended introductions."[1] Second, that said, the "portrait of Jesus' execution could not be painted with a single color."[2] A number of metaphors, symbols, and images were employed by the NT authors to highlight distinctive features of the saving significance of Jesus' death — and how that death is related to his personhood, earthly life, resurrection, and ascension.

The metaphors employed to highlight and explain the death of the Messiah were drawn from various cultural and religious sources familiar to the contemporary culture. They include the court of law (e.g., justification), world of commerce (e.g., redemption), personal and communal relationships (e.g., reconciliation), cult and worship (e.g., sacrifice), as well as battleground (e.g., triumph over evil). All the metaphors related to these domains and others are interwoven, not only in the passion narrative and execution

1. Kähler, *So-Called Historical Jesus,* p. 80 n. 11.

2. Green and Baker, *Recovering the Scandal of the Cross,* p. 15.

but also in the whole history of Jesus Christ, including the pouring out of the Spirit at Pentecost.

Several of these metaphors and testimonies of course glean from the OT background. The figure of the suffering righteous one, familiar from Second Isaiah and Psalms, connected with Messiah from early on, looms large behind the Gospel narratives. The cultic life of the temple and sacrifices forms the background of some portions of the NT, including the book of Hebrews and Romans 3. The role of prophets as Yahweh's messengers and their suffering at the hands of the disobedient people, so profoundly illustrated in the life of Jeremiah, similarly helps us understand the Gospel writers' narrative. While later Christian tradition, particularly in the Christian West, has looked at Jesus' execution primarily through the lens of punishment and pain, for the writers' contemporary culture, the passion narrative is also about utmost public humiliation and rejection by God and community. These themes can also be integrally interwoven, as in the story of the rebellious and drunkard son to be stoned as the victim of God's curse (Deut. 21:18-21) or the criminal subject to hang on the tree to "purge" the land from pollution (Deut. 21:22-23). One can easily see these motifs behind the charges of demonic possession (Mark 3:20-30), blasphemy (Matt. 9:3), and drunkenness (Luke 7:34) leveled against Jesus.

There is no doubt that the impending violent death loomed on the horizon of the Jesus of the NT Gospels;[3] no wonder he had a hard time trying to convince his followers of its necessity (Mark 8:31-38 par.). Behind the impending death the Gospel authors discern the divine plan — as evidenced in the frequent use of the Greek *dei* ("must," "have to"; Matt. 16:21; Mark 8:31; Luke 9:22; and so forth). It was a death "for many," which becomes virtually a technical term (Mark 8:31; 9:31; 10:33-34; and so forth). That said, there are precious few passages on the lips of Jesus that seek to describe in any detail the theological meaning of his death. The Markan Jesus' sayings of giving "his life as a ransom for many" (Mark 10:45) and pouring out his "blood of the covenant . . . for many" (14:24) are such sayings. "Ransom" is connected with the ideas of deliverance and release drawn from the Roman slave trade and the hopes of the OT people of God under foreign tyrannies. The metaphor of covenant blood is connected with Yahweh's faithful acts in saving, freeing, and protecting his people on the basis of covenants often sealed with blood (as in Gen. 15).

3. For a helpful discussion of some familiar parables of Jesus such as that of the vineyard owner (Mark 12:1-2 and par.) and remarks including those concerning the fate of the prophets (Matt. 24:34, 37), see Finlan, *Problems with Atonement*, pp. 109-10.

It was left to Pauline traditions to offer a rich and variegated depiction of the many dimensions of the saving significance of Jesus' work for us.[4] Often Paul mixes a number of metaphors in one passage. Romans 8:3 contains no fewer than three in one sentence: sacrificial (sent in the flesh), judicial (condemning sin), and scapegoat (condemnation "in the flesh") — and perhaps even representation.[5] 2 Corinthians 5:14–6:2 is a grand example of the conflation of metaphors. While "reconciliation" — bringing together two distanced parties (as also in Rom. 5:10-11; Col. 1:20; and Eph. 2:16) — towers here as the main metaphor, others in the passage include "substitution," "representation," "forgiveness," "sin offering," "(cosmic) renewal," "righteousness," and divine "favor." Similarly, Galatians 3:10-14 offers a whole spectrum of metaphors, including "redemption" (from the curse of the law), "justification" through faith, "representation," "blessing," and reception of the Holy Spirit. At times Paul uses sacrificial images such as the Romans 3:25 "mercy-seat" instance that draws from the rich OT cultic background of the Day of Atonement (Lev. 16) as well as other Levitical sacrifices (Lev. 1–6). What is important is that the concept of sacrifice carries various meanings, including substitution related particularly to the shedding of blood, offering to God, and thanksgiving.[6] The most common biblical terms that are translated either as "to atone" or the closely related verb "to redeem" or a similar term, namely, *kipper* and *hilaskomai,* have their origin in a cultic environment and have therefore close connections with sacrificial rites.[7] The basic meaning of the terms denotes "(1) appeasement; soothing someone's anger;

4. In this and the following paragraphs I am indebted greatly to the extensive discussion in Green and Baker, *Recovering the Scandal of the Cross,* chaps. 2 and 3.

5. See further, Finlan, *Options on Atonement,* p. 25. Finlan (p. 1) lists six Pauline metaphors of atonement: sacrifice, scapegoat, redemption, justification, reconciliation, and adoption.

6. Very useful and nuanced discussions can be found in Gunton, *Actuality of Atonement,* chap. 5; and Fiddes, *Past Event and Present Salvation,* chap. 4. The meaning of sacrifice has been an occasion for heated debate since the publication in 1930 of F. C. N. Hick's *The Fullness of Sacrifice,* which totally repudiates any idea of propitiation or expiation. Blood stands for life rather than death. Christologically, its main meaning has to do with Jesus' "dedication of human life in perfect obedience. . . . He offered our human nature which He had made His own" (p. 176). In several influential publications, Vincent Taylor continued this line of argumentation against traditional understanding of sacrifice. In his mind, the restoration of fellowship and relations was the main task of sacrifices. *Jesus and His Sacrifice,* p. 295. While these viewpoints are valid, they obviously offer a reductionistic view of the various meanings of sacrifice in the texture of biblical witnesses.

7. See Lyonnet, "The Terminology of Redemption."

(2) economic satisfaction of a penalty; or (3) expiation, that is sacrificial cleansing."[8] The reference to the Passover Lamb in 1 Corinthians 5:7 comes from the same cultic word recalling the formative event in Exodus.[9] Furthermore, in some parts of his corpus Paul uses images drawn from the battlefield, cosmic or earthly, which speak of the defeat of powers (Col. 2:15), and the closely related metaphors of new creation and cosmic renewal pointing to the final victory of Christ over all powers (2 Cor. 5:16-17; Eph. 2:14-15).

To many readers of the NT it is not obvious that along with the Pauline corpus, the other main textual source is the Lukan tradition; indeed, in the original language, there is as much text from the pen of the Beloved Physician as from the apostle. The Lukan way of appropriating salvific metaphors is highly distinctive. Particularly the materials in the book of Acts are critical in that they claim to represent authentic samples of the missionary preaching of the early church encompassing both Petrine and Pauline ministries. Alongside the cross, there is a strong focus on resurrection and ascension, as well as on the pouring out and power of the Holy Spirit both within and outside the community of believers. The Pentecostal pouring out of the Spirit on all flesh (Acts 2) marks the beginning of the end — the last days. The crucified Messiah has now been made the risen and ascended Lord (*kyrios;* 2:36) who brings about forgiveness and restoration to the people of God (5:30-31). Healings as a foretaste of a holistic salvation and promises of the coming eschatological fulfillment are an integral part of the early church's preaching (Acts 3; 4; and so forth).

An even more distinctive approach to atonement is depicted in the extensive Johannine traditions with their great rhetorical devices such as speaking of the cross in terms of "lifting up" (John 3:14-15; 8:28) and glorification of the Son of Man (13:32)! Familiar OT metaphors of the sacrificial lamb (1:29) are joined with metaphors of water and cleansing (13:10-11; 15:3), which also relate to pneumatological aspects of salvation (4:13-15; 7:37-39). The epistles are fond of images of "light" and "purification" (1 John 1:5-7; 2:9; 3:3), forgiveness (1:8-9), and sacrifice for sins (2:2; 3:5). The book of Revelation uses several OT images in the cosmic context, including the victorious Lamb (Rev. 5:5, 9).

The book of Hebrews is fully embedded in the OT imagery of the temple, priesthood, sacrifices, and covenant. 1 Peter, while conversant with im-

8. Finlan, *Problems with Atonement,* p. 5.

9. A careful discussion of Paul's use of cultic imagery can be found in Finlan, *Problems with Atonement,* pp. 39-62.

ages of salvation such as the hope for the eschatological inheritance (1 Pet. 1:3-5, 13, 23), lays emphasis on what later theology calls the "moral example" view, namely, the invitation for imitation of the suffering and cross of Christ (2:12, 19, 21-25; 3:14-17 — an idea also occasionally present elsewhere, as in 1 John 3:16). A remarkable constellation of images can be found in 1 Peter 3:18-22, which blends masterfully pictures of the Innocent Sufferer put to death for others, the Preacher to the "deceased prisoners," and the Resurrected Champion who gains victory over all evil powers — and this in connection with the baptism as the symbol of regenerating purification a.k.a. Noah's ark!

Several theological conclusions emerge from the scrutiny of the NT depictions of atonement: first, to be "biblical" means honoring and embracing the rich and variegated diversity of metaphors, symbols, images, and testimonies rather than trying to pit one against the other. No single metaphor can capture the fullness of salvation. Second, the domain of atonement is far more inclusive than the cross alone. It is integrally related to the whole history of Jesus: incarnation, life, and earthly ministry; resurrection, ascension, and the giving of the Spirit. To put it another way: it is the trinitarian history of Jesus Christ. Third, the salvation offered is inclusive and holistic: enlightenment, forgiveness of sins, renewal, healing, empowerment, and release from the powers. Similarly, its scope encompasses personal, communal, and cosmic levels. Fourth, the diversity gives theology unprecedented resources in speaking of salvation in Christ in ways sensitive to cultural and religious contexts. Finally, the diversity helps us understand the rise of competing — or perhaps better: complementary — approaches to atonement present in the history of theology, the topic of the next section.

Historical Interpretations of Atonement

The Growth of Traditions

When studying the postbiblical developments of the doctrine of atonement, it is useful to remember the simple fact that, on the one hand, "The development of the Church's ideas about the saving effects of the incarnation was a slow, long drawn-out process,"[10] and that, on the other hand, at no time were any fixed statements about atonement attached to the creeds of the un-

10. J. N. D. Kelly, *Early Christian Doctrines*, p. 163.

divided church. For example, while the apostolic fathers' writings contain a number of references to Christ's work, the fathers exhibit no desire to come up with fixed formulae for doctrines such as the Trinity and the person of Christ. What these earliest writings are telling us are the salvific gifts of "new knowledge, fresh life, immortality," imparted to us.[11] Perhaps surprisingly, the apostolic fathers seem to be less concerned about the topics of sin and the need for atonement than many NT authors — even when they talk about the death of Christ for us and his glorious resurrection. For the apologists, to whom theological anthropology — and thus the topic of sin as well — became a much more important topic, the saving significance of Jesus was conceived predominantly in terms of fixing ignorance and error, and the incarnation was conceived as the assumption of human nature for its healing and restoration.[12]

The latter idea and the cosmic orientation of much of early theology gave rise to what Gustav Aulén, in his classic work *Christus Victor,* calls the "classic view" of atonement. According to him, for the first Christian millennium or so, Christian theology understood "the Atonement as a Divine conflict and victory; Christ — Christus Victor — fights against and triumphs over the evil powers of the world, the 'tyrants' under which [hu]mankind is in bondage and suffering, and in Him God reconciles the world to Himself."[13] Aulén names this first interpretation of atonement the classic view or *Christus Victor.* It speaks of Christ's victory and liberating work in terms of either "recapitulation" or "ransom."

Not until the beginning of the second millennium did another view come to dominate theology, namely, Anselm's satisfaction model, which responds to the problem of God's honor violated in the context of the late medieval hierarchical culture; Anselm seeks to explain the ultimate motif behind Christ's incarnation through this explanatory model. In Aulén's analysis, this view lays the foundation for the Protestant Reformers' penal substitution view in which Christ is punished in the place of humanity, thus satisfying the demands of justice so that God can pronounce forgiveness. Instead of God's honor and its restoration at the center, for the Reformers the main problem was humanity's condemnation due to sin and thus the need for Christ to offer a substitutionary sacrifice for the penalty. (As will be explained in the following, the Reformers also entertained other

11. J. N. D. Kelly, *Early Christian Doctrines,* pp. 163-64.
12. J. N. D. Kelly, *Early Christian Doctrines,* pp. 165-70.
13. Aulén, *Christus Victor,* p. 4.

explanatory models.) Anselm's view came to be challenged by the third main "atonement theory," developed by Peter Abelard and called the moral example view. Its focus is Christ's innocent suffering as an invitation to lay down our own lives for the sake of others. Understandably this view was favored by later theological traditions such as those of the Socinians and classical liberals, who had a hard time embracing the related ideas of human depravity and the wrath of God against sinners. Before engaging these views critically, let me outline briefly their leading ideas and the context out of which they emerged.

The second-century bishop of Lyons, Irenaeus, is the leading advocate of the recapitulation view, for which he also gleaned from Justin Martyr and other apologists. Cosmic in its orientation, and closely linked to incarnation, mortality rather than sinfulness is the ultimate "power" to be defeated. Behind this interpretation is a distinctive kind of understanding of the Fall. Irenaeus, as is well known, saw the Fall as an unfortunate "accident" natural to humanity-in-childhood rather than a tragic "fall from grace," a.k.a. the later Latin understanding. Incarnation then means that Christ "recapitulates" in himself all the stages of human life, including those that belong to our state as sinners — not only individual human lives, but even the whole "history of humankind" and indeed of the creation. By his incarnation and human life he reverses the course on which Adam by his sin started to lead humanity. Christ communicates immortality to those who are united to him by faith and effects a transformation in their lives (*Against Heresies* 3.17.4; 3.18.7; 3.19.1; 5.14.2). In his perfect obedience, he compensates for the disobedience of Adam (3.21.10). To sum up in one sentence: Christ "has therefore, in His work of recapitulation, summed up all things" (5.21.1).[14]

Important for Irenaeus is the parallel between Adam and Christ. Whereas the former was the beginning of disobedient humanity, the latter brought about the redeemed and renewed humanity, thus helping perfect the image of God.[15] It is significant that as Irenaeus explains the work of this author of new humanity, he stresses the importance of the anointing with the Holy Spirit: "The Spirit, therefore, descending under the predestined dispensation, and the Son of God, the Only-begotten, who is also the Word of the Father, coming in the fulness of time, having become incarnate in man for the sake of man, and fulfilling all the conditions of human nature"

14. Behind the idea of recapitulation is Eph. 1:10.

15. Ignatius of Antioch similarly says that the divine plan of salvation aims at the new man Jesus Christ. *To the Ephesians* 20.1.

(3.17.4).[16] Indeed, Irenaeus forges an integral connection between Logos ("Word of the Father") and a trinitarian Spirit Christology in a way that later theology often has failed to do. Similarly, when speaking of the overcoming of mortality, he speaks of the possibility of life incorruptible as the function of the vivifying Spirit (5.12). In other words, at the center of this approach is the teaching that "human nature was sanctified, transformed and elevated by the very act of Christ's becoming man."[17] This conviction leads to the distinctive Eastern view of salvation as *theosis,* deification, to be discussed later.

Focusing on the recapitulation view in Irenaeus is not meant to say that this metaphor of atonement was the only one employed by the bishop of Lyons, any more than other Greek-speaking theologians. At times he referred, for example, to redemption through the blood (3.5.3; 5.16.9) or reconciliation through Christ's body given up to death (5.14.1). A representative linking of the Fall and the cross is accomplished in his well-known statement that "so that as by means of a tree we were made debtors to God, [so also] by means of a tree we may obtain the remission of our debt" (5.17.3). In a highly important statement, Irenaeus first asserts that in incarnation Christ went through all phases of human life beginning from infancy and culminating in death (2.22.4).[18] What this is to say is that even when references to passion, suffering, self-sacrifice, and redemption occur, they are still part of the underlying theological anthropology and salvific framework explained above. In Athanasius's *De Incarnatione Verbi Dei* (9), this typical feature of the Christian East comes to full fruition. When speaking of the assumption of the human body by the Logos and surrender to death in order to restore incorruptibility, Athanasius employs terms such as "offering and sacrifice free from every stain" in reference to the ultimate goal, the restoration of incorruptibility and life everlasting. Death on the cross — even when connected with the idea of "debt" — is less about the later idea of "substitution" and more that "the death of all was accomplished in the Lord's body" (20).[19]

The other version of the earliest model of atonement in Aulén's typology, *Christus Victor,* employed the imagery of ransom, as is evident in Gregory of Nyssa and Origen, and has its secular background in the act of releasing slaves by payment. In Origen's exposition the ransom was paid to the

16. The sentence remains incomplete in the original, without the main verb.
17. J. N. D. Kelly, *Early Christian Doctrines,* p. 375.
18. On the basis of John 8:56-57, he surmises that Jesus reached the age of fifty.
19. J. N. D. Kelly (*Early Christian Doctrines,* pp. 379-80) agrees.

devil (Origen, *Commentary on the Gospel of Matthew* 16.8). Gregory, who of course also subscribed to the tradition of Irenaeus and Athanasius,[20] used the famous — rather: infamous — image of God paying the ransom through deceiving the devil with the trickery of a fishhook. Hidden under human nature was Christ's deity, which the devil devoured as bait and thus helped destroy his own power. Well aware of the potential objections to such rhetoric, Gregory defended the divine deception by reminding his readers that it was just recompense for the devil's own deceitful nature (Gregory of Nyssa, *The Great Catechism* 26).

At the same time — indeed, immediately following the hook allegory — Gregory also interpreted Christ's work in terms of "healing touch," a metaphor similar in many ways (*The Great Catechism* 27) to recapitulation. Importantly enough, Gregory concluded that section of his teaching with a depiction of atonement pregnant with many meanings: "Even the death on the Cross was sublime: for it was the culminating and necessary point in that scheme of Love in which death was to be followed by blessed resurrection for the whole 'lump' of humanity: and the Cross itself has a mystic meaning" (summary of *The Great Catechism* 32). This is in keeping with the emerging, open-ended, and multifaceted conception of the salvific work of Christ among the Fathers. The same can be seen in an anonymous second-century writing that, while using the ransom metaphor, also ties it to the underlying mortality-versus-immortality dynamic so characteristic of the earliest soteriologies: "He Himself took on Him the burden of our iniquities, He gave His own Son as a ransom for us, the holy One for transgressors, the blameless One for the wicked, the righteous One for the unrighteous, the incorruptible One for the corruptible, the immortal One for them that are mortal. For what other thing was capable of covering our sins than His righteousness?" (Mathetes, *Epistle to Diognetus* 9).[21]

By and large the classic view, particularly the recapitulation version, became the dominant explanatory model of the Eastern Church, the Greek-speaking church. Eastern Christianity also continued highlighting the apologists' stress on true knowledge and light.[22] On the Latin side, somewhat surprisingly there was less interest in the doctrine of the atonement during

20. See J. N. D. Kelly, *Early Christian Doctrines,* pp. 380-81, for references in Gregory and Basil the Great.

21. The term *Mathetes,* "pupil," is the pseudonym for the unknown author of this letter.

22. For references in Clement of Alexandria and Origen, see J. N. D. Kelly, *Early Christian Doctrines,* pp. 183-85.

the patristic era, even though it was in Latin theology that the doctrine of original sin came to be developed under the leadership of Tertullian and Augustine. Related to this development, Augustine was influential in interpreting Christ's death as a unique sacrifice to appease the divine wrath (Augustine, *On Faith, Hope, and Love* 33). True, Tertullian speaks of Christ's passion and death, at times in a way that employs sacrificial and substitutionary expressions; yet he fails to offer any kind of coherent interpretative framework, and often he leans toward the apologists' pedagogic view. At the same time, the Irenaean model was supported by many Latin theologians such as Hippolytus and Hilary of Poitiers.[23]

Beginning with the fourth-century Latin theologians such as Hilary of Poitiers and Ambrose, the sacrificial interpretation became stronger. Also the idea — later developed fully by Anselm of Canterbury — of the devil having rights on us was supported by Ambrose.[24] Similar to what Martin Luther did at the time of the Reformation, Augustine summed up in a creative way various previous traditions, including the role of Christ as the mediator between God and humanity, highlighting the importance of Christ's humanity as the means of mediation. When speaking of the work of salvation, like his colleagues he occasionally resorted to the recapitulation explanation and redemption from under the power of the devil — at times speaking of Christ's blood as the payment. If there is any dominant interpretative model in the Augustinian soteriology, it may lie "in the expiatory sacrifice offered for us by Christ in His passion," which of course ties in with his mediatory role. Still, Augustine also appreciated Christ's role as example.[25]

Aulén's suggestion that it was only in the beginning of the second millennium that the classic view was challenged and complemented by two rather different approaches, those of Anselm and Abelard, has to be handled with caution. As evidenced above, the earlier theologians already held a number of different ideas about atonement, including such that in hindsight came to be associated with satisfaction or moral example views.

Anselm of Canterbury's *Cur Deus Homo* offers a logical and theological reasoning for the necessity of the incarnation.[26] In the context of medi-

23. For textual references in Tertullian and Hippolytus, see J. N. D. Kelly, *Early Christian Doctrines*, pp. 177-78, and in Hilary, p. 386.

24. J. N. D. Kelly, *Early Christian Doctrines*, p. 387.

25. J. N. D. Kelly, *Early Christian Doctrines*, p. 392. For textual references, see pp. 390-95.

26. For a helpful guide to discussion, see Jasper Hopkins, *A Companion to the Study of St. Anselm*, pp. 187-214.

eval feudal society, with its hierarchy and desire for harmony, the basic problem is disorder: the order of divine justice that governs the cosmos has been disturbed by sin. Sin, rather than being a debt to the devil (2.21), is the failure to render to God his due (1.11). The happiness for which human beings have been created by the loving and compassionate God requires voluntary harmony with the will of God. The just God is not able to forgive sin without payment for the lost honor (1.12) without losing his dignity (1.13). Satisfaction is needed (1.19) that is relative to the greatness of the violation of honor, which humanity is unable to deliver (1.20, 23; 2.4). Consequently, the debt can be paid only by God, in other words, the God-man (2.6). Christ's death, which was not occasioned by his own need but was rather a voluntary self-offering as our payment, can finally pay the debt (2.19, 20). While satisfaction is at the center, the idea of offering an example of innocent, righteous suffering is also present in this logical system (2.18).[27]

This last lead was picked up by Peter Abelard in his radical revisioning of the interpretation of atonement that also asks the same question of "why" the incarnation in his "Exposition of the Epistle to the Romans."[28] Abelard responds to Anselm by insisting that God indeed has the right of ownership to humans and that it is perfectly appropriate for God to forgive without any "satisfaction" if God so wishes. Jesus' death provides a compelling example to follow. Jesus embodies God's sacrificial love. Abelard does not focus on the original sin of Adam or the debt owed to God, but rather, in Abelard's view, sin consists of wrong and mistaken intentions, evil inclinations of the mind.[29] Jesus' death and innocent suffering offer a grand model to follow and help orient our will and love in the right direction. Thus, the nomenclature "moral example view."

This view of atonement was embraced by various later movements and thinkers who rejected the whole idea of vicarious satisfaction or penalty such as the Unitarian Socinians of the sixteenth century. Faustus and Laelius Socinus focused on the prophetic ministry of the early days of Jesus and highlighted his humanity.[30] The Enlightenment thinkers found much to commend in the moral example view. It fit well with Immanuel Kant's idea of Jesus as the moral ideal and our duty as human beings to "elevate our-

27. For a useful discussion of "variations on Anselm's theory," see Driver, *Understanding the Atonement,* pp. 53-54.

28. Abelard, "Exposition of the Epistle to the Romans," pp. 276-87.

29. As explained in Abelard, "Ethics, or Know Thyself," pp. 186-91.

30. See Pelikan, *Reformation of Church and Dogma,* pp. 324-25, with references to original sources.

selves to this ideal of moral perfection."[31] Liberal Protestants, similarly, considered this interpretation appealing, as is evident in Schleiermacher's theology. While Schleiermacher's view often resembles the patristic position in highlighting the importance of the incarnation, the example motif seems to stand at the forefront.[32] Another liberal, Albrecht Ritschl, opposed vocally any notion of penal satisfaction even though he regarded the death of Christ as the foundation for the establishment of God's kingdom.[33] One of the most influential defenders of the moral example view in the early twentieth century was Hastings Rashdall, who spoke of the "moral ideal which Christ taught by His words, and illustrated by His life and death of love," the only "ideal given among men by which we may be saved."[34]

Instead of Abelard's view, the Anselmian interpretation became the dominant view during the Middle Ages, and the classic view remained less well known in the Christian West even though in the East the Irenaean understanding became the main tradition. Thomas Aquinas helped consolidate the satisfaction view in the context of the Western Church's emphasis on sacrifice and the debt of sin. Christ brings about atonement because his pure life, passion, and death are more than able to compensate for the offense of the human race. Aquinas explains Christ's death on the cross in terms of "sacrifice" or "atonement" or "redemption." Sacrifice is necessary with regard to "something done for that honor which is properly due to God, in order to appease Him." Redemption is needed because of a twofold captivity, namely, bondage to sin, which has led to the bondage by the devil and the debt of punishment.[35]

Among the Protestant Reformers, particularly the Reformed side continued in the line of the Anselmian view.[36] Similarly, Martin Luther built on the Anselmian tradition even though he also helped rediscover in a fresh way the classic view of the Fathers. The Reformers' view is often labeled the "penal substitution" view, which implies its Anselmian basis coupled with the

31. Kant, *Religion within the Limits of Reason Alone*, p. 54; see Benner, "Immanuel Kant's Demythologization," pp. 99-111.

32. See further, McKnight, *Jesus Christ in Scripture and History*, pp. 183-84 particularly.

33. Ritschl, *Christian Doctrine of Justification and Reconciliation.*

34. Rashdall, *Idea of Atonement in Christian Theology*, p. 463.

35. Thomas Aquinas, *Summa Theologica* 3.48.2-4.

36. For a detailed investigation of all Reformation views, including the Catholic, with a focus on Calvin, see D. F. Wright, "The Atonement in Reformation Theology," pp. 37-48.

need for a sacrificial-expiatory death on the cross as a way to deal with condemned humanity's lot because of sin. Before focusing on the penal substitution view, let us highlight the creative combination of atonement views in Luther. Aulén has argued convincingly that "Luther's teaching can only be rightly understood as a revival of the old classic theme of the Atonement as taught by the Fathers, but with a greater depth of treatment."[37] This combining of the two traditions is well illustrated in the two rubrics under which another influential Luther interpreter looks at the topic of atonement in the Reformer: "Christ's Work as Satisfaction to God" and "Christ's Work as a Battle with the Demonic Powers."[38] To the satisfaction dimension is related the motif of suffering for punishment for sins and having been subjected to the wrath of God. Indeed, Christ becomes the greatest of sinners, on the basis of a careful and literal reading of passages such as Isaiah 53:6, Galatians 3:13, and 2 Corinthians 5:21.[39] Luther keeps the resurrection and death of Christ closer together than do many other Protestants: the final victory over the powers requires the raising of the resurrected one.

In Calvin's Reformed theology and particularly among his followers, both in Reformed orthodoxy[40] following the Reformation and in the ensuing conservative/fundamentalistic Princeton orthodoxy at the turn of the twentieth century, the consolidation of the penal substitution hermeneutics often becomes the test of orthodoxy. Calvin sets forth his view of atonement clearly and powerfully in the second book of his *Institutes.* He explains the incarnation and cross in terms of obedience, satisfaction of God's justice, and payment for the penalty of sin (2.9.3). Christ's priestly office speaks also of his sacrifice for the atonement of sins (2.15.6). To sum up: Calvin depicts the work of redemption in terms of both penal substitution and sacrifice for expiation and propitiation (2.16). A striking illustration of the growing influence of the satisfaction cum penal substitution cum sacrificial-expiatory interpretation in Protestant theology is the rebuttal of the Socinian critique of the Calvinistic view by Hugo Grotius — the Arminian theologian! His

37. Aulén, *Christus Victor,* p. 102. As is well known, Luther occasionally exploited the trickery metaphor of Gregory and others; see *LW* 29:135.

38. Althaus, *Theology of Martin Luther,* pp. 201-17 with detailed documentation of original texts. I am well informed of the fact that Althaus also critiques harshly Aulén's threefold typology and the exact nature of the "ransom" model (pp. 18-23). I still think that for my purposes here putting Aulén and Althaus side by side is not an injustice to either.

39. Among many examples, see Luther, *LW* 26:278.

40. See, e.g., a representative statement by Franz Burmann in Heppe, *Reformed Dogmatics,* p. 473.

Defense of the Catholic Faith on the Satisfaction of Christ against Faustus Socinus begins the strong apology for the satisfaction/substitution view by affirming its status as the "catholic" doctrine and defines Christ's passion in terms of "bearing the most severe tortures, and a bloody and ignominious death, pay[ing] the penalty for our sins" required by "divine justice."[41] A number of leading Calvinistic theologians of the eighteenth and nineteenth centuries not only affirmed strongly the penal substitution view but also made it virtually the orthodox interpretation. Among them, Charles Hodge is a leading figure. On the basis of a number of Reformed and some Lutheran documents, Hodge argues that it is axiomatic that forgiveness requires "satisfaction," and that can be had only through "punishment" in terms of Christ's "sacrifice."[42] While in many ways diverting from his Reformed tradition, Karl Barth's massive discussion of the topic of atonement under the telling heading "The Judge Judged in Our Place" defends unabashedly the substitutionary nature of atonement as Christ becomes the sin-bearer and the condemned.[43]

An Assessment of Atonement Traditions

The critical assessment of atonement traditions[44] has to take place at two interrelated levels. On the one hand, each of the main "theories" should be subjected to reflection. On the other hand, the complex interrelations of the main traditions and their relation to both biblical perspectives and the challenges and concerns of the contemporary world should be carefully weighed.

41. Grotius, *Defense of the Catholic Faith,* p. 107. At the same time, Grotius's "governmental" theology also differs from the Calvinistic view in that love, rather than retributive justice, is the dominant quality of God, which also leads him to appreciate — with all his criticisms! — Abelardian-Socinian interpretation as well. For a fine comparison, see Culpepper, *Interpreting the Atonement,* p. 107.

42. Hodge, *Systematic Theology,* pp. 480-544, gives a detailed exposition and defense of this view.

43. Barth, *CD* IV/1, pp. 211-82. See also p. 185 where Barth speaks of the incarnated Christ "giving Himself up to the contradiction of man against Him, His placing Himself under the judgment under which man has fallen in this contradiction, under the curse of death which rests upon Him."

44. For useful listing and consideration of typical objections against and affirmations of atonement theories, see, e.g., Driver, *Understanding the Atonement,* chap. 2; Culpepper, *Interpreting the Atonement,* chap. 3; Bloesch, *Jesus Christ,* pp. 148-58 especially; Green and Baker, *Recovering the Scandal of the Cross,* chap. 5.

That exercise prepares us for the highly complex and delicate task of reconsidering the continuing value of the received tradition in all its diversity as well as the need to make revisions in light of current topics such as inclusivity, violence, and cultural diversity. That task puts us in sympathetic dialogue with most current constructive proposals in the theology of the atonement.

The tracing of the historical developments has revealed that while there is a lot of continuity in the development of atonement views, two major orientations emerged in the beginning of the second millennium as the classic view gave room to the satisfaction model as the main paradigm in the Christian West, to be slowly reshaped into the penal substitution model. The competing third model, the moral example view, remained a marginal alternative until the Enlightenment; for those who embraced modernism and subsequent classical liberalism, some version of this model became the way to critique and, in many cases, reject the satisfaction and penal substitution interpretations. At the same time, the moral example view has, since its inception, and even before in a nonthematic form, served well as a complementary perspective. That said, throughout history, even during the first millennium, it was usual for one theologian or theological movement to embrace (at least some main aspects of) several interpretive models. This is of course in keeping with the intertextuality of the various paradigms in the NT.

The recapitulation view helps theology make an integral connection between incarnation, life, death, resurrection, and ascension, in other words, the whole history of Jesus. It reminds theology of the obvious insight that as dramatic a problem as sin is, mortality is the ultimate problem — and that God has acted decisively to remedy that ultimate problem. The recapitulation view facilitates and empowers the project of developing a more holistic, inclusive view of salvation in terms of linkage between "spiritual" and "physical," personal and communal, as well as the human and cosmic dimensions of reality. Its obvious weakness is a thin theology of the cross, which hardly is in keeping with the focus on the passion and cross of the Gospel writers. Whereas some other models of atonement err on an overindividualistic orientation, this view should pay due attention to sin and the need for salvation at the personal level.

When it comes to the other version of the classic view, one shouldn't necessarily be put off by the infamous "tricking the devil" rhetorical device — routinely noted by most commentators. The more substantial challenge is the mistaken view of the rights of the devil. While the NT puts the fallen "world" *(kosmos)* under the power of Satan (1 John 5:19), that does not imply the "possession" of the world by Satan. Even talk about "debt" in relation to the devil is not helpful; if sin accrues a debt, it is rather a debt the creature owes to the Creator.[45] The ransom theory rightly highlights the need for personal, communal, and cosmic release from the powers that both resist the will of God and claim — illegal! — authority over the creatures and creation. In this divine cosmic drama — whether by means of recapitulation or ransom — the triune God does not remain an outsider but is rather the One who assumes responsibility as Creator and shares in the suffering and pain of the work of salvation. By implication, the hope for freedom from all sorts of powers, including sociopolitical or sexist as in liberation theologies, is grounded in the history of salvation rather than a utopia.

While not often highlighted, the Anselmian way of explaining the atonement agrees in important ways with the classic view, particularly the recapitulation version, in its integral linking of atonement to incarnation. Even if the Anselmian theory may shift the focus from incarnation to the "satisfaction payment," its instincts are in a more comprehensive view of the history of Jesus. The main contribution of the Anselmian model turns out to be its greatest liability as well: that is, the attempt to interpret atonement in light of and against the medieval hierarchic and honor-keeping culture and society. On the one hand, this is a legitimate contextualization strategy — an inevitable one, as discussed before. On the other hand, as long as that contextualization exercise is not perceived as such, namely, as a *contextualization,* it is in danger of not only subsuming the theological theme under cultural constraints, but also of making that revised understanding *the* interpretation. Later history of theology, culminating in the penal substitution version, is a testament to that potential problem. As long as, on the contrary, the model is intentionally considered as a contextualization and its strategy is taken as one of the hermeneutical devices, the theory has much to commend when handled with care. Honor — and restoration of violated honor — is indeed a critical cultural and religious theme in many non-Western cultures, including especially Hebraic culture and some aspects of the Greek culture(s). It is a truism to say that while contemporary Western cultures are guilt-oriented, many others, including the above-mentioned, are shame/honor-driven.

However, the liability of Anselm's way of conceiving of the divine honor seems to operate with a formal, abstract principle. The biblical theol-

45. Consequently, the claim that "one of the strengths of the classical view is the idea that the devil has, in a certain sense, some rights over humans" is not useful. Driver, *Understanding the Atonement,* p. 42.

ogy operates with covenant-based relational and personalistic notions of the divine honor. This helps distinguish between the abstract, judicial notion of justice in the medieval society, which lays the background for the Anselmian model, and the notion of justice in terms of living rightly and in keeping with the committed, grace-based covenant relationships of the Bible. The Anselmian viewpoint, thus, has to be reminded of the need to see the work of salvation as not stemming so much from God's offended honor making God the main object of the atonement, requiring satisfaction, as from the unbounded love of the Creator for the creatures gone astray and leaving the covenant relationship. According to the biblical witness, God is the subject of reconciliation (2 Cor. 5:18-20).[46] If the metaphor of "satisfaction" is used in this context, its meaning has to be understood through the lens of the self-giving and suffering salvific act of the trinitarian God in reaching out to the lost humanity rather than an abstract divine transaction as payment.[47] Furthermore, going back to my acknowledgment of the linking of the atonement with the incarnation, an obvious question has to be raised here: Did the Word become flesh only to face death? At least for the Gospel writers

46. See, e.g., Schwöbel, "Reconciliation," p. 16. Fairly soon in early Christian theology a shift took place away from the idea of God as the subject to God as an object of reconciliation. Even Irenaeus contributed to this shift with the emerging idea of Christ as Mediator (*Against Heresies* 5.17.1) with reference to 1 Tim. 2:5. Via Augustine and especially Anselm, the mediatorial role of Christ — particularly in his obedient suffering humanity — helped shift the emphasis from God as subject to God as object. Even when it was noted that according to Paul (2 Cor. 5:19) it is God who is the subject of atonement, the focus on the appeasement of divine wrath through the mediatorial role of Christ stayed at the center. According to Pannenberg (*ST* 2:407), "Only after the destruction of the satisfaction theory by the rational criticism of the Socinians and the adoption of this criticism by the Protestant theology of the Enlightenment did attention begin to focus more widely on the difference between the thought of reconciliation in the NT (including Paul) and later theological usage. *God* did not have to be reconciled; the *world* is reconciled by God in Christ (2 Cor. 5:19)"; see also pp. 403-6.

47. Rightly Finlan *(Options on Atonement)* notes that particularly in the Pauline theology of atonement, which in itself is a mixing of metaphors drawn from various arenas of life, which Finlan creatively names "a combined judicial-commercial-moral idea," "a combined judicial-scapegoat idea," and "a combined cultic-sacrificial-moral idea," "[s]ome idea of substitution is present in each of these concepts." He adds that in Paul and the rest of the NT epistles and Revelation, "we see a number of images that speak of salvation achieved by a kind of *transaction* taking place at the cross, a penalty-bearing, a debt-cancelling, or a redemption-purchasing" (p. 3, emphasis in original). These observations alone should caution theology against too hastily leaving behind the idea of satisfaction altogether.

(and the author of 1 Peter) — perhaps more so than for the rest of NT theologians — the earthly life and ministry mattered a lot. The cross, rather than being *everything* about the mission of the Messiah, was in *every way* linked with his life and ministry, the focus of which was the obedient service of the coming of the kingdom of his Father in the power of the Spirit.

If the original satisfaction model considers the need for atonement through the lens of the divine honor violated, the penal substitutionary version, and its development, highlights the theme of guilt, which leads to punishment and thus the need for a sacrifice. Much critique has been leveled against the penal substitution approach in recent years. Let me list some of the most obvious objections routinely presented: the view of justice focusing on penalty and satisfaction as well as God's wrath in terms of anger; the guilt- and penitence-oriented ethos as the function of the later medieval/Reformation culture; the trinitarian implications that seem to set the Son and Father over against each other, and at the same time leave no role for the Spirit; overindividualism and ignorance of communal, sociopolitical, and cosmic dimensions of salvation; dissociation from the whole history of Jesus, in terms of both his life and ministry and his resurrection and ascension; lack of ethical incentive; and the model's claim for sole orthodoxy. Furthermore, a number of contemporary critics point to the problematic of violence and scapegoating, a topic weighty enough to be taken up in the following chapter. How can we deal with this criticism, and what are the implications for whether theology should use the constellation of metaphors present in this model? That said, we should also be critical of the criticism in two respects. First, it is important to see if the criticism is rightly placed. Second, with the acknowledgment of the criticism, we have to ask what, if any, is the lasting value of the penal substitution model as one among many.

Three interrelated tasks are in order here — but before that a terminological note. The term "penal substitution" is not a useful way of naming this view primarily because of the overly "penal" and judicial connotations. A slightly different alternative term could be "vicarious substitution." After this section I will use that term. First, a sheer acknowledgment: there is much to be commended in this and similar critiques. Penal substitution advocates should carefully (re)consider the critical implications of these viewpoints. This is a matter of working toward rectifying aspects or orientations of the theory that are theologically not appropriate or that violate the principle of hospitality in a way foreign to the inner theological structure. While there is no denying the presence of punishment and even retaliation in NT passages such as Romans 2:6-11, Matthew 13:42, 50, and the book of Revelation, the NT emphasis is not on retaliation but rather on rescue and repair. Following C. F. D. Moule, penal substitution advocates should consider carefully that God "puts the wicked right" by the power of suffering rather than "by causing to suffer."[48] With regard to the penal substitution model, there is a dire need to make sure trinitarian canons will be honored, overindividualism fixed, and the exclusive mind-set qualified.

Second, the penal substitution view — like the other main models — needs to be put in proper perspective, which includes an effort to relate it to other models as well as to wider theological considerations. While guilt is part of the human problem, as evident in the discussion of theological anthropology, and therefore there is a need for penitence and repentance, guilt is not all that plagues humanity. Furthermore, guilt is not only about personal life, it also relates to communal and other structural sins as much as to sins and "debt accrued" in one's individual life. Mortality and decay as well as bondage and slavery to powers, as the classic view contends, are problems too. Forgiveness and renewal of life, rather than merely an abstract satisfaction or other kind of divine transaction, should be the focus when speaking of guilt, repentance, and forgiveness. Again, the Petrine saying is a useful guide: "And He Himself bore our sins in His body on the cross, so that we might die to sin and live to righteousness; for by His wounds you were healed" (1 Pet. 2:24 NASB).

This integral ethical result of atonement should be rediscovered when resorting to the metaphors of the penal substitution model. The term "substitution" has to be handled with care.[49] Rather than Jesus — in his humanity, as it is often depicted — offering his life in the sense of appeasing an angry Father, a biblically and theologically more appropriate way to speak of substitution is to name it "representation."[50] "God was in Christ reconciling

48. Moule, "The Theology of Forgiveness," pp. 71-72 (72). I am indebted to Finlan, *Options on Atonement*, p. 97.

49. The suggestion of J. McLeod Campbell (*Nature of the Atonement*, p. 107) that in the atoning death of Christ there is nothing substitutionary or penal — any more than, say, in the sorrow of the loving parent for the wayward child — but rather "suffer[ing] just through seeing sin and sinners with God's eyes, and feeling in reference to them with God's heart," contains a kernel of truth. It points to *real* suffering of God in Christ for the world. At the same time, it falls short because of the hopelessly thin account of *salvific* and "atoning" meaning of Christ's death. In that sense, his proposal hardly differs radically from the moral example view.

50. As Christopher Marshall succinctly puts it, the Pauline understanding of "substitutionary" does not mean "one person *representing* all others [but rather that]

the world to Himself" (2 Cor. 5:19 NASB). Christ's humanity is not so much a "substitute" as it is the divinely appointed means of total identification and representation of humanity. Indeed, because "Christ takes our place," it makes it possible for us to "take His."[51] It is important to see Christ's representation both as solidarity and as substitution.[52]

The third task is to assess what aspects of the atonement are properly highlighted in this model and whether that is done properly. Here we come to the group of terms that used to be an essential part of the texture of older theologies of atonement but subsequently have fallen under suspicion: "sacrifice," "blood," "guilt," "judgment," "penalty," and "expiation." The Bible is filled with references to sacrifices. At times, sacrificial acts required death and shedding of blood. That imagery, as discussed in the previous section, carries over to some NT examples as in Romans 3. At other times, as in the famous scapegoat ritual of the Day of Atonement, the animal upon which the sins and guilt of the people were laid was not killed but rather sent out to the wilderness.[53] This implies identification and vicarious bearing, again a metaphor familiar from the NT. Those two aspects, namely, bearing the sins and being killed, may also be combined as in 1 Peter 2:24 — which focuses, interestingly enough (in keeping with the main thrust of that book), on the renewal of life, death to sin, and life for righteousness. The penal substitution hermeneutics, however, is only one among many perspectives on the work of salvation. What about the neglected or missing theological elements of this model such as a thin trinitarian and pneumatological account? The

. . . Christ died not so much instead of sinners as on behalf of sinners, as their corporate representative." *Beyond Retribution,* p. 61, italics in original. Pannenberg (*ST* 2:429-33; see also pp. 416-37) makes a distinction between "exclusive" representation (as in Anselm), in which one dies instead of others, and the "inclusive" representation of Christ, which means Christ's death, in which we were included, opened hope for overcoming death for us even though we have to die. For an important discussion, see Sölle, *Christ Our Representative.*

51. Brunner, *The Mediator,* p. 524. The way John McLeod Campbell *(Nature of the Atonement)* developed the idea of representation, namely, in terms of Christ's vicarious repentance for humanity, is not a theologically sustainable interpretation for two reasons: first of all, it is virtually unknown in biblical and historical traditions, and second, it is in danger of paralyzing the importance of human response to the work of reconciliations. A contemporary defense of Campbell's view under the rubric "substitutionary but nonpenal" is Crisp, "Non-Penal Substitution," pp. 415-33.

52. See Christian D. Kettler, "The Vicarious Beauty of Christ," p. 17.

53. For discussion of scapegoat, see further, Finlan, *Options on Atonement,* pp. 13-14, 22-25.

same burden is to be carried by all other theories of atonement. When considered as complementary and as metaphors, there is no need to expect each theory to encompass all theological perspectives.

What about the moral example view and its historical successors? It is routinely — and rightly — noted that while the older interpretations of atonement are "objective" in terms of locating the main effect of atonement in God (however, that is being negotiated), the Abelardian view is "subjective." As any half-truth, it is just that, a *half*-truth. In both cases, it is still God — in Christ — who is acting. The objective versus subjective distinction can only be determined from the perspective of humanity's side. In other words, what is the main focus of the salvific work? Be that as it may, three things can be said of this model. First, it has biblical support both in some sayings of Jesus and in 1 Peter, among others, as explained in the biblical section. It reminds us of the integral connection between Jesus' suffering and our following in the footsteps of the Suffering Servant. Put in proper perspective, this exemplarist view has a thicker theological account than simple modeling, as a child does after his or her parent, because "above and beyond its exemplary value, there is in it a surplus of mysterious causal efficacy that no merely human love possesses."[54] Second, taken in isolation from other NT perspectives, it badly fails to account for many critical aspects of atonement such as dealing with human sin in terms of transgression against God and cosmic implications of salvation. Third, when *intentionally* taken as an independent hermeneutical approach, the moral example view may cater to — and has catered to — unorthodox views evident in Socinianism and some aspects of classical liberalism.[55]

54. Quinn, "Abelard on Atonement," p. 296; I found this passage in Migliore, *Faith Seeking Understanding,* p. 185.

55. "Newer liberal versions of the moral-influence theory are guilty of . . . [this] inadequacy. Individuals respond to God's love in neo-Christendom settings or in a vague universalism of the parenthood of God and the familyhood of humanity. The moral-influence theory leaves the work of Christ unrelated to God's community-creating intention which is so prominent in both old and new covenants." Driver, *Understanding the Atonement,* p. 49.

12. Violence, Cross, and Atonement

Criticism against the Violent Notions of Atonement

Violence is part of all religions' texture.[1] Accusations against the violent nature of traditional theories of atonement, particularly in relation to satisfaction and penal substitution models, abound and come from different perspectives.[2] It is commonly assumed that while in biblical times and later it was more acceptable to envision the work of salvation in relation to violence, in the contemporary world it is not.[3] Thus, accounts of "the nonviolent atonement"[4] — to cite the title of one recent work — have been set forth in terms of both criticism and constructive proposals. "Atonement theology starts with violence, namely the killing of Jesus. The commonplace assumption is that something good happened, namely the salvation of sinners,

1. Nelson-Pallmeyer, *Is Religion Killing Us?*

2. For important discussions of the relation of religion and its rites, particularly sacrifice, to violence, see Vries, *Religion and Violence;* Lefebure, *Revelation, the Religions, and Violence.*

3. In this respect it is highly surprising that some noteworthy, leading contemporary discussions of atonement seem to show no interest in the topic of violence, power, and inclusivity. See, e.g., Davis, Kendall, and O'Collins, eds., *The Redemption* (the lead essay by O'Collins doesn't even mention violence among "Some Crucial Issues"!); Pannenberg, *ST* 2, chap. 11. Even Moltmann, who speaks of the suffering and death of Jesus as the key issue of his theology, basically avoids the whole contemporary conversation on violence in that context.

4. Weaver, *Nonviolent Atonement.*

when or because Jesus was killed. It follows that the doctrine of atonement then explains how and why Christians believe that the death of Jesus — the killing of Jesus — resulted in the salvation of sinful humankind."[5] Violence is understood in an inclusive sense, including not only killing but also any damage, physical, psychological, emotional, social, or similar, against another person or group of persons. It thus includes any personal encounters, family life, other social groups, and the whole of humanity.[6] The main critiques against the alleged violent nature of the Christian account of the atonement usually argue from some of the following points of view.

First, for many it is simply unacceptable to contemporary culture and religion to assume a God in need of or as an agent of violence. Indeed, Abelard already protested against the "cruel and wicked" view of God — and human beings! — in the Anselmian scheme of the need for payment through blood.[7] The satisfaction model is said to pervert the picture of a loving, merciful God in producing a "sadomasochistic theology and practice based on the idea of an 'offended' God who can only be mollified through the payment of innocent blood."[8]

Second, it is a commonplace to note that violence fosters violence and should thus be abandoned. It has been argued that the notion of "retributive justice" behind the criminal justice system of the Western nations according to which the level of punishment is rationed to the severity of the evil deed, has its roots in the satisfaction view of atonement.[9] Some peace church traditions consider any resort to violence as illegitimate and counterproductive to the efforts to cultivate peace and reconciliation.[10]

The most vocal critic of violence in general and, later in his career, having been converted to Catholicism, in relation to the event of Jesus Christ in particular, is the French anthropologist, philosopher, and religious scholar René Girard. His profoundly complex and world-embracing theory can be outlined in a few brief strokes.[11] Human beings are imitators who in

5. Weaver, *Nonviolent Atonement*, p. 2.

6. Weaver, *Nonviolent Atonement*, p. 8.

7. Abelard, "Exposition of the Epistle to the Romans," p. 283.

8. Ruether, *Introducing Redemption*, p. 100 (referring with approval to other feminist writers).

9. Most vocally argued by Gorringe, *God's Just Vengeance*, chap. 1 particularly, which builds on the analyses of Nietzsche and Girard.

10. See further, Weaver, *Nonviolent Atonement*, pp. 3-4.

11. An excellent introduction to main ideas is found in *Girard Reader*. Part I gives an overview of the mimetic theory, part III discusses sacrifice and sacral violence, and

their imitation end up desiring the same things as their rivals; this "mimetic desire" often leads to violence between groups, at times to a chaotic violence. To control this chaotic violence that could destroy the whole society, collective violence is redirected at one victim, the scapegoat, usually an individual with a peculiar feature or weakness. Once this scapegoat has absorbed the blame and violent emotions of the community, violence is released and peace and reconciliation follow. Religion becomes the means to control and direct the scapegoat mechanism and thus becomes an essential element in the development of culture. Myths of cultures and religions help keep the founding sacrificial event in the collective memory, but mythic narrative, rather than revealing violence as violence, makes it a sacred act for the benefit (salvation) of the culture; the victim as the bearer of collective blame has been rightly removed.

The implications for the biblical narrative in general and the passion story of Jesus are of course evident; while Girard constructed his theory of religion originally without any reference to a particular religion, after his conversion to the Christian faith he made that an important theme. His basic thesis is that there is nothing sacrificial about the death of Jesus on the cross.[12] On the contrary, unlike the mythical concealing of violence, the biblical narrative exposes violence as violence and helps make an end of the cycle. Indeed, Jesus "dies, not as a sacrifice, but in order that there may be no more sacrifices."[13] S. Mark Heim, in his discussion of Girard's view, makes the important point that a major way in which the death on the cross is exposed as violence is the resurrection. In religious myths, the sacrificed one does not rise from the tomb but rather "completely disappears in memory and subsequent accounts," so that the victim of sacrifice cannot be perceived as a victim.[14]

Third, a number of feminist and other women theologians have encountered satisfaction-based models as means of legitimizing female suffer-

---

part IV deals with scapegoat. The most important of his monographs with regard to atonement themes, including his basic thesis of violence in relation to his theory of religion, is Girard, *Things Hidden,* particularly chap. 1 (which may strike the reader as deceitfully easy because of the dialogue/interview form!).

12. Girard, *Things Hidden,* p. 180; see also chap. 11, "Nonsacrificial Death of Christ," in *Girard Reader.*

13. Girard, *Things Hidden,* p. 210. A full-scale theological engagement of Girard's theory can be found in Heim, *Saved from Sacrifice.* Another helpful discussion (which also critiques Girard for lack of sophistication in his theological application to Christian tradition) is Bartlett, *Cross Purposes.*

14. Heim, *Saved from Sacrifice,* p. 126.

ing and patriarchy as well as child abuse.[15] According to Rosemary Radford Ruether, Christian theology of the cross has encouraged women, who already are usually the (falsely) legitimized victims of violence, to continue suffering, modeling the suffering Jesus, including accepting violence from their husbands. Ultimately, this "myth of suffering" is linked with the primal myth of Eve as a subordinate to her husband.[16]

Fourth, a number of scholars have tried to negotiate the allegedly violent nature of many biblical texts. Here let me focus just on the relation of Jesus to violence. Two different kinds of approaches exist: either the Bible does not teach (divine) violence or, even though it does, we should not.[17] I dismiss the latter as too cheap an alternative and scrutinize the former approach. An example of the first tactic is the careful work of the Austrian Jesuit Raymund Schwager, who argues that rather than God punishing his Son for the sins of humankind, men and women brought punishment over their own lives by rejecting the divine reign of God.[18] The highly influential work of the biblical scholar Walter Wink, known for his trilogy on the "powers," serves as another influential example of a similar approach. Wink sets forth the argument that Jesus resisted any notion of violence and "sacrifice" in the

15. For feminist critique, see Carlson Brown and Parker, "For God So Loved," pp. 1-30; Brock, "And a Little Child Will Lead Us," pp. 50-54; for womanist (black women) critique, see D. S. Williams, *Sisters in the Wilderness*, pp. 161-67.

16. Ruether, *Introducing Redemption*, pp. 95, 98-99. Chap. 7 as a whole is a discussion of a host of female theologians from various parts of the world who have subjected traditional atonement theories, including Abelard's with its idea of Jesus' suffering and death needed to give us an example, to severe criticism.

17. A scholar who admits that the Bible teaches the violence of God but whom we should not follow is Nelson-Pallmeyer, *Jesus against Christianity*. My main problem with this view is — apart from the fact that it simply contradicts Christian tradition, both biblical and historical — its troubling view of the Trinity: one has to choose between the Jesus of nonviolence and the God of violence (e.g., p. 293). Not surprisingly, for Nelson-Pallmeyer, the atonement theories are driven by "pathological portraits of God" (p. 155) and thus betray the real God (p. 277); Finlan, *Options on Atonement*, pp. 111-19, under the heading "The Slide into Antibiblicism," offers an insightful critique of Nelson-Pallmeyer's view of violence. Another consistent attempt to reject any notion of sacrifice (and thus violence) while acknowledging its presence in the Bible is Dalferth, *Der Auferweckte Gekreuzigte*, pp. 249, 293, among others.

18. Schwager, *Jesus in the Drama of Salvation;* a somewhat similar shift of the locus of violence from the divine to the earthly realm is offered by Weaver as he claims that "Jesus was killed by the earthly structures in bondage to the power of evil. . . . Jesus' death was the rejection of the rule of God by forces opposed to that rule" (*Nonviolent Atonement*, p. 44).

traditional atonement-theology sense as he inaugurated the "domination-free order" of God's reign. For Wink, "the victory of the cross" consists of "breaking the spiral of violence," echoing the approach of Girard as well.[19]

Overcoming Violence

As much weight as these criticisms carry, not all contemporary theologians are convinced that all notions of violence should be removed from the Christian account of the atonement. The affirmations derive from some criticisms of the types of arguments presented above in this section, from some kind of necessity of violence in the kind of world we live in, and also from the fact that some leading mainline theologians such as Pannenberg and Moltmann either do not tackle the violence criticism or are theologically bound to continue speaking of suffering, death, and sacrifice.

While the charge against the "sadomasochistic" God hardly deserves a serious theological response, as one can hardly find a sound theological mind in the contemporary world that really would advocate such a caricature,[20] behind the rhetoric there is the serious theological question of how to conceive the work of salvation as the joint work of the triune God. Too easily traditional models of atonement yield a picture of the suffering Son in the hands of the just and demanding Father. In keeping with trinitarian communion theology developed in the context of the doctrine of God, there is mutual love, respect, and dependency rather than domination and abuse in the inner-trinitarian relations. Subjugation, abuse, or similar perverted motives have nothing to do with this kind of God-in-communion.[21] A more systematic development of trinitarian implications of atonement will be discussed in what follows.

19. Wink, *Engaging the Powers*, with reference to titles of chaps. 6 and 7 on pp. 109, 139.

20. In that respect, I find it embarrassing to theologians as an academic guild that too often the presentation of such fancy criticisms lacks the needed nuancing. While unfortunately and regretfully, the history of Christianity certainly knows cases in which subjugation of women or abuse of children has been "theologically" justified, that tendency is as far from a mainline, seriously-to-be-taken theology as any other aberration. Mere uncritical listing of those charges hardly advances careful theological reasoning nor supports the case for any segment of humanity.

21. For beginnings, see the helpful discussion in Van Dyk, "Do Theories of Atonement Foster Abuse?" pp. 24-25 particularly.

Girard should be credited with helping Christian theology — as well as any other religious traditions willing to hear his message — to expose hidden, and at times not so hidden, violence in religions. His attempt to eliminate violence from religion, even when it fails in light of classical Christian theology, is to be congratulated. Furthermore, his willingness to work with biblical texts from both Testaments (again, even when, exegetically, his approach is wanting) should be acknowledged. Yet there are severe problems as well. His theory is of course thoroughly modernist in suggesting a grand universal narrative even though he is usually classified under "postmodern" approaches to violence.[22] His theory is based on the ontology of violence rather than on an ontology of hospitality.[23] Hence, it is unable to provide an account of a hospitable God who saves humanity, nor is it conducive to the efforts to overcome violence in societal and political arenas, as the ensuing discussion will show. The main problem with Girard is that he does away with any notion of Christ being sacrificed as he claims that "there is nothing in the Gospels to suggest that the death of Jesus is sacrifice, whatever definition (expiation, substitution, etc.) we may give for that sacrifice."[24]

It can also be argued that in reality, Girard fails to offer any real "cure" for the human problem. It is far from certain that men and women, just having realized that violence is a vicious circle, will stop resorting to it. Mere knowledge of the deadly seriousness of violence hardly helps fix the problem behind the desire for violence and murder.[25] The point of the biblical story

22. So also Boersma, *Violence, Hospitality, and the Cross,* p. 138.

23. See further, Boersma, *Violence, Hospitality, and the Cross,* p. 134.

24. Girard, *Things Hidden,* p. 180. The book of Hebrews, the most sacrifice-terminology-driven in the NT, simply got it wrong, Girard argues (pp. 227-31). Interestingly, the Jewish scholar J. D. Levenson admits that indeed Paul at times used sacrificial language such as in 1 Cor. 5:7 with reference to the paschal Lamb. *Death and Resurrection,* p. 209. See also pp. 222-23. For a highly nuanced theological discussion of sacrifice vis-à-vis the plurality of ideas and rites of sacrifices in religions, see Milbank, "Stories of Sacrifice," pp. 75-102. For the similarities and differences between the myths of sacrifice in religions and the NT, see Heim, *Saved from Sacrifice,* pp. 110-12; his main point is that the main difference is that religions speak of deities being sacrificed as *myths* while the NT claims to tell a *true* story that happened "under Pontius Pilate."

25. See Placher, "Christ Takes Our Place," p. 9. Some friendly critics of Girard, while rejecting his denial of any notion of sacrifice in the NT accounts of the cross, materially end up affirming a conception of the work of the cross in which the divine initiative of atonement is lacking. They argue that Jesus' death followed the pattern of the slaughter of sacrificial animals as a function of the violence of those who executed the slaughter, without any divine intention behind it. If sacrifice language is used in this context, it only

of Jesus' obedient self-sacrifice is that that is the ultimate and last sacrifice. Christ's sacrifice is once and for all (Heb. 7:27). No more sacrifices or shedding of blood — that has ceased to be a means of atonement (10:14; 9:14). "It is finished" (John 19:30). John Milbank argues forcefully and carefully: "The trial and punishment of Jesus itself condemns, in some measure, all other trials and punishment, and all forms of alien discipline. . . . The only finally tolerable, and non-sinful punishment, for Christians, must be the self-punishment inherent in sin."[26] Not only Jesus' death on the cross but also his life and ministry speak for the cessation and overcoming of the cycle of violence. According to Miroslav Volf, "the Crucified Messiah" absorbs aggression, challenges violence by unearthing scapegoating and struggling actively against it. Ultimately, according to Volf, Christ's cross is an act of embrace of his opponents. The death of Christ means atonement for sins. It also makes it possible for human beings to embrace enemies.[27]

It seems to me that breaking the cycle of violence must begin with honest and scandalous acknowledgment of the existence of violence in the Bible. Crucifixion was a profound event of violence.[28] Contrary to popular conceptions, all three main traditions connect atonement with violence, including the one that often is not supposed to do so, the moral example view. It is not only Jesus' life and teaching but particularly his death that inspires loving response in us. So, it seems as though the only way to avoid all notions of violence is to ignore both biblical and historical traditions.[29] This acknowledgment has nothing to do with the ultimate justification of vio-

---

denotes voluntary self-sacrifice. Schwager, *Must There Be Scapegoats?* p. 204; Hardin, "Sacrificial Language in Hebrews."

26. Milbank, *Theology and Social Theory,* p. 421; for this quotation, I am indebted to Placher, "Christ Takes Our Place," p. 14. Maximus Confessor materially says the same: "The death of Christ on the cross is a judgment of judgment." *Questions to Thallasius,* p. 43, cited in Placher, p. 14.

27. Volf, *Exclusion and Embrace,* pp. 291-95.

28. For classic historical and theological treatment, see Hengel, *Crucifixion in the Ancient World.* Hengel claims that its origins are in the Persian Empire but that it was known among many others such as Indians, Scythians, and Assyrians (pp. 23-32). *The History of Herodotus* is a well-known source of references to crucifixion in ancient times; e.g., 3.159 chronicles the crucifixion of about 3,000 leading men by Dareios.

29. Not only in contemporary theology, but also in the early history of Christian theology, there were — misguided! — attempts to absolve God of violence such as the allegorical hermeneutics or the Marcionite way of positing the difference between two gods, that of the OT and that of the NT; for a brief discussion with sources, see Boersma, *Violence, Hospitality, and the Cross,* pp. 41-42.

lence, even less its glorification. It is biblical realism in a crucified, fallen world. "The drama of salvation starts and ends with violence, and without violence its central act is unthinkable."[30]

Consequently, a more proper and nuanced account of violence is needed. While Christian tradition has reached nothing like a consensus in this matter — as the debates about, say, "just war" illustrate — Christian theology by and large has been open to the idea of the justification of limited violence under certain circumstances with a view to a higher good.[31] Leaving aside the complex network of issues about whether human beings should ever resort to violence as citizens of nations as well as the relation between personal and structural violence, for the purposes of this discussion, I suggest a minimum definition of violence: it is harm done to another human being (or group of people or even the whole of humanity) with evil intentions or at least without thinking of the best of the other. Thus, a medical doctor's amputation of a patient's leg to save his or her life is not violence. Killing, hitting, abusing, or speaking badly of my neighbor or a stranger is always and without limitations violence.[32] Furthermore, I argue that while humans have no right to violence (thus defined, and as mentioned, apart from the consideration of the "just war"), God does. I agree with Volf's argumentation of this point. Taking his cue from the vision of Revelation 19, Volf concludes: "The end of the world is not violence, but a nonviolent embrace without end," which leads to the conflation rather than separation of the images of the "victorious rider on the white horse" and the "sacrificial lamb": "The world to come is ruled by the one who on the cross took violence upon himself in order to conquer the enmity and embrace the enemy. The Lamb's rule is legitimized not by the 'sword' but by its 'wounds.' . . . With the Lamb at the center of the throne, the distance between the 'throne' and the 'subjects' has collapsed in the embrace of the triune God."[33] It goes without saying that humans have no right whatsoever to imitate violence; humans are not gods.[34]

This focused discussion of the threat of violence in the Christian doctrine of reconciliation has investigated in some detail the most common accusations against tradition and has sought to both respond to those charges

30. Volf, *Exclusion and Embrace*, pp. 290-91.

31. For an excellent brief historical and contemporary discussion, see Cole, "Good Wars," pp. 27-31; see also Boersma, *Violence, Hospitality, and the Cross*, pp. 43-44.

32. See further Boersma, *Violence, Hospitality, and the Cross*, pp. 43-52.

33. Volf, *Exclusion and Embrace*, pp. 300-301.

34. Volf, *Exclusion and Embrace*, pp. 301-2.

and, even more importantly, open up the door for a hospitable, nonviolent, and nonoppressive account of salvation. This discussion of violence, as well as related issues such as oppression and abuse of power, however, only outlined the main contours and clarified issues. A more detailed and deeper scrutiny of key theological issues related to atonement in Christian tradition, including suffering, sacrifice, and execution of the innocent Messiah, is needed to fully capture this essential topic. That is one of the many tasks of the constructive project ahead of us in the ensuing two chapters.

13. Toward a Contemporary Trinitarian Theology of Reconciliation

Many Metaphors of Reconciliation

I have insisted on the need to honor the diversity of metaphors of salvation in the biblical witness as well as in later theological tradition.[1] That is at the same time an appeal to the idea of complementarity of various interpretations of the atonement. That said, we have to assess carefully the contours of such a theological exercise. It all boils down to the basic question of whether we may adopt any metaphors we wish, for example, to meet the needs of changing circumstances, or whether some basic metaphors should be retained. In other words, is it the case that "the choice of forms of interpretation is limited by the nature of the event itself, and their content is shaped by it"?[2] The mere fact that in changing cultural and religious settings we find it hard to understand or communicate key biblical teachings is not a valid

1. Colin Gunton (*Actuality of Atonement,* pp. 61-62) makes the important observation that not only does the Bible entertain a number of different metaphors but that those metaphors are used differently in different settings and there is often a mixture of metaphors. Examples include these: when speaking of the victory of the Lion of Judah, Rev. 5:9 also speaks of sacrifice and the slave market; the book of Hebrews, full of sacrificial, cultic, and priestly metaphors, can also speak of Jesus' identification with our humanity in order to conquer death (2:14). Gunton also reminds us of the important fact that metaphors do not "operate in self-contained worlds" and are thus open to each other (p. 83).

2. Pannenberg, *ST* 2:421-22. Similarly, N. T. Wright, *New Testament and the People of God,* pp. 129-30.

theological reason for their dismissal.[3] The use of *metaphors* in this discussion is guided by the basic conviction that behind them is a "true" narrative of the life, ministry, death, and resurrection of Jesus Christ.[4] Metaphors thus understood — unlike their use in literature — cannot be taken as "largely free human inventions, vaguely grounded in what happened in Palestine in the first century of our era."[5] Metaphor is neither a way to soften the meaning of key words such as "sacrifice" to the point in which they mean virtually nothing[6] nor a way to dismiss all historical contours as in Hick's "metaphorical" Christology.[7] Acknowledging the metaphorical nature of atonement language is not to say that one can simply "pile up" metaphors as one wishes. Metaphors have to be weighed as to their importance and relevance.[8] Their

3. Pannenberg, *ST* 2:422; Farrow ("Ascension and Atonement," p. 68) issues a warning about succumbing to the temptation "to falsify the doctrine of reconciliation by putting it into the employ of this or that local cause, or by tailoring it to this or that all-too-limited-agenda."

4. The NT theologian Wright (*New Testament and the People of God,* pp. 129-30) makes the important point that "metaphors are themselves mini-stories, suggesting ways of looking at a reality which cannot be reduced to terms of the metaphor itself."

5. Gunton (*Actuality of Atonement,* p. 42) himself does not endorse the statement in the citation but rather agrees with my position. His book offers a most helpful and accessible guide to the complexities of the use of metaphor in contemporary theology and in relation to its use in science, on the one hand, and literature, on the other hand. A more technical one is Soskice, *Metaphor and Religious Language.*

6. As happens with David Wheeler's treatment of sacrifice when he says that what "dies" dies "of offended pride," as Aaron confesses over the goat and sends it away. As a result, there is a changed emotional state as "the offended party cedes their right to be aggrieved." "Cross and the Blood," pp. 11-12. A more thoughtful way of trying to negotiate the traditional idea of sacrifice is offered by a number of German biblical scholars such as Hartmut Gese and Otfried Hofius, who basically link the idea of sacrifice to Jesus' *life* rather than his death on the cross. For references and careful criticism, see Finlan, *Options on Atonement,* pp. 87-89.

7. See J. Hick, *Metaphor of God Incarnate.*

8. McFague (*Metaphorical Theology,* p. 23) speaks in this instance of some metaphors that have "staying power" and names them "models." Something similar is meant with "root metaphor"; Barbour, *Myths, Models, and Paradigms,* p. 65. I find helpful the threefold atonement typology of "prophetic," "liturgical," and "sapiential," in Clifford and Anatolios, "Christian Salvation," pp. 739-69. That typology carefully integrates biblical, historical, and contemporary viewpoints. I am far less convinced than Peter Schmiechen (*Saving Power,* pp. 4-8) that metaphors (plus, in his terminology, "titles" and "proper names") of atonement develop into "theories." Even when he defines theories fairly loosely, I think that is to imply too much of intentional "theorizing" and fixation in most atonement views. His book identifies no fewer than ten theories under four main groups:

frequency and usage in the biblical canon, alignment with Christian tradition, and theological coherence serve as appropriate criteria.[9] To put it another way, there needs to be some kind of "systematic" relating of metaphors with others. A trinitarian framework is a major framework for such relating.

Contemporary theology should exercise cautious self-criticism and not too hastily throw away essential biblical-theological elements of atonement, even when many things in the traditional Western Church's understanding call for reconsideration.[10] Contrasting the two poles of discussion going back to the end of the nineteenth century between classical liberals such as A. Ritschl and the more traditional M. Kähler, Pannenberg in his *Systematic Theology* sets the basic question in this way: "[W]hether Christ rectifies erroneous views concerning an unchangeable fact, namely the love of God (which . . . sinners cannot believe in because of their sense of guilt), or whether Christ is the author of a changed situation," only God is able to atone; it is not possible for humans. In the latter case, "the death of Christ must be seen as a real overcoming of the misery that consists of our having fallen into sin and death and the related estrangement from God."[11] Overcoming this ultimate problem in the historical work of salvation necessitates also speaking of expiation, which "removes the offense, the guilt, and the consequences" (2:411). This means that "in interpreting the death of Jesus, we must make the nature of the event normative for the evaluation, selection, and use of the interpretive models available" (2:423). It can be argued that traditional notions of sacrifice, expiation, representation, and substitution — while not encompassing everything about the death on the cross, let alone the whole salvific work of the triune God — cannot be covered by others (2:242).

---

under *"Christ died for us":* (1) sacrifice, (2) justification by grace, (3) penal substitution; under *"Liberation from sin, death, and demonic powers":* (4) liberation; under *"The purposes of God":* (5) the renewal of creation, (6) the restoration of creation, (7) Christ the goal of creation; under *"Reconciliation":* (8) Christ the way to knowledge of God, (9) Christ the reconciler, (10) the wondrous love of God (for a brief presentation of each, see pp. 8-11).

9. See further, Brümmer, *Model of Love,* pp. 22-29.

10. Revisionist Judaism has also made attempts parallel to those of, say, classical liberalism in Christianity to downplay and virtually reject biblical ideas such as sacrifice as something alien to the origins of that religion. That is visible in the nineteenth century in Hermann Cohen, "Die Versöhnungs-idee," pp. 125-39.

11. Pannenberg, *ST* 2:410. References to this work have been placed in the text in this and the following paragraph.

But again, this insight has to be put in a proper *theological* perspective to save it from the unfortunate implications of conceiving of the death of Christ primarily as appeasement of the wrath of God due to human sin. God, who raised Jesus from the dead through the Spirit, rather "showed himself to be the Victor over sin and death in reconciliation of the world" (2:412).

The salvific work of the triune God encompasses, as the first part of this volume indicated, not only the suffering, death, and resurrection of Jesus Christ, but also his incarnated life. Hence, before delving into the many details about the cross, resurrection, and ascension, a careful consideration of the relation of incarnation to atonement is necessary, and is the focus of the next section.

Incarnation and Reconciliation

Oliver Crisp sets the stage for this discussion in a succinct way: "Amongst traditional, orthodox Christian theologians it is often thought that the incarnation is the prerequisite for the atonement, that without the incarnation no atonement can take place, but that the atonement is some act distinguishable from the incarnation. Though the two are intimately related, on this way of thinking, they are discrete elements in salvation history."[12]

Over against this traditional emphasis, an alternative account of the relation of incarnation to atonement stresses continuity and the principle of mutuality: "The core idea is that these two things, incarnation and atonement, are really two parts of one whole divine event or act; indeed, that the atonement is a part of the whole that is the incarnation."[13] In our earlier discussion, along with Irenaeus, Athanasius was lifted up as a paradigm.[14] The background to this orientation, discussed above, is the close link between creation and incarnation as well as the creation of humanity and incarnation, established with a view to the holistic salvation of humankind and the cosmos.

Among the contemporary constructive theologians, Kathryn Tanner has put forth the most robust and sophisticated argument for the close link

12. Crisp, "Tanner on Incarnation," p. 111.

13. Crisp, "Tanner on Incarnation," p. 112.

14. Torrance's discussion of atonement in *The Trinitarian Faith* is an extensive engagement of Athanasius in this respect (see especially chap. 5).

between incarnation and atonement with her claim for incarnation as atonement.[15] As Crisp accurately describes it,

> [O]n this view, "the incarnation" is shorthand for the whole work of Christ that obtains in eternity, unfolding in time from the first moment at which his human nature begins to exist to his death on the cross, and beyond that too, including his resurrection, ascension and current intercession for the saints at the right hand of God the Father. When it is seen in this light, the atonement becomes something that occurs as part of this work of Christ that is the incarnation. It is not an act entirely separate from the incarnation, any more than the final movement of a great orchestral work is separate from the orchestral work as a whole.[16]

In her earlier work the Episcopalian Tanner claims that incarnation means that "we are being brought to God, assumed into the divine Trinitarian life."[17] Rather than in "vicarious punishment or an atoning sacrifice or satisfaction of God's honor or as a perfectly obedient act," the saving role of the cross comes to the fore in the assumption of sin and death by the Logos. The *Christus Victor* model is thus her choice.[18] In her later work, she similarly speaks of salvation as God's giving us access to union with God: "God wants to give us the fullness of God's own life through the closest possible relationship with us as that comes to completion in Christ."[19] The key to Tanner's emphasis on incarnation as union with God is the creation of humanity into the image of God, with which discussion she begins her *Christ the Key*.[20] Grace — and atonement — hence, rather than being any kind of "emergency" measure, is rather the "necessary" means of completing what human nature, oriented to and finding its fulfillment only in God, is lacking: "Because we have been created to have such a close relationship with the very goodness of God, with a nature that requires attachment to God to be what it is supposed to be, grace is necessary to complete our nature, to add to it what it requires for its excellent operations and well-being. Receiving

15. Tanner, *Christ the Key*. In this book, Tanner develops and clarifies the position set forth in her earlier book *Jesus, Humanity*, chap. 1.

16. Crisp, "Tanner on Incarnation," p. 112.

17. Tanner, *Jesus, Humanity*, p. 15.

18. Tanner, *Jesus, Humanity*, p. 29,

19. Tanner, *Christ the Key*, p. vii.

20. Tanner, *Christ the Key*, chap. 1.

God's grace becomes a requirement for simply being a human being fully alive and flourishing."[21]

Hence, she proposes the "incarnational model of atonement," in which salvation comes, as already mentioned, primarily through the assumption of our humanity by the Logos. Thus, the primary meaning of "atonement" is "at-one-ment."[22] The significance of the incarnation lies in its capacity to bring the human person of Jesus of Nazareth into the closest possible relationship that can exist between God and a human being. Because of the humanity of Jesus, this special relationship can extend to all human beings. The end result of this relationship is the redemption of humanity.[23]

This is the logic of Tanner's reasoning in her attempt to replace the traditional ideas of atonement in terms of God's punishment and any means of humanity to pay the debt (as in the Anselmian view)[24] with incarnation as the "primary mechanism for atonement."[25] "Jesus saves . . . as a human being," and "Salvation occurs in a human life."[26] The entire life of Jesus is at work in atonement, where God, through the Word, assumes suffering and death.[27] Redemption comes in the attachment of the human to Christ, who is righteous while the human person is not.[28]

The critical question about Tanner's proposal is obvious: In what way(s) can the incarnation just by virtue of uniting the human person with Jesus Christ be an atoning "mechanism"?[29] Tanner comes closest to explaining this in her creative use of the ancient concept of *communicatio idiomatum:* "The happy exchange of the atonement is just a case of the saving communication of idioms that the incarnation brings about. As a result of the incarnation, the characteristics of human life become the (alien) proper-

21. Tanner, *Christ the Key,* p. 60. "[T]he whole of what we are by nature achieves a new state by God's grace; grace raises our full human nature, complete on its own terms, up to another divine level of existence and functioning" (pp. 137-38). Chap. 4 of the book, titled "Trinitarian Life," the longest one, elaborates in detail the mutual roles of the Spirit and Son in the descent of God into the human sphere and the ascent of humanity into God's life.

22. Tanner, *Christ the Key,* p. 256.

23. Tanner, *Christ the Key,* pp. 144-47.

24. Tanner, *Christ the Key,* p. 87. Chap. 6 is an extensive critique of traditional atonement theories.

25. Tanner, *Christ the Key,* p. 252.

26. Tanner, *Jesus, Humanity,* p. 30.

27. Tanner, *Christ the Key,* pp. 256-57.

28. Tanner, *Christ the Key,* p. 86.

29. This question is also raised by Crisp, "Tanner on Incarnation," p. 118.

ties of the Word, and thereby the properties of the Word (its holiness, its life-enhancing power) become the (alien) properties of humanity in a way that saves humanity from sin and death."[30] The radical difference, however, between Tanner's use of the formula of exchange of the attributes and that of the Reformers (who took it from the Fathers) is that whereas for the contemporary theologian the cross has no connotations of sacrifice, penalty, vicarious suffering, and satisfaction, for the Reformation theologians those aspects laid the foundation for the possibility of the exchange. Even Torrance, whose thinking in many ways is followed by Tanner, argues that incarnation alone does not establish redemption. What is needed in addition to this is the personal act of God incarnate in the atonement, acting vicariously in his humanity in the life and death of Christ.[31] Torrance's position is of course in keeping with that of Athanasius and Irenaeus as well as the rest of the Fathers by and large.[32]

Tanner's creative and thoughtful reworking of the doctrine of atonement on the basis of incarnation is an important contribution even though it has to be deemed one-sided and wanting. First, as a corrective to traditional accounts of Christology and reconciliation, Tanner highlights the importance of the whole history of Jesus, including his earthly life.[33] Second, in keeping with this, and following the spirit of the recapitulation model, she speaks of salvation as "a form of temporal, historical process, involving struggle with the forces of sin, and the sort of changes that typify any human life, sinful or not."[34] Through his obedience and love, the Son of God recapitulates and sanctifies the life of suffering humanity. Third, her discussion of "sacrifice" and its abuses in Christian tradition is to be welcomed. The previous discussion here reiterates many of the same complaints against tradition such as the appeasing of an angry God. Rightly, she reminds us that the ultimate goal of sacrifices is to establish a "joyous communion" between God and his people.[35] However, it does not do justice to the biblical data to regard as the only

30. Tanner, *Christ the Key,* p. 254.

31. For a detailed account of Torrance's understanding of the relationship between incarnation and atonement, see Molnar, *Incarnation and Resurrection,* chap. 3. I am indebted to Crisp, "Tanner on Incarnation," p. 112 n. 5.

32. Whereas Torrance, as mentioned, builds on Athanasius, Tanner's main patristic source with regard to atonement is Gregory of Nazianzus, especially his *Fourth Theological Oration* (and also Cyril of Alexandria).

33. See further Tanner, *Christ the Key,* p. 262.

34. Tanner, *Christ the Key,* pp. 260-61.

35. Tanner, *Christ the Key,* p. 266; see also pp. 262-73.

notion of the sacrifice of the cross "Jesus' whole life . . . [as] a sacrifice of love."[36] This criticism holds even in light of the discussion above concerning the many meanings of the notion of sacrifice in the biblical tradition. Furthermore, in light of the biblical tradition and later atonement models, a good case can be made for the claim that Tanner's revisionist interpretation, as valuable as it is in many regards, fails to account for the seriousness of the human plight and of sin. In the discussion of "why incarnation?" in part I of this volume, it was concluded that even though incarnation should not be seen only — and perhaps not even primarily — as a divine emergency plan to combat the effects of the Fall, neither can that dimension be eliminated. Athanasius, Irenaeus, and others whose views are referred to in support of the link between incarnation and creation (rather than incarnation and Fall) undoubtedly held on to both "reasons" as the occasion for the incarnation. Consider Romans 5:17-19: "If, because of one man's trespass, death reigned through that one man, much more will those who receive the abundance of grace and the free gift of righteousness reign in life through the one man Jesus Christ. Then as one man's trespass led to condemnation for all men, so one man's act of righteousness leads to acquittal and life for all men. For as by one man's disobedience many were made sinners, so by one man's obedience many will be made righteous."[37] In light of this kind of biblical material, it is difficult to deny the importance of the need for atonement in terms of divine intervention and overcoming of the severe effects of the Fall, which of course presupposes the traditional notion of the incarnation but also speaks of sacrifice, perhaps even "satisfaction" of divine justice. At the least, the traditional type of recapitulation view is presupposed that, even though its focus is in the life and resurrection of the Savior rather than in the cross, still demands the suffering and death of the Messiah for the overcoming of death.

Suffering God and Crucified Messiah

At stake in the question of whether Christian theology should continue to speak of the suffering, cross, and death of Jesus "for us" is more than just human salvation; it has also to do with the whole notion of God, and therefore, the possibility of a distinctively Christian *theo*logy. No other contemporary theologian has underscored this more than Moltmann, who boldly consid-

36. Tanner, *Jesus, Humanity,* p. 29.

37. For the importance of this passage, see Crisp, "Tanner on Incarnation," p. 130.

ers "the cross of Christ as the foundation and criticism of Christian theology."[38] In the preface to *The Crucified God,* he claims that "whatever can stand before the face of the crucified Christ is true Christian theology. What cannot stand there must disappear."[39]

Jesus' willingness to suffer "for us" is depicted in the NT in the context of his obedience to his Father's will (Heb. 5:8-9); that passage speaks of the learning of obedience through suffering, a statement that "should not be seen as contrasting filial closeness to the Father" but rather as an expression of the "tension between learning obedience in time and pretemporal sonship." Jesus' obedience to the Father, then, "is not alien obedience of the slave . . . [but rather] an expression of his free agreement with the Father."[40] While the cross, as will be explained in the following, marks the culmination of obedience in self-offering, it is important to see the obedience characterizing the earthly Jesus' whole life as he distinguished himself from the Father with whom he was united and whose kingdom he served. This filial relationship found its first expression in the history of Israel under the king as Yahweh's son (2 Sam. 7:14).[41]

Jesus was put to death as a messianic pretender[42] and blasphemer who was believed to have violated the law and tradition, as well as to have usurped the status of God.[43] There was also a collision with religious authorities as he was regarded as a rebel.[44] Even though he first came into con-

38. Subtitle to his *Crucified God.*

39. Moltmann, *The Crucified God,* p. x; so also p. 65. For the significance of the cross to Christian theology's identity, see p. 24, and for the discussion of the theology of the cross in Paul, Luther, and others, see pp. 69-75.

40. Pannenberg, *ST* 2:316. No one else in contemporary theology has argued so vocally for the vicarious humanity of Jesus than T. F. Torrance; see particularly, *The Mediation of Christ.* I am also reminded here of what an Orthodox theologian is saying with regard to Jesus' obedience: "In patristic tradition, freedom and obedience are seen as inseparable. The Trinity itself is a perfect communion of love, and not only of love but, we can dare to say, also of obedience. . . . Obedience is part of the mystery of love and humility. Those who live in mutual obedience and love, as do the persons of the Trinity, share a single nature and therefore a single will in perfect harmony." Rodger, "Soteriology of Anselm of Canterbury," p. 25.

41. Pannenberg, *ST* 2:317.

42. Pannenberg, *ST* 2:312-15. That might be the reason why Paul preferred the symbol of the new Adam instead of Messiah since the latter obviously was linked with particular this-worldly messianic hopes of the people of Israel.

43. Moltmann, *The Crucified God,* pp. 128-35.

44. Moltmann, *The Crucified God,* pp. 136-45.

flict with his own people, it is clear from the Gospel narratives that the Gentile (Roman) authorities executed Jesus.[45] In the words of the postcolonialist theologian Mark Taylor, "Jesus' death on the cross is best viewed as what that event concretely was, an imperial execution."[46] This has significant theological implications: "Roman participation in the events leading to the execution of Jesus perhaps was the occasion for extending the understanding of the death of Jesus as expiation to the Gentile world represented by Rome."[47] The Christology of the Roman Catholic Aloysius Pieris of Sri Lanka links Asia's poverty and spirituality to Jesus' "double baptism" in "the Jordan of Asian religions and the Calvary of Asian poverty." This is Jesus' immersion in the Asian context and life. Jesus pointed to the ascetic John as the archetype of the true spirituality of the kingdom of God and denounced the striving for the accumulation of wealth and trust in mammon. Jesus' radical social program, in Pieris's analysis, led him finally to the cross; he was executed by the power elite. The powerful crucified him at "a cross that the money-polluted religiosity of his day planted on Calvary with the aid of a colonial power (Luke 23:1-23). This is where the journey, begun at Jordan, ended."[48] The point made here, coming from different perspectives, is that whatever "reasons" were behind the murder of Jesus, political factors, including religious-political as well as socioeconomic factors, were part of it, even though it was also part of the divine plan. The last claim is of course contested by many contemporary interpreters of the crucifixion, including many postcolonialists;[49] however, Christian tradition and theological intuitions do not allow us to reduce the crucifixion to merely an event on the human level without reference to divine initiative and plan.

Jesus' sufferings were real.[50] Yet, even more painful was the rejection, first by his own people and then ultimately by his Father. "To suffer and to be rejected are not identical. Suffering can be celebrated and admired. It can

45. For the involvement of both Jewish and Roman authorities in the trial and condemnation of Jesus, see Moltmann, *Way of Jesus Christ,* pp. 160-64.

46. M. L. Taylor, *Executed God,* p. xiv.

47. Pannenberg, *ST* 2:426.

48. Pieris, *Asian Theology of Liberation,* p. 49.

49. Thus Taylor (*Executed God,* p. 108) claims that the execution of Jesus "was not a salvific event"; it was rather "his creative and dramatic contestations with religio-imperial powers" (p. 108).

50. While the whole life and self-offering of Jesus are to be seen as suffering "for us," for the pivotal event of crucifixion there is no parallel; see further Hengel, *Crucifixion in the Ancient World.*

arouse compassion. But to be rejected takes away the dignity from suffering and makes it dishonourable suffering. To suffer and be rejected signify the cross."[51]

While the NT gives due place to the "for us" motif in the suffering of Jesus, including for the whole world (John 3:16), there is also a wider horizon, including the "birth pangs" of the whole of creation (Rom. 8:18-23). This is what Moltmann names the "apocalyptic sufferings of Christ":

> At the centre of Christian faith is the history of Christ. At the centre of the history of Christ is his passion and his death on the cross. We have to take the word "passion" seriously in both its senses here, if we are to understand the mystery of Christ. For the history of Christ is the history of a great passion, a passionate surrender to God and his kingdom. And at the same time and for that very reason it became the history of an unprecedented suffering, a deadly agony. At the centre of Christian faith is *the passion of the passionate Christ.* The history of his life and the history of his suffering belong together. They show the active and the passive side of his passion.[52]

The apocalyptic sufferings, rather than suffering for his own sake, Jesus "suffers for the world" as they are related to the kingdom whose coming he serves.[53]

Several critical qualifiers are in order to put the emphasis on suffering and the cross in proper perspective. First, theologically it is not appropriate to interpret the life and ministry of Jesus *merely* through the lens of his suffering, as has often happened in tradition. The ancient creeds might have given rise to this reductionist understanding of the scope of the salvific meaning of the whole history of Jesus Christ. Hence — in a passage immediately preceding the above-quoted paragraph on suffering — Moltmann rightly issues a plea for theology to highlight the earthly life of Jesus including his healings, exorcisms, welcoming of sinners, and acting as representative of Israel.[54] Jesus' sufferings are critical to his salvific ministry, but they are not all. Second, without in any way diminishing the significance of as-

51. Moltmann, *The Crucified God,* p. 55; materially Miroslav Volf (*Exclusion and Embrace,* p. 26) says the same.

52. Moltmann, *Way of Jesus Christ,* p. 151, emphasis in original.

53. Moltmann, *Way of Jesus Christ,* p. 153.

54. Moltmann, *Way of Jesus Christ,* p. 150.

pects of Jesus' earthly ministry other than his suffering, as Andrew Sung Park pointedly puts it: "It is not right to limit the crucifixion of Jesus Christ to the three hours of suffering on the cross. The crucifixion of Jesus must be understood as extending to his whole life. Jesus lived the life of taking up his cross everyday."[55] Third, the highlighting of the critical role of the cross in Christian faith and theology has nothing whatsoever to do with glorification of suffering in general or of Christ's suffering in particular. On the contrary, as Moltmann puts it, "the cross is the really irreligious thing in Christian faith," despite many "roses" added to the cross for mistaken religious, spiritual, and cultural reasons.[56]

Fourth, any talk about suffering, particularly divine suffering, sounds ideological and suspicious to contemporary people. This is because of its link with violence and its alleged effect on sanctifying passive suffering of many who already suffer at the hands of others.[57] Women, particularly in the Third World, may be such victims, and religion can be used — and has been used — as a pretext. Rightly, many female theologians have critiqued the (ab)use of Jesus' suffering as a pretext for condoning forced, passive suffering of women and other victims,[58] or even worse, enforcing the silence of women and children about their abuse.[59] Those unchristian acts and attitudes have nothing to do with the Christian gospel of salvation and have to be rejected categorically.[60] There is nothing in the gospel story about the voluntary obedience of the Son of God, even to the point of surrendering his life as sacrifice for the salvation of the world, that would suggest, as some feminists are mistakenly claiming, that for women to claim their value they should sacrifice themselves and refrain from pursuing their own needs.[61] The gospel's call to sacrifice one's own needs for the sake of one's neighbors in the service of the love of God is a voluntary, intentional personal decision

55. Park, *Wounded Heart of God,* p. 124.

56. These misinterpretations of the cross are discussed in detail in Moltmann, *The Crucified God,* chap. 2; quote p. 37.

57. For an exchange between Dorothee Sölle, a feminist theologian who harshly critiqued Moltmann's emphasis on the voluntary self-surrender of Jesus in his *Crucified God* and Moltmann, see Moltmann, *Way of Jesus Christ,* pp. 175-76.

58. Ruether, *Introducing Redemption,* pp. 104-5; Brock, *Journeys by Heart,* p. 56.

59. Carlson Brown and Parker, "For God So Loved," p. 2.

60. My disagreement with these female theologians has to do with the fact that, unlike them, I am not willing to renounce all talk about Jesus' redemptive suffering for its alleged necessary link with what I called above its abuse.

61. As is claimed by Carlson Brown and Parker, "For God So Loved," p. 2.

to "imitate Christ" and may lead to personal fulfillment and contentment. Even more absurd is the reasoning of some that when parents are taking the God of the Bible as their model, then God's "demanding the total obedience of 'his' son — even obedience to death" may not "prevent the parent from engaging in divinely sanctioned child abuse."[62] Not only does this reasoning have no support whatsoever in the Bible, but no sane theologian throughout history has even taught this — or even implied it.

When it comes to Christ's sufferings, there are both an active and a passive side.[63] On the one hand, the sufferings of Christ were voluntary, not imposed by others as in domestic violence or brutal wartime rape. On the other hand, Christ represents the victim rather than the perpetrator. Christ, the Suffering Servant, also resisted power structures, abuse of the weak, and any instrumental treatment of the other.[64] Suffering and pain are reprehensible and objectionable not only to women or other minorities. We all abhor them. They are not to be glorified.[65] "The pain and the frequent failure of the way of the cross are a scandal for all human beings, in every age."[66] As explained above, in the trinitarian account of the sufferings of Christ, in the anguish and death of the Son of God, there are the presence and sympathy of the Father. God's presence is most concrete and deepest in the midst of our suffering. Hence, for many "the suffering of Jesus gave . . . a sense of comfort, for God in Jesus understood their pain and grief and shared their heavy load."[67]

The Korean-born theologian Andrew Sung Park looks at the meaning of the cross through the lens of the key cultural concept of his first culture, namely, *han*. That multifaceted concept denotes suffering and pain, "a sense of unresolved resentment against injustices suffered, a sense of helplessness, . . . a feeling of acute pain and sorrow in one's guts and bowels."[68] Incarna-

62. Carlson Brown and Parker, "For God So Loved," p. 9.

63. The rejection of all notions of passive suffering in relation to Jesus because of its alleged legitimization of the passive suffering of women in the hands of the perpetrators, therefore, misses the point and has to be subjected to constructive criticism. See Ruether, *Women and Redemption*, p. 279; Carlson Brown and Parker, "For God So Loved," pp. 2-3; Heyward, *Saving Jesus from Those Who Are Right*, pp. 79-80.

64. See further, Park, *Wounded Heart of God*, p. 124.

65. This is well noted by Haight, *Future of Christology*, p. 78.

66. Volf, *Exclusion and Embrace*, p. 27.

67. J. M. Hopkins, *Towards a Feminist Christology*, p. 53; see also p. 56.

68. Joh, *Heart of the Cross*, p. xxi. (Joh attributes this definition to Han Wan Sang but gives a mistaken reference to another author; I was unable to trace the original source.) A careful discussion of the many meanings of *han* can be found in Park, *Wounded Heart of God*, chap. 1 particularly.

tion and crucifixion speak to the theme of *han:* "The all-powerful God was crucified. The cross is the symbol of God's han which makes known God's own vulnerability to human sin. . . . The cry of the wounded heart of God reverberates throughout the whole of history. God shamefully exposes the vulnerability of God on the cross, demanding the healing of the han of God. The cross is God's unshakable love for God's own creation. Like parents who give birth to and then love children, God is wrapped up in a creational love with humanity."[69]

Fully mindful of the feminist critique of violence and suffering in traditional atonement theories, another Korean American theologian, the postcolonialist Wonhee Anne Joh, is convinced that "the power of the cross also points simultaneously to the possibility of a radical form of love that can be linked with the Korean concept of *jeong.*" That crucial cultural concept "encompasses but is not limited to notions of compassion, affection, solidarity, relationality, vulnerability, and forgiveness."[70] Joh also uses the notion of *han,* mentioned above and widely used also by *minjung* theologians. Her main theological claim is that "the cross works symbolically to embody both the horror of *han* and the power of *jeong.*"[71] Hence, Joh distinguishes herself from those feminist critics such as Dorothee Sölle who categorically reject any talk of the cross as religious and theological symbol and consider it merely a political means of punishment of Jesus and all who confronted the powers that be.[72] In keeping with the in-between nature of *jeong,* Joh reports that for Korean American Christians the cross is both an empowering and a disempowering symbol: "The cross continues to empower people as it signifies radical solidarity with their experience of *han* and *jeong* as embodied in their lived immigrant experiences. However, it continues to be disempowering to many . . . because of its traditional interpretation of self-abnegation and its acceptance of sacrifice even unto death, as Jesus is

69. Park, *Wounded Heart of God,* p. 123. What I find problematic in Park's account of the cross and love of God manifested therein is that he speaks in this same context of the inability of God to "save Godself apart from salvation of humanity," in other words, apart from humanity's response to the salvific work of God (pp. 123-24). While I fully endorse the importance of human response — as a *response* — to the divine initiative of salvation, as will be carefully discussed below, I also find highly problematic the tendency to limit God's freedom in the way Park does.

70. Joh, *Heart of the Cross,* p. xiii. For a succinct account, see her "Transgressive Power of Jeong," pp. 149-63.

71. Joh, *Heart of the Cross,* p. xiv.

72. Joh, *Heart of the Cross,* p. 79.

understood to have demonstrated on the cross."[73] As implied above, theology can only critique and expose the complex and often subtle ways that the cross has been used to foster subjugation, submission, and self-negation.[74]

Although Wonhee Anne Joh sees much promise in the radical emphasis on the suffering of — and *in* — the God of Moltmann's theology of the cross in that "the event of the crucifixion . . . [is] the manifestation of God's resistance against oppression and [that] God's presence on the cross is appealing and comforting,"[75] she also joins the critics of Moltmann, including the liberationist Leonardo Boff, the Asian theologian C. S. Song, and the feminist Dorothee Sölle. With these critics, Joh wonders if Moltmann's trinitarian interpretation of the cross takes away from its horrific nature as a means of execution and makes the event too "tidy . . . [and] somehow theologically masked or contained."[76] In other words, Moltmann's view makes the killing of Jesus too much an act of divine violence rather than human violence. Hence, "Moltmann lets the work of redemption be done within the divine Trinitarian relationality. . . . [It can be asked] What has happened to the participation of humanity in redemptive work?"[77] C. S. Song radicalizes the human participation in the event of crucifixion with his stress on "crucified people" rather than "crucified God" and speaks of "human beings abandoning human beings" rather than the second person of the Trinity having been forsaken by the first person.[78] A related theme of criticism against Moltmann's focus on the trinitarian divine suffering, particularly from the liberationist perspective, is that it is too soft on the role of Jesus' suffering as the form of resistance and overcoming of suffering. Furthermore, postcolonialists and liberationists are wondering if that kind of account of the cross elicits proper action from Christians toward rectifying the causes of suffering and resisting evil.[79]

It seems to me that these kinds of criticisms against the theology of the cross — those not only of Moltmann but also of the wider Christian tradition, going back to Luther and others — are useful reminders for constructive

73. Joh, *Heart of the Cross,* p. 71.

74. Joh, *Heart of the Cross,* chap. 4, does that well.

75. Joh, *Heart of the Cross,* p. 75. Joh, along with others, also appreciates greatly Moltmann's emphasis on the love of God (p. 79 and passim).

76. Joh, *Heart of the Cross,* p. 77.

77. Joh, *Heart of the Cross,* p. 78.

78. Song, *Jesus, the Crucified People,* pp. 88-89.

79. For a detailed discussion, see Joh, *Heart of the Cross,* pp. 75-90 and chap. 5 (pp. 91-115).

theology of atonement in its search for a more coherent, inclusive, and robust account of reconciliation. At the same time, these criticisms have to be subjected to careful critical correction. My advocacy of the trinitarian account of the whole history of salvation of Jesus Christ, including the cross, also insists on its robust and deep relatedness to human, imperial responsibility for killing the innocent Jesus, as well as, as will be discussed below, the need for reconciled men and women, and the whole Christian community, to both spread the message of reconciliation and participate in the liberative work of reconciliation. At the same time, with tradition, I argue that before the cross can be a salvific event, in the most inclusive sense of the term, it has to be a divine initiative. Only God is able to save us; humans do not have that capacity. Hence, the choice between, say, considering the cross as either a political execution or a redemptive divine act is mistaken on all accounts, whether in light of biblical, historical, or systematic perspectives.

Christ as Sacrifice and Our Representative

Notwithstanding its strangeness to most (but not all!) contemporary cultures, it is important to consider carefully the continuing relevance of the metaphor of sacrifice.[80] For the first Christians, who were Jewish, the temple cult with its sacrifices as a means of atonement was very familiar, and it is no surprise that they applied that framework to the salvific work of Jesus on the cross.[81] In the NT the whole life and self-offering of Christ are depicted as sacrifice; consequently, his followers are exhorted to offer their lives as a "living sacrifice" (Rom. 12:1). The NT — in keeping with the sacrificial theology and practice of the OT[82] — employs the sacrifice metaphor in diverse and constructive ways, for example, against the culture of shame (Heb. 12:2) or in references to a sweet sacrificial fragrance (Eph. 5:2). An indication of the highly metaphorical, creative usage of the sacrifice metaphor is the presentation of Jesus not only as a sacrificial lamb (John 1:29) but also as the priest who offers sacrifice (Heb. 7:27).[83]

We owe the working out of a groundbreaking theological meaning of

80. An almost encyclopedic discussion can be found in Blocher, "Sacrifice of Jesus Christ," pp. 23-36.

81. See Lyden, "Atonement in Judaism and Christianity," pp. 49-50.

82. As helpfully delineated in Goldingay, "Old Testament Sacrifice," pp. 3-20.

83. See further Gunton, *Actuality of Atonement*, pp. 120-26 particularly.

sacrifice in Christian tradition to Saint Augustine, who first set forth the fourfold distinction of "to whom it is offered, by whom . . . what it is that is offered and for whom,"[84] and whose definition was affirmed and elaborated by Thomas Aquinas.[85] What makes sacrifices unique, Thomas surmised, is that, offered to God, the gift is made sacred in the process; in other words, the human offering whose recipient is God, is being transformed and sanctified.[86] In Christ's self-sacrifice, the giver and the gift are of course the same.[87] Indeed, as Augustine already argued, in Christ's case, all four elements of the sacrifice become one; the giver/gift remains one with humanity, for whose benefit the act is done, and with the receiver, God.[88] In the context of Christ's salvific self-sacrifice, humanity is not offering to God something to "appease" an angry God, but rather, God who was in Christ (2 Cor. 5:17) is both the giver and receiver of the final, ultimate, onetime (Heb. 10:10) gift of sacrifice. "The death of Christ as a sacrifice must therefore be an act in which Christ becomes, theologically speaking, handed over [*paradidōmi*] to God."[89]

S. Mark Heim makes the obvious observation that the rejection of the

84. Augustine, *Trinity* 4.3.19.

85. Thomas Aquinas, *Summa Theologica* 3.22.33 ad1; 48 a3 c. For a careful and useful discussion of Thomas's use of Augustinian analysis, see Simon, *Die Messeopfertheologie Martin Luthers.* I am indebted to Risto Saarinen (*God and Gift,* p. 81) for pointing me to this source; his discussion of sacrifice in chap. 4 is insightful. In a creative way, Saarinen tries to offer an apology against contemporary charges of violence in emphasizing (on the basis of a more "anthropocentric reading of the Anselmian theory") that "(1) humans and not God are the agents of sacrifice" even though God perhaps "orchestrated" the scene of crucifixion and "(2) what is required of humans is not bloodshed but mercy" with reference to the Matt. 9:13 preference for mercy rather than sacrifice (p. 88; see also p. 89). In my view, the problem here is that this apologetic may also become counterproductive in implying that, after all, God needed to be "satisfied" at the expense of something humanity (namely, the "human" Jesus) had to offer God. Furthermore, while it is right to say — and we have to say — that at the cross God did not die (*pace* Hegel and Nietzsche), instead the Son of God did; what happened at the cross was much "more" than just a death of the human being (as in martyrdom). I am not of course saying that Saarinen's proposal is teaching either one of these two mistaken notions; I am saying that, in my reading, these dangers lurk behind his suggestion.

86. Aquinas, *Summa Theologica* II/2.85.3 ad3.

87. Aquinas, *Summa Theologica* 3.48.3.

88. Augustine, *Trinity* 4.3.19. While the Augustinian-Thomistic theology of sacrifice doesn't of course say everything about the theological meaning of sacrifice, it sets Christian tradition in the right path, even apart from its relevance to the theology of the Eucharist and the giving of gifts in the church such as tithes.

89. Saarinen, *God and Gift,* p. 84.

penal substitution theory by many "now frequently entails rejection of any consideration of Jesus' death as a sacrifice, of Jesus' dying for us, of the cross as representing any kind of transaction or 'ransom,' of the passion as an event with any objective effect as opposed to being purely illustrative."[90] Some African American theologians reject all notions of sacrifice in traditional atonement theories. Karen and Garth Kasimu Baker-Fletcher wonder if all notions of sacrifice in this context merely enforce the surrogacy role assigned for black women. They suspect any sacrificial notion as a "particularly 'male' construction within our community that one must be willing to 'die' for something in order for it to be valuable."[91] Some feminists have joined the call to jettison all forms of atonement theology.[92] Heim rightly critiques the leaving behind of all notions of sacrifice because those ideas "are rooted in scripture and tradition for good reasons. We cannot understand Jesus' death without understanding that it was a sacrifice, since this is the basis for knowing what it was doing to end sacrifice."[93] The "scandal of the cross" must remain, not as a way of affirming the legitimacy of violence, let alone abuse, but rather as a way to embrace the "promise of the cross": redemption, liberation, salvation, and finally the end of violence.[94]

I fear that a total no to traditional accounts of atonement faces the danger of virtually being silent about the divine salvific initiative in Christ.[95] The womanist theologian Delores Williams's refusal to consider any notion of sacrifice and God-willed death of his Son leads to a reductionistic, human-centered view of salvation: "[I]t seems more intelligent and more scriptural to understand that redemption had to do with God, through Jesus, giving humankind new vision to see the resources for positive, abundant relational life."[96] God giving us a new vision hardly speaks of the divine ini-

90. Heim, *Saved from Sacrifice,* p. 294.

91. Baker-Fletcher and Baker-Fletcher, *My Sister, My Brother,* p. 103.

92. Carlson Brown and Parker, "For God So Loved," p. 26.

93. Heim, *Saved from Sacrifice,* p. 294; Saarinen (*God and Gift,* p. 93) materially agrees: "A consistent and straightforward non-sacrificial reading of the gospels leads to a sacrifice of central elements of Christianity, including the death of Jesus."

94. See also Volf, *Exclusion and Embrace,* pp. 25-27.

95. I wonder if this is the case with the (mature) systematic theology of the Mennonite Gordon D. Kaufman, *In Face of Mystery,* in which even the two chapters on Christology (25; 26) say very little of atonement however one understands this doctrine.

96. D. S. Williams, *Sisters in the Wilderness,* p. 165. For an important historical and theological study of the doctrine of atonement in both black theology and womanist theology, see Terrell, *Power in the Blood?*

tiative in any sense similar to classical tradition![97] Rather, what she describes as the heart of atonement is a result and gift for men and women of the salvific work of the triune God. Furthermore, one of the meanings of sacrifice in most cultures involves doing away with pollution and uncleanness. While sin has many facets, one of the underlying meanings has to do with that. Christ's sacrifice is a metaphor of dealing with that "dirt" that separates us from the all-holy God. The importance of sacrificial rites in African traditional religions has prompted some theologians to speak for the importance of the sacrifice motif in the communication of the gospel "in a way that can evoke a healthy meaning of Christ's death and resurrection."[98] In keeping with the deep communion aspect of African cultures, it is noteworthy that people gathered together around the sacrifice believe in the presence of the deity; thus "sacrifice usually brings Deity/deity and worshippers together in an intimate fashion."[99]

Because the term "penal substitution" is materially one-sided and limited, has such a checkered history, and elicits so many negative feelings, it is not useful for constructive theology. Donald Bloesch's suggestion, "vicarious substitutionary atonement," even though not likely to gain the widest support, is more appropriate in light of the fact that Jesus' suffering on the cross, which "is rightly described as the vicarious suffering of the wrath of God at sin, rests on the fellowship that Jesus Christ accepted with all of us as sinners and with our fate as such."[100] It helps avoid the loaded term "penal"[101] and instead uses terms more at home with Christian tradition throughout the centuries. It also helps set forth a more dynamic, multifaceted, and multidimensional account of salvation:

> The atonement, of course, involves much more than divine forgiveness. It entails liberation, satisfaction, expiation and propitiation. The sacrifice of Christ on the cross effects not only pardon for sin but release

97. Somewhat similarly to Williams, Mary Grey defines redemption only as "right relation" and "mutuality-in-relation," literally *"at-one-ment."* Grey, *Redeeming the Dream,* pp. 110, 126.

98. Ubruhe, "Traditional Sacrifice," p. 16.

99. Ubruhe, "Traditional Sacrifice," p. 17. Ubruhe refers to Thompson, "Anatomy of Sacrifice," p. 30.

100. Pannenberg, *ST* 2:427; for the theme of the "vicarious" death of Jesus instead of us, sinners, see also p. 374.

101. Pannenberg feels comfortable in using terms such as "penal" and "expiation" as well (*ST* 2:427).

> from the power of sin. It involves not only the propitiation of God but also the liberation of sinner. It removes not simply the sense of guilt but the very stain of guilt. The theme of reconciliation is found in the so-called subjective theories of the atonement, but they fail to do justice to expiation, satisfaction, and propitiation.[102]

Bloesch's liability is the term "wrath" in the context of the "vicarious suffering." True, the Bible speaks of the wrath of God against all ungodliness and sin, but very little in the biblical testimonies makes the vicarious death on the cross of Jesus a matter of God's wrath. Furthermore, that wrath motif has been utilized in Christian tradition in such a gross and unnuanced way that it is difficult for contemporary people to hear it in an appropriate way.

Vicarious suffering is related to Jesus' role as our representative. Jesus suffered and died for us not as an "individual" but as a representative of the community. He died for the whole world. In the words of C. S. Song, Jesus is "the crucified people."[103] In this light, the feminist critique of the lack of relatedness of Jesus in his death on the cross sounds odd.[104]

A proper way to rehabilitate the positive and necessary aspects of the substitutionary and penal substitutionary traditions is to expose their occupation with juridizing, individualizing, and de-historicizing tendencies. Perhaps it is not the sacrificial, substitutionary, and "penal" elements of the atonement tradition that necessarily endanger hospitality but rather the three orientations mentioned.[105] The presence of legal notions in the explanation of the sacrificial death on the cross is not the problem; the problem is how law and legality are understood. This juridizing tendency of atonement, owing not a little to Augustinian and Calvinistic traditions, tended to trump the trinitarian unity of the work of salvation, cast it in a semimechanistic economy of exchange, an effect of which is the typical Protestant notion of forensic justification. The result of these developments is that "God's eternal hospitality was bounded and regulated by strict legal arrangements and so lost the welcoming nature of absolute, pure hospitality."[106] An overindividu-

102. Bloesch, *Jesus Christ,* p. 157.

103. Song, *Jesus, the Crucified People.*

104. This critique is represented most vocally in Brock, *Journeys by Heart,* pp. 60, 105, and passim.

105. So also Boersma, *Violence, Hospitality, and the Cross,* p. 163; the whole chap. 7 is a constructive attempt to meet these challenges in favor of a more appropriate understanding of traditional theories.

106. Boersma, *Violence, Hospitality, and the Cross,* p. 166.

alistic account of atonement both strengthens and is the result of the juridizing effect, rampant in modern Western culture, owing also to the Reformation. Individualism fosters the conception of sin and the Fall that has thin social and cosmic implications. Too easily in sync with juridizing and individualistic tendencies is the nonhistorical orientation in which what happens on this earthly level here and now is secondary or meaningless in light of what happens in the realm of timeless eternity. The doctrine of election in the Augustinian-Calvinistic system is of course the prime example. God's dealings with his people in the OT, the life of Jesus, implications for trinitarian life, as well as the relational, communal, and cosmic elements became sidelined.

The task of the current interpreter of the atonement traditions is to balance, relativize, and make more appropriate the notions of sacrifice, substitution, expiation, and paying the penalty — conceptions that are anchored in biblical and traditional theologies and cannot be simply replaced by other metaphors. It is a scholarly consensus in contemporary biblical studies that the biblical understanding of law, founded as it is on the covenant, is based on Yahweh's faithfulness and call to a mutual relational faithfulness. This is a corrective to the typical reading of law in the Bible through the lens of the Western medieval-Reformation notion of law, including the traditional Reformed federal theology.[107] The Pauline and patristic understanding of incarnation and recapitulation in terms of community helps negotiate the individualizing effects. A proper account of the meaning of the salvific life, death, resurrection, and atonement of Jesus as the representative of the people of Israel and, in continuation, as the collective new Adam helps connect with history. The whole history of Jesus, including the subsequent pouring out of the Spirit on the new community sent out to the world, belongs to atonement with a promise of a holistic offer of salvation that encompasses all aspects of human, social, and cosmic life. Only a proper trinitarian account would insure such a comprehensive exposition.

The critics who want to completely dismiss not only the idea of sacrifice but also substitution and expiation — and even those who are willing to speak of sacrifice but not of the rest — would do well in reconsidering the continuing value of these contemporary formulations of the atonement that are firmly linked with tradition but in a way that seeks to embrace various

107. Detailed discussion with proper sources will be conducted in the discussion of soteriology, including the reworking of the highly debated law-and-gospel question.

kinds of biblical and traditional elements.[108] That said, Heim's word of advice is useful: "The challenge for the theology of the cross is to keep the first-level description of the sacrificial exchange that is being condemned and overcome in Christ's death from bleeding, literally, back into the formulation of what God is doing through that death and what Christians celebrate in faith. One check on this can be found in the relation between God and Jesus (and in the trinitarian terms between the Father and the incarnate Word) that atonement theories assume."[109]

This remark reminds us of the vital importance of a proper trinitarian framework for the consideration of atonement.[110] Only a trinitarian account helps us avoid the obvious Anselmian danger of putting the Son and Father in opposition to each other or the feminists' charge against an abuse of the Son in the hands of the Father.

The Trinitarian Work of Salvation

The salvific and *theo*logical meaning of the death on the cross can only be discerned from the perspective of trinitarian faith.[111] While hardly anyone would contest this claim, it is also true that not any kind of allegedly trinitarian interpretation is appropriate. Robert Sherman's attempt to offer a trinitarian account of atonement integrated with three classical theories in

108. Finlan (*Options on Atonement*, p. 28) helpfully notes: "Paul did plant the seeds of penal substitution, although this theme was taken much too crudely and literally by later minds, while his themes of participation, believer transformation, and deification were pushed aside. For many centuries Western Christians have been trained to think in terms of penal-substitution, and they tend to impose this concept on all NT soteriological passages. This causes Christians to see penal substitution everywhere, for instance, in Hebrew sacrifices, which they misinterpret as a form of ritualized punishment, downplaying its cleansing and gift-exchange functions." As mentioned above, even among the Fathers, who by and large went with recapitulation and *Christus Victor* views, the notions of sacrifice, propitiation, blood, and substitution are not missing, and with some of them (Western Fathers), they are quite frequent. For a helpful listing of such passages in Irenaeus, Origen, Cyril of Alexandria, Hilary of Poitiers, Augustine, and Gregory the Great, see Boersma, *Violence, Hospitality, and the Cross*, pp. 161-63.

109. Heim, *Saved from Sacrifice*, p. 309.

110. For a robust consideration of the trinitarian implications of the atonement, defending in a nuanced way the value of traditional viewpoints, see McIlroy, "Towards a Relational and Trinitarian Theology of Atonement," pp. 13-32.

111. See further Jüngel, *Justification*, p. 118.

which *Christus Victor* goes with the royal Father, vicarious sacrifice with the priestly Son, and moral example with the prophetic Spirit, while interesting as a rhetorical device, also misses the key concern behind the need to look at the atonement as the joint, unified work of Father, Son, and Spirit.[112] His is rather the work of a three-member team.[113] Even more counterproductive is Richard of St. Victor's view that "The Father punishes, the Son expiates, the Spirit forgives."[114] Here not only is the classic rule of the unity of the work of the triune God in the world challenged but also violence within the life of the Trinity is proposed. Yet another attempt to offer a more thoroughly trinitarian understanding of the atonement that raises more problems than it solves is Michael Winter's, which is based on the idea of Jesus interceding for humanity's forgiveness.[115] While Christ's intercessory role in general is a well-attested biblical truth (Heb. 7:25), the main trinitarian problem is whether the Father is reluctant to save humanity without his Son's pleading (and why does it take the Son's death to do the pleading as "divine intermediary"?).[116]

The "rule" of Saint Basil sets theology on a proper road. The Father is the "original cause," the Son the "creative cause," and the Spirit the "perfecting cause."[117] While not uniform, the works of the persons of the Trinity are

112. Sherman, *King, Priest, and Prophet.* In the introduction to the book, Sherman issues a statement that clearly points to the understanding of atonement as a unified work of the Trinity as he defines it as "the activity of God the Father in the Son through the Spirit that overcomes the bondage or desire or pride or dislocation or estrangement or alienation or evil or limitation that separates humanity from God" (p. 15).

113. A proper way of using the threefold office of Christ is just that — the threefold office of *Christ* — as is done masterfully by Torrance, *Atonement.* Even Pannenberg, who was a well-known critic of the Reformation doctrine of the threefold office of Christ, in his systematic theology (*ST* 2:444-49) rehabilitates its use as long as strict trinitarian canons are being honored.

114. Richard of St. Victor, *De Verbo Incarnato* 11, cited in Finlan, *Problems with Atonement,* p. 85. This kind of view of what happened on the cross, unfortunately, could give some legitimization for the kind of critique some women theologians have targeted against Anselm's view, namely, that the father-son analogy in the cross leads to the idea of the "punishment of one perfect child" by "the perfect father," as a result of which the father could forgive the rest of the children. Brock, *Journeys by Heart,* p. 55. In light of the trinitarian view of atonement constructed in this discussion, Brock's criticism is a caricature with no theological substance.

115. Winter, *The Atonement,* pp. 108-13.

116. For similar criticisms, see Finlan, *Problems with Atonement,* pp. 97-98. "Divine intermediary" is from Girard, *Things Hidden,* p. 183.

117. Saint Basil the Great, *On the Holy Spirit* 16.38.

united. Calvin, among others, has followed in these footsteps.[118] God who was in Christ (2 Cor. 5:19) — maybe we could speak of the Son here as the "form" of atonement[119] — took the initiative and reconciled the world to himself; through the life-giving Spirit the crucified Son was raised to new life, and through the mediation of the Spirit the salvific benefits are communicated to humanity and to the creation.

When it comes to the cross, the trinitarian account begins from the cry of dereliction. Boldly running against much of contemporary theology's reservation about the cross and violence, Moltmann proposes the cry of dereliction as the way to the truly authentic theology for our world:

> Basically, every Christian theology is consciously or unconsciously answering the question, "Why hast thou forsaken me," when their doctrines of salvation say "for this reason" or "for that reason." In the face of Jesus' death-cry to God, theology either becomes impossible or becomes possible only as specifically Christian theology. Christian theology cannot come to terms with the cry of its own age and at the same time always be on the side of the rulers of this world. But it must come to terms with the cry of the wretched for God and for freedom out of the depths of the sufferings of this age. Sharing in the sufferings of this time, Christian theology is truly contemporary theology. Whether or not it can be so depends less upon the openness of theologians and their theories to the world and more upon whether they have honestly and without reserve come to terms with the death-cry of Jesus for God.[120]

The ultimate "reason" for the death of Israel's Messiah for the world was godforsakenness. This differentiates Jesus from Socrates, the Stoics, the Zealot martyrs and other "noble martyrs" of Israel,[121] and even Christian martyrs. Jesus died in anguish and with crying (Mark 14:33; 15:37 par.; Heb. 5:7), not only because of physical pain, as real as that was, but also because of

118. Calvin, *Institutes* 1.13.18: "[T]o the Father is attributed the beginning of action, the fountain and source of all things; to the Son, wisdom, counsel, and arrangement in action, while the energy and efficacy of action is assigned to the Spirit."

119. As does Schwöbel, "Reconciliation," p. 33.

120. Moltmann, *The Crucified God,* p. 153. For a highly nuanced account of the joint work of the Son and Father, including the mutual "giving up" and willingness to suffer, see also Pannenberg, *ST* 2:438-41.

121. For the important theme of "noble martyrdom" in the Greek world and Israel, see Finlan, *Options on Atonement,* pp. 15-17; Finlan, *Problems with Atonement,* pp. 52-55.

rejection. "'E'lo-i, E'lo-i, la'ma sabach-tha'ni?' which means, 'My God, my God, why hast thou forsaken me?'" (Mark 15:34).[122] As much as this cry is the expression of deepest human anguish, on the lips of the dying Jesus of Nazareth, the Son of God, it is also the "climax of his self-distinction from the Father."[123] As obedient Son, rather than "count[ing] equality with God a thing to be grasped" (Phil. 2:7), he accepted the fate of humanity and thus let death expose his finitude.[124] At the same time, the "divine absence from the world reached its peak of intensity in the dereliction of the Son on the cross."[125] Sinners want to escape from the presence of God in their affirmation of independence from their Creator. Jesus' death on the cross means suffering in our stead; he takes the fate of the God-fleeing sinners. That way, the "judgment in the cross of the Son became for the world its access to salvation."[126]

This tells us that the God of the dying Son Jesus Christ does not shy away from the suffering of either his Son or of the world but rather makes the suffering his own and so overcomes it in hope. All suffering becomes God's so that God may overcome it.[127] At the cross, the Father suffers in deserting his Son.[128] The Son suffers the pain of being cut off from the life of the Father, and the Father suffers the pain of giving up his Son. By doing so, God "also accepts and adopts [suffering] in himself, making it part of his own eternal life."[129] Therefore, the cross is not only an event between God and humanity. "What happened on the cross was an event between God and God. It was a deep division in God himself, in so far as God abandoned God and contradicted himself, and at the same time a unity in God, in so far as God was at one with God and corresponded to himself."[130] Thus, the cross belongs to the inner life of God, not only occurring between God and estranged humanity.[131] "God's being is in suffering and suffering in God's be-

122. Curiously, Luke has the confident "into thy hands I commit my spirit" in place of this cry of dereliction (Luke 23:46).

123. Pannenberg, *ST* 2:375.

124. Pannenberg, *ST* 2:374.

125. Pannenberg, *ST* 2:392.

126. Pannenberg, *ST* 2:392.

127. Moltmann, *The Crucified God,* p. 246.

128. Moltmann, *The Crucified God,* p. 243.

129. Moltmann, *Trinity and the Kingdom,* p. 119; materially, Pannenberg, *ST* 2:391 and 1:314, says the same. The criticism by Leonardo Boff (*Passion of Christ,* p. 114) is based on misunderstanding: Moltmann is not advocating this view of the cross as an instance of the Father murdering the Son and thus failing to put an end to violence.

130. Moltmann, *The Crucified God,* p. 244.

131. Moltmann, *The Crucified God,* p. 249.

ing itself," because God is love.[132] Here is the motive for God's willingness to suffer, namely, love. Rather than a neutral observer of world events, God is "pathetic" in that "he suffers from the love which is the superabundance and overflowing of his being."[133] Perhaps the best parallel in human life is the self-sacrificial, persistent, and caring love of the mother. Far from this are the classical notions of God's aseity, inability to suffer and be vulnerable. "As mothers' hearts rend with their children's suffering more readily than with their own, so God's unsurpassed love for humans is narrated scripturally as a love both that *is* and that *gives up* the beloved one who dies in compassion for us."[134]

At the same time, the deity of the Father is at stake at the cross: "The passion of Jesus Christ is not an event which concerned only the human nature that the divine Logos assumed, as though it did not affect in any way the eternal placidity of the trinitarian life of God. In the death of Jesus the deity of his God and Father was at issue."[135] That said, it is not correct to speak of the "death of God" on the cross;[136] "[w]e can say only of the Son of God that he 'was crucified, dead, and buried.'"[137] Perhaps the best we can do here is to stick with the ambiguity of Christian tradition when it comes to the exact "subject" of the suffering on the cross.[138] Theology has to avoid the Scylla of Monophysitism (and patripassianism) of speaking of the "death of God" and the Charybdis of making the death on the cross so "external" to the divine life that it virtually becomes only the death of the "human nature" of Jesus of Nazareth (perhaps as a "penalty payment" to an angry Father!).[139]

132. Moltmann, *The Crucified God,* p. 227.

133. Moltmann, *Trinity and the Kingdom,* p. 23.

134. See further, Cahill, "The Atonement Paradigm," pp. 429-30, emphasis in original; see also p. 428.

135. Pannenberg, *ST* 2:314; materially, Moltmann says the same, *The Crucified God,* p. 151.

136. As does Hegel, *Lectures on the Philosophy of History,* pp. 125-31; he cites a line from a hymn by J. Rist (1641): "God has died; God himself is dead" (p. 125). This idea materially was of course picked up and made a theme by Nietzsche (among others, *The Gay Science,* bk. 3, #108). For a careful discussion, see Jüngel, *God as the Mystery,* pp. 63-104.

137. Pannenberg, *ST* 1:314.

138. See helpful notes by Pelikan, *Emergence of the Catholic Tradition,* p. 265.

139. It seems to me that Pannenberg borders on the danger of making the death on the cross too much a matter of merely the human nature of the Son — because of his focus on the humanity, rather than divine *Logos,* as the subject of the incarnate Son. He writes: "To be dogmatically correct, indeed, we have to say that the Son of God, though he suffered and died himself, did so according to his human nature" (*ST* 1:314). In the con-

Here the benefits of a responsible and nuanced use of the Chalcedonian two-nature Christology can help. The traditional distinction between the human nature and the divine nature in the one person has the advantage of considering the work of Christ as fully human and divine as both natures contribute to it in a distinctive way. In this respect, the current approaches of those, like Pannenberg, who instead of the hypostatic union consider the work of the historical (human) Jesus as the acting subject — who is the divine Son as anticipation of the eschaton as established in his resurrection — have a different emphasis in relating the death only to the human nature. The classic approach more robustly looks at the work of reconciliation as an integrally divine and human work in one person, even if it is not able to clarify all the details.[140] At the same time, it is of utmost importance to speak of the cross as the supreme manifestation of the suffering of God, and of the cross, therefore, as an event that in some way touches the divine life. And to honor trinitarian canons, we need to speak of not only the suffering of the Son but also of the Father's suffering with the Son, his "sym-pathy."[141] This also means that God who "was in Christ" (2 Cor. 5:19) brings "into the passion history of this world the eternal fellowship of God, and the divine justice and righteousness that creates life."[142]

Here there is a mutually conditioning relationship between the holiness and love of God. Love and holiness cannot be set in opposition any more than can love and justice. They all belong simultaneously and uncompromisingly to the mystery of atonement. More strongly and consistently than his Reformed predecessors, including Calvin, Barth saw the basic motivation for the atonement in the holy love of God.[143] As Tillich rightly points out, there is no conflict between the love and justice of God.[144] Daniel Migliore writes, "The grace of God includes judgment, and the judgment of

text of Pannenberg's overall Christology, this seems to violate the *communicatio idiomatum* principle.

140. I acknowledge here the careful discussion of Pannenberg's Christology in McClean, "Anticipation," pp. 201-8 and passim.

141. Pannenberg, *ST* 1:314; Moltmann, *The Crucified God*, pp. 190, 242-45; Moltmann, *Way of Jesus Christ*, pp. 178-79.

142. Moltmann, *Spirit of Life*, p. 130.

143. See McCormack, *For Us and Our Salvation*. Similarly, P. T. Forsyth already set forth a thick account of God's holiness and love as the basis for the atonement in *The Cruciality of the Cross*.

144. Tillich, *Systematic Theology*, 2:174.

God serves the purpose of grace."[145] P. T. Forsyth reminds us, there is no separating attributes of God without truncating the integrity of God's being: "An attribute of God is God Himself behaving, with all His unity."[146] That said, it is also important to underscore the underlying biblical conviction that "the heart of God does not harbor in exact parallel fashion love and wrath, mercy and justice, election and reprobation, hospitality and violence."[147] While God expresses wrath against sin, injustice, and cruelty, God *is love.* Whereas God may have to use violence to further salvific purposes, God *is* love.

When we see atonement as the unified work of the triune God, it becomes evident that "God does not love us because Christ died for us, but that Christ died for us because God loves us, and his sacrifice is an expression of this love. The cross of Christ was not given by man to change God, but given by God to change man." Culpepper continues, "Far from effecting any change in the attitude of God toward man in the sense of turning hostility into love or making a friend of an enemy, the cross of Christ gave expression to the love of God for man which was in God's heart from all eternity, working out in history God's eternal purposes in Christ."[148] The principle of inner-trinitarian mutuality characterizes the cross.[149]

Atonement is the joint work of Father, Son, and Spirit. Its patrological and christological implications are usually in the fore, whereas many atonement expositions have little to say of the Spirit. In the NT, the destiny of Jesus leading to the cross and beyond via resurrection and ascension to the right hand of the Father is linked with the ministry of the Holy Spirit (John 16:7-11; 7:39). Heim's Girardian-driven interpretation helps shed light on one crucial aspect of the Spirit's work here. In reference to John 15:26-27, he reminds us that "the work of the *paraclete* is to testify by the side of victims, to

145. Migliore, *Faith Seeking Understanding,* p. 187.

146. Forsyth, *Work of Christ,* p. 117.

147. Boersma, *Violence, Hospitality, and the Cross,* p. 9.

148. Culpepper, *Interpreting the Atonement,* p. 131. I don't find helpful the opinion of Bloesch (*Jesus Christ,* p. 147) that reconciliation "consists not only in a change of attitude on the part of the human but also in change of attitude on the part of God." Indeed, I am not quite sure what he means with this idea.

149. For an important discussion from a feminist perspective of mutuality, see Heyward, *Saving Jesus from Those Who Are Right.* A trinitarian account of the cross, based on the idea of mutuality, would help correct her misunderstanding of the relationship between Father and Son being based on authoritarian obedience (pp. 77, 79; see also 58-59, among others).

be their advocate and to 'prove the world wrong.'" In light of the testimony of the *paraclete* concerning "sin and righteousness and judgment," the violence and perversion are exposed: "Sin becomes an excuse for persecution, righteousness becomes defined as submission to scapegoating, and judgment uses violence against violence. The historical task of the Holy Spirit . . . is to prove this wrong, by testimony to Christ"[150] and by Christ's innocent self-offering at the cross. Importantly, Heim also reminds us how often after the ascension of Christ the Holy Spirit is mentioned in his role as the "advocate" of those facing suffering, violence, and death, as with Stephen at the moment of martyrdom (Acts 7:55-56), or Peter and John when arrested (4:8-11), or Paul on the way to his final destiny (20:22-23). The promise in Luke 12:10-12 of the aid of the Holy Spirit in the midst of persecution gains a new significance in light of this perspective.[151]

Seen from the perspective of inner-trinitarian relations, what applies to all other joint works of the Trinity also applies to atonement: "Everything in the conduct of the Son and the work of the Spirit ultimately serves to glorify the Father and enhance the irruption of his kingdom into the world."[152] The Father is "dependent" for his deity on the obedient ministry of the Son as much as the Son is dependent on the Father for raising him up with the power of the Spirit to new life. According to the biblical testimonies, the Holy Spirit's role is to glorify the Son (John 16:14), testify as the Spirit of the truth to Jesus (15:26), and teach and remind the disciples of all that Jesus taught (14:26).

Theologically, it is significant that these Johannine sayings are set in the context of the culmination of Jesus' earthly ministry, the context of the Last Supper, the context of suffering, death, and resurrection. "Basic for the glorifying of the Son by the Spirit" — which serves the glorification of the Father — "is the Easter event. . . . The life-giving work of the Spirit relates primarily in this context to Jesus himself, for by the Spirit he was raised from the dead (Rom. 8:11; cf. 1:4 and 1 Pet. 3:18). . . . As the Creator of new life from the resurrection, the Spirit leads to knowledge of the sonship of Jesus in the light of the confirmation and vindication of his pre-Easter work (1 Tim. 3:16)."[153] In terms of its salvific effects, the glorifying work of the Spirit serves the consummation of redemption and atonement since it brings about the "overcoming of mortality and consummation by participation in the eternal life

150. Heim, *Saved from Sacrifice*, pp. 153-54 (154).
151. Heim, *Saved from Sacrifice*, pp. 154-56.
152. Pannenberg, *ST* 2:395.
153. Pannenberg, *ST* 2:395.

that by the Spirit unites the Son to the Father and that has already come as the future of creation in his resurrection from the dead."[154] The linking of the believers with the salvific works of the Son has been the focus of traditional pneumatology with its accounts of *ordo salutis.* Rightly it can be said, "An exposition of atonement which leaves out Pentecost, leaves the atonement unintelligible — in relation to us."[155] This is something that has to be said, and will be discussed in detail in the context of *ordo salutis.* However, to say only that is to say too little. The Spirit's role in salvation goes far beyond the "subjective" communication to Christians of the benefits of the "objective" work of the Son, as the discussion above has sought to illumine.

The trinitarian drama of salvation is not yet exhausted by what was said of Jesus' earthly ministry in the context of incarnation, including his teaching, healings, exorcisms, and pronouncing of forgiveness, nor by the highlighting of various aspects of his suffering, rejection, and death. The trinitarian account of atonement also includes resurrection, ascension, and the Pentecostal pouring out of the Spirit, to which we next turn.

Raised to New Life

Resurrection is an integral part of the salvific work of the triune God.[156] Resurrection is a trinitarian moment. Kevin J. Vanhoozer zooms in on the trinitarian significance of resurrection:

> "The Lord has risen" (Luke 24:34). What in Greek is a single word joyfully proclaims the climax of the drama of redemption. "The Lord has risen" contains *in nuce* the resolution of the dramatic tension built up over centuries: How would God make good on his promise? How could God keep covenant with covenant breakers? How would God bless all the nations through the seed of Abraham? "The Lord has risen." There is a density in this statement that calls for thought and "thick description." While the explicit subject of this sentence is Jesus Christ, the implied subject is God the Father who raised him. And while the explicit predicate is resurrection, the implicit predicate is Jesus' crucifixion.[157]

154. Pannenberg, *ST* 2:396.

155. Moberly, *Atonement and Personality,* p. 151.

156. See Torrance, *Space, Time, and Resurrection,* p. 46.

157. Vanhoozer, *Drama of Doctrine,* p. 41. Vanhoozer rightly notes that his way of

Not only is the resurrection the joint work of the Father and Son, but also of the Spirit, in that the Spirit proceeds "from this event [of the cross] between the Father and the Son" and thus is the "boundless love which proceeds from the grief of the Father and the dying of the Son" and reaches out to humanity.[158] As the bond of love, the Spirit represents divine unity in the midst of deepest separation. "What proceeds from this event between Father and Son is the Spirit which justifies the godless, fills the forsaken with love and even brings the dead alive."[159]

There is a profound contradistinction in the death-resurrection dialectic. As Torrance puts it, we can speak of the "mutual involution of mortality and immortality, death and life, the crucifixion and the resurrection of Christ."[160] There is also a deep tension between God's condemnation of sin and his eternal love for humanity. Resurrection is a remarkable evidence of God's steadfast and loving clinging to sinful humanity in the midst of and beyond death and judgment.[161]

In the preaching and theology of the early church, the linking of the cross with the resurrection (and ascension) becomes a key theme: Acts 2:23-24; 3:14-15; 4:10; 5:30; 10:39-40; Romans 6:3-11; 8:34; 1 Peter 1:19-21; 3:18, 21-22.[162] Two familiar passages in Paul embody this integral linkage between the cross-and-resurrection/resurrection-and-cross: first, Christ has not only died for us, "indeed much more," he has been raised (Rom. 8:34).[163] Unlike many later interpreters of atonement, for Paul resurrection always loomed large as the ultimate horizon of salvation as he "articulates both a redeeming death theology and an apocalyptic resurrection theology."[164] Resurrection

---

speaking of the "subject" and "predicate" materially says the same as Jenson, *Systematic Theology,* p. 194.

158. Moltmann, *The Crucified God,* p. 245.

159. Moltmann, *The Crucified God,* p. 244.

160. Torrance, *Space, Time, and Resurrection,* p. 48; see also Moltmann, *Way of Jesus Christ,* pp. 213-14.

161. See further, Torrance, *Space, Time, and Resurrection,* p. 67; see also p. 73.

162. For an important discussion of the meaning of resurrection as the culmination of the Passover in some NT passages (John 19:36; 1 Cor. 5:7) and a number of the Fathers, including Irenaeus, Clement of Alexandria, Eusebius of Caesarea, Cyril of Jerusalem, Gregory of Nazianzus, Tertullian, Lactantius, and Augustine, see Maxwell, "The Resurrection of Christ," pp. 27-31.

163. Many translations miss the important expression, *māllon dé;* RSV puts it too lamely: "who died, yes, who was raised from the dead." See further, Moltmann, *Spirit of Life,* pp. 137-38.

164. Finlan, *Problems with Atonement,* p. 74.

and cross belong together. "The risen Christ *is* the historical and crucified Jesus, and *vice versa*."[165] Second, Christ "was put to death for our trespasses and raised for our justification" (Rom. 4:25). Resurrection is evidence of God's vindication of the condemned and executed Jesus.[166] At the same time, it was a confirmation of Jesus' life, ministry, and claims.[167]

The NT makes the important soteriological link between resurrection and reconciliation that later theology too often has missed — especially Western theology. The Protestant doctrine of justification, when understood merely or primarily as a forensic declaration, suffers not only from the lack of pneumatological empowerment but also from the neglect of resurrection. The Pauline statement that Christ was "raised for our justification" (Rom. 4:25) is not only about vindication, it is also about justification. It means the release of the sinner from under judgment due to sin and forgiveness, which is more than just the word of pardon. It means both "emancipation from the thralldom of guilt and reaffirmation as God's dear children in Jesus Christ."[168] Torrance illustrates this link between resurrection and justification with the help of the Gospel story of the healing of the paralytic who was let down through the roof in front of Jesus (Mark 2:12 par.). Jesus' command for the man to "rise up" utilizes the most typical word for resurrection in the NT *(egeiro)*. For the early church, he surmises, the forgiveness and healing offered meant nothing less than the manifestation of the "full reality in the healing and creative work of God upon the whole man" effected as a result of resurrection.[169] It is highly significant that in Acts this linkage between forgiveness and physical healing remained intact — linked with the resurrection and ascension of Christ and the pouring out of the Holy Spirit (Acts 3:12-16; 4:8-12). In the raising of Jesus the Spirit of God who is the spirit of life is working in a mighty way overcoming death and decay.

The soteriological and "spiritual" meaning of the resurrection of Christ is not meant to compromise its historical and "physical" nature. On the contrary, it is necessary for Christian theology to continue affirming that even as a miraculous event, the raising of Christ belongs to this world, time, and space; otherwise, resurrection does not mean the redemption of human

165. Moltmann, *The Crucified God*, p. 160, emphasis in original.

166. Under the heading "The Verdict of the Father," Barth (*CD* IV/1, pp. 283-357) offers a massive explanation of this theme.

167. See further, Pannenberg, *ST* 2:344-45.

168. Torrance, *Space, Time, and Resurrection*, p. 61.

169. Torrance, *Space, Time, and Resurrection*, p. 62.

life on this earth.[170] Indeed, it means the redemption of space and time as well. On the basis of the hypostatic union principle, Christian theology affirms that "in the risen Christ . . . there is involved an hypostatic union between eternity and time, eternity and redeemed and sanctified time, and therefore between eternity and new time."[171] In the section on eschatology, we have to discuss the details of this question.

As mentioned above, the dynamic of the resurrection has two sides. We have to take a closer look at that dynamic and put it in proper perspective. On the one hand, resurrection confirms the validity of Jesus' earthly life and his claims; on the other hand, it is an eschatological event that points to our resurrection (1 Cor. 15:12-23). A proper "theology of hope" can only be developed from the perspective of resurrection.[172] These two effects of the resurrection, which Moltmann names "endorsement" and "fulfillment," belong together and mutually condition each other:

> If we wished to confine ourselves to the endorsement, "resurrection" would be no more than an interpretative theological category for his death; and all that would remain would be a theology of the cross. If we were to concentrate solely on the fulfillment, the Easter Christ would replace and push out the crucified Jesus. But if . . . the earthly Jesus is "the messiah on the way," and the Son of God in the process of his learning, then Easter endorses *and* fulfils this life history of Jesus which is open for the future. At the same time, however, resurrection, understood as an eschatological event in Jesus, is the beginning of the new creation of all things.[173]

Resurrection is an eschatological event. It points not only to the future of our own hope for resurrection but even beyond, to the future of this world and creation.[174] Hence, we can say with Moltmann that in this event

170. See further, Torrance, *Space, Time, and Resurrection,* pp. 86-87. This is of course not to settle the question of how to best negotiate the nature of the resurrections in other known historical events. That question was addressed above in the context of resurrection in relation to Jesus' identity.

171. Torrance, *Space, Time, and Resurrection,* p. 98.

172. Moltmann, *The Crucified God,* p. ix.

173. Moltmann, *Way of Jesus Christ,* p. 171. Elsewhere Moltmann (*The Crucified God,* p. 162) uses the terms "ontic-historical" and "noetic-historical" when speaking of reading the history of Jesus both forward and backward in a mutually conditioning way (p. 162).

174. See further, Russell, "Eschatology and Physical Cosmology," p. 275 particularly.

Christian theology sees "not the eternity of heaven, but the future of the very earth on which his cross stands." Even more: "It sees in him the future of the very humanity for which he died."[175] Resurrection links creation, atonement, and future hope: "God's *No* to all evil and its privation of being falls together with his *Yes* in the final affirming of the creation as that which God has made and declared to be good."[176] As such, raising the crucified who was put to death instead of sinful humanity is a profound evidence of the faithfulness of God to his creation.

While eschatological, referring to the future hope, resurrection is also a powerful sign and energy of hope for today's struggle for equality and justice. While a universal hope, it is always applicable and at work in particular occasions. The African American theologian Garth Kasimu Baker-Fletcher rightly notes that resurrection represents the liberation of the "self from the shackles of Euro-dominated death" and the "release of our inner captive so that we might rise to new life as self-affirming Afrikans." This black Christian's hope then is not an attempt "to negate the purported universal significance of Christian salvation and resurrection teachings."[177] In other words, this black "Xodus" Christology "focuses on the universal significance of the particular Christ who is black."[178]

Ascension, the Cosmic Rule, and Consummation of Salvation

By and large contemporary theology, with the exception of the Eastern Orthodox tradition, has ignored the topic of the ascension.[179] In the Eastern Church this feast was known as *analepsis,* "taking up," and also as the *episozomene,* "salvation," denoting that by ascending into his glory Christ completed the work of our redemption.[180] The cosmic Christology of many church fathers highlighted the importance of ascension. The lack of attention in much of Protestant theology is markedly different from the early church, for which, as mentioned above, atonement, resurrection, and ascension

175. Moltmann, *Theology of Hope,* p. 21; so also p. 194.

176. Torrance, *Space, Time, and Resurrection,* p. 58.

177. G. K. Baker-Fletcher, *Xodus,* p. 88.

178. As paraphrased by Weaver, *Nonviolent Atonement,* p. 118.

179. In older theologies, ascension occupies a larger place; see, e.g., Aquinas, *Summa Theologica* 3.57-59.

180. For the importance of ascension in Orthodox theology, see Florovsky, "And Ascended into Heaven," pp. 23-28.

played a critical role in preaching and teaching. Curiously enough, among the NT Evangelists, only Luke mentions ascension,[181] and in his theology it plays a significant role (Luke 24:50-53; Acts 1:9-11; 2:32-36; 5:30-32). In the rest of the NT, ascension is mentioned quite frequently in various contexts (Phil. 2:6-9; 3:20; Eph. 4:8-10; 1 Tim. 3:16; 1 Pet. 3:22; Heb. 2:9; 12:2).[182]

Over against the ascension motif, the NT and Christian tradition also include a descent motif. True, the biblical basis is scanty,[183] which may be one of the reasons why in contemporary theology, by and large, this ancient doctrine of the descent into hell has been relegated to the margins.[184] Except for the two references in 1 Peter (3:18-20; 4:6), which in themselves have stirred a lot of exegetical debate, we are left with very little.[185] The descent motif is present in contemporary religions of the NT period. The descent of Christ into hell is part of the Apostles' Creed. Pelikan offers an important interpretation of this line's function in the creed: "The descent into hell then assumed the function that the Greek fathers had assigned to the death and resurrection, the triumph celebrated by Christ over the devil and his legion."[186] To appreciate the theological meaning of the descent, we need to see its integral link to death and suffering on the one hand, and to resurrection and ascension on the other hand. The going-down movement symbolizes profoundly the ultimate end of humiliation. The proclamation and releasing work are dramatic expressions of the victory over death and underworld after the Pauline statement, "death is swallowed up in victory" (1 Cor. 15:54). "Jesus, as the human face of God, was not simply a temporary and fleeting vision on this earth. He was the divine attempt to bridge the primordial alienation between God and humanity. All people everywhere, regardless of their respective location in space and time, had through him the

181. Except for the longer ending of Mark, in 16:19.

182. Joseph Fitzmyer, S.J., seems to downplay the presence of the idea of ascension in the NT ("Ascension of Christ and Pentecost," p. 409). For more balanced treatments, see Donne, "Significance of the Ascension," pp. 555-68; Dunn, "The Ascension of Jesus," pp. 301-22.

183. Interestingly enough, extracanonical literature is pregnant with explicit references to the descent, including *Gospel of Nicodemus* and *Odes of Solomon.*

184. For details, see Schwarz, *Christology,* p. 290.

185. The debate was already acknowledged by Luther, *LW* 30:113, in his commentary on 1 Peter. Exegetical disputes include the diversity of opinions about items such as the identity of the "spirits in prison," ranging from the sons of God in Gen. 6:4 to the souls of the preflood generation.

186. Pelikan, *Emergence of the Catholic Tradition,* p. 151.

opportunity to be confronted with the gospel, God's word of salvation."[187] With the inclusion of this statement in the creed, the church meant "not only to indicate that Christ has triumphed over all possible dimensions, even over that dimension where death usually reigns, but also to express something of the divine compassion."[188]

Systematic argumentation, as repeatedly mentioned, is an attempt to discern inner-theological and material connections between Christian truth claims. To consider atonement in a proper perspective, as the work of the triune God — as an event and a process — expands the horizon of interpretation beyond the resurrection of the crucified Messiah. His lifting up to the right hand of the Father — "to receive the crown for the work of Redemption"[189] — and vestment with cosmic rule in the anticipation of the consummation of salvific purposes toward humanity and creation are already present in the history of Jesus Christ as anticipation. Even a cursory look at the state of humanity amidst wars, violence, injustice, and godlessness reminds us of the obvious fact that the reconciliation of the world, while absolutely finalized (Heb. 9:26), still awaits its culmination. The author of the book of Hebrews saw this clearly: "Christ, having been offered once to bear the sins of many, will appear a second time, not to deal with sin but to save those who are eagerly waiting for him" (9:28). Importantly, this biblical passage that speaks of the finality of Christ's sacrifice (9:26), speaks of the continuing intercessory ministry of the ascended Christ (9:24), as well as the hope of his return (9:28).[190] Thomas Aquinas offers a standard exposition of the topic of ascension. He surmises that ascension is the "cause of our salvation" seen from both the human and the divine view. By virtue of ascension, our "souls are uplifted to Him" as far as ascension fosters faith, hope, and love, as well as because it helps increase reverence for him; no more do we know him "after flesh" but rather in his glorified state (2 Cor. 5:16). From the divine point of view, Thomas lists the following "effects": preparing the place for us (John 14:2-3); interceding for his own (Heb. 7:25); and giving gifts (Eph. 4:10).[191] Thomas also discusses extensively the ascended Lord's "judiciary power," universal rule over all humankind and angels.[192] In Protestant theology, the Heidelberg Catechism lists materially similar kinds of

187. Schwarz, *Christology*, p. 294.
188. Schwarz, *Christology*, p. 294.
189. Cyril of Jerusalem, *Catechetical Lectures* 14.23.
190. See further, Pannenberg, *ST* 2:443-44.
191. Aquinas, *Summa Theologica* 3.57.6.
192. Aquinas, *Summa Theologica* 3.59.

benefits of the ascension, including the pouring out of the Spirit.[193] The NT and patristic theology make the relation between ascension and Pentecost an integral topic.[194]

Barth made ascension an integral part of his Christology in general and the exposition of reconciliation in particular.[195] Not only can Barth's fourth volume of *Church Dogmatics* be called "one of *the* major works of ascension theology,"[196] but much of his theology, christologically focused as it is, assumes and builds on the themes of ascension and exaltation.[197] Ascension is a real event of history rather than myth.[198] It points "forwards and upwards"[199] and thus is the "proleptic sign of the parousia."[200] Barth explains the meaning of ascension in terms of the dynamic of presence and absence:

193. "First, that he is our advocate in the presence of his Father in heaven; (a) secondly, that we have our flesh in heaven as a sure pledge that he, as the head, will also take up to himself, us, his members; (b) thirdly, that he sends us his Spirit as an earnest, (c) by whose power we 'seek the things which are above, where Christ sitteth on the right hand of God, and not things on earth.'" Heidelberg Catechism, Q. 49, in *Historic Creeds and Confessions,* p. 22.

194. John 15:26; 16:7; Acts 1:4-11; 2:1-4: Acts 2:1-4; Eph. 4:10; for references in the Fathers, see Kapic and van der Lugt, "Ascension of Jesus," pp. 28-29. For a discussion of the relation of the Johannine (John 20:19-23) and Lukan (Acts 1–2) traditions to each other and the integral relationships, see Kesich, "Resurrection, Ascension and the Giving of the Spirit," pp. 249-60.

195. Sympathetically and critically building on Barth, there is also an important discussion to be found in Torrance, *Space, Time, and Resurrection,* chaps. 5; 6; 7. For my purposes, it is not important to go into the debate as to how closely Torrance follows Barth; commentators differ on this; for a helpful discussion, see Burgess, *Ascension in Karl Barth,* chap. 6.

196. Farrow, "Karl Barth on the Ascension," p. 127, emphasis in original. Discussions of ascension can also be found at the end of *CD* III/2.

197. *CD* IV/2, § 64 is titled "The Exaltation of the Son of Man"; for the importance of ascension to all of Barth's theology, see further, Burgess, *Ascension in Karl Barth,* pp. 16-17, 23-24. In a sense, Barth thinks he is following the lead of the Evangelists and other NT writers in that while they do not talk much about ascension (any more than resurrection), they seem to presuppose it everywhere: "In the later apostolic preaching both events [resurrection and ascension], like the Virgin Birth at the beginning of the Gospel narrative, seem to be presupposed. . . . Even in the Easter narratives the empty tomb and the ascension are alike in the fact that they are both indicated rather than described" (*CD* III/2, p. 452).

198. Barth rejects Bultmann's description of ascension as "naturemiracle" as "hair-splitting" (*CD* III/2, p. 451), yet at the same time he warns us that we should not try "to visualise the ascension as a literal event, like going up in a balloon" (p. 453).

199. Barth, *CD* III/2, p. 453.

200. Barth, *CD* III/2, p. 454.

> He showed Himself quite unequivocally to be the creature, the man, who in provisional distinction from all other men lives on the God-ward side of the universe, sharing His throne, existing and acting in the mode of God, and therefore to be remembered as such, to be known once for all as this exalted creature, this exalted man, and henceforth to be accepted as the One who exists in this form to all eternity. The most important verse in the ascension story is the one which runs: "A cloud received him out of their sight" (Ac. 1:9). In biblical language, the cloud does not signify merely the hiddenness of God, but His hidden presence, and the coming revelation which penetrates this hiddenness. It does not signify merely the heaven which is closed for us, but the heaven which from within, on God's side, will not always be closed.[201]

Speaking in his theology boldly of both the humiliation and exaltation of Jesus Christ, Barth, however, makes every effort not to view these "two states," as in older theology, as two subsequent moments. Rather, he views them dynamically as "two opposed but strictly related moments in that history which operate together and mutually interpret one another."[202] In assuming human flesh, the Son of God "descends" all the way to the death of sinners; in being united with the Son of God, the Son of Man "ascends." Barth here holds tightly to the Chalcedonian formula that simultaneously he is Son of God and Son of Man.[203] With regard to resurrection, it was concluded that on the basis of the hypostatic union principle, in the risen Christ God's time and our time come together. Ascension takes this development even further and completes the process of the "taking up of *human time* into God." Similarly, in the risen and ascended Christ, "the life of human beings is wedded to eternal life."[204]

Between now and eschatological consummation, participation in the redeemed life happens in this world, particularly in the community of Christ.

201. Barth, *CD* III/2, p. 454; see also a useful reflection (not related to Barth), Kerr, "The Presence of Absence," pp. 1-5.

202. Barth, *CD* IV/2, p. 106.

203. See further, Burgess, *Ascension in Karl Barth*, pp. 28-29.

204. Torrance, *Space, Time, and Resurrection*, p. 98. Hence, like resurrection, Christian theology should underscore the "physicality" of the ascension to secure the redemption of the whole of humanity. This emphasis can be seen in early theology, for example, in John Chrysostom, *Homilies on the Acts of the Apostles* 2, and John of Damascus, *Exposition of the Orthodox Faith* 4.2; see further, Kapic and van der Lugt, "Ascension of Jesus," pp. 27, 29-30.

The church is the body of the crucified one as well as the risen one. Thus, again, the integral link between ascension and ecclesiology. Ascension is not only a soteriological topic, it is also an ecclesial one.[205] Barth's theology points out the connection with the church as he includes the discussion of the church in the context of reconciliation in parts IV/2 and IV/3. The ecclesiological implications of ascension will be developed in our discussion of the church.

In the NT, particularly in Philippians, Colossians, Ephesians, and Hebrews, as well as in patristic theology,[206] the cosmic implications of the resurrection and ascension are present in a way that later theology by and large lost sight of. Particularly modern Protestant theology after the Enlightenment developed radically in the other direction with its quest of the historical Jesus and subsequent developments. Even Barth with his profound focus on ascension did not work out the implications embryonic in his theology. Speaking of the "third form of existence" of Christ along with the earthly-historical and in his church, Barth cautiously considers the meaning of Christ's existence as *Pantocrator* based on Colossians 1:16-20 and Calvin's cosmically oriented view of the Holy Spirit:

> Does He really exist only as the One He alone is with God, and then as the One He is with and in His community? Does He not already exist and act and achieve and work also as the *Pantocrator,* as the κεφαλὴ ὑπὲρ πάντα, as the One who alone has first and final power in the cosmos? Concealed though He may be in the cosmos and not yet recognised by it as by His community, does He not already exist in it with supreme reality, with no less reality than He does at the right hand of God the Father or in His community? In this respect we may recall the striking doctrine of Calvin . . . concerning the Holy Spirit as the principle of life which rules not merely in the history of the saved community but also in the whole created cosmos as such.[207]

Barth continues his reflections by wondering whether the "future coming forth of Jesus Christ from heaven, from the hiddenness of God, mean also and at the same time His coming forth from His hiddenness in world-occurrence."[208] Moltmann's Christology makes full use of the cosmic implications of the ascension doctrine and makes it a leading theme. In his

205. Farrow, "Ascension and Atonement."
206. See further, Moltmann, *Way of Jesus Christ,* pp. 46-51, 280-87.
207. Barth, *CD* IV/3.2, p. 756.
208. Barth, *CD* IV/3.2, p. 756.

vision, the ascended Christ as the *Pantocrator* encompasses not only the "conquest of enmity and violence and in the spread of reconciliation and harmonious, happily lived life,"[209] but also the world of nature and evolution. His chapter on ascension is titled "The Cosmic Christ," in which he also discusses Christ as the "Ground" and "Redeemer" of evolution.[210]

What about the risen Lord? What is the meaning of the ascension for liberation Christology that focuses on the Jesus of history? In Boff's vision, the risen and ascended Christ has penetrated the world in a much more profound manner — now ever-present according to his own promise (Matt. 28:20). Boff also refers to the Pauline idea of Christ as the "pneumatic body," spirited body (1 Cor. 15:44). The resurrection has revealed the cosmic dimension of Christ, for in him all creation has come into existence and he is the goal of all. From this perspective, the significance of the incarnation comes into a new light. For Boff, the main focus of incarnation is the completion of creation rather than the remedy for sin, which has been the focus of classical theology. "The eternal person of the Son was always acting in the world from creation, but his presence was concentrated in Christ and was spread throughout the cosmos after the resurrection. Jesus is portrayed as the focal being in whom the total manifestation of God takes place within creation."[211]

The rediscovery of ascension as an integral part of the salvific work of the triune God may also help the church's proclamation in various cultural and religious settings and contexts. In different settings the need of salvation is expressed and felt differently, and these differences go beyond semantic differences. In many African and Asian contexts, the question is about power over evil forces. In Confucian settings, as in Chinese contexts, the leading motif is often the cultivation of the person and community in search of harmony. And so forth. The missiologist Herbert Hoefer rightly notes that what "is striking is that each answer to such issues of present living draws upon the fact of Jesus as ascended Lord." However, Western theology has ignored ascension with its focus on the cross. Resurrection and ascension help theology and missiology to offer a response that goes beyond guilt and touches on important issues such as honor, shame, immortality, and meaning.[212] The discussion of soteriology will further develop these insights.

209. Moltmann, *Way of Jesus Christ,* p. 279.

210. Moltmann, *Way of Jesus Christ,* chap. 6; see also Farrow, *Ascension and Ecclesia,* pp. 191-221 especially.

211. La Due, *Jesus among the Theologians,* p. 175.

212. Hoefer, "Gospel Proclamation of the Ascended Lord," pp. 43-48.

14. Reconciliation as the Church's Mission in the World

Reconciliation and the Restoration of Relationships

Casting the doctrine of atonement in a proper trinitarian framework and in the context of God's faithfulness to his creation helps us widen and make more inclusive the work of atonement by focusing on the multifaceted meaning of the term "reconciliation" — healing and bringing together broken relationships. Of all the metaphors of salvation, reconciliation has the potential of being the most inclusive and comprehensive, encompassing ideas such as "cosmic reconciliation, the Hebrew notion of *shalom,* the meaning of the cross, the psychological effects of conversion, the work of the Holy Spirit, the overcoming of barriers between Christians, the work of the church in the world, peacemaking, movements towards ethnic reconciliation and the renewal of ecological balances between humanity and its natural environment."[1] Underlying many of these facets of reconciliation is the motif of restoration of relationships.[2] The goal of reconciliation is "the restoration of the sin-broken fellowship of humanity with its Creator, the source of its life." This does not mean that the limited human independence given to creatures is eliminated, but rather that it is positively affirmed by

1. Langmead, "Transformed Relationships," p. 6.

2. See further, Gunton, *Actuality of Atonement,* p. 143. Strangely enough, reconciliation as the function of healing broken relationships has not enjoyed the central place in the theology of atonement. For the tracing of historical developments in modern theology beginning from Hegel, to F. C. Baur and M. Kähler, to A. Ritschl, and finally to Barth, see Schwöbel, "Reconciliation," pp. 26-32.

God.[3] Affirming independence from God, humanity gets stuck with the slavery of sin and finally death, separation from God. The work of the triune God in reaching out to his creatures aims at restoring and reaffirming their limited, God-given independence after the model of Jesus. This taking up — adoption into the filial Sonship that we see perfectly in Jesus — happens through the Holy Spirit. Hence, "Through the Spirit reconciliation with God no longer comes upon us solely from outside. We ourselves enter into it."[4] The Spirit mediates the gulf between the past work of the cross and the present life of the believers as reconciled persons as well as that between now and the eschatological consummation.[5] Whatever else the atonement is about, it is about restoring relationships, and that is a continuous process. Forgiveness is a good example. Rather than being merely about "canceling the debt," forgiveness is about restoring a broken relationship and effecting a new covenant-based relationship of mutual love and commitment.[6]

A good way to test the usefulness of the trinitarian relation-oriented approach is to look at the satisfaction model, which for many reasons mentioned above has fallen out of favor. Its view of sin is juridical and retributive, and fails to render to God what is due. Where relationality fades into the background and where problems begin in the contemporary reading of the Anselmian narrative is the "transformation of the relation into one that can be built upon a system of debt, guilt, and payment of satisfaction."[7] This economic approach fosters and concentrates on an external, impersonal notion of salvation rather than repairing a broken relationship between the Creator and creature. Behind this economic framework of owing to God is not a free, grace-filled, unconditional parent-child relationship but rather an instru-

3. Pannenberg, *ST* 2:449-50.

4. Pannenberg, *ST* 2:450.

5. See further, Schwöbel, "Reconciliation," p. 20.

6. See further, Fiddes, *Past Event and Present Salvation*, p. 15.

7. Henriksen, *Desire, Gift, and Recognition*, p. 270. As an extreme example, feminist Julie Hopkins (*Towards a Feminist Christology*, p. 51) surmises that satisfaction atonement, when linked with the long Christian tradition of sanctioning sex as something sinful by its very nature, coupled with the Augustinian teaching on original sin's transmission through sex, makes women culpable for Jesus' death; in that view, women are the "vessels" through which in childbearing the transmission of sin happens and thus they are primarily guilty for Jesus' death! Now women have two choices for making satisfaction for their guilt, either be passive and obedient or, like men, become celibate and ascetic. Although the reasoning of Hopkins is hardly followed by many and its historical basis is weak, it illustrates in a radical way the potential weaknesses of a one-sided satisfaction view.

mentalized economic exchange. "This externalization of the process of satisfaction and atonement seems to render Christ's witness and ministry as being of little or no relevance to this process of atonement."[8] While Anselm thus rightly underscores the need for incarnation as the divine initiative for our salvation, and the seriousness of sin, particularly as a way to distort our relation to God, his satisfaction model also fails to give much meaning to Jesus' life and ministry in its focus on the death (even the meaning of obedience of life is derived from the need to have an innocent "payment" on the cross). In addition, its view of sin as merely violation of honor is hardly biblical.[9]

Reconciliation is more than self-sacrifice, redemption, and substitution — even though for its validity it assumes those aspects.[10] Alongside the cross, it includes resurrection, Christ's cosmic rule, and the founding of Christian community for the sake of proclaiming and embodying the gospel of reconciliation. The language of reconciliation "refers both to an event in the past and to an enduring relationship in the present, which is claimed to be eschatologically ultimate."[11] Reconciliation also forges an important link between creation, atonement, and consummation. "If the God of redemption who is revealed in Jesus Christ is the same as the Creator of the world and the human race, then we must view his saving work as an expression of his faithfulness to his creative work."[12]

In Paul, the main passages about reconciliation are about communal and racial reconciliation, as well as the cosmic restoration of relations.[13] In the first chapter of Colossians (vv. 16-22), having lifted up Christ as the principle and agent of creation, Paul speaks of his role as the head of the church

8. Henriksen, *Desire, Gift, and Recognition,* p. 272.

9. Henriksen, *Desire, Gift, and Recognition,* p. 273. That said, I also consider the conclusion through the lens of the Girardian hermeneutics of the Anselmian theory one-sided at best and erroneous at worst: "Christ did not die as he did in order to cancel the punishment that humanity deserved by means of the infinitely undeserved suffering of his innocent divinity. Hence, to see the legal apparatus present at the crucifixion as there because God has a satisfaction case to prosecute and a punishment to enforce on humanity is totally wrong" (p. 273).

10. In the main passages on reconciliation in Paul to be discussed in the following (e.g., Col. 1:16-22 and Eph. 1:13-22), metaphors of sacrifice, blood, representation, and substitution occur along with restoration of relationships.

11. Schwöbel, "Reconciliation," p. 19.

12. Pannenberg, *ST* 2:297; see also Fiddes, *Past Event and Present Salvation,* pp. 17-22.

13. 2 Cor. 5:18-20; Rom. 5:9-10; Col. 1:19-22; Eph. 2:16; see further, Fee, "Paul and the Metaphors for Salvation," pp. 60-62.

and then bursts into a glorious hymn: "For in him all the fulness of God was pleased to dwell, and through him to reconcile to himself all things, whether on earth or in heaven, making peace by the blood of his cross. And you, who once were estranged and hostile in mind, doing evil deeds, he has now reconciled in his body of flesh by his death" (vv. 19-22a). This is a remarkable vision of reconciliation encompassing creation, atonement, God's communal intentions, and new creation — viewpoints not too often highlighted in Christian atonement tradition. The second chapter of Ephesians, similarly, puts the vision of reconciliation into the widest possible horizon: Christ, "our peace, who has made us both one, . . . making peace, . . . [would] reconcile us both [Jews and Gentiles] to God in one body through the cross, thereby bringing the hostility to an end" (Eph. 2:14-16). All this has been brought to culmination in the church, the body of Christ, which is "the dwelling place of God in the Spirit" (vv. 19-22).[14] Other passages could be added from Paul. The remarkable statement in Galatians 3:28 of the racial (Jews and Gentiles), societal (free and slaves), and sexual (female and male) "one[ness] in Christ" is but the culmination of the great narrative of atonement and reconciliation that begins from the crucified Christ and the reception of the Spirit with miracles (vv. 1-5) and moves to the promise to Abraham to unite Jews and Gentiles (vv. 6-12), to the blending of metaphors of atonement of death and life as well as curse and blessing (vv. 13-14).[15]

Reconciliation, thus, is a metaphor that in a most inclusive way speaks of the various dimensions of the salvific work of the triune God. In many ways it supports and also strengthens the ancient recapitulation view. Irenaeus's appropriation of the Pauline idea in Ephesians 1:10, "to unite all things in him, things in heaven and things on earth" as the time was fulfilled, can be read in the wider context of that epistle, namely, that God "has put all things under his feet and has made him the head over all things for the church" (1:22), has "made us alive together with Christ (by grace you have been saved)" (2:5), as "in Christ Jesus you who once were far off have been brought near in the blood of Christ. For he is our peace, who has made us both one, and has broken down the dividing wall of hostility" (2:13-14). Recapitulation, linked with reconciliation, yields a breathtaking horizon of salvation including the personal level (saved by grace, made alive), the ecclesiological level (head of the church), the racial level (the separated brought together), the political level (all things put under his feet), and the

14. See also Schwöbel, "Reconciliation," pp. 20-22.

15. For a detailed study, see D. A. Campbell, "Reconciliation in Paul," pp. 39-65.

cosmic level (all things in heaven and earth) — and all this in the real history of this world (time fulfilled).[16]

While "reconciliation" as one of the key metaphors of salvation is a widely used concept in theology, originally it derived from the secular Hellenistic language of diplomacy.[17] Even though an event and process initiated and brought about by the triune God, its relevance goes beyond the restoration of hostility between individuals and God. It has everything to do with reconciliation of relationships between humans and between groups of humanity, including in the sociopolitical arena. Recent conflicts in South Africa and elsewhere in that continent, in the former Yugoslavia and elsewhere in eastern Europe, and between Western and Muslim countries have brought the need for reconciliation into a new focus.[18] Reconciliation between persons, people groups, and nations requires both truth telling and love, remembering and forgetting, giving and receiving. The church's role, based on the gospel of reconciliation, will be discussed when we consider the tasks of the missional church.

Missionary Proclamation of the Gospel of Reconciliation

While Christ's death for us was final (Heb. 10:10), the process of salvation is continuous: "Salvation happens here and now. It is always in the present that God acts to heal and reconcile, entering into the disruption of human lives at great cost to himself." Thus we should speak of "salvation as event and process."[19] On the divine side, the triune God, who completed the work of atonement, continues to suffer for the salvation of the creation.[20] On the human side, the finished work of reconciliation to which we cannot add anything (Heb. 10:10) continues in the church's missionary proclamation of the gospel.

16. This linkage in Ephesians was inspired by Farrow, "Ascension and Atonement," p. 83.

17. Aletti, "God Made Christ to Be Sin," p. 104. That said, "the Pauline usage of the terminology represents a real innovation in *Religionsgeschichte*." Kim, *Paul and the New Perspective*, p. 218.

18. See, e.g., "Final Document 1," Second European Ecumenical Assembly (EEA2), Graz, Austria, June 23 to 29, 1997 (www.ccee.ch/ressourcen/download/20080529135416.doc; accessed November 1, 2011).

19. Fiddes, *Past Event and Present Salvation*, p. 14.

20. Fiddes, *Past Event and Present Salvation*, p. 22. In Moltmann's theology, of course, the continual suffering of God for the salvation of the world is a profound theme.

It is highly important to discern the integral relationship between the profound statement about the reconciliation of the world by God and the sending out of Christians to issue the appeal to all men and women to be "reconciled to God." According to the NT, God has committed to us "the message of reconciliation" (2 Cor. 5:19). N. T. Wright reminds us that the "call of the gospel is for the church to implement the victory of God in the world through suffering love. The cross is not just an example to be followed; it is an achievement to be worked out, put into practice."[21]

Pannenberg — who is often doing theology through the ordering of the topics of discussion[22] — makes a significant point in ending his chapter on reconciliation with the discussion of "the gospel" and the need for the church to proclaim the missionary message of reconciliation.[23] The missionary proclamation of the gospel is needed to mediate the benefits of the finished work of Christ to men and women. That said, one has to formulate the integral connection between the finished work of Christ and the mandate of proclaiming the message of the gospel of reconciliation — most profoundly evidenced in Paul's teaching in 2 Corinthians 5 — carefully. On the one hand, we must correct the one-sided emphasis on the nature of the atonement as finished work in a way that makes the human response meaningless; on the other hand, we have to critique also views in which the work of atonement will be completed only with the human response to the proclamation. Barth and Pannenberg, respectively, serve as paradigms here.

As is often the case, Barth was constructing his own view in radical response to alternatives he saw as faulty. Here he was debating the views of G. Thomasius and Rudolf Bultmann. Barth quotes the statement from the kenotic theologian of the nineteenth century:

> It is only with the objective reconciliation by which humanity has become the object of the grace of God that the actual possibility, that is, the right and power to be reconciled with God, is won for the individual members of the race. But this possibility has to become actuality. That which Christ has worked out once and for all for the whole race, that

21. N. T. Wright, *Evil and the Justice of God,* p. 98. I am indebted for this reference to Chan, "The Gospel and the Achievement of the Cross," p. 31.

22. As noted in the context of the doctrine of the triune God where he places the discussion of the Trinity before that of the unity. The same happens in the doctrine of *ordo salutis,* which he places in the middle of the discussion of the church.

23. Pannenberg, *ST* 2:454 and passim.

> which is available for everyone in Him, now has to come to every individual, so that there is a real fellowship of men with God. This is the purpose of the whole objective mediation of salvation, and with it it reaches its goal.[24]

Barth rejects the distinction between an "objective" and a "subjective" atonement and places stress one-sidedly on the already changed situation of humanity. Even worse to Barth is Bultmann's downplaying the objective effect of reconciliation: "By Christ there has been created nothing more than the possibility of . . . [life], which does, of course, become an assured actuality in those that believe."[25] On the other side, Pannenberg argues that "the reconciliation of the world has taken place in the death of Christ (2 Cor. 5:19), even though it is completed only by the Spirit in believers."[26] This may suggest that apart from the human response, the work of salvation is not fully finished.

Theologically, a middle way between Barth and Pannenberg is to be sought. Proclamation, rather than completing the work of reconciliation, helps mediate and actualize its benefits. Only in this light can we affirm what Pannenberg says, namely, that the "proclamation is itself part of the making of reconciliation" as Christians, in Christ's stead, appeal to all people to be reconciled with God (2 Cor. 5:20).[27] Here the gospel comes to the fore as the "power of God for salvation" (Rom. 1:16), as in it the life-giving power of the Spirit is at work for reconciliation. Indeed, in the apostolic proclamation of the gospel, "the eschatological future [is] inbreaking of the rule of God."[28] As a result, not only the awareness but also the life and conduct of men and women will be changed.[29]

24. From G. Thomasius, *Christi Person und Werk,* vol. 3, 2 (1888), p. 206, as quoted in Barth, *CD* IV/1, p. 285.

25. From *Theology of the New Testament* (ET, 1952), vol. I, p. 252, as quoted in Barth, *CD* IV/1, p. 285. On the contrary, Paul Tillich (*Systematic Theology,* 2:170) maintains the distinction as he speaks of the "two sides of the process of atonement," namely, "divine act and human response," both of which are needed.

26. Pannenberg, *ST* 2:454.

27. Pannenberg, *ST* 2:455; similarly Rae, "A Remnant People," pp. 93-95.

28. Pannenberg, *ST* 2:459.

29. Heim, *Saved from Sacrifice,* pp. 29-33, includes a number of testimonials from various parts of the world of changed lives as a result of hearing and responding to the message of reconciliation. In an irenic and ecumenical spirit, Heim chronicles testimonials of even that kind of preaching of atonement that he himself finds theologically — and with a view to violence — highly problematic.

In a way, Barth later came to that conclusion. In the context of transitioning from the finished work of Christ — which absolutely altered the state of sinful humanity — to anticipation of the discussion of the church, he states: "But the alteration of the human situation as it is brought about by this man and His direction in the act of His lordship works itself out in the fact that there were and are and will be a Christian community and Christians in the world."[30] This insight helps us make the important link between the doctrine of atonement and ecclesiology, a theme to be developed in that discussion. The linking with the church also saves theology of atonement from the dangers of individualism so rampant in our cultures of the Global North. The danger of forgetting that it was in the first place the "world" that was reconciled by God inspired the chiding remark by P. T. Forsyth about individuals entering "into private negotiations with God about their salvation."[31]

Taking a cue from Gregory of Nyssa's use of the metaphor of the divine "trickery" of the devil, a kind of "economic exchange," the postcolonial Marion Grau seeks to develop a "Christology of divine commerce." Although Grau develops this imagery for somewhat different purposes than mine, it seems fair to me to utilize his model to illustrate the mutual conditioning of the divine initiative and the necessary human response in reconciliation.[32] Whereas in Gregory's metaphor the divine commerce is solely executed by God and his Son as the "bait," Grau's

> reconstruction . . . does not envision redemption as one-sided, unilaterally omnipotent "done deal," with God/Christ as the singular agent and omnipotent purveyor of salvation. Rather, divine commerce recon-

30. Barth, *CD* IV/2, p. 378; I am grateful to Rae ("Remnant People," p. 94) for pointing me to that passage.

31. As paraphrased by Rae, "Remnant People," p. 102; Forsyth, *Work of Christ*, p. 100. For the importance of linking salvation and ecclesiology in the theology of Paul, see Fee, "Paul and the Metaphors for Salvation," pp. 44-46. For the importance of communal and ecclesiological aspects of reconciliation in patristic theology, see Daley, "'He Himself Is Our Peace,'" pp. 169-72.

32. Grau's main purpose is to help "pastors and teachers to address the painful complexity of our economic ties to exploitation in a context of neoimperialism." In that process, he utilizes two key concepts of the postcolonial theorist Homi Bhabba: ambivalence and mimicry. Grau, "Divine Commerce," pp. 164-84. Another current theologian who has developed an economic interpretation of salvation, with reference to tradition's use of the divine "trickery," from a feminist point of view, is Ray, *Deceiving the Devil.*

structs redemption as divine investment into a creation that responds and interacts with God in a mutual, ongoing process of *redemption continua.* The metaphor of divine commerce highlights exchanges between divine and human subjects, using an economic concept to indicate the deep relationality and co-creativity of the cosmos, the ties that bind all in the divine economy of creation.[33]

One of the ways of responding to the work of reconciliation is to continue working for liberation of the oppressed and marginalized.

Reconciliation and Liberation

John Milbank has harshly critiqued Girard because of the ontology of violence that does not leave room for the politics of hospitality. Focusing on cultural and anthropological roots and development of violence, Girard has not offered much advice about political promises.[34] As Boersma poignantly remarks, "Milbank hears Girard as saying no to the violence of the earthly city but doesn't hear him saying yes to the hospitality of the city of God."[35] I fear the Chinese theologian C. S. Song misses the point when he seeks "to work toward the abolition of the cross" because of its cruel nature and thus its incapacity to help tackle the issues of the real world.[36]

Having highlighted above the importance of Christ's cross as the divine gift, self-donation for sinners, I would like to expand here the idea of gift in terms of "divine self-donation for the enemies and their reception into the eternal communion of God." With this theme, Miroslav Volf develops and reorients Moltmann's stress on the "passion of God" as a way of solidarity and cosuffering. This means the deepening of the "social significance of the theme of divine self-giving: as God does not abandon the godless to their evil but gives the divine self for them in order to receive them into divine communion through atonement, so also should we — whoever our en-

33. Grau, "Divine Commerce," pp. 165-66. Since I am using Grau's model in a particular way, for my own purposes, I neglect the fact that his original way of reasoning is dangerously close to the view Barth rightly opposed, namely, that instead of an "objective" reconciliation executed by the triune God, the completion of reconciliation is dependent on human beings.

34. See, e.g., Milbank, *Theology and Social Theory,* p. 395.

35. Boersma, *Violence, Hospitality, and the Cross,* p. 144.

36. Song, "Christian Mission," pp. 130-48.

emies and whoever we may be."[37] Volf sees in the liberationist Jon Sobrino's notion of solidarity as "struggling on the side of" this same theme of self-donation: an active mode of solidarity is more than cosuffering, as much as it is that also; it is giving one's self as a gift. This is what "Jesus the liberator" does.[38] This is what I see happening, even though in a different framework, in the classic work of Walter Rauschenbusch, *A Theology for the Social Gospel.* Having first discussed the social gospel in relation to personal sin, he looks at "the salvation of super-personal forces" and only then moves to consider the relation of the social gospel to atonement.[39] Conservative Christians to whom any talk about "social gospel" borders on anathema should take another look at this linking of personal and structural sin and the work for liberation and reconciliation on the basis of atonement brought by the triune God.[40]

For Christian theology, it is essential to acknowledge that the work for liberation on various levels belongs to the gospel also because history is one. There are not two histories, "secular" and "sacred." Men and women live and find their destiny in one history, created and made possible by God. Hence, Christ's "redemptive work embraces all the dimensions of existence and brings them to their fullness. The history of salvation is the very heart of human history."[41] Consequently, in Christian theology there is also an integral link between liberation, salvation, and creation as God is confessed to be the "All-determining Reality" (Pannenberg) as Creator, Provider, and the One who brings about the consummation of creation. Following Gutiérrez's terminology, we can thus speak of creation as the first salvific act, political liberation as "self-creation of man," and "salvation . . . [as] re-creation and complete fulfillment."[42] And since "the work of Christ is a new creation . . . in Christ (Gal. 6:15; 2 Cor. 5:17)," to salvation and liberation also belong eschatology. What is begun in creation will be redeemed and sanctified at the eschaton. When Gutiérrez says that "eschatological promises . . . [are] historical promises," they ought not to be understood in classical liberalism's reductionistic, immanentist way that strips out the transcendent, divine dimensions of salvation, but rather in a way that affirms the redemption and

37. Volf, *Exclusion and Embrace,* p. 23.

38. Volf, *Exclusion and Embrace,* p. 24; Sobrino, *Jesus the Liberator,* p. 231.

39. Rauschenbusch, *A Theology for the Social Gospel,* chaps. 10; 11; 19, respectively.

40. For an important discussion of the theme "liberation and salvation," see Gutiérrez, *A Theology of Liberation,* chap. 9.

41. Gutiérrez, *A Theology of Liberation,* p. 153.

42. See further, Gutiérrez, *A Theology of Liberation,* pp. 153-60.

renewal of this-worldly realities as part of the coming of the new creation.[43] That theme will be fully developed in our discussion of eschatology.

Feminists have rightly critiqued traditional atonement theories for their "abstractness" with no or little attention to inequality, oppression, exploitation, sexism, abuse, and similar sociopolitical problems.[44] Liberation theologians have complained about the lack of social and political initiative and potential in traditional atonement theologies.[45] They have contended that violent accounts of atonement, on the one hand, lack needed ethical incentive and, on the other hand, have helped marginalize certain segments of humanity, particularly women, the poor, and other minorities. Particularly Anselm's and to a lesser extent Abelard's views have been found wanting, at times even counterproductive to the work of liberation.[46] Behind different visions of salvation between traditional and liberation theologies lies the important issue of how to understand the main human dilemma, in other words, the doctrine of sin.[47] In the contemporary world there is a need to rediscover a robust theology of sin that would support a holistic and inclusive account of salvation, including personal, social, and cosmic levels.

To combat this perceived lacuna, liberationists of various stripes have issued a call to leave behind merely rationalistic, abstract ways of doing theology and embrace a biased, particular point of departure. They seek "an answer to the following question: 'what relation is there between salvation and the historical process of the liberation of man?'"[48] Gutiérrez rightly remarks that this question in itself is not a new one but rather essentially traditional. "Theological reflection has always at least implicitly addressed itself to" this question that can be posed in different ways. "We are dealing here with the classic question of the relation between faith and human existence, between faith and social reality, between faith and action, or in other words, between the Kingdom of God and the building up of the world."[49] What makes the questioning new and novel in contemporary theology is its

43. See further, Gutiérrez, *A Theology of Liberation*, pp. 160-68; quotes on pp. 158 and 165.

44. Brock, *Journeys by Heart*, p. 57.

45. E.g., Maimela, "Atonement in the Context of Liberation Theology," p. 45.

46. Cone, *God of the Oppressed*, pp. 211-12. While more sympathetic to Abelard's view, liberationists have critiqued its individualistic rather than communal orientation; see Maimela, "Atonement in the Context of Liberation Theology," p. 47.

47. See further, Maimela, "Atonement in the Context of Liberation Theology," p. 51.

48. Gutiérrez, *A Theology of Liberation*, p. 45.

49. Gutiérrez, *A Theology of Liberation*, p. 45.

urgency and intentionality. Not only treating it implicitly, but making it a theological theme, contemporary theology seeks a more holistic and comprehensive account of the many dimensions of salvation brought about by Jesus Christ.

For African American/black theologians, the work of liberation means taking "blackness" as the beginning and goal of theology.[50] At times this approach, ironically — and counterproductively — has led to exclusivism. The violent rhetoric of the younger Cone was just that, *violent:* "If Jesus Christ is white and not black, he is an oppressor; and we must kill him."[51] Even as rhetoric, this kind of violence is unacceptable and should be rejected.[52] The limitation of hospitality to only one race, the blacks (as well as, alternatively, whites or others), has to be rejected as violence. This is not to deny the legitimacy — or necessity — of acknowledging the black experience as a particular point of view for understanding and appropriating the gospel of reconciliation.[53] Stripped of violence, Cone's approach to liberation does not radically differ from, say, the way Moltmann links suffering, cross, resurrection, and liberation. Speaking of the oppressed, Cone says, "God not only fights for them but takes their humiliated condition upon the divine Person and thereby breaks open a new future for the poor, different from their past and present miseries."[54] From the perspective of "black experience," the doctrine of God looks up to Jesus' death and resurrection through which "God has freed us to fight against social and political structures while not being determined by them." In Jesus' resurrection, it becomes evident that God's liberating work is not only for Israel, but for all who are enslaved.[55] The fight is not meaningless since "God is the sovereign ruler and nothing can thwart his will to liberate the oppressed."[56] The Brazilian liberationist Jon Sobrino agrees: the cross and the suffering of all

50. For affirming the blackness of God and Jesus, see, e.g., G. K. Baker-Fletcher, *Xodus*, pp. 88-89.

51. Cone, *Black Theology of Liberation,* p. 111.

52. The mature Cone has softened his rhetoric and acknowledged its source in reaction to injustice and oppression of the blacks in then predominantly white society.

53. Building on his teacher Paul Tillich's idea of the symbolic nature of all God-talk, Cone explains (*Black Theology of Liberation,* p. 7): "The focus on blackness does not mean that *only* blacks suffer as victims in a racist society, but that blackness is an ontological symbol and a visible reality which best describes what oppression means in America."

54. Cone, *God of the Oppressed,* p. 128.

55. Cone, *Black Theology of Liberation,* p. 3.

56. Cone, *God of the Oppressed,* p. 145.

"crucified people" help us most appropriately to understand the meaning of the resurrection of Christ.[57]

Liberationists rightly remind Christian theologians of an often-too-narrow outlook on salvation and insist that sociopolitical aspects not be overlooked. In Gutiérrez's terminology, traditional theology errs in viewing salvation as exclusively "quantitative," that is, as "guaranteeing heaven" for the greatest number. According to him, in the Latin American context, there is an urgent need to reinterpret salvation in qualitative terms, as a way of social, political, and economic transformation. The careful analysis of Gutiérrez leads him to the conclusion that the Christian sense of salvation has three interrelated facets:

1. Personal transformation and freedom from sin,
2. Liberation from social and political oppression, and
3. Liberation from marginalization (which may take several forms, such as unjust treatment of women and minorities).

Speaking of the "multidimensionality of salvation," the Asian American Pentecostal theologian Amos Yong helps us expand the scope of the salvific work of the triune God, including liberation at various levels, in the widest possible framework:[58]

1. Personal salvation: individuals transformed into the image of Jesus
2. Family salvation: salvation of the individual linked with his/her own kin
3. Ecclesial salvation: communal dimensions of being and living as saved
4. Material salvation: healing of body and mind, finances, livelihood
5. Social salvation: healing and reconciliation of relationships and communities in terms of
    a. racial reconciliation
    b. class reconciliation
    c. gender reconciliation

57. Sobrino, *Jesus the Liberator,* p. 14. Importantly, it is often the case that Christians — the oppressed, marginalized, and weak — may fail to acknowledge the significance of resurrection in their devotion to the suffering and death of Christ. This kind of account comes from the life of the black churches in the South African context, but it may be true more widely; Mofokeng, *The Crucified among the Crossbearers,* pp. 27-28.

58. Yong, *Spirit Poured Out on All Flesh,* pp. 91-98.

6. Cosmic salvation: redemption of all creation and interconnectedness of human beings and environment
7. Eschatological salvation: transformation and renewal of all creation, coming of the new creation

Many Christians are asking, should the Christian church attempt to be political? The answer to this legitimate question is simply this: the "church is political by default even if it is not political on purpose"![59] Lack of attention to peace, equality, integrity of all persons, and similar values that spring from the gospel of salvation is a political gesture even though, unfortunately, most churches pay little attention to such a lack. The task of the Christian church is to cooperate with God in shaping the society in light of the values of the coming kingdom of God, the kingdom of equality, justice, and peace. To accomplish this noble task, the church has to give preference to the poor and marginalized. Even though final, all-encompassing justice and peace may not come until the full arrival of the kingdom, the followers of Christ are called to do whatever is in their power to reach the noble goal. It is here that the "church finds its full identity as a sign of the reign of God to which all human beings are called but in which the lowly and the 'unimportant' have a privileged place."[60]

How does the Christian theology of liberation relate to the liberationist efforts in other religions? The Roman Catholic Gustavo Gutiérrez of Peru and the engaged Vietnamese Buddhist Thich Nhat Hanh provide an inspiring case study.[61] Both liberationists speak of the importance of awareness and transformation of consciousness.[62] Gutiérrez expresses the liberationist

59. Keller, Nausner, and Rivera, eds., *Postcolonial Theologies,* "Introduction," p. 5.

60. Gutiérrez, *A Theology of Liberation,* p. xlii.

61. In this section, I am indebted to the insightful discussion in Lefebure, *The Buddha and the Christ,* chap. 8.

62. For the importance of awakening to life, see, e.g., Hanh, *Our Appointment with Life,* p. 35. For Hanh the Heart Sutra, which Mahayana Buddhists use for daily chanting, expresses the core vision of the universe: all things are "inter-are," that is, all things and all beings interpenetrate and reflect all other things and beings. Hanh, *Heart of Understanding,* p. 3. The ending mantra of the sutra is a powerful tool for transformation and liberation as it challenges the entire community of beings to go "to the other shore," to the land of liberation. See the insightful discussion in Lefebure, *The Buddha and the Christ,* p. 161; the whole chap. 7 is a useful discussion of this Vietnamese Buddhist's life and work of liberation. One of the key motifs in Gutiérrez's transformation of consciousness is the use of the category of "ideology," unmasking concealed and suppressed motifs that lie behind abuse of power in various forms; see his *A Theology of Liberation,* pp. 234-35.

agenda and passion for justice in asking: "How are we to speak of the God of life when cruel murder on a massive scale goes on . . . ?"[63] Less passionate but equally committed and solid is Hanh's vision of liberation, which he anchors deeply in his own spiritual tradition: "'Awakened' people are certainly going to form small communities where material life will become simple and healthy. Time and energy will be devoted to the enrichment of spirituality. These communities will be Zen monasteries of a modern style where there will be no dogma. In them the sickness of the times will be cured and spiritual health will be acquired."[64]

Both liberationists seek to interpret their canonical writings in a way that facilitates consciousness and initiative for liberation. Gutiérrez is famous for a nonideological activist reading of the Bible, "rereading of history and the Bible from the perspective of the poor."[65] Not unlike his Vietnamese counterpart, the Peruvian priest sees it necessary to combine contemplation and practice as they "feed each other; the two together make up the stage of silence before God."[66] Echoing the Christian liberationist hermeneutics, Hanh warns Buddhists of reading the Scriptures mainly for the description of reality; instead, "the doctrine serves only as a method, as a guide, to the practitioner in . . . the experience of reality."[67]

Christ's cross and resurrection are not innocent politically; on the contrary, they imply political claims. Even though crucifixion was a fairly common way of execution, in Jesus' time it was reserved particularly for revolutionaries and self-made messiahs. "The cross already said, with all its violent symbolic power, that Caesar ruled the world, and that those who stood in his way would be both shamed and obliterated."[68] Resurrection — the "political dynamite"![69] — and ascension claim that if Jesus is the Lord, then Caesar is not![70] The *Christus Victor* model contains tremendous potential for linking atonement with sociopolitical liberation. Often liberationists build on that legacy as is manifested, for example, in a typical statement by

63. Gutiérrez, *On Job*, p. 102.

64. Hanh, "The Individual, Society, and Nature," p. 42.

65. Gutiérrez, *The Power of the Poor in History*, p. 20.

66. Gutiérrez, *Essential Writings*, p. 52.

67. Hanh, *Zen Keys*, p. 47.

68. N. T. Wright, "Redemption from the New Perspective?" p. 79.

69. N. T. Wright, *The Resurrection of the Son of God*, p. 730.

70. N. T. Wright, *The Resurrection of the Son of God*, p. 225. For a succinct, well-documented discussion of the political implications of atonement, see N. T. Wright, "A Fresh Perspective on Paul?" pp. 21-39.

Cone: "Fellowship with God is now possible, because Christ through his death and resurrection has liberated us from the principalities and powers and the rules of this present world."[71] In his salvific work Christ not only conquers principalities and powers but also issues a judgment on unjustified human violence, cruelty, oppression, and tyranny. Christ, the Suffering Messiah, is on the side of the sufferers. He both opposes violence and empowers those in need of power and persistence for the work of liberation. Speaking from the South African context, liberationist G. O. Abe expresses this vision in a powerful way: "The true gospel message of Jesus Christ should inspire theologians, especially Africans to rescue the afflicted and liberate the oppressed, the victims of injustice. All forms of dominant inhuman and unchristian attitudes and structures which cause human suffering and agony should be analysed and vigorously combated for effective salvation of all."[72] The Roman Catholic Robert Schreiter, who has for years spoken to the urgency of reconciliation in the work of the church and her mission, reminds us that reconciliation without justice is a false reconciliation because it tries to ignore the suffering of the oppressed.[73]

The ancient idea of *Christus Victor*, the powerful Christ who rose from the dead and defeated the opposing powers, is obviously relevant to the African search for power. What is also distinctively African about *Christus Victor* is his ability to overcome the spell and threat of spirits, magic, disease, and death. Several other key christological titles such as Redeemer, Conqueror, and Lord have parallels in African cultures.

Christus Victor is also relevant in many contemporary cultures in which — unlike the Enlightenment-based Global North — the demonic is a real issue. Witchcraft and the occult are such issues, and are not unknown to the cultures of early Christianity either.[74] Against the predictions of Western theologians,[75] Christians in the Global South, even after the coming of modernity, continue to face the demonic in various forms in their contexts, and many of them believe the gospel relates to it. The Nigerian Paul Omieka Ebhomielen

71. Cone, *God of the Oppressed,* p. 209.

72. G. O. Abe, "Redemption, Reconciliation, Propitiation," p. 11; for another account of an inclusive liberationist vision of salvation, see Maimela, "Atonement in the Context of Liberation Theology," pp. 51-53.

73. Schreiter, *Reconciliation,* pp. 18-25.

74. There is wide interest in anthropology, sociology, and religious studies in the resurgence of witchcraft: Geschiere, *The Modernity of Witchcraft;* Meyer, *Translating the Devil.*

75. See, e.g., Parrinder, *Witchcraft,* pp. 202-3.

has investigated the application of the *Christus Victor* framework to the demonic in Africa and concluded that there is great potential application of God's power and victory over the forces of evil, including its effects such as fear and insecurity, as well as the idea of cosmic redemption along with personal and social redemption.[76] He also argues that the cross, when viewed through the lens of *Christus Victor,* makes more sense to Africans. Behind the death of the innocent sacrifice is the conflict or struggle between God and evil rather than the Anselmian view of satisfaction: "In Christ, the divine love struggled with evil in order that the divine will might be realized."[77] Not only incarnation and death on the cross, but the whole life of Jesus is a matter of conflict, including his teaching, healings, exorcisms, and temptations. For Africans, the world is a "battleground," a key idea in Aulén's depiction of the earliest model of atonement.[78] Ebhomielen makes the important theological point by underscoring the importance of placing the cross into the whole salvation history of Christ; the "proper vision about Christ is the wholistic one, in which the entire life of incarnation, death, and resurrection are taken together."[79]

Particularly in the younger churches of Africa, African Instituted Churches and various types of Pentecostal-charismatic churches, prayers, liturgies, and "techniques" to protect from and provide deliverance from the "powers" are an integral part of Christian life. It is common in the deliverance sessions in these churches to hear people shout victory in the name of Jesus and the Lord's authority over all powers and principalities, including physical, mental, and material.[80] How much these practices owe to and genuinely reflect the traditional *Christus Victor* framework is an open theological question in need of careful study and reflection. The point made here is that one of the potential applications of the *Christus Victor* motif is in the combat of the demonic in various forms.

An important part of the missionary task of the church as it lives out and proclaims the gospel of reconciliation involves relations with other living faiths. The last chapter of this volume will take up the discussion started at the end of part I. The introduction to that chapter offered a careful explanation of principles and procedures guiding this interfaith exercise, and so these will not be repeated here.

76. Ebhomielen, "Gustaf Aulen's *Christus Victor* View," pp. 276-82.

77. Ebhomielen, "Gustaf Aulen's *Christus Victor* View," p. 283.

78. Ebhomielen, "Gustaf Aulen's *Christus Victor* View," p. 289.

79. Ebhomielen, "Gustaf Aulen's *Christus Victor* View," p. 287.

80. For a careful account, see Onyinah, "Deliverance as a Way of Confronting Witchcraft," pp. 181-202.

15. Christian Salvation among Religions

The Messiah of Israel and the Savior of the Nations

With his announcement of the imminence of God's righteous rule dawning in his own ministry, "Jesus came to move the covenant people to conversion to its God."[1] This, however, poses an open question to the Jewish people. Jesus did not do away with the first commandment but rather radicalized it — to the point that he let his life be consumed in the service of his Father and asked his followers to put aside everything that would hinder total devotion to his Father (Matt. 6:33). "How radically does the faith of Judaism take the first commandment in relation to all other concerns, even its own religious tradition?"[2] Christian theologian Pannenberg asks his Jewish counterparts. Even though the relation of Christ's ministry, passion, and particularly cross to Jewish faith needs much careful consideration, as an expression of the capacity of God to bring good out of evil (Gen. 50:20), in the estimation of Christian theology one has to conclude that it was only after the rejection of his own people that Jesus' death on the cross made him the "Savior of the nations."[3] Ironically, the Messiah of the covenant people died for the people outside the covenant, in other words, the Gentiles. This is not to deny the validity of Jesus' death for the people of Israel; it is rather a *Christian* theological statement about the universal efficacy of the salvific work of Israel's Messiah.

1. Pannenberg, *ST* 2:311.
2. Pannenberg, *ST* 2:311.
3. Pannenberg, *ST* 2:312; so also Moltmann, *Way of Jesus Christ*, p. 34.

Hence, decisive for the church's relation to the people of Israel is the delicate matter of putting the cross in a proper perspective: "If the church has developed an interpretation of the cross that sees it as the point of God's rejection of Israel, of Israel's rejection of Jesus, of the loss of Israel's inheritance, and of transference to the church, then it must reckon with the fact that Jesus died for the Jewish nation before he died for the scattered children of God beyond Israel's boundaries."[4] Ironically, had not the messianic people rejected their Messiah, "Christianity would have remained an intra-Jewish affair."[5] In other words: whatever universal effects the cross of Christ has, they do not invalidate the fact that as a Jew he died for the salvation of the Jews, not only for the Gentiles. That said, Christian theology is convinced that "[w]hat began with Judaism must finally end with the nations, and Christians are the go-between,"[6] and that hope includes the consummation of the divine plan that "all Israel will be saved" (Rom. 11:26).

It is significant that the influential Jewish philosopher of religion Franz Rosenzweig in his mature work *The Star of Redemption* came to affirm the role of the Christian church in the preaching of the gospel to the Gentiles. The contemporary Jewish ecumenist Lapide continues that reasoning.[7] Where the Christian theological standpoint focused on the universal and unique salvific role of Jesus Christ has to challenge this Jewish reasoning involves the idea of Judaism and Christianity as two roads to the Father. "I am the way, and the truth, and the life; no one comes to the Father, but by me" (John 14:6). This is not to deny but rather to confirm the biblical notion that "salvation is from the Jews" (John 4:22). Nor is it to introduce supersessionism.

The cross as a cultural-religious symbol is highly offensive to Judaism.[8] The only exception in the twentieth century has been the appropriation of the cross by Eastern European Jews as the symbol of Jewish "crucifixion" at the hands of oppressors. However, even that picture is more complicated. In Eastern Europe, Jesus has been a symbol not only of the victim but also of the perpetrator![9]

4. J. G. Kelly, "The Cross," pp. 166-67.

5. Braaten, "Introduction," p. 18.

6. Braaten, "Introduction," p. 19.

7. F. Lapide, *Jewish Monotheism and Christian Trinitarian Doctrine,* p. 71: "the coming-to-believe of Christendom was without doubt a God-willed messianic act, a messianic event on the way to the conversion of the world to the One God."

8. Flannery, *The Anguish of the Jews;* Cohn-Sherbok, *The Crucified Jew.*

9. Susannah Heschel, "Jewish Views of Jesus," in *JWF,* p. 157.

What has contributed harmfully — and continues to do so — to the mutual relations is the "supersessionist ideologies of Christian identity" vis-à-vis the nation of Israel and the Jewish people.[10] The NT's attitude to the Jewish people, and particularly the implications of the telling of the narrative of Jesus in terms of the conflict with the Jewish people, is a highly complicated and complex issue. To its own detriment and to the detriment of common mission, rather than reaching out to the Jewish people in seeing the passion story of Jesus as the way of identification in solidarity with the suffering of the messianic people, the Christian church has interpreted the passion stories of the Gospels in terms of hostility toward Israel.[11] In doing so, the church has missed the opportunity of seeing Jesus' death as a means of "bearing in his own body the judgment he foresaw as coming upon Israel, sacrificing himself as the Maccabean martyrs had done before him, on behalf of the people."[12]

The Atonement in Jewish Estimation

An important task here is the comparison between Jewish and Christian theologies of atonement, a topic that, surprisingly, has not loomed large in the agenda of mutual talks. Both sides have much to learn from each other. The idea of vicarious atonement after the Christian interpretation, with a view for the salvation of the world rather than for the benefit of the nation as in the Maccabean martyrs' case, "seems strange and foreign to Jews who believe that the problem of sin had already been dealt with in the Torah."[13] This is because, first of all, Jewish theology does not hold to the Christian tradition's view of the Fall (in any of its main forms of interpretation), which would necessitate the divine initiative such as the death on the cross.[14] Second, the transcendent goal of salvation in the afterlife is not as central either in the OT or in later forms of Judaism as it is in Christian tradition, even though the idea of divine reward and punishment after death is not to be ignored in rabbinic and most other Jewish traditions. Following the Torah and its commandments, as the chosen people, and thus testifying to God's unity

10. J. G. Kelly, "The Cross," p. 168. For a useful, succinct discussion of anti-Semitism in relation to atonement, see Finlan, *Options on Atonement*, pp. 61-69.

11. See Schüssler Fiorenza and Tracy, eds., *The Holocaust as Interruption.*

12. J. G. Kelly, "The Cross," p. 177; see also pp. 171, 176.

13. Kogan, *Opening the Covenant*, p. 116.

14. See further, Kepnes, "Turn Us to You," pp. 293-319.

and holiness, is the way of "salvation" in Judaism.[15] That said, Jewish scholar Michael S. Kogan rightly remarks that it was on the basis of Hebrew Scriptures such as Isaiah 53:4-6 that Christian theology came to interpret the vicarious suffering of their Messiah.[16]

Hence, the search for continuities — in the midst of radical discontinuities — between the Christian and Jewish views of atonement is more than an attempt to find a pedagogical contact. It has to do with the material and systematic structures of both traditions. A complicating factor here is that even contemporary Jewish theology tends to operate with the Christian idea of atonement that is one-sided and limited, implying that it is mainly about "the shedding of blood" and sacrifice as well as focused (almost exclusively) on the salvation of individuals. In other words, the kinds of trinitarian, more comprehensive, and multifaceted ramifications in Christian theology developed in this work and widespread in various kinds of contemporary Christian writings seem to be unknown even among the most acute and informed Jewish interpreters.[17] The Christian side has much to learn about the complex and rich matrix of the idea(s) of atonement in Jewish and OT traditions.

There is no denying that particularly the early Christian views and early rabbinic views evolved in close connection with the Old Testament atonement traditions. The concept of sacrifice is one of the important connecting links between the two religions. It is of utmost importance for a proper understanding of the roots of Christian theology and salvation and

15. Kogan, *Opening the Covenant,* pp. 11-13. Two clarifying notes have to be added. First, as in some Christian forms of liberalism, many contemporary liberal Jews either do not believe in the afterlife in the traditional sense, or if they do, they are not concerned about it. Second, the overly general description of "salvation" in Jewish tradition is not to be hastily labeled "salvation by works" after traditional Christian polemics. The "new perspective" in Christian NT studies has shed new light on this typical Christian interpretation. A detailed discussion will take place in the context of soteriology.

16. Kogan, *Opening the Covenant,* p. 116. This observation holds even in light of the different use of these kinds of Scriptures by Jewish tradition in which they mainly speak of the "vicarious" suffering of the people of God in the hands of enemies. Behind this interpretation is also the well-known fact that the term "messiah" in the OT seems to denote at times the whole people of God or at least a collective group rather than an individual. The same of course applies to terms such as the "(Suffering) Servant of God" of Second Isaiah. For an important discussion, see Batnitzky, "On the Suffering of God's Chosen," pp. 203-20.

17. See, e.g., Kogan, *Opening the Covenant,* pp. 18, 19, 22, 27-29, and passim (published in 2010 and showing an extraordinarily deep and wide knowledge of not only Christian tradition but also contemporary Christian theology).

for Christian-Jewish dialogue to acknowledge that, despite the reality that because of the popular myths of a god dying and rising to new life, "the gentiles may have understood Jesus' death in such mythic terms . . . the sacrificial concept of Jesus' death was not developed in response to gentile ideas but, rather, as a Jewish conception of the righteous one who reconciles us to God by his sacrifice of suffering and death."[18] In both religions, sacrifice is an atoning act that also calls for human response.[19] The OT prophetic literature, which both traditions embrace, time after time targets worshipers who merely do the cultic acts without repentance, mercy, and works of justice.

How would Jewish tradition interpret such key NT statements as "Behold, the Lamb of God, who takes away the sin of the world!" (John 1:29)? In other words: "How can Jews understand the Christian proposition that Jesus Christ's crucifixion is an atonement for the original sin of Adam that brings salvation to Christians and restores a condition of harmony for the world?"[20] According to Steven Kepnes, Jews may gain insight into its meaning through the lens of the biblical notions of purity and impurity, sacrificial offices and systems, including the rituals of the sanctuary, as well as the temple. Reference to the Lamb who takes away sin, of course, is based on the slaughtering of lambs for the expiation of sins. Christ's self-sacrifice also connects with Jewish liturgical days such as Yom Kippur.[21]

Differences, however, are noteworthy. Even though Jesus may be called metaphorically the High Priest,[22] in Jewish faith the high priest conducts the sacrificial act whereas in Christian faith Jesus is the sacrifice, the sacrificial Lamb. This is not to say that Jewish faith doesn't know substitutionary suffering for others; of course it does, both in terms of the "Suffering Servant" of Second Isaiah and of righteous martyrs, as during the Maccabean era. Still, the onetime finished self-sacrifice of Jesus after the Christian interpretation is markedly different from the continuing sacrificial cult administered by the priesthood in Judaism. Not only the finality of the sacrifice of Jesus but also its

18. Lyden, "Atonement in Judaism and Christianity," p. 51. A discussion of the Jewish origins can be found in R. J. Daly, *Origins of the Christian Doctrine of Sacrifice.*

19. Lyden, "Atonement in Judaism and Christianity," pp. 47-48, 50. For the significance of the disappearance of temple sacrificial rites in 70 C.E. for the process of internalizing the meaning of sacrifices in terms of confession and forgiveness, see Büchler, *Studies in Sin and Atonement.*

20. Kepnes, "Turn Us to You," p. 297.

21. Kepnes, "Turn Us to You," pp. 297-301.

22. Interestingly, this title occurs only in the book of Hebrews, which among all the NT writings makes most use of the cultic and sacrificial heritage of Judaism.

universality marks it as different from the understanding of the Jewish tradition. Jesus' sacrifice, even as the work of the triune God, is contingent on the relation to his person, a claim without parallel in Judaism and a stumbling block to its monotheism. The role of the Messiah in Judaism is to serve as the agent of reconciliation, but not as the one who reconciles — only Yahweh can do that. Finally, a foundational difference has to do with the offer and object of the sacrifice. Whereas in Judaism people offer the sacrifice to Yahweh, in Christian theology (2 Cor. 5:17) it is God who reconciles to world to himself.[23] All this is to say that both differences and similarities should be acknowledged in hopes of better rediscovering the central meaning of atoning theologies of both religions as well as for continuing mutual dialogue and invitation.

One can see that Judaism and Christianity express the same basic ideas about atonement but in different ways. Their views about this idea do not create an incommensurable rift between the two religions, as it once may have seemed; rather, we find significant similarities that connect the two in spite of their differences. If the views of Judaism and Christianity are as close as they seem to be at this point, then there must be hope that a comparison of their respective views will lead to greater understanding, new recognition of commonalities, and a way to mutual appreciation.[24]

That said, one must be mindful of the dangers of bad apologetics. The profound differences between the two religious traditions in relation to understanding atonement should not be artificially softened nor eliminated. Rather, in the spirit of mutual learning and love as well as integrity of confession and identity, a new exploration of the possibility of the common ground should be explored. The search for the common ground does not mean denying either religion the right to share its own testimony or to try to persuade the other. This allowance may seem like an unfair admission to the Christian church in light of the fact that, unlike the Jewish faith, the Christian faith is missionary by nature. This, however, is the legacy of the message and mandate of the church founded by the Jewish Messiah. If God was in Christ and reconciled the world to himself, then the "ambassadors" are sent out to make the plea that all people, whether Jews or Gentiles, "be reconciled to God" (2 Cor. 5:19-20).

23. Lyden, "Atonement in Judaism and Christianity," pp. 50-53. An interesting way to try to find connections between the Christian theology of reconciliation and the Jewish prayer book *(siddur)*, which focuses on sacrifice as well, is offered by Ochs, "Israel's Redeemer Is the One to Whom and with Whom She Prays."

24. Lyden, "Atonement in Judaism and Christianity," p. 53.

This also means that, rightly configured, the church has the continuing mandate to share testimony to Christ also with the Jewish people. This is not to ignore the unique and special place given to Israel in the divine economy. On the other hand, neither is this to deny the foundational biblical conviction that "there is salvation in no one else" (Acts 4:12), and the gospel of Christ "is the power of God for salvation to every one who has faith, to the Jew first and also to the Greek" (Rom. 1:16).[25] The Jewish theologian Michael S. Kogan puts succinctly the dynamic tension facing Christian theology with its belief in Christ as the Messiah: "to be faithful to the New Testament command to witness for Christ to all peoples and to convert all nations, while, at the same time, affirming the ongoing validity of the covenant between God and Israel via Abraham and Moses."[26]

At the center of this tension lies the obvious but important fact that "historically Christianity has been theologically exclusive and humanistically universal, while Judaism has been theologically universal and humanistically exclusive." Christian theological exclusivism, however, is qualified by the equally important conviction that Christ died for all and that therefore, all people from all nations can be beneficiaries of this salvific work.[27] To make progress in this foundational issue, there is a challenge to both parties. Kogan formulates it well: if the Jews desire for Christians to affirm the continuing validity of the covenant after the coming of Jesus Christ, then the Jews are confronted with this challenge: "Are Jews really ready and willing to affirm that God, the God of Israel and of all humanity, was involved in the life of Jesus, in the founding of the Christian faith, in its growth and spread across much of the world, and in its central place in the hearts of hundreds of millions of their fellow beings?" Kogan answers yes to this question, and he is of the opinion that those of his fellow Jews who do not are no more "enlightened than those Christians who still refuse to affirm the Jews' ongoing spiritual validity as a religious people."[28] The implications of this complicated issue have to be worked out in detail in the volume on ecclesiology.

25. Contra Moltmann (*Way of Jesus Christ,* pp. 35-37), who argues that the Bible contains no expectation for the conversion of Israel to Christ/Messiah and therefore, the church should refrain from mission to Israel and expecting Jews' conversion.

26. Kogan, *Opening the Covenant,* p. xii.

27. Kogan, *Opening the Covenant,* pp. xii-xiii.

28. Kogan, *Opening the Covenant,* p. xiii; see also p. 13; on p. 32 Kogan makes the striking statement that the fact that, of the "many billions [who] worship Israel's God, only some 15 million of them being Jews," means that "[t]his is either some gigantic accident or the partial fulfillment of God's commission to Abraham."

The Christian Theology of the Cross in Light of the Islamic Interpretation

Not only with regard to the source of salvation but also, consequently, with regard to the means of salvation, there is a sharp difference between Christianity and Islam: "The cross stands between Islam and Christianity. Dialogue cannot remove its scandal, and in due course a Muslim who might come to believe in Jesus has to face it."[29] One of the reasons the suffering Messiah does not appeal to Muslims is that "paragons of success and vindication" such as Abraham, Noah, Moses, and David are much more congenial with the vision of God's manifest victory on earth. Says M. Ali Merad, "in the Quran, everything is aimed at convincing the Believer that he will experience victory over the forces of evil." Furthermore, "Islam refuses to accept this tragic image of Passion. Not simply because it has no place for the dogma of the Redemption, but because the Passion would imply in its eyes that God had failed."[30]

The single most important dividing issue between Islam and Christian faith is the crucifixion. Muslim tradition does not speak with one voice regarding what happened on the cross or necessarily even of its theological meaning. Yet it is true that "almost all Muslims believe that the crucifixion did not occur or that a substitute was executed in Jesus' place (popularly, Judas of Iscariot fills this role). Jesus, then, did not die. Instead of dying, rising and ascending as in the Christian sequence of events, he was born, lived[,] then was raised to heaven like Enoch and Elijah in the Bible, without dying."[31] Furthermore, the whole of Muslim theology unanimously "denies the expiatory sacrifice of Christ on the Cross as a ransom for sinful humanity."[32] In the Islamic view, such a sacrificial, atoning death is not needed because of the lack of the doctrine of the Fall and sinfulness as in Christian tradition.[33]

Christian theology has been aware of and interested in Muslim interpretations of the crucifixion from the beginning of the encounter. As early as the seventh Christian century (the first Islamic century), John of Damascus, in the last chapter of *De Haeresibus (On the Heresies),* discusses the key

29. Bebawi, "Atonement and Mercy," p. 185.

30. Merad, "Christ according to the Qur'an," pp. 14, 15, quoted in Leirvik, *Images of Jesus Christ in Islam,* p. 4.

31. Bennett, *Understanding Christian-Muslim Relations,* p. 51.

32. Ayoub, "Towards an Islamic Christology," p. 94.

33. See, e.g., Zebiri, *Muslims and Christians Face to Face,* pp. 216-17.

Qur'anic passage (4:157).[34] Attacks against the Christian teaching of the crucifixion have played a significant role in Muslim anti-Christian polemics and continue to do so, as illustrated in the widely influential pamphlet by the Indian–South African Ahmed Deedat, *Crucifixion or Cruci-fiction?*

The Qur'an contains only one explicit reference to the alleged crucifixion of Jesus, 4:156-59:

> (156) And because of their disbelief and of their speaking against Mary a tremendous calumny;
>
> (157) And because of their saying: We slew the Messiah, Jesus son of Mary, Allah's messenger — they slew him not nor crucified him, but it appeared so unto them [or: "but a semblance was made to them"];[35] and lo! those who disagree concerning it are in doubt thereof; they have no knowledge thereof save pursuit of a conjecture; they slew him not for certain.
>
> (158) But Allah took him up unto Himself. Allah was ever Mighty, Wise.
>
> (159) There is not one of the People of the Scripture but will believe in him before his death, and on the Day of Resurrection he will be a witness against them —

The most common interpretation of the Qur'anic account of Jesus' crucifixion is that while it appeared that the "Messiah, Isa son of Marium" was killed on the cross, he was not; rather, "Allah took him up to Himself" (4:157-58).[36] By and large, Muslim tradition denies the killing of Jesus.[37] The typical explanation is that one of the disciples took his place and was killed while Jesus was taken by Allah.[38] This "substitutionist theory" is by far the

34. The last chapter of *De Haeresibus* (100/101) is unusually long. See further, Merrill, "Of the Tractate of John of Damascus on Islam," pp. 88-89.

35. Translation of N. Robinson, *Christ in Islam and Christianity*, p. 106.

36. For a careful analysis of this key verse, which is used in Islamic theology to reject the Christian interpretation of crucifixion (and resurrection), see Busse, "Jesu Errettung vom Kreuz in der islamischen Koranexegese von Sure 4:157," pp. 160-95. For a lucid, nontechnical discussion of various interpretations of this and related key passages, see Bennett, *Understanding Christian-Muslim Relations*, pp. 51-52.

37. According to S. H. Nasr (*Islamic Life and Thought*, p. 210), the denial of the cross is one of the foundational differences between the two religions.

38. Or then the Jews killed another person but claimed he was Jesus. There is yet another version, a minority opinion, according to which Jesus died on the cross but it had no spiritual effects after the Christian interpretation; see Beaumont, *Christology in Dialogue with Muslims*, pp. 9-10.

most common view in Muslim commentaries and popular piety.[39] Jews, "the people of the book" (4:159), wrongly believed they had killed the Messiah.[40] Most Muslim commentators believe that verse 159 refers "to the still future death of Jesus, who had been raised alive into heaven and would return to kill the Antichrist."[41] On the basis of 3:55 and 4:159, Jesus has a role to play on the Day of Judgment. The most common Muslim opinion is that Jesus will return to earth before the last days, marry, have children, fight victoriously the forces of evil, and then face a natural death. Hadith teaches that in his return, Jesus will destroy the cross;[42] after all, the cross is abhorrent to Muslim intuitions. In sum: on the one hand, Muslim tradition denies that Jesus was put to death on the cross (4:159); on the other hand, it teaches that Jesus will die later (4:159; 19:33), but before his "natural" death he will return for a certain ministry.

On the crucial verse 4:157, whereas John of Damascus simply dismissed the Qur'anic teaching that allegedly denies the crucifixion, some thirty years after his death, the Nestorian (Mar Timothy) Catholicos Timothy I[43] responded to the Muslim caliph that Jesus died only according to his human nature. Timothy appealed to two important Qur'anic verses, both of which traditionally have been understood as referring to Jesus' death (though, of

39. For a brief account, see Leirvik, *Images of Jesus Christ in Islam,* pp. 67-69. Although by far the most widely held opinion, the substitution theory itself has passed through several stages of development, from at first identifying the substitute as a volunteer, later as a criminal ("punishment substitutionism"), and finally as Simon. Ayoub, "Towards an Islamic Christology," pp. 97-99. The important fourteenth-century Muslim theologian in Damascus, Ibn Kathir, suggests as the substitute a person by the name of Sergius, whose identity remains unknown. The excerpt can be found in *JBC,* p. 120; see also pp. 119-23.

40. There is a long tradition in Islamic theology that attributes the mistaken Christian understanding to erroneous transmission of the texts; see Whittingham, "How Could So Many Christians Be Wrong?" pp. 167-78.

41. N. Robinson, *Christ in Islam and Christianity,* p. 106. My discussion on crucifixion is deeply indebted to this source even when it is not explicitly mentioned.

42. *Sahih al-Bukhari* (vol. 3, book 34, no. 425): "Narrated Abu Huraira: Allah's Apostle said, 'By Him in Whose Hands my soul is, son of Mary (Jesus) will shortly descend amongst you people (Muslims) as a just ruler and will break the Cross and kill the pig and abolish the Jizya (a tax taken from the non-Muslims, who are in the protection of the Muslim government). Then there will be abundance of money and no-body will accept charitable gifts.'" http://www.usc.edu/schools/college/crcc/engagement/resources/texts/muslim/hadith/bukhari/; accessed January 11, 2011.

43. For his encounter with Caliph al-Mahdi, see Bennett, *Understanding Christian-Muslim Relations,* pp. 89-101.

course, not in the context of crucifixion): 19:33 and 3:55.[44] He believed that on this basis it was established that Jesus died and rose again. The caliph's response was something to be expected: Jesus' death lies in the future.[45]

Christian apologetic has advanced two different positions as a response to the standard Muslim denial of Jesus' death on the cross.[46] The first one is illustrated in Timothy's position — as softly and ironically as he put it — namely, that the Qur'an is inconsistent in, on the one hand, affirming the death of Jesus (19:33; 3:55) and, on the other hand, denying it (4:157). The second apologetic way of argumentation has advanced the thesis that, indeed, the Qur'an is not denying the crucifixion. This position rests on three interrelated arguments: (1) Not only the two passages mentioned, but also other passages in the Qur'an affirm the death of Jesus (5:17, 75, 117). (2) What 4:157 denies is the indestructibility of the divine nature but not the death on the cross of Jesus according to his human nature. This was indeed Timothy's Nestorian position, and this interpretation was also affirmed, for example, by Paul of Antioch in the twelfth century.[47] This reasoning is in keeping with the standard Muslim view according to which the soul of martyrs is not really "killed" but rather taken up to God, and thus martyrs are "alive" with God (3:169). (3) On the basis of the biblical teaching that makes Jesus' death a matter of his voluntary submission rather than something forced upon him by humans (John 10:17, 18), the Qur'an (4:157) is merely denying the arrogant claim by the Jews of having killed Jesus.[48] In sum: this second line of Christian apologetics is saying that indeed, the Qur'an is consistent and thus

44. Qur'an 19:33: "Peace on me the day I was born, and the day I die, and the day I shall be raised alive!" (The context determines that this speaks of Jesus since this is one of the two suras of Mary, the main sources of Jesus' life in the Qur'an.)

Qur'an 3:55: "(And remember) when Allah said: O Jesus! Lo! I am gathering thee and causing thee to ascend unto Me, and am cleansing thee of those who disbelieve and am setting those who follow thee above those who disbelieve until the Day of Resurrection. Then unto Me ye will (all) return, and I shall judge between you as to that wherein ye used to differ." The phrase translated here "ascend unto Me" is usually taken to mean "cause you to die."

45. N. Robinson, *Christ in Islam and Christianity,* p. 107.

46. This paragraph is based on N. Robinson, *Christ in Islam and Christianity,* pp. 108-9.

47. "By this statement the Quran gives evidence for the divine nature of Christ which is the Word of God neither pain nor scorn can touch." Cited in N. Robinson, *Christ in Islam and Christianity,* p. 108 (without original reference).

48. This view is also supported by the common Christian interpretation of biblical teaching that it was the Romans rather than the Jews who put Jesus to death.

affirms the death of Jesus, at least when it comes to his human nature.[49] It goes without saying that this interpretation hardly has convinced many Muslims.

Two major exegetical questions surround the interpretation of 4:157-58, namely, the meaning of "Allah took him up unto Himself" (v. 158) and "a semblance was made" (v. 157, following Robinson's rendering). The former has to do with what really happened to Jesus if he was not put to death on the cross. The latter relates to the question of who, instead of Jesus, was crucified. Muslim commentary literature on these passages is endless, and Christian apologetics has also engaged them widely from the beginning.

The Arabic word *tawaffā*[50] means literally "to receive" but has been interpreted also as "to die" when Allah is the subject. Indeed, this verb appears twice in relation to Jesus (5:117; 3:55), and three times in reference to Muhammad's fate (40:77; 13:40; 10:46). It might be significant that in many current translations the three passages relating to Muhammad are interpreted as denoting dying, as in 10:46: "Whether We let thee (O Muhammad) behold something of that which We promise them or (whether We) cause thee to die, still unto Us is their return, and Allah, moreover, is Witness over what they do" (10:46). On the contrary, in both cases in which reference is made to Jesus' fate, the literal meaning of "to receive" (or its equivalent) is used in translations.[51] According to Robinson, the Christian interpretation, which goes back all the way to the seventh Christian century, as discussed, making *tawaffā* mean death also in the case of Jesus, has some strong support behind it. The remaining twenty-four references in the Qur'an are all in some way or another associated with death, along with the three instances relating to Muhammad's fate. Furthermore, even those classical commentators who as

49. There have been interesting attempts on the Christian side to explain the Qur'anic passage 4:156-59 in terms of sectarian Christian implications and debates such as that between the Nestorians and Monophysites. Whereas the former, as mentioned, attributed the death only to the human nature, Monophysites, in their insistence on one nature, can only speak of the death on the cross in terms of the divine nature suffering. Another sectarian interpretation, appealing to Muslim tradition as well, is the ancient Gnostic tradition in which it was not Jesus but rather Simon the Cyrene who was crucified. N. Robinson, *Christ in Islam and Christianity,* pp. 110-11.

50. N. Robinson, *Christ in Islam and Christianity,* devotes the whole of chap. 12 to the detailed discussion of the use of this term in the Qur'an and relevant Muslim commentaries.

51. For a brief, detailed discussion, see N. Robinson, *Christ in Islam and Christianity,* pp. 113-15.

a rule denied the death of Jesus on the cross still acknowledged that normally the verb denotes death.[52] That said, Robinson contends that in light of the Qur'anic and commentary literature, the issue is still complicated and far from settled. The complications include the observations that only in the five passages that relate to Muhammad and Jesus, "the verb is used in the active voice with God as the subject and with one of his prophets as the object."[53] Whatever the final exegetical or lexical conclusion, Islamic theology has firmly settled the issue contrary to the Christian view.

Regarding the meaning of "a semblance was made to them" in 4:157, Muslim theology agreed with Robinson's conclusion almost unanimously: "Despite differences of opinion about the details the commentators were agreed that 4:157 denies that Jesus was crucified. The most widespread view was that it implies that the Jews erroneously crucified Jesus' 'semblance' and not Jesus himself."[54]

Kenneth Cragg offers a comprehensive, highly nuanced judgment of the state of affairs of the dispute between Muslim theology and Christian theology regarding the cross and its meaning. The crucifixion entails three interrelated aspects, namely, "the act of men in wrong, the act of Jesus in love, and the act of God in grace." According to Cragg, whereas Muslim theology affirms the first two aspects, "[w]hat the Quran, and with it the whole corporate mind of Islam, denies is the third dimension, i.e., God's act. It is this which is totally precluded by every category of theology and faith." To bring home that point, Cragg pointedly expresses the Muslim judgment: "'God was *not* in Christ reconciling the world to himself': he was with Jesus withdrawing him to heaven."[55] That judgment is valid even though there is some resonance between the Anselmian focus on law and legal demands and Islam. In Islam, disobedience brings about punishment. However, the difference lies in how death is related to punishment. Whereas in much of traditional Christian theology death is a result of sin, in Islam it is not: death is natural.[56] And apart from that question, Islam does not know the Christian kind of doctrine of atonement for others' sins.[57]

52. N. Robinson, *Christ in Islam and Christianity,* p. 125.

53. N. Robinson, *Christ in Islam and Christianity,* p. 113.

54. N. Robinson, *Christ in Islam and Christianity,* p. 140, at the end of the chapter-long detailed study of this expression in the Qur'an and commentary literature.

55. Cragg, *Jesus and the Muslim,* pp. 167-68.

56. Bebawi, "Atonement and Mercy," pp. 191-92.

57. See further, Eggen, "Africa and Vasco da Gama's Voyage," p. 336.

Salvation and Savior in Buddhist Perspectives

A foundational difference between the Buddhist and Christian visions is that "Savior has no place in the Buddhist worldview. An individual must control and be responsible for his or her own destiny."[58] One is one's own refuge, and no one else — not even Buddha — can save one from the law of *kamma*.[59] The leading Tibetan Buddhist scholar and practitioner José Ignacio Cabezón succinctly summarizes the reasons for the Buddhist repudiation of the role of Jesus as Savior as in Christian tradition. Buddhists "balk at the idea that any deity is capable of granting salvation to others simply through an act of will. Given Buddhists' metaphysical commitments, then, there can be no God who is the creator of the universe, who is originally pure and primordially perfect, who is omnipotent and who can will the salvation of beings. Jesus, therefore, *cannot be* the incarnation of such a God."[60]

The death on the cross of the Savior for the sins and salvation of others is an idea totally unknown in all traditions of Buddhism.[61] The generic idea of redemptive or "vicarious" suffering on behalf of others is not unknown in Buddhism — think, for example, of the commonly known story in Thai (Theravada) Buddhism of the sixteenth-century Queen Srisuriyothai's self-sacrifice to save her people under the threat from the king of Burma or the annual ritual of *loikrathong,* which seeks to embody the sending away of the sins of the past year utilizing candles and miniature rafts. Nevertheless, any notion of somebody suffering (death) to atone for sins or even taking up the other person's suffering onto himself is utterly foreign to the Theravada tradition.[62] Resorting to such a vicarious act done by another person, even a divinity, would mean shrinking from one's own responsibility to deal with one's *kamma.* In Mahayana Buddhism, the Boddhisattva — unlike the *Theravada Arahat (ariya-puggala)* — is willing to postpone his own entrance into the *nibbana* to help others reach the goal. Even that, however, is

58. Boonyakiat, "A Christian Theology of Suffering," p. 114; see also Gross, "Meditating on Jesus," p. 45.

59. For differences between Mahayana and Theravada in this respect, see J. R. Davis, *Poles Apart,* pp. 98-104.

60. Cabezón, "Buddhist Views of Jesus," in *JWF,* p. 23.

61. For a typical criticism against the idea of atoning death, see, e.g., the criticism of the seventeenth-century Chinese monk and scholar Ouyi Zhixu (in *JBC,* p. 230): "Why does the Lord of Heaven have to buy human beings free from their sins with his own body, rather than being able to forgive the sins directly?"

62. See further, Simmer-Brown, "Suffering and Social Justice," pp. 107-9 particularly.

the function not of a "savior" but rather of a "good neighbor," even when the Boddhisattva may grant his own merit to help the other.[63]

What about Pure Land Buddhism? Is the path outlined by this Buddhist tradition compatible with the Christian view of salvation? In the Indian religious traditions from which Buddhism also emerged, there are two determinative metaphors of salvation. The "monkey path," depicted by a baby monkey clinging tightly to the back of the mother on a dangerous walk, signifies self-power; whereas the "cat path," illustrated by the kitten being held by the mother by the nape of the neck, speaks of other-power. The Pure Land tradition of Mahayana Buddhism developed both in the Japanese (known also as Shin Buddhism) and Chinese contexts represents the latter. The main savior figure is Boddhisattva Dharmakara, who, through the rigorous and pure practice of forty-eight vows, reached enlightenment and became Amitabha Buddha. He opened the path of salvation in primordial times by establishing the Western Pure Land and made it possible for all sentient beings reborn in that land to reach enlightenment, "salvation."[64] "The Buddha embodied his virtue in his Name for all beings, enabling them to enter the Pure Land at death. Through their faith in, and meritorious recitation of the Name, they are saved by its power."[65] Significant in relation to Christ and his self-offering in Pure Land thought is the emphasis on the contingency of Boddhisattva Dharmakara's enlightenment in the Pure Land on the condition of the inclusion of others.[66] This orientation goes beyond the foundational Buddhist idea of interdependence and even the Mahayana emphasis on Boddhisattva postponing his or her own "stepping into the river" of enlightenment in order to help other sentient beings.

As is well known, with all his great reservations of all human religiosity, Barth felt deep sympathies for the Pure Land tradition, the existence of

63. For differences between Mahayana and Theravada in this respect, see J. R. Davis, *Poles Apart,* pp. 98-104.

64. Boddhisattva is a Buddha-in-the-making aiming at enlightenment. Indeed, there is more than one Pure Land in those traditions. Wherever there is an enlightened Buddha, there is Pure Land. The Western Pure Land created by Boddhisattva Dharmakara is the main Pure Land and combines teachings and features of others.

65. Bloom, "Jesus in the Pure Land," in *JWF,* p. 33; see also p. 32.

66. The eighteenth vow expresses this clearly: "If, when I attain Buddhahood, sentient beings . . . who sincerely and joyfully entrust themselves to me, desire to be born in my land, and call my Name even ten times, should not be born there, may I not attain perfect Enlightenment." Inagaki, *The Three Pure Land Sutras,* p. 243; I am indebted to Bloom, "Jesus in the Pure Land," in *JWF,* p. 33 n. 5.

which was "a providential disposition" parallel to Reformed Christianity based on the logic of grace. He considered carefully the form of Pure Land developed by Shinran with an appeal to faith.[67]

That said, the difference between Pure Land and Christian tradition is also remarkable and should be duly acknowledged. Alfred Bloom puts it succinctly:

> The Christian understanding is rooted in the principle of sacrifice with a background of the ancient Hebraic temple sacrificial system. In this mode Jesus becomes the Lamb of God sacrificed for the sins of all humanity. As the theology develops, God, present in the incarnated Christ, becomes both the sacrifice and the sacrificed. Sacrifice is raised to the level of a cosmic event and relationship. . . . In the case of Dharmakara the model is that of selfless giving in which the Boddhisattva perceives the plight of sentient beings and pledges to resolve it through his devoted, selfless effort. . . . It involves an existential decision on the part of the Bodhisattava to work for a solution to the human condition.[68]

The main argumentation of Bloom holds even though, as argued above, Christian theology of reconciliation operates with a number of interrelated and complementary metaphors, not only sacrifice. Yet, in comparison with other religious traditions, the sacrifice model's influence is significant.[69]

For several Buddhist commentators Jesus' "self-negation" culminating in the cry of dereliction at the cross, as the ultimate expression of anguish, serves as a paradigm that reveals some commonalities between the two religious traditions. Soho Machida sees the cry "E'loi, E'loi, la'ma sabachtha'ni?" (Mark 15:34) as "the ultimate expression of anguish that came out of Jesus' mouth when he touched the darkness of sin (karma) that is at the core of human existence."[70] As tragic as the passion was, it was also the "beginning of hope."[71] Similarly, Nishida Kitarō, in *The Logic of the Place of Nothingness and the Religious Worldview,* considers self-negation as the only

67. Barth, *CD* I/2, pp. 340-42 (342).

68. Bloom, "Jesus in the Pure Land," in *JWF,* p. 34.

69. For Barth's listing of differences between Pure Land ("Japanese Protestantism") and Christian theology, see *CD* I/2, pp. 342-43 particularly. "It does not have the character of a real solution" (p. 342). Among the main differences for Barth was the lack of notions of holiness and wrath in relation to God/Amitabha.

70. Machida, "Jesus, Man of Sin," pp. 65-66.

71. Machida, "Jesus, Man of Sin," p. 67.

means for a human being to encounter the Absolute. There is a mysterious mutual conditioning between death and life — not unlike in some Christian interpretations: "This absolute negation does not mean mere death, which is death in relative opposition to life. . . . We must die to human life and death; therein lies absolute life. The absolute death is absolute life, and absolute negation is absolute affirmation."[72]

In terms of Christian contextualization, the description of Jesus by the Nestorian monk Jingjing ("Adam" in Syriac) from the time of the Tang Dynasty, titled the "Luminous Religion" (1781), provides a fascinating example. What is highly significant about this tale is that there is no mention whatsoever of the cross or resurrection, both themes not being well received by the Chinese Buddhist (and Confucian) audience:

> Hereupon our Tri-une (Eloah) divided His Godhead, and the Illustrious and Adorable Messiah, veiling His true Majesty, appeared in the world as a man. Angels proclaimed the glad tidings. A virgin brought forth the Holy One in Tâ Ts'in. A bright star announced the felicitous event. Persians saw its splendor and came with tribute. He fulfilled the Old Law, as it was delivered by the twenty-four holy ones. He announced great plans for the regulation of families and kingdoms. He appointed His new doctrines, operating without words by the cleansing influence of the Tri-une. He formed in man the capacity of correct faith. He defined the measures of the eight (moral) conditions, purging away the dust (of defilement) and perfecting the truth (in men). He threw open the gate of the three constant (virtues), thereby bringing life to light and abolishing death. He hung up the bright sun to break open the abodes of darkness. By all these things the wiles of the devil were defeated. The vessel of mercy was set in motion to convey men to the palace of light, and thereby all intelligent beings were conveyed across (the intervening space). His mighty work being thus completed, at noonday. He ascended to His true (place). He left behind Him the twenty-seven standard books. These set forth the great conversion for the deliverance of the soul. They institute the washing of His Law by water and the spirit, cleansing away all vain delusions, and purifying men till they regain the whiteness of their pure simplicity.[73]

72. Kitarō, *Last Writings,* p. 68; I am indebted to Machida, "Jesus, Man of Sin," p. 66.

73. This text is to be found in Lopez, "Jesus in Buddhism," in *JBC,* p. 265; its original source is Legge, *Christianity in China,* pp. 5, 7.

This account is fascinating not only in its Chinese contextual nature but also in its rich usage of Christian symbols of salvation and atonement — yet, as mentioned, without any hint of the death and raising to new life of the Messiah. Is this yet another "atonement" theory similar to those in the Christian tradition that do not attempt to say everything but only some things about salvation? Abelard's moral example theory comes to mind as a fitting counterexample.

The "Spiritualization" of Sacrifice in Hinduism

Raja Ram Mohun Roy, who had a high regard for Jesus as an ethical teacher (but fell short of affirming his divine incarnation), expresses the Hindu opposition to the Christian idea of atonement in his correspondence with an anonymous Christian priest. Against the Christian minister's reasoning that Jesus can be called a "Saviour of men" only if "he died in their stead to atone for their sins" rather than just helping them live an ethical life, Roy contends that the title "Saviour" is "applied frequently in the divine writings to those persons who had been endued with the power of saving people, either by inculcating doctrines, or affording protection to them although none of them atoned for the sin of mankind by their death." In support, Roy refers to OT Scriptures such as Obadiah 21, Nehemiah 9:27, and 2 Kings 13:5, which use the term translated in many renderings as "savior." Furthermore, Roy notes that Jesus himself at times refers to his salvific work on the basis of "the inculcation of the word of God," as in John 14:3, 5:24, and 6:63. For Roy, the conclusion follows that, on the one hand, there is no way to attribute any "atoning" power to Jesus' influence and that, on the other hand, it wouldn't diminish Jesus' significance for him to be revered as a "Divine Teacher."[74] Apart from exegetical challenges such as the interpretation of the OT references to "savior" and the meaning of the Johannine references to the "word" in Jesus' work,[75] Roy accurately expresses the radical difference between the two faiths regarding the topic of "salvation." This reasoning is not limited to Hindu interpreters of Jesus such as Roy who do not believe in the divine in-

74. *English Works of Raja Ram Mohun Roy,* vol. 3, part I, pp. 172-75, reproduced in *JBC,* pp. 162-64.

75. Even in Christian hermeneutics, the references in the OT to "savior" do not mean the NT understanding of the agent of atonement for sins. The Johannine references to the "word" employed by Roy have to be read in the context of the Johannine and NT understanding of the Word of God (and Logos).

carnation of Jesus, but includes even those who do share the same Hindu view of "atonement."

In other words, the biblical idea of Jesus as the Lamb of God (John 1:29) sacrificed for the sins of the world is foreign to all Hindu strands as long as it is cast in the Christian framework. That said, as mentioned earlier, the idea of self-sacrifice for the sake of others and their well-being is very much part of Hindu thought. The sacrificial lamb imagery can only make sense if it is understood in its "cosmological" — we could probably also say metaphorical — sense and linked with the basic Vedic principle of *rita* (right order). This multifaceted term denotes cosmic order as well as moral order, and in relation to sacrifices, also the right order of sacrifices.[76] Sacrifices offered to gods *(vedi)* were the basic means of securing the order in ancient Hinduism. Indeed, "sacrifice" *(yajña)* is named in *Rig Veda* the "center of the universe."[77] The NT and early Christian atonement theories include perspectives that are related to these kinds of cosmic ramifications of the cross. However, in Christian tradition they are integrally related to the biblical narrative of the triune God breaking the power of evil and resistance to divine purposes in Christ reconciling everything in heaven and earth with God.

One aspect of salvation in Christian theology has to do with forgiveness. That is not a totally foreign idea to Hinduism even though it is not a central one. Bhagavad-Gita (18.66) says, "Relinquishing all Dharmas take refuge in Me alone; I will liberate thee from all sins; grieve not." To properly understand this statement, one has to stick with the Hindu view of what "sin" is, namely, "that which keeps the mind attached to sense perception and objects of the senses. Such attachment produces restlessness, which clouds perception of the soul."[78]

The idea of grace is not unknown in Hinduism, either.[79] The divine initiative of God to "come down" in the form of the avatars, as discussed above, is itself a manifestation of grace, so much so that Rudolf Otto dared

76. In the Rig Veda, *Rita* controls all the operations of the universe including the actions of the gods. In the Upanishads, *Rita* operates in the ethical realm through karma, the principle related to samsara.

77. *Rig Veda* 1.164.35: "This altar is the earth's extremest limit; this sacrifice of ours is the world's centre." Trans. Ralph T. H. Griffith (http://www.sacred-texts.com/hin/rigveda/rv01164.htm; accessed February 2, 2011); see Ravi Ravindra, "Jesus Is Not an Idol," in *JWF*, pp. 97-98.

78. Ghosh, *Mejja*, p. 177, cited in Bharat, "Hindu Perspectives," p. 256.

79. See further, Kulandran, *Grace in Christianity and Hinduism*, pp. 140-42 particularly.

to speak of "India's religion of grace."[80] Hence, Bhagavad-Gita contains well-known sayings that speak of grace, such as this one from the last chapter, fittingly titled "The Way of Liberation in Renunciation" (18.56, 58, 62):

> 56. Even doing all actions always, taking refuge in Me, — by My grace he attains to the eternal, immutable State. . . .
> 58. Fixing thy mind on Me, thou shalt, by My grace, overcome all obstacles; but if from self-conceit thou wilt not hear Me, thou shalt perish. . . .
> 62. Take refuge in Him with all thy heart, O Bhârata; by His grace shalt thou attain supreme peace (and) the eternal abode.

Even more pointed is 9.30-31:

> 30. If even a very wicked person worships Me, with devotion to none else, he should be regarded as good, for he has rightly resolved.
> 31. Soon does he become righteous, and attain eternal Peace, O son of Kunti boldly canst thou proclaim, that My devotee is never destroyed.

It is significant that these sayings open up the way of devotion *(Bhakti mārga)* along with the way of knowledge *(Jñāna mārga)* and way of action *(Karma mārga)*.[81] It is often noted that the *bhakti* tradition is the closest to Christian faith with relation to grace.[82] Nowhere else is this "grace-based" doctrine taught more clearly than in *Charama Sloka,* the last verse of Gita (18.66): "Relinquishing all Dharmas take refuge in Me alone; I will liberate

80. Otto, *India's Religion of Grace,* p. 17: "What is the good conferred in salvation by Christianity? Communion with a living God. What is the means of salvation? Grace, *gratia* and *gratia sola,* which lays hold of the lost, rescuing and redeeming him. Now these are the very slogans and distinctive terms of the *Bhakti* religion (Vaishnavism)." Similarly, Monier Williams (*Brahmanism and Hinduism,* p. 96) says of Vaishnavism that it has "more common ground with Christianity than any other form of non-Christian faith."

81. In keeping with the Upanishadic tradition, Bhagavad-Gita of course gives preference to the way of knowledge, the way to realize one's identity with Brahman, as in 12.5-7: "Greater is their trouble whose minds are set on the Unmanifested; for the goal of the Unmanifested is very hard for the embodied to reach. But those who worship Me, resigning all actions in Me, regarding Me as the Supreme Goal, meditating on Me with single-minded Yoga, — to these whose mind is set on Me, verily, I become ere long, O son of Prithâ, the Saviour out of the ocean of the mortal Samsâra."

82. See the classic study by Otto, *India's Religion of Grace.*

thee from all sins; grieve not."[83] It might be important to contemporary interests that, especially in Vaishnavism, the consorts of God are usually the conduits of grace. Commonly called *Sakti* (lit. power), among the consorts of Vishnu the most important in this respect is Srī or Lakshmī. Somewhat similarly to folk Catholicism, she is the mediatrix between humanity and God. The significance of the female consorts is enhanced in light of the fact that in Hindu theism the (male) gods tend to withdraw into distance, thus making space and creating need for a mediator.[84]

Again, the Christian interpreter has to exercise caution in not reading too much or different content into these kinds of sayings. Hinduism by and large is not a religion of grace in the sense that Christian faith is. It is highly significant that immediately following the "last verse," the next one says categorically (18.67): "This is never to be spoken by thee to one who is devoid of austerities or devotion, nor to one who does not render service, nor to one who cavils at Me." In keeping with this there are numerous sayings in Gita in which to the *bhakta,* the devotee, a number of strict exhortations and requirements are set forth in order to pursue the way of knowledge, action, and "obedience" (see, for example, 12.13-19). The late native bishop of South India, Sabapathy Kulandran, rightly concludes:

> The author [of Gītā] seems to want to make it clear that he does not wish to take the doctrine of *Bhakti* away from the ancient haunts of religion, the shades of over-spreading trees, where the sages from of old have practiced religious exercises. The *Bhakta* seems to be the same old seer, who by the realization of his identity with the Brahman has risen to a state of detachment from the world, except that he is now being asked in addition to have devotion to Krishna also [the focus of Gītā]. . . . The Gītā, no doubt, proclaims the doctrine of Grace; but it proclaims it in the context of Hinduism.[85]

This observation is in keeping with the wider contextual difference between these two religions — and it has to be acknowledged for the sake of fruitful dialogue. Whereas in Christian tradition the emphasis is "on the God who is offering salvation," in Hinduism, even in Shaivanism, let alone in

83. Verse 66 is not literally the last verse; twelve others follow. The expression "last verse" means something like "final" in the sense of giving the highest teaching.

84. See further, Kulandran, *Grace in Christianity and Hinduism,* p. 153.

85. Kulandran, *Grace in Christianity and Hinduism,* p. 143.

Saivism and other traditions, it is "on the effort of the individual seeking salvation."[86] Put otherwise: "In the Christian doctrine of Grace, therefore, we confront an act of God," whereas in the Hindu view, liberation is a matter of human initiative and accomplishment.[87] Ultimately, the Christian view of salvation is linked with the salvific work of the triune God in the context of the cross.[88]

Even though Hindu and Christian traditions employ the idea (and the former also the ritual) of sacrifice, they are so different as to be virtually incommensurate with each other. With regard to the notion of sacrifice, there is, however, a common denominator that facilitates dialogue: the effort to "spiritualize sacrifice." The Jesuit Francis X. Clooney has compared these two ways of spiritualizing sacrifice by taking a look at how each tradition, thinking of sacrifice as a central value, has reinterpreted it "without detaching themselves from the practice altogether." This kind of comparison is less interested in the assumed similarity or dissimilarity of Jewish/Christian and Vedic/Hindu rituals; the focus is on the way the two traditions have "developed comparable patterns and trajectories in their ways of spiritualizing sacrifice."[89] This kind of exercise may also shed light on the way Christian tradition in the aftermath of the final sacrifice of Jesus and Jewish tradition after the fall of Jerusalem have attempted the same. In addition, it could help shed light on the Christian self-understanding of sacrifice in its many meanings. In the tradition of the thirteenth-century Ramänuja, the Vedänta Desika, more than a century later, outlines four characteristics of the proper service and devotion of the "Lord" (Bhagavùn): devotion to the Lord is the highest calling of the human person; service to other human beings is the best way to show devotion to the Lord; thus, total devotion to the Lord and others is the ideal, and what makes it possible to best serve the other devotees is to ac-

86. Kulandran, *Grace in Christianity and Hinduism,* p. 245.

87. Kulandran, *Grace in Christianity and Hinduism,* p. 242.

88. For useful discussion explaining the meaning of salvific mediators in Hinduism and Christianity and their differences, see chap. 2 in Brockington, *Hinduism and Christianity.*

89. Clooney, "Sacrifice," p. 364. In discerning the Hindu traditions' way of spiritualizing sacrifice, Clooney looks at the following strands: "the early Mimamsa school of liturgical theology, as expressed in the *Parva Mtmämsu Sütras* of Jaimini (ca. 200 BCE); the theocentric Vedänta of Ramänuja (1017-1137 CE); the Sanskrit- and Tamil-speaking SrTvaiçnava reflection of one of Ramanuja's successors, Vedänta of Desika (1268-1369 CE)" (p. 366). The teaching of the Upanishads is not included (which, as is well known, not only spiritualize the sacrifice but also leave it behind).

knowledge their worth; there is a mutual relationship between the Lord and devotees in that as the Lord rejoices in the honor of his devotees, the more devotion they give to the Lord, the more joyous the Lord is.[90] Clooney begins the comparison with the commonsense note that it doesn't take a Christian to say that "sacrifice 'from the heart'" is better than a mere offering or ritual. Other significant similarities include the importance of community and the community's discernment of the gracious nature of the Lord.[91]

Differences are significant as well. Whereas in Christian understanding of the spiritualizing of sacrifice God as transcendent is always the focus, in Hindu traditions God is virtually displaced because gods are considered "immanent" beings (as far as, at least, Christian conception is concerned).[92] "The sacrificial world has been rearranged around God; but the whole includes both God and what is outside God." The idea of covenant underlies Christian (and Jewish) notions of sacrifice; in Hinduism, the underlying principle is *dhamma,* or right order. Clooney's conclusion thus is: "The parallel Judaeo-Christian and Vedic-Hindu structures of spiritualization and community-orientation remain 'parallel lines': they never quite meet or cross one another, but nevertheless serve as mirrors reflecting one another."[93]

What, then, are the theological implications? One is to "demythologize" the common assumption that the desire to spiritualize sacrifice and worship is solely and uniquely a *Christian* idea. It is not, but rather is shared by some other religions as well. In terms of Hindu-Christian dialogue, this common feature of a spiritualizing tendency — notwithstanding profound theological and spiritual differences with regard to the meaning of sacrifice — may assist Christian theology in helping Hindus understand some key elements of Christ's sacrifice. Clooney suggests three such lessons from the comparison: first, Jesus' life and death are a profound manifestation of total devotion to God; second, his self-sacrifice on the cross is thus the most profound and perfect ritual enactment of that devotion; and third, Jesus Christ reveals the purest devotion of God, as on the cross God empties himself for the sake of his people.[94]

90. Clooney, "Sacrifice," pp. 373-74.

91. Clooney, "Sacrifice," p. 375.

92. Even Vishnu's primacy among the gods does not signify transcendence in the absolute sense.

93. Clooney, "Sacrifice," pp. 375-76.

94. Clooney, "Sacrifice," p. 378.

Epilogue: Continuing Methodological Miscellanea

"One of the most significant things about Jesus of Nazareth," remarks the physicist-turned-priest John Polkinghorne, "is that we have heard of him." Indeed, how do we know anything of a man who "lived two thousand years ago in a not very important frontier province of the Roman Empire. He died comparatively young, painfully and shamefully executed and deserted by the band of close followers that he had gathered around him. He wrote no book that could have conveyed his message to future generations."[1] Not only have the Christians — followers of this Palestinian carpenter confessed to be the divine Savior — heard of Jesus' name, nearly all people have! This curious fact alone necessitates careful reflection upon the meaning of Jesus the Christ not only within the narrow contours of Christian communities but also in relation to people of other faiths and no faith, as well as in relation to the whole of creation. Hence, it seemed appropriate to begin this five-volume series entitled Constructive Christian Theology for the Pluralistic World with the investigation of the meaning and significance of Christ and his work for us and for the whole world.

Christology, however, can be fully developed only in the context of unfolding the whole of Christian doctrine, which is nothing other than the discernment of the unfolding of the trinitarian plan of salvation for the world the triune God has created. The volume entitled *Triune God and Revelation* considers Christ's role as the embodiment of the divine revelation as well as the second person of the Trinity. The volume *Creation and Humanity* focuses

1. Polkinghorne, *Exploring Reality*, p. 60.

on Christ's role as the agent of creation, including the creation of human beings made in God's image, to be conformed to the image of his Son. Whereas in the present volume, the relation of Jesus Christ to the Spirit was carefully considered, in the volume entitled *Spirit and Salvation* the relation of the Spirit to Jesus Christ plays an important part of the development of the theme. In the trinitarian account of salvation, the dual work of the Son and the Spirit as a gracious gift to men and women also receives consideration. The volume *Community and Future* scrutinizes the role of Christ as the Head of his body, the church, the people of God and temple of the Holy Spirit. The community of Christ is being drawn to the trinitarian eschatological coming of the Father's kingdom whose righteous rule already arrived in the coming of the Son in the power of the Spirit, and is yet to come in its fullness. The development of Christian constructive theology is, in other words, a christologically integrated trinitarian unfolding of the salvific plan of God.

The current volume has attempted to construct a contemporary theological account of Christ and Christ's salvific work. In that enterprise, every effort has been made to take stock of the width and breadth, as well as the diversity and unity, of the great Christian tradition, both historical and current. A significant part of current theological traditions is the rapidly globalizing Christian church's emerging reservoir of insights, testimonies, and convictions from diverse and various perspectives. While one should never attempt to be encyclopedic even in systematic development of theological themes, neither should the theologian be content in sticking with what is familiar and safe. How well this discussion has been able to do justice to the whole diversity of Christian tradition is of course left to the reader to judge.

Part of that judgment process is to realize that the rich historical tradition of the Christian church, until contemporary times, has been the commodity of the whole global church. It is not the case that Augustine, Aquinas, Catherine of Siena, and Schleiermacher are only or mainly for theologians from the Global North, mainly aging white men. These fathers and mothers of faith are as much part of the roots of African, Asian, and Latin American Christian expressions — not mainly because of the role played by the missionary movement rooted in Euro-American traditions but because all contemporary Christian traditions, if they wish to be *Christian,* stand on the shoulders of not only biblical authors but also historical witnesses. One does not have to endorse uncritically their testimonies and suggestions, but neither should one neglect them.

The current nomenclature, "contextual" (or "global" or "intercultural") theology, is highly problematic even though, for the time being, it has been a necessary and useful tool to wake up academic Christian theology from the slumber of Euro-American hegemony. Now that the concept has been voiced, it is time to lay it to rest since, as mentioned several times above, it could be mistakenly understood in terms of only *some* theologies being contextually driven while others are "neutral."

The way forward in global Christian theological scholarship is, on the one hand, for academia in the Global North to invite "contextual" views as equal dialogue partners, and on the other hand, to have "contextual" theologians stop undermining and eschewing tradition as if, for example, the main source of oppression in Christian community is traditional ways of addressing God or speaking of Christ's suffering. Only when the "global" theological scholarship — the term "global" here should be understood as inclusive of geographical, racial, sexual, ecumenical, and other distinctions — will engage in a (self-)critical and constructive mutual dialogue between tradition and contemporary challenges and promises is there hope for a more balanced, robust, and vigorous theology.

An essential part of that new, emerging way of doing theology is the robust engagement of other living faiths that this volume also attempts. The present volume builds on the conviction that this kind of theological engagement cannot — and should not — begin from an empty table, so to speak. Rather, speaking from my own Christian tradition, there should be first a careful and thoughtful development of a contemporary Christian vision of God and reality before opening it up for mutual dialogue, learning, correction, and enrichment from other faith traditions. Or to be more precise: already in the process of developing one's account of contemporary Christian vision an incremental engagement of other faith traditions usually turns out to be useful. Yet this project argues that in order to put a robustly and authentically *Christian* (in this case) theology — rather than a generic religious ideology owing something to all faith traditions and representing none of them — in dialogue with Jewish, Muslim, Buddhist, Hindu, and other faiths, the working out of constructive/systematic theology has to draw from the inner logic of the tradition. By the term "inner" I do not mean insular or isolated, but rather that, in keeping with the methodology of systematic theology in search of a coherent account of reality, the doctrines and claims be based on the best of the revelatory and other traditions. Then and only then can representatives of other faiths encounter an authentically Christian doctrine. Hence, in the development of a constructive theological vision in this volume and in the rest of the project, while interfaith insights will be engaged more briefly throughout the discussion, a concentrated and focused dialogue will take place following the main outline and discussion of the Christian constructive view.

The interfaith engagement contains tremendous promise and a huge challenge to Christian theology. Polkinghorne rightly locates both the promise and the challenge:

> I am writing from within the Christian community of faith, but one must admit that exploration of sacred reality is made problematic by the diversity of the world faith traditions. Each displays a considerable stability in its traditional heartlands. Each manifests an authenticity in the spiritual way of life that it preserves and nurtures. Today's multicultural society makes us keenly aware that this is so. People of other faiths are no longer strange people, living in faraway countries and believing very odd things. They are our neighbours, living down the street, and we can see the evident integrity of their lives. The deeply troubling intolerance and violence that some minorities within the different faith communities can display do not negate the values that are affirmed and followed by the majority. Yet, each religion also makes claims about the form of its encounter with sacred reality that appear incompatible with the testimonies of other faith communities.[2]

This twofold opportunity and challenge will be kept freshly in mind as this continuing construction of contemporary Christian theology in critical and sympathetic dialogue with other living faiths takes us to other systematic topics.

2. Polkinghorne, *Exploring Reality,* pp. 127-28.

Bibliography

Abe, Gabriel Oyedele. "Redemption, Reconciliation, Propitiation: Salvation Terms in an African Milieu." *Journal of Theology for Southern Africa* 95 (1996): 3-12.

Abe, Masao. "A Dynamic Unity in Religious Pluralism: A Proposal from the Buddhist Point of View [Zen Buddhism]." In *The Experience of Religious Diversity*, edited by John Hick and Hasan Askari. Aldershot: Gower, 1985.

———. "Kenotic God and Dynamic Suyata." In *Divine Emptiness and Historical Fullness: A Buddhist-Jewish-Christian Conversation with Masao Abe*, edited by Christopher Ives, pp. 3-65. Valley Forge, Pa.: Trinity, 1995.

Abelard, Peter. "Ethics, or Know Thyself." In *The Classical Moralists: Selections Illustrating Ethics from Socrates to Martineau*, edited by Benjamin Rand, pp. 186-91. Boston: P. Smith; Houghton Mifflin, 1909.

———. "Exposition of the Epistle to the Romans (an Excerpt from the Second Book)." In *A Scholastic Miscellany: Anselm to Ockham*, edited and translated by Eugene R. Fairweather. Library of Christian Classics. Philadelphia: Westminster, 1956.

Abhedananda, Swami. *Vedanta Philosophy.* Kolkata: Ramakrishna Vedanta Math, 1959.

Ahlstrand, Kajsa. *Fundamental Openness: An Enquiry into Raimundo Panikkar's Theological Vision and Its Presuppositions.* Studia Missionalia Upsaliensia 57. Uppsala: Uppsala University Press, 1993.

Ahn, Byung Mu. "Jesus and the People (Minjung)." In *Asian Faces of Jesus*, edited by R. S. Sugirtharajah. Maryknoll, N.Y.: Orbis, 1995.

Aletti, Jean-Noël, S.J. "God Made Christ to Be Sin (2 Corinthians 5:21): Reflections on a Pauline Paradox." In *The Redemption: An Interdisciplinary Symposium on Christ as Redeemer*, edited by Stephen T. Davis, Daniel Kendall, S.J., and Gerald O'Collins, S.J. Oxford: Oxford University Press, 2004.

Alfaro, Sammy. *Divino Compañero: Toward a Hispanic Pentecostal Christology.* Princeton Theological Monograph Series. Eugene, Oreg.: Pickwick, 2010.

Alston, W. *Divine Nature and Human Language: Essays in Philosophical Theology.* Ithaca, N.Y.: Cornell University Press, 1986.

Althaus, Paul. *The Theology of Martin Luther.* Translated by Robert C. Schultz. Philadelphia: Fortress, 1966.

Althaus-Reid, Marcella. *Indecent Theology: Theological Perversions in Sex, Gender, and Politics.* London: Routledge, 2001.

Amnell, Matti T. *Uskontojen Universumi: John Hickin uskonnollisen pluralismin haaste ja siitä käyty keskustelu.* Suomalaisen Teologisen Kirjallisuusseuran Julkaisuja 217. Helsinki: STK, 1999.

Anderson, Allan H. "The Gospel and Culture in Pentecostal Mission in the Third World." *Missionalia* 27, no. 2 (1999): 220-30.

Anderson, Ray S. "The Incarnation of God in Feminist Christology: A Theological Critique." In *Speaking the Christian God: The Holy Trinity and the Challenge of Feminism,* edited by Alvin F. Kimel Jr., pp. 288-312. Grand Rapids: Eerdmans, 1992.

Ante-Nicene Fathers, The: Translations of the Writings of the Fathers Down to A.D. 325. Edited by Alexander Roberts and James Donaldson et al. 9 vols. Edinburgh, 1885-1897. Public domain; available at www.ccel.org.

Appiah-Kubi, Kofi. "Jesus Christ: Some Christological Aspects from African Perspectives." In *African and Asian Contributions to Contemporary Theology,* edited by J. S. Mbiti. Geneva: WCC Ecumenical Institute, 1977.

Aquinas, Thomas. *De Potentia.* Westminster, Md.: Newman Press, 1952.

———. *The Summa Theologica of St. Thomas Aquinas.* Second and revised edition, 1920. Literally translated by Fathers of the English Dominican Province. Online Edition Copyright © 2008 by Kevin Knight.

Aulén, Gustaf. *Christus Victor: An Historical Study of the Three Main Types of the Idea of the Atonement.* Translated by A. G. Hebert. London: SPCK; New York and Toronto: Macmillan, 1931.

Ayoub, Maḥmud [Mahmoud] M. "Jesus the Son of God: A Study of the Terms *Ibn* and *Walad* in the Qur'ān and *Tafsīr* Tradition." In *Christian-Muslim Encounters,* edited by Y. Y. Haddad and W. Z. Haddad. Gainesville: University of Florida Press, 1995.

———. "Towards an Islamic Christology, II: The Death of Jesus, Reality or Delusion (a Study in the Death of Jesus in Tafsīr Literature)." *Muslim World* 70, no. 2 (1980): 91-121.

Baillie, D. M. *God Was in Christ: An Essay on Incarnation and Atonement.* 2nd ed. New York: Charles Scribner's Sons, 1948.

Baker-Fletcher, Garth Kasimu. *Xodus: An African American Male Journey.* Minneapolis: Fortress, 1996.

Baker-Fletcher, Karen, and Garth Kasimu Baker-Fletcher. *My Sister, My Brother: Womanist and Xodus God-Talk.* Eugene, Oreg.: Wipf and Stock, 2002.

Balić, Smail. "The Image of Jesus in Contemporary Islamic Theology." In *We Believe in One God,* edited by A. M. Schimmel and Abdoldjavad Falaturi. London: Burns and Oates, 1979.

Balthasar, Hans Urs von. *Theo-Logic.* Vol. 3, *The Spirit of Truth.* Translated by Adrian J. Walker. San Francisco: Ignatius, 2005.

Bammel, Ernst. "Christian Origins in Jewish Tradition." *New Testament Studies* 13, no. 4 (1967): 317-35.

Barbour, Ian G. *Myths, Models, and Paradigms: A Comparative Study in Science and Religion.* San Francisco: Harper and Row, 1974.

Barker, Gregory A., ed. *Jesus in the World's Faiths: Leading Thinkers from Five Religions Reflect on His Meaning.* Maryknoll, N.Y.: Orbis, 2008.

Barker, Gregory A., and Stephen E. Gregg, eds. *Jesus beyond Christianity: The Classic Texts.* Oxford: Oxford University Press, 2010.

Baron, Salo W. *A Social and Religious History of the Jews.* Vol. 1. New York: Columbia University Press, 1951.

Barrett, David B., George T. Kurian, and Todd M. Johnson. *World Christian Encyclopedia.* 2nd ed. New York: Oxford University Press, 2001.

Barth, Karl. *Church Dogmatics.* Edited by Geoffrey William Bromiley and Thomas Forsyth Torrance. Translated by G. W. Bromiley. Edinburgh: T. & T. Clark, 1956-1975. Online edition by Alexander Street Press, 1975.

———. *The Epistle to the Romans.* Translated by Edwyn C. Hoskyns from the 6th ed. London: Oxford University Press, 1963 [1933].

———. "The Humanity of God." Translated by John Newton Thomas and Thomas Wieser. In *The Humanity of God,* pp. 37-68. Richmond: John Knox, 1960.

Bartlett, Anthony W. *Cross Purposes: The Violent Grammar of Christian Atonement.* Harrisburg, Pa.: Trinity, 2000.

Bartley, William Warren, III. *Retreat to Commitment.* Chicago: Open Court, 2003 [1962].

Bathrellos, Demetrios. "The Sinlessness of Jesus: A Theological Exploration in the Light of Trinitarian Theology." In *Trinitarian Soundings in Systematic Theology,* edited by P. L. Metzger, pp. 113-26. New York: T. & T. Clark, 2005.

Batnitzky, Leora. "On the Suffering of God's Chosen: Christian Views in Jewish Terms." In *Christianity in Jewish Terms,* edited by Tikva Frymer-Kensky et al., pp. 203-20. Boulder, Colo.: Westview Press, 2000.

Beaumont, Mark. *Christology in Dialogue with Muslims: A Critical Analysis of Christian Presentations of Christ for Muslims from the Ninth and Twentieth Centuries.* Carlisle, U.K.: Paternoster, 2005.

Bebawi, George H. "Atonement and Mercy: Islam between Athanasius and Anselm." In *Atonement Today,* edited by John Goldingay. London: SPCK, 1995.

Becker, Adam H., and Annette Yoshiko Reed, eds. *The Ways That Never Parted: Jews and Christians in Late Antiquity and the Early Middle Ages.* Tübingen: Mohr Siebeck, 2003.

Bede, the Venerable. *Commentary on the Acts of the Apostles.* Translated, with an introduction, by Lawrence T. Martin. Kalamazoo, Mich.: Cistercian Publications, 1989.

Bediako, Kwame. *Christianity in Africa: The Renewal of a Non-Western Religion.* Edinburgh: Edinburgh University Press; Maryknoll, N.Y.: Orbis, 1995.

———. *Jesus in African Culture: A Ghanaian Perspective.* Accra: Asampa Publishers, 1990.

Ben-Chorin, Schalom. *Die Antwort des Jona, Zum Gestaltwandel Israels.* Hamburg: n.p., 1956.

Benner, Drayton C. "Immanuel Kant's Demythologization of Christian Theories of Atonement in Religion within the Limits of Reason Alone." *Evangelical Quarterly* 79, no. 2 (2007): 99-111.

Bennett, Clinton. *Understanding Christian-Muslim Relations: Past and Present.* London: Continuum, 2008.

Berger, Peter L. *The Heretical Imperative.* London: Collins, 1980.

Berkhof, Hendrikus. *The Doctrine of the Holy Spirit.* Atlanta: John Knox, 1976.

Bevans, Stephen B., and Roger P. Schroeder. *Constants in Context: A Theology of Mission for Today.* Maryknoll, N.Y.: Orbis, 2004.

Bhabha, Homi K. *The Location of Culture.* London and New York: Routledge, 1994.

Bhagavadgita. Translated by Ramanand Prasad. EAWC Anthology, 1988. http://eawc.evansville.edu/anthology/gita.htm.

Bharat, Sandy. "Hindu Perspectives on Jesus." In *The Blackwell Companion to Jesus,* edited by Delbert Burkett. Oxford: Wiley-Blackwell, 2011.

Bird, Michael F. *Are You the One Who Is to Come? The Historical Jesus and the Messianic Question.* Grand Rapids: Baker Academic, 2009.

Blocher, Henri. "The Sacrifice of Jesus Christ: The Current Theological Situation." *European Journal of Theology* 8, no. 1 (1999): 23-36.

Bloesch, Donald. *Jesus Christ: Savior and Lord.* Downers Grove, Ill.: InterVarsity, 1997.

Bloom, Alfred. "Shin Buddhism in Encounter with a Religiously Plural World [Pure Land Buddhism]." *Pure Land,* n.s., 8-9 (1992): 17-31.

Boersma, Hans. *Violence, Hospitality, and the Cross: Reappropriating the Atonement Tradition.* Grand Rapids: Baker Academic, 2006.

Boff, Clodovis. *Theology and Praxis: Epistemological Foundations.* Translated by Robert R. Barr. Rev. ed. Maryknoll, N.Y.: Orbis, 1987.

Boff, Leonardo. *Jesus Christ Liberator: A Critical Christology for Our Time.* Translated by Patrick Hughes. Maryknoll, N.Y.: Orbis, 1978.

———. *Passion of Christ, Passion of the World.* Maryknoll, N.Y.: Orbis, 1987.

———. *Trinity and Society.* Translated by Paul Burns. Maryknoll, N.Y.: Orbis, 1998.

Bonhoeffer, Dietrich. *Christology.* Translated by John Bowden. London: Collins, 1966.

———. *Christ the Center.* Translated by John Bowden. New York: Harper and Row, 1960.

———. *Letters and Papers from Prison.* Edited by Eberhard Bethge. Translated by Reginald Fuller and others. Rev. ed. New York: Macmillan, 1967.

Bonino, José Miguez. *Room to Be People.* Philadelphia: Fortress, 1979.

Boonyakiat, Satanun. "A Christian Theology of Suffering in the Context of Theravada Buddhism in Thailand." Ph.D. diss., Fuller Theological Seminary, 2009.

Borg, Marcus J. *Meeting Jesus Again for the First Time: The Historical Jesus and the Heart of Contemporary Faith.* San Francisco: HarperSanFrancisco, 1994.

Boslooper, Thomas. *The Virgin Birth.* London: SCM, 1962.

Braaten, Carl E. "Introduction: The Resurrection in Jewish-Christian Dialogue." In *The Resurrection of Jesus: A Jewish Perspective,* by Pinchas Lapide. Minneapolis: Augsburg, 1983.

Branick, Vincent P. "The Sinful Flesh of the Son of God (Rom 8:3): A Key Image of Pauline Theology." *Catholic Biblical Quarterly* 47, no. 2 (1985): 246-62.

Brock, Rita Nakashima. "And a Little Child Will Lead Us: Christology and Child Abuse." In *Christianity, Patriarchy, and Abuse: A Feminist Critique,* edited by J. Carlson Brown and C. R. Bohn. New York: Pilgrim Press, 1989.

———. "The Feminist Redemption of God." In *Christian Feminism: Visions of a New Humanity,* edited by Judith L. Weidman. San Francisco: Harper and Row, 1984.

———. *Journeys by Heart: A Christology of Erotic Power.* New York: Crossroad, 1988.

Brockington, John. *Hinduism and Christianity.* New York: St. Martin's Press, 1992.

Brown, Colin. *Jesus in European Protestant Thought (1778-1860).* Durham, N.C.: Labyrinth Press, 1985.

———. *Miracles and the Critical Mind.* Grand Rapids: Eerdmans, 1984.

Brown, David. *The Divine Trinity.* Ithaca, N.Y.: Cornell University Press, 1985.

———. "'Necessary' and 'Fitting' Reasons in Christian Theology." In *The Rationality of Religious Belief,* edited by W. J. Abrahams and S. W. Holtzer, pp. 211-30. Oxford: Clarendon, 1987.

Brown, Raymond E. *The Birth of the Messiah: A Commentary on the Infancy Narratives in Matthew and Luke.* Garden City, N.Y.: Doubleday, 1977.

———. *The Death of the Messiah: From Gethsemane to the Grave.* Vol. 1. New York: Doubleday, 1994.

———. *An Introduction to the New Testament.* New York: Doubleday, 1997.

———. *The Virginal Conception and Bodily Resurrection of Jesus.* New York: Paulist, 1992.

Brown, Raymond E., Karl P. Donfried, Joseph A. Fitzmyer, and John Reumann, eds. *Mary in the New Testament: A Collaborative Assessment by Protestant and Roman Catholic Scholars.* Philadelphia: Fortress, 1978.

Brümmer, Vincent. *The Model of Love: A Study in Philosophical Theology.* Cambridge: Cambridge University Press, 1993.

Brunner, Emil. *The Christian Doctrine of Creation and Redemption.* Translated by Olive Wyon. Philadelphia: Westminster, 1952.

———. *Dogmatics.* Translated by Olive Wyon. 3 vols. Philadelphia: Westminster, 1950-1979.

———. *The Mediator: A Study of the Central Doctrine of Christian Faith.* Translated by Olive Wyon. Cambridge: Lutterworth, 2002 [1934].

Buber, Martin. *Der Jude und Sein Judentum: Gesammelte Aufsätze und Reden.* Cologne: n.p., 1963.

———. "The Two Foci of the Jewish Soul." In *Israel and the World: Essays in a Time of Crisis.* New York: Schocken, 1963.

Büchler, Adolf. *Studies in Sin and Atonement in the Rabbinic Literature of the First Century.* New York: Ktav, 1967.

Bujo, Bénézet. *African Theology in Its Social Context.* Maryknoll, N.Y.: Orbis, 1992.

Bultmann, Rudolf. *The History of the Synoptic Tradition.* Translated by John Marsh. New York: Harper and Row, 1963 [1921].

———. *Jesus Christ and Mythology.* New York: Charles Scribner's Sons, 1958.

———. "New Testament and Mythology." In *Kerygma and Myth: A Theological Debate,* edited by Hans Werner Bartsch, pp. 1-44. New York: Harper and Row, 1961.

Burgess, Andrew. *The Ascension in Karl Barth.* Aldershot, Hampshire: Ashgate, 2004.

Busse, H. "Jesu Errettung vom Kreuz in der islamischen Koranexegese von Sure 4:157." *Oriens* 36 (2001): 160-95.

Byrne, Brendan, S.J. "Christ's Pre-existence in Pauline Soteriology." *Theological Studies* 58, no. 2 (1997): 308-30.

Cahill, Lisa Sowle. "The Atonement Paradigm: Does It Still Have Explanatory Value?" *Theological Studies* 68, no. 2 (2007): 418-32.

Campbell, Douglas A. "Reconciliation in Paul: The Gospel of Negation and Transcendence in Galatians 3:28." In *The Theology of Reconciliation,* edited by Colin E. Gunton, pp. 39-65. London and New York: T. & T. Clark, 2003.

Campbell, J. McLeod. *The Nature of the Atonement.* With a new introduction by James B. Torrance. Carberry, Scotland: Handsel Press; Grand Rapids: Eerdmans, 1996; orig. 1856.

Caputo, John, and Michael Scanlon, eds. *God, the Gift, and Postmodernism.* Bloomington: Indiana University Press, 1999.

Carlson Brown, Joanne, and Rebecca Parker. "For God So Loved the World." In *Christianity, Patriarchy, and Abuse: A Feminist Critique,* edited by J. Carlson Brown and C. R. Bohn, pp. 1-30. New York: Pilgrim Press, 1989.

Chan, Mark L. Y. "The Gospel and the Achievement of the Cross." *Evangelical Review of Theology* 33, no. 1 (2009): 19-31.

Charlesworth, James H. *The Historical Jesus: An Essential Guide.* Nashville: Abingdon, 2008.

"Christ Seen by Contemporary Muslim Writers." *Encounter* (Rome) 87 (1982): 3-14.

Chung, Paul S., ed. and trans., with Kim Kyoung-Jae and Veli-Matti Kärkkäinen, co-eds. *Asian Contextual Theology for the Third Millennium: Theology of Minjung in Fourth-Eye Formation.* Eugene, Oreg.: Pickwick/Wipf and Stock, 2006.

Clayton, Philip. *Adventures in the Spirit: God, World, Divine Action.* Edited by Zachary Simpson. Minneapolis: Fortress, 2008.

Cleage, Albert. *The Black Messiah.* New York: Sheed and Ward, 1968.

Clifford, Richard J., and Khaled Anatolios. "Christian Salvation: Biblical and Theological Perspectives." *Theological Studies* 66, no. 4 (2005): 739-69.

Clooney, Francis X., S.J. *Comparative Theology: Deep Learning across Religious Borders.* Oxford: Wiley-Blackwell, 2010.

———. "Comparative Theology: A Review of Recent Books (1989-1995)." *Theological Studies* 56, no. 3 (1995): 521-50.

———. *Hindu God, Christian God: How Reason Helps Break Down the Boundaries between Religions.* Oxford and New York: Oxford University Press, 2001.

———. "Sacrifice and Its Spiritualization in the Christian and Hindu Traditions: A

Study in Comparative Theology." *Harvard Theological Review* 78, no. 3/4 (1985): 361-80.

———. *Theology after Vedānta: An Experiment in Comparative Theology.* Albany: State University of New York Press, 1993.

Coakley, Sarah. "What Does Chalcedon Solve and What Does It Not? Some Reflections on the Status and Meaning of the Chalcedonian 'Definition.'" In *The Incarnation: An Interdisciplinary Symposium on the Incarnation of the Son of God,* edited by Stephen T. Davis et al., pp. 143-63. Oxford: Oxford University Press, 2004.

Cobb, John B., Jr. *Beyond Dialogue: Towards a Mutual Transformation of Christianity and Buddhism.* Philadelphia: Fortress, 1982.

———. *Christ in a Pluralistic Age.* Philadelphia: Westminster, 1975.

———. *The Structure of Christian Existence.* Philadelphia: Westminster, 1967.

Coffey, David. "Spirit Christology and the Trinity." In *Advents of the Spirit: An Introduction to the Current Study of Pneumatology,* edited by Bradford E. Hinze and D. Lyle Dabney, pp. 315-38. Milwaukee: Marquette University Press, 2001.

Cohen, Hermann. "Die Versöhnungs-idee." In H. Cohen, *Jüdische Schriften,* 1:125-39. Berlin: C. A. Schwetschke & Sohn, 1924.

Cohn-Sherbok, Dan. *The Crucified Jew.* London: HarperCollins, 1992.

Cole, Darrell. "Good Wars." *First Things* 116 (October 2001): 27-31. http://www.firstthings.com/article/2007/01/good-wars-22.

Cone, James H. *A Black Theology of Liberation.* 2nd ed. Maryknoll, N.Y.: Orbis, 1986.

———. *God of the Oppressed.* Rev. ed. Maryknoll, N.Y.: Orbis, 1997 [orig. New York: Seabury, 1975].

Cook, Michael J. "Jewish Perspectives on Jesus." In *The Blackwell Companion to Jesus,* edited by Delbert Burkett. Oxford: Wiley-Blackwell, 2011.

Cousins, Ewert H. "Panikkar's Advaitic Trinitarianism." In *The Intercultural Challenge of Raimon Panikkar,* edited by Josef Prabhu, pp. 119-30. Maryknoll, N.Y.: Orbis, 1996.

Cragg, Kenneth. *The Arab Christian.* London: Mowbray, 1992.

———. *The Call of the Minaret.* Rev. ed. Maryknoll, N.Y.: Orbis, 1985 [1956].

———. "'Greater Is God': Contemporary Takbīr; Muslim and Christian." *Muslim World* 71, no. 1 (January 1981): 27-39.

———. "Islam and Incarnation." In *Truth and Dialogue in World Religions: Conflicting Truth Claims,* edited by John Hick. Philadelphia: Westminster, 1974 [published in the U.K. under the title *Truth and Dialogue: The Relationship between World Religions*].

———. *Jesus and the Muslim: An Exploration.* London: George Allen and Unwin, 1985.

———. *Muhammad in the Qur'an: The Task and the Text.* London: Melisende, 2001.

———. *The Weight in the Word: Prophethood; Biblical and Quranic.* Brighton: Sussex Academic Press, 1999.

Cranfield, C. E. B. *The Epistle to the Romans.* Vol. 1. Edinburgh: T. & T. Clark, 1975.

Crisp, Oliver D. "Did Christ Have a *Fallen* Human Nature?" *International Journal of Systematic Theology* 6, no. 3 (2004): 270-88.

———. *Divinity and Humanity: The Incarnation Reconsidered.* Cambridge: Cambridge University Press, 2007.

———. "Kathryn Tanner on Incarnation as Atonement." In *Revisioning Christology: Theology in the Reformed Tradition.* Farnham, Surrey, U.K.: Ashgate, 2011.

———. "Non-Penal Substitution." *International Journal of Systematic Theology* 9, no. 4 (October 2007): 415-33.

———. "Robert Jenson on the Pre-existence of Christ." *Modern Theology* 23, no. 1 (2007): 27-45.

Crossan, John Dominic. *The Birth of Christianity: Discovering What Happened in the Years Immediately after the Execution of Jesus.* San Francisco: HarperSanFrancisco, 1998.

———. *The Historical Jesus: The Life of a Mediterranean Jewish Peasant.* San Francisco: HarperCollins, 1991.

Cullmann, Oscar. *Christology of the New Testament.* Translated by Shirlie C. Guthrie and Charles A. M. Hall. Rev. ed. Philadelphia: Westminster, 1963.

Culpepper, Robert H. *Interpreting the Atonement.* Grand Rapids: Eerdmans, 1966.

Cupitt, Don. "The Finality of Christ." *Theology Today* 78, no. 666 (1975): 618-28.

Dalai Lama. *The Good Heart: A Buddhist Perspective on the Teachings of Jesus.* Boston: Wisdom Publications, 1996.

———. "The Good Heart." In *Jesus beyond Christianity: The Classic Texts,* edited by Gregory A. Barker and Stephen E. Gregg. Oxford: Oxford University Press, 2010.

Daley, Brian E. "'He Himself Is Our Peace' (Ephesians 2:14): Early Christian Views of Redemption in Christ." In *The Redemption: An Interdisciplinary Symposium on Christ as Redeemer,* edited by Stephen T. Davis, Daniel Kendall, S.J., and Gerald O'Collins, S.J. Oxford: Oxford University Press, 2004.

———. "Nature and the 'Mode of Union': Late Patristic Models for the Personal Unity of Christ." In *The Incarnation: An Interdisciplinary Symposium on the Incarnation of the Son of God,* edited by Stephen T. Davis et al. Oxford: Oxford University Press, 2004.

Dalferth, Ingolf U. *Der Auferweckte Gekreuzigte: Zur Grammatik der Christologie.* Tübingen: Mohr Siebeck, 1994.

Daly, Gabriel. "Theology of Redemption in the Fathers." In *Witness to the Spirit: Essays on Revelation, Spirit, Redemption,* edited by Wilfrid Harrington. Dublin: Irish Biblical Association; Manchester: Koinonia Press, 1979.

Daly, Robert J. *The Origins of the Christian Doctrine of Sacrifice.* Philadelphia: Fortress, 1978.

Davidson, Ivor J. "Pondering the Sinlessness of Jesus Christ: Moral Christologies and the Witness of Scripture." *International Journal of Systematic Theology* 10, no. 4 (2008): 372-98.

Davis, John R. *Poles Apart: Contextualizing the Gospel in Asia.* Bangalore: Theological Book Trust, 1998.

Davis, Stephen T. "John Hick on Incarnation and Trinity." In *The Trinity: An Interdisciplinary Symposium on the Trinity,* edited by Stephen T. Davis, Daniel Kendall, S.J., and Gerald O'Collins, S.J. Oxford: Oxford University Press, 1999.

———. *Logic and the Nature of God.* Grand Rapids: Eerdmans, 1983.

Davis, Stephen T., Daniel Kendall, S.J., and Gerald O'Collins, S.J., eds. *The Incarnation: An Interdisciplinary Symposium on the Incarnation of the Son of God.* Oxford: Oxford University Press, 2004.

———, eds. *The Redemption: An Interdisciplinary Symposium on Christ as Redeemer.* Oxford: Oxford University Press, 2004.

Dayton, Donald W. *Theological Roots of Pentecostalism.* Grand Rapids: Zondervan, 1987.

D'Costa, Gavin. *The Meeting of Religions and the Trinity.* Maryknoll, N.Y.: Orbis, 2000.

Dearman, J. Andrew. "Theophany, Anthropomorphism, and the *Imago Dei:* Some Observations about the Incarnation in Light of the Old Testament." In *The Incarnation: An Interdisciplinary Symposium on the Incarnation of the Son of God,* edited by Stephen T. Davis et al., pp. 31-46. Oxford: Oxford University Press, 2004.

Declaration on the Admission of Women to the Ministerial Priesthood (15 October 1976) Sacred Congregation for the Doctrine of the Faith. http://www.ewtn.com/library/curia/cdfinsig.htm.

Deedat, Ahmed. *Crucifixion or Cruci-fiction?* Durban: Islamic Propagation Centre International, 1984.

Del Colle, Ralph. *Christ and the Spirit: Spirit-Christology in Trinitarian Perspective.* New York and Oxford: Oxford University Press, 1994.

———. "Spirit-Christology: Dogmatic Foundations for Pentecostal Charismatic Spirituality." *Journal of Pentecostal Theology* 3 (1993): 91-112.

De Mesa, José M. "Making Salvation Concrete and Jesus Real Trends in Asian Christology." January 1, 1999. Available by permission of *SEDOS* on the Network for Strategic Missions: http://www.strategicnetwork.org/index.php?loc=kb&view=v&id=07429&mode=v&pagenum=1&lang=.

Derrida, Jacques. "Faith and Knowledge: The Two Sources of 'Religion' at the Limits of Reason Alone." Translated by Samuel Weber. In *Religion, Cultural Memory in the Present,* edited by Jacques Derrida and Gianni Vattimo, pp. 1-78. Stanford: Stanford University Press, 1998.

———. *Given Time: 1. Counterfeit Money.* Translated by Peggy Kamuf. Chicago: University of Chicago Press, 1995.

———. "Hospitality, Justice, and Responsibility: A Dialogue with Jacques Derrida." In *Questioning Ethics: Contemporary Debates in Continental Philosophy,* edited by Richard Kearney and Mark Dooley, pp. 65-83. London: Routledge, 1999.

Dewart, Leslie. *The Future of Belief: Theism in a World Come of Age.* New York: Herder, 1966.

Dhavamony, Mariasusai. *Christian Theology of Religions: A Systematic Reflection on the Christian Understanding of World Religions.* Studien zur Interkulturellen Geschichte Des Christentums 108. Frankfurt: Peter Lang, 1998.

Dickson, Kwesi A. *Theology in Africa.* London: Darton, Longman and Todd, 1984.

"The Doctrinal Deliverance of 1910" of the Presbyterian Church (USA). PCA Historical Center, Archives and Manuscript Repository for the Continuing Presbyterian Church. http://www.pcahistory.org/documents/deliverance.html.

Donne, Brian K. "The Significance of the Ascension of Jesus Christ in the New Testament." *Scottish Journal of Theology* 30 (1977): 555-68.

Douglas, J. W. "From Gandhi to Christ: God as Suffering Love." In *Gandhi on Christianity,* edited by R. Ellsberg. Maryknoll, N.Y.: Orbis, 1991.

Douglas, Kelly Brown. *The Black Christ.* Maryknoll, N.Y.: Orbis, 1994.

Driver, G. R. *Understanding the Atonement for the Mission of the Church.* Scottdale, Pa.: Herald, 1986.

Dufourmantelle, Anne, and Jacques Derrida. *Of Hospitality.* Translated by Rachel Bowlby. Stanford: Stanford University Press, 2000.

Dunn, James D. G. "The Ascension of Jesus: A Test Case for Hermeneutics." In *Auferstehung/Resurrection,* edited by Friedrich Avemarie and Hermann Lichtenberger, pp. 301-22. Tübingen: Mohr Siebeck, 2001.

———. *Christology in the Making: A New Testament Inquiry into the Origins of the Doctrine of the Incarnation.* 2nd ed. London: SCM, 1989 [1980].

———. "Incarnation." In *The Christ and the Spirit: Collected Essays of James D. G. Dunn,* vol. 1, *Christology.* Grand Rapids: Eerdmans, 1998.

———. *Jesus and the Spirit: A Study of the Religious and Charismatic Experience of Jesus and the First Christians as Reflected in the New Testament.* Grand Rapids: Eerdmans, 1997.

———. "Rediscovering the Spirit (1)." In *The Christ and the Spirit: Collected Essays of James D. G. Dunn,* vol. 2, *Pneumatology.* Grand Rapids: Eerdmans, 1998.

———. *Romans 1–8.* Dallas: Word, 1988.

Dupré, Louis K. *The Enlightenment and the Intellectual Foundations of Modern Culture.* New Haven: Yale University Press, 2004.

Dupuis, Jacques. *Jesus Christ at the Encounter of World Religions.* Maryknoll, N.Y.: Orbis, 1991.

———. *Toward a Christian Theology of Religious Pluralism.* Maryknoll, N.Y.: Orbis, 1997.

Dyrness, William A. *The Earth Is God's: A Theology of American Culture.* Maryknoll, N.Y.: Orbis, 1997.

Dyrness, William A., and Veli-Matti Kärkkäinen, eds. *Global Dictionary of Theology: A Resource for the Worldwide Church.* Assistant editors, Simon Chan and Juan Martinez. Downers Grove, Ill.: InterVarsity, 2008.

Ebhomielen, Paul Omieka. "Gustaf Aulen's Christus Victor View of Atonement as It Relates to the Demonic in Africa." Ph.D. diss., Baylor University, 1982.

Eckhardt, A. Roy. *Reclaiming the Jesus of History: Christology Today.* Minneapolis: Fortress, 1992.

Edwards, Denis. *Jesus the Wisdom of God: An Ecological Theology.* Maryknoll, N.Y.: Orbis, 1995.

Eggen, Wiel, S.M.A. "Africa and Vasco da Gama's Voyage: Issues and Solution." *African Ecclesial Review* 40, no. 5/6 (1998): 334-41.

Elizondo, Virgilio P. Foreword to *Mañana: Christian Theology from a Hispanic Perspective,* by Justo L. González. Nashville: Abingdon, 1990.

English Translations of the Satyarth Prakash: Literally Exposed of Right Sense (Vedic Reli-

gion) of Maharshi Swami Dayanand Saraswati "The Luther of India" Being Guide to Vedic Hermeneutics. Lahore: Virjananda Press, 1908; reproduced in *JWF.*

Erickson, Millard J. *Christian Theology.* 3 vols. in 1. Grand Rapids: Baker, 1984.

Evans, C. Stephen. *Historical Christ and the Jesus of Faith: The Incarnational Narrative as History.* Oxford: Oxford University Press, 1996.

Evans, Craig A. "Assessing Progress in the Third Quest of the Historical Jesus." *Journal for the Study of the Historical Jesus* 1 (2006). Available at http://www.craigaevans.com/Third_Quest.rev.pdf.

———. *Resurrection and the New Testament.* London: SCM, 1970.

Farquhar, J. N. *The Crown of Hinduism.* 1913. Reprint, New Delhi: Oriental Books Reprint Corporation, 1971.

Farrow, Douglas. "Ascension and Atonement." In *The Theology of Reconciliation,* edited by Colin E. Gunton. London and New York: T. & T. Clark, 2003.

———. *Ascension and Ecclesia: On the Significance of the Doctrine of the Ascension for Ecclesiology and Christian Cosmology.* Grand Rapids: Eerdmans, 1999.

———. "Karl Barth on the Ascension: An Appreciation and Critique." *International Journal of Systematic Theology* 2 (2000): 127-50.

Fee, Gordon D. "Paul and the Metaphors for Salvation." In *The Redemption: An Interdisciplinary Symposium on Christ as Redeemer,* edited by Stephen T. Davis, Daniel Kendall, S.J., and Gerald O'Collins, S.J. Oxford: Oxford University Press, 2004.

———. "St. Paul and the Incarnation: A Reassessment of the Data." In *The Incarnation: An Interdisciplinary Symposium on the Incarnation of the Son of God,* edited by Stephen T. Davis et al., pp. 62-92. Oxford: Oxford University Press, 2004.

Fiddes, Paul F. "Concept, Image and Story in Systematic Theology." *International Journal of Systematic Theology* 11, no. 1 (2009): 3-23.

———. *Past Event and Present Salvation: The Christian Idea of Atonement.* Louisville: Westminster John Knox, 1989.

"Final Document 1." Second European Ecumenical Assembly (EEA2). Graz, Austria, 23 to 29 June 1997. http://www.cec-kek.org/English/Graz1.htm.

Finlan, Stephen. *Options on Atonement in Christian Thought.* Collegeville, Minn.: Michael Glazier Books, 2007.

———. *Problems with Atonement: The Origins of, and Controversy about, the Atonement Doctrine.* Collegeville, Minn.: Liturgical Press, 2005.

Fitzmyer, Joseph, S.J. "Ascension of Christ and Pentecost." *Theological Studies* 45 (1984).

Flannery, Edward H. *The Anguish of the Jews: Twenty-three Centuries of Antisemitism.* Rev. ed. New York: Paulist, 1985 [1971].

Florovsky, Georges. "And Ascended into Heaven." *St. Vladimir's Seminary Quarterly* 2, no. 3 (1954): 23-28.

Ford, David F. "Introduction to Modern Christian Theology." In *The Modern Theologians: An Introduction to Christian Theology in the Twentieth Century,* edited by David F. Ford. 2nd ed. Cambridge: Blackwell, 1997.

Forsyth, P. T. *The Cruciality of the Cross.* New York and London: Hodder and Stoughton, 1909.

———. *The Work of Christ.* London: Hodder and Stoughton, 1910.

Fredericks, James Lee. *Buddhists and Christians: Through Comparative Theology to Solidarity.* Maryknoll, N.Y.: Orbis, 2004.

———. *Faith among Faiths: Christian Theology and Non-Christian Religions.* New York: Paulist, 1999.

Frei, Hans W. *The Eclipse of Biblical Narrative: A Study in Eighteenth and Nineteenth Century Hermeneutics.* New Haven: Yale University Press, 1974.

———. *Theology and Narrative: Selected Essays.* Edited by George Hunsinger and William C. Placher. New York: Oxford University Press, 1993.

———. *Types of Christian Theology.* Edited by George Hunsinger and William C. Placher. New Haven: Yale University Press, 1992.

Friedrich, Gerhard. "Der Brief an die Philipper." In *Die Briefe an die Galater, Epheser, Philipper, Kolosser, Thessalonicher und Philemon,* by J. Becker, H. Conzelmann, and G. Friedrich. Das Neue Testament Deutsch 8. Göttingen: Vandenhoeck & Ruprecht, 1976.

Fulkerson, Mary McClintock. "Feminist Theology." In *The Cambridge Companion to Postmodern Theology,* edited by Kevin J. Vanhoozer. Cambridge: Cambridge University Press, 2003.

Fuller, Daniel. *Easter Faith and History.* London: Tyndale Press, 1968.

Fulljames, Peter. *God and Creation in Intercultural Perspective: Dialogue between the Theologies of Barth, Dickson, Pobee, Nyamiti, and Pannenberg.* Frankfurt am Main and New York: P. Lang, 1993.

Galvin, John P. "Jesus Christ." In *Systematic Theology: Roman Catholic Perspectives,* edited by Francis Schüssler Fiorenza and J. P. Galvin, 1:256-314. Minneapolis: Fortress, 1991.

Gandhi, Mohandas K. *The Message of Jesus Christ.* Bombay: Bharatiya Vidya Bhavan, 1963 [1940].

Garber, Marjorie. *Vested Interest: Cross-Dressing and Cultural Anxiety.* New York: Routledge, 1992.

Geschiere, Peter. *The Modernity of Witchcraft: Politics and the Occult in Postcolonial Africa.* Charlottesville: University Press of Virginia, 1997.

al-Ghazali. *The Ninety-nine Beautiful Names of God.* Translated by David B. Burrell and Nazih Daher. Cambridge: Islamic Texts Society, 1992.

Ghosh, Sananda lal. *Mejja.* Los Angeles: Self-Realization Fellowship, 1980.

Girard, René. *The Girard Reader.* Edited by James G. Williams. New York: Crossroad, 1996.

———. *Things Hidden Since the Foundation of the World.* Translated by Stephen Bann and Michael Metteer. Stanford: Stanford University Press, 1987.

Godbout, Jacques. *The World of the Gift.* Translated by Donald Winkler. Montreal and Ithaca, N.Y.: McGill-Queens University Press, 1999.

Goddard, Hugh. *A History of Christian-Muslim Relations.* Chicago: New Amsterdam Books, 2000.

Gogarten, Friedrich. *Die Verkündigung Jesu Christi.* Heidelberg: Schneider, 1948.

Goldenberg, Naomi. *Changing of the Gods: Feminism and the End of Traditional Religions.* Boston: Beacon Press, 1979.

Goldingay, John. "Old Testament Sacrifice and the Death of Christ." In *Atonement Today,* edited by John Goldingay, pp. 3-20. London: SPCK, 1995.

González, Justo L. *Mañana: Christian Theology from a Hispanic Perspective.* Nashville: Abingdon, 1990.

Gorringe, Timothy. *God's Just Vengeance: Crime, Violence, and the Rhetoric of Salvation.* Cambridge Studies in Ideology and Religion 9. Cambridge: Cambridge University Press, 1966.

Gospel of Sri Ramakrishna, The: Translated into English with an Introduction by Swami Nikhilananda. New York: Ramakrishna-Vivekananda Center, 1984 [1942]; reproduced in *JBC.*

Grant, Jacquelyn. "Womanist Theology: Black Women's Experience as a Source for Doing Theology, with Special Reference to Christology." In *Constructive Christian Theology in the Worldwide Church,* edited by William R. Barr, pp. 337-54. Grand Rapids and Cambridge: Eerdmans, 1997.

Grau, Marion. "Divine Commerce: A Postcolonial Christology for Times of Neocolonial Enterprise." In *Postcolonial Theologies: Divinity and Empire,* edited by Catherine Keller, Michael Nausner, and Mayra Rivera, pp. 164-84. St. Louis: Chalice, 2004.

Green, Joel B., and Mark D. Baker. *Recovering the Scandal of the Cross: Atonement in New Testament and Contemporary Contexts.* Downers Grove, Ill.: InterVarsity, 2000.

Greenberg, Irving. "Judaism, Christianity, and Partnership after the Twentieth Century." In *Christianity in Jewish Terms,* edited by Tikva Frymer-Kensky et al., pp. 25-35. Boulder, Colo.: Westview Press, 2000.

Grenz, Stanley J. *Theology for the Community of God.* Grand Rapids: Eerdmans, 1994.

Grey, Mary. *Redeeming the Dream: Feminism, Redemption, and Christian Tradition.* London: SPCK, 1989.

Griffith, Sidney H. *The Church in the Shadow of the Mosque: Christians and Muslims in the World of Islam.* Princeton: Princeton University Press, 2008.

Griffiths, Bede. *Vedanta and Christian Faith.* Los Angeles: Dawn Horse Press, 1973.

Griffiths, Paul J. "Hindu Perceptions of Christianity in the Twentieth Century." In *Christianity through Non-Christian Eyes,* edited by P. J. Griffiths. Maryknoll, N.Y.: Orbis, 1990.

Gross, Rita M. "Meditating on Jesus." In *Buddhists Talk about Jesus, Christians Talk about the Buddha,* edited by Rita M. Gross and Terry C. Muck. New York: Continuum, 2000.

Gross, Rita M., and Terry C. Muck, eds. *Buddhists Talk about Jesus, Christians Talk about the Buddha.* New York: Continuum, 2000.

Grotius, Hugo. *Defense of the Catholic Faith on the Satisfaction of Christ against Faustus Socinus.* Translated by F. H. Foster. In *Bibliotheca Sacra,* edited by E. A. Park et al. Vol. 36. Andover: Warren F. Draper, 1897.

Gunkel, Hermann. *The Influence of the Holy Spirit: The Popular View of the Apostolic*

Age and the Teaching of the Apostle Paul. Translated by R. A. Harrisville and P. A. Quanbeck II. Philadelphia: Fortress, 1979 [orig. 1888].

Gunton, Colin E. *The Actuality of Atonement: A Study of Metaphor, Rationality, and the Christian Tradition.* Edinburgh: T. & T. Clark; Grand Rapids: Eerdmans, 1989.

———. "Two Dogmas Revisited: Edward Irving's Christology." *Scottish Journal of Theology* 41, no. 3 (1988): 359-76.

Gutiérrez, Gustavo. *Essential Writings.* Edited by James B. Nicholoff. Minneapolis: Fortress, 1996.

———. *On Job: God-Talk and the Suffering of the Innocent.* Translated by Matthew J. O'Connell. Maryknoll, N.Y.: Orbis, 1987.

———. *The Power of the Poor in History: Selected Writings.* Maryknoll, N.Y.: Orbis, 1983.

———. *A Theology of Liberation: History, Politics, and Salvation.* Translated and edited by Sister Caridad Inda and John Eagleson. Maryknoll, N.Y.: Orbis, 1986 [1973]; rev. ed. with a new introduction, 1988.

Habets, Myk. "Spirit Christology: Seeing in Stereo." *Journal of Pentecostal Theology* 11, no. 2 (2003): 199-234.

Habgood, John. Preface to *Many Mansions: Interfaith and Religious Tolerance,* edited by Dan Cohn-Sherbok. London: Bellew Publishing, 1992.

Hagner, Donald A. *The Jewish Reclamation of Jesus: An Analysis and Critique of the Modern Jewish Study of Jesus.* Grand Rapids: Zondervan, 1984.

———. "Paul in Modern Jewish Thought." In *Pauline Studies: Essays Presented to F. F. Bruce on His 70th Birthday,* edited by D. A. Hagner and M. J. Harris. Exeter: Paternoster, 1980.

Haight, Roger J., S.J. "The Case for Spirit Christology." *Theological Studies* 53, no. 2 (1992): 257-87.

———. *The Future of Christology.* New York: Continuum, 2005.

Hamerton-Kelly, R. G. *Preexistence, Wisdom, and the Son of Man: A Study of the Idea of Pre-existence in the New Testament.* Cambridge: Cambridge University Press, 1973.

Hampson, Daphne. *After Christianity.* Valley Forge, Pa.: Trinity, 1996.

Hanh, Thich Nhat. *The Heart of Understanding: Commentaries on the Prajnaparamita Heart Sutra.* Edited by Peter Levitt. Berkeley, Calif.: Parallax Press, 1988.

———. "The Individual, Society, and Nature." In *The Path of Compassion: Writings on Socially Engaged Buddhism,* edited by Fred Eppsteiner. 2nd rev. ed. Berkeley, Calif.: Parallax Press, 1988.

———. *Our Appointment with Life: Discourse on Living Happily in the Present Moment.* Translation and commentary on *The Sutra on Knowing the Better Way to Live Alone (Bhaddekaratta Sutta).* Translated by Annabel Laity. Berkeley, Calif.: Parallax Press, 1990.

———. *Zen Keys.* Translated by Albert and Jean Low. Garden City, N.Y.: Anchor Books, 1991.

Hardin, Michael. "Sacrificial Language in Hebrews: Reappraising René Girard." In *Vio-*

lence Renounced: René Girard, Biblical Studies, and Peacemaking, edited by Willard M. Swartley. Telford, Pa.: Pandora; Scottdale, Pa.: Herald, 2000.

Harnack, A. von. *History of Dogma.* Vol. 2. Translated by Neil Buchanan. 1894. Reprint, New York: Russell and Russell, 1958.

———. *What Is Christianity?* Translated by Thomas Bailey Sanders. 2nd rev. ed. London: Williams and Norgate; New York: Putnam, 1902, 1957.

Harris, Elizabeth J. "My Unfinished Business with the Buddha." In *Buddhists Talk about Jesus, Christians Talk about the Buddha,* edited by Rita M. Gross and Terry C. Muck, pp. 89-94. New York: Continuum, 2000.

Hauerwas, Stanley, Nancey Murphy, and Mark Nation, eds. *Theology without Foundations: Religious Practice and the Future of Theological Truth.* Nashville: Abingdon, 1994.

Hegel, G. W. F. *Lectures on the Philosophy of History.* Vol. 3, *The Consummate Religion.* Edited by Peter C. Hodgson. Berkeley and Los Angeles: University of California Press, 1985.

Heim, S. Mark. *Saved from Sacrifice: A Theology of the Cross.* Grand Rapids: Eerdmans, 2006.

Hengel, Martin. *Crucifixion in the Ancient World and the Folly of the Message of the Cross.* Philadelphia: Fortress, 1977.

———. *The Son of God: The Origin of Christology and the History of Jewish-Hellenistic Religion.* Translated by John Bowden. Philadelphia: Fortress, 1976.

Henriksen, Jan-Olav. *Desire, Gift, and Recognition: Christology and Postmodern Philosophy.* Grand Rapids: Eerdmans, 2009.

Heppe, Heinrich. *Reformed Dogmatics.* Edited by Ernst Bizer. Translated by G. T. Thomson. London: Allen and Unwin, 1950.

Heschel, Susannah. *Abraham Geiger and the Jewish Jesus.* Chicago: University of Chicago Press, 1998.

———. "Jesus as a Theological Transvestite." In *Judaism Since Gender,* edited by Miriam Peskowitz and Laura Levitt. New York: Routledge, 1997.

Heyward, Carter. *Saving Jesus from Those Who Are Right: Rethinking What It Means to Be Christian.* Minneapolis: Fortress, 1999.

Hick, F. C. N. *The Fullness of Sacrifice.* London: Macmillan, 1930.

Hick, John. *A Christian Theology of Religions: The Rainbow of Faiths.* Louisville: Westminster John Knox, 1995. [Published in the U.K. as *The Rainbow of Faiths: Critical Dialogue on Religious Pluralism.* London: SCM, 1995.]

———. "Critique" of "Christ beyond Creative Transformation," by John B. Cobb Jr. In *Encountering Jesus: Debate in Christology,* edited by S. T. Davis, pp. 158-60. Atlanta: John Knox, 1988.

———. *God Has Many Names.* Philadelphia: Westminster, 1982.

———. *An Interpretation of Religion: Human Responses to the Transcendent.* London: Macmillan, 1989.

———. "Islam and Christianity." A lecture delivered by Hick to the Iranian Institute of Philosophy, under the auspices of the Iranian Institute for Interreligious Dialogue in Tehran, in March 2005. http://www.johnhick.org.uk/jsite/index.php

?option=com_content&view=article&id=58:islam&catid=37:articles &Itemid=58.

———. *The Metaphor of God Incarnate: Christology in a Pluralistic Age.* London: SCM, 1993.

———. "The Non-Absoluteness of Christianity." In *The Myth of Christian Uniqueness: Toward a Pluralistic Theology of Religions,* edited by J. Hick and P. F. Knitter. Maryknoll, N.Y.: Orbis, 1987.

———. "On Conflicting Religious Truth Claims." *Religious Studies* 19 (1983): 485-91.

———. *Problems of Religious Pluralism.* London: Macmillan, 1988.

———. "A Recent Development within Christian Monotheism." In *Christians, Muslims, and Jews,* edited by D. Kerr and D. Cohn-Sherbok. Canterbury: University of Kent, 1983.

———. "Rethinking Christian Doctrine in Light of Religious Pluralism." In *Christianity and the Wider Ecumenism,* edited by Peter C. Phan. New York: Paragon House, 1990.

———. "Trinity and Incarnation in the Light of Religious Pluralism." In *Three Faiths — One God: A Jewish, Christian, Muslim Encounter,* edited by John Hick and Edmund S. Meltzer. Albany: State University of New York Press, 1989.

———, ed. *The Myth of God Incarnate.* London: SCM, 1977.

Historic Creeds and Confessions. Edited by Rick Brannan. Available on Christian Classics Ethereal Library Web site: http://www.ccel.org/ccel/brannan/hstcrcon.html.

Hodge, Charles. *Systematic Theology.* Vol. 2. Grand Rapids: Eerdmans, 1940 [1871].

Hodgson, Peter C. "Hegel's Christology: Shifting Nuances in the Berlin Lectures." *Journal of the American Academy of Religion* 53, no. 1 (1985): 23-40.

Hoefer, Herbert. "Gospel Proclamation of the Ascended Lord." *Missiology* 33, no. 4 (2005): 43-49.

Holy Qur'ān, The: A New English Translation of Its Meanings. © 2008 Royal Aal al-Bayt Institute for Islamic Thought. Amman, Jordan. This version of the Qur'an is also available online at http://altafsir. com.

Hopkins, Jasper. *A Companion to the Study of St. Anselm.* Minneapolis: University of Minnesota Press, 1971.

Hopkins, Julie M. *Towards a Feminist Christology: Jesus of Nazareth, European Women, and the Christological Crisis.* Grand Rapids: Eerdmans, 2005.

Hume, David. *An Enquiry concerning Human Understanding.* Edited by L. A. Selby Bigge. Oxford: Clarendon, 1902 [1777].

Hunter, Harold D. *Spirit Baptism: A Pentecostal Alternative.* New York: University Press of America, 1983.

Hurtado, L. W. "The Origins of the Worship of Christ." *Themelios* 19 (January 1994): 4-8.

Ibn-al-Arabi. *The Bezels of Wisdom.* Translated by R. W. J. Austin. London: SPCK, 1980.

Idinopulos, Thomas A. "Christianity and the Holocaust." *Cross Currents* 28, no. 3 (Fall 1978): 257-67.

Idinopulos, Thomas A., and Roy Bowen Ward. "Is Christology Inherently Anti-

Semitic? A Critical Review of Rosemary Ruether's *Faith and Fratricide*." *Journal of the American Academy of Religions* 45, no. 2 (1977): 193-214.

Imbach, Josef. *Three Faces of Jesus: How Jews, Christians, and Muslims See Him*. Translated by Jane Wilde. Springfield, Ill.: Templegate Publishers, 1992.

Inagaki, Hisao. *The Three Pure Land Sutras*. Kyoto: Nagata Bunshodo, 1994.

Ives, Christopher, ed. *Divine Emptiness and Historical Fullness: A Buddhist-Jewish-Christian Conversation with Asao Mabe*. Valley Forge, Pa.: Trinity, 1995.

Jamros, D. P. "Hegel on the Incarnation: Unique or Universal?" *Theological Studies* 56, no. 2 (1995): 276-300.

Jantzen, Grace M. *Becoming Divine: Towards a Feminist Philosophy of Religion*. Bloomington: Indiana University Press, 1999.

Jenkins, Philip. *The Next Christendom: The Coming of Global Christianity*. Oxford: Oxford University Press, 2011.

Jenson, Robert W. *Systematic Theology*. Vol. 1, *The Triune God*. Oxford: Oxford University Press, 1997.

Joh, Wonhee Anne. *Heart of the Cross: A Postcolonial Christology*. Louisville: Westminster John Knox, 2006.

———. "The Transgressive Power of Jeong: A Postcolonial Hybridization of Christology." In *Postcolonial Theologies: Divinity and Empire*, edited by Catherine Keller, Michael Nausner, and Mayra Rivera. St. Louis: Chalice, 2004.

John of the Cross, St. *Ascent of Mount Carmel*. Translated by E. Allison Peers. Turnbridge Wells: Burns and Oates, 1983.

Johnson, Elizabeth. "Jesus, the Wisdom of God: A Biblical Basis for Non-Androcentric Christology." *Ephemerides theologicae lovanienses* 61, no. 4 (1985): 261-94.

———. *She Who Is: The Mystery of God in Feminist Theological Discourse*. New York: Crossroad, 1993.

Johnson, Luke T. "The New Testament's Anti-Jewish Slander and the Conventions of Ancient Polemic." *Journal of Biblical Literature* 108 (1989): 419-41.

Jung, Carl. *Psychology and Religion: West and East*. Translated by R. F. C. Hull. New York: Pantheon, 1958.

Jüngel, Eberhard. *God as the Mystery of the World: On the Foundation of the Theology of the Crucified One in the Dispute between Theism and Atheism*. Translated by Darrell Guder. Grand Rapids: Eerdmans, 1983.

———. *Justification: The Heart of the Christian Faith*. Translated by Jeffrey F. Cayzer. Edinburgh: T. & T. Clark, 2001.

Juntunen, Sammeli. "The Notion of 'Gift' (Donum) in Luther's Theology." In *Luther between Paul and Present*, edited by Ulrik Nissen et al. Helsinki: Luther-Agricola Society, 2004.

Kabasele, Francois. "Christ as Ancestor and Elder Brother." In *Faces of Jesus in Africa*, edited by Robert J. Schreiter. Maryknoll, N.Y.: Orbis, 1991.

———. "Christ as Chief." In *Faces of Jesus in Africa*, edited by R. J. Schreiter. Maryknoll, N.Y.: Orbis, 1991.

Kähler, Martin. *The So-Called Historical Jesus and the Historic Biblical Christ*. Translated by Carl E. Braaten. Philadelphia: Fortress, 1964 [1896].

Kant, Immanuel. *Perpetual Peace: A Philosophical Essay* [1795]. Translation and introduction by M. Campbell Smith. London: Swan Sonneschein and Co., 1903.

———. *Religion within the Limits of Reason Alone.* Translated by Theodore M. Greene and Hoyt H. Hudson. Harper Torchbook/The Cloister Library edition. New York: Harper and Row, 1960.

Kapic, Kelly M. "The Son's Assumption of a Human Nature: A Call for Clarity." *International Journal of Systematic Theology* 3, no. 2 (2001): 154-66.

Kapic, Kelly M., and W. van der Lugt. "The Ascension of Jesus and the Descent of the Holy Spirit in Patristic Perspective: A Theological Reading." *Evangelical Quarterly* 79, no. 1 (2007): 23-33.

Kärkkäinen, Veli-Matti. "Dialogue, Witness, and Tolerance: The Many Faces of Interfaith Encounters." *Theology, News & Notes* 57, no. 2 (Fall 2010): 29-33.

———. *An Introduction to the Theology of Religions: Biblical, Historical, and Contemporary Perspectives.* Downers Grove, Ill.: InterVarsity, 2003.

———. *Pneumatology: The Holy Spirit in Ecumenical, International, and Contextual Perspective.* Grand Rapids: Baker Academic, 2002.

———. *The Trinity: Global Perspectives.* Louisville: Westminster John Knox, 2007.

Kasper, Walter. *The God of Jesus Christ.* Chestnut Ridge, N.Y.: Crossroad, 1986.

———. *Jesus the Christ.* Translated by V. Green. London: Burns and Oates; New York: Paulist, 1976.

Kaufman, Gordon D. *In Face of Mystery: A Constructive Theology.* Cambridge: Harvard University Press, 1993.

Kavunkal, Jacob. "The Mystery of God in and through Hinduism." In *Christian Theology in Asia,* edited by Sebastian C. H. Kim. Cambridge: Cambridge University Press, 2008.

Keller, Catherine, Michael Nausner, and Mayra Rivera, eds. *Postcolonial Theologies: Divinity and Empire.* St. Louis: Chalice, 2004.

Kelly, J. N. D. *Early Christian Doctrines.* Rev. ed. San Francisco: Harper, 1978.

Kelly, John G. "The Cross, the Church, and the Jewish People." In *Atonement Today,* edited by John Goldingay. London: SPCK, 1995.

Kelsey, David H. *Proving Doctrine: The Uses of Scripture in Modern Theology.* Harrisburg, Pa.: Trinity, 1999.

Kepnes, Steven. "'Turn Us to You and We Shall Return': Original Sin, Atonement, and Redemption in Jewish Terms." In *Christianity in Jewish Terms,* edited by Tikva Frymer-Kensky et al., pp. 293-319. Boulder, Colo.: Westview Press, 2000.

Kerr, Hugh Thomson. "The Presence of Absence." *Theology Today* 43, no. 1 (1986): 1-5.

Kesich, Veselin. "Resurrection, Ascension and the Giving of the Spirit." *Greek Orthodox Theological Review* 25, no. 3 (Fall 1980): 249-60.

Kettler, Christian D. "The Vicarious Beauty of Christ: The Aesthetics of the Atonement." *Theology Today* 64, no. 1 (2007): 14-24.

Khalidi, Tarif. *The Muslim Jesus: Sayings and Stories in Islamic Literature.* Cambridge, Mass., and London: Harvard University Press, 2000.

Kierkegaard, Søren. *Journals and Papers.* Edited and translated by Howard V. Hong and Edna H. Hong. Bloomington: Indiana University Press, 1967.

———. *Philosophical Fragments.* Translated by David F. Swenson. Revised by Howard V. Vong. Princeton: Princeton University Press, 1962.

Kim, Seyoon. *Paul and the New Perspective: Second Thoughts on the Origin of Paul's Gospel.* Grand Rapids: Eerdmans, 2002.

Kitarō, Nishida. *Last Writings.* Translated by David A. Dilworth. Honolulu: University of Hawai'i Press, 1987.

Klausner, Joseph. *Jesus of Nazareth: His Life, Times, and Teaching.* Translated by Herbert Danby. New York: Macmillan, 1925.

Klein, C. *Anti-Judaism in Christian Theology.* Translated by Edward Quinn. Philadelphia: Fortress, 1978.

Knitter, Paul F. "Christian Salvation: Its Nature and Uniqueness — an Interreligious Proposal." *New Theology Review* 7, no. 4 (1994): 33-46.

———. *Jesus and the Other Names: Christian Mission and Global Responsibility.* Maryknoll, N.Y.: Orbis, 1996.

———. *No Other Name? A Critical Survey of Christian Attitudes toward the World Religions.* Maryknoll, N.Y.: Orbis, 1985.

———. *One Earth, Many Religions: Multifaith Dialogue and Global Responsibility.* Maryknoll, N.Y.: Orbis, 1995.

———. "Toward a Liberation Theology of Religions." In *The Myth of Christian Uniqueness: Toward a Pluralistic Theology of Religions,* edited by John Hick and Paul F. Knitter. Maryknoll, N.Y.: Orbis, 1987.

Knox, J. *The Humanity and Divinity of Christ: A Study of Pattern in Christology.* Cambridge: Cambridge University Press, 1967.

Kogan, Michael S. *Opening the Covenant: A Jewish Theology of Christianity.* Oxford: Oxford University Press, 2008.

Kole, Cece. "Jesus as Healer?" In *Faces of Jesus in Africa,* edited by R. J. Schreiter. Maryknoll, N.Y.: Orbis, 1991.

Kotsko, Adam. *The Politics of Redemption: The Social Logic of Salvation.* London: T. & T. Clark, 2010.

Krieger, D. J. "Methodological Foundations for Interreligious Dialogue." In *The Intercultural Challenge of Raimon Panikkar,* edited by Josef Prabhu. Maryknoll, N.Y.: Orbis, 1996.

Krishnananda, Swami. *The Philosophy of the Bhagavadgita.* Rishikesh, India: Divine Life Society Sivananda Ashram, n.d.

Kulandran, Sabapathy. *Grace in Christianity and Hinduism.* Cambridge: James Clarke, 2000 [1964].

Küng, Hans. "Christianity and World Religions: The Dialogue with Islam as One Model." *Muslim World* 77 (1987): 80-95.

———. *Christianity and World Religions: Path to Dialogue.* New York: Doubleday, 1986.

———. "A Christian Response [to *Religious Practice: Rite, Myth, and Meditation*]." In *Christianity and the World Religions: Paths to Dialogue with Islam, Hinduism, and Buddhism,* by Hans Küng, with Josef van Ess, Heinrich von Stietencron, and Heinz Bechert, translated by Peter Heinegg. Maryknoll, N.Y.: Orbis, 1986.

———. *Does God Exist? An Answer for Today.* New York: Random House, 1981.

Kuschel, K.-J. *Born before All Time? The Dispute over Christ's Origin.* Translated by John Bowden. London: SCM; New York: Crossroad, 1992.

Küster, Volker. *The Many Faces of Jesus Christ: Intercultural Christology.* Translated by John Bowden. Maryknoll, N.Y.: Orbis, 2001.

Ladd, G. E. *The Presence of the Future: Eschatology of Biblical Realism.* Rev. ed. Grand Rapids: Eerdmans, 1996 [1974].

La Due, William J. *Jesus among the Theologians: Contemporary Interpretations of Christ.* Harrisburg, Pa.: Trinity, 2001.

Lampe, Geoffrey. *God as Spirit.* Oxford: Clarendon, 1977.

———. "The Holy Spirit and the Person of Christ." In *Christ, Faith, and History: Cambridge Studies in Christology,* edited by S. W. Sykes and J. P. Clayton. Cambridge: Cambridge University Press, 1972.

Langmead, Ross. "Transformed Relationships: Reconciliation as the Central Model for Mission." *Mission Studies* 25 (2008): 5-20.

Lapide, Franz. *Jewish Monotheism and Christian Trinitarian Doctrine: A Dialogue by Pinchas Lapide and Jürgen Moltmann.* Translated by Leonard Swidler. Philadelphia: Fortress, 1981.

Lapide, Pinchas. *Israelis, Jews, and Jesus.* Translated by Peter Heinegg. Garden City, N.Y.: Doubleday, 1979.

———. *The Resurrection of Jesus: A Jewish Perspective.* Minneapolis: Augsburg, 1983.

Larson, G. "Contra Pluralism." *Soundings: An Interdisciplinary Journal* 73, no. 2/3 (Summer/Fall 1990): 303-26. Reprinted in *The Intercultural Challenge of Raimon Panikkar: Essays in Honor of Raimon Panikkar,* edited by Josef Prabhu. Maryknoll, N.Y.: Orbis, 1996.

Latourette, Kenneth Scott. *A History of Christianity.* Vol. 1, *Beginnings to 1500.* Rev. ed. New York: Harper and Row, 1975.

Lee, Jung Young. "Ancestor Worship: From a Theological Perspective." In *Ancestor Worship and Christianity in Korea,* edited by J. Y. Lee. Studies in Asian Thought and Religion 8. Lampeter, Dyfed, Wales: Mellen House, 1988.

———. *The Theology of Change: A Christian Concept of God in an Eastern Perspective.* Maryknoll, N.Y.: Orbis, 1979.

———. *The Trinity in Asian Perspective.* Nashville: Abingdon, 1999.

Lefebure, Leo D. *The Buddha and the Christ: Explorations in Buddhist and Christian Dialogue.* Maryknoll, N.Y.: Orbis, 1993.

———. *Revelation, the Religions, and Violence.* Maryknoll, N.Y.: Orbis, 2000.

Legge, James. *Christianity in China: Nestorianism, Roman Catholicism, Protestantism.* London: Trübner and Co., 1888.

Leirvik, Oddbjørn. *Images of Jesus Christ in Islam.* 2nd ed. London and New York: Continuum, 2010.

Levenson, J. D. *The Death and Resurrection of the Beloved Son: The Transformation of Child Sacrifice in Judaism and Christianity.* New Haven: Yale University Press, 1993.

Levinas, Emmanuel. *Basic Philosophical Writings.* Edited by Adriaan T. Peperzak, Simon Critchley, and Robert Bernasconi. Bloomington: Indiana University Press, 1991.

———. "God and Philosophy." Translated by R. Cohen. *Philosophy Today* 22 (1978): 127-45.

———. *Of God Who Comes to Mind.* Translated by Bettina Bergo. Stanford: Stanford University Press, 1998.

Levison, J., and P. Pope-Levison, "Christology: 4. The New Contextual Christologies; Liberation and Inculturation." In *Global Dictionary of Theology,* edited by Veli-Matti Kärkkäinen and William Dyrness. Downers Grove, Ill.: InterVarsity, 2008.

Lindbeck, George A. *The Nature of Doctrine: Religion and Theology in a Postliberal Age.* Philadelphia: Westminster, 1984.

Lipner, Julius J. "Ancient Banyan: An Inquiry into the Meaning of 'Hinduness.'" *Religious Studies* 32 (1996): 109-26.

Lossky, Vladimir. *The Mystical Theology of the Eastern Church.* New York: St. Vladimir's Seminary Press, 1976.

Luedemann, Gerd. *The Resurrection of Jesus: History, Experience, Theology.* London: SCM; Minneapolis: Fortress, 1994.

Luther, Martin. *Luther's Works.* American edition. Edited by Jaroslav Pelikan and Helmut T. Lehman. 55 vols. Libronix Digital Library. Minneapolis: Fortress, 2002.

———. Weimarer Ausgabe (the Weimar edition of Luther's works). 120 vols. Weimar, 1883-2009.

Lyden, John C. "Atonement in Judaism and Christianity: Towards a Rapprochement." *Journal of Ecumenical Studies* 29, no. 1 (Winter 1992): 47-54.

Lyonnet, Stanislas. "The Terminology of Redemption." In *Sin, Redemption, and Sacrifice: A Biblical and Patristic Study.* Analecta Biblica 48. Rome: Biblical Institute, 1970.

Machida, Soho. "Jesus, Man of Sin: Toward a New Christology in the Global Era." In *Buddhists Talk about Jesus, Christians Talk about the Buddha,* edited by Rita M. Gross and Terry C. Muck, pp. 59-76. New York: Continuum, 2000.

Mackintosh, H. R. *The Doctrine of the Person of Jesus Christ.* New York: Charles Scribner's Sons, 1913.

Macquarrie, Jon. *Jesus Christ in Modern Thought.* London and Philadelphia: SCM and Trinity, 1990.

Maimela, Simon S. "The Atonement in the Context of Liberation Theology." *Journal of Theology for Southern Africa* 39 (1982): 45-54.

Makransky, John J. "Buddhist Perspectives on Truth in Other Religions: Past and Present [Tibetan Buddhism]." *Theological Studies* 64 (2003): 334-61.

Mannermaa, Tuomo. *Kaksi rakkautta: Johdatus Lutherin uskonmaailmaan.* Suomalaisen Teologisen Kirjallisuusseuran julkaisuja 194, 2. painos. Helsinki: STKJ, 1995 [1983].

———. "Why Is Luther So Fascinating? Modern Finnish Luther Research." In *Union with Christ: The New Finnish Interpretation of Luther,* edited by Carl E. Braaten and Robert W. Jenson, pp. 1-20. Grand Rapids: Eerdmans, 1998.

Marshall, Christopher. *Beyond Retribution: A New Testament Vision of Justice, Crime, and Punishment.* Grand Rapids: Eerdmans, 2001.

Martin, Ralph P. *Carmen Christi: Philippians 2:5-11 in Recent Interpretations and in the Setting of Early Christian Worship.* Rev. ed. Grand Rapids: Eerdmans, 1983.

Marxsen, Willi. "The Resurrection of Jesus as a Historical and Theological Problem." In *The Significance of the Message of the Resurrection for Faith in Jesus Christ,* edited by C. F. D. Moule. London: SCM, 1968.

Mauss, Marcel. *Essay on the Gift.* London: Routledge, 1990 [1924].

Maxwell, David R. "The Resurrection of Christ: Its Importance in the History of the Church." *Concordia Journal* 34, no. 1/2 (2008): 22-37.

Mbiti, John S. *Bible and Theology in African Christianity.* Nairobi: Oxford University Press, 1986.

———. "Some African Concepts of Christology." In *Christ and the Younger Churches: Theological Contributions from Asia, Africa, and Latin America,* edited by G. F. Vicedom, pp. 51-62. London: SPCK, 1972.

McClean, John Andrew. "Anticipation in the Thought of Wolfhart Pannenberg." Ph.D. diss., Melbourne College of Divinity, 2010.

McCormack, Bruce. *For Us and Our Salvation: Incarnation and Atonement in the Reformed Tradition.* Studies in Reformed Theology and History 1. Princeton: Princeton Theological Seminary, 1993.

McCready, Douglas. *He Came Down from Heaven: The Preexistence of Christ and the Christian Faith.* Downers Grove, Ill.: InterVarsity, 2005.

———. "'He Came Down from Heaven': The Preexistence of Christ Revisited." *Journal of the Evangelical Theological Society* 40, no. 3 (1997): 419-32.

McDonnell, Kilian, O.S.B. "The Determinative Doctrine of the Holy Spirit." *Theology Today* 39, no. 2 (1982): 142-61.

McFague, Sallie. *Metaphorical Theology: Models of God in Religious Language.* Minneapolis: Fortress, 1982.

McGrath, Alister. "Conclusion." In *Four Views on Salvation in a Pluralistic World,* edited by Dennis L. Okholm and Timothy R. Phillips, pp. 200-209. Grand Rapids: Zondervan, 1996.

McIlroy, David H. "Towards a Relational and Trinitarian Theology of Atonement." *Evangelical Quarterly* 80, no. 1 (2008): 13-32.

McIntyre, John. *The Shape of Christology: Studies in the Doctrine of the Person of Christ.* 2nd ed. Edinburgh: T. & T. Clark, 1998.

McKnight, Edgar V. *Jesus Christ in Scripture and History: Poetic and Sectarian Perspective.* Macon, Ga.: Mercer University Press, 1999.

McLaughlin, Eleanor. "Feminist Christologies: Re-Dressing the Tradition." In *Reconstructing the Christ Symbol: Essays in Feminist Christology,* edited by Maryanne Stevens. New York: Paulist, 1993.

Melanchthon, Philipp. *Loci Communes Theologici.* In *Melanchthon and Bucer,* edited by Wilhelm Pauck. Philadelphia: Westminster, 1969.

Mendelssohn, Moses. *Jerusalem; or, On Religious Power and Judaism.* Translated by Allan Arkush. Hanover, N.H.: University Press of New England, 1983.

Merad, Ali. *Christ according to the Qur'an* (*Encounter* 1980-81). Documents for Muslim-Christian Understanding 69. Rome: Pontifical Institute for Arabic and Islamic Studies (PISAI), November 1980.

Merrill, John E. "Of the Tractate of John of Damascus on Islam." *Muslim World* 41 (1951): 88-89. Available at www.answering-islam.org/Books/MW/john_d.htm.

Meshal, Reem A., and M. Reza Pirbhai. "Islamic Perspectives on Jesus." In *The Blackwell Companion to Jesus,* edited by Delbert Burkett. Oxford: Wiley-Blackwell, 2011.

Meyer, Birgit. *Translating the Devil: Religion and Modernity among the Ewe in Ghana.* Edinburgh: Edinburgh University Press, 1999.

Migliore, Daniel L. *Faith Seeking Understanding: An Introduction to Christian Theology.* 2nd ed. Grand Rapids: Eerdmans, 2004.

Milbank, John. "Stories of Sacrifice." *Contagion* 2 (1995): 75-102.

———. *Theology and Social Theory: Beyond Secular Reason.* Oxford: Basil Blackwell, 1993.

Mir, Mustansir. "Islamic Views of Jesus." In *JWF.*

Moberly, R. C. *Atonement and Personality.* London: John Murray, 1924 [1901].

Moffett, Samuel Hugh. *A History of Christianity in Asia.* Vol. 1, *Beginnings to 1500.* San Francisco: HarperSanFrancisco, 1992.

Mofokeng, Takatso Alfred. *The Crucified among the Crossbearers: Towards a Black Christology.* Kampen, South Africa: Uitgeversmaatschappij J. H. Kok, 1983.

Molnar, Paul D. *Incarnation and Resurrection: Towards a Contemporary Understanding.* Grand Rapids: Eerdmans, 2007.

Moltmann, Jürgen. *The Church in the Power of the Spirit: A Contribution to Messianic Ecclesiology.* Translated by Margaret Kohl. London: SCM, 1977.

———. *The Crucified God: The Cross of Christ as the Foundation and Criticism of Christian Theology.* Translated by Margaret Kohl. Minneapolis: Fortress, 1993.

———. *Experiences in Theology: Ways and Forms of Christian Theology.* Translated by Margaret Kohl. Minneapolis: Fortress, 2000.

———. *God in Creation: A New Theology of Creation and the Spirit of God.* Translated by Margaret Kohl. Minneapolis: Fortress, 1993.

———. "God Is Unselfish Love." In *The Emptying God: A Buddhist-Jewish-Christian Conversation,* edited by John B. Cobb Jr. and Christopher Ives. Maryknoll, N.Y.: Orbis, 1990.

———. *The Spirit of Life: A Universal Affirmation.* Translated by Margaret Kohl. Minneapolis: Fortress, 2001.

———. *Theology of Hope: On the Ground and the Implications of a Christian Eschatology.* London: SCM, 1967.

———. *The Trinity and the Kingdom of God: The Doctrine of God.* Translated by Margaret Kohl. San Francisco: Harper and Row; London: SCM, 1981.

———. *The Way of Jesus Christ: Christology in Messianic Dimensions.* Translated by Margaret Kohl. Minneapolis: Fortress, 1993 [1989].

Moore, Stephen D. *God's Beauty Parlor: And Other Queer Spaces in and around the Bible.* Contraversions. Stanford: Stanford University Press, 2001.

Morris, T. V. *The Logic of God Incarnate.* Ithaca, N.Y.: Cornell University Press, 1986.

Moule, C. F. D. "The Theology of Forgiveness." In *From Fear to Faith: Studies of Suffering and Wholeness,* edited by Norman Autton. London: SPCK, 1971.

Munck, Thomas. *The Enlightenment: A Comparative Social History, 1721-1794.* London: Arnold, 2000.

Murphy, Nancey. *Anglo-American Postmodernity: Philosophical Perspectives on Science, Religion, and Ethics.* Boulder, Colo.: Westview Press, 1997.

———. *Beyond Liberalism and Fundamentalism: How Modern and Postmodern Philosophy Set the Theological Agenda.* Valley Forge, Pa.: Trinity, 1996.

Nagao, Gajin. "The Life of the Buddha: An Interpretation." *Eastern Buddhist,* n.s., 20, no. 2 (1987): 1-31.

Nasr, Seyyed Hossein. *Islamic Life and Thought.* London: Kazi Publications, 1981.

———. "Response to Hans Küng's Paper on Christian-Muslim Dialogue." *Muslim World* 77 (1987): 96-105.

Nazir-Ali, Michael. *Frontiers in Muslim-Christian Encounter.* Oxford: Regnum, 1987. See especially chapters "Christology in an Islamic Context" and "A Christian Assessment of the Cult of Prophet-Veneration."

Nelson-Pallmeyer, Jack. *Is Religion Killing Us? Violence in the Bible and the Quran.* Harrisburg, Pa.: Trinity, 2003.

———. *Jesus against Christianity: Reclaiming the Missing Jesus.* Harrisburg, Pa.: Trinity, 2001.

Nestorius. *The Bazaar of Heracleides.* Translated from Syriac and edited by G. R. Driver and Leonard Hodgson. London: Oxford University Press, 1925. www.ccel.org.

Netland, Harold. *Encountering Religious Pluralism: The Challenge to Christian Faith and Mission.* Downers Grove, Ill.: InterVarsity, 2001.

Neufeldt, R. "Hindu Views of Christ." In *Hindu-Christian Dialogue: Perspectives and Encounters,* edited by Harold Coward, pp. 162-75. Maryknoll, N.Y.: Orbis, 1990.

Newlands, George, and Allen Smith. *Hospitable God: The Transformative Dream.* Farnham, Surrey, U.K.: Ashgate, 2010.

Newman, N. A., ed. *The Early Christian-Muslim Dialogue: A Collection of Documents from the First Three Islamic Centuries (632-900 A.D.), Translations with Commentary.* Hatfield: Interdisciplinary Biblical Research Institute, 1993.

Newman, Paul W. *Spirit Christology: Recovering the Biblical Paradigm of Christian Faith.* New York: University Press of America, 1987.

Niebuhr, Reinhold. *Nature and Destiny of Man: A Christian Interpretation.* 2 vols. New York: Charles Scribner's Sons, 1941.

Nietzsche, Friedrich. *The Gay Science.* Edited by Bernard Williams. Cambridge Texts in the History of Philosophy. Cambridge: Cambridge University Press, 2001 (1887).

Nishitani, Keiji. *Religion and Nothingness.* Los Angeles: University of California Press, 1982.

Nissiotis, Nikos A. "Pneumatological Christology as a Presupposition of Ecclesiology." In *Oecumenica: An Annual Symposium of Ecumenical Research, 1967,* edited by Friedrich Wilhelm Kantzenbach and Vilmos Vajta. Minneapolis: Augsburg, 1967.

Norris, Richard. "'Chalcedon Revisited': A Historical and Theological Reflection." In

New Perspectives on Historical Theology: Essays in Memory of John Meyendorff, edited by Brad Nassif, pp. 140-58. Grand Rapids: Eerdmans, 1996.

Nyamiti, Charles. "African Ancestral Veneration and Its Relevance to the African Churches." *African Christian Studies* (Nairobi) 9, no. 3 (1993).

———. "African Christologies Today." In *Faces of Jesus in Africa,* edited by R. J. Schreiter. Maryknoll, N.Y.: Orbis, 1991.

———. *Christ as Our Ancestor: Christology from an African Perspective.* Gwero, Zimbabwe: Mambo Press, 1984.

———. "The Trinity from an African Ancestral Perspective." *African Christian Studies* 12, no. 4 (1996): 38-74.

Nyima, Thuken Chökyi. *The Crystal Mirror.* In *Jesus beyond Christianity: The Classic Texts,* edited by Gregory A. Barker and Stephen E. Gregg. Oxford: Oxford University Press, 2010.

Ochs, Peter. "Israel's Redeemer Is the One to Whom and with Whom She Prays." In *The Redemption: An Interdisciplinary Symposium on Christ as Redeemer,* edited by Stephen T. Davis, Daniel Kendall, S.J., and Gerald O'Collins, S.J. Oxford: Oxford University Press, 2004.

O'Collins, Gerald, S.J. *Christology: A Biblical, Historical, and Systematic Study of Jesus.* New York: Oxford University Press, 1995.

———. "The Incarnation: The Critical Issues." In *The Incarnation: An Interdisciplinary Symposium on the Incarnation of the Son of God,* edited by Stephen T. Davis et al. Oxford: Oxford University Press, 2004.

———. *Jesus Our Redeemer: A Christian Approach to Salvation.* Oxford: Oxford University Press, 2007.

———. "Redemption: Some Crucial Issues." In *The Redemption: An Interdisciplinary Symposium on Christ as Redeemer,* edited by Stephen T. Davis, Daniel Kendall, S.J., and Gerald O'Collins, S.J. Oxford: Oxford University Press, 2004.

Ogden, Schubert. "Some Thoughts on a Christian Theology of Interreligious Dialogue." *Criterion* 11 (1994): 5-10.

Onaiyekan, John. "Christological Trends in Contemporary African Theology." In *Constructive Christian Theology in the Worldwide Church,* edited by William R. Barr, pp. 355-68. Grand Rapids: Eerdmans, 1997.

Onyinah, Opoku. "Deliverance as a Way of Confronting Witchcraft in Contemporary Africa: Ghana as a Case Study." In *The Spirit in the World: Emerging Pentecostal Theologies in Global Contexts,* edited by V.-M. Kärkkäinen, pp. 181-202. Grand Rapids: Eerdmans, 2009.

Ott, Heinrich. "The Convergence: Sunyata as a Dynamic Event." In *Divine Emptiness and Historical Fullness: A Buddhist-Jewish-Christian Conversation with Asao Mabe,* edited by Christopher Ives. Valley Forge, Pa.: Trinity, 1995.

Otto, Rudolf. *India's Religion of Grace.* London: SCM, 1930.

Panikkar, Raimundo. *The Cosmotheandric Experience: Emerging Religious Consciousness,* edited with introduction by Scott Eastham. Maryknoll, N.Y.: Orbis, 1993.

———. *The Intrareligious Dialogue.* New York: Paulist, 1978.

———. "The Jordan, the Tiber, and the Ganges: Three Kairological Moments of

Christic Self-Consciousness." In *The Myth of Christian Uniqueness: Toward a Pluralistic Theology of Religions,* edited by John Hick and Paul F. Knitter. Maryknoll, N.Y.: Orbis, 1987.

———. "The Myth of Pluralism: The Tower of Babel — a Meditation on Non-Violence." *Cross Currents* 29, no. 2 [1979]: 214.

———. *The Trinity and the Religious Experience of Man: Icon-Person-Mystery.* Maryknoll, N.Y.: Orbis; London: Darton, Longman and Todd, 1973.

———. *The Unknown Christ of Hinduism: Towards an Ecumenical Christophany.* Rev. ed. Maryknoll, N.Y.: Orbis, 1981.

———. "Verstehen als Überzeugtsein." In *Neue Anthropologie,* edited by H.-G. Gadamer and P. Vogler. Philosophische Anthropologie 7. Stuttgart: Thieme, 1975.

Pannenberg, Wolfhart. *Anthropology in Theological Perspective.* Translated by Matthew O'Connell. Philadelphia: Westminster, 1985.

———. "Faith and Reason." In *Basic Questions in Theology,* translated by George H. Kehm, 2:46-64. Philadelphia: Fortress, 1971.

———. "God's Love and the Kenosis of the Son: A Response to Masao Abe." In *Divine Emptiness and Historical Fullness: A Buddhist-Jewish-Christian Conversation with Asao Mabe,* edited by Christopher Ives. Valley Forge, Pa.: Trinity, 1995.

———. *Jesus — God and Man.* Translated by Paul L. Wilkins and Duane A. Priebe. 2nd ed. Philadelphia: Westminster, 1977.

———. *Systematic Theology.* Translated by Geoffrey W. Bromiley. 3 vols. Grand Rapids: Eerdmans, 1991, 1994, 1998.

———. *Theology and the Philosophy of Science.* Translated by Francis McDonagh. London: Darton, Longman and Todd, 1976.

———. "Toward a Theology of the History of Religions." In *Basic Questions in Theology,* translated by George H. Kehm, 2:65-118. Philadelphia: Fortress, 1970.

———. "What Is Truth?" In *Basic Questions in Theology,* translated by George H. Kehm, 2:1-27. Philadelphia: Fortress, 1970.

Park, Andrew Sung. *The Wounded Heart of God: The Asian Concept of Han and the Christian Doctrine of Sin.* Nashville: Abingdon, 1993.

Parratt, John. Introduction to *An Introduction to Third World Theologies,* edited by John Parratt, pp. 1-15. Cambridge: Cambridge University Press, 2004.

Parrinder, George. *Jesus in the Qur'an.* London and Oxford: Sheldon Press and One-world, 1995.

———. *Witchcraft: A Critical Study of the Belief in Witchcraft from the Records of Witch Hunting in Europe Yesterday and Africa Today.* Harmondsworth: Penguin Books, 1958.

Pawlikowski, John. *Christ in the Light of Christian-Jewish Dialogue.* New York: Paulist, 1982; Eugene, Oreg.: Wipf and Stock, 2001.

———. "Christology, Anti-Semitism, and Christian-Jewish Bonding." In *Reconstructing Christian Theology,* edited by Rebecca S. Chopp and Mark Lewis Taylor. Minneapolis: Fortress, 1994.

Peacore, Linda D. *The Role of Women's Experience in Feminist Theologies of Atonement.* Eugene, Oreg.: Pickwick, 2010.

Pearson, Birger. "I Thessalonians 2:13-16: A Deutero-Pauline Interpolation." *Harvard Theological Review* 64 (1971): 79-94.

Pelikan, Jaroslav. *The Christian Tradition: A History of the Development of Doctrine.* Vol. 1, *The Emergence of the Catholic Tradition (100-600).* Vol. 2, *The Spirit of Eastern Christendom (600-1700).* Vol. 3, *The Growth of Medieval Theology (600-1300).* Vol. 4, *Reformation of Church and Dogma (1300-1700).* Chicago: University of Chicago Press, 1971, 1974, 1978, 1984.

Peperzak, Adriaan. *To the Other: An Introduction to the Philosophy of Emmanuel Levinas.* West Lafayette, Ind.: Purdue University Press, 1993.

Phan, Peter C. *Christianity with an Asian Face: Asian American Theology in the Making.* Maryknoll, N.Y.: Orbis, 2003.

Pieris, Aloysius. *An Asian Theology of Liberation.* Maryknoll, N.Y.: Orbis, 1988.

———. "Western Christianity and Asian Buddhism." *Dialogue* 7, no. 2 (May-August 1980): 49-85.

Pinnock, Clark H. *Flame of Love: A Theology of the Holy Spirit.* Downers Grove, Ill.: InterVarsity, 1996.

Placher, William C. "Christ Takes Our Place: Rethinking Atonement." *Interpretation* 53 (1999): 5-20.

Pobee, John. *Toward an African Theology.* Nashville: Abingdon, 1979.

Polkinghorne, John. *Exploring Reality: The Intertwining of Science and Religion.* New Haven: Yale University Press; London: SCM, 2005.

———, ed. *The Work of Love: Creation as Kenosis.* Grand Rapids: Eerdmans, 2001.

Pope-Levison, Priscilla, and John R. Levison. *Jesus in Global Contexts.* Louisville: Westminster John Knox, 1992.

Prabhavananda, Swami. *Sermon on the Mount according to Vedanta.* N.p.: Vedanta Society of Southern California, 1992 [1963].

Prabhupāda, A. C. Bhaktivedanta Swami. *Bhagavad-Gita as It Is.* Abridged version. Los Angeles: Bhaktivedanta Book Trust, 1976.

Pui-lan, Kwok. *Postcolonial Imagination and Feminist Theology.* Louisville: Westminster John Knox, 2005.

Queen, Christopher S., and Sally B. King, eds. *Engaged Buddhism: Buddhist Liberation Movements in Asia.* Albany: SUNY Press, 1996.

Quine, W. V. O. "Two Dogmas of Empiricism." In *From a Logical Point of View: Nine Logico-Philosophical Essays.* Cambridge: Harvard University Press, 1953.

Quinn, Philip L. "Abelard on Atonement: 'Nothing Unintelligible, Arbitrary, Illogical, or Immoral about It.'" In *Reasoned Faith,* edited by Eleonore Stump. Ithaca, N.Y.: Cornell University Press, 1993.

Radhakrishnan, Swami. *The Recovery of Faith.* Delhi: Hind Pocket Books, 1967.

Rae, Murray. "A Remnant People: The Ecclesia as Sign of Reconciliation." In *The Theology of Reconciliation,* edited by Colin E. Gunton. London and New York: T. & T. Clark, 2003.

Rahner, Karl. "Christology within an Evolutionary View of the World." In *Theological Investigations* 5. London: Darton, Longman and Todd, 1966.

———. "Current Problems in Christology." In *Theological Investigations* 1, translated by Cornelius Ernst, pp. 149-200. London: Darton, Longman and Todd, 1965.

———. "Die deutsche protestantische Christologie der Gegenwart." *Theologie der Zeit* 1 (1936): 189-202.

———. "Dogmatische Bemerkungen zur Jungfrauengeburt." In *Zum Thema Jungfrauengeburt,* edited by K. Suso Frank et al. Stuttgart: KBW, 1970.

———. *Foundations of Christian Faith: An Introduction to the Idea of Christianity.* Translated by William W. Dych. New York: Crossroad, 1982.

———. "Jesus Christus, III.B." In *Lexikon für Theologie und Kirche,* edited by Josef Höfer and Karl Rahner, 5:956. 2nd ed. Freiburg: Herder, 1975.

———. "On the Theology of Incarnation." In *Theological Investigations* 4, translated by Kevin Smyth. Baltimore: Helicon Press, 1966.

Räisänen, Heikki. "Maria/Mariafrömmigkeit. I. Neues Testament." In *Theologische Realenzyklopädie,* ed. Gerhard Krause et al., 22:115-19. Berlin and New York: Walter de Gruyter, 1992.

———. "The Portrait of Jesus in the Qur'an: Reflections of a Biblical Scholar." *Muslim World* 70 (1980): 122-33.

Rashdall, Hastings. *The Idea of Atonement in Christian Theology.* New York: Macmillan, 1919.

Rauschenbusch, Walter. *A Theology for the Social Gospel.* New York: Macmillan, 1917.

Ray, Darby K. *Deceiving the Devil: Atonement, Abuse, and Ransom.* Cleveland: Pilgrim Press, 1998.

Ritschl, Albrecht. *The Christian Doctrine of Justification and Reconciliation.* Translated by H. R. Mackintosh and A. B. Macaulay. New York: Charles Scribner's, 1900.

Roberts, J. Deotis. *Black Theology in Dialogue.* Philadelphia: Westminster, 1987.

Robinson, John A. T. *The Human Face of God.* London: SCM, 1972.

Robinson, Neil. *Christ in Islam and Christianity.* New York: State University of New York Press, 1991.

Rodger, Simeon. "The Soteriology of Anselm of Canterbury, an Orthodox Perspective." *Greek Orthodox Theological Review* 34, no. 1 (1989): 19-43.

Rosato, Philip J. "Spirit Christology: Ambiguity and Promise." *Theological Studies* 38, no. 2 (1977): 423-49.

Rosenau, James N. *Distant Proximities: Dynamics beyond Globalization.* Princeton: Princeton University Press, 2003.

Rosenzweig, Franz. *The Star of Redemption.* Translated from the 2nd ed. of 1930 by William W. Hallo. New York: Holt, Rinehart and Winston, 1970.

Roy, Raja Ram Mohun. [Pseudonymous letter]. In Jogendra Chungder Ghose, ed., *The English Works of Raja Ram Mohun Roy.* Calcutta: Srikanta Roy, 1901. [Vol. 1, pp. 287-90 reproduced in *JBC,* pp. 159-62.]

———. *The English Works of Raja Ram Mohun Roy.* Vol. 3, *The Precepts of Jesus — a Guide to Peace and Happiness; Extracted from the Books of the New Testament Ascribed to the Four Evangelists with Translations into Sanscrit and Bengalee.* Calcutta: Baptist Mission Press, 1820. [Part I, pp. 172-75, reproduced in *JBC,* pp. 162-64.]

Rubenstein, Richard L. "Holocaust, Sunyata, and Holy Nothingness: An Essay in Interreligious Dialogue." In *Divine Emptiness and Historical Fullness: A Buddhist-Jewish-Christian Conversation with Asao Mabe,* edited by Christopher Ives, pp. 93-112. Valley Forge, Pa.: Trinity, 1995.

Ruether, Rosemary Radford. *Faith and Fratricide: The Theological Roots of Anti-Semitism.* New York: Seabury Press, 1974.

———. *Introducing Redemption in Christian Feminism.* Introductions in Feminist Theology 1. Sheffield: Sheffield Academic Press, 1998.

———. *Sexism and God-Talk: Toward a Feminist Theology.* Boston: Beacon Press, 1983.

———. *To Change the World: Christology and Cultural Criticism.* New York: Crossroad, 1981.

———. *Women and Redemption: A Theological History.* Minneapolis: Fortress, 1998.

Russell, Robert J. "Eschatology and Physical Cosmology: A Preliminary Reflection." In *The Far-Future Universe: Eschatology from a Cosmic Perspective,* edited by George F. R. Ellis. Philadelphia: Templeton Foundation Press, 2002.

Saarinen, Risto. *God and Gift: An Ecumenical Theology of Giving.* Unitas Books. Collegeville, Minn.: Liturgical Press, 2005.

Saddharma-Pundarika; or, The Lotus of the True Law. Translated by H. Kern. Sacred Books of the East 21 (1884). http://www.sacred-texts.com/bud/lotus/index.htm.

Sahas, Daniel J. *John of Damascus on Islam: The "Heresy of the Ishmaelites."* Leiden: Brill, 1972.

Samuel, Reda. "The Incarnation in Arabic Christian Theology from the Beginnings to the Mid–Eleventh Centuries." Ph.D. tutorial, Fuller Theological Seminary, School of Intercultural Studies, Spring 2010.

Schebera, Richard. "Comparative Theology: A New Method of Interreligious Dialogue." *Dialogue and Alliance* 17, no. 1 (2003): 7-18.

Schillebeeckx, Eduard. *Jesus: An Experiment in Christology.* Translated by Hubert Hoskins. New York: Seabury Press, 1979.

Schimanowski, Gottfried. *Weisheit und Messias: Die Jüdischen Voraussetzungen der Urchristlichen Präexistenzchristologie.* Tübingen: J. C. B. Mohr, 1985.

Schleiermacher, Friedrich. *The Christian Faith.* Edited by H. R. Mackintosh and J. S. Stewart. Edinburgh: T. & T. Clark, 1999.

———. *On Religion: Speeches to Its Cultural Despisers.* Translated and edited by Richard Crouter. Glasgow: Cambridge University Press, 1996.

Schmidt, James. "What Enlightenment Project?" *Political Theory* 28 (2000): 734-57.

———, ed. *What Is Enlightenment? Eighteenth-Century Answers and Twentieth-Century Questions.* Philosophical Traditions 7. Berkeley: University of California Press, 1996.

Schmidt-Leukel, Perry. "Buddha and Christ as Mediators of the Transcendent: A Christian Perspective." In *Buddhism and Christianity in Dialogue,* edited by Perry Schmidt-Leukel, pp. 151-75. Gerald Weisfeld Lectures 2004. London: SCM, 2005.

Schmiechen, Peter. *Saving Power: Theories of Atonement and Form of the Church.* Grand Rapids: Eerdmans, 2005.

Scholem, G. "Zum Verständnis der messianischen Idee." *Judaica* 1. Frankfurt: n.p., 1963.

Schoonenberg, Piet. *The Christ: A Study of the God-Man Relationship in the Whole of Creation and in Jesus Christ.* Translated by Della Couling. New York: Herder and Herder, 1971.

———. "Spirit Christology and Logos Christology." *Bijdragen* 38 (1977): 350-75.

———. "Trinity — the Consummated Covenant: Theses on the Doctrine of the Trinitarian God." *Studies in Religion* 5, no. 2 (1976): 111-16.

Schreiter, Robert J. Foreword to *The Many Faces of Jesus Christ: Intercultural Christology,* by Volker Küster. Translated by John Bowden. Maryknoll, N.Y.: Orbis, 2001.

———. "Jesus Christ in Africa Today." In *Faces of Jesus in Africa,* edited by R. J. Schreiter. Maryknoll, N.Y.: Orbis, 1991.

———. *Reconciliation: Mission and Ministry in a Changing Social Order.* Maryknoll, N.Y.: Orbis, 1992.

Schrift, Alan D., ed. *The Logic of Gift.* New York: Routledge, 1997.

Schumann, Olaf. *Jesus the Messiah in Muslim Thought.* Delhi, India: ISPCK, 2002.

Schüssler Fiorenza, Elisabeth, and David Tracy, eds. *The Holocaust as Interruption.* Concilium 175. Edinburgh: T. & T. Clark, 1984.

Schwager, Raymund. *Jesus in the Drama of Salvation.* New York: Crossroad, 1999.

———. *Must There Be Scapegoats? Violence and Redemption in the Bible.* Translated by Maria L. Assad. San Francisco: Harper and Row, 1987.

Schwarz, Hans. *Christology.* Grand Rapids: Eerdmans, 1998.

Schweitzer, Albert. *The Quest of the Historical Jesus: A Critical Study of Its Progress from Reimarus to Wrede.* Translated by W. Montgomery. London: A. & C. Black, 1910.

Schwöbel, Christoph. "Reconciliation: From Biblical Observations to Dogmatic Reconstruction." In *The Theology of Reconciliation,* edited by Colin E. Gunton. London and New York: T. & T. Clark, 2003.

Segal, Alan F. "The Incarnation: The Jewish Milieu." In *The Incarnation: An Interdisciplinary Symposium on the Incarnation of the Son of God,* edited by Stephen T. Davis et al., pp. 116-39. Oxford: Oxford University Press, 2004.

———. *Rebecca's Children: Judaism and Christianity in the Roman World.* Cambridge: Harvard University Press, 1986.

Segundo, Juan Luis. *An Evolutionary Approach to Jesus of Nazareth.* Maryknoll, N.Y.: Orbis, 1988.

Select Library of the Nicene and Post-Nicene Fathers of the Christian Church, A. 1st ser. Edited by Philip Schaff. 14 vols. Edinburgh, 1886-1890. Public domain; available at www.ccel.org.

Select Library of the Nicene and Post-Nicene Fathers of the Christian Church, A. 2nd ser. Edited by Philip Schaff and Henry Wace. 14 vols. Edinburgh, 1890-1899. Public domain; available at www.ccel.org.

Sen, Keshub Chunder. *Keshub Chunder Sen's Lectures in India.* 2nd ed. Calcutta: Brahmo Tract Society, 1886.

Sharma, Arvind. *Classical Hindu Thought: An Introduction.* Oxford: Oxford University Press, 2000.

Shedd, W. G. T. *Dogmatic Theology.* Vol. 2. New York: Scribners, 1888.

Sherman, Robert. *King, Priest, and Prophet: A Trinitarian Theology of Atonement.* New York: T. & T. Clark, 2004.

Shults, F. LeRon. "Anthropology and Christology: The *Anhypostasis-Enhypostasis* Formula." In *Reforming Theological Anthropology: After the Philosophical Turn to Relationality.* Grand Rapids: Eerdmans, 2003.

———. *Christology and Science.* Grand Rapids: Eerdmans, 2008.

———. "A Dubious Christological Formula: From Leontius of Byzantium to Karl Barth." *Theological Studies* 57, no. 3 (1996): 431-46.

———. *The Post Foundationalist Task of Theology: Wolfhart Pannenberg and the New Theological Rationality.* Grand Rapids: Eerdmans, 1999.

———. *Reforming Theological Anthropology: After the Philosophical Turn to Relationality.* Grand Rapids: Eerdmans, 2003.

Sibbes, Richard. "A Description of Christ, Matt. XII, 18." In *Works of Richard Sibbes,* edited by, and with memoir by, Alexander B. Grosart, 1:2-31. Edinburgh: Banner of Truth Trust, 1973.

Siddiqi, Muzammil. "A Muslim Response to John Hick: Trinity and Incarnation in the Light of Religious Pluralism." In *Three Faiths — One God: A Jewish, Christian, Muslim Encounter,* edited by John Hick and Edmund Meltzer. Albany: State University of New York Press, 1989.

Simmer-Brown, Judith. "Suffering and Social Justice: A Buddhist Response to the Gospel of Luke." *Buddhist-Christian Studies* 16 (1996): 99-112.

Simon, Wolfgang. *Die Messeopferthyeologie Martin Luthers.* Tübingen: Mohr Siebeck, 2003.

Skinner, Tom. *How Black Is the Gospel?* New York: Lippincott, 1970.

Smart, Ninian, and Steve Konstantine. *Christian Systematic Theology in a World Context.* Minneapolis: Fortress, 1991.

Smith, James K. A. "The Call as Gift: The Subject's Donation in Marion and Levinas." In *The Hermeneutics of Charity: Interpretation, Selfhood, and Postmodern Faith,* edited by James K. A. Smith and Henry Isaac Venema, pp. 217-27. Grand Rapids: Brazos, 2004.

Sobrino, Jon. *Christology at the Crossroads: A Latin American Approach.* Maryknoll, N.Y.: Orbis, 1978.

———. *Jesus in Latin America.* Maryknoll, N.Y.: Orbis, 1987.

———. *Jesus the Liberator: A Historical-Theological Reading of Jesus of Nazareth.* Translated by P. Burns and F. McDonah. Maryknoll, N.Y.: Orbis, 1993.

Sölle, Dorothee. *Christ Our Representative.* Philadelphia: Fortress, 1967.

Song, C. S. "Christian Mission toward Abolition of the Cross." In *The Scandal of a Crucified World,* edited by Yacob Tesfai, pp. 130-48. Maryknoll, N.Y.: Orbis, 1994.

———. *Jesus, the Crucified People.* New York: Crossroad, 1990.

Soskice, Janet Martin. *Metaphor and Religious Language.* New York: Oxford University Press, 1985.

Stinton, Diane. *Jesus of Africa: Voices of Contemporary African Christology.* Maryknoll, N.Y.: Orbis, 2004.

Stout, Jeffrey. *Ethics after Babel: The Languages of Morals and Their Discontents.* Princeton: Princeton University Press, 2001.

Strauss, David F. *The Life of Jesus Critically Examined.* 2nd ed. in 1 vol. Translated from the 4th German ed. by George Eliot. London: Schwann Sonnenschein; New York: Macmillan and Co., 1892.

Suchocki, Marjorie Hewitt. "Sunyata, Trinity, and Community." In *Divine Emptiness and Historical Fullness: A Buddhist-Jewish-Christian Conversation with Asao Mabe,* edited by Christopher Ives. Valley Forge, Pa.: Trinity, 1995.

Sugirtharajah, R. S., ed. *Asian Faces of Jesus.* Maryknoll, N.Y.: Orbis, 1993.

———. "Complacencies and Cul-de-sacs: Christian Theologies and Colonialism." In *Postcolonial Theologies: Divinity and Empire,* edited by Catherine Keller, Michael Nausner, and Mayra Rivera. St. Louis: Chalice, 2004.

Suzuki, D. T. *An Introduction to Zen Buddhism.* Edited by Christmas Humphreys. London: Rider, 1995.

Sweetman, J. Windrow. *Islam and Christian Theology: A Study of the Interpretation of Theological Ideas in the Two Religions.* London: Lutterworth, 1945.

Swinburne, Richard. *The Christian God.* Oxford: Clarendon; New York: Oxford University Press, 1994.

Tai, Susan H. C., and Y. H. Wong, "Advertising Decision Making in Asia: 'Glocal' versus 'Regcal' Approach." *Journal of Managerial Issues* 10 (Fall 1998): 318-40.

Tanner, Kathryn. *Christ the Key.* Cambridge: Cambridge University Press, 2010.

———. *Economy of Grace.* Minneapolis: Fortress, 2005.

———. *Jesus, Humanity, and the Trinity.* Minneapolis: Fortress, 2001.

Taylor, Mark Lewis. *The Executed God: The Way of the Cross in Lockdown America.* Minneapolis: Fortress, 2001.

Taylor, Vincent. *Jesus and His Sacrifice.* London: Macmillan, 1948.

Tennent, Timothy C. *Theology in the Context of World Christianity: How the Global Church Is Influencing the Way We Think about and Discuss Theology.* Grand Rapids: Zondervan, 2007.

Terrell, JoAnne Marie. *Power in the Blood? The Cross in the African American Experience.* Maryknoll, N.Y.: Orbis, 1998.

Theissen, Gerd. *Sociology of Early Palestinian Christianity.* Philadelphia: Fortress, 1978.

Thomas, D. "The Miracles of Jesus in Early Islamic Polemic." *Journal of Semitic Studies* 39, no. 2 (1994): 221-43.

Thomas, M. M. *The Acknowledged Christ of the Indian Renaissance.* London: SCM, 1969.

———. "My Pilgrimage in Mission." *International Bulletin of Missionary Research* 13, no. 1 (1989): 28-31.

Thompson, P. E. S. "Anatomy of Sacrifice: A Preliminary Investigation." In *New Testament Christianity for Africa and the World,* edited by M. E. Glasswell and E. W. Fashole-Luke. London: SPCK, 1974.

Thurman, Howard. *Jesus and the Disinherited.* Nashville: Abingdon, 1949.

Tillich, Paul. *Systematic Theology.* Vols. 1-2. Chicago: University of Chicago Press, 1951, 1957.

Tinker, George. "Jesus, Corn Mother, and Conquest: Christology and Colonialism." In *Native American Religious Identity: Unforgotten God,* edited by Jace Weaver, pp. 134-54. Maryknoll, N.Y.: Orbis, 1998.

"Tipitaka: The Pali Canon." Edited by John T. Bullitt, in *Access to Insight,* May 29, 2010. http://www.accesstoinsight.org/tipitaka/index.html.

Torrance, Thomas F. *Atonement: The Person and Work of Christ.* Edited by Robert T. Walker. Milton Keynes, U.K.: Paternoster; Downers Grove, Ill.: InterVarsity, 2009.

———. *The Mediation of Christ.* Rev. ed. Colorado Springs: Helmers and Howard, 1992.

———. *Space, Time, and Resurrection.* Grand Rapids: Eerdmans, 1998.

———. *The Trinitarian Faith: The Evangelical Theology of the Ancient Catholic Church.* Edinburgh: T. & T. Clark, 1991.

Tracy, David. "Comparative Theology." In *The Encyclopedia of Religion,* edited by Mircea Eliade and Charles J. Adam, vol. 14. New York: Macmillan, 1987.

Troeltsch, Ernst. "On the Historical and Dogmatic Methods in Theology [1898]." Translated by Jack Forstman. In *Gesammelte Schriften,* 2:728-53. Tübingen: J. C. B. Mohr, 1913. http://faculty.tcu.edu/grant/hhit/Troeltsch.pdf.

Ubruhe, J. O. "Traditional Sacrifice: A Key to the Heart of the Christian Message." *Journal of Theology for Southern Africa* 95 (1996): 13-22.

Vähäkangas, Mika. "African Approaches to the Trinity." In *African Theology Today,* vol. 1, edited by Emmanuel Katongole. Scranton, Pa.: University of Scranton Press, 2002.

———. *In Search of Foundations for African Catholicism: Charles Nyamiti's Theological Methodology.* Leiden, Boston, and Cologne: Brill, 1999.

———. "Trinitarian Processions as Ancestral Relationships in Charles Nyamiti's Theology: A European Lutheran Critique." *Revue Africaine de Théologie* 21 (1997): 61-75.

Van Dyk, Leanne. "Do Theories of Atonement Foster Abuse?" *Dialog* 35, no. 1 (Winter 1996): 21-25.

Van Engen, Charles E. "The Glocal Church: Locality and Catholicity in a Globalizing World." In *Globalizing Theology: Belief and Practice in an Era of World Christianity,* edited by Craig Ott, Harold A. Netland, and Wilbert R. Shenk. Grand Rapids: Baker Academic, 2006.

Vanhoozer, Kevin J. *The Drama of Doctrine: A Canonical-Linguistic Approach to Christian Theology.* Louisville: Westminster John Knox, 2005.

———. *The Trinity in a Pluralistic Age: Theological Essays on Culture and Religion.* Grand Rapids: Eerdmans, 1997.

Van Huyssteen, J. Wentzel. *Essays in Postfoundationalist Theology.* Grand Rapids: Eerdmans, 1997.

Vimalakīrti Nirdeśa Sutra. Translated by Robert A. F. Thurman. Pennsylvania State University. 1976. http://www2.kenyon.edu/Depts/Religion/Fac/Adler/Reln260/Vimalakirti.htm.

Vivekananda. *The Complete Works of Vivekananda.* Calcutta: Advaita Ashrama, 12th impr., 1999. [Vol. 8, pp. 159-60 reproduced in *JBC,* pp. 177-79.]

Volf, Miroslav. *Exclusion and Embrace: A Theological Exploration of Identity, Otherness, and Reconciliation.* Nashville: Abingdon, 1996.

———. "Theology, Meaning and Power: A Conversation with George Lindbeck on Theology and the Nature of Christian Difference." In *The Nature of Confession: Evangelicals and Postliberals in Conversation,* edited by Timothy R. Phillips and Dennis L. Okholm. Downers Grove, Ill.: InterVarsity, 1996.

———. "When Gospel and Culture Intersect: Notes on the Nature of Christian Difference." In *Pentecostalism in Context: Essays in Honor of William W. Menzies,* edited by Wonsuk Ma and Robert P. Menzies, p. 28. Sheffield: Sheffield Academic Press, 2008.

Vries, Hent de. *Religion and Violence: Philosophical Perspectives from Kant to Derrida.* Baltimore: Johns Hopkins University Press, 2002.

Vroom, Hendrik. *No Other Gods: Christian Belief in Dialogue with Buddhism, Hinduism, and Islam.* Grand Rapids: Eerdmans, 1996.

Waldenfels, Hans. *Absolute Nothingness: Foundations for a Buddhist-Christian Dialogue.* Translated by J. W. Heisig. New York: Paulist, 1980.

Ward, Keith. *Religion and Community.* Oxford: Clarendon, 2000.

———. *Religion and Creation.* Oxford: Clarendon, 1996.

———. *Religion and Human Nature.* Oxford: Clarendon, 1998.

———. *Religion and Revelation: A Theology of Revelation in the World's Religions.* Oxford: Clarendon, 1994.

Ware, [Bishop] Kallistos [Timothy]. "The Humanity of Christ: The Fourth Constantinople Lecture." *Journal of Anglican and Eastern Churches Association* (1985).

Weaver, J. Denny. *The Nonviolent Atonement.* Grand Rapids: Eerdmans, 2001.

Webb, Robert L. *John the Baptizer and Prophet: A Socio-Historical Study.* Sheffield: Sheffield Academic Press, 1991.

Webster, John. "Incarnation." In *The Blackwell Companion to Modern Theology,* edited by G. Jones, pp. 204-26. Oxford: Blackwell, 2004.

Weinandy, Thomas. *In the Likeness of Sinful Flesh: An Essay on the Humanity of Christ.* Edinburgh: T. & T. Clark, 1993.

Wenham, Gordon. "Christ's Healing Ministry and His Attitude to the Law." In *Christ the Lord: Studies in Christology Presented to Donald Guthrie,* edited by Harold H. Rowdon. Leicester: Inter-Varsity Press, 1982.

Werther, D. "The Temptation of God Incarnate." *Religious Studies* 29, no. 1 (1993): 47-50.

Wessels, Anton. *Images of Jesus: How Jesus Is Perceived and Portrayed in Non-European Cultures.* Grand Rapids: Eerdmans, 1990.

Wheeler, David. "The Cross and the Blood: Dead or Living Images?" *Dialog* 35 (1996): 7-13.

Whittingham, Martin. "How Could So Many Christians Be Wrong? The Role of Tawātur (Recurrent Transmission of Reports) in Understanding Muslim Views of the Crucifixion." *Islam and Christian-Muslim Relations* 19, no. 2 (April 2008): 167-78.

Williams, Delores S. *Sisters in the Wilderness: The Challenge of Womanist God-Talk.* Maryknoll, N.Y.: Orbis, 1993.

Williams, George Huntson. "Christology and Church-State Relations in the Fourth Century." *Church History* 20, no. 3 (1951): 3-33; and 20, no. 4 (1951): 3-26.

Williams, Monier. *Brahmanism and Hinduism; or, Religious Thought and Life in India.* New York: Macmillan, 1891.

Williams, Rowan. *Resurrection: Interpreting the Easter Gospel.* Cleveland: Pilgrim Press, 2002.

Williamson, Clark. *A Guest in the House of Israel: Post-Holocaust Church Theology.* Louisville: Westminster John Knox, 1993.

Wink, Walter. *Engaging the Powers: Discernment and Resistance in a World of Domination.* The Powers 3. Minneapolis: Fortress, 1992.

Winkler, Lewis. *Contemporary Muslim and Christian Responses to Religious Plurality: Wolfhart Pannenberg in Dialogue with Abdulaziz Sachedina.* Eugene, Oreg.: Pickwick, 2011.

Winter, Michael. *The Atonement.* Problems in Theology. Collegeville, Minn.: Liturgical Press, 1995.

Witherington, Ben. *Jesus, Paul, and the End of the World: A Comparative Study in New Testament Eschatology.* Downers Grove, Ill.: InterVarsity, 1992.

Wolfson, Elliot R. "Judaism and Incarnation: The Imaginal Body of God." In *Christianity in Jewish Terms,* edited by Tikva Frymer-Kensky et al., pp. 239-53. Boulder, Colo.: Westview Press, 2000.

Worthing, Mark William. *Foundations and Functions of Theology as a Universal Science: Theological Method and Apologetic Praxis in Wolfhart Pannenberg and Karl Rahner.* Frankfurt: Peter Lang, 1996.

Wrede, William. *The Messianic Secret.* Translated by J. C. G. Crieg. Cambridge: James Clarke, 1971 [1901].

Wright, David F. "The Atonement in Reformation Theology." *European Journal of Theology* 8, no. 1 (1999): 37-48.

Wright, N. T. *The Climax of the Covenant: Christ and the Law in Pauline Theology.* Minneapolis: Fortress, 1993.

———. *Evil and the Justice of God.* Downers Grove, Ill.: InterVarsity, 2006.

———. "A Fresh Perspective on Paul?" *Bulletin of the John Rylands University Library of Manchester* 83 (2002): 21-39.

———. "Jesus and the Identity of God." *Ex Auditu* 14 (1998): 42-56.

———. *Jesus and the Victory of God.* Vol. 2 of *Christian Origins and the Question of God.* Minneapolis: Fortress, 1996.

———. *The New Testament and the People of God.* Vol. 1 of *Christian Origins and the Question of God.* London: SPCK; Minneapolis: Fortress, 1992.

———. "Redemption from the New Perspective?" In *The Redemption: An Interdisciplinary Symposium on Christ as Redeemer,* edited by Stephen T. Davis, Daniel Kendall, S.J., and Gerald O'Collins, S.J. Oxford: Oxford University Press, 2004.

———. *The Resurrection of the Son of God.* Minneapolis: Fortress, 2003.

Yeago, David S. "Jesus of Nazareth and Cosmic Redemption: The Relevance of St. Maximus the Confessor." *Modern Theology* 12, no. 2 (April 1996): 163-93.

Yogananda, Paramahansa. *Man's Eternal Quest.* Los Angeles: Self-Realization Fellowship, 1975.

Yong, Amos. *The Spirit Poured Out on All Flesh: Pentecostalism and the Possibility of Global Theology.* Grand Rapids: Baker Academic, 2005.

———. *Spirit-Word-Community: Theological Hermeneutics in Trinitarian Perspective.* Reprint, Eugene, Oreg.: Wipf and Stock, 2006.

Yuketswar, Swami. *The Holy Science.* Los Angeles: Self-Realization Fellowship, 1972.

Zakai, A. "The Rise of Modern Science and the Decline of Theology as the 'Queen of the Sciences' in the Early Modern Era." *Reformation & Renaissance Review* 9, no. 2 (2007): 125-51.

Zebiri, Kare. *Muslims and Christians Face to Face.* Oxford: One World, 1997.

Zizioulas, John. *Being as Communion: Studies in Personhood and the Church.* Crestwood, N.Y.: St. Vladimir's Seminary Press, 1985.

Index of Authors

Index of Subjects